BIBLE

Teacher Edition • Grade 1

purposeful design®
publications

Colorado Springs, Colorado

Development Team

Vice President for Academic Affairs
Derek Keenan, EdD

Assistant Vice President for Purposeful Design Publications
Steven Babbitt

Assistant Director for Textbook Development
Don Hulin

Authors
Rockie Fordham
Rachel Geyer
Connie Gunther
Melissa Hardy
Anna Long
Vance Nichols
Jean Paulsen
Julia Taves
JoAnn Keenan
Maria Phillips
Nancy Sutton
Lorraine Wadman
Lisa Wood

Editorial Team
Barbara Carpenter
Ellen Johnson
JoAnn Keenan
Maria Phillips
Cindi Shipman
Nancy Sutton
Lorraine Wadman
Lisa Wood

Design Team
Claire Dunham
Susanna Garmany

Grade 1

BIBLE

Purposeful Design

Purposeful Design Publications is the publishing division of the Association of Christian Schools International (ACSI) and is committed to the ministry of Christian school education, to enable Christian educators and schools worldwide to effectively prepare students for life. As the publisher of textbooks, trade books, and other educational resources within ACSI, Purposeful Design Publications strives to produce biblically sound materials that reflect Christian scholarship and stewardship and that address the identified needs of Christian schools around the world.

References to books, computer software, and other ancillary resources in this series are not endorsements by ACSI. These materials were selected to provide teachers with additional resources appropriate to the concepts being taught and to promote student understanding and enjoyment.

Printed in the United States of America
18 4 5 6 7

Elementary Bible, Grade 1
Purposeful Design Elementary Bible Series
ISBN 978-1-58331-255-1 Teacher edition Catalog #10012

Purposeful Design Publications
A Division of ACSI
PO Box 65130 • Colorado Springs, CO 80962-5130
Customer Service: 800/367-0798 • Website: www.acsi.org

Table of Contents

Table of Contents

Table of Contents

Song Titles and Track Numbers on Music CDs

Music 1

1. The Bible
2. *Instrumental*
3. Christmas Joy / Joy to the World
4. *Instrumental*
5. Easter Rise Up
6. *Instrumental*
7. The Fish Are Gonna Bite
8. *Instrumental*
9. Garment of Praise
10. *Instrumental*
11. Give 'em to Jesus
12. *Instrumental*
13. He Forgives Me
14. *Instrumental*
15. I Can Obey
16. *Instrumental*
17. I Saw Esau
18. *Instrumental*
19. Jesus Loves Me
20. *Instrumental*
21. Joshua
22. *Instrumental*

Music 2

1. Little Bit of Love
2. *Instrumental*
3. Noah Was a Faithful Man
4. *Instrumental*
5. Oh What a Variety
6. *Instrumental*
7. Palm Sunday Celebration
8. *Instrumental*
9. Promised Land
10. *Instrumental*
11. Right to My Heart
12. *Instrumental*
13. Rolled 'em Away
14. *Instrumental*
15. Ten Commandments
16. *Instrumental*
17. Walk Like Jesus
18. *Instrumental*
19. Wanna Say Thank You
20. *Instrumental*

Foreword

Welcome to the most effective, stimulating, and wonderfully engaging Bible series for Christian schools. The Bible should be taught with the utmost care, enthusiasm, and passion, as well as a deep sense of responsibility for its eternal impact on the life of every student. Scriptures remind us just how important this responsibility is:

> The fear of the Lord is the beginning of wisdom, and the knowledge of the Holy One is understanding. Proverbs 9:10
>
> How can a young man cleanse his way? By taking heed according to Your word. Psalm 119:9
>
> All Scripture is given by inspiration of God, and is profitable for doctrine, for reproof, for correction, for instruction in righteousness. 2 Timothy 3:16

Essential to the mission of Christian schools—which is preparing children and young people for living the Christian life—is guiding students to become grounded in and shaped by God's Word. In his book *Educating for Life*, Nicholas Wolterstorff notes, "A careful, loving, devotional study of Scripture is an indispensible component of the curriculum of the Christian school—for the reason that Scripture is the basis and nourishment of that Christian way of being in the world, which, as I have argued, is the ultimate goal of our enterprise." The Bible is the foundation of the Christian schooling enterprise!

The thematic strands that flow through the Purposeful Design Elementary Bible Series are as follows:
- God tells us His great story (meta-narrative) in the Bible.
- God's Word is truth.
- The great story is the gospel of Jesus Christ and our need of saving faith through Him.
- Knowledge, wisdom, and understanding come from a life grounded in the Scriptures.
- Becoming a spiritually formed disciple of Jesus is impossible without knowing God's Word.
- Developing a vital and authentic Christian worldview requires study, worship, and disciplined practice.

Included in the series are these key features:
- The program consists of 34 lessons spanning a week in length, with a specific lesson focus for each day.
- Scripture memory is embedded in each week's lesson.
- Vivid, inspiring illustrations bring the Bible truths to life.
- Primary grades incorporate custom music CDs that relate to the lesson.
- Various Bible translations may be used throughout the series.
- PowerPoint presentations, transparencies, and "smart board" materials are included.
- Thanksgiving, Christmas, and Easter lessons are stand-alone optional lessons.
- Chapel programs are included for teacher convenience.

Each grade level in this series, Preschool through Grade 6, focuses on the foundational teachings from the Bible about the nature and character of God, the qualities of His people, and His church. During these school years, students are given an overview of the entire Bible, with an emphasis on God's attributes, biblical characters, the early Church, and what it means to know Jesus Christ and live for him.

We pray that this series will support your efforts to develop vibrant followers of Christ who will impact the world around them.

Derek J. Keenan, EdD
Vice President, Academic Affairs

Acknowledgments

The Peer Review process is an important step in the development of this textbook series. ACSI and the Purposeful Design staff greatly appreciate the feedback we receive from the schools and teachers who participate. We highly value the efforts and input of these faculty members; their recommendations and suggestions are extremely helpful. The institutions listed below have assisted us in this way.

Calvary Baptist Day School, Winston-Salem, NC
Faith Academy, Victoria, TX
Grove City Christian School, Grove City, OH
Hebron Christian Academy, Dacula, GA
Lenawee Christian School, Adrian, MI
Linfield Christian School, Temecula, CA
Manhattan Christian Academy, New York, NY
McKinney Christian Academy, McKinney, TX
Pan American Christian Academy, São Paulo, Brazil
Valley Christian School, Aurora, OH

Art Illustrations

Ron Adair
Aline Heiser
Steve Miller

Understanding Purposeful Design Bible

Background

ACSI developed its Elementary Bible Series in the early 1990s with the goal of producing a quality elementary Bible program that reflected the needs and desires of Christian school teachers, administrators, and students at that time. The Bible is timeless, but society has changed over the years, necessitating a fresh, new approach to teaching the Bible. Purposeful Design has now revised the series based upon surveys completed by Christian school educators who had regularly taught from the original series. The results of the questionnaires were then tabulated and carefully analyzed. Keeping the results in mind, a team of talented and experienced teachers from a variety of geographic areas wrote new lessons that were then suffused with updated graphics, songs, terminology, and technology.

Overview of the Purposeful Design Elementary Bible Series

Christian Worldview

The goal of the Purposeful Design Elementary Bible Series is for every student to develop a Christian worldview. A worldview is that framework from which each person views reality, makes sense of life, and interacts with the world. The Christian worldview holds that the primary reason for each person's existence is to love and serve God. People develop a Christian worldview through both the knowledge and application of Scripture. For this reason, it is essential for students to have an in-depth knowledge of Bible truths, as well as the ability to apply Scripture to their daily lives.

Themes and Concepts

Key to the development of a Christian worldview is the presentation of overarching themes that permeate all the Elementary Bible materials, regardless of the lesson topic or grade level. These themes, as follows, are woven throughout the series both directly and indirectly:

- **God tells His great story in the Bible.** God's Word displays His nature, His works, and His plan of redemption. The teaching of sound doctrine from the Bible is central to every lesson. It is this knowledge of God that establishes a solid foundation for life.

- **God's Word is truth.** Because God's Word is true, the series presents students with Bible truths, not Bible stories. Students learn that the Bible is the best source for guidance and direction in life.

- **God loves everyone.** God loves and cares for people. His desire is for all people to have a right relationship with Him. His intentions toward every person are always gracious and good.

- **Everyone needs to come to a saving faith in Jesus.** All people must experience salvation to have a right relationship with God, so the series often presents the message of repentance, personal faith, and acceptance of Jesus Christ as Savior and Lord. A personal relationship with Jesus Christ is dynamic and life-changing as each Christian faithfully grows in knowledge and in obedience to the Lord.

- **Christlike behavior, evangelism, ministry, stewardship, and apologetics are all applications of spiritual growth in Christ.** Personal faith is demonstrated by behavior. Students learn to serve others in response to God's love for them and to share the good news of salvation in their homes and neighborhoods and throughout the world.

- **Bible study, prayer, and worship are disciplines for spiritual growth.** The series emphasizes spiritual disciplines as a way to establish and reinforce a biblical worldview as students grow in their faith by consistently using these methods for growth. God's desire is that Christians be conformed to the character of Jesus Christ. This involves a transformation of the mind and heart through the work of the Holy Spirit, who gives Christians the desire to change and enables them to do the will of God.

- **Students need to know and understand spiritual concepts.** In addition to overarching themes, each weekly Bible lesson teaches and develops spiritual concepts. These concepts include salvation, grace, mercy, repentance, perseverance, faith, forgiveness, worship, thanksgiving, praise, aspects of God's divine nature, and a personal relationship to God.

Essential Student Outcomes

A strong Bible program requires that students not only acquire skills and knowledge but also grow in faith and demonstrate that faith by their behavior. For this reason, each lesson has a unique set of expected student outcomes—statements of desired student outcomes in the areas of knowledge, skills, and life application through studying the lesson. Because growth in faith is an individual matter, students will come to apply Scripture over the course of time as they grow in their relationship with God.

Translations

The Purposeful Design Elementary Bible Series can be used in conjunction with any translation of the Bible. Teachers are encouraged to use the Bible translation endorsed by their school. The New International Version (NIV), the New King James Version (NKJV), the New American Standard (NASB), and the King James Version (KJV) are all compatible with Purposeful Design Elementary Bible. In an effort to maintain a nontranslation-specific Bible series, verses or passages of Scripture are frequently referenced but seldom quoted. Unless otherwise noted, any direct quotes from Scripture that appear in the Teacher or Student Editions have been taken from the New King James Version (NKJV).

Doctrinal Differences

The Purposeful Design Elementary Bible Series adheres firmly to the doctrinal statement that all ACSI schools sign as a condition of membership. Beyond these fundamentals of the faith, a diversity of traditions, practices, and beliefs exist within the evangelical Christian community. Purposeful Design recognizes that conscientious Christians have differing views on many theological issues. The Elementary Bible Series focuses primarily on those beliefs Christians hold in common. When doctrinal differences are known to exist, teachers are given some background information on these differences and encouraged to use the opportunity to reflect the doctrinal statement of their individual school or supporting church(es).

The Purposeful Design Elementary Bible Series is organized according to grade level, from Preschool through Grade 6. Lessons for each grade level emphasize a key biblical concept in an age-appropriate and engaging way. The Bible truths presented in each grade level build on the foundational truths students have learned in previous grades. The following table provides an overview of each grade level and subject focus in the series:

Structure of the Series

Level	Subject
Preschool	Familiar Bible truths that emphasize God's love
Kindergarten	Familiar Bible truths that emphasize God's loving care
First Grade	Familiar Bible truths that emphasize God's relationship to people
Second Grade	Studies on character traits of various people in the Bible with application to students' life

Level	Subject
Third Grade	Studies in the life of Christ, the early Church, and missions from the time of Paul until now
Fourth Grade	Studies in the basic doctrines of the Church
Fifth Grade	Studies in the Old Testament that emphasize choices and their consequences

Schedule

Each grade level includes 34 weekly lessons. The series easily accommodates a four- or five-day instructional program and provides a weekly test for Grades 1 through 6. Thanksgiving (Lesson 13), Christmas (Lesson 17), and Easter (Lesson 29) are stand-alone lessons and should be scheduled at the appropriate times in the school year.

Components of the Series

Purposeful Design Elementary Bible Series instructional materials are designed to help students appropriate and apply both knowledge of the Scriptures and skills in using the Bible. These materials include:

- Teacher Edition
- Student Edition
- Resources CD, which includes blackline masters, transparency masters in Grades 1 through 6, Visual Aid illustrations in Preschool through Grade 2, PowerPoint presentations in Grades 1 through 6, song lyrics in Preschool through Grade 2, and chapel programs
- Music CDs in Preschool through Grade 2
- Printed Visual Aids in Preschool through Grade 2
- Time Lines in Grades 2 through 6

Features of the Teacher Edition

The Teacher Edition includes all the information necessary to plan and teach each weekly lesson.

Table of Contents

The table of contents lists the lesson numbers, titles, and page numbers for each lesson. The stand-alone lessons of Thanksgiving, Christmas, and Easter, listed in the table of contents, are positioned near the time of year when these lessons might fall. These lessons can be presented at the appropriate time and do not need to be taught in sequence with the other lessons.

Lesson Preparation Page(s)

Teachers can see at a glance what materials are needed for the weekly lesson by looking at the lesson Foci (Preschool and Kindergarten), Memory Verse, Glossary terms (Grades 2 through 6), song list (Preschool through Grade 2), Expected Student Outcomes, an outline of the lesson content (Grades 1 through 6), Teacher and Student Resources, and a devotional called *Teacher's Heart.* Teacher and student resources are suggested as optional materials to explore the lesson topic. Items listed in Teacher and Student Resources do not constitute an endorsement by Purposeful Design Publications but may be used to extend the lesson.

Lesson Pages

Each Teacher Edition lesson page contains the title and focus of the lesson, a main body of instructional information, and sidebars. The main text contains instruction in a step-by-step format. In Preschool and Kindergarten, each lesson page is divided into *Worship Time*, *Listening Time*, and *Activity Time* sections. Lesson pages for Grades 1 through 6 include *Introduction*, *Directed Instruction*, and *Review* sections. All grade levels contain questions in the *Review* section to test the students' comprehension and help them recall facts from the Bible truth.

The sidebars are *Memory Verse*, *Memory Work*, *Preparation*, *Application*, and *Reinforcement.* Grades 1 through 6 have an *Extension* sidebar as well.

Memory Verse suggests a Bible verse or passage for students to memorize.

Memory Work provides creative ideas for helping students memorize the weekly Memory Verse. *Memory Work* is included on the first day of each lesson, but these suggested activities are designed to be used throughout the week.

Preparation gives teachers an advance notice of supply needs to allow for ample time to acquire and assemble any materials necessary for the lesson. This sidebar lists Visual Aids and Supplemental Materials provided on the resources and music CDs.

Reinforcement is for teacher use. This sidebar contains information related to each lesson's topic and may be read to students, but it is primarily designed to provide background information or instructional strategies.

Application contains questions that are vital to helping students internalize Bible truths. Questions in this sidebar call for students to relate concepts from the Bible truth to their own life and should be asked after the review questions. Teachers should allow questions and answers during this class time to help students develop a Bible-based, Christian worldview.

Extension provides a variety of optional activities, such as games, songs, map work, PowerPoint presentations, and art projects, to reinforce and review the lesson. Extension activities can be done at any time during the school day. Many songs, sermons, videos, and other resources are available free or for a fee on the Internet. When one of these is suggested as an extension activity, teachers need to download or present them in accordance with school policy.

Bible costumes are frequently suggested in the lower grades. Simple costumes are easily made by cutting neck openings and armholes into king-size pillowcases. Headpieces may be cut from old bed sheets or hand towels.

Recipes and foods are also frequently suggested in the lower grades. Food allergies should always be taken into account when using anything edible in a lesson. Baking temperatures given are in Fahrenheit.

The Teacher Edition includes a formal assessment at the end of each lesson. Reduced Student Edition pages with the answers to each exercise appear on instructional days.

Icons

The Teacher Edition includes two types of icons that alert the teacher to specific information or activities. The *Preparation* icon ★ points out the need for the teacher to prepare a material in advance. The materials needed and directions for preparation are noted in the sidebar that bears the same icon. The *Extension* icon prompts the teacher to note the availability of an Extension activity to reinforce the Bible truth.

Features of the Student Edition

The Student Edition is a consumable workbook designed with colorful, realistic illustrations and photographs to capture the students' interest in the Bible and subject matter. Four Student Edition pages are provided for each lesson. The pages are perforated for easy removal. They are labeled at the top with the lesson number and the day of the lesson. For example, Student Edition page 2.4 refers to Lesson 2, Day 4. Each page is also paginated. Odd-numbered pages have name lines.

Supplemental Materials

The Purposeful Design Elementary Bible Series includes the following types of Supplemental Materials:

GRADE	Blackline Masters (BLMs)	Transparency Masters (TMs)	Time Line	PowerPoints (PPs)	Chapels	Visual Aids (VAs)	Music CDs with lyrics
Preschool	Y	N	N	N	Y	Y	Y
Kindergarten	Y	N	N	N	Y	Y	Y
1st	Y	Y	N	Y	Y	Y	Y
2nd	Y	Y	Y	Y	Y	Y	Y
3rd	Y	Y	Y	Y	Y	N	N
4th	Y	Y	Y	Y	Y	N	N
5th	Y	Y	Y	Y	Y	N	N
6th	Y	Y	Y	Y	Y	N	N

All but the Time Line are on the resources and music CDs located in the Teacher Edition.

- The resources CD contains the blackline masters, transparency masters, song lyrics, PowerPoint presentations, chapel programs, and Visual Aid illustrations.
- The music CDs include one track of vocals and music and another of only instrumental music for each song suggested in Preschool through Grade 2. All songs are performed by Mary Rice Hopkins.
- Preprinted Visual Aids and Time Lines are provided for classroom use.

Visual Aids are original, full-color illustrations of Bible truths provided for Preschool through Grade 2. On the back of each Visual Aid is a paraphrased version of the Bible truth. Before reading the paraphrased text, teachers are encouraged to hold up the Bible and remind students that the Bible truth comes from God's Word.

The following abbreviations have been used to facilitate identifying the Supplemental Materials needed for each lesson. **VAs** are Visual Aids, **BLMs** are blackline masters, **TMs** are transparency masters, and **PPs** are PowerPoints. Each Supplemental Material has a title and a label containing a lesson number and a letter, indicating the order in which the material is used. For example, **VA 12A The Psalms** is the first (A) Visual Aid in Lesson 12. *The Psalms* is the title of the Visual Aid. **VA 7C The Red Sea Crossing** is the third (C) Visual Aid in Lesson 7.

Blackline masters serve a variety of purposes and may include craft projects, weekly tests, teaching aids, recipes, and supplemental activities. Weekly review tests for Grades 1 through 6 are included on blackline masters, along with answer keys. To enhance student comprehension, it is suggested that teachers review the answers to the tests in class after all students have finished. Tests may be graded if desired. Because blackline masters are in electronic format, they may be projected for classroom use.

PowerPoint presentations are optional and can be used to reinforce lesson content.

Chapel programs centered on biblical themes are provided and may be used if desired.

Additional Information

A chart of abbreviations used for books of the Bible is listed below:

OLD TESTAMENT							
Genesis	Gen		2 Chronicles	2 Chron		Daniel	Dan
Exodus	Ex		Ezra	Ezra		Hosea	Hos
Leviticus	Lev		Nehemiah	Neh		Joel	Joel
Numbers	Num		Esther	Esth		Amos	Amos
Deuteronomy	Deut		Job	Job		Obadiah	Obad
Joshua	Josh		Psalms	Ps		Jonah	Jonah
Judges	Judg		Proverbs	Prov		Micah	Micah
Ruth	Ruth		Ecclesiastes	Eccl		Nahum	Nahum
1 Samuel	1 Sam		Song of Solomon	Song		Habakkuk	Hab
2 Samuel	2 Sam		Isaiah	Isa		Zephaniah	Zeph
1 Kings	1 Kings		Jeremiah	Jer		Haggai	Hag
2 Kings	2 Kings		Lamentations	Lam		Zechariah	Zech
1 Chronicles	1 Chron		Ezekiel	Ezek		Malachi	Mal

NEW TESTAMENT							
Matthew	Mt		Ephesians	Eph		Hebrews	Heb
Mark	Mk		Philippians	Phil		James	James
Luke	Lk		Colossians	Col		1 Peter	1 Pet
John	Jn		1 Thessalonians	1 Thess		2 Peter	2 Pet
Acts	Acts		2 Thessalonians	2 Thess		1 John	1 Jn
Romans	Rom		1 Timothy	1 Tim		2 John	2 Jn
1 Corinthians	1 Cor		2 Timothy	2 Tim		3 John	3 Jn
2 Corinthians	2 Cor		Titus	Titus		Jude	Jude
Galatians	Gal		Philemon	Philem		Revelation	Rev

Preparing a Lesson

❶ MEMORY VERSE

The **Memory Verse** sidebar contains the verse students are to memorize during the week of the lesson. Teachers can choose which Bible version to use based on the reference given.

❷ MEMORY WORK

Memory Work offers suggestions to help teach the Memory Verse in fun and meaningful ways that encourage active participation from students.

❸ PREPARATION

The **Preparation** sidebar gives an advance notice to acquire and assemble any materials needed to teach the lesson. Materials not assumed to be in the classroom are listed in **BLUE BOLDFACE TYPE.** Visual aids and supplemental materials provided on the resources and music CDs are listed as well. The star icon is a quick visual reminder to alert teachers to sections needing prepared materials.

❹ EXTENSION

The **Extension** sidebar appears in most lessons to offer optional enrichment activities. Extension materials are listed in **BLUE BOLDFACE TYPE.** These materials are also listed on the Lesson Preparation page. The arrow icon is a reminder that an Extension activity is available and can be done at any time.

20.1

Following Jesus

Focus: The Vine, the Branches, and the Fruit

MEMORY VERSE ❶

John 15:5

MEMORY WORK ❷

- Write the Memory Verse on the board and read it with the class. Have the students suggest motions for each phrase in the verse. For example, for *I am the vine,* have students stand up as tall as possible. For *you are the branches,* have students stretch their arms out to their sides. Continue to invite students to suggest motions for the Memory Verse and to recite the verse as many times as needed until all have memorized it.

★ PREPARATION ❸

Bring a CLUSTER OF GRAPES to class. Prepare **TM-7 Vine and Branches** for display. (*Introduction*)

Select "Right to My Heart" from the music CDs. (*Introduction*)

EXTENSION ❹

1A Prepare some GRAPES for a snack. As students eat, remind them that the grapes would not be sweet without the sugar the leaves help to produce. They would not be juicy without the water from the soil that was carried upward through the vine to the branches. The branches needed to stay connected to the vine to produce the grapes.

Introduction ★ ❺

Hold up the CLUSTER OF GRAPES so that all students can see it. Display **TM-7 Vine and Branches**. Explain that the cluster of grapes came from a vine similar to what is on TM-7. Ask students if the cluster of grapes that you brought will grow and continue to live. (**No.**) Affirm that they have answered correctly. Grapes will not grow or live without the rooted section, the vine, to which they are attached. As you point out the various parts of the grapevine on TM-7, explain that the vine, branches, leaves, and grapes are all parts of the same living plant. God has designed each part of the grapevine to do a special job for the plant. Each leaf takes in sunlight and makes sugar for the plant. Each branch carries the sugar and water to the grapes and the leaves. The vine keeps the plant in place, holds the branches up, and carries water, sugar, and other nutrients to various parts of the plant. The vine produces the grapes that appear on the branches.

Teach students "Right to My Heart" from the music CDs.

Directed Instruction ❻

Explain that when Jesus wanted to teach a lesson, He often talked about common things with which His listeners would be familiar, such as grapevines. Jesus used the ordinary things to help the people understand more about God. In today's Bible truth, Jesus compares Himself to a grapevine. Read the following Bible truth:

> During His time on Earth, Jesus chose 12 men to be His disciples. The word *disciple* means *a follower*. The disciples followed Jesus to the places where He was teaching the people. The disciples listened to Jesus as He taught God's truth, and they followed Jesus' example by helping others.
>
> Jesus had a close relationship with His disciples. He told them, "I am like a vine and you, My friends, are like branches. A branch can only grow when it is joined to the vine. You will grow in faith and be able to do wonderful things to help many people when you listen to My words, copy My actions, and follow My directions for your life."

Direct students' attention back to the picture of the grapevine on TM-7. Circle the vine and remind students that Jesus compared Himself to the vine. Ask students to recount who were represented by the branches in Jesus' lesson. (**the disciples**)

The disciples were like branches because they stayed close to Jesus. When Jesus taught the disciples, they took what they learned and put it into practice, just like the branches of a grapevine take water and sugar from the vine, and grapes are formed.

Jesus told the disciples that they needed to do three things to grow in their faith. Ask students to share what those three things were. (**listen to what He taught them, copy His actions, and follow His directions**) Christians are to do these same things today. When Christians listen to God's Word, copy His actions, and follow His directions, they are able to do many

192

---

❺ Introduction

Introduction contains a variety of ideas ranging from music selections, group discussion topics and questions, to prayer topic suggestions and object lessons that will prepare students and invite them to fully engage in learning the concepts presented in the lesson.

❻ Directed Instruction

Directed Instruction gives step-by-step instructions for the lesson. The Bible truth is presented in this section. Also, fictional stories set in various locations around the world introduce students to other perspectives and applications of Bible concepts.

things to help others and to share the good news about God's plan of salvation. When showing God's love to others and telling others about Jesus results in a life being changed for God, it is called *bearing fruit*.

Review ❼

- What were Jesus' followers called? (**disciples**)
- Who is the vine in Jesus' lesson? (**Jesus**)
- Who are the branches in Jesus' lesson? (**the disciples, Christians today**)
- What does it mean to *bear fruit*? (**It means that I have shared about Jesus, and it has changed someone's life for God.**)
- What does a branch need in order to bear fruit? (**It needs to be connected to the vine.**)

Student Page 20.1

Assist students as needed to complete the page.

Notes:

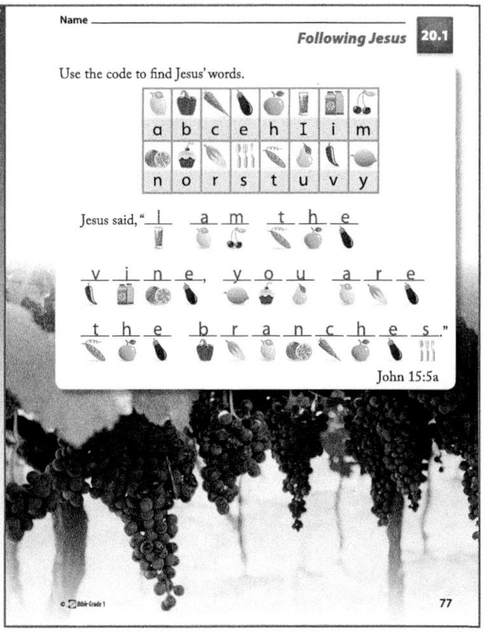

APPLICATION ❽

- What are some games that you cannot play alone? (**Answers will vary.**) Name some sports that are played with teams. (**Answers will vary.**) Is it important for Christians to work as a team with other Christians? (**Yes.**) Why? (**Answers will vary, but should include that it is important to work together to share God's Word and to help others.**)
- It is important to have a close relationship to Jesus and a close relationship to other Christians. Share some things that go wrong when people do not get along. (**Answers will vary.**)
- What is something that you can do to keep a close relationship with Jesus? (**I can read the Bible, pray, and worship regularly.**)
- What does *bearing fruit* mean and how can you bear fruit? (**Bearing fruit occurs when someone's life is changed for God. I may bear fruit when I show God's love to others and tell others about Jesus. When I listen to God's Word, copy His actions, and follow His directions, I am then able to do many things to help others and to share the good news about God's plan of salvation.**)

REINFORCEMENT ❾

Old Testament writers often used the vine to symbolize the nation of Israel. The symbolism indicated that people were connected to God through their covenant relationship with Him. Israel, however, did not bear the fruit of righteousness that should have come through its relationship with God (Isaiah 5:1–7). Jesus Christ is the true vine; He replaces the Law and restores believers into a right relationship with God (Romans 10:4).

© Bible Grade 1 193

❼ Review

Review questions focus on comprehension of key concepts from the Bible truths and/or daily lessons. Answers and suggestions help teachers guide class discussions.

❽ APPLICATION

Application questions provide an opportunity to evaluate both students' understanding of the concepts presented and their ability to apply those concepts in daily life.

❾ REINFORCEMENT

The **Reinforcement** sidebar provides additional Bible background for the lesson or supplemental information related to each lesson's theme. The information is designed for teachers, but can be shared with students.

Lesson Preparation 1.0

Creation

Expected Student Outcomes

KNOW

God creates the universe. Adam and Eve sin.

DO

Students will:

- identify the Bible as God's Word and draw a scene about Creation
- sequence the events of Creation
- identify things that were not in the Garden of Eden and discuss ways to take care of the earth
- compare and contrast pictures of life before the Fall and after the Fall

APPLY

Students will express thankfulness for God's Creation. They will recognize that everybody sins, yet God continues to love everyone.

Lesson Outline

I. God made the world (Gen 1:1)
  A. The Bible is God's Word
II. The days of Creation (Gen 1:1–31)
III. Adam and Eve (Gen 2:15–25)
  A. A beautiful garden
  B. An important job
  C. One important rule
IV. The Fall (Gen 3:1–24)
  A. Breaking the rule
  B. Leaving the garden

MEMORY VERSE

Genesis 1:1

MATERIALS

Day 1:

- Flip chart
- Globe
- VA 1A Creation
- Blocks (*Extension*)

Day 2:

- VA 1A Creation
- White butcher paper (*Extension*)

Day 3:

- VA 1A Creation
- Small treat, streamers (*Extension*)

Day 4:

- VA 1A Creation
- Apple or picture of an apple, stuffed or rubber snake

Day 5:

- VA 1A Creation
- BLM 1A Lesson 1 Test

SONGS

Oh What a Variety

TEACHER'S HEART

The first few days of school are such a busy time in a teacher's life. There are classrooms to prepare, lessons to plan, copies to run, books to organize, bulletin boards to decorate, and meetings to attend. Often the effort of a new year and the thought of a new group of students can overwhelm you and make you forget why you are a teacher. This week you will share the truth of God's Creation with young children. The almighty Creator of the universe is the same loving God who cares deeply for you.

My help comes from the Lord,
Who made heaven and earth.
He will not allow your foot to be moved;
He who keeps you will not slumber. Psalm 121:2–3

You are unique and special to the Lord, who created the mountains, the oceans, the stars, and the whole universe. The Lord, the Creator, loves you! He sees how busy you are; He sees everything weighing on your mind; He sees the work still to be done; and He sees the children soon to arrive in your classroom. Take time to reflect on the awesome power of God as you prepare for this new school year.

TEACHER RESOURCES

DeYoung, Dr. Don. *Thousands … Not Billions*. Master Books, 2005.

Ross, Hugh. *Why the Universe Is the Way It Is*. Baker Books, 2008.

STUDENT RESOURCES

Gambil, Henrietta D. *Seven Special Days*. Standard Publishing, 2005.

Lehmann, Charles. *God Made It for You! The Story of Creation*. Concordia Publishing House, 2007.

1.1 Creation

Focus: God Made the World

MEMORY VERSE

Genesis 1:1

MEMORY WORK

Have students practice the Memory Verse throughout the week using the following directions:

- Display a FLIP CHART with the Memory Verse and reference written on it. Use a different color to write the word *heavens* and the word *earth*. Recite the verse together using different tones of voice for the highlighted words.

PREPARATION

Write this week's Memory Verse on a FLIP CHART. (*Memory Work*)

Have a GLOBE on hand. (*Introduction*)

Select **VA 1A Creation**. (*Directed Instruction*)

EXTENSION

1A Throw some BLOCKS randomly on the floor. Tell students that the blocks could become a building. Wait a few moments while the class watches the blocks. When nothing happens, dramatically sigh and toss the blocks again. Watch for a few moments. Tell students that you will have to make the blocks into a building since they would not build themselves. Now use the blocks to make a building. Lead a discussion about how much planning and design are involved when building a building. Remind students that God carefully designed the world they live in, and that the world did not come into existence by accident or chance.

Introduction ★

Invite students to spend time exploring their Bible. Explain that the Bible is truth, and allow students to turn the pages. While students look at the most important book they will ever hold in their hands, talk with them about how important God's Word is and share the fun of discovery when they find an interesting picture or familiar passage. Help students understand that the Bible is God's gift and that they will enjoy reading more and more of it as they are able.

Have students turn to the front of their Bible. Help them find **Genesis 1:1**. Point out that this is the first thing God put in the whole book. Ask students to place their finger on the verse. Read the verse to the class. Hold up the GLOBE. Emphasize that the very first thing God tells all people in His special book is that He made everything. God wants people to know that the earth and everyone on it were created by Him and belong to Him. Exclaim and rejoice with your students that they serve a big God.

Directed Instruction ★

To help students understand that there was nothing before Creation, darken the room and ask them to cover their eyes. Be aware that some students may feel afraid in the dark and need to hear comforting words. Read the following with a calm voice:

> This is pretty dark, isn't it? Once the world was darker than this. Now keep your eyes closed and sh … sh … sh. Just listen! Do you hear how quiet it is? (Pause for a few seconds, allowing students time to appreciate the quietness.) Once the world was quieter than this. In fact, there was no sound at all. There was no light at all. No sun, no stars, no Earth, or trees. No land animals or fish or birds or people! There was nothing … nothing but God.

Inform students that God's Word explains how God created the world. Display **VA 1A Creation.** Tell students that whenever you read a Bible "story," you will call it a *Bible truth* because God's Word is always true. Read the Bible truth from the back of VA 1A.

Emphasize that God carefully designed the world. Explain that the earth did not create itself or happen by accident. Pray with students to thank God for the beautiful world He created.

Student Page 1.1

Read the directions. While students draw, ask them to describe what they are drawing. (**Answers will vary.**)

Review

- Why is the Bible the most important book you will ever have? (**Answers will vary, but should include that the Bible is God's Word.**)
- Where in the Bible would you look if you want to read about how God created the world? (**in Genesis or in the first part of the Bible**)

- What did God create first? (**light**) Second? (**sky**) Third? (**plants**) Fourth? (**sun, moon, and stars**)
- On which day did God create water animals and birds? (**He created them on the fifth day.**) On which day of Creation did God create land animals and people? (**on the sixth day**)
- Besides Creation, what are some other things that you can find in the Bible? (**Answers will vary, but may include Bible truths such as the account of Noah and the ark, Jesus, and the disciples.**)

Notes:

DAY 1

Name ____________________

Creation **1.1**

Draw a scene about Creation in the empty circle.

Drawings will vary.

APPLICATION

- What do you think the world was like before God added things to the water, sky, and land? (**Possible answers: empty space, no people, no animals**)
- Why do you think God created everything else before He created people? (**Answers will vary, but should include that He wanted us to have the things we need to live.**)
- How do you know that the earth was carefully designed and not an accident? (**In the Bible, God explains how He carefully created the earth.**)

REINFORCEMENT

When young children share prayer requests, they often get carried away. They share far more requests than most people can remember, and some students may make up stories in order to participate. Students need to be taught how to share prayer requests in a classroom setting. Teachers can model appropriate ways to share requests by praying aloud, by encouraging students to pray for the most pressing needs, and by writing down requests.

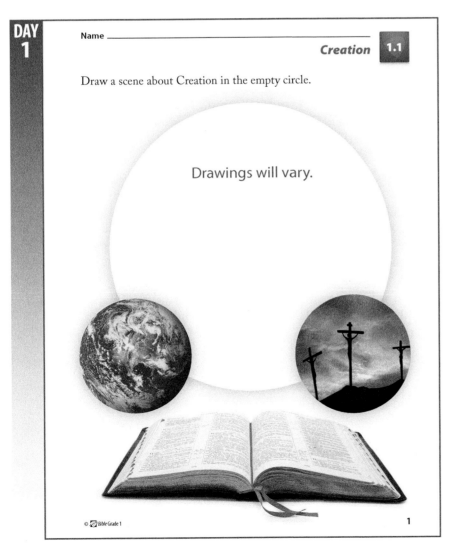

1.2 Creation

Focus: The Days of Creation

★ PREPARATION

Select **VA 1A Creation**. (*Introduction*)

Select "Oh What a Variety" from the music CDs. (*Directed Instruction*)

EXTENSION

2A Give each group of five or six students a large piece of **WHITE BUTCHER PAPER** and crayons. Gather each group on the floor around their paper. Talk with students about the many different things God created. Instruct students to draw and color God's Creation. Post the pictures in the room or hall for a few days.

Introduction ★

Use **VA 1A Creation** to review the account of Creation with students. Point out the many different plants and animals God created. Ask students if God made everything look the same. (**No, God created everything with great variety.**) Invite students to name and describe the different places or outdoor environments that they have experienced, such as the desert or seashore. Encourage students to describe the kinds of birds, fish, and other animals found in different parts of the world. Ask students to tell why polar bears do not live in the desert. (**God designed them for the cold parts of the world.**) Choose a volunteer to explain why it is that whales do not live on the land. (**God designed them to live in oceans.**) The world God created is not dull. There are many different types of plants and animals. The earth is full of variety!

Directed Instruction ★

Ask students to stand. Teach students the following fingerplay to help them remember the days of Creation:

On the first day God made daylight and night. (**Shield eyes with hand for light; cover eyes for night.**)
On the second day God made the beautiful sky. (**Wave arms over head.**)
On the third day God gathered the seas and formed dry land. (**Make gathering motions toward the floor.**)
God put all the trees and other plants on the dry land. (**Raise arms high and spread fingers.**)
And God saw that … (**Students shout, "It was good!"**)
On the fourth day God created the sun, (**Arch arms above head.**) moon, (**Make smaller arch above head.**) and stars. (**Wiggle fingers high over head.**)
On the fifth day God made the animals that live in water. He made different water animals such as sharks, starfish, and minnows. (**Act out the creatures mentioned.**)
Also, on the fifth day God created the birds of the air. He created different birds such as eagles, ducks, and penguins. (**Act out the birds mentioned.**)
On the sixth day God created all of the land animals. He created animals such as lions, horses, and elephants. (**Act out the animals mentioned.**)
On the sixth day God created people. (**Stand tall and show strong muscles.**)
On the seventh day God rested. (**Sit peacefully.**)

After so much activity, flop down in your chair and exclaim that you are tired and need a nap. Ask students if they think this is the way God felt after all that work. (**No, God never gets tired.**) Stress that although God never gets tired, people need to take time from their work to rest and spend time with Him.

Sing "Oh What a Variety" from the music CDs. The lyrics are on the resources CD.

Student Page 1.2

Help students sequence the events of Creation. Call out a number from one through six. Ask students to put their finger on the corresponding picture for that day of Creation. Tell the students to write that day's number in the oval beside the picture. Continue in this manner until all six days have been identified. Read the sentence in Exercise 2 and direct the students to trace the gray words.

Review

- What animals did God put in the sky He created? (**birds**) In the water He created? (**water animals**) On the land He created? (**plants, land animals, people**)
- Why did God make plants before He made animals and people? (**Answers will vary, but should include that plants serve as food for animals and people.**)
- Why did God rest? (**God was teaching us to rest and spend time with Him.**) Was He tired? (**No, God never gets tired. He is always watching us and taking care of us.**)

DAY 2

1.2 ***Creation***

1. Number the days of Creation.

3

5

4

1

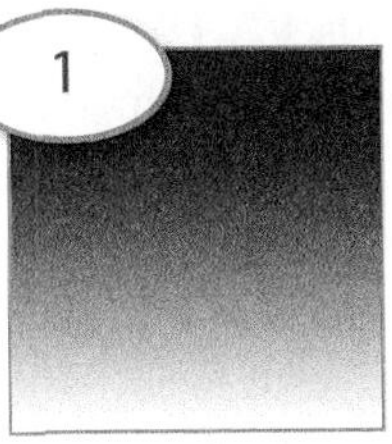

6

2

2. On the seventh day, God rested.

2

© Bible Grade 1

APPLICATION

- When a beaver builds a dam, it builds the same kind of dam beavers have been building for thousands of years. A robin always builds a robin's nest, and a beehive always takes the same basic form. God designed people to learn about what He had created and then use those materials to make new things. What kind of houses do animals build? (**Possible answers: Tree squirrels build nests; spiders build webs; gophers dig holes.**) How are people's houses different from animal homes? (**Answers will vary, but should include that people build many different kinds of houses.**)
- What do you think is the most important difference between people and all the other creatures that God made? (**Answers will vary, but should include that people were created to have fellowship with God. People are creative.**)

REINFORCEMENT

Because God worked for six days of Creation, students might conclude that God rested because He was tired. Being tired and resting is a concept that young children understand, but Psalm 121 promises that God neither slumbers nor sleeps. Reinforce for students the truth that God is always watching over and caring for them.

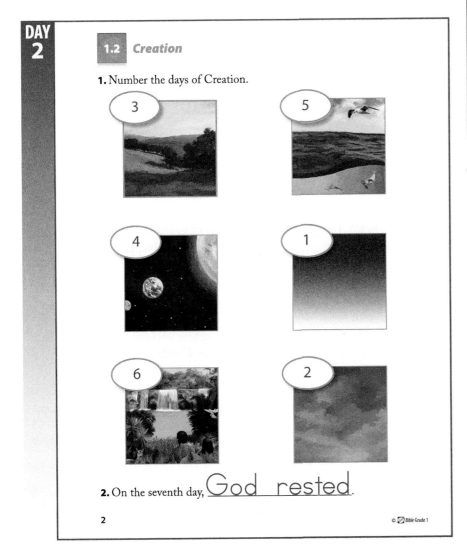

1.3 Creation

Focus: Adam and Eve

★ PREPARATION

Select **VA 1A Creation**. (*Directed Instruction*)

EXTENSION

3A Take students on a prayer walk outside. Encourage students to say thank you for specific things that God created.

3B Invite a parent to come in while students are away from the classroom. Ask the parent to place a SMALL TREAT on each desk, hang STREAMERS in the doorway, or turn on some music. When students return, have the parent dramatically tell students how special they are and explain that the special treat is just for them. Talk with students about how it feels to have an unexpected treat. Remind students to thank the parent. (Note: If the small treat is a food item, keep students' allergies in mind.)

Introduction

Ask students if they can point out the special preparations you did just for them before school began. (**Answers will vary.**) Are there special bulletin boards, decorations, or name tags? Was there a little gift on the desk when they arrived? Were the books organized just right? Share some of the special plans you made for the year. Are there field trips, celebrations, or projects you are already planning? Share your heart. Tell them that they are your students, they are special, and you work hard just for them.

Directed Instruction ★

Hold up your Bible. Tell students that God made special plans for Adam and Eve in a similar way to how you made plans for your students. Remind them that the Bible tells about the ways that God made the Garden to be a special place for Adam and Eve.

Read and discuss the following Bible verses:
Genesis 2:8–9: God purposefully designed the Garden of Eden to look beautiful for Adam and Eve.

Genesis 1:27–30: When He created people in His own image, God did not mean that people look like Him, rather people have emotions and thoughts in a way that the animals do not.

Genesis 2:19–20: God put Adam in charge of the earth and even let him name the creatures.

Genesis 2:15–17: Taking care of God's Garden was an important job. But God also gave Adam one rule to obey. Adam and Eve were not to eat the fruit from the Tree of the Knowledge of Good and Evil. God gave Adam this rule to allow them to freely choose to obey Him.

Show students **VA 1A Creation**. Ask them to point out all the special, beautiful things God made just for Adam and Eve. Explain that when God told Adam and Eve to be fruitful and multiply, He meant that they should have many children who would grow up and also have children to fill the earth. Ask a volunteer to tell the class what God said about the Tree of the Knowledge of Good and Evil. (**He told Adam not to eat the fruit of that tree.**) Review God's rule regarding this tree and remind students that Adam and Eve could eat anything else in the Garden.

Explain that Adam and Eve were not wearing clothes because they did not need to. They were not ashamed of their bodies. Even though it may seem silly now, being naked was normal for them.

Student Page 1.3

Talk with students about things that would not be found in the Garden of Eden. Instruct them to make an *X* on the things God did not put in His Garden. Have students use the blank ovals to draw two things they would find in the Garden. Remind students that God told Adam and Eve to take care of the earth. Assign students to complete the page by drawing something that they could do to take care of the earth, such as watering plants, picking up trash, or caring for a pet.

Review

- What was the special thing God did to prepare for Adam and Eve? (**He made the Garden of Eden special just for them.**)
- What were the important jobs that God gave Adam and Eve? (**to take care of the Garden, to name the animals, to be in charge of the earth**)
- What was the one important rule that God gave Adam? (**Do not eat the fruit from the Tree of the Knowledge of Good and Evil.**)

Notes:

APPLICATION

- Have you ever done something extra special for someone? What was it, and why did you do it? (**Answers will vary, but should include because I wanted to show my love.**)
- How do you think God feels about you? (**He loves me.**)
- God told Adam not to eat from the Tree of the Knowledge of Good and Evil. Why do you think He made that rule? (**Answers will vary, but should include that God wanted Adam and Eve to freely choose to love and obey Him.**)

DAY 3

Name ______________________________

Creation **1.3**

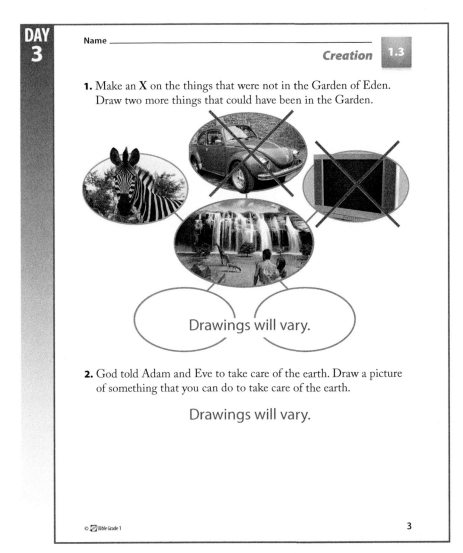

1. Make an X on the things that were not in the Garden of Eden. Draw two more things that could have been in the Garden.

Drawings will vary.

2. God told Adam and Eve to take care of the earth. Draw a picture of something that you can do to take care of the earth.

Drawings will vary.

© *Bible* Grade 1 3

1.4 Creation

Focus: The Fall

★ PREPARATION

Select **VA 1A Creation** and post it in the classroom. (*Directed Instruction*)

Prepare three pieces of paper with large lettering. These will be used as name tags. On the first write *Adam*, on the second write *Eve*, and on the third write *tree*. Obtain an **APPLE** or a **PICTURE OF AN APPLE**, a **STUFFED OR RUBBER SNAKE**, and a large piece of paper to cover VA 1A Creation. The cover is needed so that students will not refer to VA 1A when they work on Student Page 1.4. (*Directed Instruction*)

Introduction

Ask students if they know what the word *tempt* means. (**to try to get someone to do the wrong thing**) Consider sharing a simple story from your own childhood about how you were tempted and how you gave in to the temptation. Emphasize that you had a choice and made a decision to do the wrong thing. Explain the consequences of your actions and that even though your parents were upset, they still loved you very much.

Directed Instruction ★

Choose one student to be *Adam*, a second student to be *Eve*, and a third student to be *the tree*. Affix a paper name tag to each student and have those students face the class. Give *the tree* an **APPLE** or a **PICTURE OF AN APPLE** to hold. While narrating, weave the **STUFFED OR RUBBER SNAKE** around *Eve* and *the tree* in a dramatic fashion. Read the following Bible truth based on Genesis 3:1–24:

> One day in the Garden of Eden, Eve heard a voice. She saw a snake, and it was talking to her! What was happening? Satan, God's enemy, was very clever and disguised himself as a snake so he could trick Eve. The snake said, "Has God said you should not eat from every tree in the Garden?"
>
> Eve said, "We may eat the fruit from the trees in the Garden except for the tree in the middle of the Garden. God said we should not eat it or even touch it or we will die."
>
> The snake tempted Eve by saying, "Oh, no. You won't die. God just doesn't want you to eat the fruit from this tree because He knows that if you do, you will become just like Him. You will know the difference between good and evil."
>
> Eve thought about what the snake said. She looked at the fruit and ate it. She gave the fruit to Adam, and he ate it. Immediately, Adam and Eve knew they had done wrong. They both had disobeyed God!
>
> God came to walk in the Garden with Adam and Eve to spend time with them. But Adam and Eve hid. They were ashamed because they had disobeyed God. *Disobeying God* is called *sin* and they had committed the first sin. God knows everything. He knew Adam and Eve were hiding, and He knew why they were hiding. "Adam, where are you?" God called. Adam said, "I heard you coming, and I was afraid because I was naked; so I hid."
>
> God asked Adam, "Who told you that you were naked? Have you eaten from the Tree of the Knowledge of Good and Evil?" By asking this question, God was giving them a chance to tell Him the truth. Instead of telling God the truth, Adam blamed Eve, and Eve blamed the snake.
>
> Because they disobeyed, God told Adam and Eve that life would change. Now they would work harder to grow their own food. There

would be weeds and thorns in the ground. There would be pain, sickness, and suffering—all because Adam and Eve disobeyed God.

Tape a piece of paper over **VA 1A Creation**. Stress that God still loved Adam and Eve and He still loves us, even when we make wrong choices.

Student Page 1.4
Discuss the pictures on the page and allow students to work independently.

Review

- Was it the snake's fault that Eve ate the fruit? (**No, she chose to eat it.**)
- Was it Eve's fault that Adam ate the fruit? (**No, he made his own choice.**)
- What good things did Adam and Eve have before they disobeyed God? (**a close friendship with God, peace and harmony, plenty of food**)
- What was life like after Adam and Eve disobeyed God? (**Their relationship with God was broken; they had to leave the Garden; they had to work harder to grow their own food; they had pain and sickness.**)

APPLICATION

- Can you think of a time when you disobeyed your mom or dad? (**Answers will vary.**) Did your mom or dad stop loving you when you disobeyed them? (**Of course not!**)
- Did God still love Adam and Eve even after they sinned? (**Yes, God always loves us, even when we do things that are wrong.**)

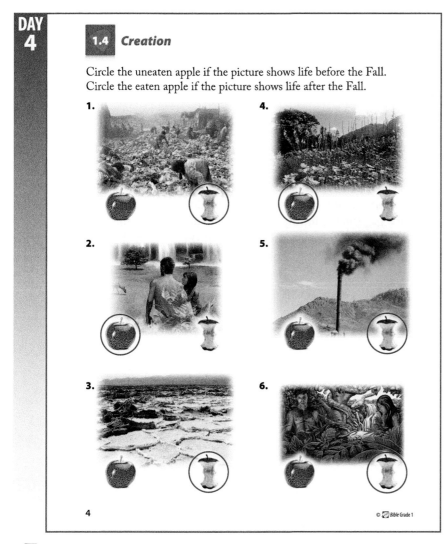

DAY 4

1.4 ***Creation***

Circle the uneaten apple if the picture shows life before the Fall.
Circle the eaten apple if the picture shows life after the Fall.

1.

4.

2.

5.

3.

6.

4

1.5

Creation

Focus: Review and Assessment

★ PREPARATION

Select "Oh What a Variety" from the music CDs. (*Lesson Review*)

Select **VA 1A Creation**. (*Lesson Review*)

Make one copy of **BLM 1A Lesson 1 Test** for each student. (*Directed Instruction*)

REINFORCEMENT

In the first grade level of the Elementary Bible Series, assessments in the form of written tests are presented as an option. Students who are unfamiliar with written assessments may feel anxious about taking tests at first. Others may find pencil-and-paper tasks difficult at this grade level. In order to reduce anxiety and yet obtain a true measure of what students have learned from the lesson, consider the following testing strategies:

1. Read the test to the students and allow them to dictate the answer for you or an aide to write.
2. Allow students to take tests with a partner.
3. Consider informally assessing student knowledge by asking students to retell the Bible truth in their own words or to act out the Bible truth.
4. Encourage students who have difficulty memorizing longer verses to say the Memory Verse in short phrases, after you provide the first word of each phrase.

Lesson Review ★

Repeat the fingerplay from Lesson 1.2 and sing "Oh What a Variety" from the music CDs.

Use **VA 1A Creation** to review the Bible truths in this lesson. Cover the following concepts:

- The Bible is God's Word. It is a special gift from God. We learn to follow God's directions by reading or hearing Bible truths.
- God created the world in six days.
- On the seventh day, God rested. God was not tired, but He rested as an example for us to rest and spend time with Him.
- Before God created Adam and Eve, He made the Garden of Eden special just for them.
- God gave Adam and Eve the job to take care of the earth. Adam was to name all the animals.
- God gave Adam one rule. He told Adam not to eat the fruit from the Tree of the Knowledge of Good and Evil.
- Satan, God's enemy, took the form of a snake in order to tempt Eve to disobey God.
- Adam and Eve disobeyed God by eating the fruit. Then they blamed each other instead of just telling God the truth.
- God told Adam and Eve that they would have to work harder to grow their own food. Then God made Adam and Eve leave the Garden. Now there would be weeds and thorns growing in the ground, and there would be pain, sickness, and suffering in the world.

Directed Instruction ★

Distribute a copy of **BLM 1A Lesson 1 Test** to each student. Read the directions and the words in the Word Bank. Read each sentence and have students complete it before moving to the next one. Explain that the first letter of each missing word has been provided. Have students complete the test by tracing the beginning letter of each answer and then writing the rest of the word. When all students are finished, direct them to put their pencil away. Discuss the test questions and provide answers for immediate feedback. Collect the test papers for assessment.

Notes:

Lesson Preparation

Cain and Abel

2.0

Expected Student Outcomes

KNOW

Cain and Abel, Adam and Eve's sons, choose how they will follow God.

DO

Students will:

- illustrate the first family as well as their own family
- identify scenes that show love for God in a selection of worship settings
- determine a possible consequence for a given choice
- review the Bible truth

APPLY

Students will ask God to help them make wise choices.

Lesson Outline

I. The first family (Gen 4)
II. Worshipping God
  A. God is worthy of our worship (Ps 8:1, 3–4a, 6–9)
  B. Our attitude in worship (Ps 9:1–2)
III. Sin and judgment
  A. Making choices (Ps 4:4a)
  B. Living with the consequences of our choices
IV. Making wise choices
  A. Source of wisdom (James 1:5)
  B. Righteous living (James 3:17–18)

TEACHER'S HEART

You began the school year with great expectation! You invested much time in preparing a nurturing place for the growth of each child. Yet despite your efforts and planning, you may have already been disappointed by the choices that some of your students have made. Like Adam and Eve, these pupils chose to go their own way rather than follow the rules. You can find encouragement, however, in the fact that the Lord sees potential in each of your students, just as He did with Adam and Eve. He knows that under your guidance, each student can flourish and grow.

Just as a vineyard caretaker lifts up new shoots that have fallen and become mired in the mud, you will need to "lift up" your students to help them be established to grow strong and true. As the vineyard caretaker is careful not to damage the stable part of the vine while tending to weaker shoots, so too must you be careful. God helps all branches in the vine bear fruit in His time. Ask God for grace and wisdom to ensure that your words do not wound the spirit or crush the heart of even the most strong-willed child. Proverbs 16:24 reminds us that "Pleasant words are like a honeycomb, sweetness to the soul and health to the bones." Have confidence that the Lord will provide you with the exact words necessary for you to effectively and lovingly minister to your students.

MEMORY VERSE

Psalm 119:30a

MATERIALS

Day 1:
- Picture of a contemporary family or TM-1 Family
- VA 2A Cain and Abel

Day 2:
- No additional materials are needed.

Day 3:
- No additional materials are needed.

Day 4:
- TM-2 Map

Day 5:
- VA 2A Cain and Abel
- BLM 2A Lesson 2 Test

SONGS

The Bible

TEACHER RESOURCES

MacArthur, John. *Before Abraham: Creation, Sin, and the Nature of God*. Thomas Nelson, 2008.
Meade, Starr. *Mighty Acts of God: A Family Bible Story Book*. Crossway Books, 2010.

STUDENT RESOURCES

Curren, Joan E. *The First Brothers*. Concordia Publishing House, 2000.
Egermeier, Elsie. *Egermeier's Bible Story Book*. Warner Press, 2007.

2.1 Cain and Abel

Focus: The First Family

MEMORY VERSE

Psalm 119:30a

MEMORY WORK

Have students practice the Memory Verse throughout the week using the following directions:

- Lead students in repeating the Memory Verse, emphasizing a different word in each repetition, for example, *I* have chosen … ; I *have* chosen … ; I have *chosen* … ; and so on.

★ PREPARATION

Display a PICTURE OF A CONTEMPORARY FAMILY or display **TM-1 Family**. (*Introduction*)

Select **VA 2A Cain and Abel**. (*Directed Instruction*)

Introduction ★

Show students a PICTURE OF A CONTEMPORARY FAMILY or display **TM-1 Family**. Elicit their observations about the picture. (**Answers will vary, but should include the number of people, the setting, and the mood of the people.**) Ask students whether all families have this number of family members. (**No.**) Ask students to state the number of children in their family. (**Answers will vary.**) Have those with no siblings stand. Count the students standing, and then direct them to sit down. Repeat with students who have one sibling, two siblings, etc., until all students have participated. Ask students if they always get along well with their brothers and sisters. (**Answers will vary, but will most likely be no.**) Tell students that today they will learn about the first family on the earth.

Directed Instruction ★

Ask students to state the names of the first two people that God created. (**Adam and Eve**) Question to see if they recall where the first people lived. (**in the Garden of Eden**) Remind students that Adam and Eve disobeyed God. Ask how they disobeyed. (**They ate fruit from the tree that God had told them not to eat from.**)

Display **VA 2A Cain and Abel**. Read the back of VA 2A for today's Bible lesson, defining *offering* as *a gift given to God*. Ask students to identify which person is Cain and which is Abel based on the text that they just heard.

Remind students that Abel willingly *sacrificed*, which means *gave up something of great value*, to honor God. Explain that Cain did not seem to care as much about honoring God. Because Cain grudgingly gave God some of his crops and not the first crops or the best crops, God rejected Cain's offering. Cain's heart was not filled with love for God.

Teach students that the word *jealous* means *to be unhappy that you do not have what someone else has*. Tell them that Cain was jealous because God had accepted Abel's sacrifice but had not accepted his. Cain allowed himself to become angry with God. Explain that God still wanted a close relationship with Cain and told him that if he changed his attitude, God would accept him. Cain refused God's offer and chose to stay jealous and angry.

As the anger in Cain's heart grew, it bubbled up into angry actions. Even though Abel had not done anything bad to Cain, Cain killed him! To make matters worse, Cain lied when God asked him what happened. Cain made poor choices and had to live with the consequences. Explain that *consequences* are defined as *the things that happen after choices are made*.

Student Page 2.1

Remind students that God gave them a special gift—their family. Review that God wants family members to make good choices and to get along with one another. Read the directions on the page and have students complete it independently.

Review

- Cain and Abel had different jobs. What job did each of them do? (**Cain was a farmer; Abel was a shepherd.**)
- Why did God reject Cain's offering? (**Cain did not have the proper attitude toward God as he brought an offering to Him. He did not bring the first or best crops of his harvest; rather, he gave God some of his leftovers.**)
- What did God tell Cain He would do if Cain changed his attitude? (**God would accept Cain.**)
- What two sins did Cain try to hide from God? (**He killed his brother; he lied to God when God asked him where Abel was.**)
- What were the consequences of Cain's choices? (**He would no longer be able to meet with God as he had before; the ground would no longer provide crops in abundance; he would have to travel from place to place and not stay anywhere for very long.**)

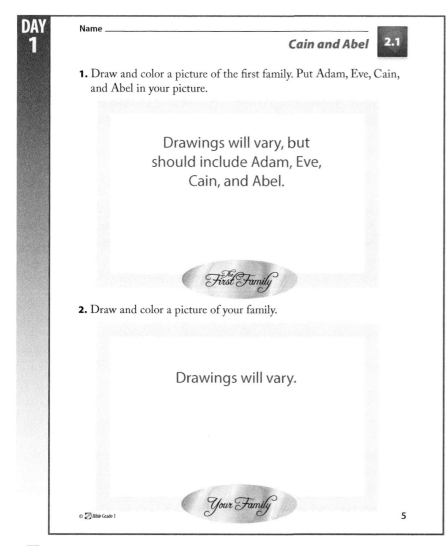

Notes:

DAY 1

Name ______________________________

Cain and Abel **2.1**

1. Draw and color a picture of the first family. Put Adam, Eve, Cain, and Abel in your picture.

Drawings will vary, but should include Adam, Eve, Cain, and Abel.

The First Family

2. Draw and color a picture of your family.

Drawings will vary.

Your Family

APPLICATION

- Remember that Cain was jealous of Abel because God accepted Abel's offering, but not Cain's. Have you ever been jealous? How did it make you feel? (**Possible answers: angry, lonely, sad**)
- Read **Isaiah 55:7**. What does God want you to do when you feel jealous? (**I should turn away from my bad attitudes and actions and ask God to help me. If I confess my sins to God, He is faithful to forgive me according to 1 John 1:9.**)
- What are some different kinds of offerings that you can bring to God? (**Possible answers: money, goods or materials, a thankful heart for my many blessings**)

REINFORCEMENT

Cain's offering was made out of obligation, out of a sense of duty, and merely as a token gift to the Creator. He offered it in the process, or course, of time—not from the first of what he had. Cain gave to God whatever he had at hand, but did not make worshipping God the priority in selecting his offering.

Abel's sacrifice was born out of faith, acknowledging that he was a sinner and asking the Creator to forgive his sin. He selected the first and the best of all that he had to present to God. Abel offered his gift in faith, trusting that God would approve of his offering (Hebrews 11:4). All that is offered to God—time, talents, and monetary gifts—should be the best available.

2.2 Cain and Abel

Focus: Worshipping God

EXTENSION

2A Take students on a tour of the worship center or the sanctuary where chapel will be held. Familiarize students with different aspects of the environment, which may include a cross, a podium, a baptistery, a choir loft, Bibles, hymnals, and chairs or pews. If the room has pictures designed in stained glass, point out familiar Bible scenes. Show students where they will sit when they come to the chapel service. Help students to develop a sense of reverence whenever they enter the sanctuary.

Introduction

Review that God created everything, including the first family of Adam, Eve, Cain, and Abel. Remind students that Abel brought a pleasing offering to God. Ask students if they have ever given an offering to God. (**Answers will vary.**) Tell them that one of the best offerings they can give Him is their worship. Define the word *worship* as *telling God that He is worthy, or deserving, of praise*. Share that today's lesson is about worshipping God.

Directed Instruction

Instruct students to listen for some of the things that God made as you read **Psalm 8:1**, **3–4a**, and **6–9**. (**the earth, the heavens, the moon, the stars, people, the land animals, the birds, the fishes**) Remind them of the great beauty that God provided for people in His Creation. Model a prayer of worship by leading students in a brief prayer of praise.

Inform students that they will be attending chapel services this year. Ask students to think about what type of activities they will be participating in when they attend chapel this year. (**Answers will vary.**) Lead students to conclude that singing, praying, listening, and reading the Bible are all ways to worship God. Tell students that when they attend chapel, they are there to worship God. Direct students to listen for the action words that describe worship after each "I will . . ." statement as you read **Psalm 9:1–2**. (**praise, tell, be glad and rejoice, sing**) Tell students that their heart's attitude during worship is very important to God. Remind students that Cain's offering would have been acceptable to God had Cain's actions shown sincere worship for the Lord.

Read the following fictional story:

> Rosa was having a bad day. When she got up, she couldn't find one of her new tennis shoes, so she had to wear her old shoes to school instead. As she unpacked her backpack, Rosa remembered that her library book was still on the kitchen table. Today was library day, but now she could not check out a new book. At lunchtime, Rosa stared angrily into her lunch bag. She did not like the burrito that Mama had prepared. Rosa felt as if the day just could not get any worse!
>
> After lunch, her teacher, Mrs. Winters, told the students that it was time to go to chapel. Most of her classmates were very excited as they walked quietly to the sanctuary, but Rosa just shuffled along. As they found their seats, Rosa sat down with a thud and crossed her arms. Although she sang the songs, Rosa was not concentrating on the words. When the guest speaker began to talk, Rosa picked up a hymnal and flipped through the pages; she was not listening to the message. When the speaker ended the chapel service with a prayer, Rosa was glad that chapel was over and that she could return to the classroom.

Ask students if Rosa truly worshipped God while she was at chapel. (**No.**) Invite students to share how they know that she did not truly worship

God. (**Possible answers: She shuffled along; she sat down with a thud and crossed her arms; she did not concentrate on the words of the songs; she did not listen to the speaker's message; she did not think about God at all; she was glad that chapel was over.**) Tell students that God is pleased when they truly praise Him, when they tell Him how much they love Him, when they are glad to be in the church or the worship center, and when they sing worship songs from their heart.

Student Page 2.2

Read the directions and discuss the pictures for Exercise 1. Check over the exercise with students and discuss the pictures, as necessary. Read each word needed for students to complete Exercises 2–10.

Review

- When you worship, what are you telling God? (**that He is worthy, or deserving, of praise**)
- What does God care about most as you worship? (**our heart attitude**)
- What activities do you participate in as you worship? (**Possible answers: singing, praying, listening to the message, reading the Bible**)

DAY 2

2.2 ***Cain and Abel***

1. Circle the pictures that show students worshipping God.

God is pleased when you worship Him with a good attitude. Color the heart next to the things that you can do to show your love for God when you worship.

2. praise God
3. chew gum
4. talk to my neighbor
5. sing
6. read the Bible
7. pray
8. sleep
9. listen
10. wiggle

6 © Bible Grade 1

APPLICATION

- Why do you want to worship God? (**Possible answers: to tell Him that I love Him, to thank Him for loving me, to praise Him for His Creation**)
- How can you prepare your heart for worship? (**Answers will vary, but should include asking God to help me to keep my focus on Him.**)

REINFORCEMENT

Music has traditionally played an important role in Christian worship, and hymns and spiritual songs have been a component of worship from the beginning of the Church. In recent years contemporary music has become popular for both corporate and personal worship.

Musician and composer, Andraé Crouch, is one Christian artist who has contributed substantially to the growing number of worship songs sung in churches today. Andraé, who got his start singing and playing the piano at his father's church before he was even 10 years old, has become an influential figure in the field of contemporary gospel music. In the early sixties, Andraé formed a group of gospel singers and eventually began recording albums. He continued to write and produce music, winning Grammy and Dove awards for both Christian and secular music. Andraé has made a lifelong commitment to worship and to bring the message of salvation to the world through his music.

2.3 Cain and Abel

Focus: Sin and Judgment

EXTENSION

3A Read **Acts 3:19a**. Get two sheets of paper and write on one *God* and on the other *sin*. Post the papers on opposite sides of the room. Tell students that *repent* means *to turn away from or to move in the opposite direction of*. To illustrate, instruct students to stand in a straight line, like soldiers, facing the paper labeled *sin*. Have students march in that direction and then tell them, "Halt!" or "Stop!" Face the students and explain how soldiers turn in the opposite direction by doing an about-face turn. Demonstrate how to make the turn by placing one foot behind the other and quickly pivoting 180 degrees to face the opposite direction. Allow students to practice an about-face turn at your command. Tell them that when they repent, or turn away from sin and move back toward God, they are making a good choice. God is pleased with repentance. Have students walk toward the paper labeled *God* before returning to their seats.

Introduction

Select a volunteer to tell what Adam and Eve chose to do that disobeyed God's rule. (**They ate fruit from the Tree of the Knowledge of Good and Evil.**) Remind students that when they choose to disobey God, they sin. Explain that when they listen to or read God's Word, God guides them to make good choices.

Inform students that whenever they make a choice, something happens. Good things usually happen when people make good choices, and bad things usually happen when people make bad choices. Provide one or two contemporary examples, such as when a boy wears his sweater, he will not get cold at recess, and when a girl does not eat her dinner, she gets hungry. Ask students to recall the consequence that Adam and Eve had for disobeying God. (**They had to work harder to grow their own food. They had to leave the Garden of Eden, the perfect place where they had lived before the Fall.**) Tell students that this made Adam and Eve very sad, but they had to live with the consequences of their choice. Today's lesson is about the consequences of Abel's choices and Cain's choices.

Directed Instruction

Review the choices that Abel and Cain made. (**Abel selected a firstborn lamb for his offering and came to God with a worshipful heart. Cain did not bring the first or best crops from his field; he killed his brother out of anger and jealousy, and then lied to God when asked about Abel.**) Ask students to tell who sinned in this week's Bible lesson, Cain or Abel. (**Cain**)

Discuss and identify the consequences of Abel's and Cain's choices. (**God accepted Abel's offering; He was pleased with Abel's worshipful heart. However, God did not accept Cain's offering. He told Cain he would have to work harder for his crops and must travel from place to place.**) Point out that Abel made good choices and had good consequences—God accepted his offering. Cain made bad choices, including refusing to change when God gave him the chance to. Cain's bad consequences were that he had to work harder for his crops, and he had to move around. Cain was sad about the consequences of his choices, but he had to accept them.

Student Page 2.3

Read the directions aloud. Review the pictures on the left-hand side of the page by describing the action that is taking place in each picture. Ask the volunteers to tell whether each child pictured is making a good choice or a bad choice. Direct students to complete the page. Review the answers together in class by asking students to explain their answer choices.

Review

- What consequence did Adam and Eve have for eating the fruit from the Tree of the Knowledge of Good and Evil? (**Answers will vary, but should include that they had to leave the Garden of Eden.**)
- Abel offered God a perfect, firstborn lamb. What was the consequence for his choice? (**God accepted Abel's offering.**)

- Cain had a poor attitude when he made his offering to God. What was the consequence? (**God did not accept Cain's offering.**)
- What consequence did Cain have for killing his brother and lying to God about what happened? (**Cain had to work harder to produce crops and was forced to move from place to place.**)

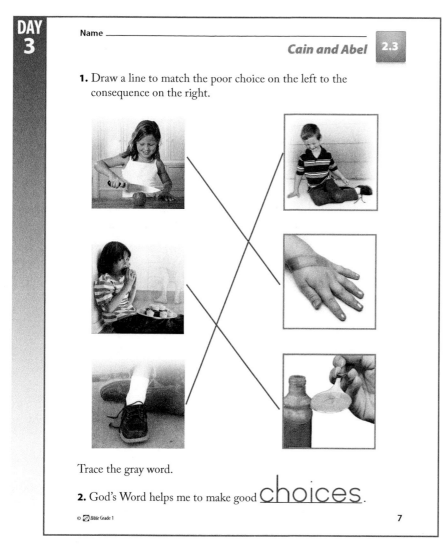

Notes:

DAY 3

Name ______________________________

Cain and Abel 2.3

1. Draw a line to match the poor choice on the left to the consequence on the right.

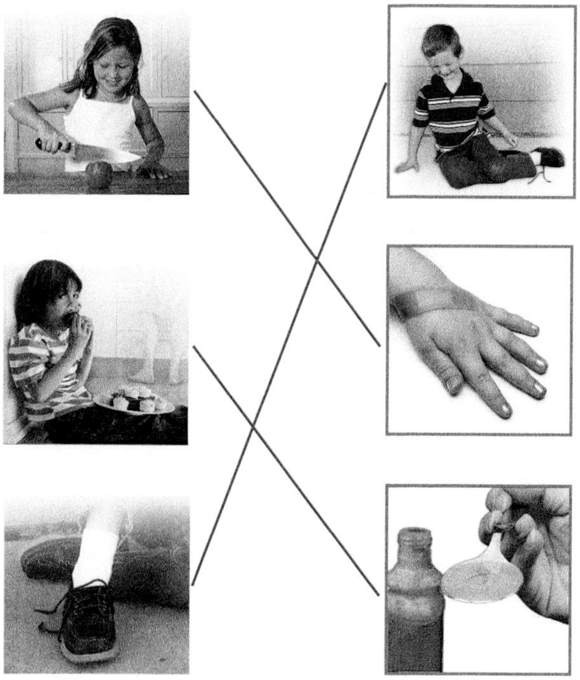

Trace the gray word.

2. God's Word helps me to make good choices.

© Bible Grade 1 7

APPLICATION

- One of the ways that Cain sinned was in allowing his anger to lead him into sin. God says that although you may feel angry at times, you should not sin (Psalm 4:4a). What are some things that you can do when you are angry so that you will not sin? (**Possible answers: I can tell my feelings to a parent; I can pray.**)
- Remind students that all choices have consequences. If Cain had made other choices, what might the consequences have been? (**Possible answers: If Cain had brought his best offering to God with a good attitude, God would have accepted his offering; if Cain had not gotten angry at his brother, he would not have killed Abel; if Cain had been thankful for the opportunity to worship God and for his garden crops, God would have allowed him to stay on his land and have good harvests.**)
- Ask volunteers to share a time when they made a poor choice and the resulting consequence of that choice. Have other students identify positive, alternate choices that could have been made. Brainstorm other consequences that might have resulted from a better choice. (**Answers will vary.**)

2.4 Cain and Abel

Focus: Making Wise Choices

★ PREPARATION

Display **TM-2 Map**. (*Introduction, Directed Instruction*)

Select "The Bible" from the music CDs. (*Directed Instruction*)

EXTENSION

4A Read the following scenarios to students and ask them to suggest wise solutions to the problems. Help students realize that God can teach them how to make wise choices and have a pure heart as they pray and read the Bible.

1. Kyra plans to go to the zoo on Friday with her dad; however Grandpa calls and says that he's sick and needs to go to the doctor on Friday to get some medicine. Kyra feels disappointed because Dad agrees to take Grandpa to the doctor, which means there will not be enough time to go to the zoo. How can Kyra show a good attitude about missing the trip to the zoo? (**Answers will vary.**)
2. Marcos is playing on the playground when Ben pushes him out of the way to go down the slide first. Marcos wants to push him back, but he knows that would be wrong. Even though Marcos is angry, what should he do? (**Answers will vary.**)

Introduction ★

Display **TM-2 Map** and give students a moment to look at the map. Then hold up a Bible. Tell students that the map and the Bible are similar. Both the map and the Bible give directions. The map shows how to get from place to place; the Bible shows how to live.

Directed Instruction ★

Explore the map together, noting the location of various buildings, the park and the lake, the railroad tracks, and the streets. Have students locate Grace Christian School, the starting point for a brother and sister, Kevin and Emily, to walk home. Identify Kevin and Emily's house. Ask the following questions:

- On which street is Kevin and Emily's house? (**Maple Street**). Guide students to see that there are two ways that the children could walk home from school.
- Which route is shorter? (**Oak Street**) Point out the route from school to home via Oak Street.
- Why might the brother and sister want to walk home on Oak Street? (**Oak Street is shorter, so they would be home faster.**)
- Explain that their mom always wants the children to walk home on Maple Street. Indicate the route from school to home via Maple Street.
- Why would their mom tell the children to walk on Maple Street instead of Oak Street? (**Oak Street is more dangerous because it is near the railroad tracks, the electric company, and Deep Lake. On Maple Street, they would pass a church, Grandma's house, and the park on the way home.**)

Conclude that the shortest or easiest way to do something may not always be the best way. Students should listen to those who love them and guide them to make good choices. Ask students for examples of other people who may offer wise advice besides parents. (**Possible answers: teachers, pastors, grandparents, guardians**) Why would God be the best one to go to for wise advice? (**God loves us very much and He knows all our needs.**)

Read **James 1:5**. Ask students to share ways that God speaks to them and helps them to make wise choices. (**Answers will vary, but should include that God speaks to them through the Bible, through the teaching of the Word, and through prayer.**) Explain that even when parents are not there to talk to, God is always listening to the student's prayers and speaking to them through His Word, the Bible. It makes Him very happy when they ask Him to guide them in making good decisions.

Read **James 3:17–18**. Remind students that both Cain and Abel brought an offering to God, but only Abel's offering showed that he had made a wise decision about what to offer, when to offer it, and how to offer it. Explain to students that when they ask God for wisdom and follow His guidance, the result is that they become more and more like Jesus—pure, peace-loving, merciful, and sincere. Their life is righteous. *Righteous* means *honoring God by doing what He says.*

Sing "The Bible" from the music CDs. The lyrics are on the resources CD. Review the words and lead students in singing the song.

Student Page 2.4

Read the directions for each exercise one by one, allowing students time to complete each exercise before moving on to the next one. Review the answers in class.

Review

- Why is the shortest or easiest way not always the best choice? (**Sometimes there are dangers along the way.**)
- Who can you go to for wise advice? (**Possible answers: parents, grandparents, guardians, teachers, pastors**)
- Who will always be there to help you make wise choices, even when your parents or other people are not around? (**God**)
- What word means *honoring God by doing what He says*? (**righteous**)
- What is the best way to live a righteous life? (**by asking God for wisdom and following His guidance**)

APPLICATION

- Think about how Cain and Abel brought their sacrifices to God when they came to worship Him. What does this Bible truth teach you about worship? (**It teaches me that my heart attitude matters to God. I cannot really worship if my attitude is wrong.**)
- How can you use what you learn in the Bible to make good decisions? (**I can remember what the Bible truth tells me about people, their actions, and their attitudes. I can learn what pleases God from His Word.**)

DAY 4

2.4 *Cain and Abel*

1. Write the name of the brother who chose to give his best to God.

Abel

Cain **Abel**

2. Circle the picture of the offering that God accepted.

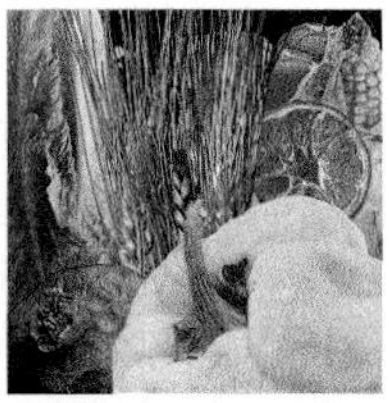

3. Color the spaces that have a star. Find the hidden word that completes the sentence. Write that word.

4. When I need help to make wise choices, I will ask God.

8 © Bible Grade 1

2.5 Cain and Abel

Focus: Review and Assessment

★ ***PREPARATION***

Select **VA 2A Cain and Abel**. (*Lesson Review*)

Duplicate **BLM 2A Lesson 2 Test** and provide a copy for each student. (*Directed Instruction*)

Lesson Review ★

Use **VA 2A Cain and Abel** to review the Bible truths in this lesson. Cover the following concepts:

- Cain and Abel, the first brothers born into the world, were the sons of Adam and Eve. These brothers both brought sacrifices to the Lord.
- Because Abel loved God, he chose to give up one of his firstborn lambs as a sacrifice to the Lord.
- Cain did not give the first or the best fruits of his fields to God. He only sacrificed his leftovers, and he did that with a poor attitude.
- God accepted Abel's offering, but He refused Cain's offering because Cain did not have a proper attitude toward God.
- All choices have consequences. Cain made bad choices. He let his jealousy and anger take over. He killed his brother and lied to God, even though God had given him a chance to do right. Cain had to live with the sad consequences of these poor choices.
- God cares most about heart attitudes when people worship.
- God is pleased when people truly praise Him by telling Him how much they love Him, by worshipping Him gladly, and by singing songs of praise from their heart.
- God is always present to help people make wise choices. He speaks to them through His Word, the Bible. Children can ask their parents, grandparents, guardians, teachers, and pastors for help in making wise choices.
- When a person has a right attitude toward God and lives in a way that honors Him, he or she lives a righteous life.

Directed Instruction ★

Distribute a copy of **BLM 2A Lesson 2 Test** to each student. Read the directions and the words in the Word Bank. Read each sentence and have students complete it before moving to the next one. Explain that the first letter of each missing word has been provided and that they are to trace over each one when writing the words. Have students complete the test. When all students are finished, direct them to put their pencil away. Discuss the test questions and provide answers for immediate feedback. Collect the test papers for assessment.

Notes:

Lesson Preparation
Noah

3.0

Expected Student Outcomes

KNOW

God is faithful to deliver Noah and his family. Noah's descendants rebel against God and He confuses their language at the Tower of Babel.

DO

Students will:
- complete a cloze activity to review the Bible truth
- identify character qualities of Noah
- complete sentences to demonstrate understanding of the Bible truth
- identify ways to bring glory to God
- review a story about showing God's love to others

APPLY

Students will conclude that sin has consequences and God keeps His promises.

Lesson Outline

I. Noah obeys God (Gen 6:5–7:24)
   A. God floods the earth
II. God's promise (Gen 8:1–9:17)
   A. Noah honors God
   B. The rainbow
III. The Tower of Babel (Gen 10–11)
   A. God gives directions
   B. The people disobey God
   C. Seeking to glorify God, not ourselves
IV. Accepting others

TEACHER'S HEART

Do you ever wonder how Noah stayed faithful in a violent and corrupt world? He was 500 years old, and was surrounded by people who had forgotten God, yet he was so faithful that he began building a boat for rain he'd never witnessed. Then Noah faithfully kept building the ark before God closed the door—confirmation that Noah's trust in God was justified.

How did Noah maintain his faith? We know only that Noah was righteous, blameless, and that he walked with God (Genesis 6:9). The task God gave Noah did not make sense until almost 100 years after it was begun. Yet, Noah walked with God by faith, not by sight (2 Corinthians 5:7). Noah did not need things to make sense in order to place his trust in God.

Are you struggling with a problem that doesn't make sense? Are you waiting for an answer to prayer that is long in coming? Are you having a hard time staying faithful in the midst of your culture? Walk with God. Give Him your time, read His Word, be in prayer, and allow God to renew your mind. God's will is perfect, even when it doesn't make sense.

MEMORY VERSE

Proverbs 3:5–6a

MATERIALS

Day 1:
- Umbrella
- VA 3A Noah
- PP-1 We Trust God (*Extension*)
- BLM 3A Ark, card stock (*Extension*)

Day 2:
- Globe
- BLM 3B Origami (*Extension*)

Day 3:
- Worksheet
- VA 3B The Tower of Babel
- Globe
- BLM 3C The Tower of Babel, card stock, envelopes (*Extension*)

Day 4:
- Globe
- Russian pancakes (*Extension*)

Day 5:
- VA 3A Noah, VA 3B The Tower of Babel
- BLM 3D Lesson 3 Test

SONGS

Noah Was a Faithful Man

TEACHER RESOURCES

Wiersbe, Warren W. *Be Basic (Genesis 1–11)*. David C. Cook, 1998.

STUDENT RESOURCES

Models of Noah's ark. Kits can be ordered online from various websites.

Stewart, Dorothy M. *It's Hard to Hurry When You're a Snail*. Lion Children's Books, 2009.

3.1 Noah

Focus: Noah Obeys God

MEMORY VERSE

Proverbs 3:5–6a

MEMORY WORK

- Explain that *to trust God* means *to count on God*. People can trust God because He has the ability, strength, and power to do all that He has promised. *To acknowledge God* means *to agree that God is in control*. Divide the class into two groups. Tell each group to jump as they say one word from the Memory Verse, alternating between the groups. The group whose turn it is to jump for the word *acknowledge* should jump three times, once for each syllable. Have both groups say the Scripture reference.

★ PREPARATION

Have an UMBRELLA on hand. (*Introduction, Directed Instruction*)

Select **VA 3A Noah**. (*Directed Instruction*)

Select "Noah Was a Faithful Man" from the music CDs. (*Directed Instruction*)

EXTENSION

1A To review the Bible lesson and to help students understand the meaning of the Memory Verse, show students **PP-1 We Trust God**.

1B Make a copy of **BLM 3A Ark** on CARD STOCK for each student. Distribute the copies. Have students write their name on the back of the ark, color the ark, and turn in their paper. Follow the directions on the blackline master. Distribute the prepared arks. Invite students to use the completed ark and animal strip to retell the Bible truth.

Introduction ★

Open your UMBRELLA as you tell students that you are preparing for rain inside the classroom. Be dramatic while you convince them that it really could rain inside. Look up to see if the rain is coming and put out your hand as if to feel for drops of rain. Show surprise when students laugh or try to tell you that you do not need the umbrella.

Directed Instruction ★

Set the umbrella near you and show students **VA 3A Noah**. Inform students that today's Bible truth is about Noah, a man the Bible says walked with God. Read the Bible truth from the back of VA 3A.

Dramatically express your belief that it is going to rain inside today. Mention that you see some students who look as if they doubt that it will rain inside. Ask students why they do not believe your statement, and choose a volunteer to explain why it probably will not rain in your classroom. (**Rain comes from rain clouds.**)

Remind students that Noah trusted God and believed that what God said would happen would really occur. Because of this trust, Noah worked on the ark even though it took many, many years. Noah followed God's directions even though he might not have understood what a flood was. Review for students that *to trust God* means *to count on God*. Ask students to suggest many things that Noah counted on God to provide. (**Possible answers: direction, food for the animals and people, safety**)

Put your umbrella away. Help students conclude that although God told Noah about the rain, God did not tell you to expect rain in the classroom. Make sure students understand that they must listen to God carefully. They do not decide when miracles will happen; God does.

Sing "Noah Was a Faithful Man" from the music CDs. Practice the song several times during the week. Consider breaking your class into groups and having each group sing one stanza. Have the students join together to sing the chorus.

Student Page 3.1

Read the directions and the text. Assist students in completing the page. Allow them to color the animals in Exercises 2–5, as desired.

Review

- Why did God flood the earth? (**The people stopped listening to God. They were wicked and evil.**)
- Why did God decide to save Noah and his family? (**Noah was the only person listening to God and doing the right thing.**)
- How did Noah know what to do? (**God told Noah exactly how to build the ark. God told Noah the kind of wood to use, the size the ark was to be, and how to keep it watertight.**)

• How long did it take Noah to build the ark? (**about 100 years**) How long did it rain? (**40 days and 40 nights**) How long was the earth covered with water? (**150 days**)

Notes:

DAY 1

Name ____________________

Noah **3.1**

1. Use the Word Bank to complete the sentences.

WORD BANK
boat
Noah
trusted
rain

God told Noah to build a big ___boat___. The big boat was the ark. Noah ___trusted___ and obeyed God. Noah worked on the ark for about 100 years! Then the ___rain___ fell. The earth was flooded. God kept ___Noah___ and his family safe.

Color two animals in each row that tell about Noah.

© Bible Grade 1 9

APPLICATION

- Why do you think the people who lived before the Flood disobeyed God over and over again? (**Answers will vary, but should include that the people did not pay attention to God's directions; they neither trusted nor acknowledged God.**)
- Is it always easy to follow God's directions and make good choices? (**It is not easy, but God will help us make good choices when we come to Him in prayer.**)
- What can you do to stay close to God? (**I can pray, read the Bible, listen to teaching, worship Him, show love for others.**)

REINFORCEMENT

Ever since the Fall, all people have been born with a sinful nature. Because God cannot tolerate sin, sinful people are separated from Him. Human beings can do nothing to bridge the separation between God and people. God, through His grace and love, sent His Son to die for all people and to pay the price for sin and restore people to fellowship with God.

First graders are concrete thinkers and understand that when a rule is broken, a consequence follows. They are able to grasp that the sins of the wicked people in Noah's day were met with the consequence of destruction. God saved Noah and his family because Noah placed his faith and trust in God. It is faith and trust in Jesus' redeeming work on the cross that saves us as well.

3.2 Noah

Focus: God's Promise

★ PREPARATION

Have a GLOBE available. (*Directed Instruction*)

EXTENSION

2A Print a copy of **BLM 3B Origami** for you and each student. Cut out the figure on each paper as indicated. This activity is designed to help students understand how difficult it was for Noah to build the ark without knowing what it would look like when it was finished. Distribute the precut figures to the students. Do not tell the students what they are making. Guide students to make the origami dove as you follow the directions on the blackline master. When the dove is completed, invite students to color the beak and add a paper olive branch. Explain that Noah sent out a dove to see if the floodwaters had receded. When the dove brought back a freshly plucked olive leaf, Noah knew that it would soon be safe to leave the ark.

Introduction

Ask students if they have ever seen a rainbow. (**Answers will vary.**) Invite a few students to share where they saw the rainbow, its size, and all its colors. Explain that they may see a rainbow whenever sunlight passes through raindrops in the clouds at just the right angle. When the white light passes through the droplets of water, the light is divided into the various colors of the spectrum.

Directed Instruction ★

Remind students that after the Flood was over, Noah gave God a sacrificial offering. God was pleased that Noah honored Him in this way. (*Honor* means *to show respect*.) Even though God knew that people would continue to sin, He was pleased with Noah's offering and He promised never to destroy the whole earth with a flood again. God placed a beautiful rainbow in a cloud in the sky! The rainbow is the sign of God's promise.

Ask students to recall how sin entered the world. Remind them that God created a beautiful world and placed Adam and Eve in the Garden of Eden. God gave His people a choice to obey Him, but they did not obey. God allows everyone to choose whether or not they will yield to Him and follow His directions. If people love Him, they will follow His directions (John 14:15).

Select a volunteer to tell you what disobedience to God is called. (**sin**) Recall that Adam and Eve decided not to follow God's directions. Remind students that God directed Cain to worship Him with a pure heart, but that Cain chose anger and jealousy over love and trust for God. Ask students to share why God was pleased with both Abel and Noah's offerings, but rejected Cain's. (**Both Abel and Noah had the right attitude; Cain did not. Abel brought God one of his best animals for a sacrifice; Noah brought a truly thankful heart for God's deliverance from the floodwaters; Cain brought his offering when he got around to it.**)

Tell students that God gave Noah and his sons directions after the Flood. His directions are written in the Bible in the book of Genesis, the first book in the Bible. Read **Genesis 9:1**. Ask students to recall the directions that God gave Noah and his sons. (**Be fruitful and multiply; fill the earth.**) Explain that being *fruitful* means *to have lots of children and grandchildren*. Show the GLOBE as you explain that the ark may have landed in what is modern-day Turkey. From there, God wanted lots of people to spread out over the entire earth.

Student Page 3.2

Read the directions and the text. Assist students in completing the exercises. Direct students to color the rainbow with the same colors God used to create the first rainbow. Tell students to overlap the colors slightly. Starting at the top, the colors are red, orange, yellow, green, blue, and purple. Write the names of the colors on the board for students to follow.

Review

- When was it safe for Noah and his family to leave the ark? (**when the land was dry**)
- What did Noah do when he left the ark? (**He built an altar and made an offering to God.**) Was God pleased with Noah's offering? (**Yes.**)
- What promise did God make to Noah? (**God promised that He would never destroy the earth again through a flood.**)
- What sign reminds you of God's promise? (**the rainbow**)

Notes:

APPLICATION

- God gave Noah and his sons very important directions. How do you know God's directions for your life? (**God has given me directions in His Word, the Bible.**)
- How can you learn more about God's directions in the Bible? (**Answers will vary, but should include listening to parents and teachers, and reading the Bible when I am able.**)
- Each time you learn about how God wants you to live, how should you follow His directions? (**I should follow His directions right away with a good attitude.**)

DAY 2

3.2 *Noah*

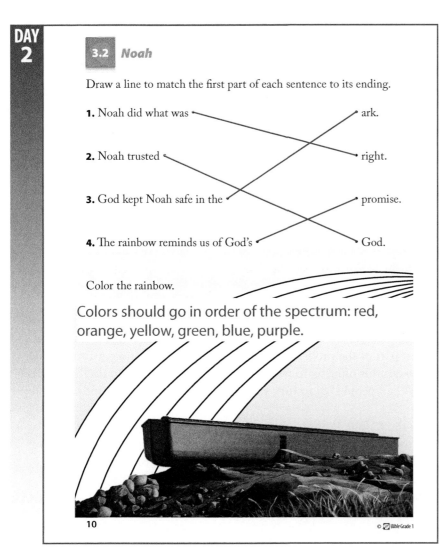

Draw a line to match the first part of each sentence to its ending.

1. Noah did what was	ark.
2. Noah trusted	right.
3. God kept Noah safe in the	promise.
4. The rainbow reminds us of God's	God.

(Answer lines drawn: 1 → right.; 2 → God.; 3 → ark.; 4 → promise.)

Color the rainbow.

Colors should go in order of the spectrum: red, orange, yellow, green, blue, purple.

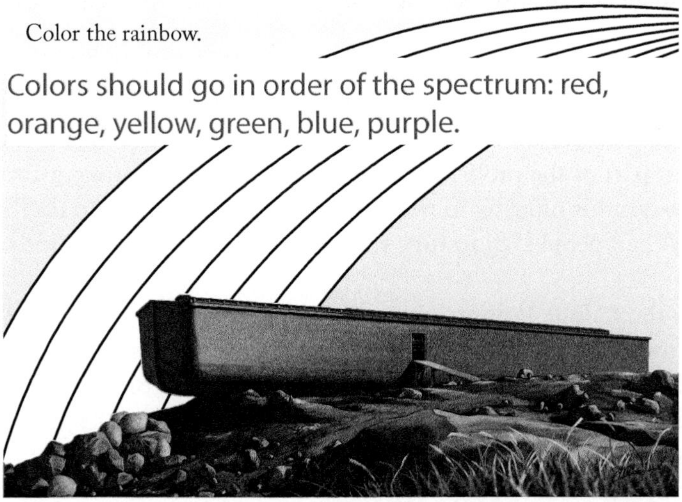

10

© Bible Grade 1

3.3 Noah

Focus: The Tower of Babel

★ PREPARATION

Cut several sheets of various colors of paper into three or four large pieces each. Angle the cuts so that the original sheets of paper can be reassembled like a jigsaw puzzle. Prepare enough pieces to give each student one cut piece. (*Introduction*)

Set aside a WORKSHEET that one of your students has done, but one on which the student has forgotten to write his or her name on the line at the top. (*Directed Instruction*)

Select **VA 3B The Tower of Babel**. (*Directed Instruction*)

Have a GLOBE available. (*Directed Instruction*)

EXTENSION

3A Print one copy of **BLM 3C The Tower of Babel** on CARD STOCK for each student. Distribute the copies. Instruct students to color the tower and cut out the puzzle pieces. Provide ENVELOPES for students to use to take their puzzle home. Review ways for students to show their family the puzzle and tell family members about the Bible truth.

Introduction ★

When God mixed up the languages at the Tower of Babel, everyone had to search to find other people whose language they could understand. To help students understand the concept of finding similarities, give each student one piece of the colored paper that you cut in advance. Students need to quickly find the others with the same color and reassemble the pieces like a puzzle.

Gather the pieces, mix them up, and pass them out again. Tell students that this time they must put the puzzles together without talking.

Help students reflect on the methods they used to quickly find each other. Ask students to share how the activity was different when they could not talk. Explain that in today's lesson students will be learning about a group of people who could not understand one another's words.

Directed Instruction ★

Hold up the WORKSHEET that has no student's name on it. Using a dramatic voice, shake your head and explain to students that you do not know who did the worksheet. Tell students that a key direction in first grade is for all students to write their name at the top of each paper. Following directions is very important to keep the class running smoothly.

Remind students that God gave people the Bible. It tells about God and includes directions on how to live. Ask students to recall what happened to Adam and Eve when they did not follow God's directions. (**Sin entered the world. Adam and Eve had to leave the Garden of Eden.**)

Display **VA 3B The Tower of Babel**. Before reading the text, challenge students to listen to God's directions. Read the back of VA 3B. Ask how the people responded to God's directions. (**The people disobeyed God by staying in one place.**) What did God do because the people disobeyed? (**He confused their language so that they would have no choice but to spread throughout the earth.**)

Remind students that the people did not follow God's directions because they were more concerned about making themselves famous and bringing glory to themselves. Their attitude was wrong, and that bad attitude was the biggest part of the problem. Similarly, Cain had the wrong attitude when he brought his offering to the Lord. He was not willing to do things God's way. When people fail to turn their hearts to God, they fall into sin.

Show the GLOBE. Point to Iraq, the approximate modern-day location of the Tower of Babel, then point out each continent on which people now live. Briefly mention some of the languages spoken on each continent. (Examples: *Africa*: Bantu, Lingala, Portuguese, French, English; *Asia*: Mandarin, Cantonese, Hindi; *North America*: English, French; *South America*: Spanish, Portuguese)

Student Page 3.3

Read both of the scenarios aloud, encouraging students to follow along. Afterward, tell them to answer the questions. Discuss the ways that each child pictured is bringing glory to God. Then, discuss various situations that your students may wish to pray about. Encourage students to share ways that God has answered their prayers.

Review

- What did God tell the people to do? (**to keep having children and spread throughout the whole earth**)
- What did the people do instead of listening to God? (**They built a city so they could stay together.**)
- Why did the people start building a tower? (**They wanted to bring glory to themselves, not to God.**)
- How tall had the people planned to build the tower? (**all the way up to heaven**)
- How did God make sure that the people followed His directions? (**He confused their language so that they could not understand each other.**)

DAY 3

Name ______________________________

Noah **3.3**

Listen to each story. Write **yes** or **no** to answer each question.

1. Amina did not like to paint pictures. She did not think that her pictures were as pretty as the other children's pictures. One day her teacher asked her to paint a picture of a flower. Amina didn't want to paint, so she prayed. "God," she said, "Help me to paint a flower." Then Amina painted a beautiful flower! She told her teacher how God had helped her to paint well.

Did Amina bring glory to God? ___yes___

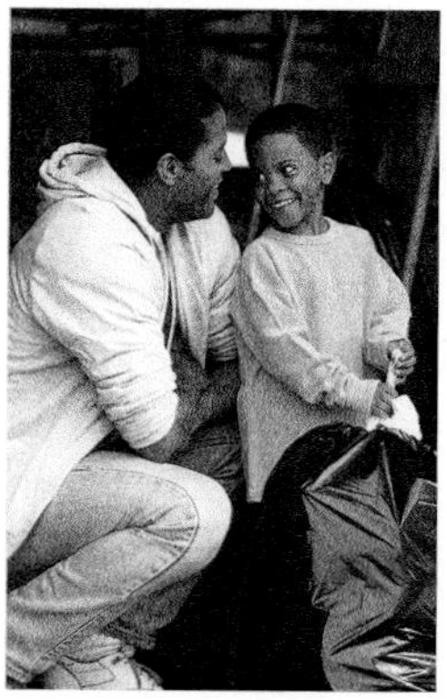

2. Keon liked to help his dad. On Saturday, Keon's dad asked Keon to help rake the leaves and put the leaves in trash bags. Keon thought that the leaves would be too heavy. Keon prayed, "Dear God, help me to lift the heavy bags of leaves to please You and to help my dad." God helped Keon! Keon lifted all the heavy bags. He told his dad how God had helped him.

Did Keon bring glory to God?

___yes___

APPLICATION

- Why do you think God chose not to punish the people for building the tower, but instead chose to scatter them throughout the earth? (**Answers will vary, but should include that He loved them and wanted to give them another chance to do His will. God had also promised not to destroy the earth through a flood ever again.**)
- Have you ever done something wrong, but not received the punishment you deserved? How did that feel? (**Possible answers: glad, thankful**)
- Even though all people have sinned, how did God make a way for people to be free from the punishment they deserve? (**Jesus died on the cross to pay for our sins. Anyone who believes in Jesus, repents of his or her sin, and trusts in Jesus will be forgiven.**)

REINFORCEMENT

There are over 6,000 languages spoken in the world today. That number seems even larger considering the fact that the entire Bible has been translated into only about 400 of those languages. Altogether, only about one-third of the world's spoken languages have any translated Scripture at all. Organizations, such as Wycliffe Bible Translators and New Tribes Mission, are working to bring the Scriptures to the approximately 350 million people in the world who do not have the Bible in their own language.

3.4 Noah

Focus: Accepting Others

★ PREPARATION

Have a GLOBE available. (*Directed Instruction*)

EXTENSION

4A Invite someone who speaks another language to visit your classroom. Ask your guest to read a familiar story or sing a familiar song in his or her language, but do not tell the students that your guest will speak a different language. Allow the students to be surprised by hearing something that sounds familiar, but different, from what they are used to. If your guest is from another country, tell students where the country is located. Ask your guest to teach the class a few words such as *good morning, hello, good-bye*, or *Jesus*.

4B *Blini*, RUSSIAN PANCAKES, are a traditional Russian food. They can be made with different types of flour and in different thicknesses. Keeping student food allergies in mind, ask a parent to make *blini* for the class. Several recipes are available on the Internet. Serve the *blini* with jam or powdered sugar for a fun enhancement to today's story.

Introduction

Begin class today by saying, "Dobroye utro" ('dō·brā 'o͞o·trä). Explain that this means *good morning* in Russian. Tell students that today they will be learning about a girl from Russia.

Directed Instruction ★

Read the following story, and instruct students to listen for the things that Sveta, the girl in the story, brought to share with her classmates:

Bethany loved being in first grade! She loved drawing pictures, learning to read the Bible, and listening to her teacher, Mrs. Howes. More than anything else, Bethany loved being with her best friend, Kim. The two girls sat right next to each other in class. They were so much alike that Mrs. Howes teased that they could be twins.

Bethany walked into class one day and noticed a new little girl in Kim's seat. Right away, Bethany knew there must be some mistake. Kim was supposed to sit there! Bethany went to the little girl and told her that she was in the wrong seat. But the little girl didn't move or even say anything! Bethany couldn't understand why the girl was silent.

Then Mrs. Howes introduced the new girl to the class. Her name was Sveta. Sveta was a girl from Russia who had been adopted by an American family. Sveta was just starting to learn English. Mrs. Howes asked Bethany to befriend Sveta and to help Sveta learn.

Bethany did her best to show Sveta what to do. She showed her how to take out her reading book, but Sveta couldn't read English. Bethany gave Sveta a new pencil to write letters in her handwriting book, but Sveta wrote her letters in the Russian alphabet.

Later in the day, Mrs. Walters, Sveta's adoptive mother, came to visit. Mrs. Walters hugged Sveta. Mrs. Walters had a box full of Russian things for Sveta to show the class.

Sveta showed the class pictures from a Russian city called *Moscow*. The buildings were so colorful; they had round tops with stripes, bright colors, and even gold! Next, Sveta showed an interesting stringed instrument called a *balalaika*. It looked a little like a guitar. Bethany wondered if Sveta would play a song for the class.

Then Sveta opened a colorful, wooden doll. Inside was a smaller, twin doll. She opened the smaller doll and inside was an even smaller doll. She kept going until there were nine matching dolls in a long row. The littlest doll was really tiny! The pretty dolls were Bethany's favorite.

Mrs. Walters saved the best for last, though. She had a plate filled with very thin Russian pancakes called *blini*. Sveta showed the class how to spread jam on a *blin*, roll it up, and eat it. Mmmmmm … delicious!

The students smiled at Sveta and thanked her for teaching them about the country of Russia. Bethany and Kim decided right then to be Sveta's new friends and to do everything they could to help Sveta learn English. Maybe they could even be triplets!

Review

- Why do the people in Russia and other countries speak different languages? (**God mixed up the languages at the Tower of Babel.**)
- Why was Sveta so quiet in class? (**She didn't speak English.**)
- Why did Sveta show her classmates Russian things? (**to teach students about Russia**)
- How will Bethany and Kim show God's love to Sveta? (**They plan to help her to learn English.**)

Student Page 3.4

Show students your country and Russia on a GLOBE. Read the directions and assist students in completing the page.

APPLICATION

- How do you think Sveta felt when she could not understand the other children? (**Possible answers: sad, lonely, afraid, confused**)
- How would you give directions to someone who does not speak English? (**Answers will vary.**)
- Why do Christians reach out to people around the world? (**Jesus told us to take the gospel into the whole world (Matthew 28:19).**)
- How does the Lord want you to behave toward people from other countries or cultures? (**We should accept others because God has accepted us (1 John 4:11).**)

REINFORCEMENT

Throughout the year, tell students about your own travels or invite guests from other cultures to your classroom. Look for opportunities to help students compare and contrast cultures different from their own. Your students will learn to respect and care for people who are different from themselves. This background will help you to explain the work of missionaries who go abroad. However, it is important to keep in mind that every Christian is called to share the gospel, no matter where he or she lives.

DAY 4

3.4 ***Noah***

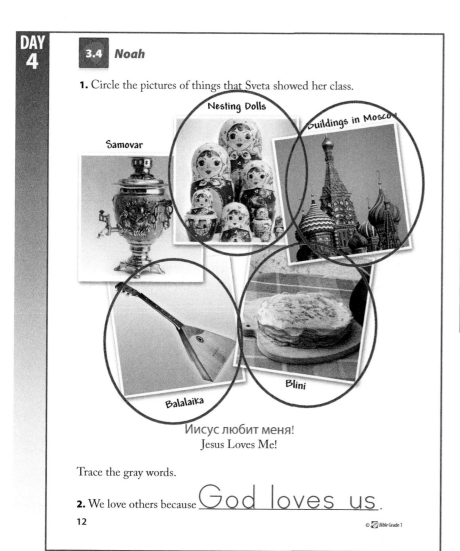

1. Circle the pictures of things that Sveta showed her class.

Иисус любит меня!
Jesus Loves Me!

Trace the gray words.

2. We love others because God loves us.

12

© Bible Grade 1

3.5 Noah

Focus: Review and Assessment

★ PREPARATION

Select "Noah Was a Faithful Man" from the music CDs. (*Lesson Review*)

Select **VA 3A Noah** and **VA 3B The Tower of Babel**. (*Lesson Review*)

Duplicate one copy of **BLM 3D Lesson 3 Test** for each student. (*Directed Instruction*)

Lesson Review ★

Use "Noah Was a Faithful Man" from the music CDs to lead a short time of worship.

Use **VA 3A Noah** and **VA 3B The Tower of Babel** to review the Bible truths. Cover the following concepts:

- The people who lived after Adam and Eve became wicked and evil. They were living for themselves instead of living for God.
- Because of the people's great wickedness, God decided to send a flood to destroy the earth.
- God saw that Noah loved and followed Him. God chose to save Noah and Noah's family along with many, many animals.
- God asked Noah to build a big boat called an *ark*. Noah trusted God and obeyed. It took him about 100 years to build the ark. Then God sent the animals, two of each kind, but seven of each kind of animal that could be used for food or as a sacrifice. Noah, his family, and the animals got on board the ark, and God closed the door.
- Rain fell for 40 days and 40 nights. Underground water burst up to flood the ground. Every land animal and person who was not on the ark died.
- After the Flood, Noah gave a sacrificial offering of thanksgiving to honor God. God was pleased with Noah's offering.
- God promised not to flood the earth ever again. God put a rainbow in a cloud in the sky as a sign of His promise.
- After the Flood, God told Noah and his family to have many children and to move all over the earth, but instead they stayed together.
- The people built a great city, and tried to build a tower all the way to heaven. The people wanted to be more famous than God and bring glory to themselves.
- God promised not to destroy the earth by a flood again, so He mixed up the languages of the people. That way they could not understand each other or work together. God's will was finally done as the people found others who spoke the same language, moved away from Babel, spread out, and filled the earth.
- Now there are people who live everywhere on the earth, speak many different languages, and live in many different ways.

Directed Instruction ★

Distribute a copy of **BLM 3D Lesson 3 Test** to each student. Read the directions and the text. Allow students to complete the test independently. Review the answers in class and collect the test papers for assessment.

Notes:

Lesson Preparation

Abraham and Isaac

4.0

Expected Student Outcomes

KNOW
God establishes His covenant with Abraham and Isaac.

DO
Students will:
- answer questions to contrast a modern relocation with Abraham's move
- read a rebus story to review the Bible lesson
- identify pictures that show trust and obedience
- complete sentences from a story about trusting God

APPLY
Students will express trust in God for His promises and plan for their life.

Lesson Outline

I. God makes two promises (Gen 12:1–7, 18:1–15)
  A. God promises blessing (Gen 12:1–3)
  B. Abraham trusts God and obeys (Gen 12:4–7)
  C. God confirms His promises (Gen 18:10)
II. Abraham demonstrates his trust (Gen 21–22)
  A. God fulfills His first promise (Gen 21:1–2)
  B. God tests Abraham's trust (Gen 22:1–2)
  C. Abraham trusts and obeys (Gen 22:6–8)
III. God continues to test Abraham (Gen 22)
  A. Abraham trusts and obeys (Gen 22:9–10)
  B. God acknowledges Abraham's trust (Gen 22:10–14)
  C. God restates his promise to Abraham (Gen 22:15–18)
IV. God's special plan for me (Jer 29:11, Lk 11:11–13)

TEACHER'S HEART

During the first few weeks of school, you have no doubt tried to determine your students' strengths and weaknesses in order to best meet their needs and teach to their learning styles. However, have you also considered that your students may be "sizing you up" as well? From the day that they first walked into your classroom, your first graders have been watching you. Are you impartial in your dealings with them? Do you follow through on your promises? Can they count on you to provide an environment that is safe both physically and emotionally? In short, can they trust you?

Abraham learned to trust God to do all that He said He would do. He moved forward in faith and confidence, trusting that God would fulfill the promises He had made to him. Help your students to better understand the true nature of God by modeling trustworthiness before them so that they can see that you, too, trust God's leadership in your daily life. Celebrate the opportunities that the Lord has already prepared for you this day so that you may help students learn to fully trust and obey the Lord!

MEMORY VERSE

Psalm 31:14

MATERIALS

Day 1:
- Sentence strips
- Cardboard box
- VA 4A God's Promise to Abraham

Day 2:
- No additional materials are needed.

Day 3:
- Jars, beans, sand
- Fine-grade sandpaper (*Extension*)

Day 4:
- Dollar bill, penny
- Floor puzzle (*Extension*)

Day 5:
- VA 4A God's Promise to Abraham
- BLM 4A Lesson 4 Test

SONGS

The Bible

TEACHER RESOURCES

Abraham and Isaac. DVD. Crown Financial Ministries, 2009.
Hunt, Gladys. *Honey for a Child's Heart*. Zondervan, 2002.

STUDENT RESOURCES

Keams, Becky Lockhart. *Abraham's Big Test*. Concordia Publishing House, 2000.
Lloyd-Jones, Sally. *The Jesus Storybook Bible*. Zonderkidz, 2007.

4.1 Abraham and Isaac

Focus: God Makes Two Promises

MEMORY VERSE

Psalm 31:14

MEMORY WORK

- Say the Memory Verse and its reference. Shuffle the sentence strips. Ask five volunteers to come forward and stand in a line. Distribute one sentence strip to each volunteer. Tell them not to talk to one another. Direct the volunteers to shift positions until they think that the strips are in the correct order. Once the volunteers are satisfied that they have correctly unscrambled the verse, ask the remaining students to check the volunteers' work by giving a thumbs-up or thumbs-down vote. Lead the class in repeating the Memory Verse.

★ PREPARATION

Prepare FIVE SENTENCE STRIPS by writing sections from the Memory Verse and its reference on the sentence strips. (*Memory Work*)

Obtain a MEDIUM-SIZED CARDBOARD BOX. (*Introduction*)

Select **VA 4A God's Promise to Abraham**. (*Directed Instruction*)

EXTENSION

1A Determine in advance a promise that you will make to the students. Create an air of excitement about the promise by discussing the activity, but do not specify a day or time. Explain that the students will need to trust you to keep your promise. Record in your lesson plan book the promise you make and when you intend to carry it out.

Introduction ★

Pack a few items from your classroom into the MEDIUM-SIZED CARDBOARD BOX as if preparing to move. As you pack, dramatically explain why each item is important and should be included. As students begin asking what you are doing, tell them that you are showing them what it takes to move from one location to another. Talk about the efforts and time necessary to take down posters, bulletin board decorations, and other items. Throughout the packing scenario, talk about the need for having a positive attitude during a move.

While packing, inquire as to whether any of the students have ever moved. Discuss the preparations that a family must make as they get ready to move. (**Answers will vary, but should include learning about the community that will be the family's new home, packing their belongings, and saying good-bye to friends.**) Conclude by telling students that someone in today's Bible lesson really did have to move!

Directed Instruction ★

Display **VA 4A God's Promise to Abraham**. Direct students to listen for the two promises that God made to Abraham as you read the back of VA 4A.

Ask students to identify important differences between how a modern family would move and Abraham's move. (**Abraham did not know where his new home was going to be or how long it would take to get there. Modern families almost always know both of those things.**)

Direct students' attention to Abraham and Sarah's home on VA 4A. Invite students to compare and contrast their home to that of Abraham and Sarah. (**Possible answers: Our homes are permanent structures made from brick, wood, or concrete; Abraham and Sarah's home was a tent made from fabric.**)

Review what Abraham and Sarah did to welcome their guests. (**Answers will vary, but should include that they baked bread, cooked meat, and prepared gifts of milk and butter.**) Ask students to describe what they do to make company feel welcome in their homes. (**Possible answers: clean the house, prepare a special meal, put out clean towels, set the table with our best dishes**)

Student Page 4.1

Read the directions and the text. Assist students in completing the page.

Review

- What was the first promise that God made to Abraham? (**All the families of the earth would be blessed through Abraham.**)
- What did Abraham have to do to receive this promise? (**He had to trust God, pack up all his family, and move to the place that God would show him.**)

- Abraham and Sarah had visitors one day. Who were they? (**three people who looked like men, but who were really the Lord and two angels**)
- The Lord made a second promise to Abraham and Sarah. What was it? (**Next year Sarah would have a son.**)
- What special message is as true today as it was in the days of Abraham? (**Nothing is too hard for the Lord!**)

Notes:

APPLICATION

- Have you ever heard a promise that sounded too good to be true, something that would probably not happen? (**Answers will vary.**)
- Has anyone ever broken a promise to you? How did you feel? (**Answers will vary.**)
- What do you know to be true about God's promises? (**God always keeps His promises.**)

DAY 1

Name ______________________________

Abraham and Isaac **4.1**

Abraham moved to the land that God showed him. Think about how Abraham moved.

Write **yes** or **no** to answer each question.

1. Did Abraham have a 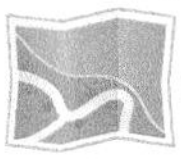 map? no

2. Did Abraham have a  GPS system? no

3. Did Abraham have a  moving van? no

4. Did Abraham stay in a  motel room? no

Do you know what Abraham did have? To find out, unscramble the words below the lines and write them in the correct order.

5. Abraham had faith in God!

God **in** **faith**

13

4.2

Abraham and Isaac

Focus: Abraham Demonstrates His Trust

EXTENSION

2A If you are physically able, select a girl volunteer to assist you with an activity that demonstrates trust. To conduct a Trust Fall, stand behind the girl. Direct her to cross her arms, close her eyes, and fall backward while relying on you to catch her. After you have caught her, ask her how she felt during the exercise. Repeat the exercise with the same student. Ask the class if they think the volunteer was more or less confident that you would catch her the second time. (**The volunteer would have felt more confident.**) Point out that even though the volunteer could not see you and did not know exactly when you would catch her, she could trust you because you had been faithful to catch her before.

Explain that Abraham could not see God and did not know how God would supply a lamb for the sacrifice. Still, Abraham trusted God because God had fulfilled His earlier promise of giving Abraham a son. Explain that the students' relationship with God works in the same way; each time they trust God, it will become easier to trust Him the next time.

Introduction

Choose a few students to review the promises that God made in Lesson 4.1. (**All the families of the earth would be blessed through Abraham; Sarah would have a son.**) Tell students that Abraham loved God and was delighted to hear God's promises. In today's lesson, however, God will ask Abraham to do something that will be very difficult.

Directed Instruction

Read the following Bible truth based on Genesis 21:1–22:8:

> The Lord kept His promise to Abraham and Sarah. They had a son the very next year and, according to God's instruction, they named him *Isaac*, which means *laughter*. Remember that Sarah laughed when she heard that she was going to have a baby in her old age.
>
> One day when Isaac was older, God spoke to Abraham. God said, "Head toward the land of Moriah, Abraham, and take your son Isaac. Remember, he's the one that I had promised to give you. Offer him as a sacrifice to me on one of the mountains that I will show you." What a strange thing for the Lord to say! Abraham had worshipped the Lord many times by sacrificing animals on altars. But now, God was telling Abraham to sacrifice his son! This must have been a very difficult thing for Abraham to hear, but Abraham knew that God had promised him that a nation would come through him and his son Isaac.
>
> Abraham rose early the next morning, saddled his donkey, and took two of his young servants with him, along with Isaac. He split wood for the fire that he would build. They walked for two days, and on the third day Abraham saw where the sacrifice was to take place. He told his servants, "Stay here with the donkey. Isaac and I will go and worship, and then we will come back to you."
>
> Abraham had Isaac carry the wood for the burnt offering. As they were walking, Isaac asked Abraham, "Father, we have the wood for the fire, but where is the lamb for the offering?" Abraham responded, "Isaac, God will provide for Himself the lamb for a burnt offering."

Explain that the Bible truth does not end here and that you will read about what happened to Abraham and Isaac in the next lesson.

Student Page 4.2

Review the major life events of Abraham, Sarah, and Isaac. Explain that the small pictures take the place of the characters' names and the animals in the narrative. Note that there are two pictures of Isaac—one as a baby and one when he was older. Read the page together.

Review

- Which promise was fulfilled by the birth of Isaac? (**the promise that Sarah would have a son**) What did Isaac's name mean? (**laughter**)

- What difficult thing did God ask Abraham to do? (**sacrifice his promised son, Isaac**)
- How was the sacrifice that God asked Abraham to make different from other sacrifices Abraham had made? (**Instead of the sacrifice of an animal, God was asking Abraham to sacrifice his son, whom God had promised to Abraham as a blessing.**)
- What did Abraham ask Isaac to do? (**carry the wood for the sacrifice**)
- Where did Abraham say he would get the lamb for the sacrifice? (**God would provide it.**)

Notes:

APPLICATION

- Have you ever had to obey your mom or dad without understanding why they asked you to do something? Share what happened. (**Answers will vary.**)
- Why do you think Isaac trusted his father? (**Answers will vary, but should include that Isaac knew that Abraham had a close relationship with God.**)
- What shows you that Abraham trusted God? (**He was obedient to prepare for the sacrifice of his son, as God had asked him to do; he told the servants that he and Isaac would come back to them; and he expressed faith that God would provide the lamb for the burnt offering.**)
- Why do you think that Abraham trusted God when God told him to sacrifice Isaac? (**Abraham had learned to trust God through the years. He had exercised his faith on many occasions.**)

DAY 2

4.2 *Abraham and Isaac*

Read the story.

God kept his promise to . They had a the next year and named him **Isaac**.

When was older, God told to go to the mountain and offer as a sacrifice. thought, "I do not understand why God would ask me to do this, but I trust Him." cut some wood and loaded it on his . Then , two servants, and all went to the place of the sacrifice. When they arrived, told the servants to stay with the while he and his son went to worship God.

had carry the wood. "We have the wood for the fire, but where is the for the sacrifice, Father?" asked. looked at and replied, "I am sure that God Himself will provide the for the offering, my son."

14

© Bible Grade 1

4.3 Abraham and Isaac

Focus: God Continues to Test Abraham

★ PREPARATION

Prepare TWO JARS by filling one with BEANS and the other with SAND. (*Introduction*)

EXTENSION

3A Share an anecdote about a time when you felt God leading you to do something that you did not fully understand, and then relate the consequences of your decision to trust God for the outcome. Help students to realize that, just as God called Abraham and you to trust His plan, He also wants students to trust Him.

3B Give each student a small piece of FINE-GRADE SANDPAPER to draw a picture of Abraham and Sarah traveling to the land God had promised. Explain that the soil might have been very dry and sandy at times. Remind students to use their crayons to draw Abraham, Sarah, Lot, their animals, and their tent on the sandpaper. Students will need to press down on their crayons to give their drawing an interesting texture. As students draw, talk about how the journey required Abraham to trust that God would lead him.

Introduction ★

Show students the JAR filled with BEANS. Encourage students to guess the number of beans in the jar. (**Answers will vary.**) Show students the JAR filled with SAND. Encourage students to guess the number of grains of sand. (**Answers will vary, but students should conclude that it is nearly impossible to know how many grains of sand are in the jar.**) Invite students to listen for what God had to say to Abraham about grains of sand.

Directed Instruction

Review events of the previous lesson, building suspense as students recall that Abraham was called to sacrifice his promised son, Isaac. Read the following Bible truth based on Genesis 22:9–24:

> When they arrived at the mountain for the sacrifice, Abraham built an altar. He put the wood in place. Next he went to Isaac, tied him up, and placed him on the altar. Abraham lifted up a knife and was about to kill his son. Suddenly, the Angel of the Lord called to him, "Abraham, Abraham! Don't touch your son or do anything to harm him, because I now know that you love God more than your only son."
>
> When Abraham looked up, he saw a ram whose horns had been caught in some bushes. So Abraham offered the ram for a burnt offering instead of his son Isaac.
>
> The Angel of the Lord called to Abraham a second time and said, "Because you were willing to give up your only son and because you were obedient, I will bless you more than you can possibly imagine. The people that will come from you will be like the stars of the heaven and as the sand on the seashore—far too many to count. From you, all the nations of the earth will be blessed."
>
> What Abraham did by obeying and being willing to offer his son to God was a picture of something that would take place in the future. Many years later, God chose to give His Son, Jesus Christ, to die for the sins of the world.

Discuss with students how difficult it must have been for Abraham to prepare the altar and lay his dear son upon the woodpile. Point out, however, that Abraham trusted God to fulfill His promises and that Abraham was obedient to do all that God had asked of him. Tell students that a *covenant* is *a promise that will never be broken* and that God had made a covenant with Abraham.

Ask whether Abraham's choice to obey was a wise choice. (**Yes.**) Remind students that all choices have consequences. Good choices usually have good consequences. What was the good consequence of Abraham's obedience to God? (**All the families of the earth would be blessed through him. The number of people born into Abraham's family line would be too many to count.**) Ask students whether they think God kept this second promise to Abraham. (Yes.) Inform students that Jesus was in Abraham's family line even though Jesus was born many, many years later. God had a plan for blessing the world by offering Jesus to die for everyone's sins.

Review

- What was Abraham willing to do in obedience to God's command? (**sacrifice his son Isaac**)
- Why did the Angel of the Lord tell Abraham not to harm his son? (**Abraham's obedience proved that he loved God more than he loved Isaac.**)
- What promise did God make to Abraham once again? (**All the families of the earth would be blessed through Abraham's family.**)
- What person from Abraham's family line sacrificed His own life many years later so that you could be forgiven of your sins? (**Jesus**)

Student Page 4.3
Read the directions and the text. Allow students to complete the page.

DAY 3

Name ____________________

Abraham and Isaac **4.3**

Abraham trusted and obeyed God. When you trust and obey your parents, you are learning to trust and obey God.

Listen to each story. Circle the correct picture.

1. Dad told Lindsay to share the laptop computer with her sister Katie, but Lindsay did not want to share. Which picture shows Lindsay obeying Dad?

2. Julie and her brother Ian were having a picture taken. Julie thought that being silly would make the picture look good, but Mom said that smiling faces would make the picture look good. Which picture shows Julie obeying Mom?

Complete the sentence.

3. When I trust and obey my parents, I am learning to trust and obey God, or Jesus.

APPLICATION

- What is the difference between trusting God and obeying God? (**When I trust God, I count on God to do what He says He will do. When I obey God, I do what God asks me to do because I trust Him. I do it right away and with a good attitude.**)
- Compare the ways that Noah and Abraham trusted and obeyed God. (**Answers will vary, but should include that regardless of the significant effort involved, both did as God asked.**)

REINFORCEMENT

Students may question the difference in terminology used between the lamb that Abraham trusted God to provide and the ram that God supplied for the sacrifice. Are these animals the same or different? They are the same. Lambs—in contrast to sheep—are considered to be less than one year old and have not yet produced offspring. A young male lamb is called a *ram lamb* and a young female lamb is called a *ewe lamb*. It is likely that the ram that Abraham offered was older than a lamb, yet it is undeniable that God provided the animal for the sacrifice.

4.4 Abraham and Isaac

Focus: God's Special Plan for Me

★ PREPARATION

• Have on hand a DOLLAR BILL and a PENNY. (*Introduction*)

EXTENSION

4A Remove one piece from a FLOOR PUZZLE and retain that piece. Ask students to work together to assemble the puzzle. As students discover that a piece is missing, talk about what part of the picture might be on the missing piece. Give one or two students pieces of paper and challenge them to make a replacement piece. Allow students to realize that their drawn pieces will not fit as well as the original piece. Add the final piece to the puzzle and tell students that as they trust God to fulfill His promises to them, He will show them His perfect plan for their life.

REINFORCEMENT

What drives people to give to others sacrificially? The Macedonian believers joyfully provided an offering for others despite their own poverty (2 Corinthians 8:1–3). The widow at the temple gave a very small offering, but it was all that she had (Mark 12:42–44). Abraham was willing to sacrifice his son of promise, Isaac. In each case, the actions were prompted by love for God and the desire to honor Him with their gifts.

God Himself set the standard for sacrificial giving. Motivated solely by love for an undeserving world, He gave His only Son that we might be redeemed. The Lord does not need sacrifices in order to accomplish His will here on Earth; rather, He is pleased, when people give to others in proportion to what they have been given.

Introduction ★

Show students a DOLLAR BILL and a PENNY and discuss the value of each one. Ask students to suggest reasons why it might be more difficult for someone to give a dollar to the Lord than it would be to give just a penny. (**A dollar has more value than a penny.**) Explain that the greater the value of something, the more difficult it may be to give it away.

Remind students that they can give not only their money and possessions to the Lord, but they can serve others as well. Help students to understand that it is not the monetary value of what they give or do in service to the Lord that matters, but rather the heart attitude that is important. Encourage them to serve sacrificially with a joyful heart and as an expression of love for the Lord.

Directed Instruction

Read the following fictional story:

Mark loved to ride his shiny blue bicycle after school. How exciting it was to glide down the hill toward the park and to feel the cool breeze on his cheeks! Mark knew that once he arrived at the park, his friends Justin and Carlos would be there, too. Today, as they did most every day, they would all ride their bikes along the path that wove past the flower garden until they arrived at the playground. He and his friends could think of nothing they would rather do than ride their bicycles!

One afternoon when Mark arrived home from the park, his mom invited him to sit down so they could talk. She explained that their church was collecting items for the Thomas family whose home had recently been damaged by a fire. Mark knew that the family had four school-aged children, including a first-grade boy, Lucas, who was in Mark's Sunday school class. How sad Mark was to hear this news! Mom and Mark talked about the family's needs. The Thomases were living in the hotel near the park. The church was conducting a clothing drive and some of the neighborhood ladies agreed to prepare meals for them. When Mark realized that most of the children's toys had been destroyed in the fire, he quickly offered to give them two toy trucks and three puzzles. Then Mark and his mom prayed, asking God to show them other ways that they might help the Thomas family.

Every day the following week, Mark thought about Lucas and how boring it must be to sit in a hotel room after coming home from school. As he continued to pray, Mark soon knew what God wanted him to do. Mark invited Lucas, Justin, and Carlos to come to his house on Saturday to play. They all ate lunch and then played football. What fun the four boys had! When it was finally time for the boys to go home, Mark had a surprise for Lucas; he let Lucas borrow his shiny blue bike so Lucas could ride in the park each afternoon until the Thomas family could move back into their home. Justin and Carlos eagerly offered to meet Lucas and show him the path that led to the playground. Lucas' eyes opened wide, filled with excitement! Mark had a broad grin; he was happy to see Lucas' joy and knew that he'd made the right choice.

Help students realize that God has a plan for each of their lives. Explain that God is pleased to answer their prayers when they trust Him.

Review

- What was Mark's favorite after-school activity? (**riding his bicycle in the park with his friends**)
- What did Mark and his mom do before they tried to decide how to help the Thomas family? (**They prayed for God's guidance.**)
- How did Mark get the idea to loan Lucas his bike? (**He prayed and God gave him the idea.**)

Student Page 4.4

Read the directions aloud. Allow students time to complete each exercise before moving on to the next one. Discuss students' answers.

APPLICATION

- What did Mark have to sacrifice when he loaned his bike to Lucas? (**Possible answers: He would not be able to ride his bike at the park; he could not be sure he would get his bike back from Lucas in the same condition as when he lent it.**)
- Read **Luke 11:11–13**. This passage assures us that God will provide what we need when we ask Him to help us. How were Mark and Abraham's experiences alike? (**Answers will vary, but should include that both Abraham and Mark asked for God's guidance, trusted God, and were obedient to God's leading; both Abraham and Mark were willing to sacrifice.**)
- Read **Jeremiah 29:11**. How does it make you feel to know that God has a special plan for your life? (**Answers will vary.**)

DAY 4

4.4 ***Abraham and Isaac***

Think about the story of Mark and Lucas. Listen to each sentence. Fill in the circle in front of the right ending.

1. Mark and his friends loved to ____.

○ skateboard ○ climb trees ● ride bikes

2. Mark heard about the fire at Lucas' house, so he and Mom ____.

○ went to the park ● prayed ○ played with puzzles

3. Mark felt that God wanted him to ____.

○ ignore Lucas ○ tease Lucas ● loan his bike to Lucas

4. When Mark acted on his decision, he made a ____.

● sacrifice ○ cake ○ park

5. Part of God's plan for my life is for me to ____.

○ ride my bike ● serve others ○ play with toys

16

4.5 Abraham and Isaac

Focus: Review and Assessment

★ PREPARATION

Select **VA 4A God's Promise to Abraham**. (*Lesson Review*)

Make one copy of **BLM 4A Lesson 4 Test** for each student. (*Directed Instruction*)

Select "The Bible" from the music CDs. (*Directed Instruction*)

Lesson Review ★

Use **VA 4A God's Promise to Abraham** to review the Bible truths from this lesson. Cover the following points:

- God promised Abraham that all the families of the earth would be blessed through him.
- Abraham had to pack up and move all his family to the place that God would show him in order to receive this promise.
- Abraham trusted God and followed God's leading.
- Abraham and Sarah were quite old when they finally settled in the land God had promised.
- Three men, who were really the Lord and two angels, visited Abraham and Sarah one day.
- God's second promise to Abraham was that Sarah would have a son the next year.
- Sarah laughed when she heard the promise because it seemed impossible.
- The Angel of the Lord gave Abraham a special message that is as true today as it was in the days of Abraham: Nothing is too hard for the Lord!
- Isaac's name meant *laughter* because his mother had laughed at God's promise.
- God tested Abraham's love for Him when God asked Abraham to offer his promised son, Isaac, as a sacrifice.
- When Isaac asked where they would get the lamb for the sacrifice, Abraham told his son that God would provide the lamb.
- Abraham was willing to sacrifice his son Isaac in obedience to God's command.
- The Angel of the Lord told Abraham not to harm his son because Abraham had proved that he loved God more than he loved Isaac.
- God provided a ram that was stuck in the bushes for the burnt offering.
- God made a covenant—a promise that can never be broken—with Abraham. God promised that many children would be born into Abraham's family line.
- The person from Abraham's family line who sacrificed His own life many years later so all people could be forgiven of their sins was Jesus. God fulfilled his promise to Abraham!

Directed Instruction ★

Distribute a copy of **BLM 4A Lesson 4 Test** to each student. Read the directions and each word in the Word Bank. Tell students that the first letter of each answer has been provided for them and to trace over each one when writing the word. Dictate sentences, one at a time, and have students write the correct answer before moving to the next exercise. Share correct answers.

Review with students that the Bible contains many promises that God made. Remind students that God will keep every promise that He has made. Sing "The Bible" from the music CDs.

Lesson Preparation

5.0

Jacob and Esau

Expected Student Outcomes

KNOW

Jacob cheats Esau out of his birthright. Jacob deceives Isaac. Jacob and Esau reconcile.

DO

Students will:

- compare and contrast characteristics of Jacob and Esau
- select appropriate words to complete a fill-in-the-blank activity
- complete sentences to review the Bible truth
- decode a word to discover an important concept from the lesson

APPLY

Students will identify some consequences of lying and recognize the need for repentance and reconciliation.

Lesson Outline

I. Jacob steals the birthright (Gen 25:20–34)
  A. Twin sons foretold
  B. Jacob cheats Esau
II. Jacob steals the blessing (Gen 27:1–43)
III. Jacob's unusual dream (Gen 27:43–29:20)
  A. Jacob flees from his brother
  B. God's covenant with Jacob
IV. Jacob returns home (Gen 29:21–33:17)
  A. Jacob's name is changed
  B. Jacob and Esau are reconciled

TEACHER'S HEART

There is a hardy vine called *kudzu*. This amazing plant grows up to 12 inches each night. If unchecked, it quickly grows up, on, and over any stationary object in its path. Kudzu is green and lush with a fragrant violet and purple cluster of blossoms. It looks beautiful, but those who are familiar with kudzu know it kills what it covers.

Isn't bitterness like kudzu? Satan disguises it to look lovely. He hides its damaging effects and consequences. Then before you realize it, it has a hold on your heart and life, numbing and killing your fellowship with God.

You can cut kudzu at the root but as long as even a small portion of the root remains, it will grow again—again choking and killing whatever is in its path. One way to get rid of kudzu is to bring in a pig and let it rout out every molecule of the root. Likewise, the only way to get rid of bitterness is to confess every molecule of it to the Lord and let Him rout it out. He wants you to be victorious! He delights in helping you! If you are being choked by bitterness, won't you accept His victory in this area of your life?

MEMORY VERSE

Psalm 34:13

MATERIALS

Day 1:
- No additional materials are needed.

Day 2:
- VA 5A Jacob Steals the Blessing
- BLM 5A Steal the Bacon (*Extension*)
- Animal hide or fake fur (*Extension*)

Day 3:
- Pillow, stone, card stock
- VA 5B Jacob's Unusual Dream
- BLM 5B Jacob's Unusual Dream, card stock, BLM 5C Angels (*Extension*)

Day 4:
- No additional materials are needed.

Day 5:
- VA 5A Jacob Steals the Blessing, VA 5B Jacob's Unusual Dream
- BLM 5D Lesson 5 Test

SONGS

I Saw Esau

TEACHER RESOURCES

Dawson, Joy. *Influencing Children to Become World Changers*. Thomas Nelson, 2003.

Elkins, Stephen. *100 Bible Stories, 100 Bible Songs*. Integrity Publishers, 2005.

STUDENT RESOURCES

Adams, Michelle Medlock. *Bible Story Color 'n' Learn*. Carson-Dellosa Publishing Company, Inc., 2009.

Auld, Mary. *Jacob and Esau*. Franklin Watts, 2003.

5.1 Jacob and Esau

Focus: Jacob Steals the Birthright

MEMORY VERSE

Psalm 34:13

MEMORY WORK

- Introduce the week's Memory Verse by writing it on the board and having students follow along as you read it. After students are familiar with the verse, invite them to suggest some motions to emphasize key words in the verse. Say the Memory Verse again, using the motions suggested by the class.

EXTENSION

1A Sometimes people are tempted to make quick decisions, like Esau did, in order to get an immediate reward. Remind students that when they are willing to be patient, the outcome is often worth the wait. Ask students to suggest some things that are better if they wait for them. (**Possible answers: waiting for a freshly baked cookie to cool before eating it, waiting until Christmas to open gifts instead of peeking ahead of time, saving money for a special toy instead of buying candy**) Distribute a large sheet of drawing paper to each student. Encourage students to draw themselves doing something that they would like to learn to do that requires patience to master. Brainstorm examples for illustrations, such as learning a difficult routine in gymnastics, or memorizing math facts.

Introduction

Ask students to recount two promises that God made to Abraham. (**God promised to bless Abraham so that all the families of the earth would be blessed through Abraham's family. Abraham and Sarah would have a son.**) Remind students that Isaac was the son that God promised Abraham. God continued to bless Abraham's son and grandsons and so on.

Directed Instruction

Read the following Bible truth based on Genesis 25:20–34:

Abraham loved his son Isaac and wanted the best for him. So when Isaac grew up and was old enough to be married, Abraham sent a servant back to Abraham's home country to find a young woman for Isaac to marry. Abraham's servant prayed about his job. He wanted the Lord to choose the young woman to marry Isaac. The Lord chose a beautiful girl named *Rebekah*, who became Isaac's wife.

Sometime later, Rebekah discovered that she was pregnant. She didn't know it, but she was going to have twins! Before they were even born, the babies wrestled with each other. Rebekah was worried, so she prayed to the Lord. The Lord said, "You will give birth to two sons who will become the fathers of two great nations. One nation will be stronger than the other. The older child's family will serve the younger child's family."

When the twins were born, their parents named the firstborn *Esau*, which means *hairy*, because he had a lot of hair on his body. They named the second boy *Jacob*. As the boys grew, Esau became Isaac's favorite because Esau was a great hunter, and Isaac loved the taste of the meat of wild animals. Rebekah favored Jacob because he took care of the sheep, tended the garden, and stayed close to home.

One day, Jacob made a pot of stew. Its delicious smell filled the air. Esau had been out hunting earlier, and now he was tired and hungry. When he smelled Jacob's stew, Esau told Jacob, "Brother, please let me have some of that stew. I'm tired and hungry." The good smell of the stew was making Esau feel hungrier and hungrier! All he thought about was his empty stomach.

Jacob saw Esau's hunger as the key to get something that he'd wanted for a long time—Esau's birthright. The *birthright* means *the land, animals, and belongings given to the oldest son when the father died*. Jacob was not the firstborn, and he had always been jealous of his brother because Esau would receive what their father owned.

Jacob replied, "I'll trade you a bowl of my stew for your birthright."

"I'm so hungry, I'm about to die," Esau said. "What good is my birthright if I die today? You can have it." So Jacob gave Esau bread and stew, and the birthright became Jacob's.

Explain that the birthright was very special and was reserved for the oldest son. In addition to receiving privileges and wealth, the son who received the birthright had a responsibility to lead the family in the ways of God. Esau did not think about these things when he made his foolish trade.

Review

- Who were the parents of Esau and Jacob? (**Isaac and Rebekah**)
- What three things did the Lord tell Rebekah when she prayed to Him? (**She would have twin sons; these two sons would be the leaders of two great nations; the older son would serve the younger one.**)
- What did Esau get in exchange for giving Jacob his birthright? (**a bowl of stew and some bread**)

Student Page 5.1

Remind students that Jacob and Esau were twin brothers, but they were very different. Esau, the older twin, was a very hairy man. He preferred to hunt wild game. Jacob, the younger son, preferred to stay at home near the tents with his mother. He took care of the sheep, tended the garden, and cooked. Complete the page together.

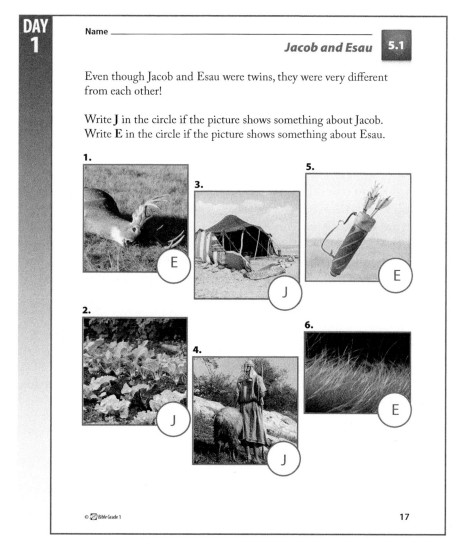

DAY 1

Name ______________________________

Jacob and Esau **5.1**

Even though Jacob and Esau were twins, they were very different from each other!

Write **J** in the circle if the picture shows something about Jacob.
Write **E** in the circle if the picture shows something about Esau.

1.

E

3.

J

5.

E

2.

J

4.

J

6.

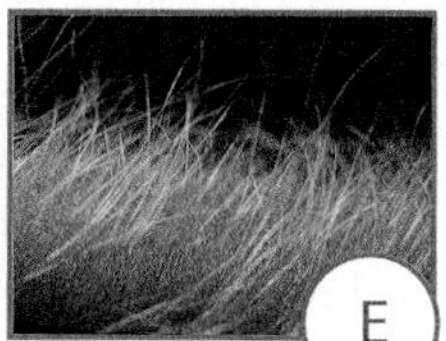

E

APPLICATION

- Which poor choice did Esau make that showed he really did not care about his birthright? (**He chose to trade his birthright to his brother.**)
- God promised to bless all the people on the earth through Isaac and his sons. Do you think that Esau took God's promise seriously? (**No.**) How do you know? (**Esau did not take God's promise seriously because he did not care about the land that God had promised to give to Abraham and his family. He was willing to give it all to Jacob in a trade for a bowl of stew and some bread.**)
- What consequence did Esau have as a result of giving up his birthright? (**He gave up his right to the land God had promised.**)
- What promises has God given you? (**Answers will vary, but should include that God has promised me eternal life through His Son, Jesus; He promises to give me guidance through His Word; He promises to hear my prayers.**)

REINFORCEMENT

In ancient Jewish tradition, a father generally bestowed the birthright on his eldest son. In addition to a double portion of the father's property, this position of honor, prestige, and recognition of authority also carried with it a special responsibility—to inherit the position of spiritual head of the family. The one to whom the birthright had been given became the spiritual leader of the family and accepted the duty of guiding family members to live righteously before God. The birthright could be removed by God or the father of the firstborn son.

5.2 Jacob and Esau

Focus: Jacob Steals the Blessing

★ PREPARATION

Select **VA 5A Jacob Steals the Blessing**. (*Directed Instruction*)

Select "I Saw Esau" from the music CDs. (*Directed Instruction*)

EXTENSION

2A Using rules provided on **BLM 5A Steal the Bacon**, play the game with students during recess.

2B Invite students to hold and feel a small piece of **ANIMAL HIDE** or **FAKE FUR**. Longer fur, such as goatskin, would be more in keeping with today's lesson than rabbit skin. As students feel the texture of animal hair, ask them to recall how animal skins were involved in today's Bible lesson.

Introduction

Select two volunteers to serve as game players for this activity. The players stand on either side of a desk or small table. Put a chalkboard eraser in the center of the desk. Direct the players to put their hands behind their backs. Explain that when you give the signal, each player is to try to distract the other player and then grab the eraser without the other one noticing.

Explain that in this game, the players know the rules and have agreed to try to take the eraser. Clarify that in real life, however, God is not pleased when people secretly cheat or steal, taking things from others that are not their own.

Directed Instruction ★

Ask students to remember that when Jacob and Esau were young men, Jacob tricked his brother into foolishly selling his birthright. Esau, the older son, sold the birthright to Jacob for a bowl of stew. Next, tell students that today's lesson happened many years after the birthright was stolen. Invite students to listen and discover who will be involved in stealing something. Display **VA 5A Jacob Steals the Blessing** as you read aloud the text on the back.

Make an observation that it seemed that this family had divided into teams, with one parent and one son on each team. Ask students to share who was on the team that was involved in stealing something. (**Rebekah and Jacob**) Because Jacob was her favorite son, Rebekah was willing to help him steal the special blessing that Isaac was going to give to his firstborn son, Esau.

Point out that when Jacob told one lie to his father, he had to tell additional lies to cover the first one. Review the questions that Isaac asked and Jacob falsely answered. (**Who are you; how did you get the meat so quickly; are you really my son Esau?**)

Ask students if Rebekah and Jacob showed honor to Isaac by carrying out this plan. (**They did not honor Isaac.**) Remember that God had already promised that Jacob's family would one day rule over Esau's. Rebekah and Jacob did not have to lie and steal to receive God's blessing. That was a bad choice. They needed to trust God.

Lead students to recall the consequences of Rebekah and Jacob's bad choice. (**Esau wanted to kill his brother; Jacob had to move away from his family to be safe; family members were separated.**)

Select "I Saw Esau" from the music CDs. Review the words and lead students in singing the song.

Review

- Why did Rebekah think her plan would work? (**Isaac was old and blind.**)
- How do you know that Jacob knew he was lying to his father? (**Jacob was afraid that Isaac might find out about Jacob's trick.**)
- What did Rebekah do to help Jacob trick his father, Isaac? (**She got some of Esau's clothes for Jacob to wear; she put goatskins on Jacob's hands, arms, and neck; she prepared meat for Jacob to take to Isaac.**)
- What did Esau learn when he finally brought the meat to his father? (**Isaac had been tricked into giving Esau's blessing to his brother.**)
- Why was Esau so angry? (**Jacob had cheated him out of both his birthright and his blessing.**)

Student Page 5.2

Read the text to students and instruct them to complete the sentences using words from the Word Bank.

Notes:

DAY 2

5.2 ***Jacob and Esau***

Use words from the Word Bank to complete the sentences.

WORD BANK

Jacob	father	birthright	blessing
stew	Esau	bread	

1. ___Jacob___ tricked his brother, Esau.

2. Esau sold his ___birthright___ for a bowl of ___stew___ and some ___bread___.

3. When he sold his birthright, Esau did not honor his ___father___, Isaac.

4. Jacob lied to his father to get his father's ___blessing___.

5. ___Esau___ planned to kill Jacob!

18

© Bible Grade 1

APPLICATION

- Have you ever done something that you hoped your parents would not find out about? (**Answers will vary.**) How did keeping a secret make you feel? (**Answers will vary.**)
- Will your parents trust you if you do things that you know are wrong, but try to hide from them? (**Hiding our sin does not build trust.**)
- What could you do in the future to help build trust between you and your parents? (**Answers will vary, but should include telling the truth and confessing any sin so that our parents can forgive us and trust us again.**)

REINFORCEMENT

The family blessing differed from the birthright. When the family patriarch became elderly or frail, he would call his children to himself, lay hands on them, and confer his blessings upon them. A special blessing was generally given to the eldest son, indicating his place of prominence in the family. The father handed over to him the business and patriarchal duties of the family, thereby endowing him with physical wealth and power.

While both the birthright and blessing carried authority and prestige, God viewed the birthright as superior, placing spiritual matters above the physical.

5.3 Jacob and Esau

Focus: Jacob's Unusual Dream

★ PREPARATION

Obtain a SMALL PILLOW and a STONE OF THE SAME SIZE. (*Introduction*)

Select **VA 5B Jacob's Unusual Dream**. (*Directed Instruction*)

EXTENSION

3A Duplicate **BLM 5B Jacob's Unusual Dream** on CARD STOCK and duplicate **BLM 5C Angels** for students to recreate what Jacob saw in his dream. Encourage students to retell today's Bible lesson with their finished projects.

Introduction ★

Show students the SMALL PILLOW and the STONE OF THE SAME SIZE. Then ask students to compare and contrast the two items. (**They are the same size. The pillow is soft and light, but the stone is hard and heavy.**) Ask two volunteers to take turns and place their head on the stone and then on the pillow. Ask them to describe the difference. (**Possible answers: The stone is scratchy and hard; the pillow is cool and soft.**) Tell students that in today's story, Jacob used a stone for a pillow.

Directed Instruction ★

Read the text on the back of **VA 5B Jacob's Unusual Dream** to share the Bible truth.

Ask students why Jacob was in such a hurry to leave his family and home. (**Esau was so angry after Jacob stole his blessing that Esau said he would kill Jacob.**) Do you think Jacob had time to pack much to take with him? (**No.**) That explains why Jacob used a stone for a pillow!

In his dream, Jacob saw a ladder, or a staircase. This ladder, or staircase, was special because it reached all the way to heaven! Ask students to recall who was going up and down the ladder or staircase. (**angels**) The Bible says that one of the jobs that an angel may have is to act as a messenger. The message that Jacob received, however, was not just from a messenger angel but from God Himself!

Ask students if they remember the promise that God made to Abraham and later to his son Isaac. (**They would have many children and through their family all the families of the earth would be blessed.**) God chose this special night to extend those same promises to Jacob, too. Then God also made another promise to Jacob. What was it? (**God would protect Jacob and bring him safely home again.**)

Ask students if they have ever awakened from a dream that was so real that they thought that it was something that actually happened. Once their eyes opened, however, they figured out that they were just dreaming. It was different for Jacob. When he woke up, Jacob knew that this dream was real! God had actually spoken to him. Jacob immediately made an altar to honor God. Jacob set up his stone pillow and poured some special oil over it. Pouring oil over that stone set that place apart as special. Jacob wanted the place where God had spoken to him to be remembered, so he named the place *Bethel*, which means *house of God*. It was at Bethel that Jacob began to know God personally; he no longer just knew about Him.

Review

- Where did Jacob go when he ran away from his angry brother Esau? (**to his relative Laban's house**)
- What did God tell Jacob during his unusual dream? (**God would give him the land he was sleeping on; he would have many descendants; the**

whole earth would be blessed because of his family; God would protect Jacob wherever he went and would bring him home again.)

- What did Jacob do to his stone pillow when he realized that he had spoken with God? (**He poured some oil over the stone and made it into an altar to honor the Lord.**)
- Where did Jacob go after leaving Bethel? (**He went to Haran to the home of his relative Laban.**)
- What did Jacob agree to do if he could marry Laban's daughter Rachel? (**He would work seven years for Laban.**)

Student Page 5.3

For each exercise, read the beginning of the sentence and each choice provided as an ending. Allow students to choose an ending before moving to the next sentence. When all have finished, discuss students' answers.

Notes:

DAY 3

Name ______________________________

Jacob and Esau **5.3**

Listen to the beginning of each sentence and the choices to end each sentence. Put a ✓ by the correct ending.

1. Jacob left his home because

_____ he was going on a fun trip.

__✓__ he was running away.

_____ he was having a race.

2. Jacob used a stone

_____ for a chair.

_____ to build a house.

__✓__ for a pillow and an altar.

3. The ladder in Jacob's dream

__✓__ went from Earth to heaven.

_____ was beside a tree.

_____ was held up by angels.

4. In the unusual dream, God told Jacob,

_____ "Do not sin."

__✓__ "I am with you."

_____ "Go back home."

© Bible Grade 1 19

APPLICATION

- God promised to protect and be with Jacob wherever he went. What are some situations for which you could express thanks, knowing that you have God's protection and care? (**Possible answers: joining a soccer team, trying out for a play, learning to ride a skateboard**)
- Jacob knew about God, but until his unusual dream, he did not really know God. What is the difference between knowing about a person and actually knowing the person? (**When we know someone, we are able to have a relationship with him or her. We can't have a relationship with someone who we only know about, but do not know personally.**)
- Does God want you to know about Him or to know Him personally? (**He wants us to know Him personally, come to Him in prayer, and trust Him with all our heart.**)

5.4 Jacob and Esau

Focus: Jacob Returns Home

REINFORCEMENT

Wrestling requires intense concentration, strength, and stamina. Not only is it a sport that demands physical and mental effort, but it requires determination to persevere. Jacob, in wrestling with the Man until morning, showed that he had such determination. Even when his hip was dislocated, Jacob would not let the Man go because Jacob realized that he needed God's blessing in his life. Jacob made a huge leap spiritually from the beginning of his life as a liar and cheater to reach such an understanding. The Man identified this step of spiritual growth by changing Jacob's name, which means *supplanter*, to *Israel*, which means *prince with God*.

Introduction

Jacob loved Rachel so much that he agreed to work seven years so he could marry her. Listen to today's lesson to find out what happens next.

Directed Instruction

Read the following Bible truth based on Genesis 29:21–33:17:

At the end of seven years, Laban had a great wedding feast. Jacob was so happy. He finally was going to marry the woman he loved! After the marriage ceremony was over, Jacob found out Laban had tricked him. The girl he married wasn't Rachel, but her older sister, Leah. Jacob was very angry! He asked Laban, "Why did you lie to me? You said I could have Rachel for my wife!" Laban said, "In our country, the older daughter always gets married before the younger one. If you will work seven more years for me, I'll let you marry Rachel, too." Jacob loved Rachel so much that he agreed to do what Laban said, and he married Rachel.

Years went by. Jacob had two wives, eleven sons, and a daughter. He had many servants and animals. Jacob had lived in Haran for many years since he had first arrived, and the Lord had blessed Jacob, just as He'd promised. Then the Lord said to Jacob, "Return to your family. I will be with you." So Jacob took his family and journeyed to his father's home.

As Jacob neared home, he sent servants ahead to tell Esau that he was returning and wanted Esau's approval. When Jacob's servants returned, they told him that Esau was coming and bringing 400 men with him.

Jacob was terrified! He prayed and asked the Lord to keep his family safe. Then Jacob gathered many goats, sheep, camels, cows, and donkeys and sent them to Esau. He hoped his brother would accept this gift and forgive him for stealing the birthright and the blessing.

Jacob also sent his family ahead of him. Now Jacob was all alone. But that night a Man came and wrestled with Jacob. They wrestled until dawn, but Jacob did not give up. The Man made Jacob's hip come out of joint and said, "Let me go, it's morning." Jacob realized that this was no ordinary Man! Jacob said, "I will not let you go until you give me a special blessing."

The Man said, "What is your name?" and Jacob told him. The Man replied, "You will no longer be called *Jacob*. From now on, your name will be *Israel*." From that day forward, *Jacob* was called *Israel*. His *descendants*, which means *family members that would come after him*, would one day be called *the children of Israel*, or *Israelites*.

Jacob was no longer afraid of what might happen. He joined his family and waited for Esau and the 400 men. When Esau saw Jacob, Esau ran toward Jacob, hugged him, and kissed him. Both brothers cried. Esau had forgiven Jacob!

Student Page 5.4

Read directions to students and have them complete the exercise independently. Assist students as needed.

Review

- Why did Jacob end up marrying Leah instead of Rachel? (**Laban told Jacob that, in their country, the oldest daughter always got married first.**) Did Jacob get to marry Rachel? (**Yes, but he had to work seven more years.**)
- Do you think Jacob learned his lesson about tricking and cheating others because he had been tricked into marrying Leah? (**Yes.**)
- Why was Jacob afraid of Esau's coming with 400 men? (**Jacob thought that Esau was still angry and planned to harm Jacob and his family.**)
- Who was the Man that Jacob wrestled with? (**Possible answers: Jesus, God**) What new name did the Man give to Jacob? (**Israel**)
- How do you know that Esau had forgiven Jacob? (**He ran toward Jacob and hugged and kissed him.**)

APPLICATION

- How do you know that Jacob was a man who did not give up easily? (**Jacob worked for 14 years so that he could marry Rachel. He wrestled all night with the Man, even though Jacob's hip was out of joint.**)
- In what kind of situations might you be tempted to quit when things get hard? (**Possible answers: working on a hard math lesson, being kind when others are mean, cleaning up a very messy room**)
- What can you do to work through difficult times? (**Possible answers: I can ask a parent or teacher to help me; I can remember that God wants me to treat others the way that I would like to be treated; I can pray for a good attitude and a willing heart.**)

DAY 4

5.4 ***Jacob and Esau***

Solve the math problems. Match your answer to the letter in the Code Box. Write the letter in the box of the same color at the bottom of the page to discover the new name that God gave to Jacob.

5 + 3 = 8

2 + 4 = 6

1 + 1 = 2

2 + 1 = 3

3 + 2 = 5

4 + 3 = 7

Code Box

1 = P
2 = R
3 = A
4 = D
5 = E
6 = S
7 = L
8 = I

I S R A E L

20

5.5 Jacob and Esau

Focus: Review and Assessment

★ PREPARATION

Select **VA 5A Jacob Steals the Blessing** and **VA 5B Jacob's Unusual Dream**. (*Lesson Review*)

Print a copy of **BLM 5D Lesson 5 Test** for each student. (*Directed Instruction*)

Lesson Review ★

Use **VA 5A Jacob Steals the Blessing** and **VA 5B Jacob's Unusual Dream** as you review the Bible truths. Cover the following points in your review:

- Jacob and Esau were twin brothers. Esau was the older twin; Jacob was younger.
- Isaac, Abraham's son, was Jacob and Esau's father. Isaac favored Esau over Jacob.
- Jacob was jealous of Esau and looked for a way to get Esau's birthright. When Esau came home from hunting and was hungry, Jacob saw a way to make a trade and cheat Esau out of his birthright.
- Esau traded his birthright for a bowl of stew and some bread.
- To help her favorite son, Jacob, get the blessing of his father, Isaac, Rebekah got some of Esau's clothes for Jacob to wear; put goatskins on Jacob's hands, arms, and neck; and prepared meat for Jacob to take to Isaac.
- Isaac blessed Jacob instead of Esau.
- Esau was angry that Jacob had cheated him out of both his birthright and his blessing.
- Esau threatened to kill Jacob. Jacob had to run away. He stopped at Bethel for the night.
- During Jacob's unusual dream at Bethel, God told Jacob that He would give Jacob the land he was sleeping on, Jacob would have many children, the whole earth would be blessed because of Jacob's family, God would protect Jacob wherever he went, and God would bring Jacob home again.
- When Jacob realized that he had spoken with God, he poured special oil over the stone and made it into an altar to honor the Lord.
- After he left Bethel, Jacob went to his relative Laban's home in Haran.
- Jacob married Leah due to Laban's trickery.
- Jacob agreed to work for Laban for seven more years so that Jacob could marry Rachel, Laban's younger daughter.
- A Man wrestled with Jacob on the night before Jacob was to meet Esau again.
- The Man blessed Jacob and gave Jacob a new name—Israel. Now that Jacob had God's blessing, he was no longer afraid to meet his brother.
- Esau had forgiven Jacob. He ran toward Jacob and hugged and kissed him.

Directed Instruction ★

Distribute a copy of **BLM 5D Lesson 5 Test** to each student. Read each sentence and have students complete each exercise before moving to the next one. Share correct answers and discuss how false sentences should be made true.

Notes:

Lesson Preparation

Joseph

6.0

Expected Student Outcomes

KNOW
God turns bad experiences in Joseph's life to good.

DO
Students will:
- complete sentences to reinforce the Bible truth
- distinguish between true and false statements about Joseph's life
- decode a puzzle to find out how Joseph saved Egypt
- brainstorm and discuss ways to forgive others

APPLY
Students will conclude that godly leaders practice forgiveness. Students will exercise forgiveness in their own life.

Lesson Outline
I. Joseph the dreamer (Gen 37)
  A. Joseph's two dreams
  B. Joseph is sold into slavery
II. Joseph in prison (Gen 39–40)
  A. Joseph is a slave
  B. Joseph and the prisoners' dreams
III. Joseph saves Egypt (Gen 41:1–42:24)
  A. Joseph interprets Pharaoh's dream
  B. Joseph stores food for Egypt
IV. Joseph forgives his brothers (Gen 42:25–50:26)
  A. Joseph tests his brothers
  B. Jacob's household moves to Egypt

TEACHER'S HEART
God's love for you is unconditional and, as His ambassador, you should display unconditional love for your students—not play favorites. Hard to do? Yes, sometimes it is. But try this. First of all, in January each year, begin praying for the students who will be in your class next year. Second, when you begin the new year, pray for each of your students by name. Third, give a bit of extra attention, a pat or a hug to the not-as-easy-to-love students. Can you give these students special jobs? Can you design an assignment built for success? Can you remember to offer encouraging remarks and smiles? Fourth, ask the Lord to let you see these students through His eyes of love. Fifth, ask yourself what would have been the result if Jesus had only died for those who were cute and lovable. Would you have been included? Would anybody? And last of all, determine in your mind that you will love all your students equally. The Lord will give you the grace to do just that. Remember, love never fails (1 Corinthians 13:8). Try these six simple steps. You'll be amazed and delighted with the results. The Lord will be pleased, too! God will give you the strength to love the unlovely and help each child to grow and mature.

MEMORY VERSE
1 Thessalonians 5:24

MATERIALS
Day 1:
- VA 4A God's Promise to Abraham, VA 5A Jacob Steals the Blessing, VA 5B Jacob's Unusual Dream
- VA 6A Joseph the Dreamer
- BLMs 6A–B The Story of Joseph (*Extension*)

Day 2:
- Brightly colored coat or sweater
- VA 6B Joseph in Prison
- PP-2 Christlike Behavior (*Extension*)

Day 3:
- Pillow
- VA 6C Joseph Saves Egypt

Day 4:
- TM-3 Joseph Chart
- VA 6D Joseph Forgives His Brothers
- BLM 6C Benjamin's Sack (*Extension*)

Day 5:
- VA 6A Joseph the Dreamer, VA 6B Joseph in Prison, VA 6C Joseph Saves Egypt, VA 6D Joseph Forgives His Brothers
- BLM 6D Lesson 6 Test

TEACHER RESOURCES
MacArthur, John. *Jacob and Egypt: The Sovereignty of God.* Thomas Nelson, 2008.

STUDENT RESOURCES
Koralek, Jenny. *Coat of Many Colors.* Wm. B. Eerdmans Publishing Co., 2004.
Turnbull, Stephanie. *Egyptians.* Usborne, 2004.

6.1 Joseph

Focus: Joseph the Dreamer

MEMORY VERSE

1 Thessalonians 5:24

MEMORY WORK

- Write the Memory Verse on the board and encourage students to follow along as you read it. Then ask students to crouch down close to the floor, ready to jump up. Have students whisper the Memory Verse until everyone says the word *faithful*. At that point, tell students to jump up and complete the verse. Be sure to say this week's verse enthusiastically!

★ PREPARATION

Select **VA 4A God's Promise to Abraham**, **VA 5A Jacob Steals the Blessing**, and **VA 5B Jacob's Unusual Dream**. (*Introduction*)

Select **VA 6A Joseph the Dreamer**. (*Directed Instruction*)

EXTENSION

1A Use **BLMs 6A–B The Story of Joseph** to make a small book about the Bible truth. Direct each student to color the pictures and cut on the dotted lines. Tell students to put the pages in the correct order. Use the gray margin lines as a guide for stapling and staple the small storybook together. Encourage students to read the book to parents or friends.

Introduction ★

Choose three volunteers to help you review the sequence of events from Lessons 4 and 5. Distribute **VA 4A God's Promise to Abraham**, **VA 5A Jacob Steals the Blessing**, and **VA 5B Jacob's Unusual Dream** to each volunteer, but do not put the pictures in chronological order. Have the volunteers stand facing the class. Invite students to help you put the pictures in the correct order.

Choose a few students to review the characters of Abraham, Isaac, Jacob, and Esau and their relationship to one another. (**Abraham was Isaac's father; Isaac was Jacob and Esau's father; Jacob stole his brother Esau's birthright.**) During this review period, remind students that God made a special covenant, or promise, with Abraham. Explain that all of the people born to Abraham's children and grandchildren were part of the covenant. Remind students that Jacob had 12 sons and some daughters (Genesis 37:35). All of these children were part of the promise that God made to bring blessing to all the families of the earth. This week, students will learn more about the way God blessed Abraham's family.

Directed Instruction ★

Shake your head, sigh, and raise your hands, palms up, in a helpless gesture. Inform students that even though God blessed Jacob, Jacob failed to act wisely in something. His error was to show favoritism to one of his sons over the others. Ask students to listen for the name of the son that Jacob favored and the problems it caused. Read **VA 6A Joseph the Dreamer**.

See if students listened for the name of Jacob's favorite son. (**Joseph**) Invite students to act out Joseph's first dream. Choose a student to be *Joseph* and direct that student to stand at the front of the classroom. Ask the student to pretend to be holding a bundle of wheat. Choose 11 other students to bow down before *Joseph*.

Remind students that in Joseph's second dream the sun, moon, and 11 stars bowed to Joseph. Since the sun and the moon in the dream represented Joseph's parents, bring out the fact that it would have been very embarrassing for parents to bow down to one of their sons. Remind students that Jacob was disappointed in Joseph for even mentioning the dream.

Explain that God gave Joseph these two dreams to show what would happen in the future. Jacob and his sons should have understood that God was with Joseph. They should have trusted God's plan for Joseph's life, but they did not.

Review

- How did Joseph's father, Jacob, show that Joseph was his favorite? (**Jacob gave Joseph a special, colorful, long-sleeved coat.**)

- Why did the older brothers hate Joseph so much? (**Possible answers: Joseph was the favorite; they didn't like his dreams; they didn't want their younger brother to have a position of authority over them in the future.**)
- What did Joseph's dream about the bundles of wheat mean? (**It meant that all of the brothers would bow down and show respect to Joseph.**)
- What did Joseph's dream about the sun, moon, and stars mean? (**It meant that Joseph's family would bow down to him someday.**)
- How did Joseph's brothers feel about him? (**They hated him; they were jealous of Joseph because he was their father's favorite.**)

Student Page 6.1

Read each event of Joseph's life and pause when you come to each blank space. Allow students to share the correct word to write in the blank space. When all have finished, choose a volunteer to reread the Bible truth.

Notes:

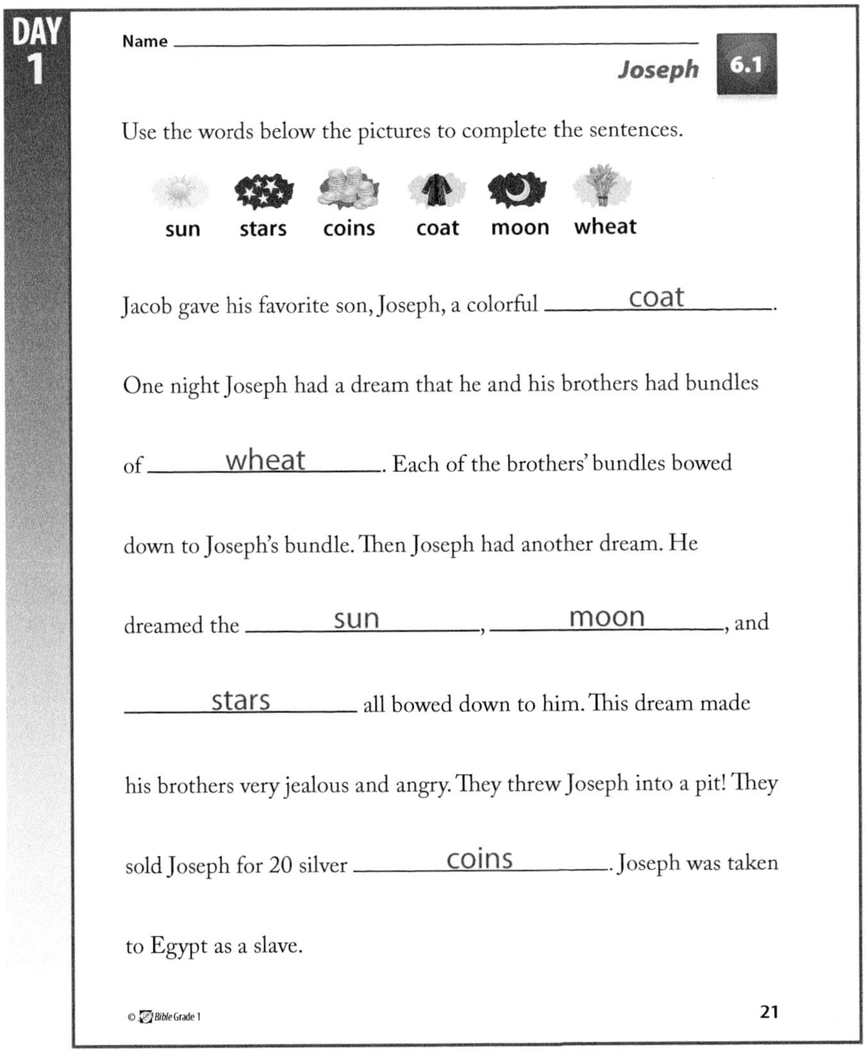

DAY 1

Name ______________________

Joseph **6.1**

Use the words below the pictures to complete the sentences.

sun stars coins coat moon wheat

Jacob gave his favorite son, Joseph, a colorful ___coat___.

One night Joseph had a dream that he and his brothers had bundles of ___wheat___. Each of the brothers' bundles bowed down to Joseph's bundle. Then Joseph had another dream. He dreamed the ___sun___, ___moon___, and ___stars___ all bowed down to him. This dream made his brothers very jealous and angry. They threw Joseph into a pit! They sold Joseph for 20 silver ___coins___. Joseph was taken to Egypt as a slave.

© *Bible* Grade 1 21

APPLICATION

- Remember that God promised to bless Abraham's family. In today's lesson, did Jacob's sons act as if they acknowledged God or His blessing? (**No.**) How do you know? (**Possible answers: Jacob's sons were jealous of Joseph; they hated Joseph; they sold Joseph as a slave; they lied to their father to cover up what they had done.**)
- How should family members treat each other? (**Answers will vary, but should include that they should love each other; they should help each other; they should forgive each other when they've hurt each other; they should tell the truth.**)
- God had a special plan for Joseph's life, and God has a special plan for your life, too. How can you learn what God's plan for you will be? (**Answers will vary, but should include that I can learn God's Word, pray to Him, and look for opportunities to serve others.**)

6.2 Joseph

Focus: Joseph in Prison

★ PREPARATION

Bring in a BRIGHTLY COLORED COAT or SWEATER. (*Introduction*)

Select **VA 6B Joseph in Prison**. (*Directed Instruction*)

EXTENSION

2A Show **PP-2 Christlike Behavior** to reinforce the concepts presented in this week's lesson.

REINFORCEMENT

When young children pray, they often find it easy to pray for things they want, but quite difficult to pray prayers of repentance. There are several reasons for this; they may be embarrassed to admit their sins, or they may feel that they do not do things that are wrong. It is important to teach students to examine their own actions and to honestly confess their sins to God and to each other, asking for forgiveness. Modeling this type of prayer for them is a great teaching strategy. Sharing about a personal time of repentance and seeking forgiveness from God opens the way for students to begin their own journey of repentance and forgiveness.

Introduction ★

Bring a BRIGHTLY COLORED COAT or SWEATER to class. Choose a volunteer to be *Joseph* and three or four volunteers to represent *the brothers* and *the slave traders*. Review the Bible truth, using the actions noted:

Jacob showed favoritism by giving Joseph a beautiful, colorful coat. (**Put the coat or sweater on *Joseph*.**)

Joseph told his family about his dreams. (***Joseph* pretends to tell about his dreams.**)

Joseph's brothers were jealous and angry. The brothers threw Joseph into a pit. (***The brothers* take off the coat or sweater. *Joseph* crouches down, as if in a pit.**)

Joseph was sent to Egypt as a slave. (**The *slave traders* lead *Joseph* away. *Joseph* looks sad.**)

Directed Instruction ★

Explain to students that people often complain about unfair things. The Bible does not say that Joseph complained. Joseph knew that God was with him. He trusted God even when unfair things happened.

Tell students that you will read about Joseph again in today's lesson. Ask them to listen for the ways Joseph handled the tough things that were happening to him. Show the picture on **VA 6B Joseph in Prison** to students. Point out that Joseph is in prison. Explain that even though bad things happened to Joseph, God was with him. Joseph understood that God could and would use all the bad things to work out for good. Teach that the word *pharaoh* means *an Egyptian king*. Read the text on the back.

Invite a few students to share their conclusions about how Joseph dealt with unfair things. (**Possible answers: He knew that God was with him; he was always honest; he worked hard and did his very best.**)

Review

- Who bought Joseph from the traders? (**Potiphar**)
- Why was Joseph sent to prison? (**Potiphar's wife told her husband a lie about Joseph, and he was sent to prison for something he didn't do.**)
- How was Joseph able to tell the butler, or cupbearer, and the baker the meanings of their dreams? (**God was with Joseph and told Joseph what each dream meant.**)
- What did Joseph ask the butler, or cupbearer, to do when he went back to Pharaoh? (**Joseph asked the butler to tell Pharaoh that he was put in prison unfairly and should be allowed to go free.**)
- What did the butler, or cupbearer, do? (**He forgot about Joseph.**)

Student Page 6.2

Read the directions and the text for each exercise. Allow volunteers to tell the class if each statement is true or not true. Give students time to write their answers.

Discuss things to put in the picture at the bottom of the page. When students have finished their drawings, invite volunteers to share their pictures with the class.

Notes:

APPLICATION

- It did not seem as if God was blessing Abraham's family when Joseph was unfairly treated. How do you feel when you are treated unfairly? (**Answers will vary.**)
- Even though Joseph was in prison, God was with him. How do you know that God is with you? (**Answers will vary, but should include that the Bible tells us that God is always with us (Matthew 28:20).**)
- Do you think that Joseph worried when he was in prison? (**Answers will vary.**)
- What should you do when you feel worried? (**I should pray and ask God for help; I should let my parents know how I feel.**)

DAY 2

6.2 *Joseph*

Write **yes** on the line if the sentence is true. Write **no** if it is not true.

1. __yes__ Jacob gave Joseph a beautiful, colorful, long-sleeved coat.

2. __no__ Joseph's brothers loved him very much, all the time.

3. __yes__ Joseph was sold as a slave and was taken to Egypt.

4. __no__ Potiphar's wife told the truth about Joseph.

5. __no__ Joseph met the pharaoh's son and grandson in prison.

6. __yes__ Joseph explained the meaning of two prisoners' dreams.

7. Draw a picture of Joseph in prison.

Drawings will vary.

6.3

Joseph

Focus: Joseph Saves Egypt

★ **PREPARATION**

Bring a PILLOW to class. (*Introduction*)

Select **VA 6C Joseph Saves Egypt**. (*Directed Instruction*)

Introduction ★

Hold your PILLOW, yawn, and behave as though you are very sleepy. Tell students that you had a bad night's sleep because bad dreams awakened you. Unfortunately, you cannot remember your dreams. Give a few students time to relate some of their own dream experiences.

Invite students to recall the way dreams affected Joseph's life. (**Joseph dreamed that one day his family would bow down to him. Those dreams caused his family to become very angry with him. God gave Joseph the meaning of the dreams that the butler and baker dreamed, and the interpretation of each dream came true.**)

Directed Instruction ★

Show students the picture on **VA 6C Joseph Saves Egypt**. Explain that students will hear about another important dream in Joseph's life. Read the text on the back of VA 6C to students.

Emphasize that the first thing Joseph said to Pharaoh was that Joseph himself did not know the meaning of the dreams, but that God told him what the dreams meant. Joseph acknowledged and honored God!

Explain to students that a *famine* means *a time when little to no food grows.* Joseph told Pharaoh that Egypt would have seven years with lots of food, but then there would be seven years without any food. During a long period of famine, many people would die from hunger. Pharaoh trusted Joseph's explanation of the dream and listened to Joseph's plans to save the Egyptian people. Then Pharaoh made Joseph a leader and put him in charge of giving people the food that had been stored.

Remind students that 10 of Joseph's brothers came to Egypt to buy food. Discuss the possible reasons why Joseph did not tell his brothers who he really was. (**Possible answers: Joseph did not know if his brothers still hated him or not; he wanted to see if his brothers had changed; he was not glad to see his brothers.**)

Review

- Why did Pharaoh ask to see Joseph? (**Pharaoh was bothered by dreams and had heard that Joseph could tell him what the dreams meant.**)
- How did Joseph honor God when he met Pharaoh? (**Joseph acknowledged that it was God who would give him the interpretation.**)
- Why did Joseph's brothers go to Egypt? (**They needed to buy food because the famine had spread to Canaan.**)
- Why did Joseph call his brothers *spies*? (**He wanted to test them and see if they had changed.**)
- Joseph gave food to his brothers. What did Joseph tell his brothers they had to do if they wanted more food? (**They had to leave Simeon in prison and bring their youngest brother, Benjamin, back to Egypt.**)

Student Page 6.3

Emphasize that Joseph was given the second highest job in Egypt. The pharaoh trusted Joseph to save Egypt during the time of the famine.

Read the directions on the page. Point out the pyramid and explain that pyramids are structures that Egyptians built. Direct students to write the first letter of each word pictured in the pyramid on the corresponding line in the puzzle. Assist students in completing the page to discover how Joseph saved Egypt from disaster. Remind students to capitalize the word *God*, because it is the name of a person, and *Egypt*, because it is the name of a place.

Notes:

APPLICATION

- In Joseph's life, God used some bad things to produce a good result. Have you ever had something bad happen to you, but something good happened as a result? (**Answers will vary.**)
- God helped Joseph to know the meaning of Pharaoh's dreams. What are some ways that God helps you? (**Answers will vary, but should include that God guides me, He is always present, He gave me my parents, and He died on the cross to pay for my sins.**)

REINFORCEMENT

Ancient Egypt was an agricultural society, and the success of the entire economy depended on the Nile River. The soil in the river valley was left fertile by the yearly receding floodwaters. The higher the floodwaters rose, the more arable land was produced. Farmers in the Nile valley grew a wide variety of grains, along with vegetables and fruits. After the harvest, animals were allowed to graze in the fields. Pharaoh had understandable cause for concern when he dreamed of thin cows and corn coming out of the Nile. Obtaining the correct interpretation of his dreams was vital to the life of the nation.

DAY 3

Name ______________________

Joseph **6.3**

Find out how Joseph saved Egypt. Fill in each blank with the first letter of the picture shown on the pyramid.

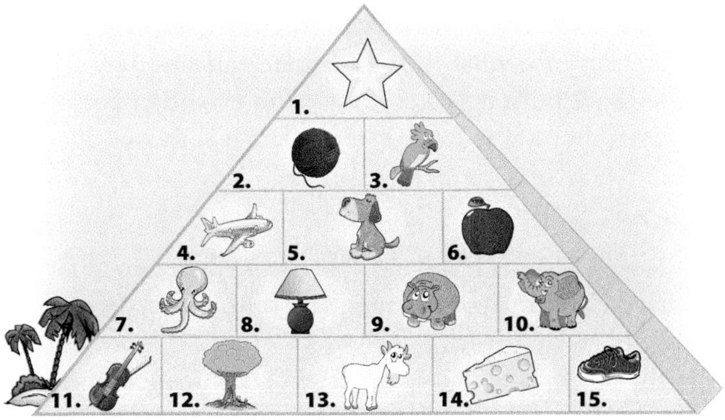

G (13)	o (7)	d (5)			
h (9)	e (10)	l (8)	p (3)	e (10)	d (5)
J (4)	o (7)	s (1)	e (10)	p (3)	h (9)
s (1)	a (6)	v (11)	e (10)		
E (10)	g (13)	y (2)	p (3)	t (12)	

© Bible Grade 1

23

6.4 Joseph

Focus: Joseph Forgives His Brothers

★ PREPARATION

Display **TM-3 Joseph Chart**. (*Introduction*)

Select **VA 6D Joseph Forgives His Brothers**. (*Directed Instruction*)

EXTENSION

4A Invite students to complete the dot-to-dot activity on **BLM 6C Benjamin's Sack**. Remind students that Joseph used the hidden cup to see if his brothers cared for each other. Ask students to verbally answer the question in the directions. (**Joseph wanted to see if his brothers had changed.**)

Introduction ★

Use **TM-3 Joseph Chart** to compare and contrast the negative things that happened to Joseph with the positive outcomes that God brought about as a result. After reading each bad thing that happened to Joseph, allow students to suggest how God used it for good. Suggested answers are provided.

Directed Instruction ★

Inform students that they are going to hear about how God used all of the bad things that happened to Joseph for a good thing. Read **VA 6D Joseph Forgives His Brothers** to students.

Help students understand that even though life was hard for Joseph, he trusted God. Just as Noah trusted God, Joseph understood that God had a plan to protect and save his family. God planned to send Joseph to Egypt to save the lives of many people.

Explain that it was not easy for Joseph to forgive his brothers because they had hurt him so badly. It was only possible for Joseph to forgive his brothers because Joseph had a close relationship with God. Joseph knew that God wants His people to forgive each other. Without a close relationship with God, Joseph might have stayed angry with his brothers and never forgiven them.

Point out that another reason that Joseph was able to forgive his brothers was that he saw that they were sorry for their sin. Explain to students that when they are sorry for what they have done and sincerely apologize to someone they have hurt, it makes it easier for the other person to forgive them. However, they are to forgive, regardless if someone apologizes or not.

Review

- How did Joseph test his brothers? (**He put a silver cup in Benjamin's sack, accused Benjamin of stealing, and told his brothers that Benjamin would have to go to prison.**)
- How did the brothers pass Joseph's test? (**They begged Joseph to let Benjamin go. They told Joseph that if they did not take Benjamin home, it would break their father's heart. Judah said he would take Benjamin's place as a slave. They showed a spirit of repentance for what they had done to Joseph many years before.**)
- Joseph told his brothers that what they did all those years ago was evil, but that God had used it for good. How did God bring good from the evil that his brothers had done? (**God sent Joseph to Egypt to save his family and to save the lives of many during the famine.**)
- What did Joseph want his family to do? (**He wanted them to move all of their families, flocks, and herds to Goshen in Egypt.**)
- What did God promise Jacob? (**God promised that He was Jacob's God and the God of Jacob's father. God told Jacob not to be afraid to go to Egypt. God told Jacob that He would bless Jacob's family there. Then**

God would bring Jacob's descendants back to Canaan, and someday Jacob's children would be as many as the sands of the sea.)**

Student Page 6.4

Divide students into pairs. For each picture, read the text, and give students time to talk with their partner about how each child pictured can forgive. Help students conclude that they should always pray for and bless those whom they have forgiven. Invite a few students to share their conclusions with the class.

Notes:

APPLICATION

- What would it feel like to be hurt and taken away from your family? (**Answers will vary.**) Would you want to forgive the people who hurt you and took you away from your family? (**Answers will vary.**)
- Share about a time when a friend hurt you. What did you do to restore your friendship with that person? (**Answers will vary.**)
- Is it always easy to forgive someone who hurts you? (**It is not always easy, but God calls us to forgive others (Colossians 3:13). God will help us to forgive others if we ask Him to.**)
- Do you have to see someone who has sinned against you before you can forgive him or her? (**No, I can forgive and then tell him or her about it in person later, if telling him or her would help the relationship.**)

DAY 4

6.4 ***Joseph***

1. Megan is sad. Her sister Beth was mean to her. Should Megan forgive Beth? Tell what Megan should do.

2. Matt pushed James on the playground, and James cut his knee. James is hurt, and he is mad at Matt. Should James forgive Matt? Tell what James should do.

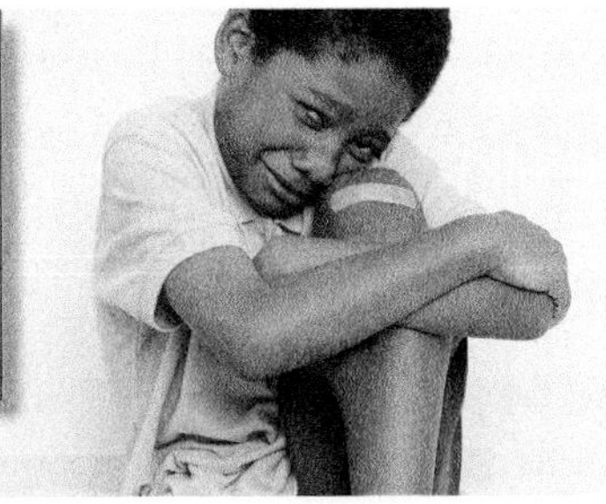

3. Luke's brother left some of their toys on the floor. Dad thinks that Luke left the toys out. Now Luke has to pick up the toys. Luke is mad at his brother. Should Luke forgive his brother? Tell what Luke should do.

24

© *Bible* Grade 1

6.5

Joseph

Focus: Review and Assessment

★ PREPARATION

Select **VA 6A Joseph the Dreamer**, **VA 6B Joseph in Prison**, **VA 6C Joseph Saves Egypt**, and **VA 6D Joseph Forgives His Brothers**. (*Lesson Review*)

Print a copy of **BLM 6D Lesson 6 Test** for each student. (*Directed Instruction*)

Lesson Review ★

Use **VA 6A Joseph the Dreamer**, **VA 6B Joseph in Prison**, **VA 6C Joseph Saves Egypt**, and **VA 6D Joseph Forgives His Brothers** to review the Bible truths from this lesson. Be sure to review the following points:

- Jacob had 12 sons, but his favorite son was Joseph. He gave Joseph a colorful, long-sleeved coat and loved him more than all his other sons.
- Joseph had dreams of the future. Joseph told his family about the dreams, but his family became angry because the dreams showed that they would bow down to Joseph one day.
- Joseph's brothers were so jealous that they hated Joseph. Because they hated him so much, Joseph's brothers threw him into a pit.
- Reuben, Joseph's oldest brother, wanted to save Joseph, but the other brothers sold Joseph as a slave. Joseph was taken to Egypt.
- In Egypt, Joseph was sold to a man named *Potiphar*. Potiphar trusted Joseph, but Potiphar's wife said that Joseph did something that he did not do. Potiphar believed his wife and had Joseph put in prison.
- In prison, Joseph met two men who had dreams that they did not understand. God told Joseph what the dreams meant, and the interpretation came true, just as Joseph had said.
- When Pharaoh, the king of Egypt, heard about Joseph, Pharaoh asked Joseph to tell him the meaning of his dreams. Joseph told Pharaoh that God gave him the meaning of the dreams.
- Because God was with Joseph, Joseph was able to give the pharaoh a plan to save all the people of Egypt.
- Pharaoh trusted Joseph so much that he gave Joseph the second most important job in Egypt. Joseph saved the people of Egypt from dying during the famine.
- The famine reached the land of Canaan, too, and Jacob sent his 10 oldest sons to Egypt to buy food.
- When Joseph saw his brothers again, he wanted to test them to see if their hearts had changed. He hid a silver cup in Benjamin's sack and threatened to put Benjamin in prison. But Joseph's brothers had changed so much that they begged him to take Judah instead of Benjamin.
- Joseph forgave his brothers for sending him away from his family. Joseph knew that God had a plan for good. God used Joseph to save Egypt and Jacob's family during the time of the famine.

Directed Instruction ★

Distribute a copy of **BLM 6D Lesson 6 Test** to each student. Read the directions and pronounce any difficult words. After collecting the test, discuss students' answers.

Notes:

Lesson Preparation

Moses

7.0

Expected Student Outcomes

KNOW

God protects Moses, calls him to serve, and uses him to lead the Israelites to the Promised Land.

DO

Students will:
- complete sentences to review the Bible truth
- evaluate the name that God told Moses to call Him
- order the events leading up to the Exodus
- discuss appropriate scriptural solutions to their own feelings of frustration or incapability

APPLY

Students will recognize that obeying God leads to deliverance.

Lesson Outline

I. Moses is born (Ex 2:1–10)
  A. The Hebrews are slaves
  B. Baby Moses is saved
II. The burning bush (Ex 2:11–4:31)
  A. God calls Moses
III. The ten plagues (Ex 7–12)
  A. Pharaoh has a hard heart
  B. God sends plagues
  C. Pharaoh lets God's people go
IV. Crossing the Red Sea (Ex 13–14)
  A. God's people leave Egypt
  B. Pharaoh changes his mind
  C. God delivers His people again

TEACHER'S HEART

Do you ever feel overwhelmed by the job that God has placed before you? Moses felt the same way! In fact, Moses felt so inadequate that he made excuses to God five times! He really didn't think he was the man for the job. However, once Moses yielded himself to God and placed his trust in Him, Moses was able to face the challenge that God had called him to. The Red Sea was in front of him and Pharaoh and his army were right behind him. Worse, his own people were blaming him for their impending doom. Moses had no idea how God was going to get him out of this situation, but he was confident God was going to do something.

God knows that you may be feeling inadequate or overwhelmed. He led you to this task and He will continue equipping you for it. Seek God's guidance, God's wisdom, and God's peace. Yield yourself to God's control. You may not know how God is going to part the sea before you, but He will part it. Do not be afraid. Stand still and see the salvation of the Lord.

MEMORY VERSE

Psalm 50:15

MATERIALS

Day 1:
- Flip chart
- VA 7A Moses Is Born
- BLM 7A Watching over Moses, cotton balls or mounting foam (*Extension*)

Day 2:
- Photographs
- VA 7B The Burning Bush

Day 3:
- No additional materials are needed.

Day 4:
- VA 7C Crossing the Red Sea

Day 5:
- VA 7A Moses Is Born, VA 7B The Burning Bush, VA 7C Crossing the Red Sea
- BLM 7B Lesson 7 Test

SONGS

Promised Land

TEACHER RESOURCES

Goldingay, John. *Exodus and Leviticus for Everyone*. Westminster John Knox Press, 2010.

Morgan, Robert J. *The Red Sea Rules: 10 God-Given Strategies for Difficult Times*. Thomas Nelson, 2001.

STUDENT RESOURCES

Stronach, John, and Bill Boyce. *The Ten Commandments*. DVD. Genius Products, 2007.

7.1 Moses

Focus: Moses Is Born

MEMORY VERSE

Psalm 50:15

MEMORY WORK

- Write the Memory Verse on the board or on a FLIP CHART. Read the verse together, then tape a piece of paper over one of the words and repeat the verse again. During the week, continue to cover more and more words until the verse can be recited from memory.

PREPARATION

Select **VA 7A Moses Is Born.** (*Directed Instruction*)

EXTENSION

1A Provide each student with a copy of **BLM 7A Watching over Moses** and a piece of light blue construction paper to make a craft that can be used to retell the Bible truth. Students will need to color and cut out the figures of baby Moses, the basket, and Miriam. Have students draw and color reeds and tall grasses on their blue paper before gluing the figures to the paper. For a three-dimensional effect, provide students with small pieces of COTTON BALLS or MOUNTING FOAM to put behind the baby before putting him into the basket.

Introduction

To illustrate the concept of slavery, choose several volunteers to act as slaves for a brief period. Using a strict voice and firm demeanor, demand that the slaves dust shelves, clean the boards, get on the floor to pick up tiny pencil shavings, or other similar classroom chores. Be tough with the slaves and try to choose chores that students dislike. Make some unreasonable demands, such as having students get down on their hands and knees to pick up litter. Let them know that they have no choice but to do what you say.

After a brief period, interview one or two of the students who pretended to be slaves and ask them how it felt to be a slave. If a student claims that the experience was fun, explain that pretending to be a slave for a few minutes may have been fun, but true slavery is not at all fun! Real slaves serve for many, many years under slave masters who are much more harsh and demanding.

Directed Instruction ★

Open the Bible to the book of Genesis. Remind students that the Bible is God's Word. Tell students that in the first book of the Bible, God taught about many things, including Creation, the Flood, His call to Abraham, and the life of Joseph. Remind students that God had made a covenant with Abraham, Isaac, and Jacob. In His covenant, God promised blessing to their family, adding that all the families of the earth would be blessed through them. God did not forget His promise; He never does!

Review that Joseph had invited his father, Jacob, and all his brothers to move to Egypt during the time of the famine. Jacob's sons had large families that had increased in number to many, many people, just as God had promised. They lived in an area of Egypt called *Goshen*.

Open the Bible to the second book, Exodus. Explain that today's Bible truth comes from Exodus. This account takes place many years after Joseph died. Show the picture on **VA 7A Moses Is Born** and read the text.

Review

- What did Jochebed and Amram do with their son Moses after he was born? (**They took care of him for three months and tried to hide him from the Egyptians.**)
- Why could the parents no longer hide Moses in their home? (**He probably cried or made other noises.**)
- What did Jochebed do since Moses was too big to keep at home? (**She made a basket and coated the bottom of it with tar to keep the water out. Then she put Moses into the basket and put the basket in the river.**)
- What was Miriam's job? (**Miriam had to keep watch over Moses and the basket.**)
- What happened to Moses while Miriam was watching him? (**Pharaoh's daughter found him and decided to make him her son.**)

Student Page 7.1

Read the directions and any unfamiliar words. Allow students to complete the page independently.

Notes:

APPLICATION

- It was very brave of Miriam to watch her baby brother and to speak to Pharaoh's daughter. Has God ever called you to do something brave? What might God ask you to do that would take courage? (**Possible answers: tell someone about Jesus, help someone in trouble, sacrifice something that is important to me**)
- Do you have jobs to do to help your parents like Miriam did? (**Answers will vary.**) Why is it important to do your jobs well? (**Answers will vary, but should include that when I do small jobs well, I will be prepared to be responsible for larger jobs.**)

DAY 1

Name ______________________

Moses **7.1**

Use the words on the basket to complete the sentences.

1. The Hebrews had to work hard as ___slaves___.

2. Then Pharaoh said to kill all the ___baby___ boys.

3. Jochebed put her baby in a ___basket___.

Use the words on the pyramid to complete the sentences.

4. Miriam was a brave ___girl___.

5. She watched over ___Moses___.

6. Miriam ___talked___ to Pharaoh's daughter.

7. God ___saved___ baby Moses.

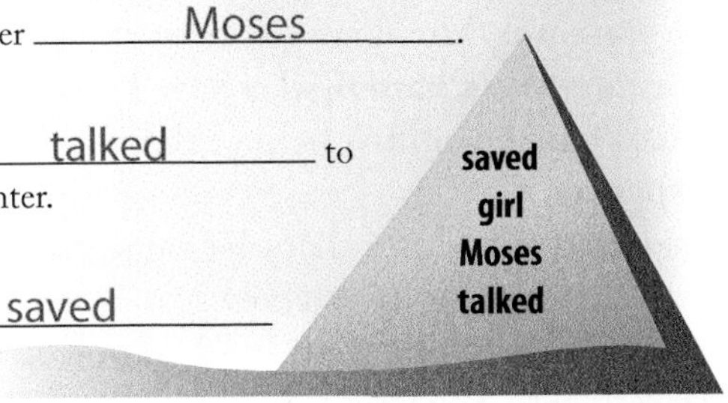

 25

7.2 Moses

Focus: The Burning Bush

★ PREPARATION

Select "Promised Land" from the music CDs. (*Introduction*)

Bring in several PHOTOGRAPHS to share with students. These should be photographs of someone taken at various times throughout the person's life. (*Introduction*)

Select **VA 7B The Burning Bush**. (*Directed Instruction*)

Introduction ★

Play "Promised Land" from the music CDs. Remind students that the Hebrews were slaves, just as the students pretended to be in Lesson 7.1. The Hebrews looked forward to being free and returning to their own land. Invite students to sing along.

Share a few PHOTOGRAPHS. Tell the approximate age of the person in each photograph. Point out that just as the person pictured grew up, Moses did too. Explain that in today's lesson, Moses is now an adult.

Directed Instruction ★

Open the Bible to the book of Exodus. Remind students that the Bible truths about Moses come from Exodus, the second book in the Bible. Recall for students that Moses was a Hebrew, and he was a descendant of Abraham, just like Isaac, Jacob, and Joseph. Read the Bible truth on the back of **VA 7B The Burning Bush**.

Ask students to share what happened when Moses became angry. (**He killed an Egyptian.**) Was Moses obeying God when he killed the man? (**No, Moses disobeyed God by doing that.**) Remind students that all choices have consequences. Ask students to recall the consequence that followed Moses' choice to disobey God. (**He had to run away to the desert. He could no longer live in the palace or be with the Hebrew people.**)

Express surprise that Moses saw a bush that was burning, but it was not being burned up by the fire. Then God spoke from the flames within the bush! Ask students to share how they might have felt if they were there in the desert with Moses. (**Answers will vary.**)

Reinforce that Moses did not believe he could do what God wanted. He was not sure that he could convince the Hebrew people to accept him as their leader because he was not a strong speaker. Finally, Moses decided to trust God, and he went back to speak to the leaders of the Hebrew people.

Review

- Why did Moses run away from Egypt? (**He killed an Egyptian, and he was afraid that he would be punished.**) Where did Moses go, and what did he do there? (**He went to the desert where he took care of sheep.**)
- What did Moses see while watching the sheep? (**He saw a bush that was on fire, but it did not burn up. God spoke from the flames.**)
- Why do you think Moses was worried about going back to Egypt? (**Possible answers: Pharaoh may have known about Moses' crime; the children of Israel wouldn't believe that God really sent him; he wasn't a strong speaker.**)
- What did God tell Moses that His name was? (**I AM**)
- Why was God freeing the Hebrews from slavery in Egypt? (**Answers will vary, but should include that they had prayed to be set free. God wanted them to return to the land that He had promised to Abraham.**)

Student Page 7.2

Read the directions and allow students to complete the page independently.

Notes:

APPLICATION

- God had a special plan for Moses. He has a special plan for your life, too. How can you learn more about God's plan for your life? (**Possible answers: I can listen to God's Word, pray, obey my parents and teacher, and do my best in everything I do.**)
- Why do you think that God chose Moses to lead His people even though Moses had killed a man? (**Answers will vary, but should include that we are all sinners, yet God still chooses to use us.**)
- God said that His name is I AM. What do you think that means? (**Answers will vary, but should include that God exists right now, just as He did in Moses' time and will for all eternity.**)

DAY 2

7.2 *Moses*

God told Moses His name. God said, "My name is I AM." God's name is a reminder that God has always been and will always be.

1. Color the sheep that have the letters in God's name, I AM.

Unscramble the words below the lines. Write the words in the correct order.

2. ___I AM___ called Moses to
AM I

___go to Pharaoh___.
to Pharaoh go

26

7.3 Moses

Focus: The Ten Plagues

★ PREPARATION

Select "Promised Land" from the music CDs. (*Introduction*)

REINFORCEMENT

The Bible records that in order to convince Pharaoh to let the people go, God sent 10 plagues upon the land of Egypt. Did these events really happen? Absolutely! An early nineteenth century papyrus that dates from the end of the Middle Kingdom in Egypt was taken to the Leiden Museum in Holland where it was interpreted in 1909. The papyrus, the *Ipuwer Papyrus*, is believed to be an eyewitness account from the perspective of an Egyptian living at the time. In the papyrus, the author describes the plagues in amazing detail, exactly paralleling the account in Exodus.

Introduction ★

Play "Promised Land" from the music CDs. Remind students that the Promised Land in the song refers to the land that the Hebrew people were promised by God. Abraham, Isaac, and Jacob had lived there. Jacob and his descendants had lived there before they moved to Egypt. Because the Hebrew people were slaves, they longed to go to the Promised Land where they would finally be free!

Directed Instruction

Read the following Bible truth based on Exodus 7–12 and have students put up one finger for each plague:

God was ready to free His people from their slavery, but Pharaoh was not ready to let them go. Even after Moses and Aaron showed Pharaoh the signs God gave them, Pharaoh refused to let God's people leave Egypt. So God sent 10 plagues, which were diseases and problems, to the Egyptians to convince Pharaoh to let the Hebrew people go free.

1. God told Moses to have Aaron raise his walking stick and strike the river's water. It turned into blood! All the fish died! The Egyptians could not drink from the river now!
2. God sent frogs up out of the water. Frogs were everywhere—in the houses, in the bedrooms, on the beds, on the people, in their ovens, and even in their food bowls!
3. God sent tiny little bugs called lice or gnats to bite the people and their animals.
4. God sent thousands of biting flies that filled the Egyptians' homes and covered the ground. The flies came and bit the Egyptians, but not the Hebrews.
5. God sent a terrible sickness to kill the Egyptian horses, sheep, and other animals. But the Hebrew animals stayed healthy.
6. God told Moses to throw ashes into the sky. When the ashes settled back down, the Egyptians and their remaining animals broke out with painful sores called boils.
7. God sent hail with very large, heavy hailstones, which are pieces of ice that fall from the sky. He warned Pharaoh to bring the animals and people inside. Any living thing left outside would die because of this hail. The hail even destroyed the trees!
8. God sent hungry grasshoppers. Wind blew all day and night from the east. The next morning, the grasshoppers ate whatever grain was left in the fields. But the Hebrews still had grain.
9. God made it so that it was dark for three days, even in the daytime. The Egyptians couldn't see one another; but the Hebrews had light where they lived.

Still ... Pharaoh refused to let God's people go!

10. God sent the tenth and final plague, and it was worse than all the rest. At midnight, all the firstborn sons of the Egyptians died, even Pharaoh's oldest son died. The firstborn of their animals died, too. But

none of the Hebrew children or animals died. God gave them very special instructions so death would pass over their homes. God told them to prepare a special meal to eat. The meal was called the Feast of the Passover because death passed over all the Hebrew homes.

After all of this happened, Pharaoh finally told the Hebrews to leave Egypt. The people of God traveled toward Canaan, which was also called the Promised Land, the land that God had promised to His people.

Review

- What terrible things happened to the Egyptians because Pharaoh was so stubborn that he would not obey God? (**God sent 10 plagues.**)
- What was the worst plague of all? (**The firstborn sons of all the Egyptians and the firstborn of all their animals died.**)
- How did God protect the Hebrew children from death? (**God gave them special instructions that they obeyed.**)

Student Page 7.3

Assist students as needed to complete the matching exercises.

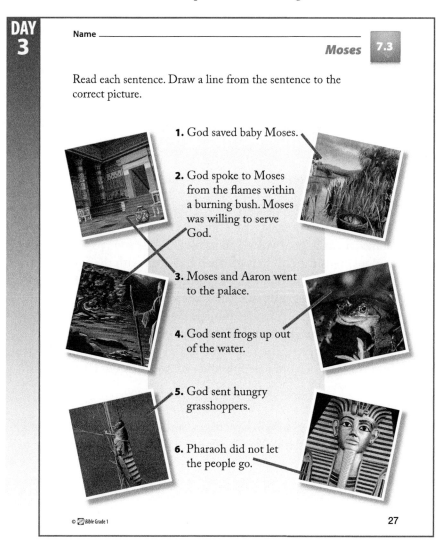

DAY 3

Name ______________________________

Moses 7.3

Read each sentence. Draw a line from the sentence to the correct picture.

1. God saved baby Moses.

2. God spoke to Moses from the flames within a burning bush. Moses was willing to serve God.

3. Moses and Aaron went to the palace.

4. God sent frogs up out of the water.

5. God sent hungry grasshoppers.

6. Pharaoh did not let the people go.

APPLICATION

- What do you think finally convinced Pharaoh to let God's people go? (**Answers will vary, but should include the death of Pharaoh's firstborn son and the fact that Pharaoh saw that when God wants something to happen, it happens!**)
- Pharaoh was very, very stubborn! Even though his people were suffering, he still would not let the Hebrew people go. Are you stubborn sometimes? Does your stubbornness ever cause you to disobey God? (**Answers will vary.**)
- What should you do when you are in a stubborn mood? (**Answers will vary, but should include that I should pray and ask God to help me with my attitude. Then, I should decide to be more willing and giving.**)

7.4 Moses

Focus: Crossing the Red Sea

★ PREPARATION

Select "Promised Land" from the music CDs. (*Introduction*)

Select **VA 7C Crossing the Red Sea**. (*Directed Instruction*)

EXTENSION

4A Sometime during the school day, perhaps when you are taking your class to lunch, leave early. Lead your students on a route that is different from one you normally take. Make sure to lead them in a circle or in a way that makes no sense. When they begin asking questions and telling you that you are going the wrong way, just tell them that they must trust you. Lead students to a solid wall of the room they need to enter and tell them to go in. When students tell you that it is impossible to enter a room without using the door, explain that the Hebrew people must have felt the same way when they came to the Red Sea. They could not understand how God could get them across!

Introduction ★

Play "Promised Land" from the music CDs. Invite students to move and sing along with the music. After listening to the music, ask students why they were celebrating. (**Answers will vary, but should include that God always keeps His promises and that He set the Hebrews free so they could leave Egypt for the Promised Land.**) Explain that in the same way, Christians can celebrate because Jesus died on the cross to set them free from sin.

Directed Instruction ★

Remind students that the tenth and worst of all the plagues was the death of the firstborn son of the Egyptians and the firstborn of all their animals. Even Pharaoh's oldest son died! The only way the Hebrews were able to avoid this plague was to follow God's instructions. Then death passed over their homes. When Pharaoh finally let the people go, they had to be ready to move quickly and follow Moses out of Egypt. Show the picture on **VA 7C Crossing the Red Sea** and read the text on the back.

Explain that although the Hebrew people were obedient to God's instructions to avoid the tenth plague, they still had not learned to trust God. Once they saw the Red Sea in front of them and the Egyptian army behind them, they stopped trusting God! Ask students to recall what the children of Israel said when they were faced with this problem. (**We're all going to die!**)

Remind students that God had done many powerful things that the people had seen with their own eyes. Tell students that the children of Israel had learned about God from their parents and grandparents. The Hebrews knew about God's promise to Abraham, Isaac, and Jacob. The people even knew about the way God used Joseph to save his family during the famine and bring his family to Egypt.

Express amazement in your voice and gestures while you recount all of the miraculous signs the children of Israel had seen with their own eyes. They saw a river turned into blood, frogs, tiny bugs, and biting flies all over people and animals in Egypt except their own people. They saw terrible sicknesses that killed the Egyptian animals, hailstones fall from the sky, grasshoppers eat all the grain, and darkness cover the land. God protected the families and animals of the Hebrews. But even after they saw all these wonderful things, the Hebrew people still did not trust God completely.

Review

- How did the Hebrews know where to go in the desert? (**God provided a bright pillar of cloud to follow by day and a pillar of fire in the sky to follow by night.**)
- Was Pharaoh glad to let the people go? (**No, he changed his mind and started chasing them with his army.**)

- Did the children of Israel trust God at the Red Sea when the Egyptian army was coming to attack them? (**No, the children of Israel were frustrated, scared, and mad at Moses. They blamed him for the danger.**)
- What powerful thing did God do to deliver the people? (**God parted the sea, and the people walked across on dry land.**)
- Did Pharaoh and the army have dry land to cross? (**No, the sea closed in on them, and they drowned.**)

Student Page 7.4

Talk about how it feels to be stuck or frustrated and what Christians should do when experiencing those feelings. Lead a class discussion about each of the scenarios presented on the page and ask students to offer their solutions to the class.

Notes:

DAY 4

7.4 ***Moses***

Listen to the short stories. Think about how each boy or girl is feeling. What should the children do? Talk about your ideas in your group.

1. Caleb is taking piano lessons. He has to practice for 20 minutes each day. Caleb cannot always find the right notes. He wants to play the piano well. What should Caleb do?

2. Miko doesn't like to eat vegetables, but her mom says that they will make her grow strong. Miko wants to please her mom. What should Miko do?

3. Ivan finds it hard to read and write. Homework is difficult for him, but he wants to do well in school. What should Ivan do?

28

APPLICATION

- It seemed that the Hebrew people were trapped by the Red Sea and that they could not pass through. Do you ever feel stuck or unable to do something? (**Answers will vary.**)
- What should you do when you feel stuck or frustrated? (**I should remember to stay close to God, encourage myself with His truth, and pray for His help.**)
- In today's Bible lesson, how was Moses like Abraham? (**Moses and Abraham both trusted God. Moses did not immediately understand how God was going to save the people, but he moved forward in faith. Abraham trusted God. He had never seen the land that God told him to move to, but he moved forward in faith.**)

REINFORCEMENT

Orthodox Jewish families today still celebrate *pesach*, or Passover, as they were commanded to do in Exodus 12:14–20. The holiday begins after sundown on the fourteenth day of the month of Nisan on the Hebrew calendar, which is in March or April on the western calendar, and it continues for the next seven to eight days. Jews follow several dietary restrictions during this period, including the avoidance of all foods with yeast. The highlight of the celebration is the seder meal, a traditional meal with specific foods served to commemorate the first Passover on the night when death passed over the Hebrew families who had faithfully followed God's instructions.

7.5

Moses

Focus: Review and Assessment

★ PREPARATION

Select **VA 7A Moses Is Born**, **VA 7B The Burning Bush**, and **VA 7C Crossing the Red Sea**. (*Lesson Review*)

Make one copy of **BLM 7B Lesson 7 Test** for each student. (*Directed Instruction*)

Lesson Review ★

Use **VA 7A Moses Is Born** to review the Bible truths from this lesson. Cover the following points:

- The Hebrews were living peacefully in Goshen, an area of Egypt, when a new pharaoh became worried that they would become more powerful than the Egyptian people.
- The new pharaoh forced God's people to become slaves.
- Much later, another pharaoh began killing all of the baby Hebrew boys.
- Moses' mother, Jochebed, saved Moses by putting him in a basket and placing the basket in the river.
- Moses' sister, Miriam, watched over Moses while he floated in the water.
- When Pharaoh's daughter found the baby and needed someone to take care of him, Miriam talked to Pharaoh's daughter and told her that Jochebed could take care of the baby.

Use **VA 7B The Burning Bush** to review the Bible truths. Cover the following points:

- When Moses saw an Egyptian beating a Hebrew slave, he became angry and killed the Egyptian.
- Moses fled to the desert and lived there for 40 years as a shepherd.
- While Moses was tending his sheep, God spoke to him from within the flames of a burning bush. God told Moses to go back to Egypt and lead the Hebrew people out of Egypt.
- Moses obeyed God. His brother, Aaron, went with him to speak to Pharaoh.
- When Moses and Aaron showed Pharaoh all of the signs God gave them, Pharaoh still refused to let the people go.
- God showed His power by sending 10 plagues against the Egyptians. The last plague was the worst; the firstborn son of all the Egyptian families and the firstborn of their animals died. Pharaoh finally let the Hebrew people go.

Use **VA 7C Crossing the Red Sea** to review the Bible truths. Cover the following points:

- Moses led the people across the desert toward the Red Sea.
- When Pharaoh regretted letting the Hebrew people go, he changed his mind. He took his whole army and chased after the Hebrew people.
- God parted the Red Sea and the Hebrew people walked across on dry ground.
- When the Egyptians tried to follow in their chariots, God made the wheels fall off! All the Egyptians drowned.

Directed Instruction ★

Distribute a copy of **BLM 7B Lesson 7 Test** to each student. Read each exercise and allow students to respond before moving on to the next exercise. When all students have finished taking the test, review the answers in class and collect the test papers for assessment.

Lesson Preparation

The Ten Commandments

8.0

Expected Student Outcomes

KNOW
God provides manna, quail, and the Ten Commandments for His people.

DO
Students will:
- complete a scrambled word activity to identify key items in the Bible truth
- examine the Ten Commandments and their applications for today
- determine which commandments are broken by certain behaviors
- review the Bible truth by matching key terms to their descriptions

APPLY
Students will thank God for meeting their physical and spiritual needs.

Lesson Outline

I. God meets physical needs (Ex 15:22; 16:4–5, 13)
  A. God provides water
  B. God provides manna
  C. God provides quail
II. God meets spiritual needs (Ex 20:1–17)
  A. The Ten Commandments
III. God provides His laws (Ex 20:1–17)
  A. More about the Ten Commandments
IV. The golden calf (Ex 31:18–32:35)
  A. The people make an idol
  B. Sin and consequences
  C. The people repent (Ex 34:1–28)

TEACHER'S HEART

How many times have you heard it said of an individual, "Oh him? Well, he marches to the beat of a different drummer," when what should have been said was, "Oh him! He thinks the rules don't apply to him. He does what is right in his own eyes." The Bible declares that in the days of Noah, every man, except Noah, did what was right in his own eyes. Look at the destruction that kind of thinking and behavior has brought to the world!

Today's society wants you to think that rules are bad. More and more people want to do what is right in their own eyes. Regardless of past history, they want to go their own way, make their own rules, and worst of all, they want God to be totally out of their life. Christians, however, have the truth of God's Word. You know from your own experience that following God brings blessing, and refusing to follow God brings ultimate defeat. As you teach about the Ten Commandments this week, ask God to strengthen your heart and help you impress upon your students their need for God's rules in their life.

MEMORY VERSE

1 John 5:3a

MATERIALS

Day 1:
- 3" × 5" index cards
- Half-gallon container
- Honey-flavored breakfast cereal (*Extension*)

Day 2:
- Board game and printed instructions
- TM-4 The Ten Commandments
- Board games (*Extension*)
- BLM 8A The Ten Commandments Puzzle (*Extension*)

Day 3:
- TM-4 The Ten Commandments
- PP-2 The Ten Commandments (*Extension*)

Day 4:
- VA 8A The Ten Commandments
- Flip chart (*Extension*)

Day 5:
- VA 8A The Ten Commandments
- BLM 8B Lesson 8 Test

SONGS

Ten Commandments

TEACHER RESOURCES

"The Ten Commandments and You." *Rose Book of Bible Charts, Maps, and Time Lines*. Rose Publishing, Inc., 2005.

STUDENT RESOURCES

Dobson, Shirley. *God's Ten Best: The Ten Commandments Coloring Book*. Gospel Light, 2002.

Nolan, Allia Zobel. *The Ten Commandments for Little Ones*. Harvest House Publishers, 2009.

8.1 The Ten Commandments

Focus: God Meets Physical Needs

MEMORY VERSE

1 John 5:3a

MEMORY WORK

- Write the Memory Verse on the board, and write each word from the Memory Verse on a 3" × 5" INDEX CARD, one word per card. Write the Scripture reference on another card. Distribute the cards to various students. Review any unfamiliar words. Read the Memory Verse, instructing students who hold cards to stand up when they hear the word that is on their card. State the Scripture reference, and have the student with that card stand up. Then have the entire class repeat the verse and reference. Redistribute the cards to other students and practice the Memory Verse again.

★ PREPARATION

Have a HALF-GALLON CONTAINER on hand. (*Directed Instruction*)

EXTENSION

1A Although it is impossible to know exactly how manna tasted, the Bible describes its taste as being like wafers made with honey (Exodus 16:31). Taking food allergies into account, provide each student with a small serving of HONEY-FLAVORED BREAKFAST CEREAL to experience a taste similar to manna.

Introduction

Ask students if they have ever taken a long walk, perhaps in the mountains or desert. (**Answers will vary.**) What might a person take along on a long walk? (**Answers will vary, but should include water and food.**)

Remind students that Moses was leading the children of Israel on a long walk. The people had to leave Egypt in a hurry. Pharaoh came after them with his army. God parted the Red Sea, and the children of Israel were able to cross on dry land. The children of Israel did not have time to pack for the trip before they left Egypt, so they did not have much food or water for the long journey to the Promised Land. Tell students to listen to how God provided for His people in today's lesson.

Directed Instruction ★

Read the following Bible truth based on Exodus 15:22–16:26:

> Once the Hebrews were safely across the Red Sea, they continued to travel through the desert toward the Promised Land. They walked and walked! The desert was very dry. First, the people got thirsty. Then, they got hungry. It didn't take long before the people started complaining!
>
> It was hard to find enough water and food for thousands and thousands of people. Moses needed God's help! God provided freshwater for the Hebrews to drink. He also provided special food for them to eat. God sent *little, thin, white flakes* called *manna*. The manna appeared on the ground in the morning. The people picked up manna every day for five days. On the sixth day, they collected enough manna to eat for two days. That way, they didn't need to work on the seventh day, the day that God had said to rest. God also sent small birds called *quail* to the camp so the people would have meat.

Explain that even though the Hebrews complained, Moses trusted God. He knew that God could provide food and water for the people. Moses had a close relationship with God, just like Abraham and Joseph had had many years before. Moses prayed for the people. God provided for them.

Remind students that the children of Israel were walking through the desert. There was probably very little shade, and it was hot in the daytime! Have students imagine what it would be like to be thirsty for a long time. Ask students to tell what God provided first for His people. (**water**)

Show students a HALF-GALLON CONTAINER, and ask students to tell the name of the special food that God provided. (**manna**) Explain that God told the people to gather enough manna to fill the container one time per day for every person for the first five days, and two times on the sixth day. Marvel that God provided such a large quantity of food for thousands and thousands of people in the desert!

Reiterate that the people had specific instructions about the collection of manna. They could not be greedy and collect too much manna, or it would turn smelly and wormy. Moses knew the people might forget that it was God who had provided for their needs when they lived in the desert, so Moses asked Aaron to save some of the manna in a jar as a reminder. The jar of manna was one item that was kept in *a special, gold-covered box* called *the ark of the covenant*. The Hebrews carried this box as they traveled.

Review

- What did the children of Israel do when they felt thirsty and hungry? (**They complained to Moses.**)
- Who did Moses turn to first when he heard the people complain? (**God**)
- What did God provide to meet the people's physical needs? (**water, manna, and quail**)
- Why did God tell the people to gather a double portion of manna on the sixth day? (**so they would not have to work on the seventh day, the day God said to rest**)

Student Page 8.1

Assist students as needed in completing the page.

DAY 1

Name ____________________

The Ten Commandments **8.1**

Read each sentence. Unscramble the letters below each line. Write the word to complete the sentence.

1. Moses led the children of Israel across the Red Sea. Then the people were out in the ___desert___.
eesrdt

2. The people were thirsty. God gave them ___water___.
tewar

3. The people were hungry. The first food that God gave them was ___manna___.
nnmaa

4. Then the children of Israel wanted meat. Moses prayed, and God gave them ___quail___.
ilqua

5. To help the people remember God's care, Moses kept some of the manna in a ___jar___.
raj

29

APPLICATION

- Point out that as slaves in Egypt, the people had not been accustomed to observing a day of rest—a Sabbath day. Why is it important to have a day dedicated to rest and worship? (**Answers will vary, but should include that rest gives us time to be thankful to God and enjoy His relationship with us, and to enjoy our relationships with family members or friends.**) What do you do when you worship God? (**Answers will vary.**)
- Have students recall God's instructions regarding the collection of manna. Why was it so important for the people to follow God's instructions exactly? (**If they collected too much manna and kept it overnight, it would become spoiled and wormy. If they did not collect a double portion of manna on the day before the Sabbath, then they would go hungry.**)
- God's people needed to trust and obey Him. How can you show the Lord that you trust and obey Him? (**Answers will vary, but should include doing as the Bible says even if we don't fully understand why, since God knows everything.**)
- God provided water, manna, and quail for the children of Israel. What types of things has God provided for you? (**Possible answers: food, water, housing, clothing**)

8.2 The Ten Commandments

Focus: God Meets Spiritual Needs

★ PREPARATION

Provide a BOARD GAME and PRINTED INSTRUCTIONS. (*Introduction*)

Display **TM-4 The Ten Commandments**. (*Directed Instruction*)

Select "Ten Commandments" from the music CDs. (*Directed Instruction*)

EXTENSION

2A Allow students to play BOARD GAMES during a free period, reminding them to follow the rules so that they will all enjoy the games.

2B Print one copy of **BLM 8A The Ten Commandments Puzzle** for each student. Have students glue or tape their puzzle pieces to a sheet of construction paper to keep the pieces in place.

Introduction ★

Take out a BOARD GAME that may be new to your students and pretend that you are going to play. Offer rules about how to play the game, but state silly rules that are obviously incorrect. When students protest, take out the game's PRINTED INSTRUCTIONS and begin reading them, as if discovering the correct way to play. Conclude that when everyone understands the rules, the game is fair and more fun for everyone. Assure students that they will understand the rules before actually playing the game.

Directed Instruction ★

Ask students to share what they do when they want to talk to a friend. (**Answers will vary, but should include making a phone call or visiting in person.**) Continue by asking what students do when they want to talk to God. (**pray**) Explain that Moses and God were good friends. They were such good friends that God invited Moses to meet Him on Mount Sinai so they could talk!

Tell students that God knew His people would need rules for living, just as young people today need rules for classroom behavior or rules to play games. So, when Moses and God talked on Mount Sinai, God gave Moses a wonderful gift for the people, the Ten Commandments. Display **TM-4 The Ten Commandments**, and read the text. Explain that students will have an opportunity to reread the commandments in tomorrow's lesson.

Talk about the meaning of the word *commandment*. Ask a volunteer to share what a commandment is. (**Answers will vary, but should include that a commandment is a rule; it is something that one should do.**) These were very important rules from God for the children of Israel to obey, but they are also rules for Christians today.

Play "Ten Commandments" from the music CDs. Use the song throughout the week to reinforce the Bible truth.

Student Page 8.2

Read the text and each scenario presented. As students are working, discuss the commandments, especially emphasizing the positive purposes of God. For example, "You shall not take the name of the Lord your God in vain" can be explained as God wanting His name to be held in respect because it is part of who He is. Remind students that before returning to Egypt, Moses asked God to tell him His name. God said His name is I AM; not I WAS or I WILL BE. God exists eternally! His name shows His nature.

Review

- What were the Ten Commandments? (**a set of rules for living that God gave His people**)
- Where did God give Moses the Ten Commandments? (**on Mount Sinai**)
- Why did God give Moses the Ten Commandments? (**because God loved the people and wanted to show them the right way to live**)

• How did the Ten Commandments help to satisfy the Hebrews' spiritual needs? (**Answers will vary, but should include that God wanted to provide a way for the children of Israel to know Him and know how to be in relationship with Him.**)

Notes:

DAY 2

8.2 ***The Ten Commandments***

Listen to each story. Decide which commandment was broken by a poor choice. Write the number on the line provided.

1. Carly's parents would not let her go to her friend's house. Carly went to her room, slammed the door, and pouted. She thought her parents were being unfair!

__5__

2. Ken heard older boys in the neighborhood using God's name to curse, so Ken started to talk just like them.

__3__

3. Lauren and her sisters played sports each weekend. This left little time for chores, errands, and family time. Her parents chose to not go to church because the family was so busy.

__4__

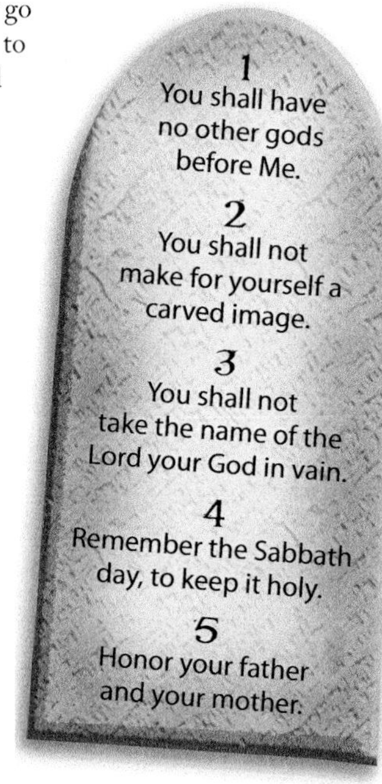

1
You shall have no other gods before Me.
2
You shall not make for yourself a carved image.
3
You shall not take the name of the Lord your God in vain.
4
Remember the Sabbath day, to keep it holy.
5
Honor your father and your mother.

4. Alex liked money so much that nothing was more important to him than getting rich. Money was all Alex could think about.

__1__

30

© Bible Grade 1

APPLICATION

- Why do you think that God gave Moses the Ten Commandments? (**Answers will vary, but should include that God wanted the children of Israel to know how to live their lives in a way that pleased Him and in a way that would make life fulfilling for them.**)
- What other kinds of rules do you need to obey today? (**Possible answers: classroom rules, traffic rules, rules for games and sports**)
- Share some good things that happen when you follow rules. (**Answers will vary, but should include that I please God, my parents, my teacher, and my friends, and I get along better with other students when I follow the rules. Following rules makes living more fair for everyone.**)

REINFORCEMENT

Whenever a contract is signed, both parties receive a copy and then usually go their separate ways. The Ten Commandments represented a covenant, or contract, between God and His people. Some scholars believe that the two, God-inscribed, stone tablets were actually two copies of the covenant, one copy for Moses and one copy for Himself. However, God gave both copies to Moses. How amazing the possibility is then in light of the fact that God had Moses keep both tablets! This could be seen as a note of grace and love indicating that God would be dwelling with His people.

8.3 The Ten Commandments

Focus: God Provides His Laws

★ PREPARATION

Display **TM-4 The Ten Commandments**. (*Directed Instruction*)

Select "Ten Commandments" from the music CDs. (*Directed Instruction*)

EXTENSION

3A During a recess period, take students outside and walk along the fence that encloses the school yard. Explain that when they play within the fence, they are safe from unfriendly dogs or other dangers. The fence provides protection even if they do not see any dangers in the area. Relate that God's commands provide protection for them, too. Christians show God that they love Him when they willingly obey His commandments (John 14:15).

3B Show the presentation **PP-2 The Ten Commandments** to review the Bible truth.

Introduction

Ask students to recall the name for God's rules for His people. (**the Ten Commandments**) Where did God give the Ten Commandments to Moses? (**on Mount Sinai**) Why did God provide these rules for Moses and the people? (**because God loved the people and wanted to show them the best way to live**)

Directed Instruction ★

Remind students that disobedience to God is called *sin*. There are four different ways that people commit sin. Read the following list and have students hold up one finger for each way that people sin: People sin by 1) what they do, 2) what they say, 3) what they think, and 4) what they do not do, but they know they should do. Explain that when the children of Israel failed to obey any of the commandments, then they would be aware of their sin. Use **TM-4 The Ten Commandments** to review each of the commandments, and inform students that the commandments were originally written in Hebrew.

1. *You shall have no other gods before Me.* Explain that this commandment is broken when anyone or anything becomes more important than God. Many people consider money, fame, power, or other people as things that are more important than God.

2. *You shall not make for yourself a carved image.* Remind students that even though most people do not make carved images or worship them, that this commandment also reminds Christians not to place trust in material things or aspects of God's Creation.

3. *You shall not take the name of the Lord your God in vain.* Explain that this commandment is broken not only through the misuse of God's name in cursing or swearing, but when God's name is not held as holy, or when one professes the name of Christ as Savior and Lord, but acts differently.

4. *Remember the Sabbath day, to keep it holy.* Remind students that God commanded a day of rest. He also wants those who love Him to honor Him by joining other Christians in worship and praise.

5. *Honor your father and your mother.* Guide students to understand that not only does defiant disobedience break this commandment, but having a poor attitude toward parents is also sin. Additionally, children sin when they fail to honor their parents even when they are away from home.

Continue reading through each commandment from TM-4. Ask students to share how the commandment might be broken either through action or thought, or simply by failing to do what is right. Discuss the commandments, especially emphasizing the positive purposes of God. For example, "You shall not commit adultery" can be explained as God wanting a husband and wife to be faithful to each other. God does not want people to lie or steal because He wants people to be able to trust one another.

Play "Ten Commandments" from the music CDs so students can practice memorizing the commandments.

Student Page 8.3

Read each scenario presented and complete the page together.

Review

- Which commandment teaches you to honor your father and mother? (**the fifth commandment**)
- Which commandment tells you not to lie about your neighbor? (**the ninth commandment**)
- Which commandment teaches you to remember the Sabbath day? (**the fourth commandment**)
- Which commandment teaches you not to desire other people's possessions? (**the tenth commandment**)
- What was the purpose of the Ten Commandments? (**to make people aware of sin and to show the best way to live**)

DAY 3

Name ______________________________

The Ten Commandments **8.3**

Listen to each story. Decide which commandment was broken by a poor choice. Write the number.

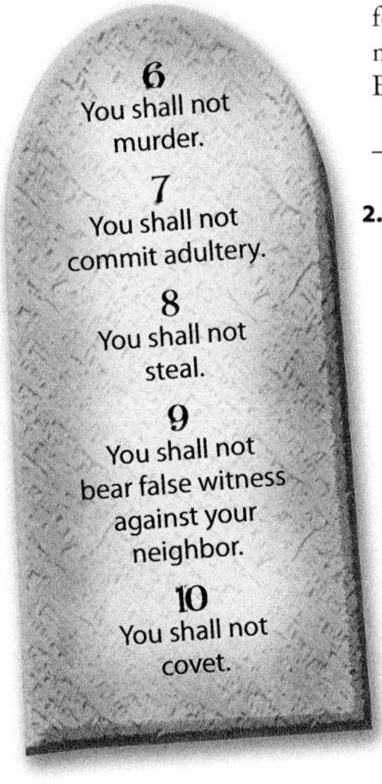

6
You shall not murder.
7
You shall not commit adultery.
8
You shall not steal.
9
You shall not bear false witness against your neighbor.
10
You shall not covet.

1. Thomas got a brand-new baseball glove for his birthday. Brian did not have a new glove. He was mad and jealous. Brian wanted Thomas' new glove.

__10__

2. Jennifer's friend Kelsey started being nice to the new girl in their class. Jennifer was afraid that Kelsey would stop being her friend. Jennifer lied about the new girl to keep Kelsey from playing with the new girl.

__9__

3. Ron saw a sparkly, green pencil under Miguel's desk. Ron knew it was Miguel's pencil, but Miguel didn't know it was on the floor. After school, Ron picked up the pencil and took it home.

__8__

4. Chelsea borrowed her sister's jacket. Chelsea never gave the jacket back to her sister.

__8__

APPLICATION

- Why do people break God's commandments? (**Possible answers: People want to do things their own way; they don't have a strong relationship with the Lord; they do not trust God.**)
- What are some of the things that keep you from trusting God? (**Answers will vary, but should include wanting my own way and not trusting that God will provide for my needs.**)
- How can you show God that you truly love Him? (**by obeying His commands**)
- What happens between you and God and between you and other people when you obey the Ten Commandments? (**Answers will vary, but should include that the relationships are stronger due to honor and trust.**)

REINFORCEMENT

The day that Moses broke the original tablets containing the Ten Commandments is infamous in the Hebrew calendar—the seventeenth day of Tammuz. Several major historic events have occurred on that day's date, including the breaching of Jerusalem's wall first by the Babylonians and later by the Romans, and the destruction of the first and second temples.

8.4 The Ten Commandments

Focus: The Golden Calf

★ PREPARATION

Select **VA 8A The Ten Commandments**. (*Directed Instruction*)

Select "Ten Commandments" from the music CDs. (*Directed Instruction*)

EXTENSION

4A Help students restate the Ten Commandments using positive, rather than negative, words. For example, to restate the third commandment, students might suggest using God's name when praying, worshipping, or praising Him. Write their responses on a FLIP CHART. Post these restated commandments in the classroom as a reminder of the actions that Christians should take.

Introduction

Ask students to share if it is difficult or easy to wait. (**Answers will vary.**) Choose a few volunteers to tell about things that they find difficult to wait for. (**Possible answers: a birthday, a visit from grandparents, parents to finish talking to other adults, vacation**) Ask if students ever get tired of waiting. (**Answers will vary.**) Explain that children sometimes find something else to do when they are tired of waiting or think that the event they are waiting for will not happen. Tell students that this is exactly what happens in today's Bible lesson.

Directed Instruction ★

Display **VA 8A The Ten Commandments** and read the text on the back.

The children of Israel had committed a great sin. What did they do? (**They made a golden idol shaped like a calf and worshipped it.**) They had to suffer the consequences for their poor choice. Moses had the idol torn down and the gold melted, ground to a powder, and sprinkled in the water. The people were made to drink it. Later, God afflicted the children of Israel, perhaps with sickness, as a punishment for the people's sin.

Finally, Aaron and the people were very sorry for their sin. They thought about all God had done for them by leading them out of the desert. They knew in their hearts that God loved them and wanted to lead them in the right way of living. They repented of their sins. Remind students that *repent* means *to turn away from or to move in the opposite direction of.*

After a time, God called Moses to come back up Mount Sinai. He told Moses to bring with him two blank tablets of stone, and God again wrote His rules for living. Moses spent time praying and asking God to forgive the people for their sins. Because God is merciful and gracious, He forgave their sins and renewed the covenant He had made with Moses' forefathers, Abraham, Isaac, and Jacob.

This time, the people had learned from their mistake and were waiting for Moses to return with the rules that God had given them. God showed His great love for the children of Israel—and for everyone—when He wrote the Ten Commandments a second time. Moses placed this set of the Ten Commandments into the ark of the covenant (Deuteronomy 10:5). Ask students to recall what was already in the ark of the covenant. (**a jar of manna**)

Play "Ten Commandments" from the music CDs and encourage students to remember the number of each commandment.

Student Page 8.4

Read the words and descriptions for students. Assist students as needed as they complete the page.

Review

- What happened when Moses started down the mountain with the Ten Commandments? (**He heard the sounds of the Hebrew people worshipping a golden calf.**)
- Why had the children of Israel made an idol, a false god? (**Possible answers: They were copying the Egyptians' way of worshipping; they thought that Moses might not return from Mount Sinai.**)
- What consequence did the people have because of their poor choice to make and worship an idol? (**The idol was torn down, and the gold dust was sprinkled on the drinking water. The children of Israel had to then drink the water. Later, God afflicted them as punishment.**)
- When the people repented of their sin, what did God do? (**God told Moses to return to Mount Sinai. God gave the people a new set of the Ten Commandments.**)

Notes:

APPLICATION

- How do you think Moses felt when he came down the mountain and saw the people disobeying God? (**Answers will vary, but should include that he felt disappointed and angry.**)
- How do you think your parents and teachers feel when they see you disobeying God? (**Answers will vary, but should include disappointed and sad.**)
- What should you do when you realize that you have sinned? (**I should repent and ask God and those I've sinned against to forgive me.**)

REINFORCEMENT

The Greek word for *idol* means *something to be seen*. The fact that the people chose to make a calf, or bull, is significant. This visible symbol had its roots in the Egyptian religion. In that ancient culture, an important object of worship was the bull. It was considered to be a means of transportation upon which a god rode in power, and, for that reason, it was also considered to be divine.

DAY 4

8.4 *The Ten Commandments*

Draw a line to match the words on the left with their descriptions on the right.

Moses	the place where God wrote on the stone tablets
golden calf	what happens after a choice is made
Mount Sinai	the leader of the children of Israel
Ten Commandments	a false god; an idol
repent	the rules that God gave to help guide His people
consequence	to turn away from sin

32

8.5 The Ten Commandments

Focus: Review and Assessment

★ PREPARATION

Select "Ten Commandments" from the music CDs. (*Lesson Review*)

Select **VA 8A The Ten Commandments**. (*Lesson Review*)

Print a copy of **BLM 8B Lesson 8 Test** for each student. (*Directed Instruction*)

Lesson Review ★

Begin with a brief period of worship. Play "Ten Commandments" from the music CDs.

Use **VA 8A The Ten Commandments** to review the Bible truth. Cover the following concepts:

- After the Hebrew people left Egypt, God parted the waters of the Red Sea so that they could cross on dry land. Once across, the people entered the desert.
- The desert was hot and dry. The people grew thirsty and hungry.
- God provided water, manna, and quail to meet the people's physical needs.
- God told the people to gather a double portion of manna on the sixth day so that they could rest on the seventh day.
- God gave His people the Ten Commandments to make people aware of sin and to show the best way to live.
- God called for Moses to meet with Him on Mount Sinai.
- Moses and God talked on Mount Sinai for 40 days.
- The people thought that Moses might not come back, so they turned away from God. They thought about what they had seen the Egyptians worshipping, so they gathered their gold to make an idol.
- *Idol* is the term for *a false god.*
- The people made their gold into the shape of a calf and began to worship the calf.
- The children of Israel broke the second commandment when they made the golden calf.
- Moses was so angry when he saw the people worshipping the golden calf that he broke the stone tablets that had the Ten Commandments written on them.
- God showed His great love for the people by writing the Ten Commandments on a second set of stone tablets.

Directed Instruction ★

Distribute one copy of **BLM 8B Lesson 8 Test** to each student. Read the sentences and the answer choices, then repeat the sentence and allow students time to select the correct answer. Collect tests for assessment. Share correct answers.

Notes:

Lesson Preparation
Joshua and Caleb

9.0

Expected Student Outcomes

KNOW
Joshua and Caleb faithfully serve the Lord as spies. Joshua leads the Israelites in the Battle of Jericho.

DO
Students will:
- determine the importance of trusting God with heart, soul, mind, and strength
- complete a cloze activity to review the crossing of the Jordan River
- analyze characteristics of key people in the account of the Battle of Jericho
- identify ways to effectively share the gospel with peers

APPLY
Students will decide to serve God rather than give in to peer pressure and conclude that God honors those who are faithful to Him.

Lesson Outline

I. Joshua and Caleb stand firm (Num 13–14)
  A. Twelve spies go into the land
  B. Two spies stand against the crowd
  C. The consequences of not trusting
II. Crossing the Jordan River (Josh 1:1–5:12)
  A. Joshua leads God's people
  B. Rahab saves the spies
III. The Battle of Jericho (Josh 5:13–6:27)
  A. Joshua follows God's instructions
  B. God gives the victory
IV. Sharing the good news
  A. Telling others about Jesus

TEACHER'S HEART

When Joshua and Caleb opposed the 10 other spies, they were facing the same test you and your students face—peer pressure. Joshua and Caleb knew and spoke the truth about what God had said and about the Promised Land, even though the other spies only saw the negatives. Joshua and Caleb knew that nothing anyone says can change the truth.

The world says that Jesus was just a good man, yet you know that He is the Son of God. The world declares that you can have it all, yet you know that all you have belongs to God. The world claims you can do anything if you put your mind to it, but you know that your strength comes from the Lord.

Don't allow the peer pressure of the world to talk you into believing lies. Be a light! Be courageous! Proclaim the truth of your life in Christ boldly, and teach your students to do the same.

MEMORY VERSE

Mark 12:30

MATERIALS

Day 1:
- Dark glasses, trench coat, magnifying glass
- Grapes, milk, bread with honey (*Extension*)
- Air-dry clay (*Extension*)

Day 2:
- VA 9A Crossing the Jordan River
- Red yarn
- Cardboard (*Extension*)
- Stones (*Extension*)

Day 3:
- Paper cones
- VA 9B The Battle of Jericho
- Shofar (*Extension*)
- BLM 9A Door Sign, cardboard (*Extension*)

Day 4:
- Stones or crumpled pieces of paper resembling stones

Day 5:
- VA 9A Crossing the Jordan River, VA 9B The Battle of Jericho
- BLM 9B Lesson 9 Test

SONGS

Promised Land
Joshua

TEACHER RESOURCES

Boice, James Montgomery. *Joshua*. Baker Books, 2006.
Wiersbe, Warren W. *Be Strong (Joshua)*. David C. Cook, 2010.

STUDENT RESOURCES

Veggie Tales: Josh and the Big Wall. DVD. Big Idea, 2008.

9.1 Joshua and Caleb

Focus: Joshua and Caleb Stand Firm

MEMORY VERSE

Mark 12:30

MEMORY WORK

- Read the Memory Verse aloud with the students. Invite them to play the game I Spy by looking for the words from the Memory Verse that have been placed around the room. Tell students who spy the words to take them down and say the Memory Verse for the class.

PREPARATION

Write several of the key words from the Memory Verse on slips of paper and post them around the classroom at a height able to be reached by students. Write the Memory Verse on the board. (*Memory Work*)

Have DARK GLASSES, a TRENCH COAT, and a LARGE MAGNIFYING GLASS on hand to use as a spy costume. (*Introduction*)

EXTENSION

1A Taking food allergies into account, ask parents to provide GRAPES, MILK, and BREAD WITH HONEY for a snack during Bible time or another time during the day. As students eat the snack, remind them that the spies brought back huge clusters of grapes from Canaan. Joshua described the land as flowing with milk and honey (Numbers 13:27).

1B Have students shape AIR-DRY CLAY into 12 small stones to be used in Lesson 9.2. Consider letting students paint the stones at a later time.

1C Play "Promised Land" for the students to listen to.

Introduction ★

Put on DARK GLASSES and a TRENCH COAT, and carry a LARGE MAGNIFYING GLASS. Tiptoe in front of your class. Look secretive by turning your head back and forth. In a whisper, inform students that today you are a spy for the Lord. You are secretly looking for godly behavior and evidence of good attitudes. Ask students to be on the lookout for godly behavior, leadership, and courage as they listen to today's Bible truth.

Directed Instruction

Read the following Bible truth based on Numbers 13–14:

> After walking in the desert for a long time, the children of Israel finally reached the border of Canaan, the Promised Land. God told Moses to send spies into the land. So Moses did as God commanded and called twelve men to spy out the land. He said, "I am sending you into the land the Lord has promised to us. It's your job to see what the land is like and report back to us about the crops, the cities, and the people who live in the land."
>
> The twelve spies went into the Promised Land. Two of those spies were Caleb and Joshua, men of great faith. The spies went from village to village. What they saw was amazing! Some of the people in the land were tall and strong. Some of the cities had high, thick walls around them. The crops were huge, and the harvest was plentiful. The spies brought back clusters of grapes that were so large that they had to be carried on a pole between two men!
>
> The spies reported back to Moses and the people. They said, "The land is rich with beautiful crops. Look at the grapes we brought back! The land the Lord promised us is wonderful. But the people are strong giants! And the cities are surrounded by thick walls! Caleb said, "We should go in and take over! God promised us this land and He will help us to take it!" Joshua agreed with Caleb, but the other spies said, "No! We can't fight those big giants. We look like little grasshoppers compared to them."
>
> The children of Israel believed the ten unbelieving spies instead of Joshua and Caleb. They didn't have the faith that God would help them conquer the land of Canaan. The Lord was very sad and angry that the people refused to trust Him. Because they would not go into the new land in the power and strength of the Lord, God said they could not go into the land until all of the people twenty years old and older died. Sadly, the children of Israel wandered in the desert for forty years, one year for each day the spies were in the land of Canaan (Numbers 14:34).
>
> However, God blessed Joshua and Caleb because they trusted Him and said and did what was right. They were faithful to God even when those around them were not. God honored Joshua and Caleb's faith by allowing them into the Promised Land.

Review

- What good things did the 12 spies report to Moses? (**rich land with good crops**)
- What things did the spies see that frightened the people? (**cities with high, thick walls and people who were giants**)
- What did Caleb and Joshua say the people should do? (**They should go in and take over. God would help them.**)
- Did the people listen to Caleb and Joshua? (**No, they listened to the 10 unbelieving spies and did not trust God.**)
- What consequence resulted from the people listening to the 10 spies instead of trusting God? (**They wandered in the desert for 40 years. Only the people who were younger than 20 years old were allowed to enter the Promised Land.**)

Student Page 9.1

Tell students that Moses described the Promised Land as flowing with milk and honey (Exodus 13:5). Remind students that the spies reported seeing huge clusters of grapes and good crops in the land. Assist students in completing the page.

DAY 1

Name ______________________________

Joshua and Caleb **9.1**

Joshua and Caleb trusted and obeyed God.
Look for the hidden letters. Write the letters. Read the words.

1. h e a r t

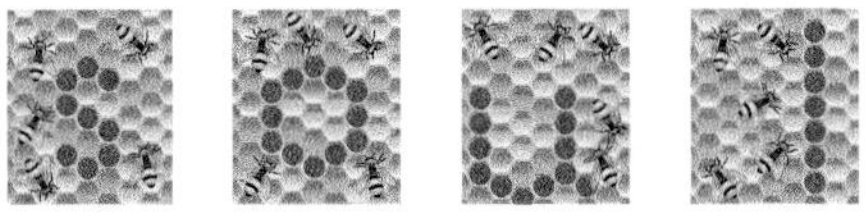

2. s o u l

3. m i n d

4. s t r e n g t h

How can you trust and obey God? Use the words to complete the sentence.

5. I can love the Lord my God with all my ___heart___, ___soul___, ___mind___, and ___strength___.

APPLICATION

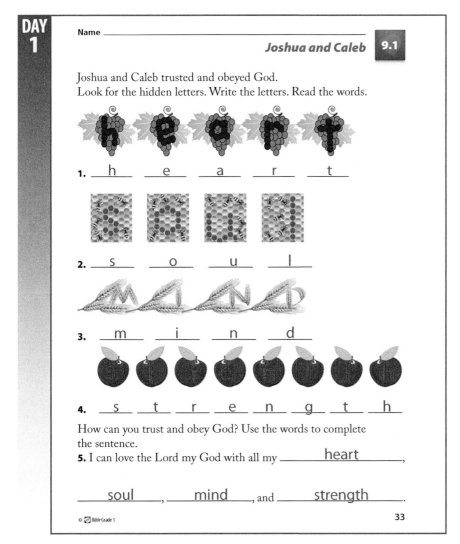

- Why were the children of Israel afraid to go into Canaan? (**They were afraid because they listened to the 10 spies who did not trust God as opposed to the two spies who did trust Him.**)
- How do you know you can trust God even when you are afraid? (**Answers will vary, but should include that God's Word tells me how God cared for Jacob even though he was afraid of Esau, and how God parted the Red Sea, even when the people were afraid that they would die. Just as God took care of His people in the Bible, He will take care of me!**)
- Caleb and Joshua stood for the Lord even though the other 10 spies did not. Have you ever chosen to do the right thing even when others were doing something wrong? How were you able to stand firm for what was right? (**Answers will vary.**)

9.2 Joshua and Caleb

Focus: Crossing the Jordan River

★ PREPARATION

Select **VA 9A Crossing the Jordan River**. (*Directed Instruction*)

Have a piece of **RED YARN** available. (*Directed Instruction*)

EXTENSION

2A If you had your students make 12 clay stones in Extension 1A of Lesson 9.1, allow the students to paint the stones and to glue the stones to a small piece of **CARDBOARD**. Have students think about something that God has done for them personally, such as giving them parents, or answering specific prayers. Explain that God wants the students to set aside a time to remember what He has done (Psalm 77:11).

2B Bring **12 STONES** to use during a prayer time, or use some of the clay stones made in Extension 1A of Lesson 9.1. Hand each stone to a volunteer and ask each volunteer in turn to share something that he or she remembers that God has done. This can be something that God did in one of the Bible truths, such as parting the waters of the Jordan River, or something that God has done in the student's personal life. Thank God for all His wondrous deeds!

Introduction

Open your Bible to Genesis. Tell students that Moses obeyed God and wrote the first five books of the Bible. Explain that the Bible truths that the class has studied so far have come from Genesis, Exodus, and Numbers, three of the first five books. Show students the title of the sixth book of the Bible, Joshua. Remind students that Joshua was one of the two spies who was courageous and had urged the people to trust God and enter the Promised Land. Explain that today's lesson comes from the book of Joshua.

Directed Instruction ★

Exclaim that the time had finally come for the children of Israel to enter the Promised Land. Share that the first obstacle to their entry into the Promised Land was a large river called the *Jordan River*. In order to take possession of the Promised Land, the people would have to show that they trusted God. Display **VA 9A Crossing the Jordan River** and read the text.

Recount that Joshua did something similar to what Moses had done many years before. He sent two spies across the Jordan. Ask a volunteer to share why Joshua might have sent two spies into the city of Jericho before attempting to take the people across the river. (**Possible answers: The people of Jericho might have sent soldiers to attack the Israelites; Joshua wanted to know what was happening on the other side of the river so that he could be ready.**) When the spies entered Jericho, they met a woman named *Rahab*. Rahab hid the spies, saving their lives. Ask students to share Rahab's understanding of God. (**Rahab had heard and believed that God was with the children of Israel and that He was powerful!**)

Call on a volunteer to hold up a piece of **RED YARN**. Ask students to share how a red cord was used in the Bible truth. (**Rahab hung the red cord from her window. When the soldiers came to take over the city, they would know not to harm the people living in that house.**) Review that the two spies returned to Joshua. They reported that the people of Jericho were afraid because they knew that the Lord was with the children of Israel. The time had come for the people to cross the Jordan!

Lead students to sequence the events of the crossing of the Jordan River. Ask students to tell who crossed first. (**the priests carrying the ark of the covenant**) Remind students that the *ark of the covenant* was *a special, gold-covered box*. The ark held the Ten Commandments, a jar of manna, and Aaron's walking stick (1 Kings 8:9, Exodus 16:33–34, Numbers 17:10, Hebrews 9:4). Ask students to share what happened when the priests carrying the ark stepped into the Jordan. (**Immediately the water formed a wall far away, leaving dry ground where the river had previously flowed.**) Who followed the ark? (**all the people**)

Ask students to explain why 12 stones were taken from the riverbed. (**The 12 stones were taken from a place where water would normally have flowed, but where God had miraculously stopped the flow of the river. They were set up as a memorial to the event that had just happened.**)

Tell students that since the children of Israel entered the Promised Land, they will be called *Israelites* more often in subsequent lessons.

Review

- What did God promise Joshua and the children of Israel? (**that He would give them every place that the bottom of their shoes touched and that He would be with them like He was with Moses**)
- Why did Rahab help the spies? (**She knew that God was powerful and that He would help the Israelites take the city. She wanted the spies to protect her family.**)
- How would the spies know which house belonged to Rahab? (**She would hang a red cord from her window.**)
- When Joshua told the people that it was time to cross the river, were they afraid? (**No, they trusted God even before they saw the water part, allowing them to cross on dry land.**)

Student Page 9.2

Read the directions and the text. Assist students to complete the page.

DAY 2

9.2 *Joshua and Caleb*

Use the words in the Word Bank to complete the sentences.

WORD BANK

Jordan	priests	stones
water	obey	

The Lord told Joshua that it was time to cross the

____Jordan____ River into the Promised Land. Crossing the river seemed impossible,

but Joshua chose to ____obey____ God. Joshua told the people, "When you see the

____priests____ carrying the ark of the covenant move, you are to follow them." The people obeyed! As soon as the priests stepped into the

Jordan River, the ____water____ stopped flowing, and the people crossed on dry land! Joshua ordered that the children of Israel make a pile

of 12 ____stones____ to remind their children of what God had done.

34

APPLICATION

- Joshua told the children of Israel to set up 12 stones from the riverbed to help them remember what God had done for them. How can you remember what God has done for you? (**Answers will vary, but should include that I can take time to think about God's blessings and thank Him every day.**)
- After 40 years in the wilderness, the people were ready to follow God's plan. God has a plan for your life, too. What can you do to follow God's plan for your life? (**Answers will vary, but should include that I can study God's Word, listen to godly teaching, pray, and spend time in worship.**)

REINFORCEMENT

Over and over in the Bible, God commands His people to remember. When the 12 Israelite men took the 12 stones from the riverbed of the Jordan and set them up as a memorial, this was one of many times that physical objects were set up to remind the Israelites of God's unfailing love. Today, Jewish families often hang a *mezuzah*, a small box containing a parchment of Scripture, on their doorposts. Whenever they enter or leave their homes, the *mezuzah* reminds the people of God's presence and their heritage.

Jesus instituted the Lord's Supper as a type of memorial, saying, "Do this in remembrance of Me" (1 Corinthians 11:24). When Christians celebrate Communion, they are obeying the Lord's command to remember.

9.3 Joshua and Caleb

Focus: The Battle of Jericho

PREPARATION

For each student, make a PAPER CONE from a piece of plain paper to be used as a horn. Roll up the paper and tape the end securely. Fold under some of the paper on the narrow end to protect the students' lips. (*Introduction, Directed Instruction*)

Select **VA 9B The Battle of Jericho**. (*Directed Instruction*)

Select "Joshua" from the music CDs. (*Directed Instruction*)

EXTENSION

3A Blow a SHOFAR for your students to hear, or invite a guest who has one to show it to the class and blow it.

3B Remind students that Joshua and Caleb agreed with what the Lord had said about the Promised Land. Later, when the Israelites were ready to settle into the Promised Land, Joshua told the people to choose whom they would serve—false gods or the Lord. Joshua openly declared what he had decided when he said, "But as for me and my house, we will serve the Lord" (Joshua 24:15d). Invite students to make a sign for the door of their home by using **BLM 9A Door Sign**. Have students color the sign and glue it to a piece of CARDBOARD.

Introduction

Distribute a PAPER CONE to each student. Tell students that the paper cones will be used later in the lesson as trumpets, but they should not blow into their trumpets just yet. Teach students that in Bible times, people made trumpets from the horns of sheep. Musicians blew into the narrow end of the horn, and a sound came out of the wider end.

Directed Instruction

Review that the Israelites had safely crossed the Jordan River on dry ground. Remind students that a big city with a high wall was on the other side of the Jordan. Ask a volunteer to tell the name of that city. (**Jericho**) Explain that the people of Jericho had built the wall as protection from enemies. There were other smaller walls or partial walls around Jericho as well. The main wall had gates to allow people to come and go, but the gates were shut tight. The people of Jericho knew that God was powerful, but they probably believed that their big wall would keep the Israelites out. Shrug your shoulders and ask students to think about how the Israelites could take over the city when it was surrounded by such a big wall.

Display **VA 9B The Battle of Jericho**. Read the Bible truth. Reenact the fall of Jericho by having students follow you around the desks and chairs in your classroom seven times, or go outside and march around an area of the playground. Remind students to be quiet as they walk around seven times, but to have their paper cones ready to use as trumpets. Students may be tempted to blow their trumpets, but remind them that Joshua and the priests followed God's instructions exactly and did not blow their trumpets too soon. After the seventh time around, allow students to shout and blow their trumpets. Cheer and praise God for His amazing victory!

Play "Joshua" from the music CDs a few times to allow students to become familiar with the words.

Review

- After Joshua led the people across the Jordan River, how did he know what to do next? (**Joshua waited for God to tell him what to do next.**)
- Whom did Joshua meet on the other side of the Jordan? (**Joshua met a Man with a sword in His hand. The Man was the Lord.**)
- What did the Lord tell Joshua to do? (**The Lord said to have all the people march around Jericho one time each day for six days, then on the seventh day, to walk around the city seven times. After the seventh time, the seven priests were each to blow their ram's horn trumpet and the people were to shout.**)
- Why was it important for the people to follow God's instructions exactly? (**Answers will vary, but should include that they could then see the wonderful outcome purposed by the Lord.**)
- Who was saved when the walls fell? (**Rahab and her family**) How was she saved? (**She hung a red cord from her window so the soldiers would know which house was hers in order to leave her and her family alone.**)

Student Page 9.3

Help students follow directions to complete the page. While students work, explain that Joshua followed every step in God's instructions carefully.

Notes:

APPLICATION

- Joshua faced two big problems—crossing the Jordan River and conquering the city of Jericho. Think about a big problem that you have had. How did you know what to do to solve the problem? (**Answers will vary.**)
- Instead of trying to handle his problems alone, Joshua brought them to the Lord. What do you do when problems come? (**Possible answers: I pray; I encourage myself with what I've learned from the Bible; I ask my parents or other godly leaders for help and advice.**)
- Walking around the walls of Jericho must have seemed pretty silly to the people of the city. Share a time when you obeyed God even though it did not make sense. (**Answers will vary.**)

DAY 3

Name ______________________________

Joshua and Caleb **9.3**

Look at the words on the bricks and the descriptions below. Choose the best word or words to fit each description. Write the underlined word.

1. people
afraid
defeated

2. Lord
all-powerful
almighty

3. Rahab
helpful
saved

4. Joshua
trusting
obedient

35

REINFORCEMENT

The horns, or trumpets, that were blown by the priests at the wall of Jericho were shofars. A shofar is an instrument made from the horn of a ram or other kosher animal. It was used in biblical times to sound the alarm for war or for other important events, such as marking the beginning of a new year. The sounding of the shofar was more than just a tradition; it also called the Jewish people to a spiritual awakening and to repentance.

9.4 Joshua and Caleb

Focus: Sharing the Good News

★ PREPARATION

Collect **12** STONES or make **12** CRUMPLED PIECES OF PAPER RESEMBLING STONES. (*Introduction*)

EXTENSION

4A Take some time to role-play appropriate ways for first graders to tell friends about Jesus. Have pairs of students take turns practicing ways to tell others what believing in Jesus means. Give encouragement and provide correction as needed.

Introduction ★

Display **12** STONES or **12** CRUMPLED PIECES OF PAPER RESEMBLING STONES. Explain that when Joshua put the stones by the river, he was building a *memorial*, which is defined as *a way to recall a memory*. He instructed the Israelites to tell their children about what God did at the Jordan River. This was done so that all the people of the earth might know that the Lord is powerful and that the Israelites might always remember to fear the Lord (Joshua 4:24). Like the Israelites, Christians need to remember God's command to share the good news with others (Matthew 28:19–20).

Directed Instruction

Read the following fictional story:

"Mom, Mom!" Jimar Johnson called as the door banged on his way into the house. Out of breath, Jimar exclaimed, "Something weird just happened."

"What's that?" asked Mrs. Johnson.

Jimar told her the whole story in a rush. His friend, Reid Anderson, had been in a bike accident and had scraped his leg badly. Reid's leg was bleeding! Jimar helped Reid get home so Mrs. Anderson could get Reid cleaned up.

"Is Reid going to be okay?" Mrs. Johnson asked.

"I think so," said Jimar.

"So … why is that weird?" asked Mrs. Johnson.

"That's not the weird part," Jimar explained. "What's weird is that I knew he was hurt, so I stopped what I was doing to pray for him. Reid didn't even understand what I was doing when I was praying! No one ever told him about God or about how to talk to Him."

Mrs. Johnson explained to Jimar that not all parents know about God or teach their children about what the Bible says. She told Jimar that some families don't go to church.

Jimar was worried and thought, "But how will Reid learn how to follow God if he doesn't go to church and people don't tell him?"

Jimar decided that he should pray even more for Reid and for the whole Anderson family. Jimar knew that God loves the Anderson family very much and that God would help him and his mother to know the best way to let the Andersons know about the Lord. He knew that God would give his mother and him the words to use when talking to the Andersons.

Review

- What happened to Reid as he was riding his bike? (**He had an accident and scraped his leg badly.**)
- How did Jimar show that he had a close relationship with the Lord? (**He stopped what he was doing to pray for Reid.**)
- What did Jimar see as being weird about this situation? (**When Jimar prayed for Reid, Reid did not know what prayer was.**)
- What decision did Jimar make about helping Reid and the whole Anderson family? (**He decided to pray for them and ask God to help him and his mother to know the best way to share the good news of Jesus with the Anderson family.**)

Student Page 9.4

Read the directions and the text on the page. Allow students to complete the exercises independently. Lead a class discussion about other ways that Jimar can share his faith with Reid.

APPLICATION

- When you play with your friends, how can you show them that you have a close relationship with God? (**Answers will vary, but should include being kind, using kind words that encourage, and helping my friends as needed.**)
- Do you have a friend who needs to know more about God? How can you share God's love with this person? (**Answers will vary, but should include telling my friend about Jesus' love for him or her, praying for and with my friend, inviting my friend to church, giving my friend a Bible or book of Bible truths.**)

Notes:

DAY 4

9.4 ***Joshua and Caleb***

Think about what Jimar can do to help Reid learn about God. Draw a line from each sentence to the correct picture.

Bible

kindness

church

1. Jimar can pray for Reid.
2. Jimar can tell Reid about Jesus' death and resurrection.
3. Jimar can give Reid a Bible to read.
4. Jimar can invite Reid to a children's Bible class.
5. Jimar can invite Reid to sit with him in church.
6. Jimar can be kind to Reid even if Reid is not kind to him.

Jesus' death

prayer

Bible class

36 © Bible Grade 1

9.5 Joshua and Caleb

Focus: Review and Assessment

★ PREPARATION

Select "The Promised Land" and "Joshua" from the music CDs. (*Lesson Review*)

Select **VA 9A Crossing the Jordan River** and **VA 9B The Battle of Jericho**. (*Lesson Review*)

Duplicate one copy of **BLM 9B Lesson 9 Test** for each student. (*Directed Instruction*)

Lesson Review ★

Use "The Promised Land" and "Joshua" from the music CDs to lead students in a brief period of worship.

Review the Bible truth of the 12 spies sent into the Promised Land. Cover the following concepts:

- Moses sent 12 spies into the Promised Land. They brought back large clusters of grapes and told Moses that the land God promised was a good land. But when the 10 faithless spies told the people that the land was full of giants and that the cities were surrounded by high, thick walls, the people became frightened and did not trust God.
- Two of the spies, Caleb and Joshua, had faith in God and told the people that the children of Israel could take the land. The people were afraid, and they refused to trust God. God judged their lack of faith and made them wander in the desert for 40 years. Only those who were younger than 20 years old would be allowed to go into the Promised Land.
- During the 40 years that they were in the desert, the people learned to trust and obey God.

Use **VA 9A Crossing the Jordan River** to review the Bible truth. Cover the following concepts:

- When Joshua led the children of Israel to the Jordan River, they obeyed willingly. As soon as the priests carrying the ark of the covenant stepped into the water, God caused the water to stop flowing.
- Joshua used 12 stones from the Jordan River to build a memorial. Every time the children asked about the stones, they were told about the miraculous way that God helped the Israelites enter the Promised Land and about God's power.
- Christians ought to remember all of the things God has done and share the good news with others.

Use **VA 9B The Battle of Jericho** to review the Bible truth. Cover the following concepts:

- The Lord told Joshua how to take over the walled city of Jericho. Joshua obeyed the Lord's instructions exactly.
- The Israelites marched around Jericho one time a day for six days. On the seventh day, they marched around Jericho seven times. When they started blowing their horns and shouting, the walls fell down.
- Rahab was saved because she had helped the spies. She hung a red cord outside her window so that the soldiers would know the location of her house and save her and her family.
- The people trusted and obeyed God. The victory belonged to the Lord!

Directed Instruction ★

Distribute a copy of **BLM 9B Lesson 9 Test** to each student. Assist the students to complete the test as needed. Review the answers in class and select volunteers to share which word or words they used to change false statements into true statements. Collect the test papers for assessment.

Lesson Preparation

Gideon

10.0

Expected Student Outcomes

KNOW

God uses Gideon to deliver His people from the Midianites.

DO

Students will:
- decode statements that show confidence in God's presence
- use pictorial clues to recall the facts about Gideon's battle
- evaluate contemporary scenarios displaying godly leadership
- recall facts about the Bible

APPLY

Students will invite God to use them for His purposes regardless of their limitations or circumstances.

Lesson Outline

I. Gideon's call to lead (Judg 6)
  A. God raises up judges
  B. Gideon asks for a sign
II. Gideon's brave army (Judg 7–8)
  A. God reduces the size of the army
  B. Gideon trusts the Lord for the victory
III. Godly leadership
  A. Characteristics of a godly leader (1 Tim 4:12)
IV. Sharing God's Word
  A. History of The Gideons International
  B. The Bible

TEACHER'S HEART

As you have become more acquainted with your students, the leadership qualities of some have become very obvious. There are children who readily volunteer for any task and often enjoy being in the limelight. Their hands are always waving, and they enjoy demonstrating their skills and knowledge to delight you and their classmates. Sitting in the shadows and on the sidelines are the students who shrink back from center stage. For these children, speaking before the class can be a challenge.

You can be instrumental in helping students develop God-honoring leadership skills. Recognize that the outgoing student who appears to enjoy center stage may have insecurities or fears. Look beyond what he or she says or does and look rather to the motivation behind the actions. Is he or she lonely and hoping to gain a friend? Does he or she have true leadership abilities that merely need to be directed or brought out? Extend opportunities to each shy student for one-on-one attention and give encouragement to develop personal strengths. What kinds of future leaders are in your classroom? Pray for them, and give God the glory as students take steps toward developing stronger leadership skills.

MEMORY VERSE

Psalm 27:1

MATERIALS

Day 1:
- BLM 10A Doorknob Hanger, card stock, glow-in-the-dark paint or markers (*Extension*)
- Handheld weights (*Extension*)

Day 2:
- Photograph of an American football team
- VA 10A Gideon's Brave Army
- BLM 10B Sword, card stock, heavy-duty aluminum foil (*Extension*)

Day 3:
- Saltshaker, flashlight

Day 4:
- Graph paper with small squares (*Extension*)
- PP-3 The Bible (*Extension*)

Day 5:
- VA 10A Gideon's Brave Army
- BLM 10C Lesson 10 Test

TEACHER RESOURCES

Arthur, Kay, David Lawson, and B. J. Lawson. *Rising to the Call of Leadership*. Random House, Inc., 2009.

Briner, Bob, and Ray Pritchard. *The Leadership Lessons of Jesus: A Timeless Model for Today's Leaders*. B&H Publishing Group, 2008.

STUDENT RESOURCES

Haidle, Helen. *What Would Jesus Do?* Zondervan Publishing Company, 2001.

Nystrom, Jennifer, and Marjorie Redford. *Gideon, Blow Your Horn*. Standard Publishing, 2009.

10.1 Gideon

Focus: Gideon's Call to Lead

MEMORY VERSE

Psalm 27:1

MEMORY WORK

- Write the Memory Verse on the board and read it chorally. Provide each student with three sheets of construction paper. Have students illustrate each of the key words within the verse. For the word *light*, have students draw a flame representing the torch of Gideon; for *salvation*, have students draw a horn to announce God's deliverance from the Midianites; for *strength* or *stronghold*, have students draw an arm with muscles flexed. Invite a few students to come to the front of the room and hold up their pictures at the appropriate times while reciting the Memory Verse.

EXTENSION

1A Duplicate **BLM 10A Doorknob Hanger** onto CARD STOCK. Provide GLOW-IN-THE-DARK PAINT OR MARKERS for students to decorate their project. As students work, remind them that they can trust the Lord to be with them when they are afraid.

1B The angel of the Lord saw that Gideon would be strong with the help of God. To demonstrate Gideon's growing strength, bring in TWO HANDHELD WEIGHTS, each weighing about five pounds. Select volunteers to hold the weights and lift their arms from their sides until their arms are level with their shoulders. Have them lower their arms, repeating until lack of strength stops them. Monitor students as they work with weights. Have them practice during the week. Remind them that, like physical strength, spiritual strength increases with continued trust in the Lord.

Introduction

Write a difficult math problem on the board. Ask a volunteer to solve the problem. When the volunteer protests that the problem is too hard, explain that today's lesson is about a servant of God who felt that the task God wanted him to do was too hard. Explain that as students trust in God and keep learning, they will be able to take on greater challenges in life.

Directed Instruction

Read the following Bible truth based on Judges 6:

Under Joshua's direction, the Israelites settled in the Promised Land. They built towns and cities. They planted crops, raised animals, and had families. The Israelites were happy; however, they only served the Lord while Joshua was alive. Trouble lay ahead!

The Israelites had not fully obeyed God when He told them to drive out all their enemies from the Promised Land. Instead, they had allowed some of their enemies to stay in the land. These evil neighbors were cruel, greedy, and ungodly. They did not worship the one, true God; instead they worshipped idols. Sadly, many of the Israelites started to worship the same idols that their neighbors worshipped.

God was very unhappy! He wanted His people to worship Him alone. During this time God raised up judges. *People who governed over Israel and decided between right and wrong* were called *judges*. It was through these judges that God delivered the Israelites from their enemies.

The Midianites were one of the enemies of the Israelites. Whenever the Israelites planted grain, the Midianites would swoop in and steal it! Soon, the Israelites did not have enough food. They had to hide food to feed themselves and their children. The Israelites got very hungry, so they cried out to the Lord, "Help us!"

God said, "I brought you up from Egypt where you were slaves. I gave you this land and helped you to drive out the people who lived here. I told you not to worship their idols. But you have not obeyed My voice!"

God was right, of course! The Israelites had not obeyed Him, and they had no way to get themselves out of this mess. God stepped in and sent an angel to a man named *Gideon*. Gideon was separating grain from the stems in a pit in the ground so the Midianites wouldn't see him and find the grain. The angel said, "Gideon, the Lord is with you. You are a strong man. The Lord has chosen you and will help you to defeat the enemy."

Gideon was unsure at first. He said, "I'm not a strong leader. In fact, my family is one of the smallest families, and I'm one of the weakest sons in the family. How can I save Israel?"

The angel turned and said to him, "The Lord will give you strength. Together, you and the Lord will defeat the Midianites." Then Gideon said, "If this is true, please give me a sign. Please don't go away until I come back with my offering." Gideon went away and soon returned with an offering of meat and grain. He put the offering on a rock under an oak tree. The angel of the Lord caused fire to come from the rock and burn up Gideon's offering! Gideon was amazed! Now he knew that the Lord had called him to the fight against the Midianites.

Review

- Why were the Israelites being troubled by enemies? (**The Israelites had not fully obeyed the Lord; they had begun worshipping idols.**)
- Why did God call Gideon to be a leader and a judge? (**God heard His people's cry; Gideon would be a strong leader with God's help.**)
- What sign did God give to prove that He had chosen Gideon? (**Fire came from the rock and burned up Gideon's offering.**)

Student Page 10.1

Read the directions, and assist students in completing the exercises.

DAY 1

Name ______________________

Gideon **10.1**

Gideon was afraid when God chose him to fight the Midianites. Gideon told God that he was not the right man for the job.

Use the code in the box to learn what the angel of the Lord told Gideon and what God wants you to know today.

1. The Lord answered, "I will be with you."

2. When I am afraid, I will remember that God is with me.

© Bible Grade 1 37

APPLICATION

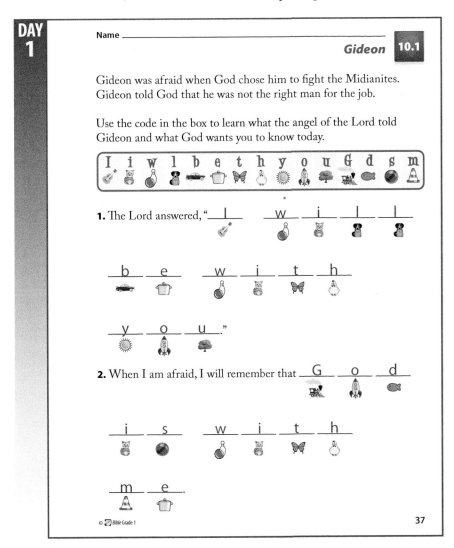

- What are some things that make you afraid? (**Possible answers: spiders, dark rooms, loud noises, big dogs**) When you are afraid or discouraged, how can you remember that the Lord is with you? (**I can say a Bible verse or sing a song to remind me that God is with me.**)
- Gideon asked the angel of the Lord for a sign to prove that God was really with him. What are some signs that God has provided to help you remember that He is with you? (**Possible answers: God's promises in His Word, my loving parents that He gave me, the beautiful world He created**)
- God has already given you many signs of how He has provided for your needs. What are some times when you might ask for God's help? (**Possible answers: to be kind to an unkind classmate, to recover from an illness, to do well on a test**)

REINFORCEMENT

The Midianites were nomads who raided the Israelites to steal their grain. The Israelites had fled to caves in the surrounding areas to hide in safety and protect their limited food supplies. Gideon was separating the stems and chaff from the grain. Normally threshing was done on the hilltops so that when the grain, stems, and chaff were tossed into the air, the lighter elements would blow away, leaving the grain to fall back into the basket. Instead, Gideon took his grain to a pit located in the lowlands to avoid being seen by the Midianites. In this pit, the separation of the good grain from the chaff would have been a frustrating task since Gideon would not have been helped by the prevailing breezes.

10.2 Gideon

Focus: Gideon's Brave Army

★ PREPARATION

Bring in a PHOTOGRAPH OF AN AMERICAN FOOTBALL TEAM that shows the quarterback. (*Introduction*)

Select **VA 10A Gideon's Brave Army**. (*Directed Instruction*)

EXTENSION

2A Print a copy of **BLM 10B Sword** on CARD STOCK for each student. Print an extra copy to use as a template. Cut out only the blade portion of the sword from your template and trace it onto HEAVY-DUTY ALUMINUM FOIL, preparing one blade-shaped piece of foil for each student. Allow students to color the hilt of the sword and glue the foil on top of the blade. As students work, explain that soldiers typically used swords during battle to defeat their enemies. Explain that a physical sword is not the only kind of weapon used to fight enemies. God has provided Christians with a weapon—His Word. Read **Hebrews 4:12**. Explain that when people read the Bible and trust God's Word, He will help them to do what is right and to make wise decisions. The truths found in the Bible will help them defeat God's enemy, Satan, who wants them to make poor choices. Believers should thank God each day for His Word and for helping them to be victorious over sin!

2B Play the game Gideon Says, modeling it after the game Simon Says. Include commands, such as drink water from the brook, lift your torch high, and blow your trumpet. Emphasize that God helped Gideon to be a good leader and that Gideon followed God's commands.

Introduction ★

Show students a PHOTOGRAPH OF AN AMERICAN FOOTBALL TEAM that depicts the American version football. Point out the quarterback. Explain that the quarterback calls the plays, and the team follows his directions. He is the leader. Ask what would happen if there were no leader of the team. (**Possible answers: Everyone would do what they wanted; there would be confusion; the team would play poorly.**) Does the quarterback also have a leader? (**Yes, the coach is his leader.**) The quarterback must listen to his coach. Leadership is important! In today's lesson, Gideon takes the lead.

Directed Instruction ★

Display **VA 10A Gideon's Brave Army**, and read the Bible truth. Review the lesson material by asking students if Gideon seemed afraid to go into battle. (**No.**) How had Gideon changed from the day that the Lord called him? (**He wasn't afraid anymore.**) What caused Gideon to become courageous? (**He trusted in the Lord.**) Why? (**because God had revealed Himself to Gideon and Gideon had grown to trust Him**) Gideon gathered a large army together. How many men joined Gideon when he was preparing for the battle? (**32,000**) All these men looked to Gideon to lead them against the Midianites, and Gideon was ready!

God decided that Gideon had too many soldiers. That sounded foolish when they were preparing to go into battle, but God had His reason. Ask students to retell why God wanted to reduce the size of Gideon's army. (**God wanted Gideon to trust Him for the victory; glory would come to God when He won the battle; Gideon might have won the battle on his own with all those men.**)

God told Gideon that any of the men who were afraid to fight could go home. Gideon's army shrank! He started with 32,000 soldiers. After the 22,000 men who were afraid left, there were only 10,000 left! That means that more than half of the army went home!

God said, "That's still too many soldiers." Why did He say this? (**He wanted the people to know that He was the Lord God; He wanted the people to trust Him for the victory.**) God told Gideon to let the men get a drink of water. Review what the two groups did as they drank. Invite two students to pantomime how each group drank. After both students have pretended to take a drink, ask volunteers to tell the class which men God told Gideon to send home. (**all the men except those who did not kneel**) How many men were left to fight the battle? (**300**)

State that the small army looked to Gideon for leadership. Ask students who Gideon looked to for leadership. (**God**) What did Gideon do that tells you he was relying on God's leadership? (**Before the battle, Gideon worshipped God, and he did what God said.**) Gideon knew that if they were to win the battle, God alone would bring the victory.

Review how Gideon divided his army into thirds and had each man carry a trumpet made of ram's horn and a clay pitcher (jar) with a torch inside. Explain that the Midianites were afraid when they heard the horns, breaking pitchers (jars), and shouting. They thought there was a great army coming to attack them! Conclude by recounting that the Israelites stood around the Midianite camp and watched the Midianites either kill one another or run away! The Lord had brought the victory!

Review

- Why did God reduce Gideon's army from 32,000 men to 300 men? (**God wanted them to know that victory was by His strength, not their own.**)
- Which men did God send home? (**those who were afraid to fight and those who knelt when taking a drink of water**)
- What weapons did Gideon's army carry into battle? (**trumpets of rams' horns and clay pitchers, or jars, with torches inside**)
- What did Gideon's army shout? (**A sword for the Lord and for Gideon!**)

Student Page 10.2

Read the directions and the text. Direct students to complete each exercise.

DAY 2

10.2 Gideon

God chose Gideon to lead an army against the Midianites. God helped Gideon to choose the right men to fight against the enemy.

Write **yes** if the sentence tells something true. Write **no** if it does not.

1. Gideon took **4,000** men into battle. no

2. Gideon watched how his men drank . yes

3. Each of Gideon's men carried a . yes

4. Each of Gideon's men carried a . yes

5. Each of Gideon's men blew a . yes

6. Each of Gideon's men used his  to destroy the Midianites. no

7. God gave Gideon's  the victory. yes

38

© Bible Grade 1

APPLICATION

- Gideon followed God's instructions exactly. Is it important to do just what God says? (**Yes, it is very important that I do all that God asks. I should repent if I don't follow God's instructions.**)
- God showed His power by using a few men to defeat a mighty army. How does God show His power in your life? (**Answers will vary, but should include that He hears my prayers, strengthens my faith, and provides for my needs.**)

REINFORCEMENT

Mosaic Law in Deuteronomy 20:5–8 allowed certain groups of people to be excused from battle. One category included those who were afraid or fainthearted, as those who were fearful might negatively affect the overall strength of the entire army.

10.3 Gideon

Focus: Godly Leadership

★ PREPARATION

Have on hand a SALTSHAKER and a FLASHLIGHT. (*Introduction*)

EXTENSION

3A Go to the playground and play a game of Follow the Leader. Allow various students to be the leader. After the game, remind students that the leaders were the ones who made the decisions that the group followed. Ask students to share their thoughts about the qualities of the best leaders, such as those who gave clear directions, or those who were decisive or creative. Ask students to name leaders in real life today. (**Possible answers: parents, teachers, pastors, those holding public office**)

Introduction ★

Show students a SALTSHAKER and ask what salt is used for. (**Answers will vary, but should include that salt makes things taste better.**) Ask students if they would sprinkle salt on their food if it tasted like playground sand. (**No.**) Turn on the FLASHLIGHT. Ask students to share times when they would use a flashlight. (**Answers will vary.**) Explain that the flashlight would be useless if the light were covered or if the batteries were dead.

Jesus said that Christians are like salt and light in the world (Matthew 5:13–14). Like Gideon, Christians are called to lead others. They are called to influence the world. To *influence* means *to gently change the way people think by what you say and do*. Ask students if their words and behavior shows others that they are Christians. (**Answers will vary.**)

Directed Instruction

Review that at the beginning of this week's lesson, Gideon was threshing grain while hiding from the Midianites. Ask students what Gideon said to the angel of the Lord when he was called to lead God's army. (**He was not a strong leader; he was from the smallest family, and he was the weakest son in the family.**) Gideon knew that he was weak and fearful on his own. With God's help, though, Gideon overcame his fear and believed that God would do what He had promised. A godly leader trusts God!

Once Gideon accepted the call from the angel of the Lord to lead the army, he began to prepare for the battle. This was a big job, but Gideon was obedient to do what God asked of him. Some people might have thought that Gideon was a foolish leader. Instead of having a large army, Gideon sent men away! Sometimes it is hard to do the right thing, especially when it does not make sense to others. Gideon was willing to do what God asked. A godly leader will stand up for what is right and do what God wants him or her to do!

Even though Gideon's army only had 300 soldiers, he showed strength as he led the men into battle. He told them that the Lord would win the victory. Gideon's faith in the Lord was seen by all the men and then they, too, trusted God as they went to war. A godly leader influences others to trust in the Lord's ways!

Ask students to name some of the faithful leaders that they have studied in previous lessons. (**Possible answers: Noah, Abraham, Joseph, Moses, Joshua, Caleb**) Each leader made a difference! Abraham obeyed God's commands. Moses influenced others and encouraged them to trust in the Lord. Joshua and Caleb stood against the lack of faith others had in God.

Read **1 Timothy 4:12**. Explain that godly leaders do not have to be adults. First graders can lead others in many ways, influencing those around them by demonstrating godly behavior.

Review

- Why did Jesus say that Christians should be like salt and light? (**Salt improves the flavor of food; light allows people to see. Salt and light make a difference. Christians need to make a difference.**)
- What are four characteristics of a godly leader? (**A godly leader trusts God, obeys God's commands, stands for what is right, and influences others to trust in the Lord's ways.**)
- Who are some godly leaders from the Bible that you have studied? (**Possible answers: Noah, Abraham, Joseph, Moses, Joshua, Caleb, Gideon**)

Student Page 10.3

Discuss each scenario. Encourage students to identify the godly leadership characteristics of the children pictured.

Notes:

APPLICATION

- Gideon trusted God even though what God told him to do did not make sense. Tell about a time that you had to trust God even though you did not completely understand what was going to happen. (**Answers will vary.**)
- Would someone who regularly disobeys God's commandments and does not repent make a good leader? Why or why not? (**No, a good leader obeys God's commands.**)
- What kind of a leader would you like to follow? (**Answers will vary, but should include a leader who trusts God, obeys His commands, and stands for what is right.**)

DAY 3

Name ______________________________

Gideon **10.3**

Talk about each picture and discuss how each first grader shows leadership that honors God.

1. Marisol is a cheerleader. She made up two cheers about Jesus and taught them to her friends. Now they cheer for the Lord!

2. DeVon says his Memory Verse to his aunt and uncle. He tells them about the Bible and encourages them to follow God.

3. Greg worships the Lord with his whole heart. He hopes that his brother will follow his example and worship the Lord in the same way.

10.4 Gideon

Focus: Sharing God's Word

EXTENSION

4A Invite a Gideon to your class to tell students what The Gideons International is doing in your community. Help students determine how many copies of God's Word are distributed by The Gideons International every minute, hour, and day. More than two copies of the Bible are given every second—over 120 Bibles per minute! In one hour, over 7,200 Bibles are distributed. In a day, over 172,800 copies of the Bible are distributed throughout the world. Create a visual display for the students to help them better visualize these numbers. Using GRAPH PAPER WITH SMALL SQUARES, color the number of blocks that represent the number of Bibles placed every second, minute, and hour.

4B Display **PP-3 The Bible** to reinforce the information about the Bible presented in the lesson.

REINFORCEMENT

Today, The Gideons International not only distributes Bibles to hotels and motels, but also gives Bibles to military members, jails, hospitals, and nursing homes. Wives of Gideons—the Auxiliary—are also busy taking copies of God's Word to medical offices, detention centers for women, and domestic violence centers. About 1.6 billion Bibles and New Testaments have been placed worldwide since 1908. There are over 290,000 Gideons and Auxiliary members in more than 10,000 local groups throughout the world. On average, more than two copies of God's Word are distributed per second. Every 4.5 days, over one million Bibles and New Testaments are distributed.

Introduction

Write the numbers *27*, *39*, and *66* on the board. Hint that students need to keep listening for these numbers in today's lesson.

Directed Instruction

Share this truth about The Gideons International, a missions organization:

> More than 100 years ago, in the fall of 1898, two traveling businessmen first met in a hotel in Wisconsin. In those days when the hotel was crowded, guests were sometimes asked to share a room with someone else. Mr. Nicholson and Mr. Hill agreed to share a room and soon discovered that they were both Christians. That night, they studied the Bible together, prayed, and asked God to show them how they could form some kind of group for Christian businessmen.
>
> Mr. Nicholson and Mr. Hill met again in the spring of 1899 while traveling. They still wanted to form a group for Christian businessmen, so they agreed to hold the first meeting on July 1, 1899. Joining them for that meeting was a third man, Mr. Knights. The men wanted to focus on sharing the Gospel and serving the Lord. All three men prayed that God would help them select the right name for their group. As they finished praying, it was Mr. Knights who said, "We shall be called *Gideons*!"
>
> Mr. Knights had been reading about Gideon in the book of Judges. He recalled how, at first, Gideon felt that he was not important and could not do anything special for God. The angel of the Lord, however, assured Gideon that he would be a good leader with the help of God. Just like Gideon, these men agreed that—though they were not special on their own—they were confident that God was with them and would bless their group.
>
> Since most of the Gideons were traveling businessmen in those days, the men thought and thought about how they could help other travelers to learn God's Word. They decided to put a Bible in each bedroom of those hotels. In 1908, the very first Bible was placed in a hotel in Montana.
>
> It has been more than 100 years since The Gideons International was organized. Since that time, there are now Gideons in more than 190 countries around the world. They distribute Bibles in over 90 languages. God has surely blessed the work of this mission organization as it provides Bibles to people around the world so that they can learn about Jesus!

Tell students that Bibles have been placed in thousands of hotel rooms by the Gideons. Open your Bible, and explain that it is divided into two parts, the Old Testament and the New Testament. Point to the numbers on the board. There are 39 books in the Old Testament. One of them is the book of Judges, the book that contains the Bible truth about Gideon. There are 27 books in the New Testament. Explain that the New Testament tells about Jesus' birth and work on the earth, and also God's work in His Church and future events.

Review

- How many men asked God to help them begin a mission organization called *The Gideons International*? (**three**)
- The Gideons are a group of missionaries. What is a missionary? (**someone who tells others about Jesus**) The Gideons are missionaries who want to share the truths found in the Bible.
- What do members of The Gideons International do? (**They give away Bibles and New Testaments all around the world.**)
- How many testaments are in the Bible? (**There are two—the Old Testament and the New Testament.**)
- How many books are in the Old Testament? (**39**) The New Testament? (**27**) In all? (**66**)

Student Page 10.4

Assist students in completing the page.

DAY 4

10.4 ***Gideon***

The Gideons International gives away millions of Bibles and New Testaments every year. These Bibles have helped many, many people come to know the Lord.

Look at the books of the Bible below. Write the correct number to make each sentence true.

1 2 27 39 66

1. The Bible is divided into __2__ main parts.

2. There are __39__ books in the Old Testament.

3. There are __27__ books in the New Testament.

4. The Bible contains __66__ books in all.

5. God wants to be number __1__ in your life!

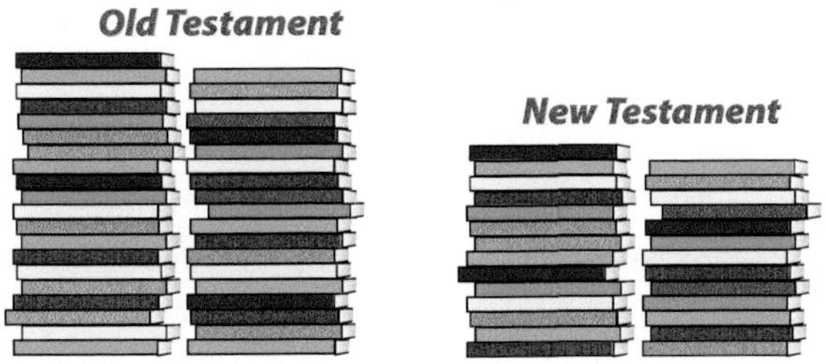

40 © Bible Grade 1

APPLICATION

- A *missionary* is defined as *someone who tells others about Jesus.* The men who started The Gideons International were missionaries. Do you need to be an adult to be a missionary? (**No.**) How can you help share the good news about Jesus with others? (**Possible answers: invite my friends to attend worship services with me, share the story of God's love with my friends, show love to others just like Jesus shows His love to me**)
- Gideon led the Israelites to victory because he trusted the Lord. The men who began The Gideons International trusted that God would bless the work of their organization, too. Why do you think they had such confidence? (**They were sharing God's Word, and God wants people to know the good news about Jesus.**)

10.5 Gideon

Focus: Review and Assessment

★ PREPARATION

Select **VA 10A Gideon's Brave Army**. (*Lesson Review*)

Duplicate a copy of **BLM 10C Lesson 10 Test** for each student. (*Directed Instruction*)

Lesson Review ★

Use **VA 10A Gideon's Brave Army** to review the Bible truth from this week's lesson. Cover the following points:

- God told the Israelites to drive out their enemies from the Promised Land. The Israelites did not obey.
- The Israelites began to worship idols like their enemies did. This did not please God.
- God raised up judges to govern and lead the people.
- The Midianites were enemies of the Israelites. They stole the Israelites' food.
- God chose Gideon to be a judge and to fight against the Midianites.
- Gideon was unsure at first about leading the Israelites. He needed a sign from God. God gave him a sign.
- Gideon trusted God and followed God's instructions.
- God reduced Gideon's army from 32,000 men to 300 men because He wanted the people to know that He was the Lord God and to trust Him for the victory.
- Gideon's brave soldiers carried trumpets of rams' horns and clay pitchers, or jars, with torches inside for weapons when they faced the Midianites.
- Good leaders trust God, obey God's commands, stand up for what is right, and influence others to trust in the Lord.
- Members of The Gideons International give away many, many Bibles and New Testaments.
- The Bible is divided into two main sections: the Old Testament and the New Testament.
- There are 39 books in the Old Testament and 27 books in the New Testament.
- The Bible contains 66 books in all.
- God can use anyone to do His work, no matter what his or her age.

Directed Instruction ★

Distribute a copy of **BLM 10C Lesson 10 Test** to each student. Read each exercise to students, and allow them to circle their answer choice before moving to the next exercise. Review answers with students. For each false statement, have students suggest ways to make the statement true.

Notes:

Lesson Preparation 11.0

Ruth

Expected Student Outcomes

KNOW
Ruth is devoted to God and loyal to Naomi.

DO
Students will:
- complete sentences that indicate Ruth's loyalty to Naomi
- evaluate the choices made by Ruth, Orpah, and Boaz
- conclude that love can be shown through service
- review the attitudes and actions of biblical characters presented previously

APPLY
Students will selflessly help others.

Lesson Outline

I. Ruth is loyal (Ruth 1)
  A. Elimelech moves his family
  B. Ruth stays with Naomi
II. Ruth is a loving servant (Ruth 2–4)
  A. Ruth takes care of Naomi
  B. Ruth marries Boaz
III. Serving others (1 Pet 4:10–11)
  A. Show God's love through service
  B. First graders can serve God
IV. Pleasing God (Col 3:23)
  A. Doing your best for God

TEACHER'S HEART

This week you will teach your students about God Jobs. These are little jobs you do for others without being asked, without expecting payment, and without obligation. They are small things that encourage in a way that shows God's love. First graders love to help and need to see that they can serve God every day.

While you help your students look for ways to shower God's love on others, look for your own little God Jobs. Is there a fellow teacher who could use a boost? Perhaps you could pick up recess duty or grade a stack of papers. Can you encourage a friend with a cup of coffee or a short note? Could you leave an anonymous treat on the principal's desk or ask your students to make cards for the music teacher? God loves you deeply, and He gave you many ways to shower His love on others. When you do that, you are administering God's grace and showing God's deep love for others (1 Peter 4:8–10). Try looking for a way to administer His grace to someone this week.

MEMORY VERSE

Galatians 6:10

MATERIALS

Day 1:
- History book
- VA 11A Ruth Is Loyal
- Chart paper, sentence strips

Day 2:
- VA 11B Ruth Serves with Love
- Unpopped popcorn kernels, paper cups (*Extension*)
- BLM 11A Ruth, card stock, uncooked barley (*Extension*)

Day 3:
- Chart paper (*Extension*)

Day 4:
- VA 7A Moses Is Born, VA 7B The Burning Bush, VA 9A Crossing the Jordan River, VA 9B The Battle of Jericho, VA 10A Gideon's Brave Army, VA 11A Ruth Is Loyal

Day 5:
- VA 11A Ruth Is Loyal, VA 11B Ruth Serves with Love
- BLM 11B Lesson 11 Test

TEACHER RESOURCES

Hybels, Bill. *The Power of a Whisper: Hearing God, Having the Guts to Respond.* Zondervan, 2010.

Mears, Henrietta C. *What the Bible Is All About*. Regal Books, 2007.

STUDENT RESOURCES

Rich, Richard. *The Story of Ruth Video on Interactive DVD*. DVD. Nest Entertainment, 2005.

Sanders, Karen. *Ruth and Naomi.* Concordia Publishing House, 2007.

11.1

Ruth

Focus: Ruth Is Loyal

MEMORY VERSE

Galatians 6:10

MEMORY WORK

- Call for the same number of volunteers as there are words in the Memory Verse to stand. Choose one more volunteer to be a servant. Explain that the servant's job is to distribute a prepared piece of paper to each volunteer. Once the papers have been distributed by the servant, recite the verse again, and have each volunteer hop in place when his or her word is recited. Collect the pieces of paper, and repeat the activity.

★ PREPARATION

Write each word of the Memory Verse on a separate piece of paper. Write the verse on the board. (*Memory Work*)

Obtain a HISTORY BOOK with pictures relating to your country's history. (*Introduction*)

Select **VA 11A Ruth Is Loyal**. (*Directed Instruction*)

Prepare a piece of CHART PAPER with the title *Ruth Pleased God.* Write each of these words on a SENTENCE STRIP: *stay, family, live, God.* (*Directed Instruction*)

EXTENSION

1A To illustrate how out of place Ruth may have felt when she arrived in Israel, plan a trip to a place that is foreign to your students. Arrange to visit an upper grade classroom when that class is out of their room. As students sit in unfamiliar surroundings, review today's Bible lesson. Discuss what Ruth sacrificed in leaving her home in order to be loyal to Naomi.

Introduction ★

Show students the HISTORY BOOK. Explain that the book contains information about important people and events that have already taken place. Point out pictures of people in the text and discuss why the lives of those people are important to study. For example, show a picture of a political leader and explain who he or she was, what type of leadership he or she provided, and when he or she was in leadership. Relate that students often study history to learn how the actions taken by people in the past affect the students' life today.

Directed Instruction ★

Hold up your Bible as you remind students that God's Word teaches about many important people. Explain that the Bible includes examples of people who made poor choices as well as examples of those who chose wisely. Choose a volunteer to give an example of people in the Bible who made poor choices. (**Possible answers: Esau made a poor choice to trade away his birthright; Pharaoh made a poor choice in refusing to let the Israelites go.**) Ask the volunteer to speculate why God's Word includes examples of people who chose to do the wrong thing. (**Answers will vary, but should include that we can learn to avoid making poor choices by learning from their mistakes.**)

Remind students that the Bible also has many examples of people who did the right thing—people like Noah, Abraham, Joseph, Moses, Joshua, and Gideon. Their stories are told in the books of Genesis, Exodus, Leviticus, Numbers, Deuteronomy, Joshua, and Judges. Restate the names of the first seven books in the Bible, and invite students to recite them with you.

Open your Bible to the book of Ruth. Share that Ruth was such a remarkable lady that the Bible has a book all about her life. Display **VA 11A Ruth Is Loyal**. Read the title, and explain that to be *loyal* means *to be faithful to someone, even when it is difficult*. Invite students to listen for ways that Ruth was loyal as you read the text.

Express surprise that, unlike several of the heroes of the Bible studied so far, Ruth did not lead the Israelites, speak with God directly, or win battles. However, there are many things that Ruth did that were very special. Call students' attention to the CHART PAPER. Hold the prepared SENTENCE STRIPS in your hand, have a roll of tape nearby, and explain that Ruth's love was special for the following reasons:

- She cared enough about Naomi to stay with her and go with her to a strange land. Invite a student to tape the word *stay* on the chart.
- Ruth chose to stay with Naomi instead of going back to her own family. Have a student tape the word *family* on the chart.
- Ruth left her family in Moab to live where Naomi lived. Choose a student to tape the word *live* to the chart.
- Ruth promised that Naomi's God would become Ruth's God. Invite a student to tape the word *God* to the chart.

Review

- Why did Elimelech and Naomi move from Bethlehem in Israel to Moab? (**There was a famine in Israel, and they wanted to provide food for their sons.**)
- What happened to the family in Moab? (**The men of the family died, leaving Naomi, Orpah, and Ruth alone.**)
- Why did Orpah decide to stay in Moab? (**Answers will vary, but should include that even though she cared for Naomi, Orpah wanted to stay where she felt more comfortable and could live with her family.**)
- Why was Ruth loyal to Naomi? (**Ruth had an extra special kind of love for Naomi. Ruth knew that Naomi was old and would need lots of help.**)
- What part of Ruth's decision was the most important? (**Ruth decided to follow Naomi's God, the one, true God.**)

Student Page 11.1

Read the directions and assist students as needed in completing the page.

APPLICATION

- Why would it have been difficult for Ruth to move away from her home? (**Possible answers: She would have had to leave her family and friends; she might have had to learn a new language; she would not have known anyone except for Naomi.**)
- Have you ever had to move or change schools? How did that feel? (**Answers will vary.**) How did you make friends or try to fit in? (**Answers will vary.**)
- What does it mean to be loyal to family and friends? What are some ways to do this? (**Answers will vary.**)

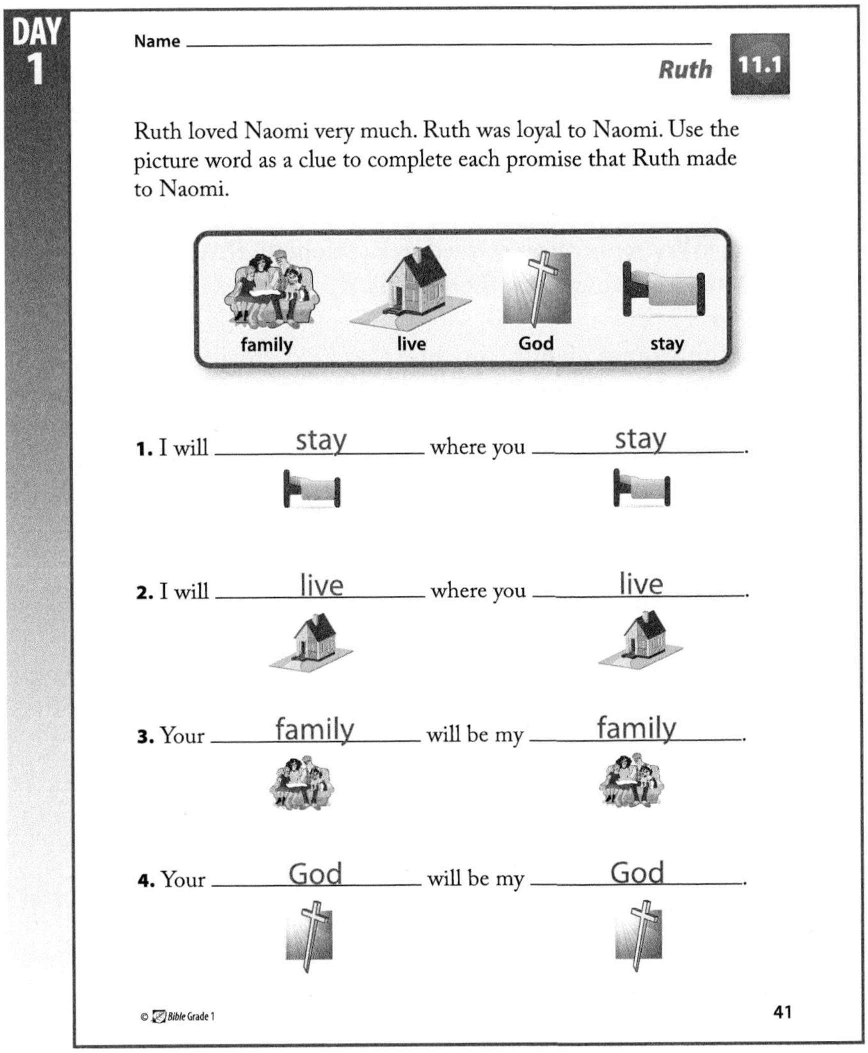

DAY 1

Name ______________________

Ruth 11.1

Ruth loved Naomi very much. Ruth was loyal to Naomi. Use the picture word as a clue to complete each promise that Ruth made to Naomi.

family | live | God | stay

1. I will ___stay___ where you ___stay___.
2. I will ___live___ where you ___live___.
3. Your ___family___ will be my ___family___.
4. Your ___God___ will be my ___God___.

© Bible Grade 1 41

11.2 Ruth

Focus: Ruth Is a Loving Servant

★ PREPARATION

Make two paper signs. Print *Moab* on one sign and *Israel* on the other. Post these on opposite sides of the classroom. (*Introduction*)

Select **VA 11B Ruth Serves with Love**. (*Directed Instruction*)

EXTENSION

2A Use this activity to help students appreciate the difficulty Ruth had in gleaning enough grain to feed herself and Naomi. Choose an area of the room and pour TWO CUPS OF UNPOPPED POPCORN KERNELS on the floor in that area. Give each student a SMALL PAPER CUP. Have students pretend to be gleaning as they pick up all the kernels.

2B Make a copy of **BLM 11A Ruth** on CARD STOCK for each student. Provide each student with a small amount of UNCOOKED BARLEY. Invite students to color the picture and glue barley at the top of each stalk of grain. As students work, inform them that barley was the grain that Ruth would have been gleaning at that time (Ruth 3:2). Barley is a small grain, and it would have taken Ruth a lot of time-consuming work to glean enough barley to provide food for both herself and Naomi.

Introduction ★

Choose three students to role-play Naomi, Orpah, and Ruth. Have them begin at the side of the classroom near the *Moab* sign. As you review the Bible truth, have your characters act out the scene. Ask students to tell you why the women were living in Moab. (**Naomi and her husband, Elimelech, had moved from Israel to the country of Moab because of a famine, a time when little to no food grows.**) Remind students that Elimelech and the two sons had died in Moab. Ask students to recall what Naomi decided to do. (**Naomi decided to go back to Israel.**) Both Ruth and Orpah loved their mother-in-law. Naomi wanted the young ladies to stay in Moab and marry again. Orpah decided to stay in Moab, so she hugged Naomi and went home. (Tell *Orpah* to go to her seat.) Ask students to recall what Ruth decided to do. (**Ruth chose to travel with Naomi to Bethlehem in Israel.**) Have the other two volunteers move to the area where the *Israel* sign is posted. Remind students that Ruth was not only loyal to Naomi, she made a choice to worship the one, true God.

Directed Instruction ★

State that even though Ruth and Naomi trusted God and returned to Bethlehem in Israel, life was not easy. Divide the class into two groups. Display **VA 11B Ruth Serves with Love**, and instruct one group of students to listen for the difficulties Ruth and Naomi faced. Instruct the other group to listen for the ways God provided for the women as you read the text on the back of VA 11B.

Have students in the first group recount the difficulty Ruth and Naomi experienced. (**When they first arrived in Bethlehem, Ruth and Naomi had no one to help provide for their needs.**)

Have the second group identify the ways that God provided for Ruth and Naomi. (**Ruth went to Boaz's field. He learned that she was the daughter-in-law of his relative Elimelech. Boaz knew that God wanted him to take care of his relatives, so he protected Ruth and made sure that she had plenty to eat as well as plenty to take back to Naomi. Boaz also pleased God by following God's rule to become a kinsman-redeemer.**)

Provide details about the meaning of *kinsman-redeemer*. *Kinsman* means that he was *a male relative*. *To redeem* means *to get or win something back*. A *kinsman-redeemer* was *a man who was willing to take on the responsibility of marrying a widow of one of his family members*. By marrying the widow, the kinsman-redeemer brought her back into the family.

Point out that Ruth and Boaz made godly choices. God gave them a son named *Obed*, who had a son named *Jesse*, who had a son named *David*. David was the one who killed Goliath, was a great king, served God, and even wrote some of the Bible. Several hundred years later, a descendant of Ruth, Mary, had a son named *Jesus*! Jesus redeemed the world by dying on the cross to restore people's relationship with God. Everyone has the choice to accept or reject His redemption.

Review

- What was life like for Naomi and Ruth when they first arrived in Israel? (**They were very poor and did not have anyone to help provide for their needs.**)
- How did they get enough to eat? (**Ruth worked hard to glean as much grain as she could from the fields.**)
- How did Boaz help Ruth? (**Boaz told Ruth to stay in his fields; he made sure she had enough to eat; he helped Ruth glean enough to feed Naomi; he made sure that she was safe.**)
- How did Boaz follow God's rules for taking care of Ruth and Naomi? (**Boaz became Ruth's kinsman-redeemer and married her. He loved Ruth and kept her and Naomi safe for the rest of their lives.**)
- Which king was Boaz and Ruth's great-grandson? (**King David**) Who was the most important person in Ruth and Boaz's family line? (**Jesus, the Redeemer**)

Student Page 11.2

Assist students as needed in completing the page.

DAY 2

11.2 Ruth

Read each riddle. Draw a line to match each riddle with its answer.

1. I lived in Moab with my husband, sons, and my sons' wives. When the men died, I wanted to move back home. Who am I?

2. I did not go to Bethlehem with Naomi. Who am I?

3. I left with Naomi to take care of her and to worship the one, true God. Who am I?

4. I followed God's laws and became Ruth's kinsman-redeemer. Who am I?

5. I am God's Son. I redeemed all of the people in the world. Who am I?

Orpah

Ruth

Naomi

Jesus

Boaz

42

APPLICATION

- People who are selfish put their own wants first. People who are selfless think of others first. Was Ruth selfish or selfless? Give a reason for your answer. (**Ruth was selfless. She put Naomi's needs above her own.**)
- When Boaz acted as a kinsman-redeemer, was he being selfish or selfless? (**He was being selfless. He did what was right by taking care of Ruth and Naomi.**)
- Have you been more selfish or more selfless today? How can you become more selfless? (**Possible answers: I can ask God to help me think of others first; I can help others at school and at home.**)

REINFORCEMENT

Gleaning means *to go back over a field that is already harvested and pick up any usable parts of the crop that remain.* God instructed the Israelites to leave behind fallen grapes or parts of a crop that were missed the first time around. This was God's way to provide for strangers, the fatherless, poor, and widows (Leviticus 19:9–10, Deuteronomy 24:19–21). When Ruth went to glean in the fields, she was performing a time-honored task to feed herself and Naomi, both widows.

11.3 Ruth

Focus: Serving Others

EXTENSION

3A Place a piece of **CHART PAPER** labeled *God Jobs* in your classroom. Encourage students to write, or illustrate, selfless acts of service that they have done either at home or at school during the day. For example, a student may write *I picked up trash at lunch*. You may choose to have students keep their acts of service anonymous or to write their names next to their entries on the chart.

Introduction

Help students to restate the meaning of *sacrificed* from previous lessons. (**gave up something of great value**) Remind students that Abel sacrificed a valuable lamb to show God his love and that Abraham was willing to sacrifice his son to show his love for God. Ask students to tell what Ruth sacrificed for Naomi. (**Ruth gave up her home and family to stay with Naomi. She was willing to pick grain off the ground to make sure that Naomi had enough food.**)

Directed Instruction

Explain that it pleases God and blesses others when His children give up something to show people His love. Read each fictional story to students. After each story, discuss how the child involved sacrificed something to share God's love.

In Bible class, Mrs. Walker taught her students about something she called *God Jobs*. She told the boys and girls that God Jobs are any kinds of jobs that are done to show love for God. Mrs. Walker read 1 Peter 4:10 to the class. In that verse, the Bible teaches that Christians should use their abilities to serve others and show them God's love. Her students promised to watch for people who were doing God Jobs and report to the class. They promised to do God Jobs whenever they had the chance.

1. Candice noticed that, after lunch, Josh was late for recess. When she asked him why, he told her that his mom comes to school three times a week to help in the lunchroom. If the kids left trash on the floor, it was Josh's mom who picked it up. He stayed to help her.
2. Dane and his dad love watching football games together. This week, the game was starting, but Dane couldn't find his dad anywhere. He finally found him outside; he was raking the neighbor's leaves! His dad explained that their neighbor was sick with the flu. Dane found another rake and spent the afternoon helping in the neighbor's yard.
3. One morning, Lily arrived at school early. The quiet halls seemed very different without all the students around. She noticed that there was a group of teachers gathered by the office. They were praying. Later, she learned that the teachers always arrive at school early to pray about the day's activities and for all of the students.
4. On Friday, Eric was on his way home from school when he noticed a neighbor struggling to carry grocery bags and two little babies from her car to her house. Remembering what Mrs. Walker said about God Jobs, Eric put his books on the sidewalk and started carrying the grocery bags into the neighbor's house. Eric missed some playtime, but he smiled when he saw how grateful his neighbor was for his help.

Review

- What God Job did Josh do in the lunchroom? What sacrifice did he make? (**Josh helped pick up trash, giving up some of his recess time to show God's love to his mom.**)

- What God Job did Dane do? What sacrifice did he make? (**Dane and his dad raked their neighbor's leaves. They gave up watching the football game.**)
- What God Job did the teachers at Lily's school do? What sacrifice did they make? (**The teachers arrived early to pray for their students. They had to come to school earlier than usual to be able to pray about the day's activities and for the students.**)
- What God Job did Eric do? What sacrifice did he make? (**Eric helped his neighbor take in groceries. He gave up some playtime.**)

Student Page 11.3

Allow students to discuss the scenarios on this page with a partner. Invite partners to report their discussions to the class.

Notes:

DAY 3

Name ______________________________

Ruth **11.3**

Look at each picture. Tell something that you would do to help.

1.

3.

2.

4.

5. Choose a picture to write about. List its number here: _____ Write about how you would help the person or people in the picture.

Answers will vary.

____

____

____

APPLICATION

- Is there a God Job that someone does to serve you? (**Answers will vary, but should include jobs that parents do because they love their children, whether or not the children show appreciation for their parents' efforts.**)
- Is there a God Job you already do without being asked? (**Answers will vary, but should include some type of chore.**)
- Name one thing you can do today that will show God's love to someone. (**Answers will vary.**)
- Read **1 Peter 4:10**. Tell what this verse means in your own words. (**God has given me different gifts, skills, or abilities. I should use what God has given me to help others.**)

11.4 Ruth

Focus: Pleasing God

★ PREPARATION

Select **VA 7A Moses Is Born**, **VA 7B The Burning Bush**, **VA 9A Crossing the Jordan River**, **VA 9B The Battle of Jericho**, **VA 10A Gideon's Brave Army**, and **VA 11A Ruth Is Loyal**. *(Directed Instruction)*

EXTENSION

4A Give each student a piece of white construction paper. Tell students to draw a picture of another classmate doing something that pleases God. Help students understand that you will turn these drawings into a special book that will be available in your classroom library all year. Guide the students to think of the ways that their classmate pleases God. Write a caption for each page as follows: *(Name of student) pleases God by (task)*. Have an artistic student design a cover for the book. Add a back cover and laminate the covers for durability.

Introduction

Hold up your Bible and explain that God's Word tells about the right attitude to have when working. Read **Colossians 3:23**. Ask a volunteer to tell what the right attitude toward work should be. (**Christians should work as if the task they are doing is for the Lord.**)

Directed Instruction ★

Select six volunteers to hold **VA 7A Moses Is Born, VA 7B The Burning Bush, VA 9A Crossing the Jordan River, VA 9B The Battle of Jericho, VA 10A Gideon's Brave Army**, and **VA 11A Ruth Is Loyal**. Have the volunteers stand so that the pictures are in chronological order. Discuss how each person, or group, pictured pleased God. Point out Miriam on VA 7A. Ask students how Miriam pleased God. (**She watched her baby brother and spoke boldly to Pharaoh's daughter. She went to get her mother, Jochebed, to take care of the baby.**)

On VA 7B, remind students that Moses has grown up. Ask students to tell what God told Moses to do. (**God told Moses to go to Pharaoh to gain freedom for the children of Israel.**) Call on a volunteer to tell how Moses pleased God. (**Moses did what God said. Moses was courageous in facing Pharaoh, and he led the children of Israel wisely.**)

On VA 9A, point out Joshua (on the far left) and the priests who were carrying the ark of the covenant. Ask how this group of people pleased God. (**They did exactly what God told them to do. They were faithful to complete their task.**)

For the review of VA 9B, ask students to share how all the children of Israel pleased God when they walked around the city of Jericho. (**They did what God commanded. Their choice to obey God led to a victory and brought glory to God.**)

For the review of VA 10A, ask students to name the hero who defeated a huge army with only 300 men and the help of the Lord. (**Gideon**) What was it about Gideon's attitude that pleased God? (**Gideon trusted God. He was outnumbered, but he knew God would give him the victory.**)

Show VA 11A. Point out Ruth and ask students to tell the special way that Ruth pleased God. (**Ruth acted selflessly when she stayed loyal to Naomi.**)

Review

- Who obeyed her mother and watched her baby brother in the Nile River? (**Miriam**)
- Who followed God's instructions exactly and walked around the city of Jericho, leading to the fall of its wall? (**Joshua and the children of Israel**)

- Who defeated the Midianites with a small force of soldiers and the help of the Lord? (**Gideon**)
- Who was selfless, left her homeland, and was loyal to her mother-in-law and to the Lord? (**Ruth**)
- Which of the people who have been mentioned trusted and obeyed God? (**all of them**)

Student Page 11.4

Help students to number the pictures in chronological order. Once students are finished, review the names of the first eight books of the Bible.

Notes:

APPLICATION

- Boaz chose to do the right thing. He married Ruth and loved her unconditionally. That means that she did not have to do anything to earn Boaz's love. How was Boaz's love for Ruth like Jesus' love for you? (**Jesus loves me unconditionally. I do not do anything to earn His love.**)
- Think about the way you love and serve others. Do you love and serve them unconditionally, or do you help only the people who will repay you? (**Answers will vary.**)

REINFORCEMENT

When Boaz first met Ruth, she was not only in great need, but a newcomer to the land as well. At first glance, there would have been little for a landowner like Boaz to gain from offering protection to such a poor woman. However, as Boaz heard more about Ruth's excellent character and reputation, he began to take an interest in her and consider how to help her and Naomi.

The kinsman-redeemer was part of the system of inheritances in the laws written down by Moses. The purpose of the kinsman-redeemer law was to protect widows. The kinsman-redeemer may have been called to make sacrifices in order to follow this law. First, he may have had to purchase the land of the deceased, an unexpected expenditure. Second, the firstborn son from the marriage would count as the son of the deceased as well as the kinsman-redeemer, in order for the deceased's name not to be forgotten.

DAY 4

11.4 ***Ruth***

1. Number the pictures in the order that they happened.

2. All of the people pictured pleased God. Share with your classmates some ways that you have chosen to please God.

44 © Bible Grade 1

11.5 Ruth

Focus: Review and Assessment

★ PREPARATION

Select **VA 11A Ruth Is Loyal** and **VA 11B Ruth Serves with Love**. (*Lesson Review*)

Make one copy of **BLM 11B Lesson 11 Test** for each student. (*Directed Instruction*)

EXTENSION

5A Take down the God Jobs chart that the students have been developing. Talk about some of the jobs that the students have done, commending them for their selfless acts of service. Use the praise songs from the music CDs that students particularly enjoy and lead a time of worship and praise. Include a prayer time, thanking God for the special way your students showed their love for Him in service this week.

Lesson Review ★

Use **VA 11A Ruth Is Loyal** to review some of this week's Bible truths. Cover the following concepts:

- Elimelech and Naomi moved from Bethlehem in Israel to Moab because there was a famine, and they wanted to provide for their sons. They lived there for many years. The boys grew up and married women from Moab.
- After a while, Elimelech and both sons died. Naomi decided to move back to Israel. Orpah, one daughter-in-law, decided to stay in Moab. Ruth, the other daughter-in-law, was loyal to Naomi and would not leave her.
- The most important part of Ruth's decision to stay with Naomi was Ruth's decision to follow the one, true God.

Use **VA 11B Ruth Serves with Love** to review more of this week's Bible truths. Cover the following concepts:

- Life was hard in Bethlehem for the two widows. They had no one to provide food for them.
- Ruth chose to go into the fields and pick up leftover grain that the harvesters had missed. She gleaned as much as she could to feed herself and Naomi.
- Boaz, the man who owned the field where Ruth was gleaning, noticed her. Boaz was related to Elimelech, Naomi's deceased husband. Boaz took care of Ruth and kept her from harm. Later, Boaz became her kinsman-redeemer.
- King David was the great-grandson of Ruth and Boaz.
- Jesus, the Redeemer, was also born into the same family line, but much, much later.

Directed Instruction ★

Distribute a copy of **BLM 11B Lesson 11 Test** to each student. Read each exercise, and allow students to respond before moving on to the next exercise. When all students have finished taking the test, review the answers in class, and collect the test papers for assessment.

Notes:

Lesson Preparation

The Psalms

12.0

Expected Student Outcomes

KNOW
The Psalms contain expressions of the heart of God's people.

DO
Students will:
- identify types of psalms
- sequence the events in David's life
- write sentences to praise God
- describe how Jesus is like a good shepherd
- define *confession*, *praise*, and *requests* as related to prayer

APPLY
Students will praise, worship, pray, and turn to God for comfort.

Lesson Outline

I. Introduction to the book of Psalms
  A. Different kinds of psalms (Ps 95:1–7, Ps 150)
II. David the psalmist (Ps 57)
  A. David's background
III. The Good Shepherd's Psalm (Ps 23)
IV. A prayer of David (Ps 86:1–13a)
  A. A pattern for prayer

TEACHER'S HEART

Music has many purposes. It can soothe the spirit, renew the heart, and communicate God's love to others. Music, especially singing, is an important part of Christian worship today, just as it was in David's time.

Children love to sing as part of their worship experience. They do this often in chapel. During chapel one week, some students sang about shining the light of Christ. Then the song leader posed the question, "Students, how can we make our faces shine?" The response she was seeking was that when children come to know Jesus as their Savior, He gives them joy that shows on their faces by their smiles.

The students raised their hands, and the song leader called on a first grader who was obviously confident that he had the right answer. The leader pointed to the boy and said, "Yes, please tell us how we can make our faces shine." The little boy scooted back in his seat and sat up tall. Very seriously he said, "We could put baby oil on our faces!"

The song leader accepted his answer, but all the teachers at chapel were silently amused. Such a simple answer—and so sincere—yet doesn't the psalmist, David, say something similar in Psalm 23? "You anoint my head with oil; my cup runs over." As you think of this sweet reminder from God's Word, won't you smile and let the joy of your salvation shine on your face today?

MEMORY VERSE

Psalm 86:11

MATERIALS

Day 1:
- Hymnal or songbook
- VA 12A The Psalms
- PP-5 The Psalms (*Extension*)

Day 2:
- Stringed instrument
- TM-5 Family Tree
- Chart paper (*Extension*)

Day 3:
- VA 12A The Psalms
- BLM 12A Shepherd's Maze (*Extension*)

Day 4:
- TM-6 Psalm 86:1–13a
- BLM 12B Prayers (*Extension*)

Day 5:
- VA 12A The Psalms
- BLM 12C Lesson 12 Test

SONGS

Garment of Praise

TEACHER RESOURCES

Keller, W. Phillip. *A Shepherd Looks at Psalm 23*. Zondervan, 2008.
Phillips, John. *Exploring Psalms, Vol. 1*. Kregel Publications, 2002.

STUDENT RESOURCES

Haidle, Helen. *The Lord Is My Shepherd*. Seed Faith Books, 2006.
Wilson, Anne, illus. *The Lord Is My Shepherd*. Wm. B. Eerdmans Publishing Co., 2003.

12.1 The Psalms

Focus: Introduction to the Book of Psalms

MEMORY VERSE

Psalm 86:11

MEMORY WORK

- Write the Memory Verse on the board and read it with students. Identify the action words in the verse. Ask students to help you draw four stick figures on the board to illustrate the actions. Consider the following suggestions: for the word *teach*, remind students that God is willing to teach them His ways. Draw a stick figure with its hands open, as if holding a Bible. For the word *walk*, show a stick figure with its legs outstretched as if walking. For *unite my heart* or *give me an undivided heart*, make a heart on a stick figure and draw a line to a larger heart labeled *God's heart*. Teach students that *fear* means *showing respect for God*, not being afraid of Him. Draw the fourth stick figure on its knees or with its hands folded in prayer.

★ PREPARATION

Have a HYMNAL or a SONGBOOK available. Browse through it to determine how it is organized. Possible divisions may include calls to worship, seasonal songs, songs of praise and worship, or national songs. (*Introduction*)

Select **VA 12A The Psalms**. (*Directed Instruction*)

Select "Garment of Praise" from the music CDs. (*Directed Instruction*)

EXTENSION

1A Show **PP-5 The Psalms** to reinforce this week's lesson.

Introduction ★

Hold up the HYMNAL or the SONGBOOK, open it, and ask for someone to share what a hymnal is and what it is used for. (**Answers will vary.**) If students are unfamiliar with musical notation, explain that the musical notes indicate the tune for the song. Show students the sections of the hymnal or the songbook that you have previously identified. Point out that the songs were written by different composers at various times. Explain that the songs are most often sung by Christians during worship services at church.

Directed Instruction ★

Share that there are songs in the Bible. Hold up the Bible, and open it to the book of Psalms. Tell students that many of the words in this book are song words. Demonstrate how students can easily locate Psalms by opening the Bible to the middle. Say the books of the Bible in order, stopping at Psalms, and have the students repeat after you.

Share that there are 150 different psalms in the book of Psalms and that they were written by several different authors and composers. Many of the psalms had tunes that went with them so that people could sing them as part of their worship, but some psalms were not set to music. They were prayers that were written for people to read and think about. Tell students that all psalms are poems.

Explain that the people who wrote the psalms expressed many different feelings as they wrote. Select a few volunteers to share types of feelings that people can have. (**Possible answers: joy, happiness, anger, sadness, excitement, fear**) Some of the psalms express joy and happiness, but some convey sad or anxious feelings. Ask students why God might have included poems that express feelings in His Word. (**God knows we have these feelings. He wants His people to turn to Him in both the good times and the bad times of life.**) Read Psalm **95:1–7**. Ask students to tell what kinds of feelings are evident in this psalm. (**joy, thanksgiving**)

There are several different kinds of psalms, but one kind is a psalm of praise. Psalms of praise were written and sung during happy times or when remembering the goodness of God. Read **Psalm 150** as an example of a psalm of praise.

Display **VA 12A The Psalms**, and read the text on the back. Explain that God can turn even difficult times into times of worship (Isaiah 61:3). Use the music CDs to teach students "Garment of Praise." Sing the song several times throughout the week.

Student Page 12.1

Read the directions and any difficult words. Then, read the finished sentences together.

Review

- What are psalms? (**They are poems that are found in God's Word.**)
- How many psalms are there in the book of Psalms? (**150**)
- What is a psalm of praise for? (**to praise God when I'm happy or when I'm thinking about His goodness**)

Notes:

APPLICATION

- Have you ever prayed to God when you were feeling sad? What did you talk to Him about? (**Answers will vary.**)
- Have you ever forgotten to praise God when you were having fun? What can you do to remind yourself to praise Him when you are feeling happy? (**Answers will vary, but should include setting aside time for prayer every day.**)

REINFORCEMENT

The book of Psalms is divided into five major sections, or books. Some biblical historians assert that these five books of psalms may have been grouped this way to correspond to the first five books of the Bible—Genesis through Deuteronomy—known as *the Torah*, *the Law*, or *the Pentateuch*. The book of Psalms has been called *The Pentateuch of David*. The following are interesting facts:

- Psalm 117 is the shortest book of the Bible. It only has two verses.
- Psalm 119 is the longest book of the Bible. It has 176 verses.
- There are 31,173 total verses in the Bible, and Psalm 118:8 is the center verse. It says, "It is better to trust in the Lord than to put confidence in man."

DAY 1

Name ____________________

The Psalms 12.1

There are 150 psalms in the book of Psalms. Psalms often tell the feelings of God's people.

Use words from the Word Bank to correctly fill in the blanks. The first letter of each word is gray for you to trace.

WORD BANK

worship	poems	music
Bible	prayers	

1. The book of Psalms is in the middle of the Bible.
2. Some psalms are prayers.
3. Some psalms have been set to music.
4. Some psalms are songs for worship.
5. All of the psalms are poems.

45

12.2 The Psalms

Focus: David the Psalmist

★ PREPARATION

Bring in a **STRINGED INSTRUMENT**, such as a guitar or violin. (*Introduction*)

Prepare **TM-5 Family Tree** for display. (*Directed Instruction*)

EXTENSION

2A Remind students that many of the psalms were prayers. Write a class prayer to begin or end the school day. Use **CHART PAPER** to write down ideas for what to include in the prayer. Consider including praise to God, thanksgiving, confession, and requests. You may wish to post the finished prayer in your classroom. As your students learn more from the Bible and grow spiritually, consider revising your classroom prayer and plan on writing other prayers together.

Introduction ★

Show students a **STRINGED INSTRUMENT**, such as a guitar or a violin. Explain that people have been making instruments similar to these for thousands of years. Allow a volunteer to touch the strings to produce a sound. Tell students that when David was young, he played the harp, a stringed instrument (1 Samuel 16:23). Remind students that many of the psalms were set to music to be sung. Many of the tunes for these songs would have been played on stringed or wind instruments.

Directed Instruction ★

Display **TM-5 Family Tree**. Show students the family line of Boaz and Ruth. Explain that David was the youngest son of Jesse, who was Ruth and Boaz's grandson. David was only a young man when God chose him to be the next king. David grew to be a godly leader. Review the following godly leadership qualities:

- A godly leader trusts God!
- A godly leader will stand up for what is right and do what God wants him or her to do!
- A godly leader influences others to trust in the Lord's ways!

David had all these qualities. When David was growing up, he took care of his father's sheep. As a young man, David served King Saul by playing the harp for him. Later, David trusted God to help him defeat the giant, Goliath. But after David defeated the giant, people started to sing songs about David's victory being greater than King Saul's victory (1 Samuel 18:7). These songs made King Saul very jealous and angry. King Saul tried to kill David! David had to run for his life! David was forced to live in hiding from King Saul for many years.

Ask students to consider how they might feel if they had to run away from home and hide to keep from being harmed. (**Possible answers: frightened, worried, sad, alone**) David probably felt many of these same feelings. Tell students that David had opportunities to kill King Saul, but he did not. David did what was right.

David wrote several psalms about his experience of hiding. In these psalms of lament, David shared his fears with God. Explain that Psalm 57 is one of the psalms that David wrote. Read **Psalm 57:1–2**. Ask students to identify what David asked God to do. (**David asked God to be merciful to him or to have mercy on him.**) Explain that David was asking God to keep him safe from King Saul. Read **Psalm 57:9–11**. Ask students to share how David ends this psalm. (**He praises God.**) David was able to praise God even though he was in great danger!

Remind students that a godly leader influences others to trust in the Lord's ways. David's psalms influenced others. When Christians today read the psalms and see how David trusted God even when he was running for his life, they are reminded to trust and depend on God.

After King Saul died, David became the next king of Israel. Many, many years later, Jesus, the Savior, was born in King David's family line.

Review

- Who were David's great-grandparents? (**Boaz and Ruth**)
- Why did David have to hide? (**King Saul was trying to kill him. David hid for many years.**)
- How did David feel when he was hiding? (**He was probably afraid, but he still praised God.**)
- What can Christians learn from reading Psalm 57? (**Christians can learn to trust and depend on God.**)

Student Page 12.2

Read the directions, and complete Exercise 1 together. Provide assistance as needed for students to write their own sentences of praise in Exercise 2.

Notes:

APPLICATION

- Which words would you use to praise God? (**Answers will vary.**)
- How can you remember to pray when you are sad or when you are afraid? (**I need to make prayer a part of my everyday life so that when I go through sad or fearful times, I will not need to remind myself to pray.**)

DAY 2

12.2 *The Psalms*

1. Number the sentences in order to tell about David's life.

__6__ David became the king of Israel.

__4__ David ran away from King Saul.

__1__ David was a shepherd boy.

__2__ David played his harp for King Saul.

__3__ David killed the giant, Goliath.

__5__ David hid from King Saul for many years.

2. Write two sentences of praise. Use some or all of the words below in your sentences.

happy joy heaven God Lord sing wonderful praise Jesus glad

Answers will vary.

46

12.3 The Psalms

Focus: The Good Shepherd's Psalm

★ PREPARATION

Select **VA 12A The Psalms**. (*Directed Instruction*)

EXTENSION

3A Make a copy of **BLM 12A Shepherd's Maze** for each student. Instruct students to complete the maze by taking the shepherd to his lost sheep. Direct students to color the picture.

Introduction

Ask students to raise their hand if they have a pet. Mention that pets can require a lot of care. Invite students to share what they do to care for their pets. (**Answers will vary, but should include bathing, brushing, feeding, cleaning the pet's cage or other pet areas.**) Have students tell what kinds of pets they have and list them on the board. Point out the fact that sheep would not often be on a list of pets because sheep are farm animals. Many cities do not allow people to keep sheep as pets. Even though sheep were not really pets in Bible times either, they were very important to their owners since they provided both meat and wool to the shepherd and his family. Today's lesson tells about how a good shepherd takes care of his sheep.

Directed Instruction ★

Choose a volunteer to hold **VA 12A The Psalms** for the class to see. Remind students that there are 150 psalms in the book of Psalms, but that the focus for today's lesson is on Psalm 23. Psalm 23 is a psalm of praise written by King David. In Psalm 23, David said that God is like a good shepherd. David said that he is like a sheep. Challenge students to look closely at the picture and listen for things that a shepherd provides for the sheep as you read **Psalm 23**. After reading, make a list of provisions suggested by students. (**Possible answers: green pastures, still waters, guidance, comfort, a table or food, a cup or drink, anointing, goodness, love, mercy**)

Explain that there are many ways that people are like sheep. First, people need to eat healthy foods. Sheep are grazing animals that usually eat grass for good health. Sheep would enjoy getting into a wheat or barley field to eat because grain is like candy for them, but too much grain upsets a sheep's stomach. The shepherd leads the sheep away from grains and brings them to green grasses. Jesus, the Good Shepherd, leads his followers away from things that will harm them to things that are good for them.

Sheep need water. Sheep do not like fast-moving water; it scares them. If they can drink from a quiet stream, they will relax and lie down to rest. Rest is very important for sheep! Jesus gives rest.

Sheep have stomachs that have four parts. They eat their food very quickly. Later they bring it back up to their mouth and chew it some more before swallowing it for the last time. This is called *ruminating*. Sheep spend about a third of their lives ruminating, but they need peace and quiet before they will do it. They will not lie down if they are afraid. The shepherd knows where to take them so they can relax and be peaceful. Jesus gives peace.

Sheep are nervous animals. They tend to stay in a group rather than wander off alone because there is safety in numbers. Sheep have few natural defenses against wild animals, so they are easily scared and have to depend on their shepherd. The shepherd might use his staff to fight off an enemy that might try to harm his sheep. Jesus gives protection.

Sheep know their shepherd by voice and by sight. A good shepherd will have spent a lot of time with his sheep. He knows all of them very well. He leads them to safety by gently putting his staff along the side of the lead sheep and guiding it in the right direction. The shepherd uses his staff for another job, too. If one of his sheep falls into a ditch, the shepherd can use the end of his staff to lift the sheep that has fallen. Jesus is always present. He gently leads His followers, His sheep, and lifts them up when they fall.

Review

- Who leads the sheep to the best grazing and drinking places? (**the shepherd**)
- Why are still waters important to sheep? (**They need still waters so they can relax to ruminate.**)
- What is the best protection that sheep have from wild animals? (**the shepherd**)

Student Page 12.3

Discuss each picture. Read the text. Assist students to complete the page.

DAY 3

Name ______________________________

The Psalms **12.3**

Psalm 23 tells about a good shepherd. Think about the psalm. Write the letter of the picture by the correct sentence.

The Lord is my shepherd. I shall not want.

1. ___B___ He makes me to lie down in green pastures.

2. ___D___ He leads me beside the still waters. He restores my soul. He leads me in the paths of righteousness for His name's sake.

3. ___C___ Yea, though I walk through the valley of the shadow of death, I will fear no evil for You are with me.

4. ___A___ Your rod and Your staff, they comfort me.

5. How is Jesus like a good shepherd?

Answers will vary.

____

© Bible Grade 1 47

APPLICATION

- Who is your good shepherd? (**Jesus**) Who are His sheep? (**those who love Jesus**)
- How is Jesus like the shepherd in Psalm 23? (**He cares deeply for me; His Word guides me; He is always with those who trust Him.**)
- Share a time when you felt afraid. How did the Lord help you to overcome your fears? (**Answers will vary.**)

REINFORCEMENT

Sheep have a tendency to look for comfortable, low areas in the pasture in which to lie down. If a sheep rolls over on its back, it is said to be *cast* or *cast down*. This is a very precarious position for a sheep! It is unable to right itself and flails about frantically. While cast down, the sheep is easy prey for a predator. Additionally, it is unable to ruminate properly, and gases build up in its system, causing a bloated condition. If the watchful shepherd does not assist him, the sheep will probably die.

12.4 The Psalms

Focus: A Prayer of David

★ PREPARATION

Prepare **TM-6 Psalm 86:1–13a** for display. (*Directed Instruction*)

EXTENSION

4A Post three paper signs in your classroom. On one sign, write *praise*; on the second, write *confession* and *repentance*; and on the third, write *request*. Read the scenarios on **BLM 12B Prayers** and have students stand by the sign that represents each aspect of prayer.

Introduction

Ask students to raise their hand if they have a good friend. Have one or two volunteers share the name of their friend and why that person is a good friend. (**Possible answer: My good friend is loyal, honest, kind, giving, and funny.**) Ask students to tell some things that friends do together. (**Answers will vary.**) Do friends enjoy spending time together? (**Yes.**) Can friends be honest with each other and count on each other? (**Yes, friends should tell each other the truth and they can count on each other to help when there is a need.**)

David communicated with God as a very good friend. The book of Psalms contains many of David's prayers. Today's lesson is about one of David's prayers.

Directed Instruction

Display **TM-6 Psalm 86:1–13a**, and read verses 1–4. Explain that Psalm 86 is not a psalm of praise; it is a different kind of psalm. It is a psalm of lament. Psalms of lament were written when people were sad, afraid, or angry. *Lament* means *to feel deep sadness*. As the writers of these psalms cried out to God, God comforted them. Psalms of lament often start out sadly, but end with hope and joy.

Explain that friends can be honest with each other. David was very unhappy when he wrote this psalm of lament to the Lord. David shared that he was poor and needy. David did not try to pretend that he was happy when he was really very unhappy. Ask students if they can be honest with God when they pray. (**Yes, it is important to honestly tell the Lord about my problems, trust Him, and pray to Him often.**)

Even though David does not repent of a sin in Psalm 86, he does say that God is ready to forgive. It is important for Christians to tell God what they did that was wrong and that they are sorry. *Telling God about a sin* is called *confession*. When Christians confess their sins to God and turn away from habitually doing them, they receive God's forgiveness!

Read **Psalm 86:5–7**. God is ready to hear the prayers of His people at any time, but sometimes Christians forget to pray or praise Him when things are going wrong. Even though David had problems, he still praised God! Read **Psalm 86:8–10**. Remind students to praise God when they pray.

David had a long conversation with God before he ever asked Him for anything! Read **Psalm 86:11–13a**. David's request was not a selfish one; he did not ask for riches or to be famous. Choose a volunteer to tell what David asked God for in his prayer. (**to teach him His ways so he could live a life pleasing to God; to help him make wise choices and honor God**) Remind students to include fewer self-directed requests when they pray.

Review

- What should be included in your prayers? (**confession and repentance, praise, request**)
- What can you expect God to do when you pray? (**to hear and answer my prayers**)
- Did David make a selfish request when he prayed? (**No, he did not ask for riches or to become famous.**) What did David ask for? (**He asked God to teach him His ways.**)

Student Page 12.4

Read the directions and each sentence for students. When students have completed the page, discuss the answers.

Notes:

APPLICATION

- Why do you think that David was able to talk to God as if He were a close friend? (**David had a close relationship with God. He built the relationship through continued trust in God.**)
- Even though God will always hear your prayers, will He always answer your prayers the way you want Him to? (**No, God answers our prayers in His time and in a way that is best for us.**)

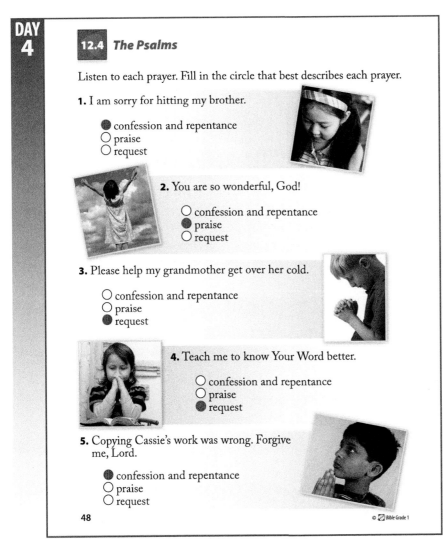

DAY 4

12.4 ***The Psalms***

Listen to each prayer. Fill in the circle that best describes each prayer.

1. I am sorry for hitting my brother.

● confession and repentance
○ praise
○ request

2. You are so wonderful, God!

○ confession and repentance
● praise
○ request

3. Please help my grandmother get over her cold.

○ confession and repentance
○ praise
● request

4. Teach me to know Your Word better.

○ confession and repentance
○ praise
● request

5. Copying Cassie's work was wrong. Forgive me, Lord.

● confession and repentance
○ praise
○ request

48 © *Bible* Grade 1

12.5 The Psalms

Focus: Review and Assessment

★ PREPARATION

Select "Garment of Praise" from the music CDs. (*Lesson Review*)

Select **VA 12A The Psalms**. (*Lesson Review*)

Duplicate one copy of **BLM 12C Lesson 12 Test** for each student. (*Directed Instruction*)

Lesson Review ★

Begin with a brief time of worship and prayer. Sing "Garment of Praise" from the music CDs. Remind students that Christians can worship God during sad times as well as glad times. Close your worship time in prayer. Remember to include prayers of confession and repentance, praise, and requests.

Use **VA 12A The Psalms** to review this week's Bible truth. Cover the following concepts:

- The book of Psalms was written by many different authors over a long period of time.
- The book of Psalms is in the middle of the Bible. There are 150 psalms in the book.
- All psalms are poems.
- Psalms express the feelings of the people who wrote them.
- Some psalms were set to music so that people could sing them.
- Some psalms were prayers.
- David, a king of Israel, wrote many psalms including Psalm 23 and Psalm 86.
- Psalm 23 is known as the Good Shepherd's Psalm. It compares God to a loving shepherd and His people to sheep.
- Psalm 86 is a psalm of lament. It tells about a sad time in David's life.
- David shared his sad feelings with God in Psalm 86.
- Christians should honestly share their feelings with God.
- Prayer should include confessing sin, repenting, praising God, and requesting His provision for needs.

Directed Instruction ★

Distribute a copy of **BLM 12C Lesson 12 Test** to each student. After students have completed the test, discuss correct answers.

Notes:

Lesson Preparation

Thanksgiving

13.0

Expected Student Outcomes

KNOW

Solomon leads God's people in worship, praise, and thanksgiving.

DO

Students will:
- write words to review the events of Solomon's dedication of the temple
- unscramble words and decode a sentence about why to praise God
- circle the correct words to complete a psalm
- write a letter to God to express thanks and praise

APPLY

Students will express gratitude to God for His goodness and mercy.

Lesson Outline

I. The temple (2 Chron 7)
II. Glorifying God (Ps 136)
  A. Worship
  B. Praise
  C. Thanks
III. A psalm of thanksgiving (Ps 100)
  A. Psalms: poems, prayers, songs
  B. Reference to Solomon's temple
IV. Giving thanks (1 Chron 16:8)
  A. Thanking God and others

TEACHER'S HEART

Have you ever felt you were the poster child for the proverb *Hope deferred makes the heart sick* (Proverbs 13:12)? You've believed and hoped and prayed that something would happen … maybe even been promised by others that something would occur … and yet the answer, the promised thing, is still nowhere to be seen. Maybe it's a personal goal or a relationship or a health issue or a financial matter or worse yet, all of them rolled into one. What do you do when your heart is so grieved it's sick?

Start and end with Jesus, the promised Savior. He knows that you are besieged at times with a spirit of heaviness—a paralyzing, depressing cloak that tries to swallow you whole and separate you from others. Isaiah 61 says that Jesus would give you the garment of praise for the spirit of heaviness. Just like you put on clothes no matter how you feel, He says to put on the garment of praise. Begin praising God for His promises, for how He has blessed you, for how He calls you as His own, for how He watches over you. God is bigger than everything you're going through. He is more powerful than despair, greater than your fears, stronger than your enemy. Trust Him. Praise Him. And then wait. You'll see the leaves of hope sprouting again as the Lord brings about the work He wants to accomplish.

MEMORY VERSE

Psalm 106:1

MATERIALS

Day 1:
- VA 13A Solomon Leads in Thanksgiving
- Pomegranate (*Extension*)

Day 2:
- Uncooked rice, paper or plastic cups (*Extension*)

Day 3:
- VA 13A Solomon Leads in Thanksgiving
- Maracas made in *Extension 2B* (*Extension*)

Day 4:
- Envelope, stamp, and note paper (or a thank-you note along with its envelope that you have received)

Day 5:
- VA 13A Solomon Leads in Thanksgiving
- BLM 13A Lesson 13 Test

SONGS

Wanna Say Thank You

TEACHER RESOURCES

Kendall, R. T. *Just Say Thanks.* Strang Communications, 2005.

The Temple: The Temple Throughout Bible History, Rose Publishing, 2005.

STUDENT RESOURCES

Hunt, Karen. *The Rumpoles and the Barleys: A Little Story About Being Thankful*. Harvest House Publishers, 2008.

Simon, Dr. Mary Manz. *My First Read and Learn Book of Prayers*. Scholastic, 2007.

13.1 Thanksgiving

Focus: The Temple

MEMORY VERSE

Psalm 106:1

MEMORY WORK

- Divide the class into three groups. Assign Group 1 the first line of the Memory Verse, Group 2 the second line, and Group 3 the third line. Have Group 1 stand, say its line, followed by Groups 2 and 3. Once the groups have mastered their line, change the assignments so that each group has a chance to practice the other lines until the entire Memory Verse is learned by all students.

★ PREPARATION

Select **VA 13A Solomon Leads in Thanksgiving**. (*Directed Instruction*)

EXTENSION

1A Hold up a POMEGRANATE for students to view. Explain that Solomon had the craftsmen decorate the two main pillars of the temple with 100 pomegranates. Cut open the pomegranate and share the seeds with the students.

1B Take the students on a tour of a church to discuss the different areas of the church and the events that take place in those areas, especially the lobby and the sanctuary.

1C Look online for a replica of Solomon's temple to share with the class.

Introduction

Ask students what they would ask for if they could have anything in the world. (**Answers will vary.**) Explain that in today's lesson they will learn about someone who asked God for something really special.

Directed Instruction ★

Display **VA 13A Solomon Leads in Thanksgiving**. Tell students that what they are seeing is the temple. Explain that the word *temple* is defined as *a building in which the Israelites worship God together*. Discuss the different features of the temple: the outer court where the people gathered to worship, the inner court (or court of the priests), and the Holy of Holies (where only the high priest could go). Tell students that the ark of the covenant was kept in the Holy of Holies, a very small space that was in the innermost section of the temple. Remind students that the Ten Commandments were inside the ark of the covenant. Draw attention to the altar (for animal sacrifices) in the outer court and let students know that the large laver, a basin that the priests used for washing, was also in the outer court. Point out the musician in the foreground blowing the shofar, a ram's horn, calling all to come and worship.

Read the back of VA 13A for today's Bible lesson. Inform students that King David had been a shepherd as a boy, tending his father's sheep, and that God had chosen David to become king. David had killed a bear and a lion as a young boy, had killed the giant Goliath as an older boy, and had worshipped God through psalms that he wrote. David had a son named *Solomon*, who became king after David. Inform students that King David had wanted to build the temple, but that God had told David it would be a job for Solomon to do.

Remind students that when Solomon became king, he knew he did not have the knowledge and experience to rule wisely. He also realized that there were so many people to rule that he could not count them all. He understood that what he needed more than anything to be a good king would be to have the knowledge and wisdom to lead the people. Solomon did the right thing by asking God for help. God was so pleased with Solomon's request that He not only answered Solomon's prayer, but also blessed him with riches and a long life.

Review with students that after Solomon prayed and thanked the Lord for the temple, God filled the temple with His presence. Make sure students understand the difference between *presence* and *presents*. God's presence was so amazing that not even the priests could enter the temple for a while (2 Chronicles 7:2). Remind students that God warned His people to follow Him always. If they ever stopped following Him, they were to pray, repent, and ask for forgiveness.

Student Page 13.1

Read the directions and the text on the page. Have students complete the page.

Review

- What was the gift that Solomon asked for? (**wisdom and knowledge to rule the people**)
- What did Solomon build? (**the temple**) How was it different from other buildings? (**Possible answers: It was used for worship; it had an altar; it was filled with the Lord's presence.**)
- What did God tell the people to do if they turned away from following Him? (**They were to pray, repent, and ask for forgiveness.**)

Notes:

APPLICATION

- How was the temple like a church? (**God's people worshipped in the temple. Christians worship in churches today.**) How was the temple different from a church? (**The temple was for the time before Jesus came to Earth; a church building is a place where Christians worship.**)
- Why was God pleased with Solomon's request for wisdom? (**Solomon didn't ask for money and riches for himself; he asked for something that would help God's people.**)

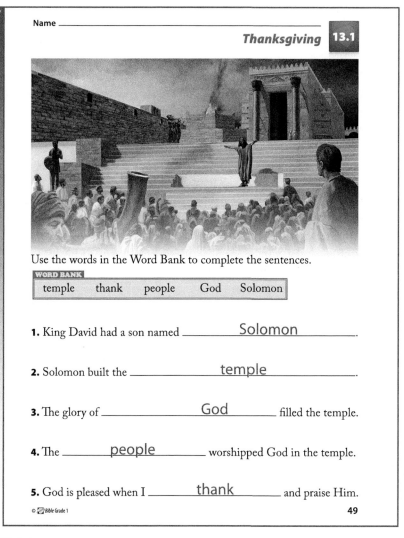

DAY 1

Name ______________________

Thanksgiving 13.1

Use the words in the Word Bank to complete the sentences.

WORD BANK

temple	thank	people	God	Solomon

1. King David had a son named ____Solomon____.
2. Solomon built the ____temple____.
3. The glory of ____God____ filled the temple.
4. The ____people____ worshipped God in the temple.
5. God is pleased when I ____thank____ and praise Him.

13.2 Thanksgiving

Focus: Glorifying God

EXTENSION

2A Let the students have a few minutes of quiet time to think of one thing they will do at home to thank each parent or caregiver. Encourage students to express their thankfulness when they return home.

2B Have students make maracas by placing a small amount of **UNCOOKED RICE** in one **SMALL PAPER OR PLASTIC CUP** and taping a second cup upside down and on top of the first cup. Let the students shake the maracas while you sing your favorite praise song together. Save the maracas to use in Lesson 13.3 for *Extension 3C*.

Introduction

Explain to students that *to glorify God* means *to give Him honor*. Solomon glorified God by building the temple. The Israelites glorified God by worshipping Him. We glorify God through our worship, too. One way Christians worship is through responsive reading. In responsive reading, people take turns reading the Bible. A leader begins by reading the first verse and the worshippers read the next verse.

Use **Psalm 136** as a responsive reading with your students. Read the first phrase of the psalm and have the students answer with the second phrase, which is the same throughout the psalm.

Directed Instruction

Tell students that there are many words Christians use to talk about being thankful and devoted to God. Three of those words are *worship*, *praise*, and *thanks*. Explain that Christians glorify God as they worship Him, praise Him, and give Him thanks.

Many people worship God by bowing down, kneeling, raising their hands, or bowing their head during prayer. Have students share times when they have worshipped God in any of these ways. (**Answers will vary.**)

Share with students that *to praise God* is *to tell Him and others of how great He is*. Praise is an important part of prayer. Ask students to share times or ways in which they have praised God. (**Answers will vary, but should include God's goodness toward people, His power, His love, and His mercy to us.**)

Inform students that *to thank God* is *to express appreciation to Him for what He has done, what He is currently doing, and what He will do in our lives*. Give students an opportunity to talk about something they are thankful for. (**Answers will vary, but should include God's love and provision through special times, people, and events.**) Share that worshipping, praising, and thanking God are habits that Christians develop and keep doing throughout life. Many times the words *praise*, *worship*, and *thanksgiving* mean the same thing.

Remind the students that after Solomon worshipped the Lord and thanked Him for the temple, fire came down from heaven, and the glory of the Lord filled the temple. The children of Israel were so amazed that they bowed down and praised the Lord, saying:
The Lord is good,
His love endures forever!

Then the music leaders played their trumpets and other musical instruments as a way to praise and give thanks to God. Explain that Solomon set an example of being thankful to God. It is very important to get together with other Christians to worship, praise, and thank the Lord.

Review

- What is the purpose of worshipping, praising, and thanking God? (**Possible answers: It brings Him glory; it honors Him as the most important part of our lives; it shows that we trust Him to guide us; it indicates that we appreciate what He has done.**)
- What are some ways that people show they are worshipping God? (**They bow down, kneel, raise their hands, or bow their head during prayer.**)
- What does it mean to praise God? (**It means declaring His greatness and power. We praise Him for who He is.**)
- What does it mean to thank God? (**It means to tell Him we're grateful for what He has done.**)
- How often should you thank God—once a year, twice a week, or every day? (**every day**)

Student Page 13.2

Read the directions and the text on the page. Have students complete the page.

DAY 2

13.2 Thanksgiving

Use the Word Bank to help unscramble the words. Write the words correctly to complete the sentences.

WORD BANK		
worship	thank	praise

1. k n t h a — I ___thank___ God for my parents.
2. s e p r a i — I ___praise___ God for His love.
3. r o w p i s h — I ___worship___ God when I bow my head in prayer.

Use the codes below to learn a reason to praise God. Write the reason on the lines.

4. ___God's___ ___love___ ___lasts___ ___forever___.

GOD LOVES YOU!

50

© Bible Grade 1

APPLICATION

- Read **Hebrews 13:15**. Ask students why the author wrote that praising God is a sacrifice. (**Sometimes we must choose to praise God even when we don't feel like it—such as when we're sad, upset, or tired.**)
- Read **1 Thessalonians 5:18**. Ask students if they are supposed to thank God only when life is good. (**No, even in times of trouble, we should thank God.**) Explain that the key word that begins this verse is *in* not *for*. We do have an enemy that causes us trouble, but even in the midst of the trouble, we should keep thanking God.

REINFORCEMENT

People in many countries of the world celebrate thanksgiving for a day or more. Jews celebrate *Sukkoth*, also called *the Feast of the Tabernacles* or *Feast of Booths*. It begins five days after *Yom Kippur*, the Day of Atonement on the fifteenth of the Hebrew month of *Tishri* in September or October. This coincides with early autumn, or harvest season in the northern hemisphere. Sukkoth celebrates the time when the Israelites lived in tents in the wilderness during the Exodus from Egypt. Modern Jews commemorate this event by erecting huts made of branches, gathering four types of plants, and offering prayers of thanksgiving to God.

13.3 Thanksgiving

Focus: A Psalm of Thanksgiving

★ PREPARATION

Select **VA 13A Solomon Leads in Thanksgiving**. (*Directed Instruction*)

EXTENSION

3A Invite a Christian musician, lyricist, composer, and/or choir director to share with your class about his or her vocation and how the Lord inspires his or her work.

3B Ask an architect familiar with Scriptures regarding the building of the temple to explain the construction process that took place.

3C Select "Wanna Say Thank You" from the music CDs and explain how the song glorifies God. Play the song again and have students sing, shake the **MARACAS** made in *Extension 2B*, or clap in time to the music.

Introduction

Write the word *spontaneous* on the board and tell students that you want to share a really big word with them. Break the word into syllables and read it together. Explain that *spontaneous* means *instantly, without planning, suddenly, just because*. Demonstrate a spontaneous hug with one of your students. Then let the class know that just like that spontaneous hug, God likes spontaneous thanksgiving and praise. It is not necessary to wait until God does something extra special before giving Him thanks and praise! It is good to give Him thanks and praise at any and all times (Psalm 92:1).

Share with the class that there are many reasons to thank and praise God. Possible reasons include the facts that He made us, He loves us, He provides for us, and He is always good. Remind students that it is important to be in the practice of thanking God, but it is also important to give the Lord spontaneous praises.

Directed Instruction ★

Display **VA 13A Solomon Leads in Thanksgiving**. Explain that the people would have had to enter gates to come into the courts of the temple. Read **Psalm 100**. Describe how the psalm explains to come through the gates or doorways with thanks and into the courts with praise.

Tell students to imagine that the classroom is the outer court of the temple and the doorway is the gate of the outer court. Open the classroom door and step just outside. Enter the room, thanking God. Praise Him once you are in the classroom. Inform students that Psalm 100 also shows how we are to enter into God's presence—joyfully and with thanksgiving and praise—whether in church, chapel, or when praying at home.

All psalms are poems, and many of them were set to music. Psalm 100 is a song of praise to the Lord. This psalm shows us that not only can we speak our praises to God, we can sing them to Him. (While we do not know who wrote the words or music for Psalm 100, the Bible tells us in 1 Kings 4:32 that Solomon wrote 1,005 songs.)

Remind students that after Solomon dedicated the temple to the Lord, the musicians praised the Lord in the temple, singing and using trumpets and other musical instruments. King David, Solomon's father, had started the practice of having musicians praise God by playing musical instruments (1 Chronicles 6:31–47). Some of the instruments were made of wood. There were harps, stringed instruments, tambourines, sistrums or castanets (instruments that were shaken like a rattle), and cymbals (2 Samuel 6:5).

Student Page 13.3

Read the directions, and then tell students to listen carefully as you read **Psalm 100** again. After you read verse 1, have them complete Exercise 1. Then read verse 2. Let them answer Exercise 2. Next, read verse 3. Prepare them to listen as you read verse 4 so that they can answer Exercises 3–4.

Finally, read verse 5 and give students time to answer Exercise 5. Review the answers in class.

Review

- Is it true that you are only supposed to give God praise and thanks at certain times? (**No. We should thank and praise God at all times.**)
- Is it true that Psalm 100 is a song of thanksgiving to God. (**Yes.**)
- Is it important for Christians to come to worship with an attitude of thanksgiving to God? (**Yes, it is very important to have the right attitude when coming to worship.**)
- How is entering the gates and courts of the temple similar to going to your church building? (**Answers will vary, but should include that entering the gates and outer court of the temple is similar to entering through the doorway into the sanctuary of the church.**)
- Tell how Psalm 100 might have been sung in the temple. (**Answers will vary, but should include that some of the temple musicians may have played their musical instruments while a choir may have sung the words.**)

DAY 3

Name ______________________________

Thanksgiving **13.3**

Psalm 100

Circle the correct word. Write it on the line.

1. Make a ___glad___ noise to the Lord.
sad (glad)

2. Come before God and ___sing___.
bird (sing)

3. Enter His gates with ___thanks___.
(thanks) books

4. Enter His courts with ___praise___.
hills (praise)

5. The Lord is good. His love lasts ___forever___.
(forever) a day

© Bible Grade 1 51

APPLICATION

- Have you ever spontaneously given thanks to God? Share what you did to thank Him. (**Answers will vary.**)
- If you had the chance to write, sing, or play a song of praise to the Lord, what would you put in your song? (**Answers will vary.**)
- Tell about your favorite song of worship or praise.

REINFORCEMENT

One of the best-loved Thanksgiving hymns is "Now Thank We All Our God." It was written in the 1600s by Martin Rinkart, a Lutheran pastor. Rinkart lived in Eilenburg, Saxony, during the Thirty Years' War. At one point, the city of Eilenburg was surrounded by the Swedish army. Famine and plague took the lives of hundreds of residents and refugees in the city. Pastors in the city conducted dozens of funerals daily. Eventually the strain became so great that the pastors themselves began to die, and soon Rinkart was the only one left. With faith and courage, Rinkart left the safety of the city gates to plead with the Swedish commander for mercy, and mercy was shown. Soon afterward, the war ended, and Rinkart wrote this hymn of thanksgiving. What is amazing is that even after so much misery, Martin Rinkart was able to express his trust and gratitude to God! The following excerpt is from "Now Thank We All Our God."

> Now thank we all our God, with heart and hands and voices, who wondrous things has done, in whom this world rejoices; who from our mothers' arms has blessed us on our way, with countless gifts of love, and still is ours today.

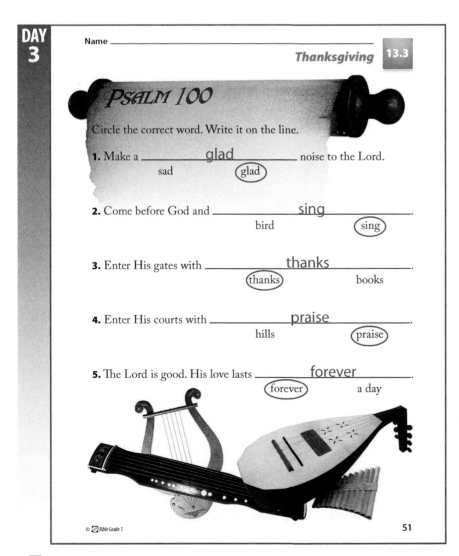

13.4 Thanksgiving

Focus: Giving Thanks

★ PREPARATION

Bring an ENVELOPE, STAMP, and NOTE PAPER to class (or a thank-you note along with its envelope that you have received). (*Introduction*)

EXTENSION

4A Have students write letters to your school staff, thanking them for their work, kind actions, and encouragement, using the format that you wrote on the board. Students may also enclose drawings or small gifts. Mail or distribute the letters to the staff.

4B Show students how to write a quick thank-you note via e-mail.

Introduction ★

Show students the ENVELOPE, STAMP, and NOTE PAPER (or a thank-you note along with its envelope). Explain that one way of expressing thanks to others is by writing them a brief letter or note. Share with students that writing a thank-you note is very important. First, a thank-you note is a way to show our appreciation to the person who blessed us. We thank that person for what he or she did for us or said about us and include how the kindness and generosity made us feel special. Second, writing thank-you notes helps us practice being grateful. Having a grateful attitude toward others is a wonderful quality to develop throughout life!

Inform students that after writing the letter, they will want to make sure that the recipient receives it. Demonstrate folding the paper, placing it inside the envelope, placing the stamp on the envelope, and writing the person's address on the envelope. Let students know that they would then place the envelope in a mailbox to be delivered.

Directed Instruction

On the board, show students the components of a letter as given below, including the greeting, the body, the closing, and the signature. Guide students through the process of letter writing by simply completing the different sections. State that the greeting is a way to indicate who the letter is for. The body of the letter contains what you want to say to the person. The closing is a way to indicate the end of the letter and can also contain a form of affection. The signature is given so that the person who receives the letter will know who the letter is from.

> *Dear ________________,*
>
> *Thank you for ______________________________________*
>
> *______________________________________. Your kindness means so much to me. You help me to see God's goodness.*
>
> *Love,*
>
> *________________*

Let two or three students come to the board to fill in the greeting, what they are thankful for (in the body of the letter), and the signature. Discuss what they have written with the class. Then, if you plan to complete *Extension 4A*, replace what the students have just inserted with blank lines, so that the components of the letter resemble the format above.

Student Page 13.4

Read **1 Chronicles 16:8** at the top of the page. Remind students how important it is to give God thanks, to pray to Him, and to let others hear about all the wonderful ways He has answered their prayers. Have students complete the letter to God, thanking and praising Him for something He has done in their own life. Help students with spelling as needed.

Review

- Why is it important to tell someone thank you? (**Answers will vary, but should include that giving thanks is a way to show our appreciation to the person who blessed us.**)
- Why is it important to tell others what God has done as well as to give thanks to God? (**so that others can also see how great God is and, in turn, give Him thanks**)
- What are various ways to say thank you? (**Possible answers: I appreciate you; that was very kind of you; I am so grateful.**)

Notes:

APPLICATION

- Describe a time when you thanked someone for something. How did giving thanks make you feel? (**Answers will vary, but should include that it makes us happy to hear about the joy that giving thanks brings to others.**)
- How does thanking and praising God help you to grow closer to Him? (**Answers will vary, but should include that thanking God helps me to remember all that He has done for me.**)

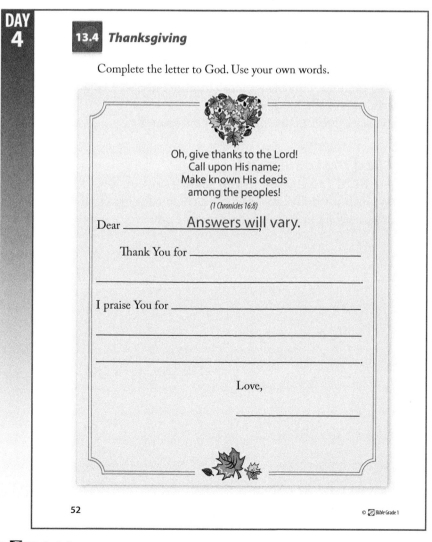

DAY 4

13.4 *Thanksgiving*

Complete the letter to God. Use your own words.

Oh, give thanks to the Lord!
Call upon His name;
Make known His deeds
among the peoples!
(1 Chronicles 16:8)

Dear ______ Answers will vary. ______,

Thank You for ____________________

____________________.

I praise You for ____________________

____

____________________.

Love,

____

52

© *Bible* Grade 1

13.5

Thanksgiving

Focus: Review and Assessment

★ PREPARATION

Select "Wanna Say Thank You" from the music CDs. (*Lesson Review*)

Select **VA 13A Solomon Leads in Thanksgiving**. (*Lesson Review*)

Make one copy of **BLM 13A Lesson 13 Test** for each student. (*Directed Instruction*)

Obtain MUSTARD SEEDS for use in Lesson 14.

Lesson Review ★

Begin your review with a short period of worship, praise, and thanksgiving. Sing "Wanna Say Thank You" from the music CDs.

Use **VA 13A Solomon Leads in Thanksgiving** to review the Bible truth. Cover the following concepts:

- King David had a son named *Solomon*. Solomon became king when he was a young man.
- God told Solomon that he could have anything he wanted. King Solomon did not make a selfish request; he asked God for wisdom to rule the people.
- God was pleased with King Solomon's request. God gave King Solomon wisdom, riches, and a long life. He chose King Solomon to build the temple.
- King Solomon built the temple as a permanent place for people to worship, praise, and thank God together.
- As soon as the temple was dedicated, God's presence filled it. It was amazing!
- Psalm 100 is a song that teaches people how to praise and thank God. Entering a church or our own personal devotional time is similar to entering the temple—coming through the gates with thanksgiving and into the courts with praise.
- Praising and thanking God is important to do, regardless of how a person feels.
- Thanking God not only brings glory to Him but also tells others of the wonderful things He has done.
- Christians ought to thank and praise God every day.

Directed Instruction ★

Distribute **BLM 13A Lesson 13 Test** to each student. Read the directions and pronounce any difficult words. Have students complete the test. Review the answers, and then collect for assessment.

Notes:

Lesson Preparation
Elijah and the Widow

14.0

Expected Student Outcomes

KNOW
A widow shows hospitality to Elijah. God uses Elijah to raise her son from the dead.

DO
Students will:
- match the beginning and ending of sentences to review God's omnipotence and provision
- unscramble words to discover an acrostic to remind students to fully rely on God
- fill in the blanks to review the Bible truth
- consider ways to show hospitality in various settings

APPLY
Students will follow God's direction and practice hospitality.

Lesson Outline

I. Prophet Elijah obeys God (1 Kings 17:1)
  A. God pronounces judgment on King Ahab
  B. God provides for Elijah during the drought
II. The widow shows hospitality (1 Kings 17:7–14)
  A. Elijah's request of the widow
  B. The widow's response to Elijah
  C. A promise of provision for the widow
III. God shows His might (1 Kings 17:15–24)
  A. God keeps His promise to the widow
  B. God uses Elijah to resurrect the widow's son
IV. Showing hospitality (Ps 23:5–6, Heb 13:16, 1 Pet 4:9, Phil 2:4)
  A. Identifying aspects of hospitality
  B. Applications of hospitality

TEACHER'S HEART

The Scripture says that Christians should never forget to show hospitality to strangers and, as a result, some have entertained angels unaware (Hebrews 13:2). What a wonderful thought!

Did you notice the Scripture didn't say to entertain strangers if you are a good cook or if you have a lot of room in your home? No! It simply says to show brotherly kindness by fixing a meal or a bed for those who need it. Your hospitality can be an encouragement and refreshment to a weary missionary or pastor; or, it may be what keeps a fellow teacher from giving up or giving in to burnout. When you show hospitality in Jesus' name, the lives you touch will never be the same. Your actions will impact others, and your own life will be enriched by serving others.

MEMORY VERSE

Philippians 2:4

MATERIALS

Day 1:
- Sentence strips
- An overly ripe piece of fruit
- VA 14A Elijah and the Widow
- BLM 14A Ravens (*Extension*)

Day 2:
- VA 14A Elijah and the Widow
- Flour, oil, bowl (*Extension*)
- Plastic frogs (*Extension*)

Day 3:
- Mustard seeds
- VA 14A Elijah and the Widow

Day 4:
- Cookies, juice (*Extension*)

Day 5:
- VA 14A Elijah and the Widow
- BLM 14B Lesson 14 Test

TEACHER RESOURCES

Clough, Sandy. *The Art of Tea and Friendship: Savoring the Fragrance of Time Together.* Harvest House Publishers, 2003.

Ehman, Karen. *A Life That Says Welcome: Simple Ways to Open Your Heart & Home to Others.* Baker Publishing Group, 2006.

STUDENT RESOURCES

Lucado, Max. *Hermie and Friends—Scripture Memory Songs: Verses About Sharing*. CD. Tommy Nelson, 2006.

Thoreson-Snipes, Nanette. *Elijah Helps the Widow*. Concordia Publishing House, 2001.

14.1 Elijah and the Widow

Focus: Prophet Elijah Obeys God

MEMORY VERSE

Philippians 2:4

MEMORY WORK

- Write the Memory Verse on the board and read it chorally. Spread the prepared sets of SENTENCE STRIPS facedown on a table or desktop. Group the class into teams of two or three students per team. Only two teams compete at a time. At your signal, the teams turn the strips of the same color over and arrange the phrases into the correct order as quickly as possible. Have each team recite the Memory Verse once it is in the correct order.

★ PREPARATION

Obtain SENTENCE STRIPS of two colors. Cut the strips into shorter pieces as needed. You will need about six pieces of each color. Segment the Memory Verse into phrases of about three to four words per phrase. Write each phrase and the reference for the verse on a separate sentence strip. Make an identical set of phrases on the second color. (*Memory Work*)

Bring in an OVERLY RIPE PIECE OF FRUIT such as an apple or a banana. (*Introduction*)

Select **VA 14A Elijah and the Widow**. (*Directed Instruction*)

EXTENSION

1A Print a class set of **BLM 14A Ravens**. Explain that the birds are ravens. God sent ravens to provide for Elijah. Have students use the ravens to write or draw pictures of various ways that God provides for their physical and spiritual needs. Display the ravens in the classroom.

Introduction ★

Display an OVERLY RIPE PIECE OF FRUIT, such as a brown banana or a shriveled apple. Ask students if the fruit looks good to eat. (**No.**) Share that you do not think you will eat the fruit because it will probably taste bad, and that you will not put it back into a bag with fresh fruit. This is because spoiled fruit makes fresh fruit ripen and begin to spoil faster. Explain that people who do not love or trust God can be like spoiled fruit in a bag of fresh fruit. They can influence others to turn away from the Lord.

Directed Instruction ★

Open your Bible to the book of 1 Kings. Explain that the Bible truth for this week is found in this book. Say the books of the Bible in order through 1 Kings and pause from time to time as students repeat after you.

Tell students that many years had passed since King David had ruled. Many kings had come and gone over time. Now King Ahab was ruler over the country of Israel, but he was not a good king. Ahab made a lot of bad choices! He married a woman named *Jezebel*. Queen Jezebel worshipped an idol called *Baal*. Remind students that an idol is a false god. Jezebel influenced King Ahab so that he began to worship Baal, too. That was a very wicked thing to do!

Display **VA 14A Elijah and the Widow**. Point out Elijah in the picture, and write his name on the board. Explain that Elijah followed God's ways. He was a prophet of the Lord. A *true prophet* means *someone who had special knowledge from God*. Point out that the woman in the picture was a widow, a woman whose husband had died. Have students listen for the message that God gave Elijah. Read the text on the back of VA 14A.

Review the Bible truth by reminding students that God called Elijah to go to King Ahab and give him a message. Elijah might have been afraid to speak boldly to the wicked king, but he was obedient to God. God gave Elijah courage to speak the truth. Ask students to recount what Elijah told King Ahab. (**If King Ahab did not stop worshipping Baal, there would be no rain or dew.**)

The king did not listen to Elijah, so the Lord did just as He had promised. Ask students to state how long the people of the land had to go without rain or dew. (**several years**) God knew that King Ahab would not listen to Elijah's message and that Ahab would angrily blame Elijah for the drought, so God protected Elijah and provided for Elijah's needs. Choose a volunteer to recount how Elijah ate and drank. (**God provided water at a brook. Ravens brought food each morning and evening.**) Ask students to share another time when God sent food to His people. (**God had provided food and water to the Israelites in the wilderness.**)

Explain that Elijah was thankful for God's provision. He probably had a lot of time to pray and thank God while he was hiding from the king. Eventually, though, the brook dried up. Ask a student to share what God told Elijah to do next. (**go to the city and speak with a widow**) This may have seemed like a strange direction from God, but Elijah did not question it. He believed God and showed his trust in God by obeying His commands.

Review

- What did Elijah tell King Ahab? (**If Ahab did not stop worshipping Baal, there would be no rain or dew until the Lord commanded it.**)
- Where did Elijah get something to drink? (**God provided water from a brook.**)
- How did God provide meat and bread to Elijah? (**Ravens brought food each morning and evening.**)
- What did God tell Elijah to do when the brook dried up? (**go to the city and speak with a widow**)

Student Page 14.1

Read the directions and the text. Assist students as needed to complete the page.

DAY 1

Name ____________________

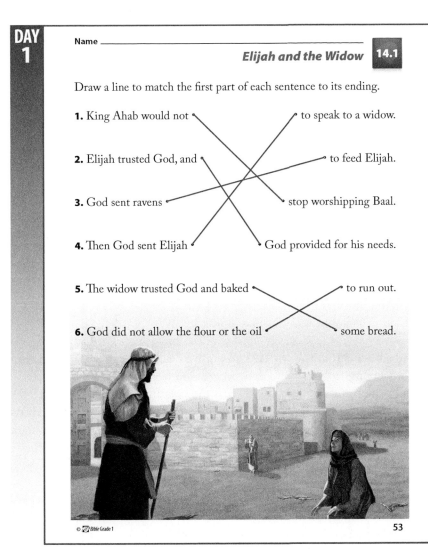

Elijah and the Widow **14.1**

Draw a line to match the first part of each sentence to its ending.

1. King Ahab would not — stop worshipping Baal.

2. Elijah trusted God, and — God provided for his needs.

3. God sent ravens — to feed Elijah.

4. Then God sent Elijah — to speak to a widow.

5. The widow trusted God and baked — some bread.

6. God did not allow the flour or the oil — to run out.

© Bible Grade 1 53

APPLICATION

- King Ahab married a woman who led him to make poor choices. Why is it important to choose godly friends? (**I need to stay away from those who would lead me into making poor choices.**)
- King Ahab's poor choice to worship an idol caused his whole country to experience a drought. Has one of your poor choices affected someone else? Tell about your choice and its consequence. (**Answers will vary.**)
- With God's help, Elijah spoke boldly before the evil king. Is it easy to do what is right? (**Not always.**) How can you have the courage to speak up for what is right? (**I can ask God to give me courage and strength.**)

REINFORCEMENT

Elijah's words to King Ahab were received as more than just a simple warning. In that pagan culture, Baal was believed to be the god of storms, rain, and fertility. In pride and arrogance, King Ahab disregarded Elijah's word from the Lord and continued to worship Baal, possibly thinking that his god would reign supreme. It is interesting to note that God chose to use a drought to demonstrate the powerlessness of Baal, the god of rain!

14.2 Elijah and the Widow

Focus: The Widow Shows Hospitality

★ PREPARATION

Select **VA 14A Elijah and the Widow**. (*Directed Instruction*)

EXTENSION

2A Show students a **HANDFUL OF FLOUR** and **ONE OR TWO TABLESPOONS OF OIL**. Pour the flour and oil into a **BOWL** and knead the dough so that students can see how the flour and oil could be shaped into a loaf. Ask students whether they would be willing to share this with someone else if it was all they had, and there was no chance of getting anything more to eat. Let students discuss how they would feel and what they would do. Tell students that hunger was a big problem in Elijah's time, but that it is also a problem for many people in the world today. Encourage students to pray for the needs of hungry people around the world.

2B Purchase a **SMALL PLASTIC FROG** for each student from a party supply store. Explain that the letters in the word *frog* are the first letters in the words **f**ully **r**elying **o**n **G**od. The frog is a visible reminder that they can turn to God to meet their needs.

Introduction

Write the letters *F.R.O.G.* on the board. Explain that these letters are initials, the first letters of words. Erase the periods between the initials and ask a student to read the word. (**frog**) Explain that the initials are the first letters of the words in the phrase **f**ully **r**elying **o**n **G**od. *Fully relying on God* means *trusting and depending on God for His provision.* Both Elijah and the widow trusted God to provide for their needs. The initials F.R.O.G. and the word *frog* can remind Christians to rely on God.

Directed Instruction ★

Display **VA 14A Elijah and the Widow**. Review that the prophet Elijah was both hungry and thirsty. He did not have any food or water, so he had to rely on God. Recount how the ravens had fed Elijah and how he had drunk water from a brook before the brook ran dry.

As he entered the town, Elijah saw a widow gathering sticks for her fire. Ask a student to tell the class what a widow is. (**a woman whose husband has died**) Because this woman's husband was dead, she may not have had anyone to provide for her needs. She would have been one of the first people to run out of food during the drought. God directed Elijah to speak to this widow. God's direction may not have made sense to Elijah, but he listened to God and obeyed.

When Elijah approached the widow, he first asked for a little drink of water. The widow was ready to show hospitality to Elijah by giving him a drink. Explain that hospitality has nothing to do with a hospital. *Hospitality* means *showing kindness to guests*. As the widow went to get the water, Elijah made a second request; he asked her to bring him a little bit of bread. The widow was collecting the firewood so that she could bake and eat one last, small loaf of bread. Then she and her young son would be completely out of food. They would starve to death after that. She wanted to show hospitality to Elijah, but sharing the last bit of food that they had left was asking a lot!

Review how Elijah comforted the widow when he gently said, "Do not be afraid." He promised her that if she would make some bread for him, the Lord God of Israel would take care of her needs!

Remind students that the widow had quite a decision to make. Should she show hospitality to Elijah and depend on God to provide for her needs, or should she turn Elijah away? Discuss the possible outcomes of each choice. Ask students to tell what the woman finally decided to do. (**to show hospitality to Elijah**) Just as Elijah had said, God never let her flour bin or the oil jar run out! God showed His power by supplying exactly what the woman and her son needed each day until rain returned to the earth.

The woman was willing to fully rely on God and follow His directions. She learned that God could be trusted to keep His promises and that God is pleased when a person shows hospitality to others.

Review

- Why was the widow in danger of starving? (**There had been a drought in the land for years. Because she was a widow, she may have had no one to provide her with food. She only had a little flour and oil left.**)
- What is hospitality? (**Hospitality is showing kindness to guests.**)
- How did the widow show hospitality to Elijah? (**She gave him a drink of water and later gave him some bread.**)
- How did the widow's gift of bread show that she fully relied on God? (**That was all the food that she had. She gave bread to Elijah, trusting that God would provide for her needs after that.**)
- How did God show His power and provision in this Bible truth? (**God sent Elijah to someone who was willing to trust God and provide for Elijah. The widow's flour and oil did not run out until rain fell again.**)

Student Page 14.2

Write the words *oil*, *flour*, *God*, and *food* on the board and read them together. Explain that the scrambled letters on the page will spell these words when they are written correctly. Assist students as needed in completing the page.

DAY 2

14.2 *Elijah and the Widow*

Unscramble the letters to complete the sentences.

1. Elijah had no water and no f o o d. (o f o d)

2. The widow only had a little f l o u r. (o r u f l)

3. The widow had only a small jar of o i l. (i o l)

4. Both Elijah and the widow had faith in G o d. (G d o)

Write the letters from the green spaces on the lines below.

5. f. r. o. g.

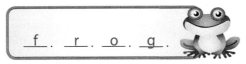

6. These initials stand for **f**ully **r**elying **o**n **G**od. Elijah and the widow relied on God. Tell how God provided for their needs. Color the picture.

Answers will vary, but should include that the flour and oil did not run out. Coloring will vary.

54

APPLICATION

- The widow showed hospitality to Elijah. How do you show hospitality to others? (**Answers will vary.**)
- Was sharing bread with Elijah a sacrifice for the widow? (**Yes.**) How did the widow's sacrifice show her trust in God? (**That was all the widow and her son had to eat. By giving the bread to Elijah, the widow had to trust God for her next meal.**)
- Tell about a time when you had to trust God. (**Answers will vary.**) Is it always easy to trust Him? (**No, it's not always easy to trust God, but as I trust Him, I see how He provides for me.**)

REINFORCEMENT

The widow's faith, demonstrated through her sacrificial gift of all that she had, initially saved herself and her son from starvation. Later, however, her entire household was fed by means of the widow's oil and flour (1 Kings 17:15). The widow's household may have included servants or other close relatives. Not only did God provide for the widow's immediate needs, but He rewarded her faith abundantly, bringing blessing to others as well.

14.3 Elijah and the Widow

Focus: God Shows His Might

★ PREPARATION

Obtain some **MUSTARD SEEDS**. You can buy them at a feed and seed store or online if they are not available in your local grocery store. (*Introduction*)

Display **VA 14A Elijah and the Widow**. (*Directed Instruction*)

EXTENSION

3A During an art period, allow students time to draw and color whatever they wish. After one or two minutes, stop students from drawing and hold up a few of the unfinished pictures. Explain that you do not know what the finished pictures will be, but that the artists know what each picture will be. Relate this to the fact that God knows the beginning to the end. Those who follow Him should trust Him, just like Elijah and the widow did.

3B Invite students to plant some of the **MUSTARD SEEDS**. Remind students that, like the plants, their faith will grow as they trust God more and more.

Introduction ★

Open a container of MUSTARD SEEDS and give one seed to each student. Inquire what the students think might grow from such a small seed. Explain that even though the seed is small, it develops into a large plant.

Write the word *miracle* on the board and sound it out together. Explain that *miracle* means *something that only God can do*. The growth of this seed into a mustard plant is like a miracle. People cannot make plants. Plants come from seeds, which come from God. God is the Creator of all life. Only God can make plants grow; He is all-powerful.

Directed Instruction ★

Display **VA 14A Elijah and Widow**. Remind students of the first three miracles that God performed in the Bible truth. Have students put up one finger for each miracle. First, God stopped the rain from falling for years because King Ahab and many of his people refused to stop worshipping Baal. Second, God provided for Elijah's needs by sending ravens to feed him. Third, God did not allow the widow's flour or oil to run out.

Tell students that after the widow showed hospitality to Elijah, and God provided her with flour and oil, she invited Elijah to stay in a room in her home as a guest. Ask students to tell who else lived in the house. (**the widow's little boy**) Remind students that one day, the boy became sick. Choose one or two volunteers to tell what their mothers would do when their children get sick. (**Possible answers: take their temperature, dispense medicine, make an appointment to see a doctor**)

Suddenly, the boy's mother noticed that he was not breathing! Elijah found that the boy had died. Imagine how sad the widow was! Her husband was dead, and now her only child was dead. She might have wondered why God had provided her with the flour and oil if He knew her son would die!

Elijah had compassion on the widow when he saw her sorrow. What he did next was very unusual. He picked up the dead boy and carried him to his own bed. Then Elijah prayed to the Lord, asking that He would return life to the child. God heard the cries of Elijah and miraculously raised the boy from the dead! Elijah rejoiced as he took the boy to his mother and said, "Here is your son. He is alive!" The widow's faith in God was made even stronger after this! She knew that Elijah was a man of God and that his words were true.

Review

- Why did the widow offer a room where Elijah could stay? (**She was showing hospitality.**)
- What tragic thing happened to the widow's son? (**Her son had gotten sick and died.**)
- What did Elijah do to help the boy? (**He put the child on his own bed and prayed to the Lord.**)

- What did the widow understand when God brought her son back to life? **(that Elijah was a man of God and his words were true)**

Student Page 14.3
Read the directions and complete the page together.

Notes:

APPLICATION

- Jesus used a mustard seed as an example to show how just a small step of faith can lead to spiritual growth (Luke 17:6). In this Bible truth, did the widow's faith in God grow? (**Yes.**) What are some ways that you can grow in faith? (**I can listen to God's Word, pray to Him, and trust Him to provide for my needs.**)
- The widow wondered about why God allowed her little boy to die. Have you ever wondered about something that has happened in your life? (**Answers will vary.**)

REINFORCEMENT

The raising of the widow's son is an example of several steps in faith. In Luke 4:24–26, Jesus taught that prophets are rejected by their own countrymen, and the Israelites had largely rejected Elijah's message, yet Elijah trusted God. Jesus pointed out that the widow lived in Zarephath in Sidon, a Canaanite town. Elijah took a step in faith when he obeyed God, left his own country, sought out the widow, and stayed in a Gentile home. When the widow's son died, Elijah picked up the dead child and stretched his own body over the child's body three times. In doing this, Elijah defiled himself by touching a dead body, but he chose to minister to the widow in her time of need. Because of Elijah's earnest prayers on behalf of the child, God was glorified, the widow was encouraged, and Elijah himself became bolder for what he would face ahead. The prophet of God was assured that he could trust God for anything!

DAY 3

Name ______________________

Elijah and the Widow **14.3**

God showed His power and love for Elijah and the widow through His miracles.

Use words from the Word Bank to complete the sentences.

The widow showed hospitality to Elijah, and the Lord provided for her needs. Her flour and oil did not run out. She baked bread for Elijah and gave him a room in her home.

WORD BANK
alive
truth
sick
prayed
died
miracle

One day, the widow's son got ____sick____. He was so sick that he ____died____. The widow was very, very sad! She spoke to Elijah. Elijah took the boy to his own room and ____prayed____ to the Lord. The Lord answered Elijah's prayer with a ____miracle____. The boy was ____alive____ again! Now the widow knew that Elijah spoke the ____truth____.

14.4 Elijah and the Widow

Focus: Showing Hospitality

★ PREPARATION

On the board, draw this graphic organizer and make the ovals large enough to write several words inside each one. (*Introduction*)

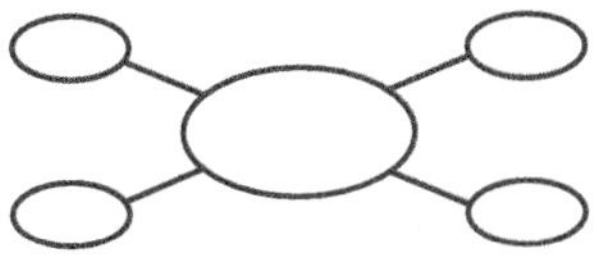

EXTENSION

4A Plan a special event with your students. Invite parents or school personnel into the classroom to share in a time of fellowship. You may wish to plan a short program that would include reciting Memory Verses or reading psalms. Remind students that showing hospitality requires thinking of the guest first. Instruct students in customs of hospitality and good manners such as offering seats to guests, serving refreshments, and making the guests feel comfortable. Offer COOKIES and JUICE to the guests and ensure that they feel honored. After guests have gone, ask students how they felt or what kind of attitude they had when showing hospitality. Discuss what went well, what did not go well, and what changes students would make in the way they showed hospitality.

Introduction ★

Write the word *hospitality* in the center oval of the graphic organizer and read it together. Review that hospitality is showing kindness to guests. Explain that the Bible teaches Christians to show hospitality to strangers (Hebrews 13:2). Caution children, for their safety, to get their parents' permission before they show hospitality to strangers. State that there are at least four things to think about when showing hospitality. As you teach the lesson, fill in the graphic organizer with various aspects of hospitality.

Directed Instruction

Teach students that showing hospitality is important for a number of reasons. Read and discuss **Psalm 23:5–6**. Remind students that God shows hospitality to people by providing for their needs. Ask a volunteer to tell how God met Elijah's needs when Elijah lived in the wilderness. (**God sent ravens to feed Elijah. Elijah was able to drink from a brook.**) Write the words *provides for the needs of others* in one of the smaller ovals of the graphic organizer.

Read and discuss **Hebrews 13:16**. Point out that hospitality often involves making sacrifices and that God is pleased when Christians give to others. Ask students to recount how the widow made a sacrifice when she showed hospitality to Elijah. (**The widow gave Elijah the last of her food.**) Write the words *pleases God* in an oval on the graphic organizer.

Read and discuss **1 Peter 4:9**. Highlight that God does not want His children to have a grumbling spirit when showing hospitality. True hospitality should be done with a good attitude! Remind students that Abraham showed hospitality to the angels who visited him. Abraham gladly provided them with something to eat and listened attentively to their words. Write the words *requires a good attitude* in an oval of the graphic organizer.

Read and discuss **Philippians 2:4**. Emphasize that true hospitality begins by thinking about the needs of others and taking action to meet those needs. When Christians show hospitality, they often consider the needs of others to be more important than their own needs. Review the words *selfish* and *selfless*. Explain that Ruth is a good example of someone in the Bible who showed hospitality selflessly. Ask a volunteer to recount how Ruth was selfless. (**Ruth put Naomi's needs ahead of her own.**) Remind students that they are called to show hospitality to others. They should always be ready to do that. Write the words *puts others first* in the last oval of the graphic organizer.

Review

- List some reasons why hospitality is important. (**Hospitality provides for the needs of others, it pleases God, it requires a good attitude, and it puts others first.**)
- Whom does God use to show hospitality? (**God calls His people to show hospitality.**)

- When should you be ready to show hospitality? (**at all times**)
- To whom should you show hospitality? (**to followers of Jesus and other family guests**)

Student Page 14.4
Read and discuss each scenario. Have students circle the better answer and underline the choice that shows hospitality.

Notes:

APPLICATION

- Tell about a time when you had to make a sacrifice in order to show hospitality. (**Answers will vary.**)
- Why is it important to have a good attitude when showing hospitality? (**The Bible says that we should not grumble or complain when sharing with others. Our attitude is important to God.**)
- Think about someone to whom you can show hospitality. Tell about what you would do. (**Answers will vary.**)

DAY 4

14.4 *Elijah and the Widow*

Circle the better answer. Underline words that show hospitality.

1. Beth's friend moved away. Beth still feels sad. Now a new girl is moving into the house where Beth's friend had lived. How can Beth show hospitality?
   - make a picture to welcome the new family
   - feel sad and do nothing

2. Victor likes to play soccer with his friends, but he does not want his new soccer ball to get dirty. How can Victor show hospitality?
   - keep his soccer ball at home
   - share his soccer ball with his friends

3. Ting's teacher asked her to help a new student, but Ting is shy. How can Ting show hospitality?
   - be friendly and talk to the new student
   - ask her teacher to get someone else to help the new student

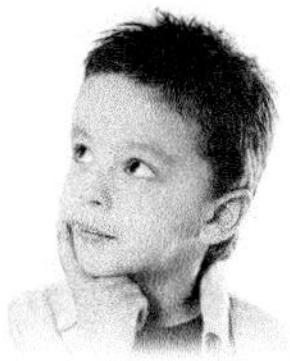

4. Nathan's grandmother needs a soft bed when she comes to visit. Nathan has a soft bed. How can Nathan show hospitality?
   - be grumpy about giving up his bed
   - be happy to let his grandmother use his bed

56

14.5 Elijah and the Widow

Focus: Review and Assessment

★ ***PREPARATION***

Select **VA 14A Elijah and the Widow**. (*Lesson Review*)

Print a copy of **BLM 14B Lesson 14 Test** for each student. (*Directed Instruction*)

Lesson Review ★

Use **VA 14A Elijah and the Widow** to review the Bible truth. Cover the following concepts:

- King Ahab, the king of Israel, married an evil woman who led him into the worship of Baal, a false god.
- Elijah was a true prophet, someone who had special knowledge from God.
- Elijah told King Ahab that if he did not stop worshipping Baal, there would be no rain or dew until the Lord commanded it.
- Because King Ahab refused to listen to God's message, there was no rain in Israel for years.
- God provided water at a brook for Elijah to drink.
- God had ravens bring meat and bread to Elijah each morning and evening.
- When the brook dried up, God told Elijah to go to the city and speak with a widow.
- The widow was in danger of starving to death because she was almost out of flour and oil. She did not have a way to get more food.
- By asking the widow for some bread, Elijah showed that he trusted God to provide for his needs and those of the widow, as He promised.
- The widow showed that she was willing to rely on God when she shared what little food she had with Elijah.
- The widow continued to show hospitality when she offered a room where Elijah could stay.
- The widow's son became sick. The boy stopped breathing and died.
- Elijah carried the boy to the room that he was using and prayed.
- God answered Elijah's prayers and brought the boy back to life.
- The widow knew Elijah was a man of God and his words were true.

Directed Instruction ★

Distribute a copy of **BLM 14B Lesson 14 Test** to each student. After students complete it, discuss correct responses.

Notes:

Lesson Preparation

Elijah Opposes False Prophets

15.0

Expected Student Outcomes

KNOW

Elijah challenges the prophets of Baal and is victorious.

DO

Students will:
- differentiate between true and false statements to review the Bible truth
- sequence events in the Bible truth
- use Bible verses to contradict modern-day lies
- determine practical ways to share their faith with others

APPLY

Students will pray in faith and speak boldly about the Lord to others.

Lesson Outline

I. Elijah is bold (1 Kings 18:1–45)
   A. Elijah challenges the false prophets
   B. False prophets fail
   C. The only true God answers
II. Know the truth
   A. Elijah looked to God (1 Kings 18:30–39)
III. Hold fast to the truth
   A. Using Scripture to counter lies
IV. Speak the truth boldly
   A. Sharing your faith with others

TEACHER'S HEART

Have you ever wondered how the Israelites could have witnessed the power of God and yet have turned to idolatry? They had such an amazing history; the Lord was with them! How could they have turned from Him?

It's interesting to note that the Israelites had not completely abandoned worship of the Lord, but had merely added the worship of Baal to their religious practices. They bowed to the culture of their neighbors and adopted their practices. Elijah knew the double-mindedness of the Israelites when he challenged them in 1 Kings 18:21 by asking, "How long will you falter between two opinions? If the Lord is God, follow Him; but if Baal, follow him." The people needed to make up their minds! God would not tolerate a rival!

Think about your students. They are constantly bombarded by media messages that encourage cultural standards that differ from God's standards. It's so easy for first graders to become confused and try to mix what they have been taught about God with what they absorb from the surrounding culture. How can you help them to stand firm and grow in their faith? It is a difficult task, yet through prayer and your example, they can be bold for the Lord!

MEMORY VERSE

Psalm 25:4

MATERIALS

Day 1:
- VA 14A Elijah and the Widow
- VA 15A Elijah Opposes False Prophets
- Paper clips, container (*Extension*)

Day 2:
- Candles, pitcher, matches or lighter
- VA 15A Elijah Opposes False Prophets
- Sentence strips
- Magnet, safety pins (*Extension*)
- BLM 15A God Sends Fire, card stock, brass paper fastener (*Extension*)

Day 3:
- BLM 15B Bible Truths
- String, paper cups (*Extension*)

Day 4:
- No additional materials are needed.

Day 5:
- VA 15A Elijah Opposes False Prophets
- BLM 15C Lesson 15 Test

TEACHER RESOURCES

MacArthur, John. *A House Divided: Elijah and the Kings of Israel.* Thomas Nelson, 2009.

Swindoll, Charles R. *Elijah: A Man of Heroism and Humility.* Thomas Nelson, 2008.

STUDENT RESOURCES

Bugtime Adventures: You're All Wet (The Elijah Story). DVD. Vision Video, 2005.

Smith, Julie. *Elijah, God's Brave Prophet.* David C. Cook, 2008.

15.1 Elijah Opposes False Prophets

Focus: Elijah Is Bold

MEMORY VERSE

Psalm 25:4

MEMORY WORK

- Write the Memory Verse on the board and read it chorally. Assign each student a partner. Have students take turns saying the verse to their partner until they have memorized it.

PREPARATION

Select **VA 14A Elijah and the Widow**. (*Introduction*)

Select **VA 15A Elijah Opposes False Prophets**. (*Directed Instruction*)

EXTENSION

1A Open several boxes of PAPER CLIPS until you have 450. Give each student a handful of paper clips until all have been distributed. Instruct students to make groups of 10 paper clips on their desk. Help students work together until all of the paper clips have been incorporated into a group. Carry a CONTAINER around to each student. Ask the student to drop each group of 10 into the container, one group at a time. Have the class count by tens, out loud, as the groups are dropped. Ask students to shout out when the number 450 is reached. Remind students that God is real and powerful! It only took one faithful man to stand up against 450 evil men. Raise the container so students can see it. Slowly and dramatically pour the paper clips out onto a desk or another container. Have students cheer for the Lord.

Introduction ★

Display **VA 14A Elijah and the Widow** and point out Elijah. Remind students that Elijah was a true prophet of God. God spoke to Elijah and Elijah told the people what God said. Review that the land of Israel was ruled by wicked King Ahab. Ask a volunteer to tell what made Ahab so wicked. (**Ahab worshipped Baal, a false god.**)

Point out a chair near you. Ask students what would happen if you prayed to the chair. (**The chair would not hear you or answer your prayer!**) Explain that idol worship was as foolish as praying to a chair. Idols were not real. They could not help the Israelites, but the Israelites continued to be drawn into idol worship. In today's lesson, God will show the people how foolish they had been to worship Baal.

Directed Instruction ★

Explain that King Ahab and Queen Jezebel were merely two of the people in Israel who worshipped Baal. Many of the Israelites had stopped worshipping God and turned to praying to Baal. Some of these idol worshippers were false prophets of Baal. These false prophets claimed to be able to talk to Baal and speak for Baal. This was not true; the false prophets told the people lies and wanted the people to turn away from the only true God.

Show students **VA 15A Elijah Opposes False Prophets**. Read the text on the back. Tell students that because God loved His people, He wanted to end the drought and famine in Israel. However, God would not tolerate King Ahab's continued worship of Baal. Recount how God had sent Elijah to speak to King Ahab before, but Ahab would not repent and turn back to the Lord. This time, Elijah proposed a contest to show the king and the people that the Lord God was the only true God. Ask a volunteer to tell the details of the contest. (**Two altars were set up, each with an animal sacrifice. If Baal sent fire to burn his sacrifice, he would be the god of Israel. However, if God sent fire to burn His sacrifice, then the people would know that He was the only true God.**)

Remind students that there were 450 false prophets involved in this contest and only one, true prophet of God. Ask students how they would feel if they were so outnumbered. (**Possible answers: frightened, alone, anxious**) Elijah showed boldness when he allowed the false prophets to go first in the contest. *Boldness* means *bravery*. Elijah was not afraid of Baal, a false god, because he knew the truth that the Lord God was the one true God and that the Lord God was with him.

Student Page 15.1

Read each statement with students and help them complete the exercises. Remind students of the importance of knowing what is true.

Review

- Why did Elijah hold a contest? (**to prove who was really God—the Lord God or Baal**)
- What did the 450 false prophets of Baal do on Mount Carmel? (**They built an altar and started calling out to their god to send fire. When nothing happened, they started shouting, jumping around, and dancing.**) Did their god ever answer? (**No, nothing happened.**)
- What did Elijah do when it was his turn? (**He built an altar with 12 stones, put wood on the stones, put an animal sacrifice on the wood, and poured water over it three times! Then he prayed to God.**)
- Did God answer Elijah? (**Yes! The whole altar burned up right away. Even the stones, the water in the ditch, and the dirt burned!**)
- What did the people do when they saw God's power? (**The people fell on their faces and said, "The Lord, He is God!"**)

Notes:

DAY 1

Name ____________________________________

Elijah Opposes False Prophets **15.1**

Elijah held a contest to show the king and the people that the Lord God was the only true God. Read each statement.

Circle God's altar if the statement is true.

Circle Baal's altar if the statement is not true.

1. King Ahab would not stop worshipping Baal.
2. Two altars were set up on Mount Carmel.
3. There were 500 false prophets of Baal.
4. Baal could hear the prayers of the false prophets.
5. Elijah had water poured over God's altar.
6. Elijah prayed, and God sent fire from heaven.
7. The people turned back to the Lord.

© Bible Grade 1 57

APPLICATION

- Have you ever done what was right when others were doing something wrong? How did that feel? (**Answers will vary.**)
- What gave Elijah the strength to be bold when he was so outnumbered? (**Answers will vary, but should include that Elijah had a close relationship with God. He knew that the Lord was the only true God.**)
- How can Christians today be bold for the Lord? (**They need to know the truth of God's Word and share that truth with others.**)

REINFORCEMENT

Despite years spent witnessing God's power and provision, the Israelites still turned to idolatry. There were several Baals worshipped throughout the Middle East at different times, but in most cases Baal was a fertility god, represented by storms and rain, and worshipped for his supposed ability to help produce children and bountiful crops. He was considered the most powerful of the gods in ancient Canaanite mythology. Although God warned the Israelites several times (Deuteronomy 6:14–15), they were often influenced by the societies around them and fell into idolatry (Numbers 25:3). Worship of Baal grew in Israel during the time of the judges (Judges 3:7, 8:33). Later, King Ahab established Baal worship as the state religion and built a temple to Baal in Samaria. Ahab and Jezebel actively worshipped the gods of Canaan (I Kings 16:32).

15.2 Elijah Opposes False Prophets

Focus: Know the Truth

Introduction

Show students the TWO CANDLES and the PITCHER OF WATER. Place one of the candles into the pitcher and allow it to soak for a minute or two. Invite students to guess which candle will light—the wet candle or the dry candle. Remove the candle from the water, and immediately use the MATCHES or LIGHTER to light the wick while it is still wet. When it does not light, inform students that wet things will not normally catch on fire.

Share that Elijah showed great boldness when he had water poured over God's altar! Remind students that Elijah did this not once, but three times, assuring that everything was soaking wet. For God to light the fire with everything covered in water was a powerful miracle! Elijah did this to convince the people that God was the only true God!

Directed Instruction

Display **VA 15A Elijah Opposes False Prophets** and review the details of the contest. Share that Elijah trusted God so much that he allowed the prophets of Baal to go first. Elijah let the false prophets pray to their god for many hours. Ask students to share what the false prophets did to get their god's attention. (**They called on their god, shouted, jumped up and down, and danced around their altar.**) The morning passed and, of course, Baal did not answer. The afternoon came, but nothing happened as a result of the false prophets' prayers.

Choose eight volunteers to hold the SENTENCES STRIPS that you prepared. Explain that now it was Elijah's turn, and things were quite different. Ask students to share what Elijah did first. (**He built an altar using 12 stones.**) Have the student with the strip reading *12 stones* to come to the front of the room. Continue by asking what happened next. (**Elijah dug a ditch around the altar.**) Call for the student who has *ditch around altar* to come up. Ask students what Elijah did next. (**He had wood piled on the stones of the altar.**) Ask the student with *wood on altar* to come forward. What happened next? (**An animal sacrifice was placed on the wood.**) Have the student with *animal on wood* join the others. Remind students that Elijah had four waterpots filled with water before he took the next step. Ask what Elijah had done with the water. (**He had the waterpots filled and the water poured over the sacrifice, wood, and stones of the altar. He repeated this three times.**) Invite the student with *soaked three times* to come forward.

Pause in your review of the Bible truth at this point. Share that the next step was the most important step of all for Elijah. He prayed! He did not have to jump around or shout to make God hear. Elijah simply trusted God and prayed in faith. Call for the student who has *prayer to the Lord.* Ask students to share what happened when Elijah prayed. (**God answered Elijah's prayer with fire.**) Have the student with *fire from heaven* come forward. After God demonstrated His power, what happened next? (**The people repented and returned to the Lord.**) Call on the student with *people repent.*

PREPARATION

Obtain TWO CANDLES of similar size and shape. Fill a PITCHER with water. Have MATCHES or a LIGHTER ready. (*Introduction*)

Select **VA 15A Elijah Opposes False Prophets**. (*Directed Instruction*)

Prepare EIGHT SENTENCE STRIPS with the following phrases: 12 stones, ditch around altar, wood on altar, animal on wood, soaked three times, prayer to the Lord, fire from heaven, people repent. (*Directed Instruction*)

EXTENSION

2A Students may wonder how the Israelites turned from the worship of God to the worship of Baal. One reason that the Israelites did this was that the beliefs of the neighboring Canaanites rubbed off on them. To help students remember this concept, bring in a MAGNET and TWO SAFETY PINS. First, show students that the magnet will pick up the pins easily, but that one pin will not attract the other. Rub the magnet over one of the pins to magnetize it. Then show students how contact with the magnet changed the nature of that pin. Use the magnetized pin to attract the pin that was not magnetized. Remind students that the beliefs of others may influence them if they do not learn God's Word and do what it says.

2B For a hands-on activity, print **BLM 15A God Sends Fire** on CARD STOCK for each student. Students will also need a BRASS PAPER FASTENER. Allow students to color, cut out, and assemble the altar. Have them use the craft to retell the Bible truth.

Conclude the lesson with prayer. Remind students that when they pray, they should pray as Elijah did. Elijah did not make a great show to get God's attention, but he prayed in faith, believing that God would hear and answer his prayer.

Student Page 15.2
Read the directions and the sentences. Assist students in completing the page.

Review

- What was different about the way that Elijah prepared his altar from the way that the false prophets prepared their altar? (**Elijah used 12 stones for his altar. He had the altar soaked with water three times.**)
- What was different about the way Elijah prayed from the way the false prophets prayed? (**Elijah prayed in faith. He trusted God. The false prophets made a great show and tried to get Baal's attention.**)
- What was different about God's answer to prayer and Baal's answer to prayer? (**God sent fire from heaven. Baal was an idol, a false god, so nothing happened.**)

APPLICATION

- Has anyone ever lied to you? How did you feel when you discovered that you had been deceived? (**Answers will vary.**)
- Why might the Israelites have believed the lies of the false prophets? (**Possible answers: The people had forgotten the Word of the Lord; the false prophets put on a convincing show; the neighboring countries worshipped Baal; it was a popular belief at the time.**)
- What is the best way to know the real truth about God? (**The best way to know the truth is to study God's Word.**)

DAY 2

15.2 *Elijah Opposes False Prophets*

Elijah gathered the Israelites on Mount Carmel to prove that the Lord was the real God.

1. Number the sentences to show how Elijah prepared the altar.

_2_ Elijah piled wood on top of the stones.

_1_ Elijah had an altar built with 12 large stones.

_3_ Elijah had a sacrifice put on the wood.

2. Number the sentences to show what Elijah did next.

_3_ Elijah had water poured over the altar three times.

_1_ Elijah dug a ditch around the altar.

_2_ Elijah had four waterpots filled with water.

3. Number the sentences to show what happened when God showed His power.

_1_ Fire came from heaven.

_3_ The people turned back to God.

_2_ The fire burned up the sacrifice, the wood, the stones, the water, and even the dirt!

58 © Bible Grade 1

15.3 Elijah Opposes False Prophets

Focus: Hold Fast to the Truth

★ PREPARATION

Duplicate as many copies of **BLM 15B Bible Truths** as needed so that each student will have one card. Cut the cards apart. (*Introduction, Directed Instruction*)

EXTENSION

3A Elijah listened to the truth of God's Word and God spoke to Elijah. Explain that Christians today learn God's Word by reading the Bible and listening to godly teaching.

For a listening activity, make a set of string phones with a length of STRING and TWO PAPER CUPS. Poke a very small hole in the bottom of each cup. Push one end of the string into one of the cups and tie a knot to hold it. Push the other end of the string into the bottom of the other cup and tie a knot. Have two students hold the cups and keep the string taut between them. Have one student speak into one of the cups while the other student holds the opposite cup to his or her ear. The vibration of the string will carry the sound from one cup to the other. Students must be quiet, take turns talking, and listen carefully. Remind students to always listen carefully to God's Word!

Introduction ★

Distribute a card from **BLM 15B Bible Truths** to each student. Help students read the paraphrased Bible verse on each card. Remind students that the Bible is true and that knowing God's Word helps Christians to tell what is true from what is not true.

Directed Instruction ★

Open your Bible to the book of Exodus. Remind students that the book of Exodus is in the Old Testament. Read **Exodus 20:3–4**. Explain that you have just read the first two commandments. Ask students to restate those two commandments of God. (**You shall have no other gods before Me; You shall not make for yourself a carved image.**) Remind students that the Israelites disobeyed the first two rules God gave them by worshipping Baal and making statues to represent God. They chose to believe the lie that Baal was not only real, but had more power than the Lord, so they broke the Lord's commandments.

Explain that there are many lies in the world today, but that Christians should use the truth of God's Word to stand firm against those lies. It is not always easy to do the right thing. It can be hard to stand for what is right when others are choosing to disobey God! However, God calls those who love Him to obey Him (John 14:15).

Tell students that you will read some scenarios. Have students listen carefully because there is something in each scenario that is not true. For each lie, there is a Bible verse that will counter it. If students think they have the card with the verse that counters the lie in the scenario, have them raise their hand and share their verse. Read the following scenarios:

- Blaine's brother, Karsen, told Blaine that it was okay to steal candy from the store because the store has a lot of candy and will not miss some. (**card number 2**)
- Josh told his mother that he would clean up his room, but he did not do it. (**card number 1**)
- Tabari promised Rachel that he would play with her, but he did not. He told Rachel that it was not important to keep his promise. (**card number 6**)
- Janae told Sara that it was okay to write her spelling words as carelessly as she wanted to because no one cares about her schoolwork. (**card number 4**)
- Simone told her sister that she could talk back whenever the teacher tried to correct her. (**card number 5**)
- Jackson told Keenan that when someone slaps you, you should slap him back even harder. (**card number 3**)

Review

- Why is it important to know God's Word? (**God's Word helps Christians to know what is true and what is not true.**)

- What should Christians do if they hear something that is not true according to God's Word? (**They should use the truth of God's Word to stand firm against lies.**)
- Is it always easy to stand firm for what is right when others are doing wrong? (**No, it can be hard to stand for what is right, but God's Word says to do just that.**)

Student Page 15.3

Have a different volunteer read the verse on each small Bible pictured. Complete the page together.

Notes:

APPLICATION

- Have you ever had to use a Bible truth to stand firm against a lie? Tell about that time. (**Answers will vary.**)

REINFORCEMENT

One of the best-known Christian apologists was C. S. Lewis, a British author, lecturer, and professor of English literature. Although he professed Christianity as a child, Lewis abandoned his faith and, for many of his early years, proclaimed himself to be an atheist. Through the faithful witness of friends, J. R. R. Tolkien and Hugo Dyson, Lewis became a follower of Jesus Christ. In 1944, Lewis broadcast seven radio talks in defense of the Christian faith. These talks were eventually published in book form as *Mere Christianity*, a powerful treatise on Christian beliefs.

DAY 3

Name ____________________

Elijah Opposes False Prophets **15.3**

False prophets do not tell the truth. The Bible tells the truth.

The sentences near the bottom of the page are not true. Write the letter of the Bible verse that corrects each untrue sentence.

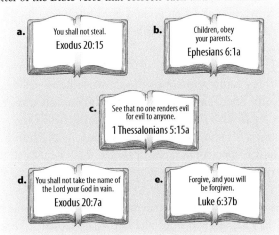

a. You shall not steal. Exodus 20:15

b. Children, obey your parents. Ephesians 6:1a

c. See that no one renders evil for evil to anyone. 1 Thessalonians 5:15a

d. You shall not take the name of the Lord your God in vain. Exodus 20:7a

e. Forgive, and you will be forgiven. Luke 6:37b

1. Using God's name to curse is no big deal. Everybody does it. D

2. It is okay to take a toy from the store without paying for it. A

3. You do not have to forgive people who hurt you. E

4. It is not important to obey your parents. B

5. If someone is mean to you, you should be mean in return! C

 59

15.4 Elijah Opposes False Prophets

Focus: Speak the Truth Boldly

REINFORCEMENT

William R. "Bill" Bright, the founder of Campus Crusade for Christ, had a burning passion for young people to come to know the Lord Jesus as their Savior. Dr. Bright began his ministry on the campus of UCLA in Los Angeles, California, in the early 1950s. Bright was quick to realize that students needed a concise, practical presentation of the gospel message, both for their own understanding of God's plan of salvation and to help them share their faith with others. Out of this need, Dr. Bright developed and printed booklets entitled *The Four Spiritual Laws*, emphasizing God's love, mankind's sin, Christ's sacrifice, and the need for faith in Christ. *The Four Spiritual Laws* has been translated into about 200 different languages and distributed to over 2.5 billion people.

Introduction

Write a few addition problems on the board with answers that are obviously wrong, such as 5 + 5 = 6. Ask a volunteer to come to the board and make an *X* next to all the problems with the wrong answers. When all the problems have been marked as being wrong, act as if you are very disappointed. Tell students that you really wanted your answers to be right, but wrong answers can never be right. Explain that thinking something is true or really wanting something to be true does not make it true. There is only one correct sum for an addition problem. There is only one, true God.

Directed Instruction

Hold up your Bible. Remind students that God's Word is true. When the 450 false prophets told the people that Baal was a powerful god, they lied! The people made a poor choice in believing the false prophets. The sad consequence was a drought and famine that lasted for over three years.

Explain that when people choose to accept Jesus as their Savior and become Christians, they have chosen to follow the truth of God's Word. They know that God's Word says that whoever believes in Jesus will have everlasting life (John 3:16). However, there are some people who do not believe the truth about Jesus. Some people have heard the truth about Jesus, but they have chosen not to believe in Him. Other people do not believe in Jesus because no one has ever told them the wonderful good news.

Lead a discussion about how Christians can be like Elijah. Elijah did two things. Elijah showed King Ahab what a poor choice he had made to worship Baal. Elijah showed the people that the Lord was the only true God.

Ask students if they know someone who may not know that faith in Jesus leads to everlasting life. (**Answers will vary.**) Talk about ways to share the truth about Jesus with someone who has never heard the good news. Include suggestions for sharing Bibles or invitations to church. Remind students that their respectful behavior can also be a way to share their faith and that they should never be rude when telling others about Jesus.

Explain that an important part of Christians sharing their faith is to pray for the person they know who does not know the Lord. Take time to pray. If possible, seat your students in a circle. Tell them that you will start the prayer and then you will call on another student to continue the prayer. The student will continue the prayer by praying for a person that he or she knows outside of the school setting who does not follow Jesus. Allow students to pass if they do not have someone in mind. When everyone has had a turn to pray, close your prayer time with a worship song.

Review

- Where do you learn the truth about God? (**from the Bible**)
- Why should Christians be like Elijah? (**Christians should stand firm for the truth of the Bible and tell others about everlasting life through Jesus.**)
- What is one way to share your faith with others? (**Possible answers: Give a Bible or an invitation to church; demonstrate respectful behavior to others.**)
- What should Christians always do as part of sharing their faith? (**They can pray for others.**)

Student Page 15.4

Divide the students into groups of two. As you read each scenario, have the partners decide how the child pictured might share Christ in the situation. Any or all of the answers provided could be used.

Notes:

APPLICATION

- Think about someone you know who does not know the Lord. Tell about how you would share the good news with that person. (**Answers will vary.**)
- Think about your behavior. Are you kind? Do you show love for others in such a way that they would want to hear about your faith? (**Answers will vary.**)

DAY 4

15.4 ***Elijah Opposes False Prophets***

Answers will vary, but all responses provided are acceptable.

1. Yoon sees his friends in the park. Yoon wants to share the good news about Jesus with his friends. Circle some ways that Yoon can share his faith.

Yoon can pray for his friends.

Yoon can invite his friends to go to church.

Yoon can be kind to his friends and explain that God loves them.

2. Traci wants her best friend, Autumn, to know about Jesus. Circle some ways that Traci can share her faith with Autumn.

Traci can pray for Autumn.

Traci can give Autumn a book of Bible truths for children.

Traci can tell Autumn about what she has learned in Bible class.

3. Taye wants his neighbor, Hudson, to learn about Jesus. Circle some ways that Taye can share his faith with his neighbor.

Taye can explain that Jesus died on the cross for everyone.

Taye can invite Hudson to go to church with him.

Taye can pray for Hudson.

60

© Bible Grade 1

15.5 Elijah Opposes False Prophets

Focus: Review and Assessment

★ PREPARATION

Select **VA 15A Elijah Opposes False Prophets**. (*Lesson Review*)

Print a copy of **BLM 15C Lesson 15 Test** for each student. (*Directed Instruction*)

Lesson Review ★

Use **VA 15A Elijah Opposes False Prophets** to review the Bible truth. Cover the following concepts:

- King Ahab and Queen Jezebel worshipped the false god, Baal.
- God punished Israel for its idol worship with a drought and famine. This lasted for over three years.
- God wanted to end the drought. He wanted His people to repent of their sins.
- God sent Elijah to speak to King Ahab. Elijah asked for a contest between Baal and the Lord God. The contest was to see who would send fire from heaven—Baal or God.
- There were 450 false prophets of Baal involved in the contest, but Elijah was the only one, true prophet of the Lord.
- The false prophets set up an altar to Baal. They cut wood and put an animal sacrifice on the wood.
- The false prophets prayed to Baal for hours. Nothing happened!
- Elijah teased the false prophets about their god. The false prophets shouted louder, but still nothing happened.
- At the end of the day, Elijah had 12 stones built into an altar to the Lord.
- Elijah put wood and an animal sacrifice on the altar. He dug a ditch around the altar. Then Elijah had four waterpots filled with water. The water was poured over the sacrifice, the wood, the stones, and into the ditch. This was done three times.
- Elijah prayed in faith to the Lord. The Lord answered immediately!
- God sent fire from heaven to burn the animal, the wood, the stones, the water in the ditch, and even the dirt!
- The Israelites saw that the Lord was the only true God. They repented of their sins and returned to worshipping the Lord.

Directed Instruction ★

Distribute a copy of **BLM 15C Lesson 15 Test** to each student. After all have completed the test, discuss the answers in class.

Notes:

Lesson Preparation
Josiah

16.0

Expected Student Outcomes

KNOW
Young King Josiah seeks God and reads His Word.

DO
Students will:
- differentiate between wise and foolish choices
- examine ways to incorporate Bible reading into their daily routines
- identify some of the promises found in God's Word
- review a story about how God's Word leads to knowledge

APPLY
Students will practice regular Bible reading.

Lesson Outline

I. Josiah the young king (2 Chron 34–35, 2 Kings 22:1–23:30)
  A. Josiah seeks the Lord
II. God's Word is found (2 Chron 34:8–15)
  A. The temple is cleaned
  B. Hilkiah finds God's Word
III. God's Word is read (2 Chron 34:16–35:19)
  A. Josiah hears God's Word
  B. The people hear God's Word
  C. Celebration of Passover is restored
IV. Choose to read God's Word
  A. Read God's Word to learn His promises

TEACHER'S HEART

This week's Bible lesson focuses on Josiah, a young boy who sought to learn about God and follow His ways. Josiah came from the line of David, and the Bible compliments him as someone who did what was right in the eyes of the Lord (2 Chronicles 34:2). However, both his father and grandfather did evil in the sight of the Lord (2 Chronicles 33:2, 22). Josiah did not grow up in an environment that fostered a love for God or modeled obedience to God's ways. So how did Josiah make a quantum spiritual leap to do what was right in God's eyes? The Bible shows us that Josiah chose to seek the God of David. That bears repeating—Josiah made a choice to seek after and follow God. God placed people around Josiah to help him learn.

Some students in your classroom may not have parents who teach them about God or read the Bible to them. In some ways, they are like Josiah, seeking God without the help and influence of godly parents. You are a spiritual guide to the students in your classroom. Just like Hilkiah, the priest, you can guide your students to the truths in the Bible. Your passion for God's Word can inspire your students to love and read the Bible. Use every opportunity to reference Bible verses that apply to classroom situations. Help your students see and know God through His Word!

MEMORY VERSE

Psalm 119:18

MATERIALS

Day 1:
- VA 16A Josiah
- BLM 16A Bible Reading Chart (*Extension*)

Day 2:
- VA 16A Josiah
- Cleaning items
- 3" × 5" index cards (*Extension*)

Day 3:
- VA 16A Josiah
- Matzo (*Extension*)

Day 4:
- Books about other countries
- Globe
- BLM 16B Bible Cover (*Extension*)

Day 5:
- VA 16A Josiah
- BLM 16C Lesson 16 Test

SONGS

The Bible

TEACHER RESOURCES

Fee, Gordon D. and Douglas Stuart. *How to Read the Bible for All Its Worth*. Zondervan, 2003.
Water, Mark, ed. *Reading Through the Bible in One Year Made Easy*. Hendrickson Publishers, 2003.

STUDENT RESOURCES

Britt, Stephanie. *My Little Bible*. Thomas Nelson, 2005.
Henley, Karyn. *Day by Day Begin-to-Read Bible*. Tyndale Kids, 2007.

16.1 Josiah

Focus: Josiah the Young King

MEMORY VERSE

Psalm 119:18

MEMORY WORK

- Write the Memory Verse on the board and read it together. Explain that God's Word is full of wonderful things for students to learn about God. Discuss some of the wonderful things that students can read about in the Bible, such as God's promise of salvation for all who believe. Remark that this week's Memory Verse is all about seeing wonderful things in God's Word. Explain that since God has graciously given them eyes to see, students will use their eyes to practice this week's verse. Have all the students with a particular eye color—brown, green, blue, or hazel—recite the verse. Then have students blink or close one eye and say the verse. Ask students to open their eyes as wide as they can while reciting the Memory Verse.

★ PREPARATION

Select **VA 16A Josiah**. (*Directed Instruction*)

EXTENSION

1A Print a copy of **BLM 16A Bible Reading Chart** for each student. Explain to students that daily reading of God's Word will help them know more about the Lord—about how kind, loving, and mighty He is. Encourage students to make the wise choice to read or listen to God's Word daily. Have students take the chart home and mark the chart after they have read the Bible or have listened to a parent read the Bible to them.

Introduction

Ask students to imagine what it would be like to be given the opportunity to do any job they want when they turn eight years old. Invite students to discuss which job they would like to do and why. (**Answers will vary.**) Allow several volunteers to share their ideas. Discuss realistic possibilities for jobs that eight-year-olds could do, such as acting or performing, helping a parent at work, or doing janitorial jobs.

Explain that in today's Bible lesson, students will learn about an eight-year-old boy who was given a huge job to do. He was not asked if he wanted the job, and he did not have the choice to turn down the job. Encourage students to listen to today's Bible truth to learn who the boy was and why he is mentioned in the Bible.

Directed Instruction ★

Open your Bible to the book of 2 Kings. Explain that the Bible truth for this week is found in this book and in the book of 2 Chronicles. Recite the names for the books of the Bible in order through 2 Chronicles, and pause from time to time as students repeat after you.

Briefly explain the following terms used in the Bible truth: *the Book of the Law* was most likely *a collection of the books written by Moses*. This was the portion of God's Word that had been written at that point in time. The word *priest* refers to *a spiritual leader in the temple*. Hilkiah was the priest when today's Bible truth took place.

Hold up **VA 16A Josiah** and remind students to listen carefully for the things that the young king did. Read the text on the back.

Guide students to understand that Josiah had not planned on becoming king at such a young age, but when his father died, Josiah became the king because he was the king's son. Josiah's father had not taught him about God or even shown him how to be a godly leader. Josiah was not at all ready to become the king! Explain that God provided Hilkiah, the priest, and others to be available to teach Josiah about God. Ask students to list people who help them to learn more about God. (**Possible answers: parents, grandparents, Bible class teachers, pastors**)

Point out that Josiah made a good choice to learn about God. He spent the early years of his reign learning about God. Have students tell some of the things they will probably study for the next several years. (**Possible answers: reading, language arts, math, social studies, science**) Remind students that studying the Bible will help them throughout their lives!

Because Josiah studied and followed God's Word, the Bible says that he did what was right in the sight of the Lord. Even though Josiah was young, he made wise choices. No one made him learn about God; he chose to study so that he could become a godly leader. Remind students that they can be like Josiah and make the wise choice to learn about God.

Review

- How old was Josiah when he became king? (**eight years old**)
- Why did he become king at such a young age? (**His father died, and he was the oldest son of the king.**)
- Who might have helped Josiah learn about God? (**Possible answers: Hilkiah the priest, other teachers**)
- Which of Josiah's relatives showed a good example of following God? (**King David**)

Student Page 16.1

Assist students in completing the page.

Notes:

APPLICATION

- How do you think Josiah felt when he became king at the age of eight? (**Answers will vary.**)
- How would you feel if you knew that you would have to rule your country when you turned eight years old? (**Possible answers: excited, scared, nervous**)
- If you had to rule your country, who could you go to for help in making wise decisions? (**Answers will vary.**)
- Josiah made a wise choice to learn about God. What are some wise choices you could make today that could help you learn about God? (**Answers may vary, but should include listening to the Bible lesson every day and reading the Bible as their skill develops.**)

DAY 1

Name ______________________________

Josiah **16.1**

King Josiah learned to make wise choices when he was young.

Read each sentence. Think about the choice that was made. Was it a wise choice or a foolish choice? Some sentences are true, but they tell of foolish choices. Underline the letter after each wise choice.

1. King Josiah learned God's Word. B
2. King Josiah followed King David's example. I
3. Many people worshipped idols. T
4. King Josiah got rid of all the idols. B
5. The people did not take care of the temple. R
6. King Josiah gave money to fix the temple. L
7. The people forgot God's laws. K
8. King Josiah read God's laws and obeyed them. E

Use the letter that is beside each wise choice to make the word that completes the sentence.

9. I can make wise choices by studying the ______BIBLE______ and doing what it says.

16.2 Josiah

Focus: God's Word Is Found

★ PREPARATION

Select **VA 16A Josiah**. (*Directed Instruction*)

Have on hand some **CLEANING ITEMS** such as mop, broom, dustpan, and cleaning cloth or sponge. (*Directed Instruction*)

Make a scroll by taping four pieces of paper together and rolling them up. Keep the scroll out of the students' sight until the appropriate time in the lesson. (*Directed Instruction*)

EXTENSION

2A Before class, write out several Memory Verses from previous Bible lessons on **3" × 5" INDEX CARDS**. Hide them around the classroom. Let students search and discover the hidden verses from God's Word. Help each student read the Bible verse that he or she found.

Introduction

Pretend that you have lost your teacher's edition for the first-grade Bible series. Talk about how you feel and the importance of what was lost. Encourage students to help you figure out where it could be and then invite students to help you find your lost book. Describe how you feel about finding it and knowing it will help the students to learn about God today.

Explain to the class that today's Bible lesson will focus on something the people of Judah had lost. In fact, they did not even know they had lost it. The people had lost something very important—God's Word!

Directed Instruction ★

Show **VA 16A Josiah** to the class. Use the picture to review the key points of the Bible truth. Ask students how old King Josiah was when he began to reign. (**Josiah was only eight when he became king.**) Who helped Josiah become a godly leader? (**Hilkiah, the priest, and other teachers**) What did Josiah learn from Hilkiah? (**He learned God's Word and how to follow God's ways.**)

Open your Bible to **2 Chronicles 34:8** and read the verse aloud. Help students to figure out how old Josiah was in the eighteenth year of his reign. (**8 + 18 = 26 years old**) Explain that even though several true prophets of the Lord continued to warn the people not to worship idols, many people still did. Josiah knew that worshipping idols was against two of God's commandments, and it was very, very wrong!

Because the people had chosen to worship idols, they paid little attention to keeping the temple, God's house, clean and in good repair. King Josiah realized the importance of worship in the life of God's people, so he sent people to clean up the temple.

Ask for volunteers to hold each of the **CLEANING ITEMS** that you brought to class. Instruct these students to pretend to be cleaning the temple. Ask the class what types of jobs might have been done to clean up the temple and have the volunteers act out the suggestions. (**Possible answers: sweeping, dusting, mopping, scrubbing the walls and the floor**)

King Josiah provided money to Hilkiah to make all of the repairs and get God's temple fixed and ready to be used for worship. Discuss some of the ways people take care of churches today and get them ready for worship services. (**Possible answers: Some people vacuum and dust; other people make repairs to the building and grounds.**) Thank your volunteers and let them return to their seat.

While the work on the temple took place, Hilkiah found something in the temple. Read **2 Chronicles 34:14**. Hold up the scroll that you prepared in advance. Explain that God's Word was first written on long sheets of paper or possibly animal skins that were rolled up. The book that Hilkiah found probably looked something like the example that you showed the class.

Remind students that the entire Bible had not been written yet, and this was the only portion of God's Word that was available at that time. Ask students to imagine how King Josiah might have reacted to finding God's Word. (**surprised, pleased**)

Review

- Why did the temple need to be cleaned? (**The people had worshipped idols and had not cared for God's house.**)
- About how old was Josiah when he ordered the temple cleaned? (**26**)
- What important item was found in the temple? (**the Book of the Law**)
- What did the Book of the Law look like? (**long sheets of paper or animal skins that were written on and rolled up**)
- After Hilkiah found the Book of the Law, he sent it to King Josiah. How did King Josiah learn what was in it? (**Someone read it to him.**)

Student Page 16.2

The pictures show ways that children can read the Bible. Discuss ways to learn God's Word that are not pictured, such as listening to Bible truths on CDs, reading the Bible online, or watching Bible truths on DVDs.

DAY 2

16.2 ***Josiah***

It is important for you to begin the habit of reading the Bible when you are young, just as King Josiah did.

Look at each picture and listen to the sentences below. Write the number of the sentence in the corner of the matching picture.

1. Alaina's mom reads the Bible to Alaina every night when Alaina is in bed.
2. Every day, Niki reads some words in the Bible by herself.
3. Annie's dad reads the Bible each evening at dinnertime.
4. Celina's mom and dad read the Bible to Celina and her younger brother at bedtime.
5. Armando's mom and dad read the Bible and pray together.
6. What is your favorite time to read the Bible?

Answers will vary.

APPLICATION

- Have you ever lost something important to you and then found it? How did finding it make you feel? (**Answers will vary.**)
- How do you think Hilkiah, the priest, felt when he found the Book of the Law? (**Possible answers: surprised, delighted**)
- Josiah had learned about God and wanted to honor God's house by cleaning it. Could Josiah's desire to worship and restore God's house have helped in discovering the Book of the Law? (**Yes, because if Josiah had not cared for the temple, the Book might not have been discovered.**)

REINFORCEMENT

Biblical scholars are not in complete agreement about what was included in the Book of the Law of Moses that was found as Hilkiah cleaned and restored the temple. Many scholars believe it was the book of Deuteronomy and most likely all five books commonly known as *the Pentateuch*—Genesis, Exodus, Leviticus, Numbers, and Deuteronomy. In either case, it was clear that the people had fallen away from the only true God. They neither worshipped Him nor obeyed His commandments.

16.3 Josiah

Focus: God's Word Is Read

★ PREPARATION

Select **VA 16A Josiah**. (*Directed Instruction*)

EXTENSION

3A Play an alphabet game that emphasizes reading the Bible. Begin by reminding the class that God's Word is full of wonderful things to read and discover. Play the game by saying the phrase, "I'm going to read my Bible and I'll read about … " Have the first student to play stand and say the first letter of the alphabet. Invite the class to call out a person or a thing from the Bible that begins with that letter, for example, *Adam*, *Abel*, *ark*, or *angels*. Then have the class repeat the phrase and the next student call out the second letter in the alphabet, B. Encourage multiple answers for each letter. Continue playing until you go through the alphabet or time is finished.

3B Invite a guest who is knowledgeable in the Jewish tradition of Passover to visit. Remind your students to show hospitality as your guest explains the various elements of the Passover seder. If possible, have some MATZO, unleavened bread, available for students to taste.

Introduction

Ask students to raise their hand if they have been reading the Bible at home. Encourage students to begin a lifelong habit of daily Bible reading.

Remind the class that King Josiah and his people did not know God's Word before the Book of the Law was found in the temple. Have students estimate how many Bibles they might have at home. (**Answers will vary.**) Help students understand that having a Bible is great, but they have to read it to get the benefit from it! Tell students that the Book of the Law was probably lost because no one was reading it!

Ask students to tell about something new that they have learned from reading the Bible. (**Answers will vary.**) Have students listen carefully to discover what Josiah and his people learned from reading the Bible.

Directed Instruction ★

Display **VA 16A Josiah** and review the Bible truth. Explain how upset King Josiah became when he discovered that his people had not been following God's ways. He understood that God punished disobedience and wanted to know what God's punishment would be. Ask students to share how they would feel if they knew they had done something that deserved punishment. (**Possible answers: upset, disappointed, scared**)

God's prophetess told King Josiah the people would not be punished in his lifetime because Josiah tried to do what was right and worship God. Ask the students to imagine how the king might have reacted to that news. (**Possible answers: relieved, surprised, joyful, thankful**) Invite students to pretend they had just heard the good news that they would not be punished. Ask a few volunteers to act out their reactions.

Ask students to recount the next thing Josiah did. (**He read the Book of the Law to all of the people.**) Unlike today, King Josiah could not send copies of the Book of the Law to all of his people—there was only one copy! The people of Israel learned about God when King Josiah read the Book of the Law to them. King Josiah knew it was important that the people in his kingdom hear about God so they could learn about God and follow God's ways. For many years, the people had not obeyed God's laws because they did not know what God's laws were! Now they could hear what God wanted them to know and to do.

Once King Josiah and the people learned God's laws, they began to obey them together. God's Word told of a feast that His people should hold every year to remember that God led His people out of Egypt. King Josiah and all of the people began to worship the Lord by celebrating the Feast of the Passover—the meal that celebrated how death passed over the Hebrews' homes. The people remembered all that the Lord had done in the past.

King Josiah was able to learn many things about God and God's ways from hearing God's Word. Remind students that as they read God's Word, their eyes will be opened to see the amazing promises that God has for them!

Review

- How did King Josiah first discover that his people were disobeying God? (**His teachers taught him truth about God. Josiah compared this to what the people were doing.**)
- How did King Josiah learn that his people were disobeying God's Book of the Law? (**Someone read the Book of the Law to him.**)
- Why did God choose not to punish the people in King Josiah's lifetime? (**because King Josiah tried to do the right thing and worship God**)
- What feast did the people begin to celebrate? (**the Feast of the Passover**)
- Why was it important to celebrate Passover? (**It was a reminder of how God caused death to pass over the Hebrews before they left Egypt.**)

Student Page 16.3

Tell students that God's Word contains many promises for them. Read the Bible verses and the sentences. Complete the page together.

DAY 3

Name ____________________

Josiah 16.3

You can discover many wonderful things in God's Word if you look!

To find a hidden picture in the box below, listen to each Bible verse and the sentence. When you hear the missing word, color the space in the box with that word.

1. Psalm 50:15: I can ____ on the Lord to help me, and He will! (call)

2. Psalm 32:8: The Lord will ____ me and watch over me. (teach)

3. Proverbs 29:25: The Lord will keep me ____. (safe)

4. 1 John 1:9: The Lord will ____ my sins. (forgive)

5. 1 John 5:14–15: The Lord ____ my prayers. (hears)

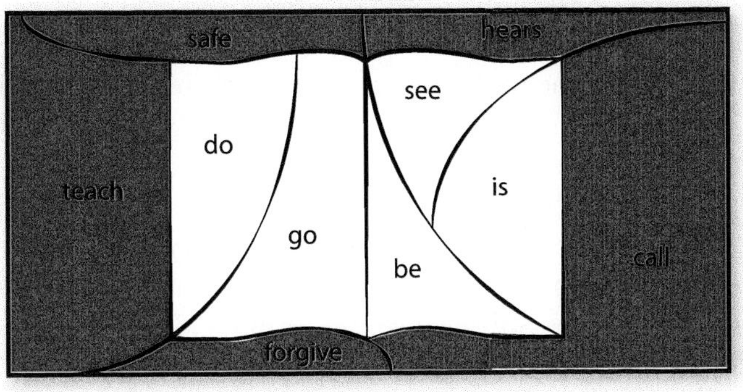

Complete the sentence.

6. I discover God's promises when I read God's ____Word____.

© Bible Grade 1 63

APPLICATION

- How do you think King Josiah felt when he realized that God punished disobedience? (**Possible answers: frightened, worried, sad**)
- How do you think King Josiah felt when the prophet said the people would not be punished? (**Possible answers: relieved, glad**)
- How do you think the people felt when they heard God's Word being read to them for the first time? (**Possible answers: happy, excited**)
- King Josiah and the people learned from God's Word and changed their ways to obey God. What have you learned from God's Word that has changed how you live or what you do or say? (**Answers will vary.**)

REINFORCEMENT

Passover is sometimes referred to as *the feast of unleavened bread* because of the absence of leavened bread during the celebration. The use of unleavened bread signifies the quick departure of the Israelites from Egypt since they did not have time for the yeast to act upon the dough before they would be freed by the pharaoh. In the New Testament, the term *Passover lamb* was a reference to Jesus Christ (1 Corinthians 5:7).

Josiah restored the Passover celebration to both the northern and the southern kingdoms of Israel and Judah. This celebration probably included a much larger audience than recorded in 2 Chronicles 30:23–27 when King Hezekiah had last held a Passover feast.

16.4 Josiah

Focus: Choose to Read God's Word

★ PREPARATION

Obtain a variety of BOOKS ABOUT OTHER COUNTRIES. (*Introduction*)

Have a GLOBE available. (*Directed Instruction*)

EXTENSION

4A Provide a copy of **BLM 16B Bible Cover** to each student. Allow students to design a cover for a Bible. Students may copy their design onto a larger piece of paper that would fit over the cover of their Bible.

Introduction ★

Display a variety of BOOKS ABOUT OTHER COUNTRIES. Pick up a book and show several pictures to the class. Read an interesting fact about the country featured in the book. Tell students that when they read about other countries, they learn about people from around the world.

Directed Instruction ★

Read the following fictional story:

Emma looked out the front window as the new neighbors moved in across the street. She was very excited to see a girl who looked about her own age. As Emma listened, she could hear the family talking, but she didn't understand any of the words the people said. Emma's mother came into the room and saw the puzzled look on Emma's face. Her mother explained that their new neighbors had just arrived from a country called *China*. The parents spoke some English, but the children spoke only Chinese. Emma felt sad that she would not be able to talk with the little girl and that she did not know anything about China.

Emma's mother brought out a book about China. Together they looked at the pictures and read the words. Mother read about pandas, animals that live in China. She showed Emma pictures of paper lanterns; the Great Wall of China; high, pointed mountains; beautiful silk banners; and colorful fireworks. Emma learned that the language of China is written in characters or little pictures instead of alphabet letters. Then Mother read the words Chinese people say to greet one another, *Ni hao* (nē hou). Over and over, Emma practiced saying the words.

Emma felt happy that her mother had read to her about China. She asked her mother to take her to meet the neighbors. Emma and her mother helped to carry boxes out of the moving van. The Chinese mother told them that her daughter's name was Ming. Emma smiled at the little girl and said, "Ni hao, Ming."

Ming had a very surprised look on her face and quickly replied, "Ni hao." Then she pointed to a colorful, plastic ball in one of the boxes that they'd just taken out of the van. Emma smiled her biggest smile. The two new friends picked up the ball and began to play. Now Emma was happy that she took time to learn a little bit about China.

Tell your students that, just like Emma learned about China from the book her mother read to her, King Josiah and the people learned about God when the Book of the Law was read to them. Ask the students to imagine what life for Josiah and his people might have been like if they had never read God's Word. (**Possible answers: continued idol worship, missed out on God's blessings, punished for disobedience**)

As King Josiah learned all he could about God, he wisely chose to obey. God's Word explains how to worship God in a way that pleases Him. Josiah learned about the Passover feast and his people began to celebrate it.

Review

- What country was Emma's new friend from? (**China**)
- How did Emma learn about China? (**She and her mother read a book about China.**)
- How did King Josiah and the people learn about God? (**The Book of the Law was read to them.**)
- Why did King Josiah want his people to hear God's Word? (**He wanted his people to know and obey God's Word.**)
- What did King Josiah learn from the Book of the Law? (**Possible answers: Josiah learned about God's laws; he discovered that the people had not kept God's laws; he learned that the people had forgotten to celebrate the Passover.**)

Student Page 16.4

Show students the country of China on a GLOBE. Remind students of the things that Emma and her mother had read about in the book about China. Assist students in completing the page.

APPLICATION

- Josiah wanted all the people to hear God's Word. Who are some of the people who encourage you to read the Bible? (**Answers will vary.**)
- Why do you read the Bible? (**Answers will vary, but should include that I read my Bible to learn what God would want me to do in all circumstances.**)
- What are some things you have learned from God's Word? (**Answers will vary.**)
- King Josiah listened to God's Word so he could learn from it. What are some things you would like to learn from the Bible? (**Possible answers: Bible truths, God's promises, ways to please God**)

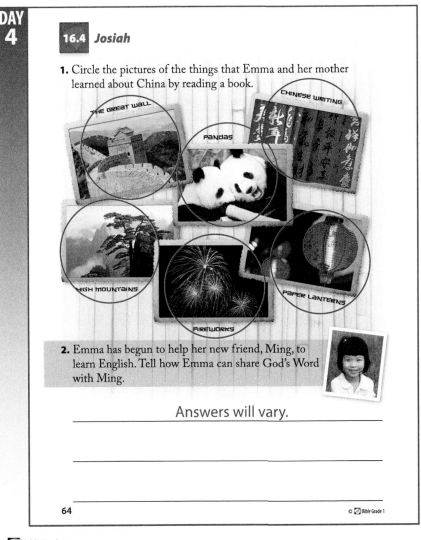

DAY 4

16.4 ***Josiah***

1. Circle the pictures of the things that Emma and her mother learned about China by reading a book.

2. Emma has begun to help her new friend, Ming, to learn English. Tell how Emma can share God's Word with Ming.

Answers will vary.

64

16.5 Josiah

Focus: Review and Assessment

★ PREPARATION

Select "The Bible" from the music CDs. (*Lesson Review*)

Select **VA 16A Josiah**. (*Lesson Review*)

Duplicate a copy of **BLM 16C Lesson 16 Test** for each student. (*Directed Instruction*)

Lesson Review ★

Have a brief period of worship. Sing "The Bible" from the music CDs. Invite several students to take turns acting out some of the Bible truths that you have studied so far this year. Take time to celebrate all of the things the students have learned from God's Word.

Use **VA 16A Josiah** to review the Bible truths in this lesson. Cover the following points:

- Josiah was only eight years old when he became the king of Judah.
- King Josiah loved God and followed God like King David, his relative from long ago.
- The Bible records that King Josiah did what was right in the eyes of the Lord.
- During the early years of his reign, Josiah studied, prayed, and learned about God. He began to see that his people did not follow God.
- Many of the people in King Josiah's kingdom worshipped idols and did not worship God.
- When Josiah was 20 years old, he began to remove all the idols throughout the land.
- The temple needed to be fixed and cleaned. King Josiah provided money to have the temple cleaned and repaired.
- While cleaning the temple, Hilkiah, the priest, found the Book of the Law of Moses.
- When the Book of the Law was read to him, King Josiah was upset to learn how much the people were not following God's ways.
- King Josiah asked what the punishment would be for the people's disobedience toward God.
- God did not punish the people in Josiah's lifetime because Josiah tried to do what was right and worshipped God.
- King Josiah read the Book of the Law to all of the people.
- King Josiah and the people learned about the Feast of the Passover, a meal that celebrated how God caused death to pass over the Hebrews' homes.
- Josiah and all of the people worshipped the Lord by celebrating the Passover each year. The people continued to obey God's Word.

Directed Instruction ★

Give each student a copy of **BLM 16C Lesson 16 Test**. Read each question to the students and allow time for each student to mark an answer. Share correct answers.

Notes:

Lesson Preparation

Christmas

17.0

Expected Student Outcomes

KNOW

The angel Gabriel foretells the birth of Christ. The Messiah is born. The shepherds and wise men worship Him.

DO

Students will:

- complete a cloze activity to review the Bible truth
- determine accurate statements about the presentation of Jesus in the temple
- match the messages given by angels to those who received the messages
- use facts from the Bible truth to complete a dot-to-dot activity
- consider the gifts that they have received from the Lord and how they can give gifts to show their love for Him

APPLY

Students will recognize that God loves them and sent His Son, Jesus, as a gift. They will worship Him.

Lesson Outline

I. Jesus is born (Lk 1:26–2:20)
  A. God prepares the way
  B. Joseph and Mary's responses to the angels' messages
  C. The shepherds' response to the angel's message
II. Jesus is presented in the temple (Lk 2:21–39)
  A. Simeon and Anna's responses to the Messiah
III. The wise men
  A. The wise men follow a star (Mt 1:18–2:15)
  B. King Herod's response to the news
IV. The greatest gift
  A. Students' response to the Christmas message

TEACHER'S HEART

The Christmas season is so busy! It is a time of decorating homes and classrooms, wrapping gifts, and practicing for Christmas programs. Often, it gets so busy that you can miss the message of Christmas, the message that God sent His only Son to die for your sins and the sins of the entire world. Romans 5:8 says, "But God demonstrates His own love toward us, in that while we were still sinners, Christ died for us." What an amazing gift!

First graders can miss the Christmas message, too. They can be so overloaded with television and print advertisements for all the latest toys that they can begin to believe that Christmas is all about getting more and more material things. As you share the Christmas message with your students, emphasize God's plan of salvation and the spiritual blessings that come from trusting in Him. Encourage your students to make room in their heart and life for the Christ child!

MEMORY VERSE

Isaiah 9:6

MATERIALS

Day 1:

- BLM 17A Stars, Part 1; BLM 17B Stars, Part 2
- Baby items
- VA 17A Jesus Is Born
- BLM 17C Nativity Puzzle, card stock (*Extension*)

Day 2:

- No additional materials are needed.

Day 3:

- Star ornament
- Air-dry clay (*Extension*)
- Used Christmas cards (*Extension*)

Day 4:

- Wrapped gift box
- Birthday cake (*Extension*)

Day 5:

- VA 17A Jesus Is Born
- BLM 17D Lesson 17 Test

SONGS

Christmas Joy/Joy to the World

TEACHER RESOURCES

Collins, Ace. *Stories Behind the Best-Loved Songs of Christmas*. Zondervan, 2001.

Ellis, Gwen. *Read and Share DVD Bible: Christmas*. DVD. Thomas Nelson, 2009.

STUDENT RESOURCES

Kingsbury, Karen. *We Believe in Christmas*. Zonderkidz, 2008.

Miller, Claire. *The Christmas Message*. Concordia Publishing House, 2006.

17.1 Christmas

Focus: Jesus Is Born

MEMORY VERSE

Isaiah 9:6

MEMORY WORK

- Write the Memory Verse on the board. Read it chorally. Divide the class into five groups and distribute one star from **BLMs 17A–B Stars** to each group. Explain that some of the words in the Memory Verse are on the yellow stars. Choose a student in each group to hold the group's star. Be sure that everyone in the group can read the word(s) on their star. Read the verse and pause when you come to the word(s) that are on each star. Have the group with those word(s) stand and say the word(s) that are on their star. Invite groups to exchange stars and repeat the activity.

PREPARATION

Copy **BLMs 17A–B Stars** onto yellow paper and cut out the stars. (*Memory Work*)

Obtain a few BABY ITEMS, such as a bottle, blanket, baby clothes or baby toys. (*Introduction*)

Select **VA 17A Jesus Is Born.** (*Directed Instruction*)

EXTENSION

1A Obtain a recording of "Unto Us a Child Is Born" from *Handel's Messiah*. Allow students to listen to the recording during the week. (Note: The words are in the King James Version of the Bible.)

1B Duplicate a class set of **BLM 17C Nativity Puzzle** on CARD STOCK. Have students color and cut apart the puzzle pieces and then reassemble the puzzle. State that each part of God's plan fits together in the birth of Christ.

Introduction ★

Display various BABY ITEMS. Ask students if they have ever had a new baby in their home. Allow a few volunteers to share some fun things about the baby. Explain that all babies are special, but that in today's lesson, they will learn about the most special baby who was ever born.

Directed Instruction ★

Open your Bible to Matthew and show your open Bible to the students. Explain that all the Bible truths that the students have studied so far have been found in the Old Testament, but now they will be learning about the life of Jesus. The Bible truths about the life of Jesus are found in the New Testament. Tell students that the first four books of the New Testament are Matthew, Mark, Luke, and John. Invite students to repeat the names of the first four books after you.

Hold up **VA 17A Jesus Is Born**, and read the text on the back. Explain that this Bible truth is also called *the Christmas story*. Ask students to imagine what Mary must have thought when the angel Gabriel told her she was the one God had chosen to be the mother of Jesus! Mary might have said, "Why would God pick me? I'm just a poor girl. How will all this happen? It seems amazing!" The angel told Mary that God was sending His Son to Earth as part of His plan of salvation. Explain that the phrase *plan of salvation* means *God's plan to send His Son to die on the cross to pay for the sins of all people*. God was doing this because he loves people dearly, and wants to rescue them from their sins.

Remind students that God spoke to Joseph, too. God selected the name for His Son, and then sent an angel to tell Joseph he should name the baby *Jesus* (Matthew 1:21). Names were very important to the people in Bible times because names had meanings. God announced that Jesus would save people from their sins! Joseph agreed to do as the angel commanded.

In God's plan, Jesus was to be born in Bethlehem. Remind students that Bethlehem was the same town where Boaz and Ruth, King David's great-grandparents, lived. How difficult the journey must have been for Mary when she was so close to giving birth!

The little town of Bethlehem usually had just a hundred people in it, but with all the people returning to be counted, there were thousands of people in this village now. There was no hospital in Bethlehem. There was not even a room available in the inn, so Mary had to have her baby in a stable! Ask students to recount what Mary did after Jesus was born. (**She wrapped Him in strips of cloth and laid Him in a manger.**)

God sent His messenger, an angel, to announce the good news of the Savior's birth. But the angel did not go to the king in the royal palace or even to the priests in the temple to tell the news. The angel went to a group of ordinary shepherds! Jesus was born for all people, rich and poor.

What a celebration! The sky was suddenly filled with many angels, all praising God! The shepherds left their sheep in the fields and went quickly to Bethlehem! There they found everything just as the angel had said it would be. What they saw changed their lives! These shepherds told everyone they met about the birth of the Savior! What good news!

Review

- What special news did the angel Gabriel bring to Mary? (**Mary would be the mother of the Savior.**)
- Why did Joseph and Mary travel to Bethlehem? (**to be counted**)
- Why did God send His Son to Earth? (**to save people from their sins**)
- Who were the first people to hear the good news of the Savior's birth? (**shepherds in the fields**)
- What did the angel tell the shepherds? (**He told the shepherds that they would find a baby wrapped in soft cloths and lying in a manger.**)

Student Page 17.1

Assist students in completing the page.

DAY 1

Name ______________________________

17.1

Christmas

Use the words at the bottom of the page to complete the sentences.

Joseph and Mary took a long trip to Bethlehem to be counted. When they reached Bethlehem, they had to stay in a ____stable____ because there was no room in the inn. That very night, the baby Jesus was born! Mary wrapped Him in soft cloths and laid Him in a ____manger____.

Out in the fields, some shepherds were watching their sheep. An ____angel____ told them that the Savior had been born! The angel told them to go to Bethlehem. They left their ____sheep____ and went to Bethlehem. They found the baby and praised God!

manger sheep stable angel

65

APPLICATION

- The celebration of Jesus' birth is called *Christmas*. What are some things that you plan to do to celebrate this special time of year? (**Answers will vary.**)
- Christians often sing Christmas carols or songs when they worship during this time of year. What is your favorite Christmas carol or song? What do the words tell you about the Lord? (**Answers will vary.**)
- Why do you think that God announced the birth of His Son to some shepherds instead of to the people in the royal palace? (**Answers will vary, but should include that Jesus came for everyone—great and small, rich and poor.**)

17.2 Christmas

Focus: Jesus Is Presented in the Temple

EXTENSION

2A The lyrics of traditional Christmas carols provide an excellent review of the week's lessons. Consider singing the first verses of several carols with the class.

2B Sing "Christmas Joy/Joy to the World" from the music CDs. Consider singing the song several times during the week.

2C During the Christmas season, there are many familiar objects that can be used to teach or review the Bible truth. One of these is a candy cane. The shape of a candy cane is like a shepherd's crook, the staff used by shepherds to recover stray sheep. The shape will remind students of the shepherds out in the fields who heard the angel's message. The candy cane can be turned so that it resembles the letter *J*, the first letter in *Jesus*. Candy canes are white with red stripes. The red stripes remind students of the price paid by Jesus on the cross to bring about God's plan of salvation for the entire world.

Introduction

Tell students to stand on one foot beside their desk. (You choose the length of time for the class to do this.) While they are standing, remind them that the promise of a savior had been made by God thousands of years before the birth of Jesus. The Jews had waited a long time. For some students, standing on one leg can feel like a long time. Ask students if they agree. (**Answers will vary.**) Then tell them to imagine how the Jews must have felt waiting from one generation to the next for God's promise of a savior to be fulfilled.

Directed Instruction

Write the words *Jewish*, *Jews*, and *Gentiles* on the board. Explain that the words *Jewish* and *Jews* refer to *the people who were descended from the Hebrew people*. Define *Gentiles* as *people who were not Jews*. Explain to students that Joseph and Mary were both Jewish.

Read the following Bible truth from Luke 2:21–39:

> Following the law of Israel, Joseph and Mary took baby Jesus to the temple in Jerusalem to be presented to God. There in the temple, they met a very old man named *Simeon*.
>
> Simeon loved God with his whole heart and was filled with the Holy Spirit. God revealed to him that he would not die before he had seen the Messiah with his own eyes. *Messiah* means *God's promised Savior*. Today was the day that Simeon would see the baby! When he saw baby Jesus, Simeon was filled with peace and gratitude. He took the baby in his arms and praised God, saying:
> *Now, Lord, as You have promised, I am ready to go home to be with You. I have seen the Messiah, the Child who will bring Your plan of salvation to all people. He will be a light to show Your truth to the Gentiles, and He will bring glory to Your people, the children of Israel.*
>
> Joseph and Mary were amazed at the things Simeon said! Jesus was the one who would bring salvation to everyone, even to Gentiles.
>
> Simeon was not the only one in the crowd at the temple who recognized Jesus. Anna was an elderly prophetess who served in the temple. The Holy Spirit told her that Jesus was God's Son. Anna told many people that Jesus was the Messiah. Later, Joseph and Mary returned to Bethlehem.

Remind students that the promise of a savior had been given to God's people thousands of years before Jesus' birth. Abraham, Jacob, Moses, Joshua, Gideon, Ruth, King David, King Josiah, and many other faithful people had been waiting for the promised Savior.

Ask students if they think that Simeon and Anna were in the same part of the temple that day by chance. (**No, God planned for them to see baby Jesus.**) Simeon helped Joseph and Mary understand more about God's plan for Jesus. He said the Savior had come to save not just the Jews, but all people from their sins!

Review

- What were the names of the two elderly people who met Joseph, Mary, and baby Jesus in the temple? (**Simeon and Anna**)
- What did Simeon and Anna know about the baby Jesus? (**They knew that He was the promised Savior, the Messiah.**)
- What did Simeon tell Joseph and Mary about God's plan for Jesus? (**Simeon told them that Jesus had come to save all people.**)
- What did Anna do after she had seen the Messiah? (**She rejoiced and told many people that the Savior had come.**)

Student Page 17.2

Remind students that both Simeon and Anna rejoiced when they saw baby Jesus. Read each of the statements in Exercise 1. Have students lightly color only the boxes that contain statements found in the Bible truth. Assist students in completing the page.

DAY 2

17.2 *Christmas*

1. Color the boxes that tell about Joseph and Mary presenting Jesus to God in the temple.

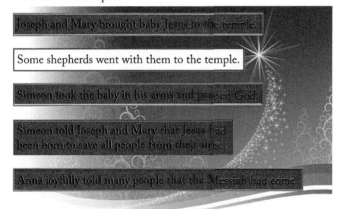

Joseph and Mary brought baby Jesus to the temple.

Some shepherds went with them to the temple.

Simeon took the baby in his arms and praised God.

Simeon told Joseph and Mary that Jesus had been born to save all people from their sins.

Anna joyfully told many people that the Messiah had come.

Read each story. Discuss the answers in class.

2. Ramón is tired of waiting to open his Christmas gifts. How can Ramón be like Simeon and wait patiently with a good attitude?
Answers will vary.

3. Pierre and Philippe celebrate Christmas in their home in Haiti. How can they be like Anna and share the good news of the Savior?
Answers will vary.

66

APPLICATION

- Have you ever had to wait for something for a long, long time? Was it easy to wait? (**Answers will vary.**)
- Simeon and Anna waited for a long time for God's promised Savior, the Messiah. They trusted God to keep His promise. How can you show that you trust God? (**I can take all my needs to Him in prayer and trust Him to provide for me.**)
- Simeon told Joseph and Mary that the Messiah would save all people from their sins. Think of someone to whom you can tell the wonderful news that Jesus came to save all people from their sins. (**Answers will vary.**)

REINFORCEMENT

The ancient Jews searched the Scriptures for hints that would reveal the identity of the Savior. The genealogies of the Old Testament were more than just a family tree; they were public records that were kept in the temple. Jesus' lineage proved that He was not only a descendant of Abraham, the father of the Israelite nation, but was also from the royal line of King David. Given the importance of genealogies in the Old Testament, it is interesting to note that there are no genealogies included in the New Testament except for those of Jesus. This fact emphasizes that Gentiles are grafted into the family of God by faith in Christ alone, not by their ancestry.

17.3 Christmas

Focus: The Wise Men

★ PREPARATION

Select "Christmas Joy/Joy to the World" from the music CDs. (*Introduction*)

Have a STAR ORNAMENT on hand. (*Introduction*)

EXTENSION

3A Provide each student with a ball of AIR-DRY CLAY to make a small nativity scene. Remind students that the wise men should not be included in the scene. The Bible explains that Jesus was not a tiny baby when the wise men came to worship Him; rather, He was a young child. Additionally, there may have been a whole caravan of wise men—not just three—who arrived in Jerusalem, because the king would not have been concerned with such a small group of travelers.

3B Cut out pictures from USED CHRISTMAS CARDS that depict various scenes from this week's lesson. Ask students to select their favorite card to use as an illustration for writing a sentence or two about that portion of the Christmas story. Assemble the pictures and written work into a booklet and cover it with heavy paper. Keep the book in your classroom library for students to reread the Christmas story.

Introduction ★

Worship the Lord by singing "Christmas Joy/Joy to the World" from the music CDs.

Display a STAR ORNAMENT. Ask students to tell some words that describe stars in the night sky. (**Possible answers: twinkling, glittering, sparkling**) Explain that a star is sometimes placed at the top of a Christmas tree because it is a reminder that God provided a special star to announce His Son's birth. Have students listen for how people received this news.

Directed Instruction

Share the following Bible truth from Matthew 1:18–2:15:

> God announced the birth of His Son to the world by placing a special star in the sky. Wise men from a faraway country saw the star and came to Jerusalem. They knew that this star announced the birth of a king, so they asked King Herod where the child could be found. King Herod talked to his helpers and told the wise men to go to Bethlehem. King Herod asked the wise men to send word when they had found the child. King Herod lied, saying he wanted to worship the young child. However, King Herod had no plan to worship Jesus; he wanted to kill Him.
>
> The star that they had seen in the east led the way to the house where the wise men saw Joseph, Mary, and the young child Jesus. The wise men gave the family gifts of gold, frankincense, and myrrh. Then God sent a dream to warn the wise men not to return to evil King Herod, so they returned to their country by a different way.
>
> An angel of the Lord appeared to Joseph in another dream and said, "Get up and take the young child and Mary and go to Egypt. Stay there until I tell you to leave because Herod will kill the young child if he finds Him. Joseph obeyed the angel of the Lord. Joseph, Mary, and Jesus stayed in Egypt until King Herod died.

Explain that God announced His Son's birth for the entire world to see! Ask students to share who came to look for the new king. (**wise men**) The wise men were intelligent men who were probably familiar with God's Word (from the Old Testament). They knew that a king would be born in Israel. When they noticed a bright star in the heavens, they understood that God's promise to send a savior was about to be fulfilled. They left their own country and traveled many, many miles, following the star.

The wise men stopped at King Herod's palace because they probably thought that the new king would be a son of King Herod. But wicked King Herod did not like the news that a new king had been born. He wanted to be the only king in Israel.

God's bright star came to rest over the house where Joseph, Mary, and Jesus lived. When the wise men arrived, they immediately bowed down before Jesus and presented Him with three very expensive gifts: gold, frankincense, and myrrh. These were the very best offerings that they had!

Student Page 17.3
Read the messages from angels and allow students to identify who received each message. Assist students in completing the page.

Review

- Who were the wise men? (**They were intelligent men who had studied the knowledge of the time and knew God's promise to send a savior.**)
- How did the wise men know where to find Jesus? (**God had placed a special star in the sky. They followed the star. When they arrived in Jerusalem, King Herod's helpers told them to go to Bethlehem because the Bible said the Messiah would be born there.**)
- Did the wise men return to King Herod? (**No.**) Why not? (**God warned them in a dream not to return to the evil king.**)
- How did Joseph know to take the young child and His mother, Mary, to Egypt? (**In a dream, an angel of the Lord told Joseph that Jesus was in danger.**)

DAY 3

Name ______________________________

Christmas **17.3**

Angels are God's messengers. Draw a line from each angel's message on the left to the person or people who received the message.

1. You will find the baby wrapped in cloths and lying in a manger. — shepherds

2. You will be the mother of the promised Savior. — Mary

3. Move your family to Egypt. — Joseph

Find the words that correctly complete each sentence. Connect the dots in the order of the sentences. Color the picture.

4. The wise men followed a ____.

5. The wise men brought ____.

6. The wise men worshipped ____.

7. The wise men were warned in a ____.

8. The wise men did not return to ____.

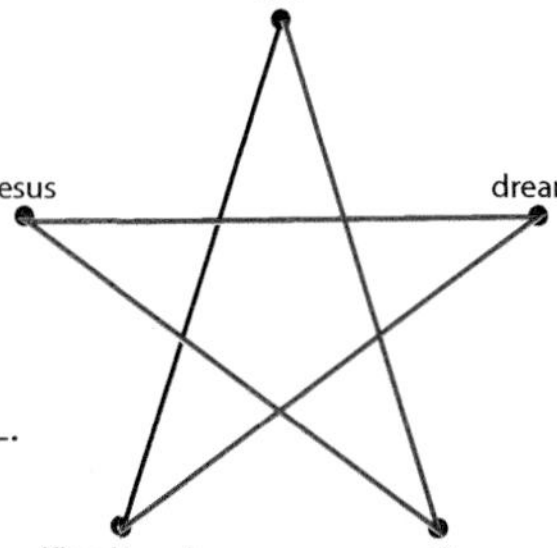

APPLICATION

- The wise men studied and knew the promises of God. How do you learn about God's promises? (**I can read the Bible; I can listen to others who can teach me about the Bible.**)
- When the wise men found the young child, they offered Him expensive gifts. What gifts can you offer the Lord? (**I can do my best work for Him; I can help others; I can obey my parents and others who have authority over me.**)
- The wise men worshipped Jesus as a king. How can your worship bring honor to your King? (**When I worship with a good attititude, I honor the Lord.**)

REINFORCEMENT

Frankincense and myrrh, two of the gifts presented to Jesus by the wise men, were rare and costly herbs. These gifts are significant for several reasons. They were both associated with healing, an attribute of the Messiah, who was foretold to be a healer in both the physical and spiritual sense (Ezekiel 34:16, Isaiah 61:1). Frankincense was used to make incense, an important element in Hebrew worship as it was to be constantly burnt before the Lord (Exodus 30:8). It was also used to relieve pain, anxiety, and fear. Myrrh was used extensively for embalming. Some myrrh also contained antiseptic and wound-healing properties. The gift of myrrh foreshadowed Jesus' sacrificial death and burial.

17.4 Christmas

Focus: The Greatest Gift

★ PREPARATION

Select "Christmas Joy/Joy to the World" from the music CDs. (*Introduction*)

Place a WRAPPED GIFT BOX somewhere in the classroom. (*Introduction*)

EXTENSION

4A Sing "Happy Birthday" to Jesus and celebrate with a BIRTHDAY CAKE. Remind students that when they go to a birthday party, the gifts are given to the one celebrating, not to the guests. Help students acknowledge that the true focus of the season should be on the Lord Jesus.

Introduction ★

Sing "Christmas Joy/Joy to the World" from the music CDs. Then, pretend to discover the WRAPPED GIFT BOX. Innocently ask various students if it is from them. Have students suggest what might be in the box. Tell students this reminds you of a story about two girls named *Kayla* and *Alyssa*.

Directed Instruction

Read the following story, emphasizing that it is fictional:

> Kayla had been looking through the toy catalog for weeks! In just three weeks it would be Christmas, and she had a long list of things that she really wanted. Kayla had reminded her mother a number of times recently that she had made her bed each morning without being asked and had done her homework as soon as she got home, so she thought she deserved the new computer game that just came out. Kayla's mother did not have much to say about Kayla's comments, so Kayla decided that some of the gifts already under the tree probably included the game that she wanted so much.
>
> Meanwhile, Kayla's friend, Alyssa, and Alyssa's father were shopping for Christmas presents, but these presents were not for family members. These gifts were for a mission project sponsored by their church. Church members bought toothbrushes, toys, socks, and colored pencils and packed them into brightly wrapped shoe boxes. A booklet about Jesus was added to the box and then the shoe boxes were shipped to children living in countries throughout the world!
>
> Alyssa had been saving some of her own money to buy a stuffed toy for herself, but she wanted to please Jesus by sharing some of her money with others. She asked her father if she could pay for several of the items to put into the shoe box. Alyssa's father was so proud of her!

Ask students if they noticed a difference between Kayla's and Alyssa's attitudes. (**Yes.**) How were the two girls different in the way they thought about gifts? (**Kayla thought about a gift that she wanted to receive; Alyssa thought about how she could give.**) Which girl was selfish and which girl was selfless? (**Kayla was selfish; Alyssa was selfless.**)

Ask students to recall the reaction of various people in the Bible to the arrival of the Savior. Choose a volunteer to tell who greeted the news of the Savior's birth with joy. (**Joseph, Mary, the shepherds, Simeon, Anna, and the wise men**) Why were they filled with joy? They understood that the greatest gift that could ever be given was Jesus! Jesus was the one who would free people from their terrible sins, so they would not be separated from God, and enable believers to go to heaven.

Ask students to tell the name of someone who was not pleased with the news. (**King Herod**) Explain that there were different responses to the good news of the Savior's birth. Some people received the news with great joy, but King Herod did not.

Explain that people today should receive God's gift of forgiveness of sins and eternal life with great joy! Invite students who would like to receive the gift of salvation to speak to you privately. Lead the class in a time of prayer.

Review

- What did Kayla want for Christmas? (**a computer game**) Why did Kayla think that she would get that gift? (**She felt that she deserved it.**)
- Why were Alyssa and her father shopping? (**They were looking for gifts to fill a shoe box that would be sent to a child somewhere in the world.**)
- Tell what Alyssa did because she wanted to please Jesus. (**She wanted to share from what she had and asked her father if she could buy some things for the shoe box with her own money.**)

Student Page 17.4

Read any difficult words on the page and allow students to complete the page independently. When all have finished, discuss student answers.

Notes:

DAY 4

17.4 *Christmas*

1. What gifts have you received from Jesus? Circle the words that tell about His gifts to you.

(eternal life) (joy) (peace) (hope) (His Word) (prayer) (forgiveness) (love)

2. What can you give back to the Lord? Circle the words that tell about gifts you can give to Him.

(praise) (worship) (a good attitude) (a heart filled with joy) (gifts for others with needs)

68

© Bible Grade 1

APPLICATION

- What is the greatest gift that you can ever receive? (**the gift of salvation—spending eternal life with Jesus**)
- How can you show your love for Jesus during this Christmas season? (**Answers will vary, but should include that I can give to others selflessly, worship Him, tell others about Him, and have a kind and loving attitude.**)
- An angel told the shepherds about Jesus' birth. The wise men followed a star to find their way to Jesus. How does God speak to you today? (**God speaks to me through the preaching, teaching, and reading of His Word, and when I worship, study the Bible, and pray.**)
- What do you think the world would be like if Jesus had not come, and people were separated from God forever? (**Answers will vary.**)

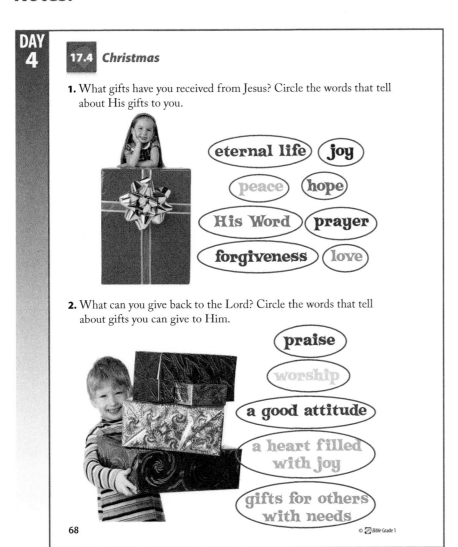

17.5 Christmas

Focus: Review and Assessment

★ PREPARATION

Select "Christmas Joy/Joy to the World" from the music CDs. (*Lesson Review*)

Select **VA 17A Jesus Is Born**. (*Lesson Review*)

Print a copy of **BLM 17D Lesson 17 Test** for each student. (*Directed Instruction*)

Lesson Review ★

Sing "Christmas Joy/Joy to the World" from the music CDs for a brief time of worship. Invite several students to share a favorite part of the Christmas story and why it is meaningful to them. Take time to celebrate Jesus' birthday with joyful songs of praise.

Use **VA 17A Jesus Is Born** to review the Bible truths in this lesson. Cover the following points:

- The angel Gabriel told Mary that God had chosen her to be the mother of God's Son.
- Joseph, Jesus' earthly father, was told to name the baby *Jesus*.
- Angels spoke to Joseph, Mary, and the shepherds.
- Joseph and Mary traveled to Bethlehem to be counted.
- God sent His Son to Earth to save people from their sins.
- An angel gave the good news to the shepherds and told them where to find the baby. Then, the sky became filled with many angels praising God.
- The shepherds left their sheep, found the baby, and worshipped Him. They told everyone about God's special gift.
- Joseph and Mary went to the temple to present Jesus to God.
- Two elderly people met Joseph and Mary. God had told Simeon and Anna that the baby Jesus was the Messiah, God's promised Savior.
- Simeon said that in God's plan, Jesus had come to forgive all people for their sins.
- Anna told everyone she saw that the Messiah had been born.
- One of God's special announcements of His Son's birth was a bright star.
- The wise men knew the promises of God. They followed the star to Jerusalem.
- King Herod tried to trick the wise men because he wanted to kill the new king, Jesus.
- The wise men followed the star to the house where the young child was staying. They presented gifts of gold, frankincense, and myrrh to Jesus.
- Joseph took Jesus and Mary to Egypt to escape from King Herod.
- Jesus' gift of salvation is the most valuable gift that anyone can ever receive.
- Worship, love, and a joyful heart are gifts that Christians should give to Jesus in response to what He has given them.

Directed Instruction ★

Give each student a copy of **BLM 17D Lesson 17 Test**. Read each question to the students and allow time for students to write their responses. Share correct answers when all have finished the test.

Notes:

Lesson Preparation

The Boyhood of Jesus

18.0

Expected Student Outcomes

KNOW

Young Jesus grows and pleases His Heavenly Father.

DO

Students will:

- unscramble sentences that describe ways to influence others by example
- solve a puzzle to discover where Jesus was found in Jerusalem
- differentiate between wise and unwise choices
- suggest wise choices that will please God

APPLY

Students will seek to do right according to God's standards.

Lesson Outline

I. Joseph's obedience (Mt 2:13–23)
  A. Escape from Herod
  B. Out of Egypt
II. Jesus' wise choices (Lk 2:39–52)
  A. Celebrating the Passover in Jerusalem
  B. Jesus is missing
  C. Jesus is found
III. Understanding wisdom
  A. Jesus' wisdom
  B. Knowledge or wisdom
IV. Grow in wisdom like Jesus
  A. Good choices please God

TEACHER'S HEART

Some days you probably encounter situations where you wish you had the gift of wisdom that God granted Solomon. Although that was a special blessing to the person who would build God's temple, the Bible doesn't say that the gift was only for one person. James 1:5–6 reminds Christians that God gives wisdom generously to all who ask Him in faith. By using the principles found in Scripture, you will be able to make wise decisions.

Wisdom can nurture relationships and help overcome relational problems. The world has answers, but they don't equal the answers that come from God's Word. Let today be the day that you seek God's wisdom with the faith that God can and will guide you. Acting on that wisdom may require courage and boldness. You may have to step out of your comfort zone and make some difficult decisions, but God will bless you for seeking His will!

This week will present challenges and opportunities to model righteous actions and reactions for your students. Just as your students will grow in wisdom and favor with God and men, you will be growing closer to God as you read His Word, meditate on it, and put its principles into practice.

MEMORY VERSE

Luke 2:52

MATERIALS

Day 1:
- VA 18A The Boyhood of Jesus
- Books about Egypt, globe (*Extension*)

Day 2:
- Suitcase
- VA 18A The Boyhood of Jesus
- BLM 18A Find Jesus Maze (*Extension*)

Day 3:
- BLM 18B Wisdom and Knowledge
- VA 18A The Boyhood of Jesus

Day 4:
- Measurement tools
- Balloons (*Extension*)

Day 5:
- VA 18A The Boyhood of Jesus
- BLM 18C Lesson 18 Test

TEACHER RESOURCES

Countryman, Jack. *God's Wisdom for Your Every Need*. Thomas Nelson, 2009.

God's Little Instruction Book for Teachers. Honor Books, 2003.

STUDENT RESOURCES

George, Elizabeth. *God's Wisdom for Little Girls: Virtues and Fun from Proverbs 31*. Harvest House Publishers, 2000.

George, Jim and Elizabeth. *God's Wisdom for Little Boys: Character-Building Fun from Proverbs*. Harvest House Publishers, 2002.

18.1 The Boyhood of Jesus

Focus: Joseph's Obedience

MEMORY VERSE

Luke 2:52

MEMORY WORK

- Write the Memory Verse on the board and read it together. Define the words *wisdom*, *stature*, and *favor*. *Wisdom* means *using what you know in the best way*. *Stature* means *height*, and *favor* means *being seen as good*. Explain that students will learn more about wisdom and favor later in this week's lesson. Remind students that Jesus grew in age and size just like any other child. To practice the Memory Verse, have students crouch down and slowly stand up (as if growing in height) as they say the verse.

★ PREPARATION

Select **VA 18A The Boyhood of Jesus**. (*Directed Instruction*)

EXTENSION

1A Provide several BOOKS ABOUT EGYPT, and show the location of Egypt on the GLOBE. Talk about some of the things students know about ancient Egypt. Explain that most of the people in Egypt today are not Christians. Take time to pray for the Christians and missionaries in Egypt.

Introduction

Ask students who rode in a car to school today to share something that they used to stay safe in the car. (**Answers will vary, but should include a car seat or a seat belt.**) Choose a volunteer to tell the class how a car seat or seat belt could protect a child from being hurt in an accident. (**If the car were to stop abruptly, the restraint would keep a child from hurtling forward, striking something in the car, or being thrown from the car.**) Explain that just as parents want to keep their children safe, God wanted to keep His Son safe too.

Directed Instruction ★

Display **VA 18A The Boyhood of Jesus** and explain that the boy pictured is Jesus. Like all children, He grew from a baby into a boy. During Jesus' boyhood, He fulfilled His Father's plan. Read the text on the back.

Review the account of the wise men's visit. Inform students that the wise men studied the discoveries and knowledge that had been written down at that time. They lived in a country some distance from Israel. The wise men had seen a bright star in the sky and knew that the star announced the birth of a new king in Israel, so they traveled to find the king. Expecting the king to be born in the palace, the wise men went to see Herod, the king of Israel. But King Herod did not have a new baby son. King Herod began to wonder who the new king might be. Then he began to get angry. He did not want any king in Israel except for himself!

Herod's anger caused him to want to kill all of the baby boys in the area around Jerusalem. Ask students why Herod wanted to do this. (**Possible answers: fear that one of them would take his throne, jealous that a baby would be king, worried that others might worship the new king instead of him**) God knew of Herod's evil plan and warned Joseph in a dream.

Joseph wanted to please God and protect young Jesus, so he took Mary and Jesus to Egypt. Because Joseph obeyed the dream that God gave him, Jesus was safe from King Herod. Herod's kingdom did not include Egypt, so he could not harm any of the baby boys in Egypt. Ask students what happened to allow the family to return to Israel. (**King Herod died.**) Inform students there were few ways that people living in Bible times could quickly learn about the news from other countries, so Joseph did not know that King Herod had died. An angel appeared to Joseph in another dream and told him it was safe to leave Egypt and to return to Israel.

Joseph and Mary left Egypt, but they did not return to Bethlehem where Jesus had been born. Instead, they went to the city of Nazareth, their hometown. God knew the plans He had for Jesus long before Jesus came down to the earth. Many years before Jesus was born, prophets had said that the Messiah, God's promised Savior, would come out of Egypt (Hosea 11:1), that Jewish women would weep for their children (Jeremiah 31:15), and that the Messiah would be from Nazareth in Galilee (Isaiah 9:1–2). Jesus fulfilled everything that was said about Him in the Bible.

Review

- How did Joseph know that God wanted him to leave Bethlehem after the wise men visited Jesus? (**God warned Joseph in a dream.**)
- Why did Joseph, Mary, and Jesus need to leave? (**King Herod wanted to kill Jesus.**)
- Where did the family go? (**to Egypt**)
- When did they know it was safe to return to Israel? (**when King Herod died and after another dream from God**)
- When the family left Egypt, where did they go? (**back to Israel, to Nazareth**)

Student Page 18.1

Complete the page together. It may be easier for students to unscramble the words if they write a small number above each word in the scrambled sentence to show the correct order. Guide students to write the words in the order that they have numbered them. Demonstrate by completing Exercise 1 on the board as an example.

DAY 1

Name ________________________________

The Boyhood of Jesus **18.1**

Joseph trusted God when he obeyed God's direction to take Jesus and Mary to Egypt.

How can you show others that you trust in God? Put each group of words in order to make a sentence. Write the sentence.

1. I kind. can be

I can be kind.

2. I tell can truth. the

I can tell the truth.

3. I read can Bible. my

I can read my Bible.

4. I pray for can others.

I can pray for others.

APPLICATION

- What might Joseph have thought when the angel told him to take Mary and Jesus to Egypt? (**Possible answers: Egypt is too far from home; I do not have a house in Egypt; I do not know when I can return to Israel.**)
- Why was it important for Joseph to obey the message that God sent in the dream? (**Answers will vary, but should include that Joseph's obedience kept Jesus safe.**)
- What choices have your parents made to keep your family safe? (**Answers will vary.**)
- Jesus may have been old enough to remember what it was like to move back to Israel. How do you think He felt about moving? (**Answers will vary, but should include that Jesus willingly obeyed His earthly parents.**)

REINFORCEMENT

The journey from Bethlehem to Egypt would have been a distance of about 45 miles. Jesus' family would not have been the only Jews in Egypt. Many Jews had fled to Egypt during the time of Jeremiah and had built a temple in this foreign land. Herod's territory extended only to the border of Egypt. The exact amount of time that young Jesus lived in Egypt is not clear, but the best estimates are from two to four years.

18.2 The Boyhood of Jesus

Focus: Jesus' Wise Choices

★ PREPARATION

Bring in a SUITCASE. (*Introduction, Directed Instruction*)

Select **VA 18A The Boyhood of Jesus**. (*Directed Instruction*)

EXTENSION

2A Make a copy of **BLM 18A Find Jesus Maze** for each student. Discuss the fact that Jesus was able to be calm and happy because He knew that being in the temple was pleasing God. Allow time for students to trace through the maze and color the picture.

Introduction ★

Bring out the SUITCASE. Have students share reasons why someone would use a suitcase. (**Possible answers: going on a trip, vacation, moving**) Explain that each year the Jewish people who lived away from Jerusalem would travel to Jerusalem for some of the important Jewish celebrations. Remind students that the Jewish people were the Hebrews' children, grandchildren, great-grandchildren, and so on.

Directed Instruction ★

Choose a volunteer to hold **VA 18A The Boyhood of Jesus**. Choose another volunteer to take the suitcase. Slowly read **Luke 2:39–52** to the class. Tell the volunteer that each time you come to a word that indicates movement, such as *went*, *returned*, *traveled*, he or she should gently move the suitcase. This will help emphasize the long walk from Nazareth to Jerusalem. After reading the passage, thank your volunteer and set the suitcase aside while you continue the lesson.

Explain that the Feast of the Passover was the meal that celebrated how death passed over the Hebrews' homes. Ask the students to recount who restored the celebration of the Passover in Israel. (**King Josiah did. He learned about the celebration when the Book of the Law was found in the temple.**) The Jews celebrated the Passover by going to the city of Jerusalem. Invite students to tell about some trips they have taken to celebrate important events such as Christmas, Easter, weddings, anniversaries, births, graduations, or birthdays.

The journey from Nazareth to Jerusalem probably would have taken three days. Ask the students what things Jesus might have taken on the journey and how they would have been carried. (**Extra clothing and food may have been carried in a pack or tied to a donkey.**) Since the town of Nazareth had many Jewish people living there, a crowd of people probably traveled together. Encourage students to imagine taking a long walking trip with hundreds of their neighbors and relatives.

After the Passover was finished, the large group traveled back to Nazareth. Jesus' parents discovered that He was missing. Ask students how it could be that Joseph and Mary traveled for a day without realizing Jesus was missing. (**The group traveling home was large, so Joseph and Mary might have thought that Jesus was walking home with another relative or a friend.**) Allow time for students to talk about any personal experience of being left behind somewhere. Ask students to share how they felt while they waited to be reunited.

Joseph and Mary returned to Jerusalem to look for Jesus. They may have worried about finding Him in the city. But Jesus did not worry because He knew God's plan for His life. He wisely chose to spend time in God's house, the temple, talking with the religious teachers. He also made another wise decision to return home with Joseph and Mary.

Review

- How old was Jesus when He traveled to Jerusalem with Joseph and Mary? **(He was 12 years old.)**
- Why did the family go to Jerusalem? **(They celebrated the Feast of the Passover.)**
- Why did Jewish people celebrate the Passover? **(They wanted to remember and celebrate what God had done to deliver them from slavery in Egypt.)**
- When did Joseph and Mary discover Jesus was missing? **(It was at the end of the first day of the walk back home to Nazareth.)**
- How did they react when they could not find Jesus? **(They were worried and headed back to Jerusalem to look for Him.)**

Student Page 18.2

Read the directions for the first exercise. Tell students the letters they find in the puzzle will fill in the blanks of the sentence. Have students complete the rest of the page.

DAY 2

18.2 *The Boyhood of Jesus*

1. How old was Jesus when He went to Jerusalem? Choose the number that tells Jesus' age. Look in the puzzle for that number. Each time you see that number, circle the letter below it. Then, write the correct letters in order on the blank lines below.

10	8	11	6	12	4	9	12	7	10
X	N	A	O	(T)	R	S	(E)	W	Y
5	12	9	8	10	12	4	11	7	13
U	(M)	Z	I	K	(P)	B	J	C	E
6	8	10	12	11	9	7	5	4	12
D	S	A	(L)	R	N	O	T	V	(E)

Joseph and Mary found Jesus in the t e m p l e.

2. Draw a picture of Jesus talking to the religious teachers in the temple.

Drawings will vary.

70 © Bible Grade 1

APPLICATION

- How do you think Jesus' parents felt when they realized Jesus was missing? **(Answers will vary, but should include that they may have felt worried or scared, but still trusted God.)**
- Do you think Jesus was scared when He realized that Joseph and Mary had left for home without Him? Why or why not? **(Answers will vary, but should include that as God's Son, Jesus knew God's plan and was assured of God's protection.)**
- Jesus and the Jewish people celebrated Passover to remember what God had done. How do you remember the ways God has helped you and your family? **(Answers will vary, but should include praying often, and thanking God and mentioning the things that He has done to help me and my family.)**

REINFORCEMENT

Both Joseph and Mary may have gone to Jerusalem annually to celebrate the Passover. According to Jewish tradition, the men were obliged to attend three Jewish feasts each year: the Feast of the Passover, the Feast of Pentecost, and the Feast of Tabernacles (Deuteronomy 16:16). For Jewish women, attendance was voluntary, so Mary set a good example of devotion to God by attending. The trip from Nazareth to Jerusalem was about 60 miles, at least a three-day walk.

18.3 The Boyhood of Jesus

Focus: Understanding Wisdom

★ PREPARATION

Print **BLM 18B Wisdom and Knowledge**. Cut the cards apart. (*Introduction*)

Select **VA 18A The Boyhood of Jesus**. (*Directed Instruction*)

EXTENSION

3A Play the game Simon Says, substituting the words *Wisdom Says* as you name wise things to do and simple actions. For example, say, "Wisdom says, 'If you listened to the Bible truth today, put your hands on your head.'" Have students who listened to the Bible truth put their hands on their head. Randomly name some unwise things, but do not start with the words "Wisdom Says." For example, say, "If you did not do your chores today, clap your hands." Students should only do the actions connected with the wise choices.

3B Ask parent volunteers to come and help lead prayer centers for some of the people who help students grow spiritually, such as pastors, parents, and Bible teachers. A prayer center can be simple; a student desk and a few chairs will suffice. Talk with your parent volunteers ahead of time to determine the person to pray for at each center. Invite students to go in small groups to the different prayer centers and pray.

Introduction ★

Choose six volunteers. Write the words *wisdom* and *knowledge* on the board and direct the students to read them together. Explain that knowledge comes from studying and learning about a certain topic. Knowledge is used to make wise choices. Godly wisdom involves using knowledge to follow God's ways. For example, knowing how to read is knowledge, but choosing to read the Bible shows godly wisdom. Hold the cards that you made from **BLM 18B Wisdom and Knowledge**. Read each scenario to one of the volunteers. Ask each volunteer if the situation demonstrates using knowledge in a wise or unwise way. Discuss answers.

Directed Instruction ★

Show **VA 18A The Boyhood of Jesus** to the class. Review the Bible truth by asking students what is happening in the picture and why. Conclude that Jesus was found in the temple, exactly the best place for Him to be learning and talking about God. Jesus knew that part of His mission was to fulfill God's plan and grow in wisdom.

One way that Jesus grew in wisdom was by spending time in God's house, the temple. When He became separated from Joseph and Mary, Jesus did not waste the time. Instead, He spent time in the temple and talked to the religious teachers. Jesus listened to them and asked them questions.

Invite students to suggest some questions that they would ask if they were sitting in the temple with the religious teachers. (**Answers will vary.**) Jesus gave some amazing answers that showed He understood about God. Ask students if they have ever surprised adults with something they knew or could do well. (**Answers will vary.**)

Jesus also showed wisdom by being obedient to His parents and returning home with them. He might have wanted to stay and talk with the religious teachers, but Jesus made the wise choice to go with His parents. Ask the students why Jesus might have wanted to stay in Jerusalem. (**Possible answers: to talk with the religious teachers some more, to read some of the scrolls, to stay in a big city**)

Turn in your Bible to **Deuteronomy 5:16** and read the verse aloud. Explain that Jesus had knowledge of how God's Word tells children to act toward their parents. Jesus took the knowledge He learned from the Scriptures and wisely applied it to His situation. Jesus obeyed the fifth commandment, just as children today should do. When Jesus' parents were ready to leave for Nazareth again, He went with them.

Some people have a lot of knowledge that comes from learning many facts. Wisdom is different from having knowledge or being smart. People who have wisdom are able to use their experiences and things they have learned from the Bible to make decisions about what is right or wrong. Really smart people don't always make wise choices, and some people who don't seem smart can show a lot of wisdom.

Review

- Where did Mary and Joseph find Jesus? (**in the temple in Jerusalem**)
- What was Jesus doing in the temple? (**spending time with the teachers, listening to them, asking them questions, giving amazing answers**)
- Why did Jesus finally leave Jerusalem? (**He obeyed His parents and went home with them.**)
- What wise choices did Jesus make when He was in Jerusalem? (**He talked with the religious teachers; He spent time in the temple; and He went home when His parents returned to get Him.**)

Student Page 18.3

Read the statements and have students differentiate between wise and unwise choices. As you complete the page together, ask students to suggest ways to turn the unwise choices into wise choices.

APPLICATION

- Jesus was listening to the religious teachers and asking them questions. If you could choose a godly person to question, who would it be? Why? (**Answers will vary.**)
- What wise choice have you made today? (**Answers will vary.**)
- Would you rather have knowledge or wisdom? Why? (**Answers will vary.**)

Notes:

DAY 3

Name ______________________________

The Boyhood of Jesus 18.3

Jesus made wise choices, and you can too! Decide if each sentence shows a wise or unwise choice. Check the correct box.

	Wise	Unwise
1. Listen to your teachers.	✓	
2. Talk during someone's prayer.		✓
3. Obey your parents.	✓	
4. Push your friend.		✓
5. Tell a lie.		✓
6. Go to church.	✓	
7. Study God's Word.	✓	

18.4 The Boyhood of Jesus

Focus: Grow in Wisdom Like Jesus

★ PREPARATION

Bring in a variety of MEASUREMENT TOOLS, such as a ruler, a measuring cup, a scale, a compass, a meterstick, or a stopwatch. (*Introduction*)

Tape masking tape across the floor of the classroom to use as a measurement line. Write the number zero at one end of the masking tape and the number 10 at the other end. Write intermediate numbers on the tape at the appropriate intervals. (*Directed Instruction*)

EXTENSION

4A Bring in THREE BALLOONS. Write each of the following words on a separate piece of paper: *wisdom, stature, favor.* Place one piece of paper in each balloon. Blow up the balloons and tie them closed. Use this game to reinforce the three areas in which Jesus showed growth. Have the class stand in a large circle. Give one balloon to a student and have the balloon passed around the circle while the class repeats the Memory Verse. At the end of the verse, the student holding the balloon pops it and reads one of the words that tells how Jesus grew.

Introduction ★

Have a volunteer choose one of the MEASUREMENT TOOLS. Ask the volunteer what type of things could be measured using that tool. For example, a ruler can measure length, a measuring cup can measure liquids or powders used for baking, and a stopwatch measures time. Choose additional volunteers and continue in the same manner.

After you have talked about the types of measurement tools that you brought, ask students to tell why people measure things. (**Measurements help people to accurately tell the size, weight, quantity, or amount of various things.**) All measurement involves comparison to a standard. Guide students to see that the best tool to measure something depends upon what is being measured; a measuring cup will help to measure a quantity of sugar, but a ruler will not help at all.

Directed Instruction ★

Read **Luke 2:51–52**. Ask students to name the three areas in which Jesus grew. (**wisdom, stature, favor**) Review what the students learned about the wisdom Jesus showed. (**He spoke with the religious teachers, asked questions, and amazed the teachers.**)

Discuss how as children grow in age, they will also grow in size. Help students estimate the size that Jesus might have been when He was 12 years old—the age of a sixth or seventh grade student today. Let students guess how tall they might grow to be. Remind students that they have no control over the size that they will grow to be, but they do have control over the wisdom that they use and the way they grow in their relationships.

Remind students that favor is being seen as good. Talk about how making right choices will help build good relationships with God and others. Jesus' relationship with God grew by being in the temple, talking with religious teachers, and studying the scrolls containing God's Word. His relationship with others grew by interacting maturely with religious teachers and obeying His parents by going home with them.

Hold up your Bible. Explain that God gave students the perfect way to measure things in their lives—the Bible. Jesus knew the Scriptures, and He made choices based on the principles in God's Word.

Read the following actions and let the students stand on the tape to rate their answers on a scale of zero to ten, where zero is very foolish and ten is very wise. (**If you have a large class, you may need to make two lines at opposite ends of the room.**) Choose volunteers to tell why they rated each answer as they did.

- acting kindly toward someone who was mean to you
- doing your best on your schoolwork
- choosing good things for your eyes to see
- serving others
- spending time in Bible study and prayer

Conclude by reminding students that the Bible provides Christians with the standard for making wise choices. As students grow in faith and the knowledge of God's Word, they will grow in wisdom as well.

Review

- How did Jesus grow in His relationships? (**He pleased both His heavenly Father and His earthly parents.**)
- What guide did God give Christians to help them make wise choices? (**the Bible**)
- How can you use the Bible as a good measurement for your life? (**I can read my Bible to be sure that I am doing what is right in God's eyes.**)

Student Page 18.4

Read each exercise with students and have them fill in the circle that shows a wise choice. When all have completed the page, ask students to share additional wise choices that they might make if they found themselves in similar situations.

APPLICATION

- How did Jesus show that He grew in wisdom? (**Answers will vary, but should include that Jesus obeyed His earthly parents and talked with religious teachers.**)
- How did Jesus show that He grew in favor with God and men? (**Answers will vary, but should include that the religious teachers were amazed by Him and He spent time in the temple, focusing on God.**)
- What choices have you made that will please God? (**Answers will vary.**)
- How can you help your relationship with God grow? (**Answers will vary, but should include reading the Bible, spending time in prayer, and learning from godly leaders.**)

DAY 4

18.4 *The Boyhood of Jesus*

Fill in the circle in front of the wise choice.

1. At the park, a little boy tried to take Simon's ball. What should Simon do?

- ○ He should push the boy and tell him not to take the ball.
- ● He should ask the boy to join him in a game.
- ○ He should get mad and go home.

2. LaShondra is not supposed to use her mom's phone, but she wants to play with it. What should LaShondra do?

- ○ She should make a phone call.
- ● She should leave her mom's phone alone.
- ○ She should play a game on the phone.

3. David and Kami watched TV, but the show started to use bad language. What should they do?

- ● They should turn off the television and play a game.
- ○ They should watch the show until it is over.
- ○ They should watch the show but say "beep" at the bad words.

72 © Bible Grade 1

18.5 The Boyhood of Jesus

Focus: Review and Assessment

★ *PREPARATION*

Select **VA 18A The Boyhood of Jesus**. (*Lesson Review*)

Make one copy of **BLM 18C Lesson 18 Test** for each student. (*Directed Instruction*)

Lesson Review ★

Use **VA 18A The Boyhood of Jesus** to review the Bible truths in this lesson. Cover the following concepts:

- Because the wise men told King Herod they had seen a sign that meant a new king had been born, Herod became angry.
- God sent a dream to Joseph and directed him to take Mary and Jesus to Egypt because King Herod wanted to kill all the baby boys living in the area around Jerusalem.
- After King Herod died, God sent another dream to let Joseph know that it was safe for Jesus to leave Egypt.
- Joseph, Mary, and Jesus moved to the town of Nazareth.
- When Jesus was 12 years old, He went with His parents to Jerusalem to celebrate the Feast of the Passover. This was a very special occasion that occurred each year. Jews traveled to Jerusalem for the celebration.
- The journey from Nazareth to Jerusalem would have taken about three days to walk.
- After the Passover celebration had ended, the group started to walk home. At the end of the first day's walk, Joseph and Mary realized that Jesus was not with the group.
- Joseph and Mary returned to Jerusalem to look for Jesus.
- Joseph and Mary found Jesus in the temple.
- Jesus was busy listening to the religious teachers in the temple and asking them questions.
- At first, the religious teachers thought that Jesus was just an ordinary boy, but they were amazed at Jesus' understanding and wisdom.
- Jesus reminded Mary that He was God's Son, and He would be where His Father would want Him to be.
- Jesus obeyed His earthly parents and went home with them.
- Jesus grew in wisdom, stature, and favor with God and men.
- Jesus showed wisdom as He talked with the religious teachers and in His choice to obey His earthly parents when it was time to leave with them.
- Jesus showed that He grew in His relationship with God by spending time in the temple talking about God.
- The Bible is God's tool to determine if a choice is wise or unwise.
- When Christians make wise choices based on the Bible, God is pleased.

Directed Instruction ★

Give each student a copy of **BLM 18C Lesson 18 Test**. Read the text to the class. Allow time for students to write the correct word on the blank. Emphasize copying the word correctly, including capitalization. After all of the students have completed the test, review the correct answers.

Notes:

Expected Student Outcomes

KNOW
God speaks to people through His Word.

DO
Students will:
- match phrases to review the Bible truth and find a word in a hidden picture that describes God's Word
- circle and write words to complete sentences about God's Word
- listen to Scripture verses and restate the importance of believing in God, treasuring His Word, loving Him, and obeying Him
- write their Memory Verse

APPLY
Students will express that God's Word is inspired, true, profitable, and eternal. They will acknowledge that knowing God's Word leads to growth in faith.

Lesson Outline
I. Jesus reads Scripture (Lk 4:16–22)
II. Attributes of God's Word
  A. True (1 Kings 17:24; Jn 1:17, 17:17; Ps 33:4, 119:160)
  B. Inspired and profitable (2 Tim 3:16–17, 2 Pet 1:21)
  C. Eternal (Heb 13:7–8)
III. God's provision through His Word
  A. Guidance (Ps 119:105)
  B. Promise of eternal life (1 Jn 5:13)
IV. The importance of memorization (Ps 119:11)

TEACHER'S HEART
Why not be the source of someone's encouragement this week? You will find that you will be encouraged as well. As you study this week's lesson, write a verse and the principle it teaches on a colorful piece of 3" × 5" paper. Add a note, such as "Isn't it nice to know that God's Word is true?" Slip it into someone's message box, post it on the bulletin board in the teacher's lounge, or put it on another teacher's desk. You may want to add an apple or other treat with the note. For example, consider taping a piece of candy to the paper and include the message, "Here is a sweet treat from God's Word for you today. His promises are eternal." Or, use a faster method by e-mailing or instant messaging your thoughts. Add emoticons for flair. Be someone's encourager. The rewards will be wonderful for both you and the other person.

MEMORY VERSE
Psalm 119:11

MATERIALS
Day 1:
- Gift bag, tissue paper
- VA 19A Jesus Reads God's Word
- PP-4 The Bible *(Extension)*

Day 2:
- Unwrapped Bible from Lesson 19.1
- BLM 19A Bible Template (*Extension*)

Day 3:
- BLM 19B God's Guidance (*Extension*)

Day 4:
- Index cards
- Treasure chest or box (*Extension*)

Day 5:
- VA 19A Jesus Reads God's Word
- BLM 19C Lesson 19 Test

SONGS
The Bible

TEACHER RESOURCES
Addington, Gordon. *Discovering the Bible: Your Daily Bible Reading Companion*. NavPress, 2010.
The One Minute Bible Day by Day: A Year of Readings. B&H Publishing Group, 2009.

STUDENT RESOURCES
ESV Seek and Find Bible. Crossway Books, 2010.
Reeves, Eira. *Day by Day Bible: Daily Devotions for Reading with Children*. Hendrickson Publishers, 2005.

19.1 God's Written Word

Focus: Jesus Reads Scripture

MEMORY VERSE

Psalm 119:11

MEMORY WORK

- Choose volunteers to hide the copies of the Memory Verse in the classroom while the rest of the students cover their eyes. Invite students to look for the hidden strips of paper and read the verse when they find each strip. Then write the verse on the board and read it chorally.

PREPARATION

Cut a sheet of paper into five strips and write the Memory Verse on each strip. (*Memory Work*)

Inside a colorful GIFT BAG place a Bible wrapped in TISSUE PAPER. (*Introduction*)

Select **VA 19A Jesus Reads God's Word**. (*Directed Instruction*)

EXTENSION

1A If you have a red-letter edition of the Bible, show the words that Jesus spoke. Emphasize that Jesus taught the way to be joyful in this life.

1B Display **PP-4 The Bible** to reinforce the lesson.

Introduction ★

Display the prepared GIFT BAG that contains the Bible wrapped in TISSUE PAPER. Build suspense and excitement about what the gift could be. Have a volunteer carefully unwrap the present to find the Bible inside. Tell the volunteer to show the Bible to the class.

Explain that the Bible is a special gift from God. It is His Word, written for all people. Let students know that God inspired the writers of the Bible to know what to write. Inspired means that God guided the thoughts of the writers. They were led by Him to include the accounts of what happened and what was said. They wrote down the events of the past, the present, and what God said would happen in the future. Remind students that God's Word helps them to know Him and to know what to do in all kinds of situations. Relate how John, one of Jesus' disciples, said that Jesus did so many things during His time on the earth that the world itself could not contain all the books that could be written about what He did (John 21:25).

Directed Instruction ★

Have students open their Bible to the beginning of the New Testament. Remind them of some of the differences between the Old Testament and the New Testament. For example, share that the Old Testament contains the lessons they have studied earlier this year. It tells of the creation of the heavens and the earth; the creation and fall of mankind; Noah and the ark; Abraham, Isaac, and Jacob; and various prophets and kings. It records how God related to man before Jesus was born. Describe how the New Testament tells about Jesus' birth and work on the earth, and also God's work in His Church and future events. It also relates what heaven is like. Most important, the New Testament shows that when people place their trust in Jesus, they are no longer separated from God. Emphasize again that it is very important to study what is in the Bible to learn who God is, how He loves people, and the plans He has for everyone.

Inform students that Jesus read and knew God's Word. Display **VA 19A Jesus Reads God's Word**. Point out the scroll—long pieces of paper that were rolled up to make a type of book. Remind students that Hilkiah, the priest, had found a scroll containing the Book of the Law in the temple many years before. Explain that, in the picture, Jesus is in the synagogue, a building in which Jewish people worshipped God. Explain that since God knows everything, He talked about Jesus in the Old Testament before Jesus was even born. Read the Bible truth from the back of VA 19A.

Review

- Where did Jesus go to worship and to read the Scripture? (**to the synagogue**)
- What book in the Bible was Jesus reading from? (**Isaiah**)
- Who was Jesus reading about? (**Himself, the coming Messiah**)
- Why did the people not believe Jesus? (**They were unwilling to believe Jesus was the Messiah.**)

Student Page 19.1

Read the directions and the text on the page. Have students complete the page. Encourage students to use a colored pencil to color the hidden picture.

Notes:

DAY 1

Name ______________________________

God's Written Word **19.1**

Draw a line that connects the beginning of each sentence to its correct ending.

1. Jesus went to the • • book of Isaiah.

2. He stood up • • synagogue to worship.

3. He read from the • • because it is true.

4. Jesus told the people that He • • to read.

5. I can believe the Bible • • was reading about Himself.

Use a blue crayon or marker to color all the shapes that have a dot. Write the hidden word to complete the sentence.

6. God's Word is ______truth______.

in blue

APPLICATION

- Why is the Bible such a special gift? (**It is God's Word that is written for everyone so that all can know Him.**)
- How can you learn more about God? (**by reading His Word**)

REINFORCEMENT

Prison Fellowship's founder Chuck Colson is an influential Christian leader in evangelical circles today. However, Colson's early life was not characterized by devotion to Christ. In fact, it was quite the opposite. In the 1970s, Colson served under President Richard Nixon as one of his top advisors. Colson gained a reputation as a "tough guy," a ruthless man who would do practically anything to ensure the success of the Nixon administration. However, in 1973, Colson's involvement in obstruction of justice brought him to a low point in life.

A friend advised Colson to seek the Lord, and Colson did just that. After reading *Mere Christianity* by C. S. Lewis, Colson came to faith in Christ and began studying the Bible. Following his conversion, he served a prison term for his crime, but left prison with a new passion—to help those behind bars to come to know Christ. Since that time, Colson has written numerous books, appeared on television, spoken on radio programs, and started many programs to assist prison inmates and their families.

19.2 God's Written Word

Focus: Attributes of God's Word

★ PREPARATION

Reuse the unwrapped Bible from Lesson 19.1. (*Introduction*)

EXTENSION

2A Have students write an encouraging note to someone at the school, such as the principal, teacher, secretary, maintenance or lunchroom worker, or another student. Provide construction paper to all students to write their notes on. Tell them to include a special Scripture verse in their notes. When the notes are finished, assist the students in delivering the notes. Remind students that they are doing what a Christian should when they are sharing Bible verses with others.

2B Make a copy of **BLM 19A Bible Template** for each student. Have students write this week's Memory Verse on the writing lines. Instruct students to cut out the Bible shape and then glue it to a piece of construction paper. When the glue is dry, assist students in folding the construction paper in half to make a folder resembling a Bible.

Introduction ★

Hold up the unwrapped Bible that you used in Lesson 19.1. Ask students to describe its color, size, and shape. Explain that they have just described what they can see and feel about the book; however, there are other things about God's Word they can know.

Directed Instruction

Tell students to listen as you read the following fictional story aloud to find out other ways to describe the Bible:

> Kylie hugged a tattered copy of the Bible close to her heart. Today was sharing day in Mrs. Johnson's first-grade class. Kylie was hoping to be able to share the Bible and a very special letter that she kept inside.
>
> Mrs. Johnson called Kylie to the front of the room to share. "This was my great-grandmother Mimi's Bible," Kylie explained to the class as she held up the Bible. "She got it when she was just a little girl, so it is about 100 years old now. Great-grandmother Mimi went to heaven when I was just a baby. Before she went to heaven, she gave the Bible to my mom to keep for me. It had a letter inside. Now that I am in first grade, I can read the Bible and the letter." Kylie read this letter to the class:
>
> *Dear Kylie,*
>
> *This was my Bible when I was just a little girl. I read the whole Bible and memorized many of the verses. I learned to know and trust Jesus as my Lord and Savior because of the words that I read in my Bible. Do you know that the Bible is God's letter to you, written down by many people? His words are true. I have followed God's Word, the Bible, all my life, and God has given me many blessings. One of my blessings is you, Kylie. I want you to know God just as I do. God will speak to you as you read His Word. Don't forget to spend time reading your Bible every day.*
>
> *Your loving great-grandmother,*
> *Mimi*

Remind students of the words they used earlier to describe the Bible, such as those describing its color, size, and shape. Kylie's great-grandmother described it in other ways. Explain her descriptions as follows:

1. The Bible is God's letter to people.
2. The Bible is true because God said it.
3. The Bible brings blessings when God's instructions in it are followed.

Tell students that just as Kylie's great-grandmother spoke to her through a letter, God speaks to people through the Bible. His Word lasts forever!

Review

- What did Kylie bring to show her class? (**a Bible**) Why was it special? (**It had belonged to her great-grandmother Mimi.**)
- Why did Kylie's great-grandmother want her to read the Bible? (**Answers will vary, but should include that she wanted Kylie to know God by reading His Word.**)
- Is God's Word true or make-believe? (**true**) How long will God's Word last? (**forever**)
- Who told the writers of the Bible what to write? (**God**)
- How does reading God's Word help you? (**It helps me to know God.**)

Student Page 19.2

Read the directions and the text on the page. Have students complete the page.

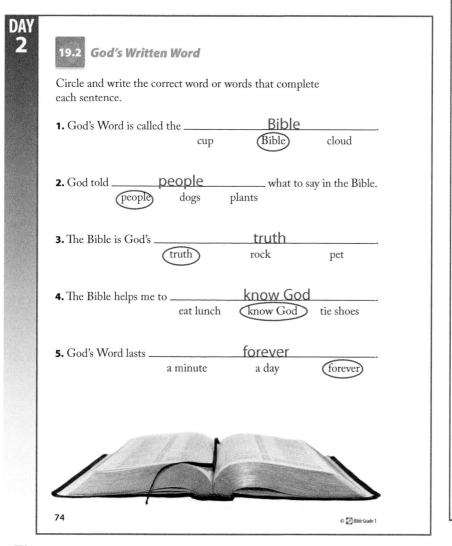

Notes:

DAY 2

19.2 ***God's Written Word***

Circle and write the correct word or words that complete each sentence.

1. God's Word is called the ___Bible___.
cup (Bible) cloud

2. God told ___people___ what to say in the Bible.
(people) dogs plants

3. The Bible is God's ___truth___.
(truth) rock pet

4. The Bible helps me to ___know God___.
eat lunch (know God) tie shoes

5. God's Word lasts ___forever___.
a minute a day (forever)

74

© Bible Grade 1

APPLICATION

- The Bible was very important to Great-grandmother Mimi. Is your Bible important to you? Why? (**Answers will vary.**)
- Since God's Word was true 100 years ago, will it still be true 100 years from now? (**Yes.**)
- Share some ways your Bible is different from other books. (**Answers will vary, but should include that the Bible is true, inspired by God, profitable, and it lasts forever.**)

REINFORCEMENT

Bible students today will find a number of English versions of the Bible available to aid in their study of God's Word. One of the oldest versions is the King James Version (KJV). This translation was authorized by King James I of England. The translation work was accomplished from 1604 to 1611. The KJV became the standard Bible for English-speaking Protestants. The prose of the KJV has influenced much of English literature over the past 300 years. As language and culture changed, some scholars sensed the need for more up-to-date language. The New King James Version was commissioned in 1975. Respected Bible scholars, church leaders, and lay Christians worked to produce this new translation of the Bible that would maintain the beauty of the language used in the original KJV.

The New International Version (NIV) is an original translation not based on previous English translations, but developed by over 100 scholars working from the best existing Hebrew, Aramaic, and Greek texts. The goal of the translators of the NIV Bible was to provide accuracy in contemporary language.

19.3 God's Written Word

Focus: God's Provision Through His Word

★ PREPARATION

Select seven pieces of colored construction paper. Tear the edges of the paper to make stepping-stones. Write each of the following words on a separate stepping-stone: *God's, Word, guides, me, down, apple, eight.* Tape each stepping-stone to the floor so that students can step easily from *God's* to *Word* to *guides* to *me*. Randomly place the additional words nearby. (*Introduction*)

EXTENSION

3A Ask a librarian to provide a large selection of **BIBLE STORYBOOKS** written at a comfortable reading level for your students. Plan a trip to the library. Students will enjoy sharing these books and reading them independently. Allow each student to select a book and practice reading it. Lead the students in a discussion about how wonderful it is that they can read. Be sure to remind them that now that they can read God's Word all by themselves, they should do so daily.

3B Make a copy of **BLM 19B God's Guidance** for each student. Have students complete the page to reinforce their understanding of what God's Word teaches them.

Introduction ★

Invite students to play a game to reinforce that God's Word provides guidance. Divide the class into groups of four. Stand facing the prepared stepping-stones and direct one group to form a single line behind you. Say "God's Word guides me" as you step on the paper stones that form that sentence. Tell students to say each word as they step on it. Remind them not to step on the words that are not in the sentence. Give each group of four a turn. Explain that they will be learning about how God's Word guides them.

Directed Instruction

Remind students that Jesus provided an example for Christians to follow when He read the Scripture in the synagogue. Christians should read or listen to the Bible as a part of their daily time with the Lord.

Student Page 19.3

Read **John 3:16** and explain that the Bible guides people to *believe* in God's Son, Jesus, so that they will have eternal life. Direct students' attention to the first row and have them lightly color the correct stone. Have them circle the letter above the stone.

Read **Psalm 119:11** and explain that the Bible guides people to *hide* and *treasure* God's Word by learning and obeying what it says so that they will not sin against God. Direct students' attention to the second row. Tell them to lightly color the two stones that state what God guides them to do. Have them circle the letters above the two stones. Next, have them draw a line from the stone colored in Exercise 1 to the first of these stones. Then, have them draw a line to connect the two selected stones in the second row.

Read **James 2:8** and explain that the Bible guides people to *love* others, regardless of how unkind others may be. Direct students' attention to the third row of stepping-stones. Tell them to lightly color the stone that states what God guides them to do according to this Scripture. Have them circle the letter above the stone. Next, have them draw a line from the second stone colored in Exercise 2 to this stone.

Read **Ephesians 6:1** and explain that the Bible guides children to *obey* their parents. Direct students' attention to the fourth row of stepping-stones on their page. Tell them to lightly color the stone that states what God guides them to do in this passage. Have students circle the letter above the stone. Then have them draw a line from the stone colored in Exercise 3 to this stone.

Emphasize the key points of the activity—to believe in Jesus for eternal life, to hide and treasure God's Word, to love God and others, and to obey God and parents. Tell students to look at their colored stones, line by line. Have them write the circled letters in order to answer Exercise 5. Discuss with students how hiding and treasuring God's Word in their minds and hearts help them to know, believe, and obey Him.

Remind students that God knows everything. Reinforce that following God's Word provides guidance in their life and promise of eternal life. Direct students to complete the page.

Review

- Why did God give you His Word? (**to help me to know Him, to guide me, to keep me from sin**)
- What does it mean to hide and treasure God's Word? (**read it, memorize it, do what it says, value it above anything else**)
- What does the Bible promise to those who believe and accept what it says? (**eternal life**)

Notes:

APPLICATION

- The Bible teaches you to love others. Does that mean you must love those who are unkind to you? (**Yes, I must. Just because someone mistreated me does not mean that I should mistreat him or her.**)
- Why is it important to follow God's Word? (**I follow God's Word because God loves me and knows what is best for me.**)

DAY 3

Name ____________________

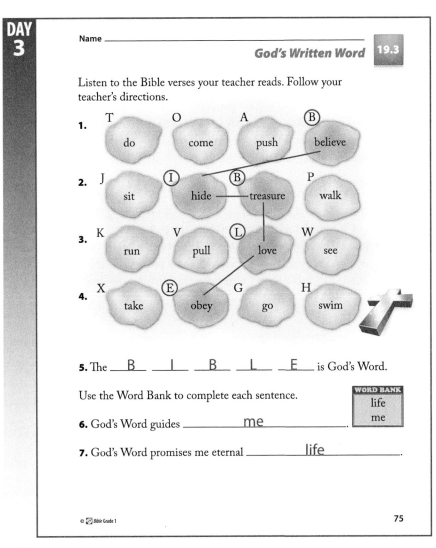

God's Written Word **19.3**

Listen to the Bible verses your teacher reads. Follow your teacher's directions.

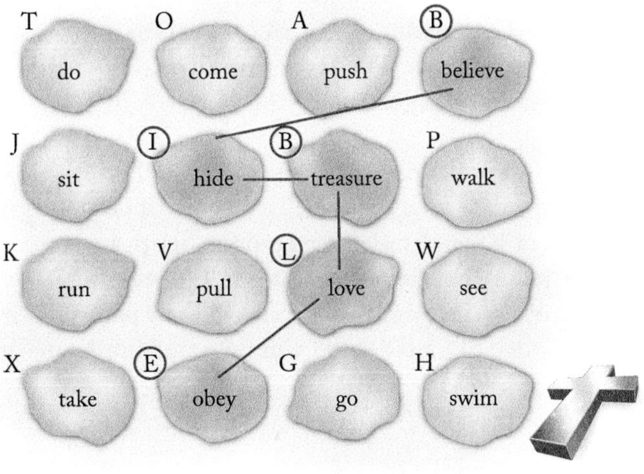

5. The __B__ __I__ __B__ __L__ __E__ is God's Word.

Use the Word Bank to complete each sentence.

WORD BANK
life
me

6. God's Word guides ______me______.

7. God's Word promises me eternal ______life______.

19.4 God's Written Word

Focus: The Importance of Memorization

★ PREPARATION

Select "The Bible" on the music CDs. (*Introduction*)

Hide FIVE INDEX CARDS containing the following words: kindness, peace, forgiveness, wisdom, comfort. Write five sentences on the board so that each sentence instructs how to find a different hidden card for a treasure hunt. (*Directed Instruction*)

EXTENSION

4A Have a treasure hunt and leave clues around the playground or classroom. Let the treasure be a Bible that is hidden in a TREASURE CHEST or a BOX.

4B Teach the students the chorus of "The B-I-B-L-E" in sign language.

Drop hand down slightly.
The
B
I
B
L
E
YES
THAT'S
THE BOOK
FOR
ME
I
STAND
ALONE
ON
THE WORD
OF GOD

Introduction ★

Sing "The Bible" on the music CDs. Ask volunteers to share some of the ways that the Bible is different from all other books. (**The Bible is God's Word, the Bible truths last forever, the Bible provides guidance, and the Bible helps Christians to know God.**) Inform students that they will be participating in a treasure hunt about the Bible, God's Word.

Directed Instruction ★

Choose five students to read aloud each sentence you have written on the board, follow the directions, and locate each INDEX CARD. When all five students have located their card, have them bring the cards to you. Discuss how God's Word is a treasure in itself. Explain that not only is God's Word a treasure, but through His Word, He leads everyone to treasures, such as kindness, peace, forgiveness, wisdom, and comfort.

Relate how the sentences on the board gave direction in how to find the hidden, written treasures. Read each sentence aloud before erasing the board. Ask students to repeat the directions from memory to see if they remember the procedure used to find each card. Share that memorizing God's Word is a tool that helps them to know God's direction for their life, to know Him better, and to live a life that pleases Him.

Read the following Scripture verses to the students and ask them to identify the treasure(s) mentioned:

- **Psalm 46:11** (**His presence, His protection**)
- **Psalm 25:8** (**His goodness, His righteousness**)
- **John 1:17b** (**His grace, His favor toward us, His truth**)
- **Proverbs 3:5–6** (**His guidance**)

Discuss with the students that by memorizing Scriptures such as these, they can encourage themselves and others with God's truth at any time. One benefit of having students memorize Scripture is that the knowledge stays with them. They do not need to wait to search in the Bible for an answer because the memorized verses will be a part of their knowledge base. Knowledge of God's Word will help students to make wise choices.

Review

- How is God's Word a treasure? (**It leads me to Him and to His treasures that I need in life.**)
- What treasures do you find in God's Word? (**Possible answers: faith, truth, joy, love, life, hope, kindness, peace, forgiveness, wisdom, comfort**)
- Why is it important for you to memorize God's Word? (**Possible answers: so I can know God better and live to please Him, so I can have His answers with me at all times**)

Student Page 19.4

Read the directions and the text on the page. Have students complete the page. Conclude the lesson by having students cover their Memory Verse and say it aloud.

Notes:

APPLICATION

- Tell about a time when God's Word comforted you. (**Answers will vary.**)
- Share something you do that helps you memorize Bible verses. (**Answers will vary.**)
- Have any of your Memory Verses helped you to solve a problem or to know more about God? Explain how those verses have helped you. (**Answers will vary.**)

DAY 4

19.4 ***God's Written Word***

1. God's Word contains many treasures. Find the correct pathway to the treasure box.

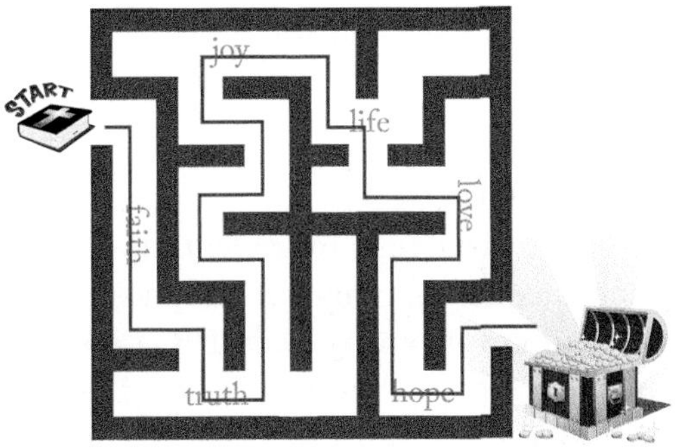

2. Write the words from the maze that name some of God's treasures.

faith truth joy

life love hope

3. Write the words of Psalm 119:11.

Psalm 119:11

19.5 God's Written Word

Focus: Review and Assessment

★ PREPARATION

Select **VA 19A Jesus Reads God's Word**. (*Lesson Review*)

Print one copy of **BLM 19C Lesson 19 Test** for each student. (*Directed Instruction*)

Lesson Review ★

Have a brief period of worship. Sing any of the worship songs that you have practiced from the music CDs. Invite students to join you in prayer to thank God for His Word, the Bible.

Use **VA 19A Jesus Reads God's Word** to review the Bible truth. Cover the following points:

- Jesus went to the synagogue in His hometown of Nazareth to worship.
- During worship time, Jesus was invited to read the Bible.
- The Bible was written on a scroll, long sheets of paper that were rolled up.
- Jesus read from the Old Testament book of Isaiah.
- Long ago, God gave His Word, the Bible, to certain people to write down. This allows people to be able to read it and know Him.
- Isaiah was a prophet. He was one of the people to whom God gave His Word. He wrote down what God told him to write hundreds of years before Jesus was born.
- Jesus explained that the words Isaiah had written about the Messiah, the promised Savior, had come true. Jesus told the people that He was the Messiah and that He was reading about Himself.
- God's Word is true and lasts forever.
- Living according to God's Word brings blessings to people.
- Some of these blessings include comfort and guidance. God's promises comfort Christians.
- God's Word guides people in the right way to live and promises eternal life through Jesus to those who trust in Him as Savior.
- Memorizing God's Word is a way to keep His Word available at all times. Memorizing verses from the Bible also helps Christians know God better and live a life that pleases Him.

Directed Instruction ★

If you have been dictating the tests to students up to this point in the school year, inform students that this test and those in the future will not be dictated. Distribute a copy of **BLM 19C Lesson 19 Test** to each student. Read the directions and pronounce any difficult words. Have students complete the test. Review the answers in class, and then collect the test papers for assessment.

Notes:

Expected Student Outcomes

KNOW
Jesus calls disciples to follow Him and obey His Word.

DO
Students will:
- use a code to review Jesus' teaching in John 15
- complete an activity about the calling of the first disciples
- determine various ways to fulfill the Great Commission
- differentiate between the fruit of the Spirit and leading others to faith

APPLY
Students will acknowledge their need to follow Christ and obey His Word. They will practice telling others about Jesus.

Lesson Outline

I. The vine, the branches, and the fruit (Jn 15:1–8)
  A. Jesus, the vine
  B. Jesus chooses disciples, the branches
  C. Bearing fruit
II. Fishers of men (Lk 5:1–11, Mt 4:18–22)
  A. Jesus calls Peter, Andrew, James, and John
  B. Catching people
III. The Church begins to grow (Lk 10:1–20)
  A. Jesus sends out many disciples
  B. Jesus gives the Great Commission (Mt 28:18–20, Mk 16:15–20)
IV. Fruit and fish
  A. The fruit of the Spirit (Gal 5:22–23)
  B. Sharing your faith

TEACHER'S HEART

First graders love stories! They listen intently and often remember their favorite stories for a long time. Not only do the students remember the stories, but as they mature, they come to an understanding that some stories can be meaningful on more than one level.

Jesus often used real-life illustrations to teach spiritual concepts. He pointed out a vine and taught about how the branches were able to bear fruit because of their connection to the vine. He compared Himself to the vine and the Church to the branches. In another illustration, Jesus used the metaphor of catching fish to describe reaching people with the gospel.

By providing illustrations that His listeners could understand, Jesus was able to teach a great deal about the kingdom of God. As you teach this week, consider how to convey spiritual concepts in such a way that your students can begin to understand these truths. You will be blessed, and your students will be, too!

MEMORY VERSE

John 15:5

MATERIALS

Day 1:
- Cluster of grapes, TM-7 Vine and Branches
- Grapes (*Extension*)

Day 2:
- Items used for fishing
- VA 20A The Disciples Follow Jesus
- BLM 20A Fishers of Men (*Extension*)

Day 3:
- Untied shoe

Day 4:
- Paring knife, apple
- PP-6 Tell the World About Jesus (*Extension*)

Day 5:
- VA 20A The Disciples Follow Jesus
- BLM 20B Lesson 20 Test

SONGS

Right to My Heart
The Fish Are Gonna Bite

TEACHER RESOURCES

Lucado, Max. *Live to Make a Difference*. Thomas Nelson, 2010.
Maxwell, John C. *Equipping 101: What Every Leader Needs to Know*. Thomas Nelson, 2003.

STUDENT RESOURCES

McDonough, Andrew. *The Gardener and The Vine*. Zonderkidz, 2010.
Nystrom, Carolyn. *Fish, Peter!* Kregel Publications, 2004.

20.1

Following Jesus

Focus: The Vine, the Branches, and the Fruit

MEMORY VERSE

John 15:5

MEMORY WORK

- Write the Memory Verse on the board and read it with the class. Have the students suggest motions for each phrase in the verse. For example, for *I am the vine*, have students stand up as tall as possible. For *you are the branches*, have students stretch their arms out to their sides. Continue to invite students to suggest motions for the Memory Verse and to recite the verse as many times as needed until all have memorized it.

★ PREPARATION

Bring a CLUSTER OF GRAPES to class. Prepare **TM-7 Vine and Branches** for display. (*Introduction*)

Select "Right to My Heart" from the music CDs. (*Introduction*)

EXTENSION

1A Prepare some GRAPES for a snack. As students eat, remind them that the grapes would not be sweet without the sugar the leaves help to produce. They would not be juicy without the water from the soil that was carried upward through the vine to the branches. The branches needed to stay connected to the vine to produce the grapes.

Introduction ★

Hold up the CLUSTER OF GRAPES so that all students can see it. Display **TM-7 Vine and Branches**. Explain that the cluster of grapes came from a vine similar to what is on TM-7. Ask students if the cluster of grapes that you brought will grow and continue to live. (**No.**) Affirm that they have answered correctly. Grapes will not grow or live without the rooted section, the vine, to which they are attached. As you point out the various parts of the grapevine on TM-7, explain that the vine, branches, leaves, and grapes are all parts of the same living plant. God has designed each part of the grapevine to do a special job for the plant. Each leaf takes in sunlight and makes sugar for the plant. Each branch carries the sugar and water to the grapes and the leaves. The vine keeps the plant in place, holds the branches up, and carries water, sugar, and other nutrients to various parts of the plant. The vine produces the grapes that appear on the branches.

Teach students "Right to My Heart" from the music CDs.

Directed Instruction

Explain that when Jesus wanted to teach a lesson, He often talked about common things with which His listeners would be familiar, such as grapevines. Jesus used the ordinary things to help the people understand more about God. In today's Bible truth, Jesus compares Himself to a grapevine. Read the following Bible truth:

> During His time on Earth, Jesus chose 12 men to be His disciples. The word *disciple* means *a follower*. The disciples followed Jesus to the places where He was teaching the people. The disciples listened to Jesus as He taught God's truth, and they followed Jesus' example by helping others.
>
> Jesus had a close relationship with His disciples. He told them, "I am like a vine and you, My friends, are like branches. A branch can only grow when it is joined to the vine. You will grow in faith and be able to do wonderful things to help many people when you listen to My words, copy My actions, and follow My directions for your life."

Direct students' attention back to the picture of the grapevine on TM-7. Circle the vine and remind students that Jesus compared Himself to the vine. Ask students to recount who were represented by the branches in Jesus' lesson. (**the disciples**)

The disciples were like branches because they stayed close to Jesus. When Jesus taught the disciples, they took what they learned and put it into practice, just like the branches of a grapevine take water and sugar from the vine, and grapes are formed.

Jesus told the disciples that they needed to do three things to grow in their faith. Ask students to share what those three things were. (**listen to what He taught them, copy His actions, and follow His directions**) Christians are to do these same things today. When Christians listen to God's Word, copy His actions, and follow His directions, they are able to do many things to help others and to share the good news about God's plan of salvation. When showing God's love to others and telling others about Jesus results in a life being changed for God, it is called *bearing fruit*.

Review

- What were Jesus' followers called? (**disciples**)
- Who is the vine in Jesus' lesson? (**Jesus**)
- Who are the branches in Jesus' lesson? (**the disciples, Christians today**)
- What does it mean to *bear fruit*? (**It means that I have shared about Jesus, and it has changed someone's life for God.**)
- What does a branch need in order to bear fruit? (**It needs to be connected to the vine.**)

Student Page 20.1

Assist students as needed to complete the page.

Notes:

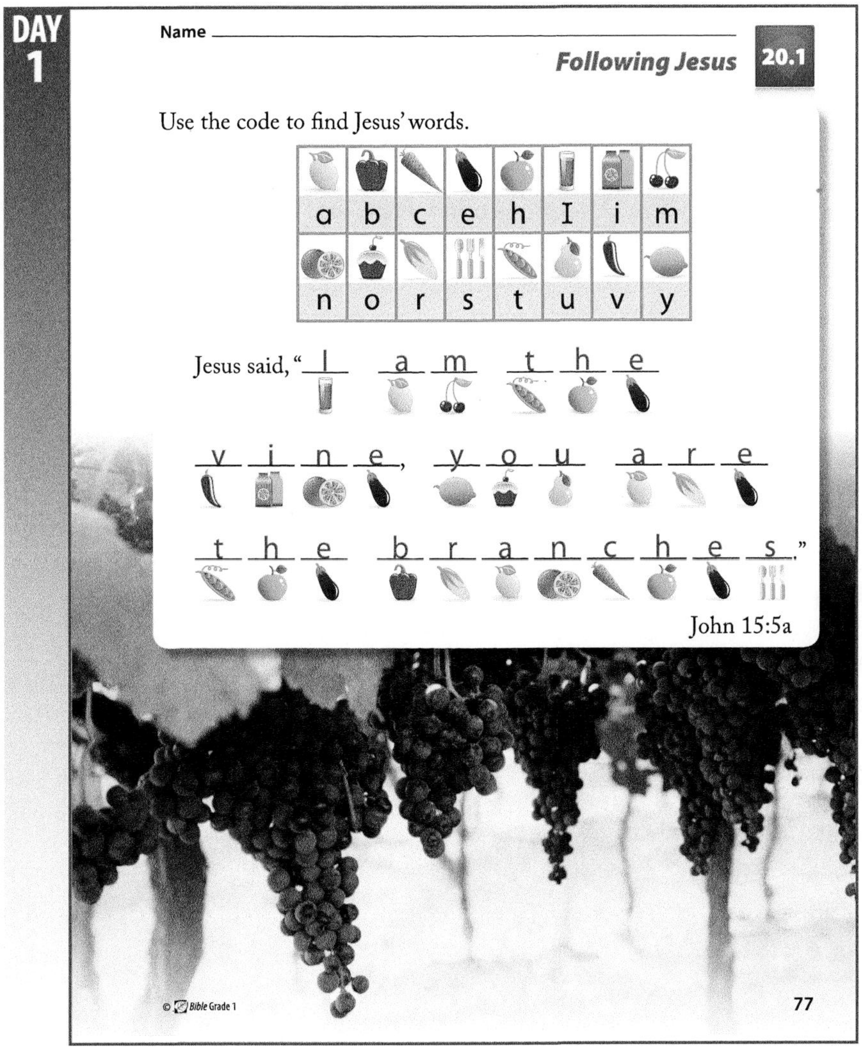
DAY 1

Name

Following Jesus 20.1

Use the code to find Jesus' words.

a	b	c	e	h	I	i	m
n	o	r	s	t	u	v	y

Jesus said, "I am the vine, you are the branches."

John 15:5a

© Bible Grade 1

77

APPLICATION

- What are some games that you cannot play alone? (**Answers will vary.**) Name some sports that are played with teams. (**Answers will vary.**) Is it important for Christians to work as a team with other Christians? (**Yes.**) Why? (**Answers will vary, but should include that it is important to work together to share God's Word and to help others.**)
- It is important to have a close relationship to Jesus and a close relationship to other Christians. Share some things that go wrong when people do not get along. (**Answers will vary.**)
- What is something that you can do to keep a close relationship with Jesus? (**I can read the Bible, pray, and worship regularly.**)
- What does *bearing fruit* mean and how can you bear fruit? (**Bearing fruit occurs when someone's life is changed for God. I may bear fruit when I show God's love to others and tell others about Jesus. When I listen to God's Word, copy His actions, and follow His directions, I am then able to do many things to help others and to share the good news about God's plan of salvation.**)

REINFORCEMENT

Old Testament writers often used the vine to symbolize the nation of Israel. The symbolism indicated that people were connected to God through their covenant relationship with Him. Israel, however, did not bear the fruit of righteousness that should have come through its relationship with God (Isaiah 5:1–7). Jesus Christ is the true vine; He replaces the Law and restores believers into a right relationship with God (Romans 10:4).

20.2 Following Jesus

Focus: Fishers of Men

★ PREPARATION

Bring in an **ITEM USED FOR FISHING**, such as a fishing rod, a reel, a sinker, a bobber, a net, or a tackle box. (*Introduction*)

Select "The Fish Are Gonna Bite" from the music CDs. (*Introduction*)

Select **VA 20A The Disciples Follow Jesus**. (*Directed Instruction*)

EXTENSION

2A Print a copy of **BLM 20A Fishers of Men** for each student. Have students complete the craft and invite them to use the craft to retell the Bible truth.

Introduction ★

Show students an ITEM USED FOR FISHING, and ask them if they have ever seen an item like this and what it is used for. (**fishing**) What else might someone need when fishing? (**Possible answers: bait, a hook**) What could be used for bait? (**Possible answers: minnows, worms**) Explain that some people today fish for fun, and some fish for their food, but in Bible times, fishing was an important job.

Teach students "The Fish Are Gonna Bite" from the music CDs. Explain that today's Bible truth is about some fishermen.

Directed Instruction ★

Most fishermen who lived during the time of Jesus did not use a fishing pole or bait. They used large nets. One type of net was called *a cast net*. This was a large, circular net that was about 20 feet across. The net had weights all around the edge. A skilled fisherman had to throw the net out over the water and trap fish underneath it. As the weights sank into the water, the fisherman pulled the net back into his boat or to the shore to trap the fish.

Fishermen had many other tasks besides just catching fish. They had to wash the nets, mend any nets that tore on the rocks, and repair their boats. They had to sort the fish and take them to the marketplace. Fishermen were hard workers! Sometimes they even worked all night, especially during hot weather. Four of Jesus' disciples were fishermen.

Display **VA 20A The Disciples Follow Jesus** and read the text on the back.

Share with students that Jesus had called both Peter and his brother, Andrew, to be disciples. Both brothers were experienced fishermen, but Jesus was not. Peter was probably very surprised when Jesus told him to go out into deep water instead of going back to the shore. Ask a volunteer to recount what Jesus told Peter to do when they had reached the deep water. (**Jesus told him to get ready to catch fish.**) Do you think that Peter expected to catch any fish? (**No.**) Why? (**Peter had been fishing all night but had not caught any fish. Jesus was not a fisherman, so Peter did not think He would know where to find the fish.**) Peter showed respect for Jesus by doing as He asked.

When Jesus asked Peter to do something, He blessed Peter for his obedience. Peter and Andrew, and their fishing partners, James and John, caught more fish than they could pull into their boats! "Who is this very special man? Where did He get such power?" they thought in amazement. Peter was afraid of such power at first, but Jesus told him not to be afraid. From that time on, they would be catching people.

Review

- Why did Jesus get into Peter's boat to teach the people? (**The people were crowding around Him.**)
- What did Jesus ask Peter to do? (**go into deep water, let down the nets, and get ready to catch fish**)
- What did Jesus tell the disciples that they would be catching instead of fish? (**They would be catching people!**)
- What did Jesus mean by *catching people*? (**He meant that the disciples would be leading people to have faith in Jesus as Savior.**)

Student Page 20.2

Assist students as needed to complete the page.

Notes:

APPLICATION

- Jesus chose four ordinary fishermen to follow Him and to do His work of sharing the message of salvation. Tell how you learned about God's plan of salvation. (**Answers will vary, but should include the influence of godly parents and grandparents, teachers, and pastors.**)
- *Catching people* means *leading people to have faith in Jesus as their Savior*. What are some ways you can lead your friends to Jesus? (**Possible answers: I can invite my friends to Bible class, give them a Bible or a book of Bible truths, ask them to come to church with me, or offer to pray for their needs.**)

DAY 2

20.2 ***Following Jesus***

Fill in the circle beside the word or words that best complete each sentence.

1. Jesus chose ___ men to be His followers.
○ 5
● 12
○ 7

2. Jesus' followers were called ___.
● disciples
○ desks
○ doors

3. The first disciples chosen by Jesus were ___, ___, ___, and ___.
○ Matthew, Mark, Luke, John
○ Peter, Paul, Andrew, John
● Peter, Andrew, James, John

4. Jesus told them, "From now on, you will catch ___."
○ fish
○ colds
● people

5. Catching people means ___ people to Jesus.
○ asking
○ finding
● leading

78

REINFORCEMENT

The Sea of Galilee was relatively small at only eight miles wide and 13 miles long, yet 250–300 boats found their way into its waters daily in search of fish. Jesus saw more than just fishermen as he called Peter, Andrew, James, and John to help Him spread His message to the nations. He saw men who could communicate His message. The fishermen spoke Aramaic as their native language but would also have known Hebrew and possibly Greek—the language necessary for conducting business in the marketplace. Jesus may have observed that fishermen were patient and not easily discouraged. The fishermen who repeatedly looked for fish in the Sea of Galilee would one day seek out people for the kingdom of God.

20.3 Following Jesus

Focus: The Church Begins to Grow

★ PREPARATION

Bring in an UNTIED SHOE, preferably one with long laces. (*Introduction*)

Select "Right to My Heart" from the music CDs. (*Directed Instruction*)

EXTENSION

3A Play the game Fishing, which emphasizes teamwork. Since this is a running and tagging game, take the class to a grassy area or another area with a soft surface. Select four students to work in two pairs. Explain that each set of partners will join hands and try to catch additional students for their team by tagging them and having them join hands with the original pair, forming a chain. Only students with a free hand may tag, and the team must stay connected to do their fishing. This gets progressively more difficult as they all must run while holding hands. If the chain breaks, the team must stop and reconnect before continuing to try to tag others. When all of the students in the class have been incorporated into one team or the other, count the students in each team to see which team has the greater number of students in its chain. Discuss what actions the two teams needed to take in order to tag others.

Introduction ★

Show students the UNTIED SHOE. Ask a volunteer to remain seated, but to give you verbal directions as to how to tie the laces. Pretend to try to follow those directions, but fail to tie the laces properly. Call on a second volunteer to come and demonstrate how to tie the shoe properly. Watch the demonstration, and then tie the shoe as your second volunteer has shown you.

Explain that when Jesus was on the earth, He not only told the disciples how to live a life that is pleasing to God—He showed them how to live!

Directed Instruction ★

Read the following Bible truth:

> Jesus sent a larger group of disciples out to the towns and villages nearby. Jesus told them to go in pairs, to heal the sick, and to tell the good news that He had come to save them from their sins. The disciples were not to take any bags or sandals with them, and they were to stay in any house that welcomed them. After the disciples went to different towns, many people believed that Jesus was God's Son. When the disciples returned, they were filled with joy and excitedly told of all the miracles that had happened in Jesus' name! These miracles displayed the power of God.
>
> Jesus told His disciples, "Go to the whole world and tell everyone the good news. Make disciples for Me in every nation." This command of Jesus is called *the Great Commission*. It is *a command from Jesus to tell people everywhere the good news of salvation, to teach people to obey Him, and to tell them that He will always be with those who believe in Him.* When Christians follow the Great Commission, they are obeying Jesus' command.

Ask students to recount what happened when this larger group of disciples went out. (**People were healed, and more people believed.**) The miracles showed God's power, and people were led to have faith in Jesus! The disciples were excited to share with even more people!

Jesus told the disciples to keep up the good work, to tell people everywhere the good news, to teach them to obey Him, and to remind them that Jesus promised that He would always be with those who believed in Him. Select a volunteer to tell the class what this command of Jesus is called. (**It is called the Great Commission.**)

Christians today love Jesus and want to please Him with their life, thoughts, and actions. All Christians around the world make up what is called *the Church*. Christians in the Church today do many of the things that Christians did a long time ago. They meet together, worship God, and study God's Word and do what it says. They pray together, encourage each other, share what they have with those who have less, and try to help others. They obey the Great Commission!

Remind students to look for opportunities to follow Jesus' command. Conclude by singing "Right to My Heart" from the music CDs.

Review

- Why did Jesus send out a larger group of disciples? (**He sent them because He wanted to heal more people who were sick, and to let more people hear the good news that He had come to save them from their sins.**)
- What happened when these disciples followed Jesus' instructions? (**Many miracles happened in Jesus' name and many people believed in Jesus as their Savior.**)
- What is the Great Commission? (**It is Jesus' command to tell people everywhere the good news of salvation, to teach people to obey Him, and to tell them that Jesus will always be with them.**)

Student Page 20.3

Read each of the sentences on the fish shapes. Remind students that fishing for people involves leading people to have faith in Jesus as their Savior. Assist students as they complete the page.

DAY 3

Name ______________________________

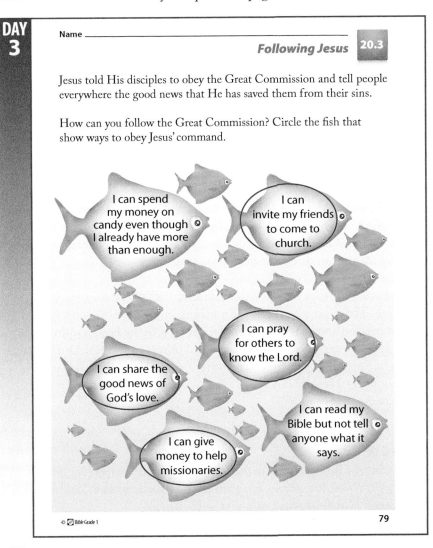

Following Jesus **20.3**

Jesus told His disciples to obey the Great Commission and tell people everywhere the good news that He has saved them from their sins.

How can you follow the Great Commission? Circle the fish that show ways to obey Jesus' command.

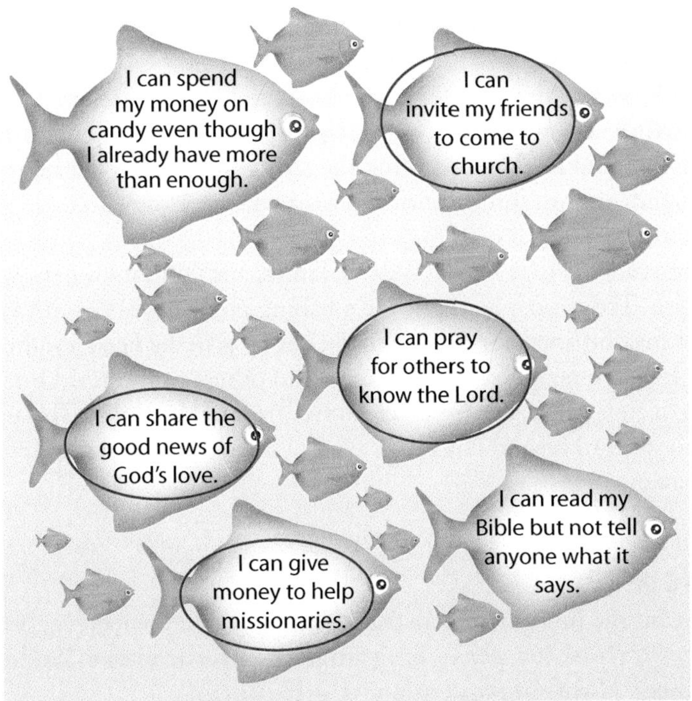

I can spend my money on candy even though I already have more than enough.
I can invite my friends to come to church.
I can pray for others to know the Lord.
I can share the good news of God's love.
I can read my Bible but not tell anyone what it says.
I can give money to help missionaries.

© Bible Grade 1 79

APPLICATION

- Jesus' disciples learned to not only hear Jesus' words, but to really listen to what He taught them. What is the difference between hearing and listening? (**Hearing is taking in sounds, but listening involves thinking about what is heard.**)
- How can you really listen to God's Word instead of just hearing it? (**I can think about it, try to understand it, and ask questions when I do not understand.**)
- All Christians around the world make up the Church. The Church is not a building; it is a group of people. What are some things that followers of Jesus do as a part of the Church? (**Answers will vary.**)

REINFORCEMENT

One of the most common languages spoken in the Roman Empire was Greek. The Greek Christians used five words to make an acrostic from the title *Jesus Christ, God's Son, Savior*, that spelled the Greek word for *fish*. This word, *ichthys*, has the same root as the word *ichthyology*, the branch of zoology relating to the study of fish.

During the first century of growth, New Testament Christians were under persecution from both the Jews and the Romans. They were subject to arrest and imprisonment for their faith in Christ. Eventually, Christians began using the sign of the fish as a code to test strangers to see if they were Christians. One person would draw a simple arc on the ground. If the second person was a Christian, he or she would complete the fish by drawing the other half, and the two could talk safely.

20.4 Following Jesus

Focus: Fruit and Fish

★ PREPARATION

Bring a PARING KNIFE and an APPLE to class. (*Introduction*)

EXTENSION

4A Display **PP-6 Tell the World About Jesus**. Use the presentation to illustrate how important each person is in helping the Church to grow.

Introduction ★

Use the PARING KNIFE to cut open the APPLE and show students the seeds. Explain that it is possible to plant these seeds and that they will grow into trees. Ask students what kind of fruit the trees will produce. (**apples**) Why would the trees not produce pears or grapes? (**Only apples grow on apple trees.**) Apple trees naturally grow apples!

Remind students that bearing fruit for the Lord involves sharing Jesus' love and power with others to the point that it changes their life for the better. Ask students to share an example of bearing fruit in their life. (**Answers will vary.**) Explain that Christians who stay connected to the vine, Jesus, naturally show His love and power to others. Christians bear the fruit of Christ.

Directed Instruction

Open your Bible and explain that Scripture describes more characteristics that Christians should have. Explain that when a person regularly demonstrates a particular attitude, it is a characteristic of that person. Encourage students to listen for nine characteristics of Christians called *the fruit of the Spirit*. Read **Galatians 5:22–23**. Have students put up one finger for each fruit as you read the passage. Write the nine fruits of the Spirit on the board. Read them together and talk about the meaning of any unfamiliar words. Tell students that longsuffering or forbearance is the same as having patience.

Explain that the fruit of the Spirit is a gift from the Holy Spirit. The Holy Spirit, God the Father, and God the Son—Jesus—are the three Persons of the Trinity. There are not three Gods, just one God. All three Persons love, care for, and want to have a relationship with everyone.

When Christians draw closer to the Lord, they will start to see more and more of these characteristics, or fruits, in their behavior. Remind students that they should be demonstrating the fruit of the Spirit out on the playground, at home, in the classroom, or wherever they go!

Remind students that Peter, Andrew, James, and John used nets to catch many fish. Today people might use a fishing pole and worms for bait. Worms may be good for catching fish, but Christians need another kind of bait to catch people. Christians can lead others to the Lord by showing them love, joy, peace, kindness, and other fruit of the Spirit. This entices them to want to hear about God's plan of salvation and accept Jesus as their Savior.

Review

- What are the nine characteristics of Christians known as *the fruit of the Spirit*? (**love, joy, peace, longsuffering or forbearance, kindness, goodness, faithfulness, gentleness, self-control**)

- Where does the fruit of the Spirit come from? (**It is a gift of the Holy Spirit to all believers in Jesus.**)
- How can Christians lead others to faith in the Lord? (**They can tell others about Jesus and show the fruit of the Spirit in their behavior.**)
- Where should Christians demonstrate the fruit of the Spirit? (**They should demonstrate the fruit of the Spirit wherever they go.**)

Student Page 20.4

Read each of the scenarios and discuss answers. Ask students to suggest additional ways that the first graders in the scenarios might display the fruit of the Spirit or share their faith in Jesus with others.

APPLICATION

- Think of someone in this class who displays a fruit of the Spirit. Tell how that person shows that fruit of the Spirit. (**Answers will vary.**)
- Which fruit of the Spirit would you like to display to others? Why? (**Answers will vary.**)

Notes:

DAY 4

20.4 ***Following Jesus***

Listen to each story about a first grader. Circle the grapes if the child is showing the fruit of the Spirit. Circle the fish if the child is leading someone to have faith in Jesus.

1. Terrell showed his little brother how to tie his shoes. Terrell had to show his brother many times before his brother could tie the shoes.

2. Livia's team lost the basketball game, but she chose to have a good attitude and not pout about the loss.

3. Santiago invited Tomás to go with him to a weekly Bible study class.

4. Mrs. Williams had difficulty hearing and often asked people to repeat what other people said. Carmen did not mind helping Mrs. Williams.

5. Natalie showed her friend a Bible craft that she had made in school. Then Natalie used the craft to tell the Bible story to her friend. Natalie explained that Jesus loves everyone!

80

20.5 Following Jesus

Focus: Review and Assessment

★ PREPARATION

Select "Right to My Heart" and "The Fish Are Gonna Bite" from the music CDs. (*Lesson Review*)

Select **VA 20A The Disciples Follow Jesus**. (*Lesson Review*)

Duplicate a copy of **BLM 20B Lesson 20 Test** for each student. (*Directed Instruction*)

Lesson Review ★

Have a brief period of worship to begin class. Sing "Right to My Heart" and "The Fish Are Gonna Bite" from the music CDs.

Use **VA 20A The Disciples Follow Jesus** to review the Bible truths in this lesson. Cover the following concepts:

- Jesus' followers were called *disciples*.
- Jesus is like the vine and Christians are like the branches.
- A branch must be connected to the vine in order to bear fruit.
- Christians need a close relationship with Jesus.
- Christians show love for God when they obey Him.
- When showing God's love to others and telling others about Jesus results in a life being changed for God, it is called *bearing fruit*.
- Jesus got into Peter's boat to speak because the people were crowding around Him while He was preaching.
- Jesus asked Peter to go into deep water, let down the nets, and get ready to catch fish.
- Peter obeyed Jesus and caught so many fish that James and John had to help him bring the fish to shore.
- Peter, Andrew, James, and John left their nets and followed Jesus as His disciples.
- When Jesus explained that the disciples would be catching people, He meant that the disciples would be leading people to have faith in Jesus as their Savior.
- All Christians around the world make up what is called *the Church*.
- Jesus' disciples told others about Him, so the Church continued to grow.
- The Great Commission is Jesus' command to tell others the good news about salvation, to teach people to accept and obey Him, and to tell those who accept Him that He will always be with them.
- *The fruit of the Spirit* refers to *characteristics that describe a growing Christian life*.

Directed Instruction ★

Distribute a copy of **BLM 20B Lesson 20 Test** to each student. Read each exercise and allow students time to answer each question. When all have finished, review correct answers with the class.

Notes:

Lesson Preparation

Loving Others

21.0

Expected Student Outcomes

KNOW
Jesus reaches out to a Samaritan woman at a well.

DO
Students will:
- read a rebus story to review the Bible lesson
- review ways to forgive and be forgiven
- indentify ways to love others unconditionally
- determine individuals with whom they can share God's love

APPLY
Students will realize that they are to love others unconditionally in response to God's unconditional love. They will thank God for His forgiveness.

Lesson Outline

I. The Samaritan woman at the well (Jn 4:5–42)
  A. Jesus offers living water to a Samaritan woman
  B. The woman believes in the Messiah
II. Forgiveness from Jesus
  A. Living water cleans inside and out
III. Loving and forgiving
  A. Jesus forgives you
  B. Forgiving yourself
  C. Asking for forgiveness from others
IV. Sharing God's love
  A. Telling others the good news

TEACHER'S HEART

The Samaritan woman didn't come to the well in the morning when most women drew water. She came late to avoid judgmental glances, whispers, and gossip. She knew what they were saying about her because she'd chosen a sinful lifestyle—a lifestyle that brought her a great deal of pain.

She met a Man at that well that day. He talked to her! In fact, He initiated the conversation! He offered her something strange—living water. Then He told her all about her sinful life, yet He didn't judge her. He understood her heart and her deep desire to be forgiven and cleansed. In the same way, Jesus knows you inside and out, and He loves you unconditionally. Jesus cleanses you from your sins and continues the work He began in your life (1 John 1:9).

This week, talk with your students about the guilty feeling they get when they know they've sinned. Share with them the joy of forgiveness and the clean feeling that comes from Jesus' living water! You belong to Jesus and He will never stop working in your life and the lives of your students.

MEMORY VERSE

Psalm 51:10

MATERIALS

Day 1:
- Cups
- Cups, container of ice water
- TM-8 Map of Israel
- VA 21A The Samaritan Woman at the Well

Day 2:
- Drinking glass, mud, plastic tub, pitcher of water
- TM-8 Map of Israel (*Extension*)

Day 3:
- Pennies
- VA 21A The Samaritan Woman at the Well

Day 4:
- Wrapper from a sweet treat

Day 5:
- VA 21A The Samaritan Woman at the Well
- BLM 21A Lesson 21 Test

TEACHER RESOURCES

Delloff, Linda-Marie, and Bernadette Glover-Williams, eds. *Women at the Well, Volume 2: Meditations for Quenching Our Thirst*. Judson Press, 2003.

Lucado, Max. *The 3:16 Promise*. Thomas Nelson, 2007.

STUDENT RESOURCES

Busch, Melinda Kay. *Jesus and the Woman at the Well*. Concordia Publishing House, 2005.

Lucado, Max. *You Are Special*. Crossway Books, 2007.

21.1 Loving Others

Focus: The Samaritan Woman at the Well

MEMORY VERSE

Psalm 51:10

MEMORY WORK

- Set the prepared THREE OR FOUR LARGE, PLASTIC CUPS in order on a table and explain that you are using drinking cups because this week's Bible truth involves a drink of water. Say the Memory Verse and have students repeat after you. Practice saying the verse a few times. Once students are familiar with the verse, remove one of the cups and recite the verse again. Continue removing the cups until all students can say the verse from memory.

★ PREPARATION

Obtain THREE OR FOUR LARGE, PLASTIC CUPS. Separate the Memory Verse into three or four phrases and use a fine-tip, permanent marker to write one phrase on each cup. (*Memory Work*)

Obtain enough SMALL CUPS for each student and yourself and a CONTAINER OF ICE WATER. (*Introduction*)

Select **TM-8 Map of Israel** (*Directed Instruction*)

Select **VA 21A The Samaritan Woman at the Well**. (*Directed Instruction*)

Introduction ★

Exclaim that you are thirsty and need a drink of water. Pour yourself a SMALL CUP of ICE WATER and pretend to enjoy it and be satisfied. Look surprised as if you have just remembered your manners and forgotten to share with the class. Pour a small cup of water for each student. Once all have had a drink, ask students if they think that small cup of water would satisfy their thirst for a month. (**No.**) Explain that not only do people need to drink water to stay physically healthy, but they need a relationship with God to be spiritually healthy.

Directed Instruction ★

Display **TM-8 Map of Israel.** Explain that Jesus and His disciples often traveled from the northern part of the country, Galilee, to the southern part of the country, Judea, and back again. Point out the towns of Nazareth and Jerusalem. Show students the Sea of Galilee where Jesus called Peter, Andrew, James, and John to become His disciples. Then point out Samaria on the map. Explain that Samaria was an area inside Israel. The people of Israel, the Jewish people, did not like the Samaritan people. So, most Jewish travelers would go around Samaria if they were traveling from Galilee to Judea. However, Jesus chose to go through Samaria.

Show students **VA 21A The Samaritan Woman at the Well** and read the text on the back. Remind students that the people of this time did not have running water. They could not turn on a faucet whenever they wanted a drink. The women in the towns would take large jars to the well, fill them with water, and carry them home. Jars filled with water were really heavy. This was hard work!

Ask students to recount what Jesus said to the woman to start the conversation. (**Please give me a drink.**) Remind students that the woman was confused when Jesus spoke to her. She wanted to know why Jesus would even talk to her when no other Jewish person would do that. Jesus showed kindness to the woman by not only speaking to her, but by offering her the gift of living water. Living water is God's free gift of life forever with Him and others who love Him.

Remind students that the woman knew that she had made some poor choices in her life and had disobeyed God. She knew that she needed forgiveness for her sins. Jesus is God, and God knows everything. Jesus knew exactly what the woman's sins were. He did not care that she was a Samaritan or that she had many sins to forgive. Jesus was ready to love her unconditionally and forgive her, just as He is ready to forgive people today. Unconditional love is not based on what a person looks like, has, does, or says.

Review

- Where did Jesus stop to get a drink? (**at a well in Samaria**)
- Why was the woman at the well surprised when Jesus talked to her? (**She was a Samaritan and Jesus was a Jew; Jews did not speak to Samaritans.**)
- What did the woman tell Jesus about the Messiah? (**When the Messiah, the promised Savior comes, He would explain the truth about God to everyone.**)
- Did the woman believe Jesus when He told her that He is the Messiah? (**Yes.**) How did she feel? (**overjoyed**)
- What did the woman do once she knew the truth? (**She went into the city and told others in the city what had happened to her at the well. The Samaritans went to listen to Jesus. Many believed that He was the Savior.**)

Student Page 21.1

Have students review the Bible truth by reading the page together.

APPLICATION

- Does Jesus know all your sins? (**Yes.**) Does He stop loving you when you sin? (**No.**)
- How does Jesus' kindness help you when you know that you have done something wrong? (**I know that Jesus loves me. I do not have to be afraid to go to Him when I have done something wrong. He will forgive me (Romans 2:4).**)
- Do you need to do anything to earn Jesus' love and kindness? (**No, God's love is unconditional!**)

Notes:

DAY 1

Name ______________________________

Loving Others **21.1**

Read the story.

One day … and His disciples were walking through Samaria. … met a … at a … . He asked the … for a drink of … . The … did not understand why … would speak so kindly to her, but she listened to Him. … offered the … living … . … knew all about the woman's sins. The … was amazed that … knew all about her. She wanted to be forgiven and to go to heaven. … told the … that He was the Messiah. The … was so excited that she left her … at the well. She told many other people in the … that she had met Jesus, the Messiah.

21.2 Loving Others

Focus: Forgiveness from Jesus

★ PREPARATION

Prepare a CLEAR DRINKING GLASS by smearing it lightly with MUD. Have a SHALLOW PLASTIC TUB and a PITCHER OF WATER ready for a demonstration. (*Introduction*)

EXTENSION

2A Before recess, allow each student to get a drink of water at the water fountain. After the class, ask students if they are thirsty again. Allow those who are thirsty to take another drink. Remind students that people have to drink water regularly in order to stay healthy and that thirst goes away only to return again. Express how glad you are that Christians have the living water that Jesus freely provides. Christians are able to go to the Lord in prayer at any time and always have His promise of life with Him forever.

2B Direct students' attention to **TM-8 Map of Israel**. Review the directions north, south, east, and west. Tell students that Israel is made up of different areas, some of which are shown on the map. Ask students to tell which direction Jesus and the disciples were traveling as they were going from Judea to Galilee; then ask them to tell you which direction they would have to travel to go back to Judea. Remind students that Jewish people usually went around Samaria when they traveled, but that Jesus loved and cared for all people, even those who were disliked by others.

Introduction ★

Invite a student to summarize the Bible truth about the Samaritan woman. Remind students that the woman knew that she was a sinner who could not live with God forever without forgiveness. Jesus was ready to forgive the woman for her sins. Once the woman understood that Jesus was the Messiah sent from God, she was thankful and rushed to tell others in the city about Jesus.

Show students the CLEAR DRINKING GLASS smeared with MUD and explain that sin is a lot like mud. It does not belong in the life of a Christian, just like mud does not belong on a glass. Sin hurts a relationship with God, and it hurts people's relationships with one another. Put the mud-smeared glass in the SHALLOW PLASTIC TUB. Talk with students about the living water of forgiveness that Jesus gives while you slowly pour WATER over the glass, rubbing as needed to rinse off the mud. Show students the clean glass and share that the glass can now be used for drinking.

Directed Instruction

Share the following fictional story about a first grader:

> Abby sat outside Principal Smith's office, waiting for her to return. She knew that Principal Smith would be disappointed to see her in trouble again. Abby wondered why she always got into so much trouble. She knew she shouldn't push her friends when she was mad, or lie to her teacher about what she'd done. She didn't want to break things when she felt frustrated, or interrupt her teacher, or draw pictures when she should be reading. Sometimes Abby did not understand how she could get into so much trouble!
>
> Abby really didn't like the way she felt when she got into trouble. She felt frustrated, sad, embarrassed, and mad at herself. These were the feelings she felt in her heart. She wished that she could give her heart a bath and make it clean just like a bath made her body clean. Then she could be clean inside and outside!

Ask students if they have ever felt like Abby. (**Answers will vary.**) Explain that the Samaritan woman who met Jesus may have felt the same way. Jesus never sinned, but He understood the bad feeling of guilt that sin often causes. He knew that the woman needed to be forgiven and have that bad feeling gone for good!

Explain to students that Christians can receive God's forgiveness through prayer. The Bible says in 1 John 1:9 that when God's people tell Him about their sin and that they are sorry they have done something wrong, He forgives them! Tell students that they will hear more about Abby in the next day's lesson.

Review

- How did Abby feel about being in trouble again? (**frustrated, sad, embarrassed, mad at herself**)

- Why was Abby in trouble so often? (**She made poor choices to lose her temper and to sin.**)
- What did Abby wish for? (**She wished that the bad feelings she felt within her heart could be clean, just like her body is clean after a bath.**)
- Did Jesus understand how Abby and the Samaritan woman felt when they sinned? (**Yes, Jesus never sinned, but He does understand. He wants to forgive us and take our guilt away.**)
- How do Christians receive God's forgiveness? (**by telling God about their sin(s) and asking for forgiveness**)

Student Page 21.2

Assist students as they complete the page.

Notes:

APPLICATION

- Think about a time when you did something that you knew was wrong. How did you feel? (**Answers will vary, but should include upset, sad, or sorry.**) How can you stop the guilty feeling? (**I can ask Jesus to forgive my sin and plan to do better the next time.**)
- How do you feel after you ask Jesus to forgive your sin? (**happy, free, peaceful**)
- What should you do if you have hurt someone else by your sin? (**I should tell the person that I am sorry and ask him or her to forgive me. I should not repeat the sin.**)

REINFORCEMENT

Early in his life, Martin Luther, one of the great reformers of the Church, did not feel God's love and forgiveness. Although he devoted himself to prayer and fasting as well as constant confession, he had no peace with God. It seemed that the more Luther sought God's forgiveness, the more he became aware of how sinful he was. It was Luther's in-depth study of God's Word that changed him. As he studied the New Testament, particularly the book of Romans, Luther gained insight into what it meant to be forgiven and have a right relationship with God. He began to teach others that forgiveness and having a close, unhindered, and personal relationship with God are gifts received through faith in Christ Jesus alone.

DAY 2

21.2 *Loving Others*

Fill in the correct circles. There may be more than one answer.

1. Kaylani hit Sean because he called her a bad name. What should they do to make things right again?

- ● They should tell each other what they did wrong.
- ● They should say they are sorry for what they did.
- ● They should ask God and each other for forgiveness.

2. Natani copied Kris' answers to the math test. What should Natani do to make things right again?

- ● She should tell Kris what she did and ask her for forgiveness.
- ● She should tell her teacher that she copied the answers.
- ● She should ask God to forgive her for cheating.

3. Ryan and Mack got into a fight at recess. What should they do to make things right again?

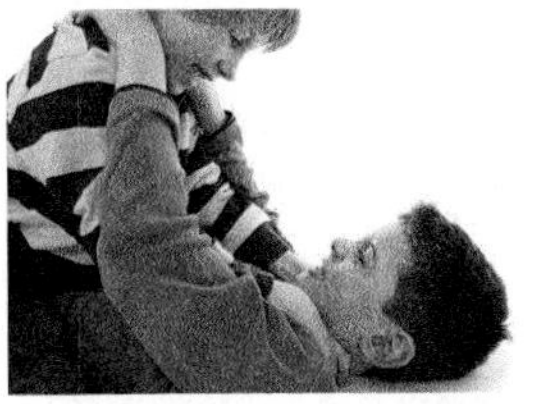

- ● They should tell each other that they are sorry for fighting.
- ● They should ask God to forgive them.
- ● They should ask each other for forgiveness.

82 © Bible Grade 1

21.3 Loving Others

Focus: Loving and Forgiving

★ PREPARATION

Have a variety of PENNIES on hand. You will need some brand new pennies and some that are old, worn, scratched, or dented. (*Introduction*)

Select **VA 21A The Samaritan Woman at the Well**. (*Directed Instruction*)

EXTENSION

3A To encourage students to know and value each other, assign each student a partner. Make sure you assign pairs in such a way that students are not partnered with their close friends. Read the following interview questions aloud, and give students a few minutes after each question to give a response to his or her partner:

1. How do you help your parents at home?
2. What is one of your talents?
3. What is the most interesting thing that you have ever made?
4. What do you like to do when you have free time?

When all students have responded, have students tell the class what they learned about their partners.

Introduction ★

Give one PENNY to each student. Retain a new penny for your own use. Ask students to describe their penny. (**Possible answers: brown, shiny, scratched, new, old, worn**) Tell students that you have a brand new penny and you are willing to trade it with someone who has an old penny. Show students your penny and select a volunteer to trade with. Once you have made a trade, ask students whether you or the student with whom you traded got the better deal. (**Answers will vary.**) Inform students that neither person benefitted from the trade because each penny is still worth one cent. It does not matter what the penny looks like, where it has been, or how old it is. It has the same value regardless.

Explain that people are so much more valuable to God than pennies! Each person is worth more to God than all the riches of the world, and no one is worth more to Him than anyone else. Christians need to follow God's example and value others.

Directed Instruction ★

Display **VA 21A The Samaritan Woman at the Well** and review the Bible truth. Remind students that the woman at the well was surprised when Jesus talked to her. Ask a volunteer to share why this was true. (**because she was a Samaritan and the Jewish people did not normally talk to Samaritans**) Explain that Jesus is different; He loves everyone and often spoke to people whom others did not like or want to be around. His kindness to the woman encouraged her to talk more with Him. He wanted her to come to faith in Him and repent of her sins. Jesus does not love people based on their appearance, age, family background, or previous poor choices. Jesus cares about all people.

Remind students that when they sincerely repent of their sins, God forgives them. However, it is important for Christians to go to the person whom they have sinned against and ask for forgiveness from that person as well. Explain that Abby, the girl in the story from Lesson 21.2, needed to learn to value her relationships and to apologize when she did wrong.

Read the following fictional story:

> By the time Principal Smith saw Abby, the little girl was completely miserable. Abby told Mrs. Smith that she needed a heart bath, because her heart felt so sad inside. Mrs. Smith smiled and explained to Abby that the sad feeling she had inside was God's way of letting her know that her heart really did need to be cleaned. The only way to do that was to ask Jesus to forgive her sins. Abby was sorry for what she had done, so Mrs. Smith helped her to ask Jesus to forgive her sins. After they prayed, Mrs. Smith reminded Abby that she also needed to apologize to the others she had hurt or disobeyed, and forgive herself. Abby promised to do so and not to be mad at herself anymore.
>
> Later on the playground, Abby decided to play with Kendall. The other children in first grade rarely played with Kendall. Kendall was shy.

Abby remembered how she had been mean to Kendall. She thought about what Mrs. Smith had said. She told Kendall that she was sorry for the way she'd treated him before. Now Abby felt really clean inside! She kept playing with Kendall, and she was glad that he wanted to play with her, even though she'd been in so much trouble. That night, Abby prayed to the Lord to forgive her for her unkindness to Kendall.

Review

- How did Principal Smith help Abby? (**Answers will vary, but should include that Mrs. Smith prayed with Abby and told Abby to ask Jesus for forgiveness for her wrong actions and to forgive herself.**)
- What happened when Abby was kind, and played with Kendall? (**She felt sorry for being mean, she apologized, she had fun.**)
- How did Abby feel when she told Kendall that she was sorry? (**She felt really clean inside.**)

Student Page 21.3

Read the directions and have students complete the page. Assist students as needed.

DAY 3

Name ______________________________

Loving Others **21.3**

Read each exercise. Decide if the actions show Jesus' love. If so, color the heart beside the exercise.

1. Taylor noticed that Luke fell at recess. Taylor helped Luke up and went to get him a bandage.
2. Mary did not want to be in the same reading group as Joel because Joel read slowly. She complained about this to others.
3. Pravaas helped his teacher put the library books on the shelves.
4. Whitney was upset because she lost a game to Lauren. Whitney called Lauren a cheater.
5. Mrs. Cook was on recess duty. The children left all of the playground toys outside when they went in. No one offered to help Mrs. Cook pick up the toys.
6. Think of something you can do to show kindness to someone. Write your idea on the lines.

Answers will vary.

APPLICATION

- Unconditional love is the kind of love that God has for His children. You do not need to do anything to earn His love. Think about how you love others. Do you treat others the way that you would like to be treated? (**Answers will vary.**)
- Do you only play with children who look, dress, or behave a certain way? (**Answers will vary.**) Is there someone who you do not play with because of the way he or she looks or acts? (**Answers will vary.**)
- Share examples of ways that you can treat others like Jesus would treat them. (**Answers will vary.**)

REINFORCEMENT

The Samaritans were descended from Jewish people who had intermarried with the people of local tribes during the time of Israel's captivity in Assyria. The Samaritans followed a religion that was a mix of Judaism and idolatry. The Jews despised the Samaritans on the grounds that mixed marriages were forbidden (Ezra 9) and also because of their idolatrous worship practices (Exodus 20). Because Samaria is located between Judea and Galilee, anyone traveling between Jerusalem and Nazareth or Cana either had to cross through Samaria or go out of his or her way to avoid it.

21.4 Loving Others

Focus: Sharing God's Love

★ PREPARATION

Have a WRAPPER FROM A SWEET TREAT on hand. (*Introduction*)

EXTENSION

4A Play the game Sharing Good News. Seat students in a circle on the floor, and join the circle. Start the game by whispering something positive about one of your students to the student next to you. For example, you might say the name of a student and that he or she is a good helper. Have the student next to you whisper that comment to the next student in the circle. When the student about whom the comment was made hears it, he or she will think of a new positive comment about another student in the circle and pass it along. Play until everyone has had a chance to hear a positive comment about himself or herself and pass one along.

Introduction ★

Show students a WRAPPER FROM A SWEET TREAT. Dramatically tell students that the treat tasted delicious! Ask a few students to share the names of snacks that they enjoy and would recommend to others. (**Answers will vary.**) Explain that when people try a new food that tastes really good, they often tell their friends to try it.

Review that Jesus offered living water to the woman at the well—God's forgiveness and life forever with Him and others who love Him. That was really, really good news! The woman was so excited that she left her waterpot at the well and rushed to share the good news with everyone in the city.

Directed Instruction

Read the following fictional story:

> Abby was a different girl after she and Principal Smith had talked and prayed together. Whenever Abby saw Mrs. Smith in the hallways or on the playground, she went over to the principal and gave her a big hug. Although Abby still got mad sometimes, she prayed whenever she felt angry, so she didn't push people any more.
>
> Abby noticed one thing at school that hadn't changed. The other first graders still weren't playing with Kendall. That made Abby sad. Kendall was a nice boy! He was smart, and he had a great imagination. Kendall thought of some great games to play. Abby thought about how much fun it would be if more children would come and play with them.
>
> Abby decided to tell others about how much fun it was to play with Kendall. She told every first grader in her class about some of the games that Kendall had invented. Abby was excited, and that made others feel excited, too. The next day, two other first graders came and joined Abby and Kendall. Kendall explained the rules of a game he had made up. Everyone played! As the week went on, more and more first graders discovered what Abby had learned and shared—playing with Kendall was really fun!

Remind students about the way the Samaritan woman told others about meeting the Messiah. She invited them to come and meet Him. Her excitement at having met and spoken to Jesus was contagious! Many Samaritans noticed the woman's excitement and went to see Jesus. Tell students that Christians are thankful because they know they are forgiven. This feeling of thankfulness and joy leads to the desire to tell others about God's free gift of salvation for all who believe!

Review

- How did Abby change after her prayer time with Mrs. Smith? (**Answers will vary, but should include that Abby was praying for help to not lose her temper.**)

- What had not changed at school? (**The first graders still would not play with Kendall.**)
- What did Abby know about Kendall? (**Kendall was smart and made up good games.**)
- What did Abby do to get others to play with Kendall? (**She happily shared what she knew about Kendall with her friends and invited them to come and play.**)
- What happened as a result of Abby's kindness? (**The first graders came to play with Abby and Kendall.**)

Student Page 21.4

Assist students as needed in completing the page.

Notes:

APPLICATION

- The Samaritan woman was excited at meeting the Messiah. Are you excited about knowing Jesus? (**Answers will vary.**)
- How can you share your excitement? (**I can invite friends to come to church, Bible class, or midweek Bible studies.**)
- How do you think Kendall felt when Abby was kind to him? (**Answers will vary.**)
- How does someone else's kindness affect you? (**Answers will vary, but should include I feel good, comforted, I want to be kind to others, too.**)

DAY 4

21.4 *Loving Others*

Jesus showed kindness to the Samaritan woman at the well.

1. Write your name in the middle oval. Write in the outer ovals the names of people to whom you plan to share kindness.

Answers will vary.

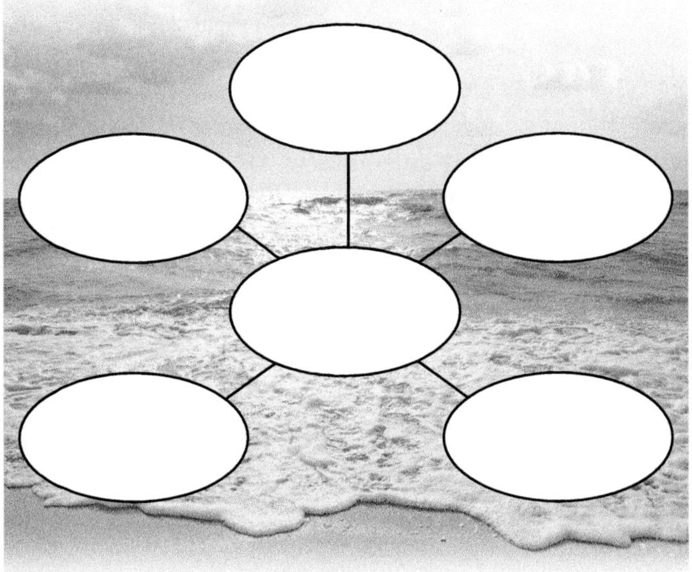

2. Think about someone you would like to talk to about God's plan of salvation. Write his or her name on the line. In class, share what you would say to that person.

Answers will vary.

84

21.5 Loving Others

Focus: Review and Assessment

★ PREPARATION

Select **VA 21A The Samaritan Woman at the Well**. (*Lesson Review*)

Make a copy of **BLM 21A Lesson 21 Test** for each student. (*Directed Instruction*)

Lesson Review ★

Use **VA 21A The Samaritan Woman at the Well** to review the Bible truths in this lesson. Cover the following points:

- While Jesus was traveling from Judea to Galilee, He stopped at a well in Samaria.
- Jesus asked a Samaritan woman for a drink of water. She was very surprised that Jesus spoke to her because most Jewish people hated the Samaritans.
- Jesus is different. He loves everyone unconditionally. Jesus loves each person no matter what that person looks like, has, does, or says. Jesus will always forgive people for their sins when they trust Him.
- Jesus told the woman all about her sins, even though He had never met her before.
- The woman was amazed that Jesus knew so much about her.
- Jesus explained that He is the Messiah and that He would give her the kind of water that would make her clean inside. Jesus promised her living water.
- Jesus was kind to the Samaritan woman. His kindness helped her to understand that He was the Messiah. He came to bring salvation to everyone!
- The woman was so excited that she left her waterpot at the well and rushed to the city to tell others that she had found the Messiah.
- Sometimes Christians can feel like the woman at the well—they have done something wrong and need to be forgiven. These are the times when they need to pray, ask Jesus to forgive them, and choose not to sin again.
- Jesus wants Christians to follow His example and love others.
- Playing nicely, using kind words, accepting others, and helping others are ways that Christians can show God's love to other people.

Directed Instruction ★

Give each student a copy of **BLM 21A Lesson 21 Test**. Assist students who need help reading any unfamiliar words. Collect the tests for assessment. Review the correct answers in class.

Notes:

Lesson Preparation 22.0

Sharing

Expected Student Outcomes

KNOW

Jesus miraculously feeds a crowd of people.

DO

Students will:

- match numbers to corresponding pictures and practice retelling the Bible truth
- choose correct endings to sentences reviewing what Jesus taught His disciples
- trace over letters describing God's character and discuss how God's character is revealed through His miraculous acts
- use a code to solve a puzzle about sharing

APPLY

Students will be willing to give what they have to meet the needs of others.

Lesson Outline

I. Feeding of the 5,000 (Mt 14:13–21, Lk 9:10–17, Jn 6:5–15)

II. The disciples learn lessons

A. Two disciples' view of Jesus' test

B. Jesus teaches trust

III. God's provision

A. Character traits of God

B. Purpose of miracles

IV. Selfless sharing

A. Stewardship

B. Giving your best

TEACHER'S HEART

Have you ever been in a situation where you felt you had little to offer the Lord so you simply pulled back and did nothing? What if the boy with the five loaves and two small fish had felt that way and decided not to give what he had? He would have lost a once-in-a-lifetime opportunity to see the Lord work through his "little offering." The boy had only five loaves and two small fish, but God satisfied the hunger of 5,000 people and collected twelve baskets full of leftovers, as well.

Have you ever wondered what the disciples did with those twelve full baskets? Better yet—have you ever wondered what He is doing with your offering of yourself to Him? What more could God do with your "twelve baskets full of leftovers"? Why not stop wondering and move on to action! Never think you have nothing to offer the Lord. You may miss seeing what He can do with your "five loaves and two small fish." May the Lord richly bless you as you are faithful to serve Him.

MEMORY VERSE

Hebrews 13:16

MATERIALS

Day 1:

- BLM 22A Memory Verse, envelopes
- Plate, rolls, fish-shaped crackers
- VA 22A Jesus Feeds Crowds of People

Day 2:

- TM-9 Pole Vault
- VA 22A Jesus Feeds Crowds of People
- BLM 22B Sharing Chart (*Extension*)
- TM-8 Map of Israel (*Extension*)

Day 3:

- Fish-shaped crackers

Day 4:

- Photograph of a child from another country, globe (*Extension*)

Day 5:

- VA 22A Jesus Feeds Crowds of People
- BLM 22C Lesson 22 Test

SONGS

Little Bit of Love (*Extension*)

TEACHER RESOURCES

Dean, Jennifer Kennedy. *Live a Praying Life: Open Your Life to God's Power and Provision*. New Hope Publishers, 2010.

Maselli, Christopher. *Miracles of Jesus Grades 1–3*. Carson-Dellosa Publishing, 2007.

STUDENT RESOURCES

dePaola, Tomie. *The Miracles of Jesus*. Puffin Books, 2008.

Life of Jesus. Laminated Wall Chart. Rose Publishing, 2004.

22.1 Sharing

Focus: Feeding of the 5,000

MEMORY VERSE

Hebrews 13:16

MEMORY WORK

- Write the Memory Verse on the board and read it chorally. Provide a copy of **BLM 22A Memory Verse** for each student. Have students cut out the loaves and fish, read the words, and put them in the correct order. Tell students to check their work by looking at the Memory Verse on the board. Tell students to paperclip their loaves and fish together. Distribute **12** ENVELOPES to students for storage of their loaves and fish.

★ PREPARATION

Divide the Memory Verse into seven phrases and write the phrases on the loaves and fish on **BLM 22A Memory Verse**. Include the Scripture reference along with the last phrase. Make a copy of the modified blackline master for each student. Have **12** ENVELOPES on hand for students to use as baskets to store the pieces for reuse. (*Memory Work*)

Prepare a SMALL PLATE with FIVE SMALL ROLLS and TWO FISH-SHAPED CRACKERS. (*Introduction*)

Select **VA 22A Jesus Feeds Crowds of People**. (*Directed Instruction*)

EXTENSION

1A Teach students "Little Bit of Love" from the music CDs to reinforce the concept of sharing with others.

Introduction ★

Display a SMALL PLATE with FIVE SMALL ROLLS and TWO FISH-SHAPED CRACKERS. Explain that you brought this for your snack and realized you should share it with the students. Go to great lengths trying to break the fish crackers and tear the bread into enough pieces for each student, but fail. Conclude that there is not enough food to satisfy everyone's hunger. (Do not distribute the pieces to your students.) Explain that Jesus once faced a similar problem of not having enough food.

Directed Instruction ★

Open your Bible to the book of Matthew. Remind students that the first four books of the New Testament are Matthew, Mark, Luke, and John. State that these books are known as *the Gospels* and Matthew is the first book in the New Testament. Invite students to repeat the names of the first four books after you.

Display **VA 22A Jesus Feeds Crowds of People** and read the text on the back. Review that Jesus, His disciples, and the people were by the Sea of Galilee. Remind students that Jesus had visited this lake once before when He called Peter, Andrew, James, and John to be His disciples. This was a place where Jesus spent a lot of time teaching others about the kingdom of God. People gathered together wherever Jesus was to hear what He had to say!

Ask students if they have ever been in a big crowd for a long time—maybe while shopping or at a sporting event. (**Answers will vary.**) While it can be fun or exciting, being around so many people can be tiring. Jesus was God's Son, but He was also a man. He got tired and He needed to rest. His disciples had been out in the countryside, sharing the good news and healing people. Jesus wanted to spend some quiet time to pray, to be with His disciples, and to continue teaching them things they needed to know. For these reasons, Jesus got into the boat and headed to a quiet place away from the crowds.

But Jesus' plan to spend some time with His disciples was interrupted. Ask students to recount how Jesus felt when He saw all of the people who had followed Him. (**He felt sorry for them.**) What did He do? (**healed the sick, taught them about the kingdom of God**) Jesus spent all day with this great crowd of people.

Explain that Jesus knew that the people were getting hungry, and He felt moved to do something about it. Ask students to tell what the little boy was willing to share. (**five loaves and two small fish**) Inform students that the boy was acting selflessly by sharing what he had. Ask students to recount the first thing Jesus did before He fed the people. (**He said a prayer of blessing.**) When everyone had been served and was full, what was left over? (**12 baskets full of pieces**) This was a miracle—something that only God can do! Remark that God is all-powerful. Explain that the account of the feeding of the 5,000 is the only miracle recorded in all four Gospels.

Review

- How did Jesus feel about the people who followed him? (**He felt sorry for them.**)
- What did Jesus do when they arrived? (**He selflessly healed the sick and taught the people about the kingdom of God.**)
- Why did the disciples want Jesus to send the people away? (**There was no food for all of the people.**)
- What did a boy offer to Jesus? (**five barley loaves and two small fish**) What did Jesus do with the boy's offering? (**He fed the entire crowd of 5,000.**)
- What is one special fact about this miracle that makes it different from all the other miracles in the Bible? (**It is the only miracle listed in all four Gospels.**)

Student Page 22.1

Assist students as they complete the page.

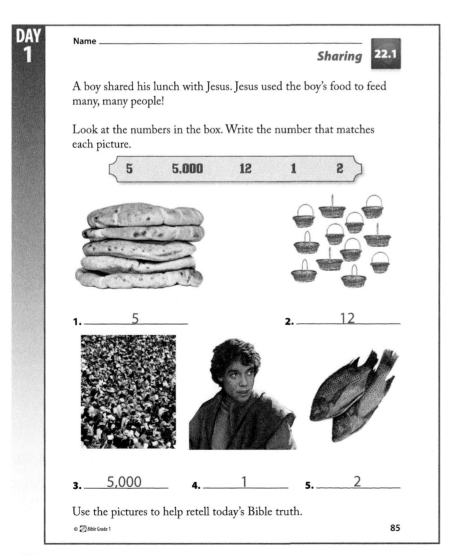

Notes:

DAY 1

Name ____________________

Sharing **22.1**

A boy shared his lunch with Jesus. Jesus used the boy's food to feed many, many people!

Look at the numbers in the box. Write the number that matches each picture.

5 5,000 12 1 2

1. 5

2. 12

3. 5,000 **4.** 1 **5.** 2

Use the pictures to help retell today's Bible truth.

© Bible Grade 1 85

APPLICATION

- Have you ever felt sorry for someone who did not have what you have? Tell about that time. (**Answers will vary.**)
- Have you ever met someone who did not have enough to eat? Would you be willing to share your food with that person? (**Answers will vary.**)
- Think about your favorite toys. Would you be willing to share those toys with someone else? (**Answers will vary.**)
- Are you thankful for what you have? Do you remember to thank God for His loving care and generous provision for your needs? (**Answers will vary.**)

REINFORCEMENT

Unlike our modern concept of a loaf of bread, the loaves mentioned in Scripture could more accurately be described as small crackers. The loaves mentioned in John 6:9 were made of barley, a grain used as food for the poor of that time. A number of these crackers would have been eaten at one time. The two small fish were likely used as a relish. The boy in the crowd had only a snack, not a full meal!

22.2 Sharing

Focus: The Disciples Learn Lessons

★ PREPARATION

Display **TM-9 Pole Vault**. (*Introduction*)

Select **VA 22A Jesus Feeds Crowds of People**. (*Directed Instruction*)

EXTENSION

2A Duplicate a copy of **BLM 22B Sharing Chart** for each student. Explain to students that sharing involves not only giving of one's belongings, but also giving of one's time, talents, and love to others. Have students tell their parent(s) to place a check mark next to each day that they observe their child sharing with others at home.

2B Display **TM-8 Map of Israel** to review the location of the Sea of Galilee. Show students the region of Galilee and the town of Nazareth. Ask which direction Jesus and His disciples would have walked if they were traveling from Nazareth to the Sea of Galilee.

Introduction ★

Display **TM-9 Pole Vault**. Explain that pole vaulting is a sport in which a runner uses a pole to throw himself or herself up and over a high bar. Comment that at one time it seemed impossible for anyone to jump over six meters, which is about twenty feet. However, in 1985, a Ukrainian man did vault over six meters. It would have been impossible for him to vault that high without good training and a coach who helped him to grow in his confidence and ability.

Unlike the man who jumped over six meters, what Jesus did in feeding 5,000 people was a true miracle—something that only God could do. Yet, Jesus was like a coach and His disciples were like team members. Jesus wanted the 12 disciples to grow in faith and do mighty things in His name!

Directed Instruction ★

Display **VA 22A Jesus Feeds Crowds of People** to review the Bible truth. As the day was getting late, the disciples made a suggestion to Jesus. Ask a student to tell what the disciples advised Jesus to do. (**send the people away to get food**) Remind students that Jesus had gone to a quiet place away from the towns. There were no grocery stores at that time. Even if Jesus were to send the people away, they would have had to walk for many miles to find a place to buy food. Ask what might have happened if all the people were sent away. (**Possible answers: Fewer people would have been healed; fewer people would have chosen to follow Jesus.**)

The disciples looked over the huge crowd of people and thought about how much it would cost to feed everyone. Philip spoke for all of the disciples: "If we had 200 denarii, it wouldn't be enough to feed all these people!" A denarius was a coin equal to what a person would receive if he or she worked all day. (*Denarii* means *more than one denarius.*) Philip had figured out that even if someone worked for eight months, all the money earned would not be enough. Philip thought about what the disciples did not have.

Andrew discovered that a boy had a little lunch of five barley loaves and two small fish. The boy was willing to selflessly share whatever he had with others. Andrew wanted to feed the people, but he could only find this small snack. He was probably rather embarrassed to even offer it to Jesus, but the boy was eager to help Jesus, so Andrew gave it to the Lord. Andrew wondered, "What good will these loaves and small fish do?"

Jesus wanted both the disciples and the crowd to understand that He is God. He took the opportunity to teach them this lesson. First, Jesus told the disciples to have the people sit down in groups. Point out that the disciples did what Jesus told them to do even though they did not understand why. Then Jesus said a prayer of blessing. Jesus wanted to thank His Father and give Him the glory for the miracle that He was about to do. The disciples served the people until everyone was full. Jesus had one last instruction for the disciples, and that was to go pick up all the little pieces of leftover food. There were 12 baskets full of leftovers!

On a hillside that afternoon, the crowd and the disciples learned more about Jesus. They saw that He is compassionate—He cares about people, and He can be trusted to provide for their needs. Best of all, Jesus showed the people that He is God!

Review

- What did Philip think about when Jesus asked him to feed the people? **(He thought about what the disciples did not have and how much food would cost.)**
- What did Andrew think about when Jesus asked him to feed the people? **(He thought about how small the boy's lunch was and how it wasn't enough to feed everyone.)**
- Why did Jesus say a prayer of blessing before He multiplied the loaves and fish? **(He wanted to thank His Father and give Him the glory for what He was about to do.)**

Student Page 22.2

Complete the page together. Then have students suggest what they might share with others in addition to sharing material goods.

DAY 2

22.2 *Sharing*

Jesus taught His disciples about Himself through His miracles. Fill in the circle next to the correct ending for each sentence. There may be more than one correct ending.

1. Jesus did miracles because
● He cared about the people.
● He wanted the people to give glory to God.
○ He wanted something to eat.

2. The disciples learned that God is
● loving and all-powerful.
○ always hungry.
● able to be trusted.

3. Jesus taught His disciples to
● trust in Him.
○ pay for food.
● use whatever they had in faith.

4. Jesus is pleased when
● Christians share what they have with others.
○ Christians act selfishly.
● Christians thank Him for His gifts.

86 © Bible Grade 1

APPLICATION

- The boy gave away his food and expected that Jesus could use it. What do you have, besides food, that you could give to others? (**Possible answers: material blessings, money, time, talents, love, care**) How might Jesus be able to use your offering? (**Answers will vary.**)
- Jesus told the disciples to feed the crowd. This would have been an impossible job for ordinary people, but Jesus is God. Have you ever had to do something really hard? Did you pray before doing that job? (**Answers will vary.**)
- Jesus instructed the disciples to have the people sit down in groups. The disciples were obedient even though they did not understand what He was about to do. Share examples of times when you have been obedient to God without understanding what would happen. (**Answers will vary.**)

REINFORCEMENT

It is estimated that Jesus fed upward of 15,000 to 20,000 people on the day of this miracle. Scripture records 5,000 due to the custom of the time, which was to count only the number of men present. If each man were accompanied by his wife and just one child, the number would have been at least three times greater.

22.3 Sharing

Focus: God's Provision

★ PREPARATION

Have enough **FISH-SHAPED CRACKERS** on hand for each student to have about 10 crackers. (*Introduction*)

EXTENSION

3A To encourage students to share with others, have each student trace his or her hand onto a sheet of construction paper and cut out the tracing. They may make several tracings. Whenever a student freely shares with another child, invite that student to write his or her name on a paper hand along with the name of the item(s) that he or she shared. Students may also share words of praise, their time, their place in line, etc. Display the hands in your classroom.

Introduction ★

Considering food allergies, provide **FISH-SHAPED CRACKERS** to each student who would like some. Allow students to eat the crackers as they work on their student page today. Remind students that Jesus had compassion on the crowds of people by the sea. He wanted to provide for their needs, just as He wants to provide for the needs of Christians today.

Directed Instruction

Remind students that a *miracle* is defined as *something only God can do.* Explain that Jesus did miracles in order to demonstrate that He was God, to meet the immediate needs of the people, and to strengthen the faith of His followers.

Student Page 22.3

Read the directions and the sentences in Exercises 1–4. Discuss the character traits listed. For Exercises 5–8, direct the students to draw a line to match each illustration with the sentence that best describes it. Afterward, discuss the character traits of God represented in each illustration. Use the following summaries to discuss the illustrations:

- Feeding of the 5,000:
  Jesus healed the sick and taught the crowds.
  Jesus challenged the disciples to feed the crowds as a test of their faith.
  A boy shared his small lunch, relying on Jesus to use his offering.
  Jesus blessed the food and gave glory to God.
  Miracles—Jesus healed the sick; Jesus multiplied the food.

- Elijah Opposes the Prophets of Baal:
  Elijah confronted King Ahab for worshipping Baal, a false god, and blamed King Ahab for the drought.
  Elijah challenged the prophets of Baal to a contest to prove that only God is the one, true God.
  Nothing happened when the 450 prophets of Baal called for fire to come burn their offering.
  Elijah dug a trench, poured water over his offering, and prayed.
  Miracle—God burned up the offering, the altar, the water, and the rocks.

- Elijah and the Widow:
  God directed Elijah to the starving widow.
  The widow shared her oil and flour even though she had no means of getting any more.
  Miracles—God provided oil and flour until the rains returned; God used Elijah to raise the widow's son from the dead.

- Gideon's Brave Army:
  Gideon was called by God to lead his people and overtake the Midianites.
  God promised to save the people from their enemies with only 300 men.
  Gideon followed God's instructions and went to battle against a much larger enemy army.
  Miracle—God overcame the Midianites with just 300 men.

Review

- What is a miracle? (**A miracle is something that only God can do.**)
- Why did Jesus do miracles? (**Jesus performed miracles to prove that He is God. He wanted people to turn to God and grow in their faith. He cares about people.**)
- How did the boy in the Bible truth participate in the miraculous feeding of the 5,000? (**He allowed Jesus to use his lunch to do a mighty work.**)

Notes:

APPLICATION

- Two of the miracles that you reviewed today had to do with God's provision of food—the feeding of the 5,000, and Elijah and the widow. Once they have had their physical needs met, people are often more willing to listen to the good news of God's plan of salvation. How can you help provide for someone's physical needs? (**Possible answers: collect food for a food drive, donate outgrown clothing, help someone with housework or homework**)
- How can you help people know the good news of God's plan of salvation? (**Possible answers: invite them to church, share how Jesus died on the cross to take away their sins, give them a Bible and offer to read the Bible with them**)
- While you can become more like Jesus as you learn about Him, you can never become completely like God. How is God greater than people? (**Possible answers: God is perfect; He is all-powerful; He is always there; He has all knowledge; He is the Creator of all.**)

DAY 3

Name ______________________________

Sharing 22.3

Read each sentence and trace the gray words. These words describe God.

1. God is caring.

2. God is generous and giving.

3. God is all-powerful.

4. God is faithful to keep His promises.

God's miracles show His character traits. Draw a line to match each sentence to the picture it describes. Talk about what each miracle teaches you about God's character.

5. Gideon leads the army of 300.

6. Elijah meets the widow.

7. Jesus feeds 5,000.

8. Elijah prays for fire.

22.4 Sharing

Focus: Selfless Sharing

EXTENSION

4A If you or your school supports a child from a Christian sponsorship agency, display the PHOTOGRAPH OF A CHILD FROM ANOTHER COUNTRY to your class. Use a GLOBE to point out the country where the child lives. Explain that children in some parts of the world benefit greatly from being supported financially. Sponsoring a child is a way for Christians to share physical possessions with those in need.

Introduction

Write the word *stewardship* on the board. Explain that *stewardship* means *taking care of everything that God has given to you and willingly sharing it with others.* This can include sharing physical things, like money, but it can also include sharing words of encouragement, as well as sharing time and assistance to those in need.

Directed Instruction

Read the following fictional story:

> Just after Mr. Garcia said amen to the blessing, José burst out, "Oh, Mom and Dad, our class started the best project today! We learned about a home for children who do not have parents. We are going to bring some of our toys to send to the children. May I give some of my toys?"
>
> Mr. Garcia said, "José, that sounds like a good idea!" José's mother smiled. "That's a great project for your class." José's older brother, Jaime, quickly said, "You know, José, I think I might have some toys I can send, too." The family talked about the project all during dinner.
>
> As soon as dinner was over, the boys went to their room and opened their toy boxes. In a few minutes, Jaime brought a nice truck, two cars, and a stuffed animal to José's room. As he set them on the bed, José placed his choices by Jaime's. José had chosen a dump truck with a broken tailgate and a car with a bent axle that made it roll in a lopsided way. They weren't very nice toys. Jaime's toys made José's toys look even worse. José shook his head and said, "Wow! You really picked some nice stuff, Jaime."
>
> Jaime grinned and said, "Well, you know I'm in a different class at school since I'm older. I thought about the Bible truth my teacher taught us last month. The Bible lesson was about the time Jesus fed 5,000 people with just five loaves and two small fish. My teacher talked about how Jesus shared dinner with the people. She said that Jesus shared His love with us, too, when He died on the cross even though He had never sinned. Thinking of that lesson made it easy for me to make my choices, especially since I trusted Jesus to be my Savior last summer. I want to give to others because Jesus first gave His life for me."
>
> José said, "I see what you mean, Jaime. Thinking about it like that makes it a lot easier for me, too. I think I'll put in these two good trucks and this car, instead. You know what, Jaime? It really is fun to share!"

Explain to students that whenever they share with others, they show God that they trust Him to provide for them (1 Timothy 6:18). Ask students to share which of the boys' first offerings pleased God more. (**Jaime's**) Why? (**Jaime offered the best toys he had.**)

Jaime said that he had help making his decisions about the toys. Ask a volunteer to recount who Jaime said helped him. (**his teacher in another**

class) Why did Jaime want to share some of his best toys with the children at the home? (**Jesus gave His love to Jaime when He died on the cross for Jaime. Jaime wanted to show Jesus' love to the children at the home.**)

Jaime shared something with his brother, too. By his example, he showed José what God wants from Christians—God wants the best they have to offer! Ask students to tell how Jaime's example influenced José. (**José changed his mind and offered his best toys, too.**)

Review

- How were the toys that José and Jaime first picked different? (**José's toys were broken; Jaime's toys were like new.**)
- What did José learn about sharing from his brother? (**Christians should share their best. Sharing can be fun, too.**)
- Why should Christians give their best to God and to others? (**Jesus gave His best when He gave His life on the cross.**)

APPLICATION

- José was not willing to share his best toys. He was acting selfishly, not selflessly. How can you overcome selfishness? (**I can pray about my attitude and choices. I can remember that Jesus was unselfish when He died on the cross for me. I can choose to share with others and then act selflessly.**)
- What two wise choices did Jaime make? (**He chose to give his best to the children's home. He also chose to put his trust in God.**) Have you made the wise choice to put your faith in God? (**Answers will vary.**)

Student Page 22.4

Assist students in completing the page.

DAY 4

22.4 ***Sharing***

Use the code to solve the puzzle about sharing.

I	i	o	n	G	r	w	s	a	h	e	d	t
20	10	8	24	12	25	15	3	13	22	11	26	2

I (20)   h (22) o (8) n (24) o (8) r (25)

G (12) o (8) d (26)   w (15) h (22) e (11) n (24)   I (20)

s (3) h (22) a (13) r (25) e (11)   w (15) i (10) t (2) h (22)

o (8) t (2) h (22) e (11) r (25) s (3).

22.5 Sharing

Focus: Review and Assessment

★ PREPARATION

Select **VA 22A Jesus Feeds Crowds of People.** (*Lesson Review*)

Make a copy of **BLM 22C Lesson 22 Test** for each student. (*Directed Instruction*)

Lesson Review ★

Use **VA 22A Jesus Feeds Crowds of People** to review the Bible truths in this lesson. Cover the following points:

- The disciples wanted Jesus to send the people away because it was getting late and there was no food for them.
- A little boy offered Jesus five barley loaves and two small fish to help feed the crowd.
- Philip focused on what the disciples did not have when he said, "Two hundred denarii would not feed this crowd."
- Andrew and the boy focused on what they did have when the boy offered all he had for Jesus' use.
- Jesus said a blessing to give God the glory for the miracle that He was about to do.
- One special fact about the miracle of Jesus feeding the 5,000 is that it is the only miracle listed in all four Gospels.
- One of God's purposes in doing miracles is to show people more about Himself.
- Christians can learn more about the character of God by studying the miracles from the Bible.
- Christians today should share their belongings, time, talents, love, care, and the good news of Jesus with others.
- Christians should give their best when they share because Jesus freely gave His best on the cross.
- When Christians lovingly share and meet people's physical needs, this builds a relationship with the people and will often lead to meeting their spiritual needs, too.

Directed Instruction ★

Distribute a copy of **BLM 22C Lesson 22 Test** to each student. Read the directions, and have students complete the test.

Notes:

Lesson Preparation

Caring for Others

23.0

Expected Student Outcomes

KNOW
Jesus heals a paralyzed man.

DO
Students will:
- match the Bible characters to the words they may have spoken
- complete a maze that highlights obstacles to faith
- review the founding of Compassion International
- complete a puzzle that reinforces forgiveness and healing

APPLY
Students will pray in faith for others and help them with compassion.

Lesson Outline

I. Jesus heals a paralyzed man (Lk 5:17–26, Mt 9:2–8, Mk 2:3–12)
II. Building faith
  A. Facing obstacles
  B. Overcoming worry, fear, and doubt
III. Compassion
  A. Rev. Everett Swanson visited Korea in 1952
  B. Compassion International is founded
IV. Forgiveness
  A. Healing in body and in spirit

TEACHER'S HEART

When the paralyzed man's friends carried him to Jesus, they did not stop at the first obstacle. They were determined to bring their friend to the very feet of Jesus. Luke tells us that Jesus was involved with teaching a group of Pharisees and other religious leaders. Intimidating? Not for this group of friends. They managed to carry the mat up a ladder or stairway to the roof, break a hole in the roof, and lower the paralyzed man into the middle of the crowd, right in front of Jesus (Luke 5:19). That was teamwork!

As a teacher, you can tend to become isolated. You spend the day in your classroom. You often eat lunch in your classroom, trying to catch up on whatever task is most urgent. You make and execute your lesson plans with very little input from others. You and other teachers can become a group of individuals who may complain about staff meetings or other duties that take you away from your classroom, your planning, and your grading.

Examine yourself. Do you feel alone and overwhelmed? Chances are you have colleagues who feel the same way. Just like the paralyzed man had friends, so do you. Join together with one or more friends to lift each other up in prayer, trusting that God has the power to give you strength for the challenges you face.

MEMORY VERSE

Galatians 6:2

MATERIALS

Day 1:
- VA 23A Jesus Heals a Paralyzed Man
- BLM 23A The Paralyzed Man and Jesus, card stock, string (*Extension*)

Day 2:
- Stuffed toy, towel
- VA 23A Jesus Heals a Paralyzed Man
- File folders (*Extension*)

Day 3:
- Globe
- Craft sticks, container (*Extension*)

Day 4:
- Erasers

Day 5:
- VA 23A Jesus Heals a Paralyzed Man
- BLM 23B Lesson 23 Test

SONGS

Little Bit of Love

TEACHER RESOURCES

Exley, Richard. *Encounters with Christ.* White Stone Books, 2005.

Wigglesworth, Smith. *Experiencing God's Power Today.* Whitaker House, 2000.

STUDENT RESOURCES

Burkart, Jeffrey E. *Down Through the Roof.* Concordia Publishing House, 2001.

Down Through the Roof. David C. Cook, 2007.

23.1 Caring for Others

Focus: Jesus Heals a Paralyzed Man

MEMORY VERSE

Galatians 6:2

MEMORY WORK

- Explain that a burden is something that is difficult to carry. When the Bible tells Christians to carry each other's burdens, it means that they should help one another in times of need. Write the Memory Verse on the board and read it together. Divide the class into teams of two or three students per team. Have each team meet together to help each other learn the verse by taking turns reciting it. Team members should encourage each other to recite the verse without looking at the board. Have each team come to the front of the room and recite the verse chorally.

PREPARATION

Select **VA 23A Jesus Heals a Paralyzed Man**. (*Directed Instruction*)

EXTENSION

1A Print a copy of **BLM 23A The Paralyzed Man and Jesus** on CARD STOCK for each student. Distribute the copies to students. Provide each student with TWO 12" PIECES OF STRING. Have students color and cut out the figures. Punch holes where indicated at the corners of the mat. Tell students to loop the string through the holes as shown. Save the craft for Lesson 23.2.

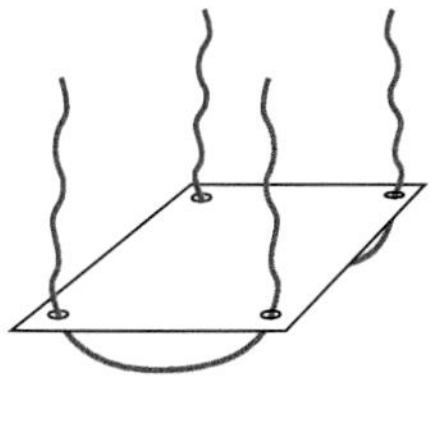

Introduction

Make a circle of chairs with the chair seats facing out. Have students sit on the floor inside the circle, surrounded by the chairs. Stand on the outside of the circle. Walk around the chairs, pretending that you are looking in. Remind students that crowds followed Jesus everywhere He went. Many times, Jesus was surrounded by people, all wanting His help.

The people knew that Jesus had the power to heal the sick. Many people had great faith and believed that if they could get close to Jesus, they would be healed (Mark 5:21–43). Point to a student in the middle of the group on the floor. Explain that if you needed to reach that student, you would have to climb over the chairs and the other students and be very careful about where you stepped. The people who wanted to see Jesus to be healed had even more trouble reaching Him! Have students return to their seats.

Directed Instruction ★ ↷

Explain that Jesus traveled all over Judea and Galilee. Soon everyone in the area knew that Jesus could heal people. One group of four friends heard about Jesus. They had faith that Jesus would heal their sick friend, if only they could get close to the Savior.

Read the Bible truth from **VA 23A Jesus Heals a Paralyzed Man**. Point out the ceiling of the house in the picture on VA 23A. Houses in that part of the world were made with flat roofs. Many of the roofs were made with wood beams stretched across the top of the room. Grass and sticks filled in the gaps between the beams and wet clay was overlaid on the top.

Ask students to imagine a crowd sitting around Jesus, listening carefully to His words. They want very much to learn about all the important things He has to teach them. The people might hear some noises coming from the roof, but they are listening to the Savior speak. Suddenly, grass, bits of dirt, and pieces of debris begin to fall from above! Choose one or two students to tell what they would do if parts of the ceiling began to fall on them. (**Possible answers: look up, scream, move out of the way**) Have a few students pretend to be people inside the house. (Students might pretend to brush dirt off of their heads, make comments indicating confusion about what was happening up on the roof, or express frustration at having dirt and dried grass land on them.)

Have students imagine that the roof is now open, and they can see the sky through the hole. There is something going on up there! A mat is being lowered through the hole to the floor below; a man is on the mat, and he looks like he is unable to move. Jesus looks down at the man with love and compassion. Everyone in the crowd can tell that Jesus cares very much about the man. Ask students to recount how Jesus healed the man. (**Jesus first told the man that his sins were forgiven. Then Jesus told him to pick up his mat and go home.**)

Tell students that the Pharisees were religious leaders who had studied the Bible, and they knew that only God could forgive sins. They did not understand that Jesus is God. When they heard Jesus forgive the man's sins, they were probably angry!

Review

- Why did the four friends go to so much trouble to get their friend to Jesus? (**They had faith in God, and they believed that Jesus would heal their paralyzed friend.**)
- How did the four friends get their friend to Jesus? (**They climbed to the roof of the house, broke through the roof, and lowered the man down to Jesus.**)
- What did Jesus tell the man that angered the Pharisees? (**Jesus told the man that his sins were forgiven.**) How did Jesus prove that He is God and could forgive sins? (**Jesus told the man to pick up his mat and walk. This was a miracle!**)

Student Page 23.1

Help students as needed to read and complete the page.

DAY 1

Name ______________________________

Caring for Others **23.1**

Four friends helped their sick friend. Jesus forgave the man and healed him.

Draw a line to match each person or group of people with the words they said or might have said.

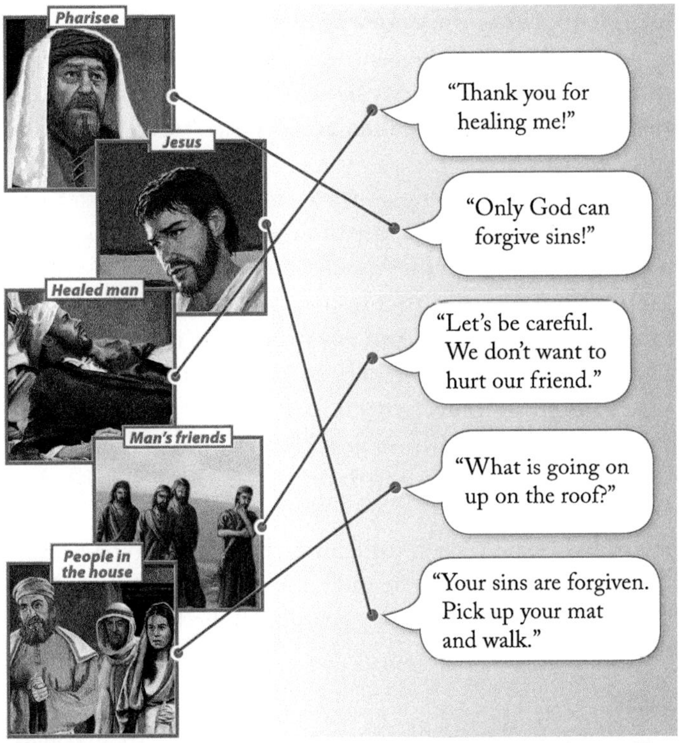

Pharisee
Jesus
Healed man
Man's friends
People in the house
"Thank you for healing me!"
"Only God can forgive sins!"
"Let's be careful. We don't want to hurt our friend."
"What is going on up on the roof?"
"Your sins are forgiven. Pick up your mat and walk."

 89

APPLICATION

- Have you prayed for a friend to receive help from the Lord? Tell about that friend and how you prayed. (**Answers will vary.**) What happened as a result of your prayer? (**Answers will vary.**)
- It is important that Christians care about their friends and pray for them. Think about a friend who needs the Lord's help. Share how you would pray for that person. (**Answers will vary.**)

23.2 Caring for Others

Focus: Building Faith

★ PREPARATION

Bring a STUFFED TOY and a TOWEL to class for a demonstration. (*Introduction*)

Select **VA 23A Jesus Heals a Paralyzed Man**. (*Directed Instruction*)

EXTENSION

2A To construct a background for the figures of Jesus and the paralyzed man made in Extension 1A of Lesson 23.1, you will need TWO MANILA FILE FOLDERS for every two students. Open two file folders and glue the outside of the right-hand side of one folder to the inside of the left-hand side of the second folder as shown. Once the glue dries, cut the file folders in half horizontally. This makes two backgrounds for the Bible figures made in Extension 1A. Have students color the backgrounds to resemble the interior of a home or a courtyard in Bible times.

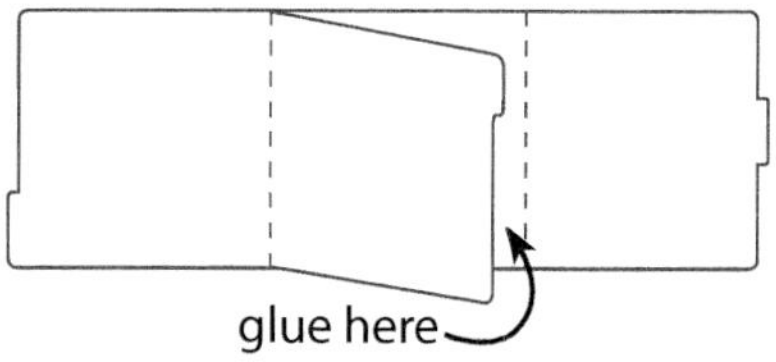

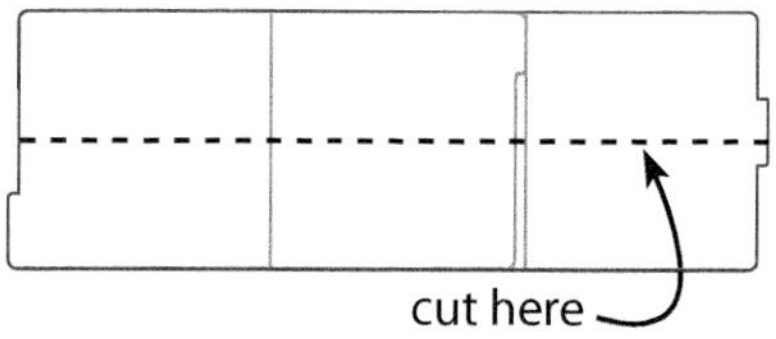

Introduction ★

Remind students that the paralyzed man's friends lowered him to Jesus' feet through a hole in the roof. Explain that this was something that had to be done very carefully or else the man would have been hurt, or someone could have fallen through the hole onto the ground below!

Call on four volunteers to try an exercise that simulates what the four friends did. Put a STUFFED TOY on top of a TOWEL placed on the floor. Invite the volunteers to pick up the corners of the towel and lift it up onto the top of a table without dropping the toy. Remind the four students that they must be careful to keep the towel steady.

After the students have had the chance to lift the toy up to the top of the table, ask students to think about how the four friends would have gotten the paralyzed man up to the roof. Explain that houses in Bible times often had ladders or stairs leading up to the roof. Taking a sick man up a ladder would have been a lot of work for the four friends, but they had faith that Jesus could heal their friend.

Directed Instruction ★

Explain that having faith in Jesus meant that the men trusted Jesus' ability to do a miracle and heal their friend. They did not let anything stop them from trusting in Jesus and from acting on what they believed.

Display **VA 23A Jesus Heals a Paralyzed Man** and discuss the problems that the four friends faced. Ask students to recount why the men could not get their paralyzed friend through the door of the house. (**There were too many people blocking the doorway.**) Why would it have been difficult to get the paralyzed man to the rooftop? (**He could not move on his own; he may have been heavy; it may have been hard to climb the ladder or stairway and safely carry the man at the same time.**)

Explain that Christians often go through difficult times in their life. During these times, there are three things can keep them from trusting God—worry, fear, and doubt. Ask students what might have happened if the men started to worry that Jesus would not heal their friend. (**They might not have opened the roof or lowered the man down.**) What might have happened if the friends had been afraid to make a hole in someone's roof? (**They might not have gotten their friend to Jesus.**) What might have happened if the friends doubted Jesus' ability to heal their friend? (**They would not have bothered to make the effort to bring him to Jesus.**)

The four friends experienced difficulties, but they also had faith in the Lord! They did not let worry, fear, or doubt get in the way of helping their friend. Each man's faith in Jesus encouraged the faith of his friends.

Review

- Did the four men have faith that Jesus would heal their friend? (**Yes, they had faith that Jesus would heal him.**)

- What problems did the men have to solve in order to get their friend to Jesus? (**They had to find a way into the house without using the door. They had to get their friend up to the rooftop and lower him without hurting him.**)
- The four friends all had faith in Jesus. How could their shared faith have been an encouragement to each other? (**Their shared faith helped them to finish what they had set out to do.**)

Student Page 23.2

Assist students as needed in completing the page.

Notes:

DAY 2

23.2 *Caring for Others*

The paralyzed man's friends did not let anything keep them from taking their friend to Jesus. They had faith in Jesus!

1. Find the correct pathway from the friends to Jesus.

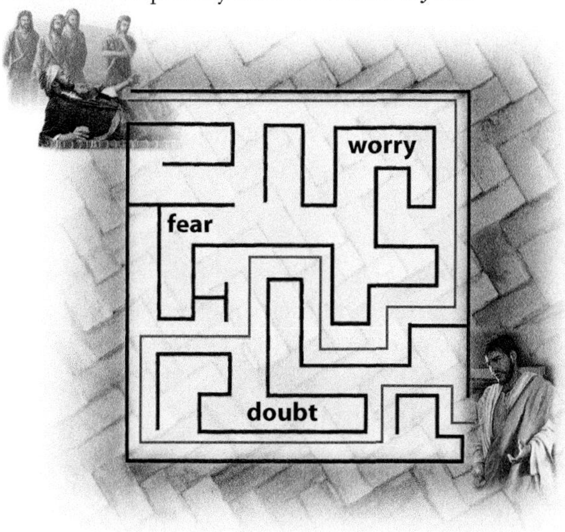

2. Write the words that tell things that could have kept the friends from reaching Jesus.

worry fear

doubt

90 © Bible Grade 1

APPLICATION

- The paralyzed man's friends faced several problems when they decided to take their friend to Jesus. Think about a problem that you have prayed about. Did friends or family members join in faith and prayer with you? (**Answers will vary.**)
- Both the paralyzed man and his friends had faith that Jesus would provide healing. Do you have faith that Jesus will provide for your needs? How can you show your faith in the Lord to others? (**I can pray for others and tell them how God loves them.**)

REINFORCEMENT

In the first century, large and small rocks were wedged together to create walls. The walls were sometimes covered in mud and straw. Roofs were flat and made with wood beams, covered with branches, and then covered with clay. Roofs could be used as workspace and were accessible by ladder or staircase. In the book of Acts, Peter used the roof for prayer (Acts 10:9). The paralyzed man's four friends carried him up a ladder or outside staircase, broke away pieces of the roof, and lowered him through the hole down to Jesus' feet.

23.3 Caring for Others

Focus: Compassion

★ PREPARATION

Select "Little Bit of Love" and other worship songs from the music CDs. (*Introduction*)

Have a GLOBE available. (*Directed Instruction*)

EXTENSION

3A Rev. Everett Swanson worked well with others. To teach your students to work together nicely, keep a set of CRAFT STICKS with the student names written on them in a SMALL CONTAINER. Draw sticks at random when assigning teams or partners.

Introduction ★

Sing "Little Bit of Love" from the music CDs.

Directed Instruction ★

Show students where South Korea is located on a GLOBE. Explain that today they will learn about a man who loved God and knew that God wants Christians to work together to help others. This man helped children in that country. Read the following aloud:

In 1952, Rev. Everett Swanson traveled to visit the country of South Korea. A war had just ended there, and Rev. Swanson planned to teach the men who had been in the army about Jesus. But God had other plans for Rev. Swanson.

Many South Korean children became orphans because of the war. This means that their parents died in the war, and these children no longer had anyone to take care of them. The children needed food, a place to live, clothing, and medical care when they were sick. The children also needed to go to school, and most of all, they needed to learn about Jesus.

Rev. Swanson met many orphans and wanted to help them, but what could he do? He didn't even live in South Korea; how could he take care of so many children with so many needs? He may not have known how to take care of orphans by himself, but he had a close relationship with God. So he prayed and trusted God to show him what to do.

Rev. Swanson went home to the United States and told his wife, Miriam, his friends Dr. and Mrs. Hemwall, and others about the orphans in South Korea. Right away, someone gave Rev. Swanson money to help the children. At this point, he knew that God wanted a group of people to work together and take care of the orphans in South Korea.

The Hemwall family helped Rev. and Mrs. Swanson get the ministry in South Korea started, and they soon learned that many Christians in the United States wanted to help, too. They set up a program so that a person who only had a little money could sponsor a child and be part of God's work in South Korea.

In just eight years, the ministry that Rev. Swanson started with a few friends was supporting 108 orphanages and thousands of children in South Korea. The children received food, clothes, medical care, education, and Bible lessons.

Sadly, Rev. Swanson died just 13 years after he started Compassion International. He learned that by working together, God's people could care for thousands of children. Fortunately, Rev. Swanson worked with so many faithful friends that after he died, they kept helping and finding new ways to take care of orphans.

Review

- What country did Rev. Swanson visit? (**South Korea**)
- What did Rev. Swanson learn when he visited South Korea? (**Many children became orphans because of the war and needed help.**)
- What kind of help did the orphans need? (**a place to live, food, clothes, medical care, education**)
- What was the most important thing the orphans needed? (**They needed to know about Jesus and God's plan of salvation.**)
- Did Rev. Swanson help the Korean orphans all by himself? (**No, he had friends who helped at first. Later, he started to meet many other people who wanted to help, too.**)

Student Page 23.3

Assist students in completing the page.

Notes:

DAY 3

Name ______________________________

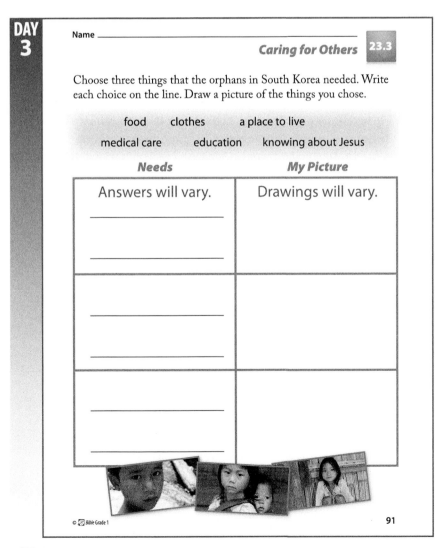

Caring for Others **23.3**

Choose three things that the orphans in South Korea needed. Write each choice on the line. Draw a picture of the things you chose.

food clothes a place to live
medical care education knowing about Jesus

Needs	***My Picture***
Answers will vary. ________ ________	Drawings will vary.
________ ________	
________ ________	

 91

APPLICATION

- How was Rev. Swanson like the paralyzed man's friends? (**Possible answers: Rev. Swanson had faith in Jesus; he wanted to help someone else; he wanted the Lord to provide for the needs of others.**)
- Why do you think that Rev. Swanson invited other Christians to help the orphans? (**because the Bible tells Christians to help others and having other people to help him meant he could help more and more orphans**)
- Rev. Swanson was able to find help providing food, clothing, and other things the children needed. How do you think he helped to provide for their spiritual needs? (**He taught them about Jesus and God's plan of salvation. He prayed for them.**)
- Think about some ways that you and your classmates could work together to help others. (**Answers will vary.**)

REINFORCEMENT

Rev. Everett Swanson founded Compassion International in 1952 to care for war orphans. Today, Compassion has over 1,000,000 sponsored children in 26 different countries. Compassion focuses on the spiritual, physical, economic, and social needs of children through child sponsorship and by forming partnerships with local churches. All of Compassion's programs are rooted in Christian child development. This long-term process can begin with prenatal care and go through leadership development for qualified young adults.

23.4 Caring for Others

Focus: Forgiveness

★ PREPARATION

Collect several types of ERASERS. (*Introduction*)

Introduction ★

Show students several types of ERASERS—pencil erasers that fit on the end of pencils, pink rubber erasers, erasers at the end of new pencils, and chalkboard or whiteboard erasers. Explain that erasers are used to erase mistakes so that the writer can start over. God has offered Christians something like an eraser—forgiveness of sins. Unlike the erasers that people use, God's gift of forgiveness erases sin completely (Ephesians 1:7).

Directed Instruction

Remind students that Jesus' first words to the paralyzed man were to tell the man that his sins were forgiven. Christians need to receive forgiveness from God. Forgiveness is powerful!

Read the following fictional story:

> Tyler clearly remembered the day of his accident. He'd been working hard and was ready to run in the Field Day race. Finally the day of the race came! Tyler's friend Mia was running in the lane next to his. The man at the starting line yelled, "Go!" The runners took off. Tyler and Mia were running right next to each other. It was difficult to tell who was in the lead. All of a sudden, Mia's foot hit a rock. She tripped and tried to keep herself from falling. She landed on Tyler, and then they both sprawled onto the dirt of the track.
>
> Teachers and parents came running! Mia was able to get up. She had scrapes on her legs and her palms were bloody. But Tyler could not get up. He had broken his leg in the fall. An ambulance came to take him to the hospital, where the doctors told him that it would take a long time for him to recover from his injuries. He would probably never be able to run again.
>
> As Tyler lay in his hospital bed, he thought angry thoughts. He blamed Mia for the accident. He blamed the doctors for not fixing his leg. He even thought about blaming God! When Mia came to visit him, Tyler told Mia that the accident was all her fault. She left the room in tears!
>
> Tyler didn't like thinking those thoughts. He did not like the way he had treated Mia, and he wished he could take back what he had said to her. He knew that he had a sinful attitude. Then Tyler had another visitor. It was Pastor Bryan. Tyler did not really want to talk to Pastor Bryan, but somehow Pastor Bryan knew that Tyler had been thinking some very sinful thoughts. Pastor Bryan told Tyler that God would forgive his sins and heal the pain in his spirit. God was ready to heal Tyler's body as well. Tyler joined his pastor in prayer. Tyler told God that he was sorry for what he had thought and for what he had said. He felt a rush of joy! His sins had been forgiven!
>
> Over the next few weeks, Tyler amazed the doctors. His leg grew stronger and stronger! His attitude was better, too. Tyler called Mia and asked for her forgiveness. She forgave Tyler for what he had said to

her and came to the hospital every day to help him exercise his leg. He was going to be able to run in no time!

Review

- How did Tyler sin? (**He blamed others for his broken leg. He said something mean to Mia.**)
- How did Tyler feel about his attitude? (**He knew that his attitude was sinful.**)
- How did Pastor Bryan help Tyler? (**Pastor Bryan told Tyler that Jesus was ready to forgive his sins.**)
- How did God help Tyler? (**God forgave Tyler's sins. God is healing Tyler's leg and making it strong again.**)

Student Page 23.4
Assist students as needed.

Notes:

APPLICATION

- Besides healing the paralyzed man so he could walk, how else did Jesus heal him? (**He forgave the man's sins.**)
- How is forgiveness of sins like an eraser? (**Jesus takes my sins away forever.**)
- How can you be forgiven of your sins? (**I can pray to Jesus, tell Him what I have done wrong, and ask Him to forgive me.**)

DAY 4

23.4 ***Caring for Others***

1. Cross out each of the letters **X**, **Y**, and **Z**. Write the remaining letters to find the answer to the question below.

*	*	H	E	*	*	F	O	R	G	A	V
E	*	T	H	E	*	*	M	A	N	S	*
*	S	I	N	S	*	*	*	A	N	D	*
H	E	A	L	E	D	*	*	*	H	I	M

HOW DID JESUS HELP THE PARALYZED MAN?

He forgave the

man's sins and

healed him.

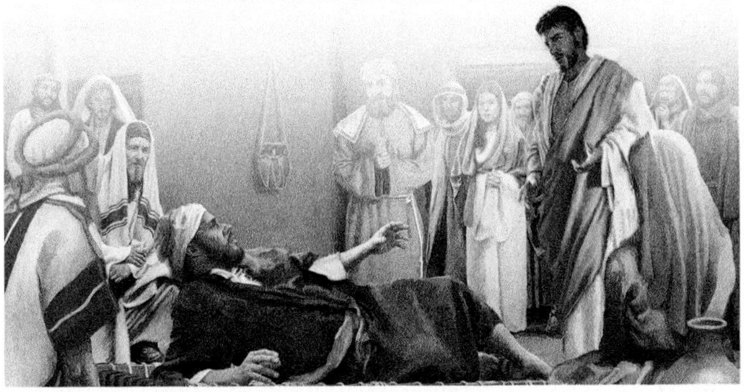

92

23.5 Caring for Others

Focus: Review and Assessment

★ PREPARATION

Select **VA 23A Jesus Heals a Paralyzed Man**. (*Lesson Review*)

Print one copy of **BLM 23B Lesson 23 Test** for each student. (*Directed Instruction*)

Lesson Review ★

Use songs from the music CDs to lead a short time of worship.

Use **VA 23A Jesus Heals a Paralyzed Man** to review the Bible truth. Cover the following concepts:

- Jesus traveled all over Galilee and Judea, healing people while He taught them about God. Crowds of people followed Him wherever He went.
- One day, Jesus was teaching in a house that was crowded with people. Many Pharisees were there to listen to Jesus teach. The Pharisees did not believe that Jesus was the Messiah.
- Four men believed that Jesus could heal their paralyzed friend, so they tried to carry their friend to Jesus. They could not get through the crowd of people.
- These four men did not let worry, fear, or doubt stop them from taking their friend to Jesus.
- The men decided to carry their friend to the roof of the house, open up a hole in the roof, and lower him through the hole. They put their friend right in front of Jesus.
- Jesus told the man that his sins were forgiven. The Pharisees were angry and told Jesus that only God could forgive sins.
- Jesus showed the people that He is God and can forgive sins when He told the man to take up his mat and walk. The paralyzed man was healed!
- When Christians tell Jesus that they are sorry for their sins, He forgives them and erases their sins completely.

Directed Instruction ★

Distribute a copy of **BLM 23B Lesson 23 Test** to each student. Collect the test papers for assessment.

Notes:

Lesson Preparation

Being Thankful

Expected Student Outcomes

KNOW

Ten lepers ask Jesus to heal them. Jesus heals all ten, but only one returns to give thanks.

DO

Students will:

- read a poem about the Bible truth and answer questions
- identify characteristics of different people in the Bible truth
- discover blessings that may be taken for granted
- evaluate actions of children in various scenarios to determine whether or not they showed mercy and grace to others

APPLY

Students will express thankfulness for God's mercy in their daily life.

Lesson Outline

I. Jesus heals ten lepers (Lk 17:11–19)
  A. Jesus meets needs
  B. The lepers act in faith
II. The lepers' response
  A. Life as a leper
  B. Nine are healed, one is thankful
III. Thankful living
  A. Focus on thanksgiving
  B. A modern example
IV. Mercy and grace

TEACHER'S HEART

As a teacher, you touch the lives of many people every day, either by actually being with them or as a result of what you say and do in your teaching. Often you hear a parent say, "I can't thank you enough for what you have done for my child!"

Then there are those times when you have endured a bad attitude from a student as he or she went through a difficult time. You gave your all to help but never received any thanks for your efforts from the student or from the parents. How discouraging this can be! While you would do it all over again, any affirmation would have been an encouragement and a blessing to you.

It is in those tough times that it is important to remember that the Lord is with you. Take heart from the promise found in Galatians 6:9, which says, "And let us not grow weary while doing good, for in due season we shall reap if we do not lose heart." Don't lose heart! The Lord Himself will thank you in due season with, "Well done, good and faithful servant … Enter into the joy of your Lord" (Matthew 25:23).

MEMORY VERSE

Isaiah 63:7a

MATERIALS

Day 1:
- Paper cones
- Thermometer
- TM-8 Map of Israel
- VA 24A Jesus Heals Ten Lepers
- BLM 24A Ten Lepers (*Extension*)

Day 2:
- BLM 24B Table Prayers (*Extension*)

Day 3:
- Binoculars or microscope

Day 4:
- VA 24A Jesus Heals Ten Lepers

Day 5:
- VA 24A Jesus Heals Ten Lepers
- BLM 24C Lesson 24 Test

SONGS

Wanna Say Thank You

TEACHER RESOURCES

DeMoss, Nancy Leigh. *Choosing Gratitude: Your Journey to Joy.* Moody Publishers, 2009.

Harvey, Jane Trufant. *Thank Him: Living Life with an Attitude of Gratitude*. Evergreen Press, 2008.

STUDENT RESOURCES

Lloyd-Jones, Sally. *My Thankful Heart: A Book About Being Grateful.* Tyndale House Publishers, 2004.

Veggie Tales Madame Blueberry: A Lesson in Thankfulness. DVD. Word Entertainment, Inc., 2003.

24.1 Being Thankful

Focus: Jesus Heals Ten Lepers

MEMORY VERSE

Isaiah 63:7a

MEMORY WORK

- Write the Memory Verse on the board and read it together. Explain that Isaiah, the writer of the book of the Bible that contains this verse, was thankful and excited about all the kind things that the Lord had done for him and for the Israelites. Encourage students to be excited about what the Lord has done in their life. Allow students to use their prepared PAPER CONE to amplify their voice as they recite the verse.

PREPARATION

Make PAPER CONES from plain paper for each student to use as a megaphone. Roll up the paper and tape the end securely. Fold under some of the paper on the narrow end of each cone to protect the students' lips. (*Memory Work*)

Obtain a THERMOMETER used for measuring body temperature. (*Introduction*)

Prepare **TM-8 Map of Israel** for display. (*Directed Instruction*)

Select **VA 24A Jesus Heals Ten Lepers**. (*Directed Instruction*)

EXTENSION

1A Duplicate one copy of **BLM 24A Ten Lepers** for each student. Invite students to color the finger puppets, cut them out, and use them to retell the Bible truth.

Introduction ★

Show students the THERMOMETER. Ask a volunteer to tell what it is used for. (**measuring body temperature**) Explain that when someone has a body temperature over 98.6 degrees Fahrenheit, he or she may have a fever and could be ill. Some illnesses are *contagious*, which means *able to be passed from one person to another*. Explain that today's lesson involves people who had a disease that was believed to be contagious.

Directed Instruction ★

Display **TM-8 Map of Israel**. Point out Galilee, Samaria, and Jerusalem. Explain that when Jesus traveled from Galilee toward Jerusalem, the most direct route was to go through Samaria. Ask students to recount how most Jewish people felt about Samaritans. (**Jews did not speak to Samaritans. They went out of their way to avoid traveling through Samaria.**) Remind students that Jesus was not like other Jewish people of His time. He loves and cares about all people!

Display **VA 24A Jesus Heals Ten Lepers** and read the text on the back.

Ask students to think back to a time when they had to stay in bed because they were sick. Explain that they probably expected to be better in a day or two and would be able to see their friends again. But in Jesus' day, there was no medicine or cure for many illnesses like leprosy. People with this disease had a very sad future with little hope of returning to their family and friends.

Ask students if they have ever been lonely. (**Answers will vary.**) The 10 lepers may have been lonely because they had to leave their families. Often, they found others who were sick like themselves. They probably all lived together near the edge of town. Imagine—a group of friends who were all sick! They had to warn others to keep away by shouting that they were sick. Ask a volunteer to share what the Law required lepers to say as a warning. (**Unclean! Unclean!**) That must have been very embarrassing.

Most people would have avoided lepers, but Jesus did not. The 10 men could see that this was Jesus, the teacher who had been healing others. They begged Him to have mercy on them. Jesus showed compassion toward the men and gave them a command. Ask a student to recount what He told the lepers to do. (**Go and show yourselves to the priests.**) That may seem like an odd command, but according to the Jewish Law, someone who had been cured of leprosy had to be examined by a priest. Only the priests had the ability to say whether or not a person was healed and could return home.

Remind students that the lepers had not yet been healed when Jesus told them to go show themselves to the priests. The men had faith that Jesus would heal them, so they quickly obeyed Him and set off to find the priests. Jesus responded to their faith by healing them of leprosy as they went on their way!

What power Jesus had! One of the men—a Samaritan—turned back to say thank you to Jesus. The Samaritan wanted to worship the one who had such power, even over sickness! Jesus was pleased that one man returned to Him, but He was amazed that the other nine did not stop to give thanks for the gift of healing they had received.

Review

- What did the 10 lepers ask Jesus to do? (**have mercy on them, heal them**)
- How did Jesus respond to the lepers' faith? (**He told them to go to the priests before they were actually healed.**)
- How many lepers were healed? (**all 10**)
- How many returned to thank Jesus? (**only one**)

Student Page 24.1

Read any difficult words on the page and allow students to complete the page independently.

DAY 1

Name ____________________________

Being Thankful **24.1**

Read the poem. Write a number word to answer each question.

As Jesus walked from Galilee
He met ten men with leprosy.
They called to Him; their cries increased.
So Jesus said, "Go to the priests."
Because of Jesus' love and power,
All ten were healed within the hour.
Nine went happily on their way.
Just one gave thanks to the Lord that day.

1. How many men had leprosy? ten

2. How many men did Jesus heal? ten

3. How many men went on their way and did not return to give thanks to the Lord? nine

4. How many men returned to thank Jesus? one

APPLICATION

- How do you feel when you give a gift to your friend and he or she really likes it? (**Answers will vary.**) Do you like being thanked for gifts you have given? (**Answers will vary.**)
- God asks for Christians to give Him thanks and praise (Hebrews 13:15, Psalm 147:7). Share some ways that you like to praise and thank God. (**Answers will vary, but should include singing songs of praise and offering thanks in prayer for specific and general blessings.**)
- Jesus was amazed that only one man returned to give thanks. How can you remember to give thanks to the Lord for all you have received? (**I can include prayers of thanksgiving in my daily prayer time.**)

REINFORCEMENT

Leviticus 14 reveals that proving oneself to be clean from leprosy demanded that the leper follow extensive legal requirements. There was an eight-day process of washing, offering sacrifices, and performing ceremonial rites. First, the priest would examine the leper's skin to determine if it was free from disease. If the person had been healed, two live birds would be brought for a cleansing ceremony. After the ceremony, the person was required to wash his or her clothes and shave off all body hair before being pronounced ceremonially clean. Then, he or she was free to enter the camp but still could not enter his or her tent for yet another seven days. On the eighth day, the person was once again required to wash, shave off all body hair, and offer both animal and grain sacrifices for his or her redemption. Finally, the former leper would be free to come back into his community!

24.2 Being Thankful

Focus: The Lepers' Response

★ PREPARATION

Select "Wanna Say Thank You" from the music CDs. (*Introduction*)

EXTENSION

2A Table prayers can become rote repetitions instead of joyful expressions of thanksgiving. Duplicate a copy of **BLM 24B Table Prayers** to teach students some new and fresh ways to thank the Lord for their food.

Introduction ★

Begin the lesson with a brief period of worship. Play the song "Wanna Say Thank You" from the music CDs. Ask students to share things that they are thankful for and make a list of those things on the board. Pray together, thanking God for the things on the list.

Directed Instruction

To help students understand what life would be like for a leper in Jesus' time, choose 10 students to role-play lepers. Have the 10 lepers stand together in one corner of the room and tell them to warn passersby of their disease by yelling, "Unclean! Unclean!" when anyone comes within two or three yards of the group. Show the lepers how far away that is. Walk slowly toward the group and signal the lepers to call out their warning as you approach. Back away from the group quickly as if you fear them or are disgusted by them. Depending on the size of your class, have several other students or all of the other students approach and pass by the group of lepers. Encourage each passerby to look at the lepers sadly or with fear. Remind the lepers to call out a warning when your volunteers get too close. Thank your volunteers and have them return to their seats.

Remind students that lepers could not work a normal job in town. They probably had to beg for a living. They could not get close to people, so they could not put out their hands to receive money. They could not even go to a store and buy food if they did get some money. They had to beg at a distance and hope that someone would leave some food for them. This was a sad way to live!

The group of 10 lepers needed a miracle! When they heard that Jesus was coming their way, they called out loudly and begged Him to have mercy on them and heal them. Jesus met their needs because He loves and cares about all people.

After being told to go to show themselves to the priests and be declared healthy, all 10 men quickly obeyed Jesus. They were so excited about this wonderful miracle! Ask a few students to share what the men might have thought when they discovered that they had been healed. (**Possible answers: Can this really be happening? I can go home! I cannot wait to see my family!**)

Leprosy was usually incurable, and yet Jesus had healed all 10 men completely. Remind students that only one leper returned to thank Jesus when he realized that he was well. This one man realized that Jesus was no ordinary man! He fell down at Jesus' feet and thanked Him. Then the man loudly praised Jesus. He worshipped Jesus for restoring his body to health! The leper may not have known it, but Jesus is God's Son. He has power over sickness and death.

Review

- How did most lepers get what they needed in order to live? (**They probably had to beg.**)
- Had the 10 lepers done anything to deserve Jesus' healing power? (**No, Jesus healed them out of His love and compassion for people.**)
- What did the one leper realize about Jesus? (**Jesus was no ordinary man.**)
- How did the leper give thanks to the Lord? (**He fell down at Jesus' feet and thanked Him.**)
- What attitudes did the other nine lepers display? (**Possible answers: ungratefulness, uncaring, thoughtlessness, forgetfulness, selfishness**)

Student Page 24.2

These exercises will be easier to complete if colored pencils are available. Read the directions and any unfamiliar words on the page. When students have completed the page, review the answers together.

Notes:

APPLICATION

- Most Jewish people would have nothing to do with a Samaritan, especially one with leprosy. How was Jesus different from most Jewish people of His time? (**Jesus loves and cares for all people.**)
- Do you only choose friends who are like you? (**Answers will vary.**) Do you avoid playing with certain boys or girls just because they are different? (**Answers will vary.**)
- How can you act in faith to show God's love to a variety of different people? (**Answers will vary.**)

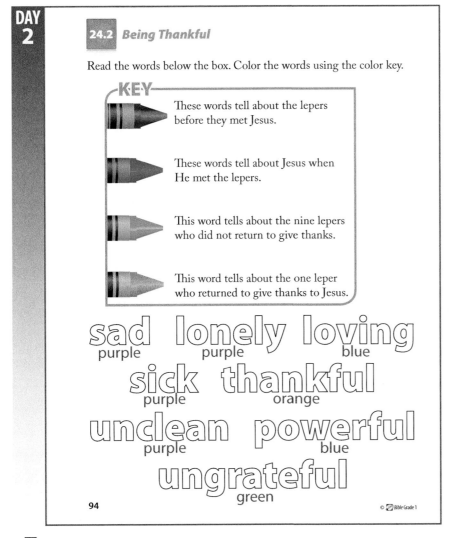

DAY 2

24.2 ***Being Thankful***

Read the words below the box. Color the words using the color key.

KEY

These words tell about the lepers before they met Jesus.

These words tell about Jesus when He met the lepers.

This word tells about the nine lepers who did not return to give thanks.

This word tells about the one leper who returned to give thanks to Jesus.

sad (purple) lonely (purple) loving (blue)

sick (purple) thankful (orange)

unclean (purple) powerful (blue)

ungrateful (green)

94 © Bible Grade 1

24.3 Being Thankful

Focus: Thankful Living

★ PREPARATION

Bring BINOCULARS or a MICROSCOPE to class. Be sure the instrument has a knob that adjusts its focus. (*Introduction*)

Introduction ★

Display BINOCULARS or a MICROSCOPE. Ask a student who has used binoculars or a microscope to tell what the device is used for. (**Binoculars make faraway things appear to be closer; a microscope magnifies tiny objects.**) Point out the knob that controls the focus on the instrument. When the instrument is in focus, everything is clear to the viewer. Good focus helps the viewer to understand what he or she is seeing.

Directed Instruction

Compare the purpose of focusing the binoculars or the microscope to the Christian's need to focus on the goodness of the Lord. Read the following fictional story, and ask students to listen to determine if the main character had his focus on himself or on the Lord:

> Gregory was having a hard day. He woke up earlier than usual because of noisy birds singing outside his window. Then his dad came in and told him that it was a bright, sunny day. It was the perfect day to play outside. Gregory didn't feel much like being cheerful. He got out of bed, stubbed his toe on the leg of the bed, and looked for some clean socks. He couldn't find any matching socks, so he pulled on two different socks. That would not have been so bad, but one of the socks had a big hole in the toe! Gregory growled! Now he was running late for school. His mother had made pancakes, but there were none left because his sister and brother had already eaten them all. Gregory had to settle for cold cereal and milk. He ran and got into the car, but he had forgotten his lunch.
>
> Later, Gregory's friend Brayden came to sit with him during lunch. Brayden noticed that Gregory did not have anything to eat, so Brayden offered him a half of his sandwich. Gregory did not like turkey and cheese. He was a little rude to Brayden when he turned down the sandwich. Nothing was going well that day.
>
> When Mrs. Woods, Gregory's teacher, asked the students to list things that they wanted to thank God for, Gregory could not think of anything to say. He focused on what had gone wrong that day. Gregory did not feel happy or thankful at all.

Review

- In what ways had God provided for Gregory? (**Answers will vary, but should include a home, a bed, a dad, a mom, a sunny day, clothing, food for breakfast, a ride to school, and a friend.**)
- How did Brayden try to help Gregory? (**He offered Gregory a half of his sandwich.**)
- What might have prevented Gregory from being able to think of something that he was thankful for? (**He was only thinking about what had gone wrong that day.**)
- If Gregory had focused on the Lord instead of on his own problems, would he have been more thankful? Why? (**Yes. When Christians look**

to the Lord and remember all that He has provided for them, they will want to respond to the Lord with a thankful heart.)

Student Page 24.3

Read any difficult words and assist students in writing student-selected names on the lines.

Notes:

APPLICATION

- Have you ever had a hard day? (**Answers will vary.**) Was it easy or difficult to focus on God's blessings that day? (**Answers will vary.**)
- How can you keep your focus on God's blessings and be grateful when you are having a hard day? (**I can pray and ask God to help me be thankful, even on hard days.**)
- Share something that you have done to become more grateful. (**Answers will vary, but should include asking God to help me count my blessings and praying thankful prayers instead of merely asking God to provide for my needs.**)

REINFORCEMENT

Jesus said to the leper who returned to Him, "Arise, go your way. Your faith has made you well." The word used for *well* in this verse is the Greek word *sozo*, which means *saved, delivered,* and *healed*. Not only did the man receive physical healing, he received spiritual healing as well!

DAY 3

Name ______________________

Being Thankful **24.3**

Gregory did not appreciate his many blessings. He did not thank the people who provided blessings to him. What about you? Do you always remember to thank others?

1. Put a check mark ✓ in the box next to any of the things that you sometimes forget to be thankful for. Write the name of someone you need to thank next to the things you checked.

- ☐ good food Answers will vary.
- ☐ someone to play with ______
- ☐ help with homework ______
- ☐ a ride to school ______
- ☐ an interesting lesson ______
- ☐ a clean classroom ______

What things will you try to remember to give thanks for each day?

Answers will vary.

2. ______ **4.** ______

3. ______ **5.** ______

24.4 Being Thankful

Focus: Mercy and Grace

★ PREPARATION

Select **VA 24A Jesus Heals Ten Lepers**. (*Directed Instruction*)

EXTENSION

4A Write the acrostic **G**od's **R**iches **A**t **C**hrist's **E**xpense on a large sheet of paper and post it in the classroom. Show students that the first letter in each word spells the word *grace*. Explain to students that Jesus showed grace to the 10 lepers by healing them. God showed His grace to everyone in that while they were still sinners, Christ died for them (Romans 5:8).

4B Remind students that they ought to extend mercy for most minor offenses, but that there are times when it is necessary to report problems to the teacher or another authority. If one student is consistently verbally or physically attacking another, that is bullying. Bullying should not be tolerated. Again, if a student sees another student engaging in a dangerous behavior, it is always important for that behavior to be reported for the safety of the student and possibly others.

Introduction

Write the words *mercy* and *grace* on the board and read them aloud. Inform students that these words tell about two of God's greatest gifts to Christians. Explain that *mercy* means *not receiving a deserved punishment. Grace* means *receiving something that is not earned.*

Directed Instruction ★

Display **VA 24A Jesus Heals Ten Lepers.** Ask a student to share what the lepers first called out to Jesus to ask Him to heal them. (**Jesus, Master, have mercy, or pity, on us!**) Explain that in Jesus' time, people often thought that sickness was God's punishment for sin. Leprosy was a particularly horrible disease because it had no cure at that time. People could suffer from leprosy for many years. The 10 lepers might have thought that their disease was a punishment for some sin they had committed. They might have thought that Jesus would not even bother to look at them. But Jesus showed the men mercy by not treating them like sinners or unwelcomed visitors from another land as other Jewish people did; Jesus showed them compassion. Jesus also showed the lepers grace by healing them. They had done nothing to deserve or earn this healing! Jesus healed them because He loved them and was responding to their faith.

Remind students that Christians ought to show mercy and grace to everyone they meet. When Christians show mercy, they do not seek to get even with someone who has harmed them, or try to get others in trouble. Christians show grace when they lovingly care for others out of compassion and concern.

Jesus demonstrated both mercy and grace during His life on the earth. The Bible says that those who have sinned deserve punishment (Romans 6:23). However, Christians do not receive the punishment they deserve for sin. Jesus mercifully took the punishment that everyone deserves by dying on the cross!

God's grace is seen in many ways. The gift of salvation is the best gift of all. Christians receive God's gracious gift of salvation through faith. Salvation is not something that can be earned by doing good things, paid for with money, traded for, or passed down from a family member. Salvation is through faith in Jesus and His grace alone (Ephesians 2:8). The gift of salvation provides the forgiveness of sins that is necessary to have a relationship with God. When Christians die, they go to live with God in heaven forever.

Review

- What is mercy? (**Mercy is not receiving a deserved punishment.**)
- What is grace? (**Grace is receiving something that is not earned.**)
- How did Jesus show mercy to the lepers? (**He looked on them with compassion and healed them.**)
- To whom should Christians show mercy and grace? (**to everyone they meet**)

• What is the best gift that God gives you through His grace? (**The gift of salvation is the best gift of all.**)

Student Page 24.4
Read each of the scenarios with students and allow them to choose the response that shows mercy or grace. Encourage students to choose one of the scenarios and discuss additional words of advice that would also show mercy or grace.

Notes:

APPLICATION

- Christians should show mercy and grace to everyone they meet. Is it easy for you to show mercy to someone who has accidentally hurt you? (**Answers will vary.**)
- What is a way to show mercy to someone who has apologized for hurting you? (**I should forgive that person.**) How can you show grace to that person? (**I can be a friend to the person I have forgiven.**)

DAY 4

24.4 ***Being Thankful***

Listen to each story. Underline the words that show mercy or grace.

1. Anita's little sister always wants to follow Anita around. Anita does not want to play with her sister all day. What should Anita say to her?

"I'll play with you for a little while today."

"Go away and don't bother me anymore!"

2. Cassidy's brother was mad at her, so he called her a bad name. That made Cassidy mad. What should Cassidy say to her brother?

"I'm telling Mom! I hope you get in big trouble."

"I don't like fighting. Let's stop it now."

3. Vanessa took Gavin's place in line. Gavin felt angry about that. What should Gavin say to Vanessa?

"I was here first, but you may have my place in line today."

"Go to the back of the line now! You know that cutting in line is against the rules."

4. Pretend that you are a friend of Anita, Cassidy, or Gavin. Discuss in class what words you could use to show mercy or grace to them.

Answers will vary.

96

24.5 Being Thankful

Focus: Review and Assessment

★ ***PREPARATION***

Select **VA 24A Jesus Heals Ten Lepers**. (*Lesson Review*)

Print one copy of **BLM 24C Lesson 24 Test** for each student. (*Directed Instruction*)

Lesson Review ★

Use **VA 24A Jesus Heals Ten Lepers** to review the Bible truth. Cover the following concepts:

- Jesus was walking through Galilee and Samaria when He met 10 men.
- The 10 men were separated from other people because they had leprosy, a skin disease.
- Lepers were required by law to live outside the village and shout, "Unclean! Unclean!" when anyone came close to them.
- The lepers knew that Jesus had the power to heal them, so they called out to Him.
- Jesus gave instructions to the 10 lepers to go show themselves to the priests. This was unusual because the lepers were not yet healed when He told them to go.
- Jesus gave the lepers these instructions because He was responding to their faith. They obeyed His instructions to go to the priests.
- The only man who came back to thank and praise Jesus was a Samaritan.
- The nine lepers did not thank Jesus for His gift of healing.
- When the Samaritan man returned to Jesus, the man praised Jesus loudly and worshipped Him.
- Christians ought to focus on God's blessings. Including prayers of thanksgiving in daily times of prayer helps Christians to be grateful.
- Jesus demonstrated mercy and grace in the healing of the 10 lepers.
- Christians are to extend mercy and grace to others.

Directed Instruction ★

Distribute a copy of **BLM 24C Lesson 24 Test** to each student. After students have completed the test, collect the test papers for assessment.

Notes:

Lesson Preparation
Giving

25.0

Expected Student Outcomes

KNOW
A poor widow gives all her money to God.

DO
Students will:
- choose the best ending for sentences that retell the Bible truth
- complete a matching activity to review Bible truths about faith
- complete sentences that identify stewardship concepts
- determine if good or poor stewardship is shown in scenarios

APPLY
Students will demonstrate responsible stewardship of their possessions and talents.

Lesson Outline

I. A widow's gift (Lk 21:1–4, Mk 12:41–44)
  A. Jesus teaches and watches people in the temple
  B. Jesus remarks about the gift of a widow
II. Demonstrating faith
  A. Prayerfully considering giving
  B. Trusting God to provide
III. Giving from the heart
  A. Sharing time, talents, and possessions
IV. Being good stewards (Mt 25:14–30)
  A. Caring for possessions
  B. Sharing love, forgiveness, mercy, and grace

TEACHER'S HEART

When you think of godly stewardship, you may think in terms of managing your time, talents, and treasures. Perhaps you count what you have and parcel it out to God in bits and pieces. The more you give God, the more generous you feel. But isn't that the way the world manages its resources, assuming ownership and then giving out of obligation or pride?

Jesus, of course, was different. He willingly gave everything He had, and as a result, you have forgiveness, mercy, grace, and salvation. God calls you to reject the patterns of the world and become a living sacrifice. Remember that your greatest gift from God is life. God has also given you the power of the Holy Spirit to renew your mind and strengthen your inner being (Romans 12:2, Ephesians 4:16).

First-grade students are not yet ready to fully understand the concept of being a living sacrifice for the Lord. However, as they grow closer to God, they grow closer to the realization that everything they have comes from God. Stewardship is all about giving back to God what is already His own.

MEMORY VERSE

Luke 6:38a

MATERIALS

Day 1:
- VA 25A The Widow's Coins
- Pennies, can
- Bulletin board paper (*Extension*)

Day 2:
- VA 25A The Widow's Coins
- Plastic coins
- Old coins or coins from different countries (*Extension*)

Day 3:
- Clock, baseball, paintbrush, sheet music, toy
- VA 25A The Widow's Coins
- PP-7 Giving to God's Work (*Extension*)
- Box (*Extension*)

Day 4:
- Jacket or sweater
- BLM 25A Things That Need Care (*Extension*)

Day 5:
- VA 25A The Widow's Coins
- BLM 25B Lesson 25 Test

TEACHER RESOURCES

Amaradio, Tony and Carin. *Faithful with Much: Breaking Down the Barriers to Generous Giving*. David C. Cook, 2008.
Young, Sarah. *Jesus Calling: Enjoying Peace in His Presence*. Integrity Publishers, 2004.

STUDENT RESOURCES

Bader, Joanne. *The Widow's Offering*. Concordia Publishing House, 2008.
Lucado, Max. *You Are Mine*. Crossway Books, 2002.

25.1 Giving

Focus: A Widow's Gift

MEMORY VERSE

Luke 6:38a

MEMORY WORK

- Write the Memory Verse on the board, stopping after the word *over.* Read the verse chorally several times. Divide the class into three groups. Begin reciting the verse and have the first group say *good measure* or *a good amount* in an exaggerated manner while pretending to scoop something out of a container. Invite the second group to say *pressed down* while they pantomime pressing downward. Assign the third group to say *shaken together* as they pretend to shake an invisible container when you reach that point in the recitation. Change groups or phrases assigned for more practice.

★ PREPARATION

Write each of the following phrases in large letters on a separate piece of white paper: *obey God, trust God, worship God, give thanks to God.* (*Introduction*)

Select **VA 25A The Widow's Coins**. (*Directed Instruction*)

Bring in NINE PENNIES and a METAL CAN for a demonstration. (*Directed Instruction*)

EXTENSION

1A Mark four sections on a LARGE PIECE OF WHITE BULLETIN BOARD PAPER and label them as: *Giving Help to My Church and Others, Family Needs, Savings,* and *Family Fun.* Invite students to draw pictures of how they use money in each section. Display their work.

Introduction ★

Remind students that Christians grow in their relationship to God as they follow His ways. Explain that you have written several practices of godly people on pieces of paper. Hold up each of the prepared papers, beginning with the paper that reads *obey God.* Invite students to suggest people they have studied from the Bible who chose to obey God. (**Possible answers: Moses, Gideon, Joseph and Mary**) Show students the words *trust God.* Choose volunteers to give examples from the Bible of people who trusted God. (**Possible answers: Noah, Ruth, King David**) Display the words *worship God* and ask for suggestions of people who made worship a priority. (**Possible answers: Abel, Solomon, Josiah**) Finally, show the words *give thanks to God.* Ask students to share examples of people who demonstrated thankfulness. (**Possible answers: King Solomon, the leper who was healed**)

Directed Instruction ★

Explain that while Jesus lived on the earth, He would sometimes see people doing things to purposely bring attention to themselves and not God. At other times, Jesus would see people doing things that would honor God. Ask students to listen for what Jesus observed while you read today's Bible truth. Display **VA 25A The Widow's Coins** and read the text on the back.

Review that when Jesus finished teaching, He sat and watched some people put money into the collection box at the temple. Remind students that Christians today also give money to the church in the form of an offering. Sometimes the offering is collected in a bag or a plate that is passed among the people in worship. Recount that while Jesus watched, some people put a lot of money into the collection box. Drop NINE PENNIES, one at a time, into the METAL CAN. Shake the can and remind students that the rich people had given quite a bit to the offering. Take the pennies out of the can.

Jesus continued to watch. He saw a poor widow come to the box. Ask a volunteer to recount how many coins she dropped into the collection box. (**two**) Drop TWO PENNIES into the metal can, one at a time so students can hear them hit the bottom. Explain that the widow had the least to give. Remind students because Jesus is God, He can see not only the gift but also the heart—the attitude and intentions—of the giver. Jesus told the disciples that the widow had given more than anyone else that day because she willingly gave all she had out of love for the Lord.

Explain that as Christians grow in their relationship to the Lord and study His Word, they will learn more about giving and want to give out of love for God and for others. Giving generously is something that all Christians should strive to do (Romans 12:10–13).

Review

- Where were Jesus and the disciples when they saw the poor widow? (**in the temple**)
- Why were they in the temple? (**Jesus was teaching the people what it really means to be members of God's family.**)
- What else did Jesus do at the temple? (**He watched people put money in the offering box.**)
- What was it about the widow that caused Jesus to compare her offering to those of the rich people? (**The widow's attitude toward giving was different from that of the rich people. She willingly gave all that she had while the rich people only gave from what they really didn't need.**)

Student Page 25.1

Students will need a colored pencil or crayon to color the coin shapes on the page. Read any unfamiliar words before allowing students to complete the exercises independently. When all students have finished the page, discuss student answers.

DAY 1

Name ____________________

Giving **25.1**

Read the sentences and the words on the coins. Color the coin that best completes each sentence.

1. Jesus and His disciples were in the ____. temple | bank | house

2. Jesus watched people put money into the ____. ball | band | box

3. Some rich people put in a lot of ____. time | money | toys

4. One poor widow put in two copper ____. rich | pans | coins

5. Jesus pointed out the widow because she gave away money that she ____. wasted | needed | covered

APPLICATION

- How does your relationship to God help you to give to others? (**I know that God loves me and will provide me with all I need. I lovingly give to others because Jesus first gave Himself to me.**)
- What should your attitude be when giving to the Church so that others may come to know Jesus and needs are met? (**I should be grateful to God for providing me with something to give, and I should be happy about giving.**)
- Does the Lord want Christians to give away all that they have? (**It would be unusual for the Lord to ask a Christian to give away all that he or she has. However, He wants Christians to use their money wisely and give freely.**)

25.2 Giving

Focus: Demonstrating Faith

★ *PREPARATION*

Select **VA 25A The Widow's Coins**. (*Introduction*)

Provide each student with a small quantity of PLASTIC COINS. (*Directed Instruction*)

EXTENSION

2A Have on hand a variety of OLD COINS or COINS FROM DIFFERENT COUNTRIES for students to use to make crayon rubbings. Instruct each student to place a sheet of plain white paper over the coin chosen for the rubbing. Remove the label from a dark crayon and have students rub the side of the crayon on the paper over the coin. It may take a few attempts for students to hold the paper still while rubbing the image. Discuss the importance of prayerfully considering how one should give and spend even small amounts of money.

Introduction ★

Display **VA 25A The Widow's Coins**. Ask a volunteer to recount where Jesus and the disciples were when Jesus was teaching. (**They were in the temple.**) What did Jesus do after He finished teaching? (**He watched people come into the temple and put money in the collection box.**) What did He see? (**Some people put in a lot of money; others put in little.**) How much money did the poor widow put into the collection box? (**two coins**) What was different about this offering from the others? (**The widow put in money that she needed in order to live; the others gave what they didn't need.**) Explain that Jesus knew the widow's situation, and realized the faith she had that God would provide for her needs.

Directed Instruction ★

Distribute the PLASTIC COINS to the students so that they do not all receive the same amount. Give one student only two plastic coins.

Direct students to count their plastic coins. As they finish, ask them to call out the totals and write the numbers on the board. Ask students to separate their money into piles that will represent various ways that Christians spend their money. Have students set aside one pile to give to God's work, one pile for family needs, and one pile for savings. (First-grade students will have a tendency to make their piles of coins all the same size. Others may want to put it all in one pile for the Lord.) Remind students that their family needs to eat, have shelter, and have savings for an emergency, so they must make three piles. It is not necessary to explain percentages or portions for each pile.

Invite students to look at each other's piles of coins. Draw students' attention to the fact that the students with the most money have the most that they could give to the Lord and they also have the most to spend on family needs. Point out that the student with only two coins could not even make three piles!

Discuss ways that the student with two coins could divide his or her coins. He or she could give both coins to the Lord or keep one coin or both coins for family needs. Point out that giving one coin to the Lord represents a much larger sacrifice for the student with only two coins. If that student were to give one or both coins away, there would be little or nothing left for family needs.

Write the word *faith* on the board. *Faith* is defined as *belief and trust in God.* Explain that giving to the Lord requires faith on the part of all Christians, but when one has little to give, more faith is required. The widow had great faith! When she gave all she had to live on to the Lord, she put her trust in Him to provide for her needs.

Tell students that giving to God's work is very important! Christians need to prayerfully consider how much they will give to their church, how much they will spend on family needs, and how much to put into savings.

All sacrificial giving requires faith. When Christians give to the Lord, providing money so that others can hear about Jesus and needs can be met, they trust Him to provide for their ongoing needs.

Review

- What is faith? (**Faith is belief and trust in God.**)
- Who demonstrated greater faith, the widow or the rich people? (**The widow did.**)
- Does giving to the Lord require faith? (**Yes.**) Why? (**When Christians give to the Lord's work—giving so that others may know Jesus and needs are provided for—they trust Him to provide for their own ongoing needs.**)

Student Page 25.2

Assist students as needed in completing the page.

Notes:

DAY 2

25.2 Giving

Each sentence shows faith and trust in God. Match the sentence on the left with the way the person or people trusted on the right.

1. Peter let down his fishing nets.	They trusted Jesus to heal their friend.
2. A boy gave his lunch to Jesus.	He trusted Jesus to feed the people.
3. Four friends brought their sick friend to Jesus.	They trusted Jesus to heal them.
4. Ten lepers begged for healing.	She trusted God to provide for her needs.
5. A poor widow put all of her money into a special box in the temple.	He trusted Jesus to provide a catch of fish.

APPLICATION

- How do you share your money with others? (**Answers will vary.**)
- What is the best way to decide how much money to share with others? (**I think about the needs that others have and then I pray and think about how much to give.**)
- Why is it important to give money to the Church? (**Possible answers: When I give to the Church, it helps others hear about Jesus; it helps others receive what they need; it helps me grow in my faith; the Bible tells me to give.**)

REINFORCEMENT

Central to the practice of the Christian faith is compassion for the poor. James stated that true religion, the worship of God, results in looking after orphans and widows in their distress and staying unspotted from the world (James 1:27). Christian teachers contribute to their students' spiritual growth by teaching them how to manage money effectively, use it to care for the poor, and avoid the temptation to build up treasures on Earth.

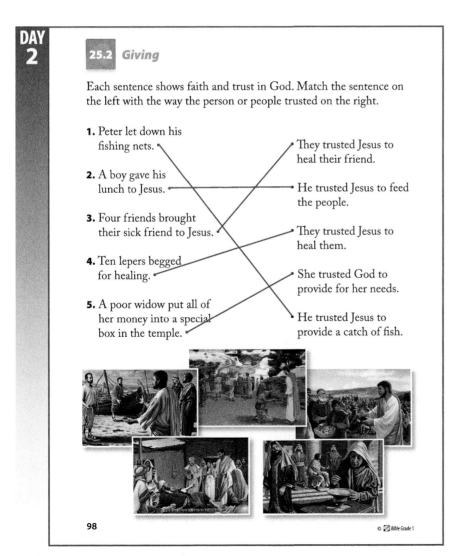

25.3 Giving

Focus: Giving from the Heart

★ PREPARATION

Have available a SMALL CLOCK, a BASEBALL, a PAINTBRUSH, a SHEET OF MUSIC, and a TOY. (*Introduction*)

Display **VA 25A The Widow's Coins**. (*Directed Instruction*)

EXTENSION

3A Display **PP-7 Giving to God's Work** to teach students about giving generously to others, including the biblical principle of tithing.

3B As a class, choose a missionary or missions organization to support, and collect a weekly offering in your classroom. Decorate a SMALL BOX with pictures that show the work of the missionary or organization. For the remaining weeks of school, continue to remind students to bring in donations. After a predetermined time period, count the money collected, congratulate the students on their faithful giving, and donate the money to the chosen recipient.

Introduction ★

Choose five volunteers to hold the SMALL CLOCK, the BASEBALL, the PAINTBRUSH, the SHEET OF MUSIC, and the TOY that you have gathered. Ask students to guess what these items have in common. (**Answers will vary.**) Explain that these items might not look like they have anything in common, but they represent blessings that God has given Christians. These blessings are time, talents, and possessions.

Have the student holding the small clock to step forward. Explain that the clock represents time. Explain that God has given everyone the gift of 24 hours every day. God desires that Christians spend time wisely.

Ask the students holding the baseball, the paintbrush, and the sheet of music to step forward. Explain that these items represent talents that some of them might have. The baseball stands for athletic skill. Ask students who have athletic skills to raise their hand. The paintbrush represents artistic skills. Have students who are artistic to raise their hand. The sheet of music symbolizes musical talent. Invite students who have musical talent to raise their hand. Remind students that God gives people many different talents and skills to share with others and to use to help others come to know Jesus. Reassure students that even if they did not raise their hand, they will discover more talents as they grow older.

Have the student holding the toy to step forward. Explain that the toy represents possessions. Christians have many different possessions that they could share with others. These possessions include money, but Christians could also share food, clothing, and other belongings. They could also open their homes to those in need.

Directed Instruction ★

Display **VA 25A The Widow's Coins**. Review the Bible truth, emphasizing that the widow put her two coins into the temple collection box to give to the Lord's work—helping others to know Jesus and to provide for those in need.

Distribute a large piece of white construction paper to each student. Explain that students will make a classroom book titled *First Graders Are God's Stewards*. Teach students that all they have comes from God, including their time, talents, and possessions. God wants Christians to use these things wisely. One way to use God's gifts wisely is to share them with others so that people can know God better and so that people can receive things they need.

Discuss ways that first graders can be good stewards, including giving money to missions, singing in a children's choir, greeting people who are entering the church, or filling a shoe box with needed supplies to send to a child in another country. Have each student draw a picture of himself or herself sharing a special talent or possession with someone else. Instruct students to take care drawing their picture, making sure to fill the whole page.

Help students write a sentence at the bottom of their picture that describes how they are giving to others. For example, Marta is painting a picture for her grandmother; Jason is teaching his brother how to play soccer.

Invite a student to decorate the cover of the book. Staple the student pages between the front cover and a piece of colored construction paper. Enjoy a shared reading time with the new book.

Review

- What are the three types of blessings that God has given Christians? (**time, talents, possessions**)
- How should Christians use these blessings? (**They should use their blessings wisely.**)
- How did the widow in the Bible truth honor the Lord? (**She put her money into the collection box in order to give to the Lord's work, and she had faith that He would provide for her needs.**)

Student Page 25.3

Assist students as needed in completing the page.

DAY 3

Name ______________________

Giving **25.3**

Choose the correct word to complete each sentence.

1. The Lord is pleased when I spend my ____time____ serving others.

2. I am being a good steward when I share my money and my other ____possessions____ with people in need.

3. When I use my special skills, or ____talents____, to help tell others about Jesus, I please God.

4. The best reason to be a good steward is to please God. List some ways you use your time, talents, and possessions to please God.

____Answers will vary.____

____

____

 99

APPLICATION

- What are some good ways to share your time with others? (**I can spend time playing with a younger child; I can pray for others; I can spend time encouraging my friends to make choices that please God; I can help my parents and my teacher.**)
- Share some talents that you have. Give examples of how you might share those talents with others. (**Answers will vary.**)
- Besides money, what other possessions could you share with people in need? (**Answers will vary, but should include canned goods, outgrown clothing, toys, and school supplies.**) (Explain that it is best to share possessions that are in good condition.)

25.4 Giving

Focus: Being Good Stewards

★ PREPARATION

Bring a JACKET or a SWEATER to class. (*Introduction*)

EXTENSION

4A Divide the class into six groups and distribute one card from **BLM 25A Things That Need Care** to each group. On each of the cards, there is a word indicating an item that needs care. Have each group meet independently and plan how they would care for the item on the card. Invite students from each group to come to the front of the room and share their conclusions.

4B To help students understand that poor stewardship often affects other people, take students on a scavenger hunt through the school campus. Challenge students to find things that did not receive proper care. In the classroom, are there broken crayons, ruined supplies, dried-up markers, or torn paper? In school halls, are there dark smears on any walls, bulletin boards with torn paper or damaged artwork? On the playground, are there deflated balls, trash, or graffiti? Point out that when someone litters, someone else usually has to clean up the mess. When one student leaves the lid off of a marker, another student cannot use it. When a classmate tears artwork on a bulletin board, it damages something another classmate has worked hard to make.

Introduction ★

Wear a JACKET or a SWEATER to class. Mention that it is not cold inside the room, and casually toss the jacket or sweater on the floor where students are likely to step on it. Tell students that perhaps you will pick it up later and that you hope it will not be too dirty. Ask students if they think that you have taken good care of your jacket or sweater. (**No.**) Invite students to share some reasons why it is important to care for clothing. (**Possible answers: Clothing that is torn or dirty is unpleasant to wear; clothing that is not cared for will need to be replaced sooner; money spent on unneeded clothing purchases cannot be used for other purposes.**) Remind students that God has given everything to them and that He expects them to use their possessions wisely and take care of their things.

Directed Instruction

Write the word *stewardship* on the board. Remind students that *stewardship* means *taking care of everything that God has given to you and willingly sharing it with others*. Teach students that Jesus spent His time teaching the disciples and the people how to live as part of God's family. Jesus taught His disciples about stewardship when He pointed out the widow in the temple, but He also taught the disciples about being good stewards on other occasions. Sometimes Jesus told parables—stories that had meanings—to help the disciples understand about the kingdom of God.

Read **Matthew 25:14–30**. Explain that in this parable, Jesus taught about using God's gifts wisely. Ask students to recount how many talents the first servant was given. (**five**) How many talents did that servant gain for his master? (**five more**) How many talents was the second servant given? (**two**) How many talents did the second servant gain for his master? (**two more**) Which servants in the parable were praised by their master? (**the two servants who used their master's money wisely**) Choose a volunteer to recount what happened to the servant who buried the money in the ground instead of using it wisely. (**The master called him lazy and threw him out!**) When Christians use their time, talents, and possessions wisely, God may give them greater responsibility (Luke 16:10). For example, learning how to play the piano well and practicing daily can lead to playing the piano during worship services and writing worship music.

Explain that an important part of being a good steward is to take care of the things that God has entrusted to one's care. Being a good steward involves keeping things clean, in good repair, and not wasting resources, such as food, water, electricity, paper products, or other supplies.

Remind students that not only are stewards charged with sharing and caring for material things, but they are to share love, forgiveness, grace, and mercy that they have received from their heavenly Father.

Review

- What does God expect Christians to do with their possessions? (**use them wisely and take care of them**)

- In Jesus' parable, did all three servants take care of their master's money? (**No, the third servant buried the money in the ground. He did not use it to benefit his master.**)
- How will God bless good stewards? (**He will give them even greater responsibility.**)
- Is it acceptable to waste resources, such as classroom supplies? (**No, it is never acceptable to waste resources.**)
- Besides material things, what else are stewards to share with others? (**God's love, forgiveness, mercy, and grace**)

Student Page 25.4

Discuss godly stewardship as you look at each picture. Complete the page together.

Notes:

DAY 4

25.4 ***Giving***

Read the sentences and look at the pictures. Decide if the child is showing good stewardship or poor stewardship of God's gifts. Fill in the correct circle.

1. Keisha recycles her family's plastic bottles, cans, and cardboard.

● good stewardship ○ poor stewardship

2. Mindy takes more food than she can eat and ends up throwing some food away.

○ good stewardship ● poor stewardship

3. Trevor makes paper airplanes instead of drawing pictures during art class.

○ good stewardship ● poor stewardship

4. Josef put a paper that he did not need in the recycle bin instead of throwing it on the floor.

● good stewardship ○ poor stewardship

100 © *Bible* Grade 1

APPLICATION

- How can you be a good steward of what God has entrusted to you? (**Possible answers: I can take only the food that I can eat; I can use paper goods wisely; I can take good care of my desk and textbooks.**)
- Why is it important to keep things clean, neat, and in good repair? (**Taking care of possessions keeps me from wasting time and money needed to replace them.**)

REINFORCEMENT

Larry Burkett, a leader in the area of personal stewardship, began his ministry as a financial counselor for Campus Crusade for Christ. As a part of his varied job-related responsibilities, Burkett spent time studying what the Bible says about money. His biblical studies into stewardship convinced him that he should teach others about a biblical approach to handling finances.

Larry Burkett left the campus ministry to form Christian Financial Concepts, a nonprofit organization dedicated to teaching the biblical principles of handling money. Over the years of his ministry, Burkett wrote books on personal finance and hosted several Christian radio shows dedicated to responsible stewardship.

25.5 Giving

Focus: Review and Assessment

★ PREPARATION

Select **VA 25A The Widow's Coins**. (*Lesson Review*)

Print one copy of **BLM 25B Lesson 25 Test** for each student. (*Directed Instruction*)

Lesson Review ★

Use **VA 25A The Widow's Coins** to review the Bible truth. Cover the following concepts:

- Jesus was with His disciples in the temple. He was teaching the people and the religious leaders who were there.
- When Jesus finished teaching, He watched people drop their offerings into the collection box.
- Rich people put in a lot of money.
- One poor widow put in two copper coins. That was all the money that she had to buy the things she needed in order to live. Jesus knew of her faith in God to provide for her needs because she gave away what she needed.
- Jesus pointed the widow out to His disciples as someone who showed great faith.
- The widow had to trust the Lord completely to provide for her needs.
- It is important to prayerfully consider how much money to give to the Lord's work so that others can learn about Jesus, as well as be given money and items they need.
- Christians are to give not only money, but also their time, talents, and other possessions.
- *Stewardship* means *taking care of everything that God has given to you and willingly sharing it with others.*
- Christians are to be good stewards of what God has given them. This includes taking care of possessions by keeping things clean and in good repair.
- It is important to share God's love, forgiveness, mercy, and grace as well as time, talents, and material possessions.

Directed Instruction ★

Distribute a copy of **BLM 25B Lesson 25 Test** to each student. When all have completed the test, discuss students' answers in class.

Notes:

Lesson Preparation
Trusting God

26.0

Expected Student Outcomes

KNOW
Peter walks on the water with Jesus.

DO
Students will:
- sequence events of the Bible truth
- write words to match clues in order to review the Bible truth
- evaluate scenarios and choose trust over fear
- read and identify verses that tell about trust

APPLY
Students will affirm that God is all-powerful and that they can trust Him.

Lesson Outline

I. Jesus dispels fear (Mt 14:22–33, Mk 6:45–52, Jn 6:15–21)
  A. The raging storm
  B. One steps out
  C. The results
II. Trust God during storms
  A. Power over problems
III. Trusting God
  A. Going it alone
IV. Keep your eyes on Jesus
  A. Trust is a choice
  B. Growing in faith

TEACHER'S HEART

Have you ever paused to notice the sky on your way to school? On some days the heavens are bright blue and are dotted with white, fluffy clouds. Sunshine fills the morning and all is right with the world! Does that describe the sky every morning? Unfortunately, no. There are also days when the sky seems to wrap its gray blanket around you. The low-hanging clouds threaten rain at any moment.

Those stormy skies often creep into the lives of every Christian. With heads down and shoulders into the wind, it's time to run for cover! The next time you find yourself facing such a storm, stop! Adjust your focus. Turn your eyes away from the swirling situation you face and look heavenward. As you fix your gaze on the Savior and trust Him, you will find strength to take first one step and then another. Will your stormy clouds disappear immediately? Probably not, but you will find comfort, direction, and peace from the Son who will shine brightly into the depths of your soul. Splash in the puddles of life with joy!

MEMORY VERSE

Deuteronomy 31:8

MATERIALS

Day 1:
- Ball
- VA 26A Peter Walks on Water
- BLM 26A Poem: Peter Walks on Water (*Extension*)

Day 2:
- VA 26A Peter Walks on Water
- Dishpan, items that will float, items that will not float (*Extension*)
- BLM 26B Jesus and Peter Figures, card stock (*Extension*)

Day 3:
- No additional materials are needed.

Day 4:
- Sidewalk chalk (*Extension*)

Day 5:
- VA 26A Peter Walks on Water
- BLM 26C Lesson 26 Test

SONGS

Give 'em to Jesus (*Extension*)

TEACHER RESOURCES

Bridges, Jerry. *Trusting God: Even When Life Hurts*. NavPress, 2008.

Ortberg, John. *If You Want to Walk on Water, You've Got to Get Out of the Boat*. Zondervan, 2001.

STUDENT RESOURCES

Cook, Jean Thor. *Jesus Calms the Storm*. Concordia Publishing House, 2003.

Taylor, Jeannie St. John. *Am I Trusting?* Kregel Publications, 2004.

26.1 Trusting God

Focus: Jesus Dispels Fear

MEMORY VERSE

Deuteronomy 31:8

MEMORY WORK

- Write the Memory Verse on the board and read it together. Explain that the word *before* in the Memory Verse means *in front of*. Invite students to share some additional prepositions that describe relative positions, such as the words *behind*, *over*, *under*, *between*, *above*, or *below*. Have a volunteer use a LARGE BALL to demonstrate some of the positions that the class has shared. Explain that the ball can only be in one place at a time, but God is not limited by time or space. Unlike the ball, God is all-powerful and ever-present. He promises to be with His children always; therefore, they do not need to be afraid as long as they keep their focus on Him.

★ PREPARATION

Have a LARGE BALL on hand. (*Memory Work*)

Select **VA 26A Peter Walks on Water**. (*Directed Instruction*)

EXTENSION

1A Print as many copies of **BLM 26A Poem: Peter Walks on Water** as needed to prepare for a short choral reading of a poem based on the Bible truth. You may choose to incorporate actions, props, or costumes to dramatize the poem. Students may want to invite their parents or another class to view their performance.

Introduction

Ask students to share some situations in which they have been afraid. (**Answers will vary.**) Remark that you have been afraid at times, too. Explain that many things in life can be frightening, such as lightning, thunder, or a strong windstorm. Ask students to raise their hand if they have ever been afraid during a storm. Explain that in today's Bible truth, the disciples were caught in a bad storm.

Directed Instruction ★

Display **VA 26A Peter Walks on Water**. Draw students' attention to the threatening sky and large waves. Remark that it was a very dangerous situation for the disciples to be out in a boat when a storm arose on the Sea of Galilee, which was a very big lake. The disciples probably would not have been able to row back to shore against the strong waves. Water would have started to fill the boat, and they could have easily sunk! This was terrifying! Tell students to close their eyes, grasp the sides of their desk or table, and imagine that they are in a small boat out on the sea. The wind is howling, and the boat is rocking back and forth. Invite students to pretend to be in the midst of a strong storm as they sway back and forth and make the sound of the wind.

Instruct students to open their eyes but to remember how they felt when they were pretending to be in a boat on a stormy sea. Read the text on the back of VA 26A.

Remind students that Peter, Andrew, James, and John had been fishermen before they became disciples. They had probably been in storms before, and they knew just how dangerous it was to be out in the middle of the sea during one of those storms. They probably rowed as hard as they could! This was a real struggle!

Right in the middle of the storm, Jesus came to them! Ask a volunteer to share what the disciples were feeling when they saw Jesus walking toward them. (**They were afraid.**) Point out that Jesus did not wait until they had made it back to land to come to be with them; He joined them when they were struggling against the huge waves.

Remind students that Peter was not sure at first that the person walking on the water was Jesus. Peter waited until he heard Jesus' voice. Oh, how Peter wanted to be with Jesus! Invite a volunteer to recount what miracle Peter asked Jesus to perform. (**Peter wanted to be able to walk out on the water to meet Jesus.**) What did Jesus say that showed Peter that he could step out of the boat? (**Jesus said for Peter to come.**)

Choose a volunteer to recount why Peter began to sink. (**He started looking at the storm instead of Jesus.**) Explain that Peter started looking all around at the strong wind and the splashing waves. He stopped paying attention to Jesus, and he began to be afraid. Shortly after Peter realized that only Jesus could help him, Jesus came to Peter's rescue. Jesus never left Peter; Peter just did not keep his eyes on Jesus!

Review

- Why were the disciples in a boat on the Sea of Galilee? (**Jesus had them go across to the other side of the sea while He stayed by Himself to pray.**)
- What happened as the disciples crossed the sea? (**A storm came up.**)
- How did the disciples feel when they saw Jesus walking on the water? (**They were terrified!**)
- What miracle did Peter ask Jesus to do? (**Peter asked Jesus to allow him to walk on the water.**)
- What happened when Peter started paying attention to the wind and looked at the waves instead of trusting Jesus? (**He began to sink down into the sea.**)

Student Page 26.1

Read any difficult words on the page and help students to sequence the events of the Bible truth.

DAY 1

Name ______________________________

Trusting God **26.1**

Number each group of sentences in the correct order to retell the Bible truth. Use numbers 1–4 for the first group of sentences. Use numbers 5–9 for the second group of sentences.

__3__ The disciples were afraid of the wind and waves.

__1__ Jesus sent the disciples across the lake in a boat.

__2__ A storm came up on the lake.

__4__ Jesus walked on top of the water!

__9__ The disciples worshipped Jesus as the Son of God.

__6__ Peter stepped out of the boat and began to walk on water.

__8__ Peter began to sink, and Jesus saved him.

__7__ Peter took his eyes off of Jesus and looked at the storm.

__5__ Peter asked to come to Jesus.

APPLICATION

- Why did Peter believe that he could walk on the water? (**Possible answers: Jesus had shown the disciples His power to do miracles before; Peter saw that Jesus was walking on the sea and wanted to be like Him; Peter trusted Jesus.**)
- What did the disciples learn about Jesus during the bad storm? (**Possible answers: Jesus had power over nature; Jesus would be with them when they needed Him.**)
- How did the miracles in the Bible truth prove that Jesus is the Son of God? (**Only God could walk on the water and empower Peter to do the same thing. Only God could calm the wind and the waves.**)

REINFORCEMENT

It was not unusual for a sudden, violent storm to descend upon the Sea of Galilee, a low-lying lake. The Sea of Galilee is 680 feet below sea level, and it is surrounded by hills. The difference in height between the sea and the surrounding land causes significant pressure and temperature changes, resulting in strong winds across the lake. The turbulent winds can stir up powerful waves, putting small fishing craft in immediate and serious danger.

26.2 Trusting God

Focus: Trust God During Storms

★ PREPARATION

Select **VA 26A Peter Walks on Water**. (*Directed Instruction*)

EXTENSION

2A Provide a DISHPAN filled with water and THREE ITEMS THAT WILL FLOAT, such as a sponge, a foam cup, and a cotton ball. Supply THREE ITEMS THAT WILL NOT FLOAT, such as a small rock, a paperclip, and a marble. Have students experiment on their own with items that float and sink. Then tell them to make a chart showing the items that float easily as well as the items that do not float easily. Remind students that people can only float on water if they are in a position for swimming or if they are wearing flotation devices. Otherwise, they will sink! Remind students that Jesus and Peter were not floating in the water; they were walking on top of the water.

2B Print one copy of **BLM 26B Jesus and Peter Figures** onto CARD STOCK for each student to make a craft to retell the Bible truth. Ask a local fast-food restaurant to donate clean french-fry baskets for students to use as a boat for their figures.

Introduction

Ask students if they have ever been swimming in a big swimming pool with both a deep and a shallow end. (**Answers will vary.**) Explain that swimming pools that have diving boards must be at least 7 ½ feet deep. Hold your hand over your head to indicate approximately how deep that would be. Ask students to tell what would likely happen if someone your height were to step off the edge of the pool at the deep end and try to walk. (**He or she would sink right to the bottom and be completely covered by the water.**) Remind students that the Sea of Galilee was far deeper than the deepest swimming pool! When Jesus and Peter walked on the water, it was a miracle!

Directed Instruction ★

Display **VA 26A Peter Walks on Water** and ask a student to recount the time of day when the Bible truth took place. (**nighttime**) In Jesus' time, there were no electric lights to guide the disciples to shore. Instruct the students to close or cover their eyes for a few seconds and explain that the night sky would have been very dark, almost as dark as closing one's eyes! Remind students that the disciples were terrified to see a man walking toward them on the water. Ask students to recount how the disciples knew it was Jesus. (**Jesus told them who He was.**)

Remind students that Peter had a close relationship with Jesus, and so he had witnessed several miracles. Peter had seen an empty fishing net overflow with a huge catch of fish. He had seen Jesus feed 5,000 people with only five loaves of bread and two small fish. Peter had seen Jesus heal many, many people. Even though Peter was probably afraid of the storm, Peter knew that Jesus was powerful. Peter also knew that he could trust Jesus. Invite a student to share what Peter did to show his trust in Jesus. (**Peter asked Jesus if he could walk on the water to Jesus. Then Peter got out of the boat and started walking right on top of the water!**)

Review the fact that Peter was experiencing a miracle! Walking on water was impossible for Peter; he could only do that through Jesus' power. Because Peter trusted Jesus and took action to step out of the boat, he was the only disciple to experience the blessing of that miracle. Remind students that when Christians place their trust in Jesus, they need to obey Him and take action to do what Jesus has told them to do.

Peter probably would have been able to walk on the sea until he reached Jesus, but he began to do something. Ask a volunteer to tell the class what Peter did instead of looking at Jesus. (**Peter started looking at the storm.**) Once Peter started to look at the waves and not at the Lord, he sank right down. Peter was in trouble! The waves were very big and the wind was very strong, and Peter needed Jesus to save him. Jesus was right there! He pulled Peter up and asked him why he had begun to doubt.

Explain that problems and difficulties in the lives of Christians are like storms. Things that Christians cannot control, such as an illness, a job loss, or an accident, can be frightening. Remind students that the storm stopped when Jesus entered the boat. Jesus has power over nature, and He has power over the problems that Christians face—even those problems that cause worry or fear.

Review

- How was it possible for Peter to walk on top of the water? (**Jesus gave him the power to do that.**)
- Why was Peter the only disciple to experience the miracle of walking on the sea? (**Peter put his trust in Jesus and was the only one who took action to step out of the boat.**)
- What did Jesus ask Peter after Peter sank into the water? (**Jesus asked Peter why he had begun to doubt.**)
- How are some problems and difficulties that Christians face like storms? (**Some problems are out of one's control and they are frightening.**)
- Who has power over the "storms" Christians experience? (**Jesus**)

Student Page 26.2

Allow students to complete the page independently.

DAY 2

26.2 ***Trusting God***

Match each clue with a word from the Word Bank. Copy each letter on a shaded line onto the boat to discover what Peter needed to do to keep from sinking.

WORD BANK
fishermen
storm
disciples
Peter
sunk

1. high winds and waves s t o r m

2. what some disciples were before they met Jesus

f i s h e r m e n

3. had gone down into the water s u n k

4. Jesus' followers

d i s c i p l e s

5. the disciple who stepped out of the boat P e t e r

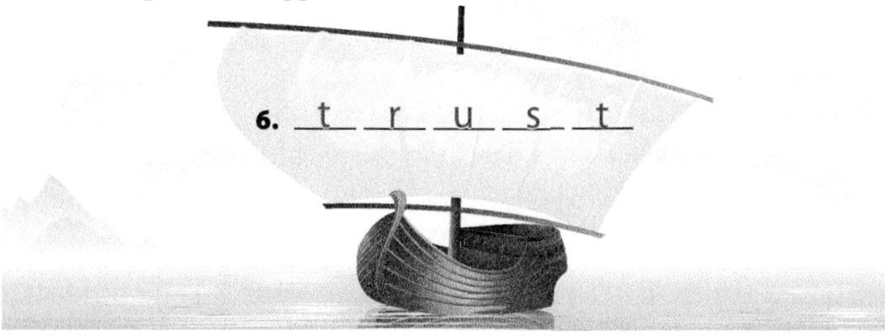

6. t r u s t

102 © Bible Grade 1

APPLICATION

- Problems and difficulties that Christians face are like storms. What will Jesus do in the midst of your "storms" when you pray to Him? (**He will be with me and help me when I go through difficult times.**)
- Have you ever had a serious problem and did not know what to do? (**Answers will vary.**) Did you trust God to help you through that problem? (**Answers will vary.**) What did you learn about God from your experience? (**Answers will vary.**)

REINFORCEMENT

When the disciples saw Jesus walking on the sea, they thought He was a ghost. Jesus responded to their fear by saying, "It is I." Those words were similar to the "I AM" response of God to Moses. The disciples would have understood what Jesus was saying—He was the one who created the wind and the waves! They had no need to fear.

In the ancient world, a rabbi's disciples did all they could to be like their teacher. If the teacher could walk on water, Peter also wanted to do that! It was for this reason that Peter asked permission before setting foot into the sea. If Jesus called Peter to come, then He would make it possible.

Jesus' words when He spoke to Peter—"Oh, you of little faith, why did you doubt?"—are not words of rebuke for getting out of the boat and attempting too much, but for trusting too little. In the Greek, *little faith* is just one word and is similar to a nickname. Jesus wanted Peter to fully believe in the love and power of I AM.

26.3

Trusting God

Focus: Trusting God

★ PREPARATION

Make signs from two sheets of construction paper, one labeled *Trust in Myself* and the other labeled *Trust in God*. Tape each sign to the front of a chair. (*Introduction*)

EXTENSION

3A Select "Give 'em to Jesus" from the music CDs. Play the song for students and ask them to listen carefully to the words. If necessary, tell students that a *burden* is defined as *a difficulty or a problem*. Ask students to identify burdens that first graders may have. Remind students that they should always pray about their problems.

Introduction ★

Place the two prepared chairs back to back at the front of the room. Ask a volunteer to come read the sign on one of the chairs and then sit down in that chair. Tell the volunteer to change seats and repeat the process. Finally, ask the volunteer to sit down in both chairs at the same time. Ask students why the volunteer could not do what you asked. (**It would not be possible to do that.**)

Point out that the student was permitted to choose the chair to sit in, but that he or she could not sit down in both chairs at the same time. Explain that just as it was impossible for the volunteer to do that, students will learn that the boy in today's story could not trust God with his problem at the same time that he was trying to solve the problem on his own.

Directed Instruction

Read the following fictional story:

> Nicholas loved to play soccer. He played as often as he could, and he took his soccer ball with him wherever he went. Once when Nicholas tried kicking the ball inside the house, his father corrected him and explained the ball should only be kicked outside.
>
> Now it was Saturday morning and Nicholas was excited! Today was the day of the big soccer game. But when Nicholas looked out his window, he saw very dark clouds. It would soon begin to rain. This storm was going to ruin his day!
>
> Nicholas was disappointed. He took his soccer ball downstairs to the kitchen. Mother was outside in the garden, and Nicholas decided to wait for her to come in and make breakfast. Then, Nicholas put the ball down on the floor and began to dribble it gently between his feet. He started to imagine himself playing in the big game and taking a shot at the goal. He kicked his ball way up into the air. Down came the ball! It hit Mother's favorite flower vase! The vase hit the floor and broke!
>
> Now Nicholas was scared! He began to think about what to do. He knew that kicking the ball in the house was the wrong thing to do. He knew that his mother would be angry about the broken vase. He never thought about praying and asking God for help to solve this problem; instead, he opened a drawer and took out some white glue. He quickly glued the vase together and put it back on the counter. Now his mother would never know!

Remind students that all choices have consequences. Nicholas' poor choice to trust in his own ability to fix the vase would have a consequence. Ask a volunteer to tell what might happen as a consequence of Nicholas' choice. (**His mother could find out that Nicholas had broken the vase. He could be punished for trying to hide the broken vase.**) Tell students that they will hear more about Nicholas in the next day's lesson.

Review

- What problem did Nicholas face? (**He kicked the soccer ball in the house and broke his mother's vase.**)
- How did Nicholas feel when he realized his mother's vase was broken? (**He felt scared.**)
- Did Nicholas' choice to fix the vase show trust in God? (**No, Nicholas trusted his own ability to solve the problem.**)

Student Page 26.3

Assist students in completing the page.

Notes:

APPLICATION

- Have you ever tried to solve a problem on your own and failed? Tell about that time. (**Answers will vary.**)
- Is it easy to trust in God when you are afraid? (**No, it is not always easy, but God wants me to trust Him and make godly choices.**)
- How can you remember to pray when you are afraid? (**I can make prayer a habit so that I will not forget to pray when I am afraid.**)

DAY 3

Name ______________________________

Trusting God **26.3**

Read each story. Mark the choice that shows trust instead of fear.

1. Ann is good at spelling, but she is very shy. Monday is the big Spelling Bee, and Ann is afraid. What should Ann do?

- ○ She should misspell a word that she knows so that she can sit down.
- ● She should pray and then do her best.
- ○ She should stay home from school.

2. Ben is afraid to jump into the deep end of the pool, but Dad says he will catch him. What should Ben do?

- ○ He should stay out of the pool.
- ○ He should go play with his little brother.
- ● He should pray, trust his dad, and jump in!

3. Lexie has a chance to ride in a hot air balloon. Her family wants her to go up with them, but she is afraid. What should Lexie do?

- ○ She should cry.
- ● She should remember how Jesus helped Peter when Peter was afraid and then trust Jesus to help her go up in the balloon.
- ○ She should stay on the ground.

26.4 Trusting God

Focus: Keep Your Eyes on Jesus

EXTENSION

Provide an exercise that helps students to learn to trust each other by having the class make a chalk mural of Peter and Jesus walking on the water. Weather permitting, go outside to a section of the playground that is paved. Explain that students will be making a chalk mural for others to see, so they have to work together and trust each other to do their jobs well. Divide the class into four groups. Give each group several pieces of SIDEWALK CHALK. Each group will be responsible for one portion of the chalk mural. Because they are working at the same time, no one group will know exactly what the other groups are making. Group one will draw a stormy sky. Group two will draw the boat and all the disciples except for Peter. Group three will draw Jesus and Peter, and group four will add the high waves. When all four groups have completed their portion of the assignment, invite students to look at the chalk mural and discuss what they learned about trusting each other as they worked on the project.

Introduction

Write the word *practice* on the board and have a student read the word aloud. Ask students to raise their hand if they are taking music lessons or are involved in a sport that requires regular practice. Choose a student who raised his or her hand to tell the class why regular practice is an important part of being able to play well. (**Answers will vary, but should include that regular practice builds skill.**)

Hold up your Bible. Remind students that the Bible truths they are learning now will provide the guidance that they need later when they face problems in life. However, reading the Bible is not the only thing that Christians can do to grow in their faith. Christians need to pray every day in order to have a close relationship with the Lord. Worship gives Christians the opportunity to thank and praise God for what He has done and is doing for them. Bible reading, prayer, and worship all help Christians to know and trust the Lord.

Directed Instruction

Read the following to continue the fictional story about Nicholas and the broken vase from Lesson 26.3:

> Whew! The vase was glued together, and Mother didn't know it had been broken. Nicholas was feeling much better. That scary feeling that he had had was gone. Nicholas played with the soccer ball, but he decided never to kick it in the house again.
>
> Mother came into the kitchen with some cut flowers and picked up the vase. She was about to fill the vase with water. Now Nicholas felt a rush of different feelings! Was the glue dry? Would Mother notice the cracks? He felt scared and guilty all at the same time! Should he tell his mother about the broken vase?
>
> Just then, Nicholas made a wise choice. He silently prayed for Jesus to help him tell the truth. When Mother turned on the water, Nicholas spoke up. He told Mother what had happened, and how he tried to fix the vase on his own. Mother looked at the vase and saw the cracks. She listened as Nicholas told her what had happened, but she wasn't angry. She told Nicholas that they would talk later about consequences for kicking the soccer ball in the house.
>
> Mother spoke gently and reminded Nicholas of the Bible truth that he had been learning in school. In that Bible passage, Peter began to doubt that he could walk on water, so he started sinking into the sea. Peter could only walk on the water as long as he kept his eyes on Jesus. When he forgot to trust the Lord, Peter began to sink!
>
> Nicholas understood. When he had a problem and didn't ask the Lord for help, things did not work out very well. From now on, Nicholas would take his problems to the Lord in prayer and follow the guidance found in God's Word.

Review

- How did Nicholas feel when Mother picked up the vase? (**scared and guilty**)
- Did Nicholas make a wise choice when he felt those feelings? (**Yes.**) Explain why. (**He prayed first and asked Jesus to help him tell the truth.**)
- What did Mother say about the vase? (**She was not angry. She reminded Nicholas to learn from the Bible. They would talk about consequences for kicking the ball in the house later.**)
- What did Nicholas understand? (**When he had a problem and didn't ask the Lord for help, things did not work out well. He needed to take his problems to the Lord.**)

Student Page 26.4

Select volunteers to read the Bible verses listed at the top of the page. Have students write each verse reference on the correct line. Discuss things that people trust in today instead of God.

APPLICATION

- Why is it good to read the Bible, pray, and worship the Lord? (**When I do these things, I grow in faith, trust, and obedience to God.**)
- How can reading the Bible help you make wise choices? (**The Bible is full of examples of how to trust God and follow His ways.**)
- How can prayer help you make wise choices? (**When I pray and ask God to help me, He will help me!**)

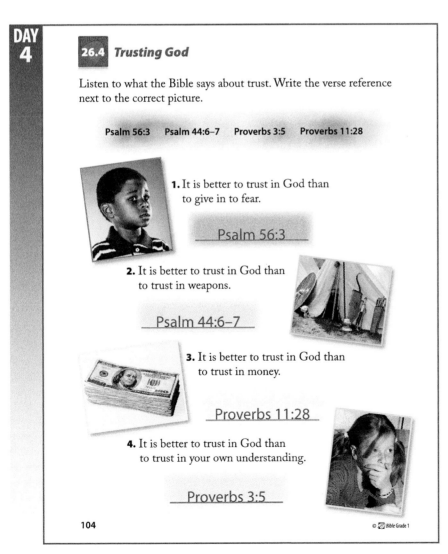

DAY 4

26.4 *Trusting God*

Listen to what the Bible says about trust. Write the verse reference next to the correct picture.

Psalm 56:3 Psalm 44:6–7 Proverbs 3:5 Proverbs 11:28

1. It is better to trust in God than to give in to fear.

Psalm 56:3

2. It is better to trust in God than to trust in weapons.

Psalm 44:6–7

3. It is better to trust in God than to trust in money.

Proverbs 11:28

4. It is better to trust in God than to trust in your own understanding.

Proverbs 3:5

104

26.5 Trusting God

Focus: Review and Assessment

★ PREPARATION

Select **VA 26A Peter Walks on Water**. (*Lesson Review*)

Make a copy of **BLM 26C Lesson 26 Test** for each student. (*Directed Instruction*)

Lesson Review ★

Use **VA 26A Peter Walks on Water** to review the Bible truth. Cover the following concepts:

- Jesus wanted to spend some time in prayer alone. He had His disciples sail across the Sea of Galilee and meet Him on the other side.
- The disciples were out in the middle of the sea at night. A storm came up.
- As the disciples were struggling to reach the shore, Jesus came to them, walking on top of the water.
- The disciples were terrified! Jesus identified Himself.
- Peter asked Jesus to allow him to walk on the water.
- Jesus invited Peter to come to Him out on the water. Peter obeyed and got out of the boat.
- Jesus gave Peter the power to walk across the water, but when Peter started to look at the storm instead of looking at Jesus, Peter began to sink.
- Peter was afraid! He called out to Jesus to save him.
- Jesus was there right away. He pulled Peter from the water. When Jesus and Peter stepped into the boat, the storm stopped.
- The other disciples knew that Jesus had done a miracle—something that only God can do. They worshipped Jesus, the Son of God.
- Christians can go through difficult times or have problems that seem like storms. Jesus will always be with them, even during hard times.
- It is important to trust God when problems arise.
- Bible study, prayer, and worship are ways Christians can grow in faith and learn to turn to God when problems arise.

Directed Instruction ★

Distribute a copy of **BLM 26C Lesson 26 Test** to each student. Be sure to read any difficult words for students before allowing them to complete the test. When all have completed the test, discuss students' answers in class.

Notes:

Lesson Preparation
Believing God
27.0

Expected Student Outcomes

KNOW
Mary and Martha learn that they can believe in God's promises. Jesus raises Lazarus from the dead.

DO
Students will:
- use pictorial clues to recall facts about Jesus' visit to His friends' home
- read a rebus story to review the Bible truth about the raising of Lazarus
- use math problems to solve a puzzle about Mary's act of faith
- determine ways that they can encourage others to grow in faith

APPLY
Students will grow in faith as they believe and trust in God, who desires the best for them.

Lesson Outline

I. Martha's special guest (Lk 10:38–42)
  A. Martha serves; Mary listens
  B. Jesus sets priorities
II. Jesus' power over death (Jn 11:1–45)
  A. Mary and Martha grow in faith
  B. Jesus raises Lazarus
III. Mary's act of faith (Jn 12:1–11, Mk 14:3–9)
  A. Mary anoints Jesus
IV. Christians' encouragement
  A. Encouraging others

TEACHER'S HEART

Poor Martha! She had a house full of hungry guests to serve. To make matters worse, there was her sister, Mary, sitting at the feet of Jesus, listening to His teaching. "What is she doing?" Martha probably thought, "Doesn't she see how much work must be done?" Finally, Martha broke down and asked Jesus to compel Mary to help her with the work.

Teachers tend to be like Martha. They love Jesus, but they are really busy people! Teaching is physically, mentally, and emotionally demanding work. Teachers are in charge and responsible, just as Martha was. They often feel like Martha felt—overwhelmed! Note Jesus' response to Martha's concern, "Martha, Martha, you are worried and troubled about many things. But one thing is needed, and Mary has chosen that good part, which will not be taken away from her" (Luke 10:41–42).

While you prepare to teach your students about the vast love Jesus has for them, remind yourself that He has a vast love for you. Remind yourself that Jesus is in charge, Jesus is responsible for getting things done, and spending time with Jesus is the one thing you need the most.

MEMORY VERSE

John 15:15b

MATERIALS

Day 1:
- Invitation
- Snack (*Extension*)

Day 2:
- Balloon
- VA 27A Lazarus
- BLM 27A Lazarus, Come Out (*Extension*)

Day 3:
- Lotion

Day 4:
- Box or basket (*Extension*)

Day 5:
- VA 27A Lazarus
- BLM 27B Lesson 27 Test

TEACHER RESOURCES

Richards, Lawrence O. *NIRV Adventure Bible for Early Readers*. Zonderkidz, 2008.
Weaver, Joanna. *Lazarus Awakening: Finding Your Place in the Heart of God*. WaterBrook Press, 2011.

STUDENT RESOURCES

Bowman, Crystal. *Jesus Raises Lazarus*. Zonderkidz, 2011.
Lord, Jill Roman. *If Jesus Walked Beside Me*. Ideals Publications, Inc., 2011.

27.1 Believing God

Focus: Martha's Special Guest

MEMORY VERSE

John 15:15b

MEMORY WORK

- Distribute a prepared copy of the Memory Verse to each student and read it together. Be sure that students can read each word on their copy of the verse. Divide the class into groups of three to four students per group. Explain that students will be assisting each other in learning the verse. Tell students to demonstrate friendship by listening to each other's recitations and by helping each other find fun ways to learn the verse.

★ PREPARATION

Write or type the Memory Verse, and make as many copies as needed for each student to have one. (*Memory Work*)

Bring an INVITATION that you have received or a blank invitation to class. (*Introduction*)

EXTENSION

1A Consider inviting the principal, librarian, another teacher, or a grandparent to read today's Bible truth. Ask a parent to provide a SMALL SNACK for students to share with their guest. Help students set and decorate a table, and then arrange the food attractively. Include instruction about letting the guest eat first, taking turns, and taking only a small portion so that there will be enough food for everyone present.

Introduction ★

Display the INVITATION and ask students to tell what it is. Choose a few volunteers to share about a time when they have given an invitation to someone. Remark that hosting a party or another special event can be fun, but it requires planning to make sure that guests feel welcome and have a good time. Explain that in today's Bible truth, Jesus was the guest of honor.

Directed Instruction

Read the following Bible truth based on Luke 10:38–42:

> Jesus had been traveling from town to town, telling people the good news of His coming kingdom. He had also been healing many sick people. When He came to the village of Bethany, near Nazareth, He went to see some special friends who lived there. These friends were Mary, Martha, and Lazarus—two sisters and a brother. They often invited Jesus to their home to eat with them and to spend time with them. They loved Jesus and He loved them. Mary and Martha were glad to serve Jesus and His disciples when they came to visit.
>
> When Martha opened the door and saw Jesus, she welcomed Him and the disciples into her home. Then Martha began to prepare and cook the food needed to serve their guests.
>
> Mary was glad to see the Lord Jesus, too. When Jesus came in and sat down to teach, Mary sat at His feet, listening to every word He said. Mary wanted to learn all she could about God.
>
> After a few minutes of hustling and bustling around, Martha noticed that Mary was not helping to prepare the meal. Martha looked around for Mary and saw her sitting near Jesus. Then Martha realized that she was going to have to do all the work because Mary was listening to Jesus teach. Martha wasn't happy! There were a lot of people in the house, and she was going to have to cook and serve all by herself!
>
> Finally, Martha couldn't wait any longer. She decided to say something to Jesus. She went directly to the Lord Jesus and said, "Lord, don't You care that Mary has left all the work to me? I am doing everything alone! Tell her to come help me."
>
> Jesus looked at her and said, "Martha, Martha, you are worried and troubled about a lot of things. What you need to do is learn from Me and trust Me. Mary understands the importance of these things. What she is learning will not be taken away from her."

What was important to one sister was not important to the other sister! Ask students to share what was important to Martha. (**making sure that her guests had food to eat**) What was important to Mary? (**listening to Jesus and learning from Him**) Remind students that when Martha shared her concerns with Jesus, Jesus helped Martha understand that cooking and preparing food were less important than learning about God!

Remind students that as they grow in faith, they will understand more about what is important to God, and they will spend more time in Bible study, worship, and prayer.

Review

- Who were Mary, Martha, and Lazarus? (**They were two sisters and a brother who were friends of Jesus.**)
- Why did Jesus go to visit this family? (**They were His friends, and they invited Him to be their guest.**)
- What did Jesus do at their home? (**He taught the people about God.**)
- What did Martha do while Jesus was teaching? (**She prepared and cooked food for Jesus and the disciples.**) What did Mary do? (**She listened to Jesus.**)
- Which sister's behavior pleased Jesus more? (**Mary's behavior**) Why? (**She was listening and learning about God.**)

Student Page 27.1

Assist students as necessary in completing the page.

DAY 1

Name ______________________________

Believing God **27.1**

Read the sentences. Write **yes** if the sentence tells something from the Bible truth. Write **no** if it does not.

1.  went to visit Mary, Martha, and Lazarus. yes

2. Martha did not welcome Jesus into her . no

3. Mary sat at Jesus' 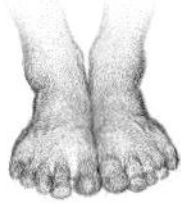 and listened to His Word. yes

4. Martha was busy making and serving . Martha saw that Mary was not helping. yes

5. Martha used the  to clean the floor. no

6. Jesus said that listening to His Word was the most important thing. Mary had put Jesus ***FIRST***. yes

APPLICATION

- If Jesus were to visit your home, what would you do to prepare for Him? (**Answers will vary.**)
- Martha and Mary had different ideas of what was important to do during Jesus' visit. If you had been in their home, would you have listened to Jesus, or would you have helped serve food? Why? (**Answers will vary.**)
- Why did Jesus tell Martha that Mary's choice to listen to Him was more important than serving food? (**Learning God's truth and developing my relationship with Him must come first in my life.**)
- What are some ways you can spend time with Jesus and learn more about Him? (**I can spend time reading my Bible, going to Bible class, praying, and worshipping Jesus.**)

27.2 Believing God

Focus: Jesus' Power over Death

★ PREPARATION

Bring a BALLOON to class. (*Introduction*)

Select **VA 27A Lazarus**. (*Directed Instruction*)

EXTENSION

2A Duplicate copies of **BLM 27A Lazarus, Come Out** for students to make a craft to reinforce the Bible truth. Students will need a large sheet of construction paper to complete the project.

2B Death is a complex concept for young children to understand, but many first-grade students have probably experienced the death of a great-grandparent, another family member, or perhaps a pet. Set aside a time when students can speak to you privately and share some of those recent experiences. Affirm the sorrow students and their family members have felt, and thank God for the comfort He gives in times of sorrow.

Introduction ★

Build suspense by blowing air into a BALLOON. Pause while inflating the balloon and ask students to recount the names of Jesus' friends who lived in the town of Bethany. (**Mary, Martha, and Lazarus**) Continue to force air into the balloon, and then pause to ask students who sat at Jesus' feet and who was worried about serving a meal. (**Mary, Martha**) Inflate the balloon until it is obvious that it might burst. Pause one last time to ask which sister had been commended by Jesus. (**Mary**) State that both Mary and Martha had been growing in faith, just as the balloon has been growing in size. Hint that Jesus will do something surprising and powerful in today's lesson. Continue to force air into the balloon until it can hold no more air. Release the balloon and let it sail around the classroom.

Directed Instruction ★

Display **VA 27A Lazarus** and read the Bible truth on the back.

Invite a student to recount what Mary and Martha did first when Lazarus became sick. (**Mary and Martha asked Jesus to come by sending Him a message.**)

Ask students to speculate about why Mary and Martha were so sure that Jesus would have healed Lazarus. (**Answers will vary, but should include that they knew Jesus well; they witnessed His power in healing other people; and they knew how much He loved Lazarus. Mary and Martha based their faith in Jesus on their close relationship with Him.**)

Using the picture on VA 27A, point out the features of a burial site in Bible times. The people used natural caves or they cut a tomb into the rock of a hillside. After someone died, the family would wrap his or her head in a cloth and wrap the body in another cloth. Then they would bind the hands and feet of the loved one in grave bands. Grave bands were strips of cloth used to tie up the wrapped body. Rather than bury their loved one in the ground, the people would place the body on a shelf inside the tomb. Instead of a door, a large stone was used to cover the opening of the tomb.

Ask students to imagine themselves as spectators to the raising of Lazarus. Martha really did not want to open Lazarus' tomb, because she thought it would stink. Have students hold their nose as if they were about to smell something offensive. Call on a volunteer to shout the words that Jesus said after the stone was rolled away. (**Lazarus, come out!**) Would Lazarus come out? Everyone knew Lazarus was dead; he had been dead four days! What Jesus commanded Lazarus to do was impossible, yet Jesus' power enabled Lazarus to come back to life and obey Jesus' command! It was an amazing miracle! Lazarus was still all wrapped in cloths and grave bands. Jesus had to tell the people to unwrap him.

Review

- Why did Mary and Martha send Jesus a message? (**They wanted Him to return to Bethany. Their brother, Lazarus, was very sick.**)
- What happened before Jesus arrived? (**Lazarus died.**)
- What did Martha say that showed her faith in Jesus' power to raise Lazarus from the dead? (**She said that God would give Jesus anything that He asked for, even the power to raise the dead.**)
- How did Jesus have the power to raise Lazarus from the dead? (**Jesus is God; He is all-powerful!**)

Student Page 27.2

Assist students in completing the page.

Notes:

DAY 2

27.2 *Believing God*

Read the story.

Lazarus, Come Out!

Mary
Martha
Jesus
Lazarus
tomb

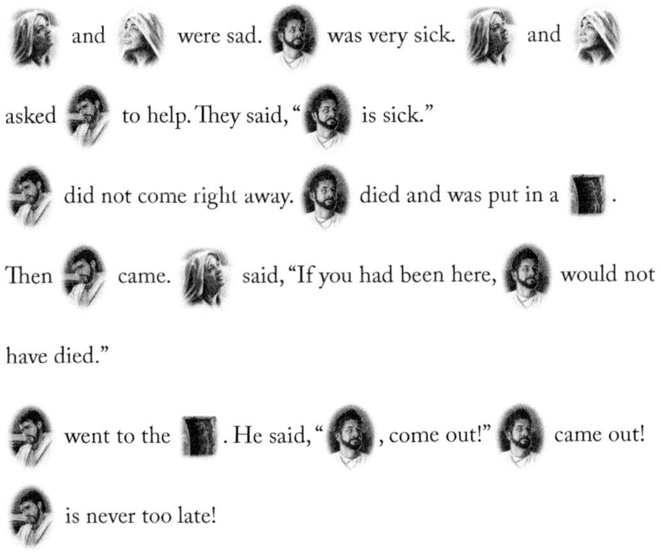
and were sad. was very sick. and
asked to help. They said, " is sick."
did not come right away. died and was put in a .
Then came. said, "If you had been here, would not
have died."
went to the . He said, " , come out!" came out!
is never too late!

106

© Bible Grade 1

APPLICATION

- Martha was too busy serving to listen to Jesus when He was a guest in her home. Have there been times when you could have listened to God's Word, but you chose to do something else? Tell how you will do things differently the next time you find yourself in the same situation. (**Answers will vary.**)
- How did Martha demonstrate her faith in Jesus in today's lesson? (**She said that God would give Jesus anything He asked for, including the power to raise Lazarus from the dead.**)

REINFORCEMENT

At the time of Lazarus, a family often had a burial cave prepared in advance. The tomb was either a natural cave or a cavern carved out of a hillside. The tomb was prepared with many niches for the burial of family members. Coffins were not used in ancient Israel; rather, the loved one was wrapped in cloth, typically linen, and carried to the tomb on a bier. The body was placed on the stone shelf and the bier was reused. As was the custom, Lazarus' head was probably wrapped in a separate cloth. Then strips of cloth bound his hands and feet.

After burial, a stone was rolled in front of the mouth of the cave to close it securely. When Jesus asked the mourners to move the stone, He was asking them to unseal the tomb in which Lazarus had been buried. Lazarus then came out dressed in grave clothes, consistent with the burial customs of the time.

27.3 Believing God

Focus: Mary's Act of Faith

★ PREPARATION

Bring some SCENTED HAND LOTION to class. (*Introduction*)

EXTENSION

3A During the year, students have learned about many people in the Bible who pleased God by their faith. To review the acts of these faithful people, direct students to sit in a circle. Name one Bible person, such as Josiah, and let each student state a fact that they remember about that person. When students have given all the facts they can remember, give the name of another person. Students who have difficulty remembering can be prompted gently or allowed to pass when it is their turn. Consider showing some of the pictures on the visual aids to help students recall details.

Introduction ★

Considering allergies, place a small amount of SCENTED HAND LOTION on each student's hands. Invite students to smell their hands and rub the lotion into their skin. Ask students to tell why people use perfumed hand lotion. (**Lotion makes hands smell nice and feel soft.**) Explain that in Jesus' time, people enjoyed pleasant fragrances just as people do today, but fragrances and perfumes were very expensive at that time.

Directed Instruction

Explain that Mary and Martha had one more meal with Jesus before He was crucified. Ask students to listen for the loving thing Mary did for Jesus as you read the following Bible truth based on John 12:1–11 and Mark 14:3–9:

> After Jesus raised Lazarus from the dead, He went to the city of Ephraim and stayed there with His disciples for a while. From there, Jesus went back to Bethany to the house of a man known as *Simon the leper*. Martha was serving a meal there. After the meal was served, Mary brought some very expensive perfume and poured it on Jesus' head. Then she poured some on Jesus' feet. She began to dry His feet with her hair. The wonderful smell of the perfume filled the house. Judas Iscariot, the disciple who would later turn against Jesus said, "Why has this expensive perfume been wasted? It could have been sold for one year's pay and the money could have been given to the poor." Judas was not really thinking about giving the money to the poor. He was the one holding the bag that contained the disciples' money, and he was a thief. He wanted the money for himself. Jesus knew Judas' heart.
>
> Jesus said, "Judas, leave Mary alone. She has kept this perfume for the day of My burial. You will have the poor with you always, but I will not be here with you always." Jesus also told the people that someday they would understand what a wonderful and important thing Mary had done to honor Him with such an expensive gift. Jesus said that Mary would always be remembered for her act of love.

Remind students that *honor* means *to show respect*. Pouring perfume on Jesus' head and feet may seem like a strange way of showing respect. Wiping someone's feet with one's hair might also seem odd, but Mary was showing Jesus her complete love and devotion to serve Him. The perfume Mary poured on Jesus' head and feet was probably her most precious possession. When Mary knelt at Jesus' feet, she showed her faith and trust in Him.

Review

- Where were Jesus and His disciples staying? (**in Bethany, at the home of Simon the leper**)

- What was Martha doing? (**serving a meal**) What did Mary do? (**She poured expensive perfume on Jesus' head and feet. She wiped His feet with her hair.**)
- Why did Judas criticize Mary's gift? (**Judas said Mary had wasted the perfume. It could have been sold and the money given to the poor.**)
- Did Jesus criticize Mary's gift? (**No, Jesus was very pleased with Mary's act of love and faith.**)
- Did the people in the house understand the importance of Mary's gift? (**No, they did not understand at the time, but Jesus said that they would understand later.**)

Student Page 27.3

Allow students to complete the page independently.

Notes:

APPLICATION

- Mary honored Jesus by pouring expensive perfume on His head and feet. By doing this, she told all the people in the house that Jesus was her Lord. How can you show others that Jesus is your Lord? (**I can show others that I honor Jesus as my Lord by my respectful behavior and good attitude.**)
- Mary's expensive gift was probably her most precious possession. Share some reasons that Mary might have chosen to give such a gift. (**Possible answers: She might have been grateful to Jesus for raising her brother, Lazarus, from the dead; she might have given the gift as an act of worship; she might have wanted to let Jesus know that she would serve Him.**)

DAY 3

Name ______________________________

Believing God **27.3**

Solve each math problem and write the answer underneath. Match the answers with the letters to fill in the sentences. Read the story. Color the picture.

1 + 1	2 + 2	3 + 3	4 + 4	5 + 5	6 + 6	7 + 7	8 + 8	9 + 9	10 + 10
2	4	6	8	10	12	14	16	18	20
h	v	g	f	o	a	i	l	t	e

Mary had so much l (16) o (10) v (4) e (20) for Jesus. She wanted to honor Jesus with a g (6) i (14) f (8) t (18). Judas said Mary had wasted her perfume! Jesus knew that Mary g (6) a (12) v (4) e (20) her gift because of her love and her f (8) a (12) i (14) t (18) h (2) in Him.

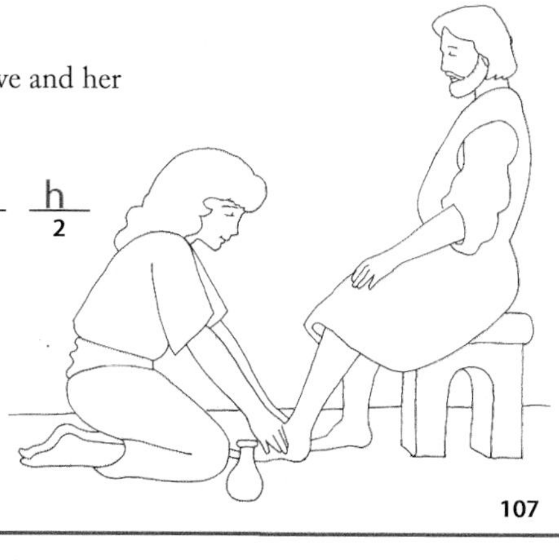

27.4

Believing God

Focus: Christians' Encouragement

EXTENSION

4A Invite students to add details and a caption to the drawings that were made in the lesson Introduction. Staple the drawings together into a booklet and place it in your classroom library. From time to time, encourage students to pray for their friends.

4B Consider placing a BOX or a BASKET for prayer requests in the classroom. Invite students to draw out the requests and to pray for each other.

Introduction

Distribute a sheet of drawing paper to each student. Invite students to choose a close friend and draw a picture of that person. The picture should show details such as the friend's favorite color, favorite activity, favorite item of clothing, or favorite pet.

When the drawings are complete, invite several students to share their work. While students share, ask questions, such as: How do you know that your friend's favorite color is blue? Use this time to help students conclude that they know their friend well because they spend time with their friend, play games with their friend, and talk with their friend.

Remind students that Mary, Martha, and Lazarus are examples of three people who had a close relationship with Jesus, similar to the relationship students have with their friends. Jesus wants all people to have a close relationship with Him. When Christians share their faith, they encourage each other to grow in their relationship with the Lord (Romans 1:11–12).

Directed Instruction

Read the following fictional story:

> Library day had come at last! This was Tara's favorite day of the week. She loved looking through the rows of bookshelves and being able to find many books that she could read all by herself. Tara decided that she would look for a funny book about talking animals. Those books were kept at the back of the children's section near the window.
>
> As Tara went back to find a book, she heard a soft sound coming from behind a shelf. Someone was crying! Tara went to see who it was. There, back by the animal stories, sat Tara's friend Kali. Kali was sobbing! Tears were running down her face, and her eyes were red. Tara immediately sat down with Kali. She wondered what could be making her friend so sad.
>
> Kali explained that her mother's military work required her to be out of the country for six months. Kali did not want her mother to leave! Six months was too long, and her mother might be in danger. Tara thought about how she could comfort her friend. Tara reminded Kali that Jesus loved and cared for Kali's mother far more than Kali did. Then Tara suggested that they pray together for Kali's mother to be safe and to come back soon. After they prayed, Kali felt much better. She thanked Tara for being a friend and for helping her remember to pray when she felt sad or afraid.

Review

- Why was Kali crying? (**Her mother's work required that she leave the family for six months. Kali did not want her mother to leave.**)
- How did Tara encourage Kali's faith? (**She reminded Kali that Jesus loved and cared for her mother. She prayed with Kali.**)

• How did Kali feel after the two girls prayed? (**She felt better and thanked Tara.**)

Student Page 27.4

Direct students to read each of the ways that they may encourage a friend to grow in faith. Have students circle the ways that they would personally choose to encourage their friends to trust God more. Ask them to share additional ideas of encouragement. (**Answers will vary.**) Discuss students' answers and allow students to complete the page independently.

Notes:

DAY 4

27.4 ***Believing God***

Answers will vary, but can include all choices.

1. How can you encourage your friends to grow in their faith? Circle each way that you will encourage others.

I WILL PRAY FOR MY FRIENDS.

I WILL SHARE BIBLE TRUTHS WITH MY FRIENDS.

I WILL PRAY WITH MY FRIENDS.

I WILL REMIND MY FRIENDS THAT GOD LOVES THEM.

I WILL INVITE MY FRIENDS TO GO TO CHURCH WITH ME.

2. Color each shape with a dot to find a hidden word. Write the word on the line to complete the words of Jesus.

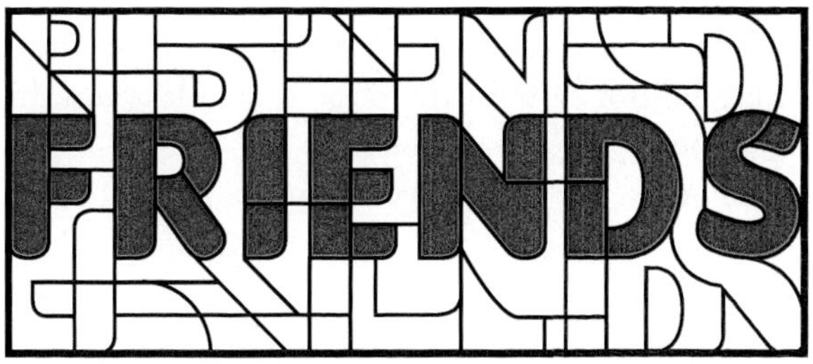

Jesus said, "I have called you friends." John 15:15

108 © Bible Grade 1

APPLICATION

- How did Tara encourage Kali to grow in faith? (**Tara reminded Kali to pray when she felt sad or afraid.**)
- How can you encourage a Christian friend to trust God more? (**Answers will vary.**)
- Have you ever received encouragement from another Christian? Tell about that time. (**Answers will vary.**)

REINFORCEMENT

When Mary broke open the bottle of perfume and anointed Jesus, she poured out a pound of nard. Spikenard, the spice used to make the perfume, was imported from the Himalayan Mountains of India and Nepal. The bottle was made of alabaster, a hard stone found in Palestine. Alabaster resembles white marble and was used to decorate Solomon's temple. At the time of Mary and Martha, alabaster was commonly used to store perfumes and oils because it kept them pure and unspoiled. Mary broke the wax seal, filled the room with the fragrance of nard, and poured out a perfume worth one year's wages. Judas objected to the cost of her gesture, but Jesus knew Mary's heart. Mary's offering was not too expensive; it was an offering fit for her Lord and King.

27.5 Believing God

Focus: Review and Assessment

★ ***PREPARATION***

Select **VA 27A Lazarus**. (*Lesson Review*)

Make a copy of **BLM 27B Lesson 27 Test** for each student. (*Directed Instruction*)

Lesson Review ★

Review the Bible truth about Mary's choice to learn from Jesus while Martha was busy preparing a meal. Cover the following concepts:

- Mary, Martha, and Lazarus were two sisters and a brother. They were close friends of Jesus.
- Jesus was often a guest in Mary, Martha, and Lazarus' home in Bethany.
- While Jesus and His disciples were in Mary and Martha's home, each sister did something different.
- Martha was busy preparing food for a meal. Mary sat at Jesus' feet and listened to Him teach.
- When Martha saw that she would have to prepare and serve the meal without Mary's help, she was not happy!
- Martha asked Jesus to tell Mary that she should get up and help.
- Jesus corrected Martha and said that Mary had made a good choice when she chose to listen to Him.

Use **VA 27A Lazarus** to review the Bible truth. Cover the following concepts:

- Lazarus became very ill. Mary and Martha sent a message to Jesus, asking Him to come quickly and heal their brother.
- Jesus delayed in coming to Bethany. During this time, Lazarus died.
- When Jesus arrived in Bethany, Martha and Mary demonstrated their faith in Him.
- Martha believed that Jesus had the power to bring Lazarus to life.
- Mary believed that Jesus could have healed her brother.
- Jesus went to Lazarus' tomb. He asked for the stone to be removed.
- Jesus prayed to His Father, God, so that the people standing nearby would believe that He was the Son of God.
- Jesus called for Lazarus to come out of the tomb. Lazarus came out! Jesus has power over death!

Review the Bible truth about Mary's gift of anointing Jesus with her perfume. Cover the following concepts:

- After Jesus raised Lazarus, He ate one last meal with Mary and Martha.
- When the meal was over, Mary took a jar of expensive perfume, broke open the jar, and poured the perfume on Jesus' head and feet. Then she wiped Jesus' feet with her hair to dry them.
- Judas, the disciple who would turn against Jesus, said that the perfume had been wasted because it should have been sold and the money given to the poor. Judas did not care for the poor at all. He was a thief and wanted some of the money.
- Jesus corrected Judas. He told everyone in the house that Mary's gift had been given in love.

Directed Instruction ★

Distribute a copy of **BLM 27B Lesson 27 Test** to each student and tell them to begin. When all have completed the test, discuss students' answers in class.

Lesson Preparation

Accepting Forgiveness

28.0

Expected Student Outcomes

KNOW

God restores Peter and places him in leadership in spite of his denials and fear.

DO

Students will:

- choose words that best complete sentences to review the Bible truth
- identify how to receive God's forgiveness and set a godly example
- unscramble words to correctly finish sentences
- fill in a chart to sequence events in a story about forgiveness

APPLY

Students will acknowledge that God by His grace restores those who repent and they will follow His example in their own relationships.

Lesson Outline

I. Peter—a crumbling rock (Jn 13:36–38, 18:15–18, 18:24–28; Mt 26:31–35, 26:69–75; Mk 14:27–42, 14:54–72; Lk 22:31–34, 22:54–62)
  A. Peter's boast
  B. Peter's sorrow
II. Peter is restored (Jn 21:1–19)
  A. Jesus calls Peter to be a leader
III. Peter boldly leads (Acts 3:1–4:23)
  A. Peter and the lame man
  B. Peter is bold for the Lord
IV. Repent and restore
  A. Repentance restores friendships

TEACHER'S HEART

A rooster crowed, and in the light of a dying fire, Peter's heart ached. He'd been up all night. Now that it was morning, he was heartsick. The realization that he'd denied the Lord flooded him with guilt. Knowing that he'd caused Jesus such pain, Peter retreated in shame and sorrow!

Isn't it just like Jesus, however, to seek out Peter and offer restoration? When Peter least expected it, the Lord appeared and offered to share a meal with His disciples. How eager Peter was to be near the Master once again! How thankful he was to be reunited in fellowship with the Lord!

What pure love Jesus has for all of life's "Peters" who stumble and fall as they travel along the road of their Christian journey. Like Peter, believers have the wonderful assurance that "If we confess our sins, He is faithful and just to forgive us our sins and to cleanse us from all unrighteousness" (1 John 1:9). As you teach this week, look for opportunities to share the offer of God's grace and forgiveness with your students.

MEMORY VERSE

1 John 1:9

MATERIALS

Day 1:
- Chart paper
- Rock

Day 2:
- No additional materials are needed.

Day 3:
- Toy puppy
- VA 28A Peter and the Lame Man
- Smooth stones, paint (*Extension*)

Day 4:
- Globe

Day 5:
- VA 28A Peter and the Lame Man
- BLM 28A Lesson 28 Test

SONGS

He Forgives Me (*Extension*)

TEACHER RESOURCES

Card, Michael. *A Fragile Stone: The Emotional Life of Simon Peter*. InterVarsity Press, 2007.

Stanley, Charles F. *The Gift of Forgiveness*. Thomas Nelson, 2002.

STUDENT RESOURCES

Keffer, Lois, and Mary Grace Becker. *Let's Hear It for the Fruit of the Spirit: 12 Instant Bible Lessons for Kids*. David C. Cook, 2005.

Peter and John action figures. Biblequest, 2007.

28.1 Accepting Forgiveness

Focus: Peter—A Crumbling Rock

MEMORY VERSE

1 John 1:9

MEMORY WORK

- Post the prepared Memory Verse in the classroom and read it together. Explain that God loves all believers and will forgive them for their sins—no matter how bad those sins are—if they are truly sorry and confess their sins to Him. Divide the class into four groups. Assign each group a color and have students recite the part of the verse that is underlined in that color. Change the color assigned to each group until all have learned the verse.

★ PREPARATION

Break the Memory Verse into four phrases and write the Memory Verse on a large piece of CHART PAPER. Use colored markers to underline each of the four phrases in a different color. (*Memory Work*)

Obtain a large ROCK, preferably one that students cannot easily lift. (*Introduction*)

EXTENSION

1A When first graders are told to apologize when they have hurt each other, their apologies are sometimes less than sincere. At times, they are still angry with each other and apologize out of obedience to the adult in charge. At the end of the school day, ask the students to think about conflicts that have occurred during the day and consider how their attitude or behavior contributed to those conflicts. Invite students to confess their sin, repent, and, if needed, sincerely apologize to the person whom they have hurt.

Introduction ★

Display the ROCK. Ask students to suggest adjectives to describe it. (**heavy, hard**) Explain that Jesus gave Simon the nickname *Peter*, which means *a rock*. Peter was not much like a heavy rock when he first began to follow Jesus. Peter was easily moved! Remind students how Peter had faith to walk on the sea during a storm, but once he took his focus away from Jesus, he sank! Encourage students to listen for the way Peter changed his mind.

Directed Instruction

Read the following Bible truth based on Matthew 26, Mark 14, Luke 22, John 13, and John 18:

> It was Passover week. Right before the time Jesus was taken to be crucified, He and His disciples ate their last meal together. Then they went out to the Mount of Olives. There Jesus said, "Tonight you will all leave Me, but after I rise again, I will go to Galilee and meet you there."
>
> Peter spoke up proudly, "Lord, I will never leave You. Even if everyone else stops following You, I will be faithful."
>
> But Jesus said, "Peter, tonight before the rooster crows, you will lie and say that you do not know Me three times."
>
> Peter insisted, "Lord, even if I lose my life with You, I will never do that." All of the disciples agreed with Peter saying that they, too, would remain faithful to the Lord.
>
> Then Jesus took Peter, James, and John, His three closest friends, to the Garden of Gethsemane to pray. While they were there, soldiers with clubs and swords came to arrest Jesus. The disciples were afraid that the soldiers would arrest them, too, so they ran away. But Peter stayed far back in the crowd and followed the solders to Caiaphas' palace where Jesus was to be tried. When they took Jesus to the trial, Peter stayed outside in the yard. A young woman came up to Peter and said, "You are a follower of Jesus."
>
> Peter said, "I don't know what you're talking about." Then Peter moved onto the porch and another woman said, "This fellow was with Jesus of Nazareth." Again Peter said, "I do not know the man."
>
> A little while later, some other men who were watching what was happening with Jesus came to Peter and said, "You really are one of Jesus' followers. You talk like one of His followers." Peter became very angry and shouted, "I do not know this man." Immediately a rooster crowed and Peter remembered what Jesus had said. Peter was so ashamed that he went away and cried because he had said that he was not one of Jesus' followers.

Ask a volunteer to tell which disciple spoke up when Jesus said that all the disciples would leave Him. (**Peter**) Jesus knew what was ahead that evening, and He made a startling prophesy. Ask a student to share what Jesus told Peter would happen later that night. (**Jesus told Peter that Peter would lie about even knowing Jesus three times before the rooster crowed.**) Peter was shocked and said that would never happen; he would die first! True to Jesus' words, all of the disciples did run away when He was arrested that night. Three times people said that they had seen Peter with Jesus, and three times Peter said that he did not know Jesus at all. Suddenly the rooster crowed, and Peter remembered Jesus' words.

Review

- Who were Jesus' three closest friends? (**Peter, James, and John**)
- What did Jesus say that the disciples would do when He was arrested? (**leave Him**)
- Did Peter leave Jesus? (**Yes.**) What did Peter do when people asked him if he were one of Jesus' followers? (**He lied about knowing Jesus.**)
- What made Peter realize that he had sinned? (**the rooster crowed**)

Student Page 28.1

Assist students in completing the page.

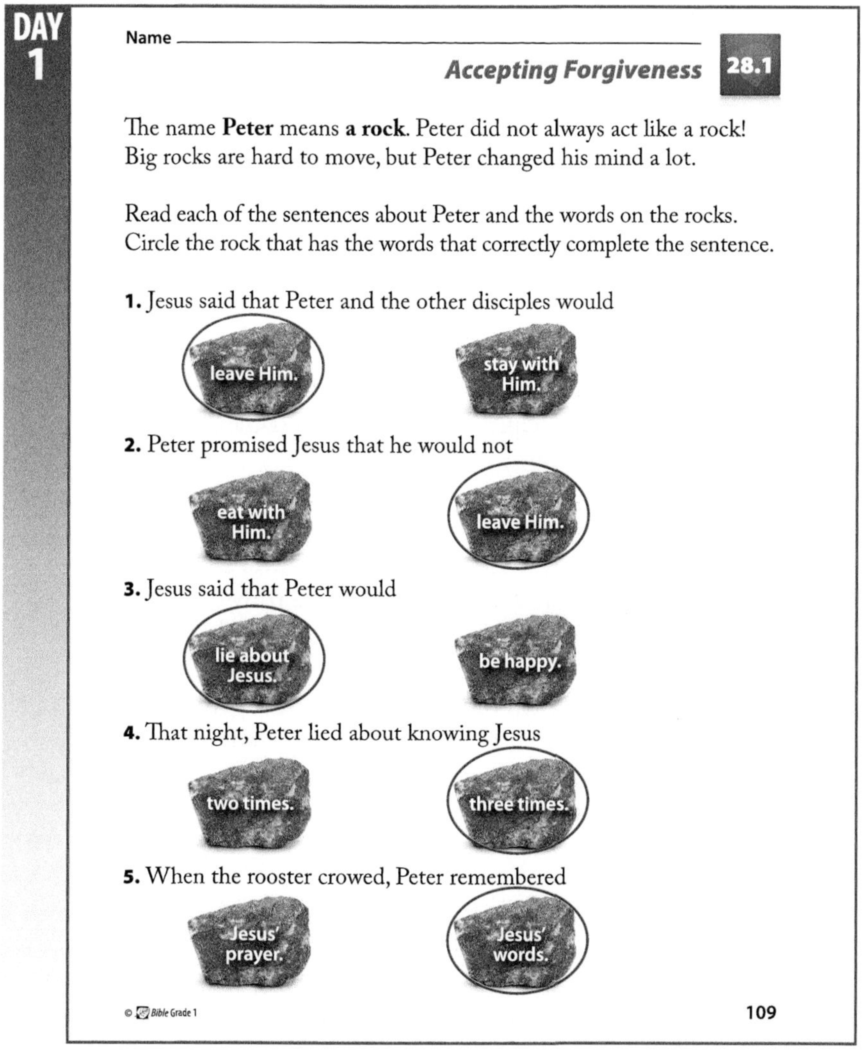

DAY 1

Name ______________________________

Accepting Forgiveness 28.1

The name **Peter** means **a rock**. Peter did not always act like a rock! Big rocks are hard to move, but Peter changed his mind a lot.

Read each of the sentences about Peter and the words on the rocks. Circle the rock that has the words that correctly complete the sentence.

1. Jesus said that Peter and the other disciples would

2. Peter promised Jesus that he would not

3. Jesus said that Peter would

4. That night, Peter lied about knowing Jesus

5. When the rooster crowed, Peter remembered

 109

APPLICATION

- Peter proudly said that he was willing to go to prison and to even die for Jesus. How did Jesus correct Peter for his proud words? (**Jesus told Peter that he would lie about knowing Him three times before a rooster crowed.**)
- Peter's lies caused him to feel sad and guilty. He needed to be forgiven! Have you ever felt sad or guilty? Tell about that time. (**Answers will vary.**)
- How do you know that Jesus will forgive you? (**The Bible tells me that Jesus will forgive me if I confess my sin and repent.**)
- Is it always easy to confess your sin? (**No, it is not always easy to say that I have done wrong, but I know that I will be forgiven when I do confess my sins.**)

REINFORCEMENT

One of the most famous men named *Peter* was Dr. Peter Marshall, renowned pastor and chaplain of the United States Senate from 1947 to 1949. Born in Scotland in 1902, Marshall had only two weeks' worth of living expenses when he came to the United States in 1927, but he dedicated himself to gaining an education with the goal of becoming a minister. Marshall's eloquent sermons were characterized by his humility and identification with the common people. He had a close fellowship with the Lord and sought to bring others into a personal relationship with Jesus Christ. Peter Marshall's wife, Catherine, wrote his biography entitled *A Man Called Peter*, which was later made into a motion picture.

28.2 Accepting Forgiveness

Focus: Peter Is Restored

★ PREPARATION

Cut three paper hearts from red or pink construction paper. Write the words *Feed, My,* and *sheep* on the hearts, one word per heart. (*Introduction*)

EXTENSION

2A To demonstrate the effects that sin has on relationships, cut three strips of colored construction paper the length of the paper and about an inch wide. On the first strip, write the word *myself.* On the second strip, write the words *my friend,* and on the third strip, write the words *my Savior.* Then tape all three strips together to form a circular chain. Hold up the chain and have students read the words on each link. Tear the strip that is labeled *myself.* The chain will be broken at this point. Explain that sin can cause broken relationship between friends. Sin also causes a broken relationship with the Lord. Tape the strip together, reconnect the chain, and explain that forgiveness, both from the Lord and from each other, can restore broken relationships. Invite students to make their own chains to demonstrate this concept to others.

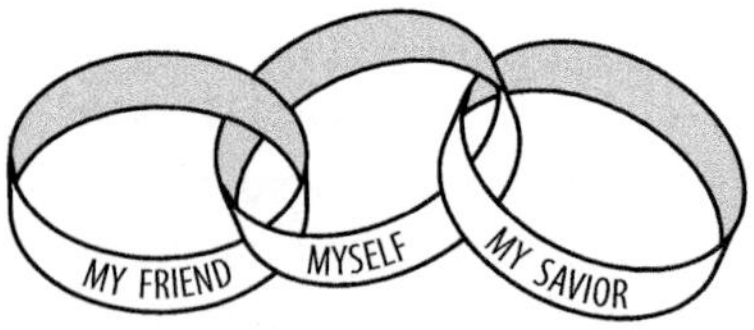

2B Teach the song "He Forgives Me" from the music CDs to reinforce the concepts of forgiveness and restoration.

Introduction ★

Choose three volunteers to come to the front of the room and face the class. Give each volunteer a paper heart with the words facing the volunteers, and arrange the three students in order so that the hearts will read *Feed My sheep* when the hearts are turned over.

Ask students to recount how many times Peter said he did not know Jesus before the rooster crowed. (**three times**) Explain that Peter sinned when he lied about knowing Jesus. He lied three times! Have volunteers turn the paper hearts to the other side. Read the words. Ask students to listen for who spoke those words and why they were spoken in today's lesson.

Directed Instruction

Read the following Bible truth based on John 21:1–19:

> Shortly after the Crucifixion, Peter and some of the disciples decided to go fishing. Even though they fished all night, they caught nothing. The next morning as they were returning in their boats, Jesus was standing on the shore. He called out to them, "Children, do you have any food?" They answered that they had no food, but they did not recognize that it was Jesus who had spoken to them. Then Jesus told them to throw their net out on the right side of the boat, and they would find some fish. They listened and obeyed, and just like that, their net was full of large fish! Later they counted the fish and found that they had caught 153 fish, and the nets had not broken!
>
> One of the disciples recognized Jesus and told Peter. Peter became so excited that he jumped into the water and began swimming toward shore. The other disciples followed in the boat, dragging the net of fish with them. As soon as they came to land, they saw fish and bread, cooking on a fire of coals. Jesus told them to bring some of the fish that they had just caught, and then He and the disciples began eating breakfast.
>
> When breakfast was over, Jesus asked Peter three times if Peter loved Him. Peter was sad that Jesus repeated the question. But just as Peter had refused to truthfully say that he was a follower of Jesus three times, Peter now answered three times that he truly did love Jesus. Jesus then told Peter to feed His sheep and care for His lambs. This meant Jesus wanted Peter to lead others to accept Jesus as Savior, and to lead, teach, and help the people who already followed Jesus. Peter returned to following Jesus, and Peter's friendship with Jesus was fully restored. Jesus let Peter know what an important part Peter was to have in leading people and helping them to grow in faith.

Review

- How many times had Peter lied about knowing Jesus? (**three**) How many times did Jesus ask Peter if he loved Jesus? (**three**) How many times did Jesus tell Peter to feed His sheep? (**three**)

- What did Jesus mean by the words *feed My sheep*? (**Peter was to lead people to trust Jesus as their Savior as well as teach and help those who already were following Jesus.**)
- Now that Peter's relationship with Jesus was restored, would Peter be a leader or a follower in the Church? (**Peter would be a leader.**)

Student Page 28.2

Assist students in completing the page.

Notes:

APPLICATION

- Why was it important for Peter and Jesus' relationship to be restored? (**Peter needed to know and love Jesus, both for his own spiritual growth and for the ability to lead others to grow in their faith. In the same way, Jesus wants a restored relationship with everyone.**)
- If you have sinned, what is the first step for you to take to restore your relationship with Jesus? (**I should honestly confess my sin and repent. Jesus will forgive me.**)
- How can you share the forgiveness that you have received from God with others? (**I can forgive others when they sin against me.**)

REINFORCEMENT

Each time Peter denied knowing Jesus, Peter became more insistent. The first time, he stood up to a simple slave girl and merely said that he did not know Jesus. The second time, he strongly stated to a girl and a man with an oath to God that he did not know Jesus. This was a very serious sin! Additionally, Peter referred to Jesus as *the man*, not the *Son of God*, as he had professed only a short time before. In his third denial, Peter became desperate and defensive when confronted by a group of people. He began calling down God's judgment on himself if he were lying. In effect, he joined the enemies of Christ who had participated in His arrest.

DAY 2

28.2 *Accepting Forgiveness*

Jesus forgave Peter. He told Peter, "Feed My sheep." This was Jesus' way of telling Peter that Peter would be a leader in the Church. Peter would lead others to know Jesus. Peter would also teach and care for people who had already accepted Jesus as Savior.

1. Color the sheep that show the only ways for Christians to receive God's forgiveness.

2. What can you do to set a good example for your classmates? Circle the words that show ways that you can be a leader.

OBEY TEACHERS
BE KIND
LISTEN WHEN OTHERS SHARE
HELP IN THE CLASSROOM
CLEAN UP
PRAY FOR CLASSMATES
PLAY WITH EVERYONE
PLAY FAIRLY

110

28.3

Accepting Forgiveness

Focus: Peter Boldly Leads

★ PREPARATION

Bring a TOY PUPPY to class. (*Introduction*)

Select **VA 28A Peter and the Lame Man**. (*Directed Instruction*)

EXTENSION

3A Jesus' restoration of Peter enabled Peter to become the "rock" that Jesus knew he would become. Jesus wants all Christians to be strong in their faith (Ephesians 6:10). To remind students to be strong, provide each student with a SMOOTH STONE. Suitable stones are usually available in craft or hobby stores. Invite each student to use PAINT or markers to put his or her name on the stone as a reminder to set a strong example of Christian behavior for others.

Introduction ★

Holding a TOY PUPPY, ask students if they have ever given a puppy a treat. (**Answers will vary.**) Discuss how the puppy begs and then waits expectantly to see what it will get.

Inform students that in Bible times, many people had to beg, too. Remind students that the 10 lepers may have counted on the generosity of others for food or clothing because they had to live away from other people. Ask students to name other people living at that time who may have had to beg for food. (**Possible answers: widows; people who were blind, ill, or otherwise unable to work**) Invite students to listen for what Peter and John gave to a beggar as you share today's lesson.

Directed Instruction ★

Open your Bible to the book of Acts. Tell students that all the Bible truths that the students have studied so far in this lesson have been found in the Gospels, the first four books of the New Testament, but now they will be learning Bible truths that took place after Jesus rose from the dead. Many of these Bible truths are found in the book of Acts. Recite the first five books of the New Testament and have students repeat after you.

Display **VA 28A Peter and the Lame Man** and read the text on the back.

Remind students that Jesus knew Peter's feelings. He knew how much Peter needed forgiveness and wanted to be restored to a loving relationship with Jesus. Jesus also knew that Peter could become a strong leader in the Church once he received Jesus' forgiveness.

When Peter understood that Jesus had forgiven him, he took Jesus' command to feed Jesus' sheep seriously. Both Peter and John took action to obey Jesus. Ask a student to recount where Peter and John were going when they met the lame man. (**to the temple to pray**) Both Peter and John spent time in prayer. They had received Jesus' power to heal and preach boldly. Have a volunteer share what happened when Peter told the lame man to stand and walk in the name of Jesus. (**the man was healed**) What did other people who saw that the man had been healed think about this miracle? (**They were amazed!**)

Review that one group of people chose to be upset instead of amazed by the man's healing. Ask students to tell who those people were. (**the temple leaders**) Recount that these leaders did not want Peter and John to tell others that they were the ones who put Jesus to death or that Jesus had risen from the dead. These leaders did not want the people to follow Jesus, even though Peter told them the truth that faith in Jesus brings forgiveness of sins. The leaders had Peter and John arrested and put in prison to try to frighten them, but once they were free, they courageously continued to preach in the name of Jesus.

Review

- What did the lame man want from Peter and John? (**money**)
- What did they offer to the man instead? (**healing in the name of Jesus**)
- What did the man do after he was healed? (**He went to the temple and praised God.**)
- What did the Jewish leaders tell Peter and John to stop doing? (**preaching about Jesus**)
- How did Peter and John demonstrate courage? (**They kept on telling others about Jesus, even though they had been ordered to stop.**)

Student Page 28.3

Complete this page together. Choose a different volunteer to read each exercise, unscramble the word at the end of the exercise, and spell each scrambled word correctly for the class.

Notes:

DAY 3

Name ______________________

Accepting Forgiveness **28.3**

Unscramble the letters below each line to make a word that correctly completes each sentence. Write the word.

1. Peter and John met a lame man who begged for money.
oeymn

2. Peter gave the man something better than gold.
olgd

3. The man praised God that he could walk.
alwk

4. The people wanted to know more about Jesus.
esJus

5. Peter and John kept on preaching boldly.
bdlyol

111

APPLICATION

- The lame man asked for money, but Peter offered healing in the name of Jesus. In what way was his healing a better gift than money? (**Money was a temporary way of helping the man; healing was lasting. The healed man could now be active in his family and community and have a full life.**)
- How did Peter share the good news about Jesus with the lame man? (**He told the lame man that he was healed through the power of Jesus.**)
- Peter was brave before the religious leaders as he proclaimed the good news about Jesus. Is it always easy to speak up for what you know is right? (**No.**) Who helped Peter to speak boldly? (**Jesus or the Holy Spirit**)
- How did Peter's preaching make a difference to the people who listened to him? (**many believed in Jesus**) In what ways can you share what you know about Jesus with others? (**Answers will vary.**)

28.4 Accepting Forgiveness

Focus: Repent and Restore

★ PREPARATION

Have a GLOBE on hand. (*Introduction*)

Introduction ★

Show students the location of the country of Ghana on the GLOBE and explain that they will hear a story about two boys who lived in Ghana, a country in western Africa.

Directed Instruction

Read the following fictional story:

> Omari and Adika were Christian boys and good friends. Like many African boys, Omari and Adika loved to play soccer. They could not afford to buy a real soccer ball, but that did not stop them from playing. They tied banana leaves together tightly until they had something that resembled a soccer ball. The boys would kick the handmade ball until it was so ragged that it fell apart, and they had to make a new one.
>
> One day some older boys came to Omari and Adika's neighborhood. These boys had a real leather soccer ball! Omari and Adika's eyes grew round with delight. Now they could play ball with something that would not fall apart. However, the older boys did not immediately invite Omari and Adika to play. They saw that Omari was tall and fast, so they called Omari to come and play with them. When Omari asked if Adika could come and play, too, the older boys would not let him! But Omari wanted to play so badly that he didn't try again to get the older boys to let Adika play. How sad Adika looked! He stood nearby and watched them play. When the game was over, Adika was so hurt that he ran home.
>
> Omari played with the older boys all week. Adika did not come to watch. At first Omari did not think about Adika, but then Omari realized something. He knew that his actions had hurt his friendship with Adika. Omari prayed that he could gain Adika's forgiveness. Then Omari made a bold decision. Omari ran to find Adika and asked him to come to where the boys were playing soccer.
>
> That afternoon Omari announced his decision to the group. If the boys would not allow Adika to play, then he would not play with them either! The boys were surprised by Omari's strong character. Then Omari put Adika in the center of the group. Right there, in front of all the other boys, Omari explained that he had not been a loyal friend to a Christian brother and asked for Adika's forgiveness. Adika did forgive him! The older boys were amazed by Omari's show of faith!

Review

- Where did the two boys, Omari and Adika, live? (**in Ghana, a country in western Africa**)
- At the beginning of the story, the two boys were friends. What happened to change that? (**Older boys invited Omari to play soccer, but not Adika. Omari played with them instead of being loyal to Adika.**)
- How was Omari like Peter? (**Omari needed Adika's forgiveness, just as Peter needed Jesus' forgiveness.**)

- What bold decision did Omari make? (**He told the older boys that if they would not let Adika play, then he would not play either.**)
- What did the older boys think of Omari's show of faith? (**They were amazed by Omari's faith.**)

Student Page 28.4
Assist students in completing the page.

Notes:

APPLICATION

- Have you ever told a friend that you were sorry? Tell about that time. (**Answers will vary.**)
- How important is it for you to say that you are sorry when you have wronged someone? (**It is very important! Words of repentance and apology help to restore relationships.**)
- Can you forgive someone who has not apologized to you? (**Yes, sometimes I should just overlook an offense (Proverbs 19:11).**)
- Omari made a bold decision to repent and to try to restore his friendship with Adika. How did his behavior influence the older boys? (**Answers will vary, but should include that the older boys saw a Christian take an action that demonstrated his beliefs.**)

DAY 4

28.4 ***Accepting Forgiveness***

Complete the chart by writing the words **friends**, **forgave**, **loyal**, **example**, and **confess** on each line to make the sentence true.

1. Omari and Adika were ___friends___.

2. Omari was not ___loyal___ to Adika.

3. Omari decided to ___confess___ his sin to Adika.

4. Adika ___forgave___ Omari.

5. Omari was a good ___example___ for the older boys.

112

28.5 Accepting Forgiveness

Focus: Review and Assessment

★ ***PREPARATION***

Select **VA 28A Peter and the Lame Man**. (*Lesson Review*)

Duplicate a copy of **BLM 28A Lesson 28 Test** for each student. (*Directed Instruction*)

Lesson Review ★

Review the Bible truth of Peter's denial of Jesus. Continue with a review of Jesus' forgiveness and restoration of Peter. Cover the following concepts:

- Soon after they had eaten their last meal together during Passover week, Jesus told His disciples that they would all leave Him, He would rise again, and He would meet them in Galilee.
- Peter proudly told Jesus that he would never leave Jesus. Jesus told Peter that he would lie about knowing Jesus three times before the rooster crowed the next morning.
- Peter did lie! The rooster's crow made Peter realize that he had sinned. He remembered what Jesus had said.
- One morning, the disciples were out fishing when Jesus came to see them. He told them to throw out their nets. They caught 153 fish, but the nets did not break.
- Jesus asked Peter if Peter loved Him three times.
- Jesus showed Peter that he was forgiven by telling Peter to feed His sheep. That meant that Peter was to be a leader in the Church.

Use **VA 28A Peter and the Lame Man** to review this Bible truth. Cover the following concepts:

- Peter and John went to the temple to pray. A lame man was near the temple gate, begging for money.
- Peter did not have any money, but offered the lame man healing in Jesus' name.
- The man was healed! He went into the temple, praising God.
- The temple leaders were not happy with Peter and John. They did not want the people to know that Jesus had risen from the dead. They put Peter and John in prison.
- When Peter and John were released from prison, the temple leaders told them not to preach in Jesus' name. Peter and John continued to preach about Jesus.
- Christians receive forgiveness from God. They are to forgive others.

Directed Instruction ★

Distribute a copy of **BLM 28A Lesson 28 Test** to each student. Be sure that students understand the directions. Have students complete the exercises according to the directions. Collect the test papers for assessment.

Notes:

Lesson Preparation

Easter

29.0

Expected Student Outcomes

KNOW

Jesus is arrested, crucified, and raised from the dead.

DO

Students will:

- order words to complete sentences about Jesus' triumphal entry
- match pictures to the text about the Last Supper and Jesus' prayer
- review events leading up to the crucifixion and share ways to show love
- unscramble letters to complete words to review Jesus' resurrection

APPLY

Students will verbalize the plan of salvation as they consider the death, burial, and resurrection of Jesus. They will pray for others as Jesus did.

Lesson Outline

I. Jesus' triumphal entry (Jn 12:12–19)
  A. Jesus fulfills Zechariah's prophecy
  B. Hosanna to the king
II. Jesus' last supper (Mt 26:17–30, Jn 17)
  A. Jesus washes the disciples' feet (Jn 13:1–11)
  B. Jesus shares bread and wine
  C. Jesus prays for all
III. Jesus' arrest, crucifixion, and burial (Mk 14:43–50, 14:53, 15:11; Lk 22:51)
  A. Cruel treatment and crucifixion (Jn 19)
IV. Jesus is risen (Mt 28:1–10, Mk 16:12–20, Lk 24:1–49, Jn 20:1–18, 1 Cor 15:3b–8)
  A. Jesus appears to Mary Magdalene and others
  B. Jesus' resurrected body (1 Cor 15:51–54)

TEACHER'S HEART

Before beginning another busy week, take some time to consider the immense love of God. It is because of this love that Jesus stared in the face of death, and yet submitted Himself to His Father's will; for love He gave thanks for the broken bread that symbolized His own broken body, for love He took the cup and gave thanks, knowing that His own blood would be poured out in order to redeem the world. Love was the motivation that moved Him to pray for you in the dark of Gethsemane, and love was the reason that He bore the Cross because He knew and trusted that even the most incomprehensible suffering was ultimately for the good.

This week you'll be looking at the events of Jesus' last week before His resurrection. It may be difficult for some students to accept the fact that Jesus died to pay for their sins, but this truth must be shared. If Jesus had not died, no one could be reconciled to God. Because of Christ's death and resurrection, Christians share in the blessed hope of eternal life.

MEMORY VERSE

Romans 6:23

MATERIALS

Day 1:
- Party horn
- VA 29A Jesus' Triumphal Entry
- PP-8 Easter (*Extension*)

Day 2:
- Matzo, VA 29B Jesus' Last Supper

Day 3:
- VA 29C Jesus' Arrest, Crucifixion, and Burial
- Polymer clay, lightweight cord (*Extension*)
- BLM 29A Easter Cube, card stock (*Extension*)

Day 4:
- Plastic Easter eggs, matzo, purple cloth, steel nail, piece of wood
- VA 29D Jesus Is Risen
- Chenille stems, ribbon (*Extension*)

Day 5:
- VA 29A Jesus' Triumphal Entry, VA 29B Jesus' Last Supper, VA 29C Jesus' Arrest, Crucifixion, and Burial, VA 29D Jesus Is Risen
- BLM 29B Lesson 29 Test

SONGS

Palm Sunday Celebration
Rolled 'em Away
Easter Rise Up

TEACHER RESOURCES

Lucado, Max. *He Chose the Nails.* Thomas Nelson, 2005.

Strobel, Lee. *The Case for Easter.* Zondervan, 2004.

STUDENT RESOURCES

The Very First Easter: The Beginner's Bible. Zonderkidz, 2009.

Veggie Tales: 'Twas the Night Before Easter. DVD. Big Idea, 2011.

29.1 Easter

Focus: Jesus' Triumphal Entry

MEMORY VERSE

Romans 6:23

MEMORY WORK

- Read the Memory Verse to students and have them repeat it after you. Explain that the word *wage* means *a payment*. People receive a payment for what they have done. Most of the time, receiving a wage, or a payment, is a good thing, but not in the case of sin. The payment for sin is separation from God forever. When Adam and Eve sinned, it caused all people to be separated from God. However, God loves people so much that He gave them a gift. The gift is His Son, Jesus, who died on the cross for everyone's sins so that they could be brought back to God. What a wonderful gift! Have students recite the verse again, emphasizing the key words *death*, *gift*, *eternal*, and *Christ Jesus*. Invite students to cheer for the Lord.

★ PREPARATION

Obtain a PARTY HORN. (*Introduction*)

Select **VA 29A Jesus' Triumphal Entry.** (*Directed Instruction*)

EXTENSION

1A Role-play the triumphal entry with the song "Palm Sunday Celebration" on the music CDs. The song is written from the perspective of the donkey. Invite students to slowly walk on their hands and knees while they sing along.

1B Show **PP-8 Easter** to review the events of the last week of Jesus' earthly life, concluding with Jesus' resurrection.

Introduction ★

Display a PARTY HORN and blow into it. Ask students to tell you what comes to mind when they see this item. (**a party, a celebration**) Have you ever had a part in planning a party or celebration? (**Answers will vary.**) How did planning the event make you feel? (**excited, happy**)

Remark that in today's lesson, people celebrated Jesus' coming to their city. This celebration was planned by God! God is all-powerful and all-knowing; God Himself told the prophet Zechariah to write about Jesus' entry into Jerusalem hundreds of years before it happened.

Directed Instruction ★

Tell students that Jewish people celebrated holidays, much as Christians do today. Passover was a very special holiday celebrated by the Jewish people every year. This holiday celebrated God's deliverance of His people from slavery during the time when they lived in Egypt. Many Jewish people traveled to Jerusalem to celebrate the Passover. Jesus and His disciples also traveled to Jerusalem for the Passover.

Display **VA 29A Jesus' Triumphal Entry**. Inform students that Christians celebrate Jesus' triumphal entry in churches today on the Sunday before Easter. This Sunday is called *Palm Sunday* because the people waved palm branches. Point out the palm branches in the picture. The people waved the branches and shouted the Hebrew word *hosanna*, which means *God saves*. Pronounce the word *hosanna* and invite students to say it after you. Read the text on the back of VA 29A.

Teach students that there were two surprising things that happened in this Bible truth. Explain that the first surprise happened when Jesus rode into Jerusalem on a donkey; He did exactly what the prophet Zechariah had written that the Messiah, the promised Savior, would do. The most surprising thing about that was that Zechariah lived hundreds of years before Jesus was even born! Jesus showed the people that His coming was part of God's plan.

The second surprise came when the people called Jesus *the king*. Jesus' disciples knew Jesus as their teacher, but it would have been very surprising to hear the people say that He was not only their teacher, but their king as well.

Review

- What did Jesus do the day before He went to Jerusalem? (**He raised Lazarus from the dead.**)
- Why were Jesus and the disciples traveling to Jerusalem? (**They were going there to celebrate Passover, a very special holiday for the Jewish people.**)
- What happened when Jesus started to ride into the city? (**Crowds of people were excited to see Jesus. They began waving palm branches and**

shouting, "Hosanna! Blessed is He who comes in the name of the Lord. Blessed is the King of Israel.")

Student Page 29.1

Complete this page together. Choose a different volunteer to read each sentence and to unscramble each set of words needed to correctly complete the sentence. It may be helpful to have students number the words in the correct order before writing them.

Notes:

DAY 1

Name ______________________________

Easter **29.1**

Put the words in order to complete each sentence.

1. Jesus showed His power over death when He raised Lazarus

__from the dead__.

dead from the

2. After Jesus raised Lazarus, He rode a

__donkey into Jerusalem__.

donkey Jerusalem into

3. The people shouted, "Hosanna! Blessed is He who comes in

__the name of the Lord__."

the Lord name of the

APPLICATION

- The people shouted praises to Jesus as their King. Is Jesus your King? Share what you do to praise Him. (**Answers will vary.**)
- Why did Jesus teach people, heal people, and serve people? (**Jesus did everything because of His love for people. He wanted all people to know the truth about His Father so that they would not have to be separated from Him any longer.**)
- Who are the people who rule over people in different countries on Earth? (**Possible answers: governors, kings, presidents, emperors**) How is King Jesus different from those people? (**Answers will vary, but should include that Jesus is all-powerful, all-knowing, and yet He invites me to pray to Him at any time and have a close relationship with Him.**)

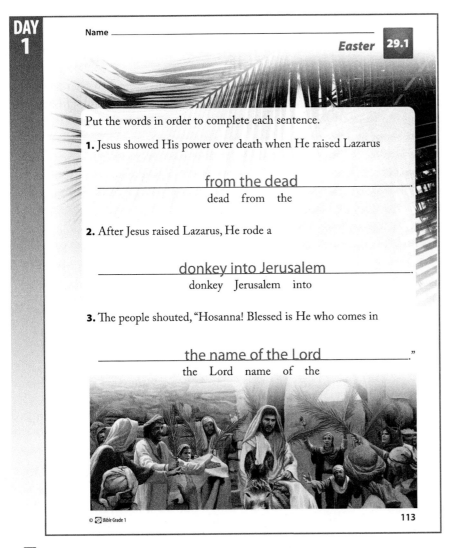

29.2 Easter

Focus: Jesus' Last Supper

★ PREPARATION

Have a PIECE OF MATZO, Jewish flatbread, on hand. (*Introduction*)

Select **VA 29B Jesus' Last Supper**. (*Directed Instruction*)

EXTENSION

2A If weather permits, take students for a walk around your campus or playground. Stop from time to time and discuss prayer needs for the people who work or play in the area. For example, you could stop at the principal's office and pray for continued godly leadership. If you are outside, you could pray for the people who live or work in the vicinity. Remind students that Jesus' prayer for His disciples was not a selfish prayer; Jesus set the example for Christians to pray unselfishly for others.

Introduction ★

Display a PIECE OF MATZO. Have students look at the matzo and explain that it is flat because it does not have any yeast in it. This flatbread was like the bread that the Hebrew slaves made before they left Egypt. This bread is used by Jewish people to remember the events of the Passover. Jesus may have used similar bread when He celebrated Passover with His disciples.

Directed Instruction ★

Remind students that Jesus and His disciples had gone to Jerusalem to celebrate the Passover. When they were all in the room where they were to eat a Passover meal, Jesus knelt down and washed the disciples' feet. That was a job for the lowest servant; it was not the job for the Messiah or for a king! Peter was surprised that Jesus would do such a dirty job. Peter did not want to let Jesus wash his feet, but Jesus explained that it was very important for Peter to receive this kindness. Jesus was showing them how important it is to serve others in love. Everything that Jesus did on Earth was done out of love.

Display **VA 29B Jesus' Last Supper**. Tell students that Jesus used the bread and wine from the meal to teach His disciples spiritual truths and to remember Him. Christians today celebrate this meal as the Lord's Supper or Holy Communion. Read the text on the back of VA 29B.

Because Jesus is the Son of God, He is all-knowing. Recount that Jesus knew who would turn against Him. Jesus knew exactly what would happen during the week of Passover. He knew that He would be betrayed by Judas, arrested, put on trial, and die on the cross. Knowing everything, Jesus still chose to go through all of the pain, death, and even being forsaken by His Father. He suffered through all of it because His loving sacrifice was the only way that people who believed in Him could have a relationship with God and live with Him in heaven forever.

Remind students that Jesus spent a lot of time in prayer. He prayed for His disciples and all the people who would come to know Him. Review these four requests by having students raise one finger for each request.

1. Jesus prayed that God the Father would protect them and keep them in unity so that they would work together and not argue with each other.
2. Jesus requested that God the Father would continue to teach them His Word, which is truth.
3. Jesus asked that the love of God would be in them.
4. Jesus requested that all believers would be with Him where He is. This prayer was very important! Many religious leaders and others would try to stop Jesus' disciples from preaching and teaching in Jesus' name. The disciples needed to help each other. What a powerful prayer!

Ask students to share who else Jesus prayed for that night. (**He prayed for people who did not know Him yet—even people who had not been born at that time.**) Were people who are alive today included in that prayer? (**Yes, Jesus wants all people to come to know Him as Savior and Lord.**)

Review

- Who washed the disciples' feet? (**Jesus**) How did Peter act when it was his turn to have his feet washed? (**Peter did not want Jesus to wash his feet. Jesus had to explain that Peter could not be part of Jesus' work unless Jesus washed Peter's feet.**)
- What did Jesus do to help His disciples remember Him? (**Jesus shared His last supper with them.**) What do Christians today call the celebration of Jesus' last supper? (**the Lord's Supper, or Holy Communion**)
- What did Jesus use to represent His body? (**a piece of bread**) What did He use to represent His blood? (**a cup of wine**)
- What were the four requests that Jesus made when He prayed for His disciples? (**He prayed that God the Father would protect them and keep them united, that He would teach them His Word (truth), that God's love would be in them, and that they would be with Jesus always.**)

Student Page 29.2

Assist students in completing the page.

DAY 2

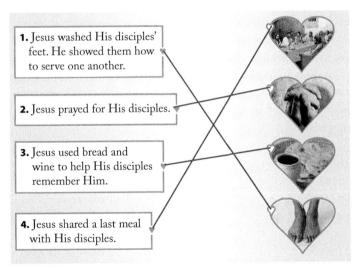

29.2 *Easter*

Jesus did everything He did because He loves all people! Read each sentence. Draw a line from the sentence to the correct picture.

1. Jesus washed His disciples' feet. He showed them how to serve one another.
2. Jesus prayed for His disciples.
3. Jesus used bread and wine to help His disciples remember Him.
4. Jesus shared a last meal with His disciples.

Write your name on the blank line. Read the sentences.

5. Jesus prayed for people who would come to know Him, even people who had not yet been born at the time of His prayer (John 17).

Jesus prayed for ____name of student____ to come to know and love Him.

114 © Bible Grade 1

APPLICATION

- What did the disciples learn about serving others when Jesus washed their feet? (**Answers will vary, but should include that no one is too important to serve and that service should be done with a loving attitude.**)
- Jesus established the Lord's Supper as a way for His disciples and all Christians to remember Him. Share some additional things that Christians do today to remember Jesus' sacrifice. (**Possible answers: Christians place crosses on churches, wear crosses as jewelry, or display pictures of Jesus.**)
- Jesus' prayer was not for Himself; it was for the disciples and for Christians throughout time. What did you learn about prayer from Jesus' example? (**I should pray for others as well as for myself and people I know.**)
- Jesus prayed that the disciples would work together to tell others about Him and not argue. Is it important for Christians today to work together? Why? (**Answers will vary, but should include that Christians cannot effectively reach people with the good news or serve others if they are not getting along.**)

29.3 Easter

Focus: Jesus' Arrest, Crucifixion, and Burial

★ PREPARATION

Select **VA 29C Jesus' Arrest, Crucifixion, and Burial**. (*Directed Instruction*)

EXTENSION

3A Provide a small amount of POLYMER CLAY to each student. Show students how to roll the clay into a cylinder, or worm shape, about three inches long and break the cylinder into two unequal pieces. Have students put the two pieces together to form a cross. Be sure that the two pieces are joined well so that the cross will not fall apart. Direct students to use the point of a pencil to put a hole into the top of their cross. Bake the clay and allow it to cool. Thread a LIGHTWEIGHT PIECE OF CORD through the hole and allow students to wear the cross to remind themselves of Jesus' sacrifice.

3B Print **BLM 29A Easter Cube** onto CARD STOCK so that each student will have a copy. Direct students to assemble the cube, roll the cube, and use the pictures to tell the events leading up to Easter Sunday.

REINFORCEMENT

"And Can It Be" is a favorite hymn of many Christians. Written by Charles Wesley in 1738, the hymn is a testimony to Wesley's own conversion to Christ. In one of the verses of the hymn, Wesley describes how he was a captive to sin. It was only through the realization that Christ had died to set him free that Wesley finally realized the peace that only Christ can give.

Introduction

Turn off the lights and close any windows or blinds to darken the classroom. Have students rest their heads on their desktop. Remind students that Jesus and His disciples had shared their final meal together. On that same night, Jesus had told them that one of them would turn against Him. He told His friends that He would have to leave them and that He would die! It was a very sad time for the disciples. Invite each student to think about the sadness he or she would feel if he or she were one of the disciples.

Directed Instruction ★

Turn the lights on and display **VA 29C Jesus' Arrest, Crucifixion, and Burial**. Remind students that Jesus never sinned; He had done nothing to deserve any kind of punishment! Yet, Jesus was willing to take the punishment that sinful people rightfully deserved because of His great love for all people. Read the text on the back of VA 29C.

Explain that the Jewish leaders were very angry with Jesus because more and more people were starting to follow Jesus instead of listening to them. The Jewish leaders refused to realize that Jesus was the Messiah, and they looked for a way to put Jesus to death. Ask a student to share how Judas treated Jesus unfairly. (**Judas did not act like a friend; he told Jesus' enemies where Jesus was praying so that they could arrest Jesus.**)

Jesus' disciples treated Jesus unkindly, too. They all ran off when Jesus was arrested! Ask a volunteer to share why that was unkind to Jesus. (**True friends stick together.**) The Roman soldiers treated Jesus cruelly. Choose a volunteer to tell what the soldiers did to Jesus even though Jesus had done nothing wrong. (**They whipped and beat Jesus; they forced Him to wear a crown of thorns; they made Him carry His cross and then forced another man to carry it for Him; they nailed Him to the cross at Golgotha and crucified Him.**)

Jesus' suffering and *crucifixion*, which means *death by being hung on a cross*, was part of God's plan of salvation. When Adam and Eve sinned, sin came into the world. Ever since that time, all people have sinned and have been separated from God. For hundreds of years God allowed the people to sacrifice animals for the forgiveness of sin, but that did not permanently fix the problem of sin. Only a sinless person's death—Jesus' death—could permanently remove sin.

Jesus knew that He would rise again, but that does not mean that He wanted to feel the terrible pain and separation that He would have to go through to pay for the sins of the whole world. He was willing to go through all of that out of love for everyone. Jesus' death on the cross paid for the sins of all the people who have ever lived. People who accept Jesus as Savior have forgiveness of sins and everlasting life with Him in heaven.

Review

- Why did the Jewish leaders want to put Jesus to death? (**More and more people were following Jesus and not following the leaders.**)
- How did the leaders know where to find and arrest Jesus? (**Judas led the Jewish leaders and soldiers to where Jesus was and then kissed Him.**)
- What happened to Jesus after He was arrested? (**Jesus was put on trial. He was sentenced to die even though He had done nothing wrong.**)
- Did Jesus want to suffer and die? (**No, He didn't want to die, but He was willing to die to follow His Father's will.**)
- What did Jesus' death on the cross provide for you and others? (**Jesus' death paid for the sins of all people for all time so that they could receive forgiveness of sins and be brought back into a loving relationship with God.**)

Student Page 29.3

Assist students as needed to complete the page.

APPLICATION

- Why did Jesus sacrifice His life for you? (**Jesus loves me so much that He died to pay the price for my sin.**)
- What part did Jesus have in God's plan of salvation? (**Jesus followed His Father's will and chose to die even though He didn't want to die.**)
- What part do you have in God's plan of salvation? (**If I confess my sins, realize that I need a savior, and place my faith and trust in Jesus, my sins will be forgiven. Then I will no longer be separated from God, I can have a relationship with God now, and live in heaven with Him forever!**)

Notes:

DAY 3

Name ______________________________

Easter **29.3**

Read the sentences. Write the letter of each picture beside the sentences that describe it.

c **1.** Jesus was arrested and taken away. When one of the disciples cut off the ear of the high priest's servant, Jesus healed the man.

b **2.** Soldiers beat Jesus. They made Jesus wear a crown of thorns and a purple robe. The soldiers made Jesus carry His cross and then nailed Him to it. Jesus let them do this to Him.

a **3.** Jesus died on the cross to pay for the sins of all people. He died for them because He loved them.

a.

b.

c.

4. Write one or two sentences telling how you can show your love for others today.

Answers will vary.

____

____

29.4 Easter

Focus: Jesus Is Risen

PREPARATION

Obtain SEVEN PLASTIC EASTER EGGS. Put a different item in each of six eggs. Use the following items: a piece of paper on which you have written the word *sin*; a PIECE OF MATZO; a piece of red paper cut into the shape of a droplet; a SCRAP OF PURPLE CLOTH; a STEEL NAIL; and a SMALL, SMOOTH PIECE OF WOOD. Leave the seventh egg empty. Be sure that the items are safe for students to touch. Hide the eggs in the room. (*Introduction, Directed Instruction*)

Select **VA 29D Jesus Is Risen**. (*Directed Instruction*)

EXTENSION

4A Invite each student to make a bouquet of three Easter lilies. Each student will need THREE GREEN CHENILLE STEMS. First, trace around the hand of each student on three pieces of white construction paper. Direct students to cut out each of their traced hands. For each flower, fold one chenille stem about an inch from both the top and the bottom. The bottom fold will protect the students' hands from the sharp point. Curve the bottom of the hand shape around the chenille stem to create a cone shape. Tape the cone closed. Staple the point of the cone onto the top fold of the chenille stem. Curl each finger of the hand around a pencil to form petals. Tie a PASTEL-COLORED RIBBON around the flowers to make a bouquet.

4B Teach students "Rolled 'em Away" and "Easter Rise Up" from the music CDs.

Introduction ★

Announce that there are SEVEN EASTER EGGS hidden in the classroom. Invite students to find all seven eggs. Explain that six of the eggs hold something symbolic of the week that Jesus died and God's plan of salvation. As the students find each egg, have them bring the unopened eggs to the front of the classroom. Set the empty egg aside temporarily.

Directed Instruction ★

Select a group of six students to come to the front of the classroom. Have each of these students open a different egg, tell the class what is inside, and share how each item was involved in the events that took place on the last week of Jesus' life on the earth.

- paper labeled *sin* (**Because people could not pay for their own sin, God sent His Son to die to pay the price.**)
- matzo (**At the Last Supper, Jesus used the bread as a symbol for His own body.**)
- red droplet shape (**Jesus was beaten and whipped for the sins of all people. It was only through the shedding of blood that all people can be forgiven of their sins.**)
- purple cloth (**Jesus was made to wear a purple robe and carry His own cross partway to Golgotha.**)
- nail (**Nails pierced Jesus' hands and feet. His side was cut by a spear.**)
- wood (**Jesus hung on a wooden cross between two other men. Those men deserved to die, but Jesus had never done anything wrong.**)

Choose another student to come to the front of the room, and give him or her the empty egg. Tell the student to show the class that the egg is empty. Exclaim that the fact that the egg is empty is actually the best surprise of all! Invite students to listen to discover how amazing it was that a tomb was empty! Display **VA 29D Jesus Is Risen** and read the text on the back.

Jesus is alive! This miracle is the greatest of all! Every year, Christians around the world celebrate the day that Jesus rose from the grave. This special day is called *Easter*. Christmas and Easter are the most special days in the year!

Inform students that the women, the two believers on the road to Emmaus, and the disciples were not the only people who saw Jesus alive. The Bible says that on one occasion, Jesus appeared to over 500 people at the same time (1 Corinthians 15:6).

Explain that Jesus' body was a heavenly body after the *resurrection*, which means *a return to life after having been dead*. He was able to appear to people as He wished—even when all the doors to the room where the disciples were gathered were shut (John 20:19). Christians, too, will receive a new body after their death (1 Corinthians 15:51–54).

Review

- Who went to the tomb on Sunday morning? (**Mary Magdalene and some other women who were followers of Jesus**)
- Who appeared to the women when the women looked for Jesus' body? (**angels**)
- What did one of the angels ask the women? (**Why are you looking for somebody who is alive in a tomb?**) What did the angel tell the women? (**He is not here, but He is risen!**)
- Who appeared to two believers on the road to Emmaus? (**Jesus**)
- Who else saw Jesus after He had risen from the dead? (**Mary Magdalene, Peter, the disciples, and over 500 people**)

Student Page 29.4

Assist students in completing the page.

Notes:

DAY 4

29.4 ***Easter***

Unscramble the letters to complete the sentences.

1. Mary Magdalene went to the tomb very e a r l y in the morning. (rylea)
2. The women brought spices and s t r i p s of cloth to finish wrapping Jesus' body. (pstris)
3. When they got to the tomb, the s t o n e was rolled back. (onste)
4. A n g e l s were there. One asked the women why they were looking for a living person in a tomb. (Aelsng)
5. The angels reminded the women that Jesus had told them He would rise a g a i n. (aagin)
6. Write the letters from the blue spaces on the lines below.

   The angel said, "He is r i s e n!"

116 © Bible Grade 1

APPLICATION

- The women and the disciples did not completely understand Jesus when He said that He would rise again. Share some reasons that they may have not understood Jesus' words. (**Answers will vary, but should include that the disciples did not have the faith that they should have had to believe that Jesus would do exactly what He said He would do.**)
- What is the happiest part of the Bible truth for you? (**I am so happy that Jesus died and rose for me! As a follower of Jesus, I will rise again too!**)
- Christians all over the world consider Easter to be one of the two most important days of the year. Why is Easter so important? (**Because Jesus rose, all who believe and trust in Him will rise again and live with Him in heaven forever.**)

REINFORCEMENT

The white lily has long been used as an Easter symbol, perhaps because the dormant bulbs appear to be dead and then come to life when the lily buds and blooms. Easter lilies became popular in the United States in the late 1800s when they were imported from Japan. After World War I, an American soldier brought back hundreds of Easter lily bulbs for his friends on the border of the Oregon-California coast. When Japan stopped exporting lilies during World War II, the Oregon-California coastal border became the Easter Lily Capital of the World. Today, at Easter, many churches cover their altars with lilies as a symbol of resurrection, new life, and the living hope all Christians share in Christ Jesus.

29.5

Easter

Focus: Review and Assessment

★ PREPARATION

Select "Rolled 'em Away" and "Easter Rise Up" from the music CDs. (*Lesson Review*)

Select **VA 29A Jesus' Triumphal Entry**; **VA 29B Jesus' Last Supper**; **VA 29C Jesus' Arrest, Crucifixion, and Burial**; and **VA 29D Jesus Is Risen**. (*Lesson Review*)

Make a copy of **BLM 29B Lesson 29 Test** for each student. (*Directed Instruction*)

Lesson Review ★

Play "Rolled 'em Away" and "Easter Rise Up" from the music CDs for a brief period of worship.

Use **VA 29A Jesus' Triumphal Entry** to review the Bible truth about Palm Sunday. Cover the following concepts:

- Jesus rode a donkey into Jerusalem. The people cut down palm branches and called Jesus their king. The prophet Zechariah wrote that the Messiah would enter Jerusalem in just this way.

Use **VA 29B Jesus' Last Supper** to review the Bible truth. Cover the following concepts:

- Jesus demonstrated servanthood by washing His disciples' feet.
- Jesus ate His last meal during Passover with His disciples.
- Jesus wanted to give the disciples something to remember Him. Jesus used bread to represent His body; He used wine to represent His blood. Christians today celebrate The Lord's Supper, or Holy Communion.
- Jesus prayed for His disciples.

Use **VA 29C Jesus' Arrest, Crucifixion, and Burial** to review the Bible truth. Cover the following concepts:

- Many Jewish leaders looked for a way to kill Jesus.
- Judas told the leaders where they could arrest Jesus.
- The Roman governor, Pontius Pilate, gave in to the Jewish leaders' demand and allowed Jesus to be whipped, beaten, and crucified.
- The Roman soldiers made Jesus wear a crown made out of thorns and a purple robe. Jesus was forced to carry His cross partway to Golgotha.
- Jesus was nailed to the cross. When Jesus knew His work on the earth was done, He said, "It is finished." Then He died and was laid in a tomb.
- Jesus' death on the cross paid for the sins of the whole world.

Use **VA 29D Jesus Is Risen** to review the Bible truth. Cover the following concepts:

- Early on Sunday morning, several women went to Jesus' tomb to finish preparing His body for burial. They saw that the stone was rolled away.
- Angels were there. One angel asked the women who they were looking for. The angel told the women that Jesus was not there; He is alive!
- Jesus appeared to Mary Magdalene. He had risen!
- Two followers of Jesus were walking to Emmaus when they were visited by a Man. It was Jesus! The followers of Jesus ran all the way back to Jerusalem and told the disciples that Jesus is alive!
- All those who believe and trust in Jesus will one day rise again!
- Christians around the world celebrate the day that Jesus rose from the grave as Easter Sunday.

Directed Instruction ★

Distribute a copy of **BLM 29B Lesson 29 Test** to each student and direct students to work independently. Collect test papers for assessment.

Lesson Preparation

Being a Leader

30.0

Expected Student Outcomes

KNOW
Stephen boldly demonstrates servant-leadership.

DO
Students will:
- identify actions of early Church leaders that helped the Church grow
- write about ways that first graders can be servant-leaders
- determine the qualities that enabled Stephen to be a godly servant-leader
- review Bible truths in which leaders demonstrated courage

APPLY
Students will realize that godly leaders serve others willingly, faithfully, and courageously.

Lesson Outline

I. The Church grows (Acts 6–7)
  A. Problems and solutions
II. Stephen is a servant-leader
  A. Sacrificial service
III. Stephen is willing and faithful
  A. A variety of gifts
  B. Serving with a good attitude
IV. Stephen is courageous
  A. Stephen speaks boldly for Christ
  B. Showing courage

TEACHER'S HEART

Stephen, the first Christian martyr, was an amazing servant-leader. He was a vessel for God to work through to show His grace to others. Stephen was willing and courageous; he sacrificed all for the Lord.

Perhaps you have surveyed your life and thought that you couldn't be used effectively by the Lord because you aren't as gifted as Stephen appeared to be. This kind of thinking can lead to burnout, and burnout will make you truly ineffective. Remind yourself that the Lord did not die for perfect vessels. He died for all people—cracked, broken, dirty vessels who need to be saved and restored. Jesus takes broken vessels, those who have chosen Him, and repairs them for His service.

The Lord has chosen you as a vessel for carrying His light! Be encouraged! Many people are won to Christ from the light that shines through cracked vessels. If you are feeling like an unusable vessel, walk around today humming that well-worn song, "This Little Light of Mine … " and look to Jesus, your source of light and strength. Let the light of His love shine through you, cracks and all!

MEMORY VERSE

Romans 12:10

MATERIALS

Day 1:
- Confetti
- VA 30A Stephen

Day 2:
- Spray cleaner, paper towels
- VA 28A Peter and the Lame Man
- VA 30A Stephen
- Plastic cups, dishpan (*Extension*)
- BLM 30A A Vessel for Service, paper bags (*Extension*)

Day 3:
- Shoe boxes, index cards (*Extension*)

Day 4:
- No additional materials are needed.

Day 5:
- VA 30A Stephen
- BLM 30B Lesson 30 Test

TEACHER RESOURCES

Benge, Janet and Geoff. Christian Heroes: *Then & Now—William Booth: Soup, Soap, and Salvation*. YWAM Publishing, 2002.

Moore, Beth. *Voices of the Faithful: Inspiring Stories of Courage from Christians Serving Around the World*. Thomas Nelson, 2010.

STUDENT RESOURCES

Howat, Irene. *Light Keepers: Ten Boys Who Changed the World*. Christian Focus Publications, 2001.

Howat, Irene. *Light Keepers: Ten Girls Who Changed the World*. Christian Focus Publications, 2001.

30.1 Being a Leader

Focus: The Church Grows

MEMORY VERSE

Romans 12:10

MEMORY WORK

- Write the Memory Verse on the board. Read the verse together. Call for the same number of volunteers as there are words in the verse to stand next to their desk. Choose one more volunteer to be a servant. Explain that the servant's job is to distribute a prepared piece of paper to each volunteer. Once the pieces of paper have been distributed by the servant, recite the verse again, and have each volunteer jump twice when his or her word is recited. Collect the pieces of paper, and repeat the activity with other volunteers and servants.

★ PREPARATION

Write each word of the Memory Verse on a separate piece of paper. (*Memory Work*)

Scatter several handfuls of CONFETTI or torn pieces of paper around the room. (*Introduction*)

Select **VA 30A Stephen**. (*Directed Instruction*)

EXTENSION

1A If you do not have a classroom helper chart, consider making one for this week. Ask students to nominate classmates for various jobs. Invite students to explain why they feel a student would be a good fit for a particular job. For example, a student might say that a certain classmate would be good at passing out papers because he or she is able to work quickly and quietly, or that a particular classmate should lead the flag salute because he or she has a strong voice.

Introduction ★

Draw students' attention to the CONFETTI scattered around the classroom and remark that you would like some help in picking it all up. Ask for a volunteer to do this. After allowing your volunteer to clean for a while, state that the volunteer is doing a good job, but that it is taking a long time. Ask students to suggest how the confetti could be removed in a more efficient manner. (**Possible answers: More helpers could be employed; they could get out the vacuum cleaner; everyone could clean the area around his or her own desk.**) Choose several volunteers to help, but assign each volunteer an area to clean. Have students pick up all the confetti.

Directed Instruction ★

Open your Bible to the book of Acts and remind students that the events recorded in Acts took place as the Church was beginning. Teach students that the early Church began with over 3,000 Christians from many different parts of the world (Acts 2:5, 40). These believers wanted to learn about the Lord from the disciples. Many of them stayed near Jerusalem. As the Church grew, there was more and more work to be done, so the disciples needed some helpers to share in their work.

Display **VA 30A Stephen** and read the text on the back.

Inform students that the believers who made up the early Church spoke different languages. Some of the people spoke Aramaic—the language that Jesus spoke—and were able to speak directly with the disciples. Other believers spoke Greek. There were even more languages spoken than just these two.

The Christians agreed that they should share their blessings, so they willingly gave their money to provide for widows. The idea was good, but it did not work well as the Church grew. Not all the widows got an equal share of the money set aside. This was probably because the widows who spoke Greek were unable to tell others what they needed.

Imagine how hard it was for the disciples to try to teach the people and still make sure that the needy widows were cared for! Remind students that the disciples directed the believers to choose seven godly men who would make sure that the widows were getting the money they needed. Ask a volunteer to say the name of one of the seven men chosen. (**Stephen**)

Explain that churches today have leaders or helpers, too. Some of these helpers are called *deacons* or *elders*. The men who are chosen to do these jobs today are to have the same qualities as the first seven deacons. They must be men with a good reputation. This means that they must live in such a way that people think well of them and know their lives truly please God. Both their words and actions should make clear that they love the Lord and trust Him as their Savior. They must be led by the Holy Spirit and be full of wisdom. This means that they will make wise choices because they want to please God (1 Timothy 3:1–7).

Review

- What did the disciples do after Jesus went back to heaven? (**They preached the good news that Jesus had risen from the dead. They taught believers more about the Lord.**)
- What did the Christians decide to do to help the widows in the Church? (**They decided to collect money for them.**)
- Did all the widows get an equal share of the money that had been collected? (**No, some of the widows did not get as much money as the others.**)
- How did the disciples solve this problem? (**They told the believers to choose seven men to be leaders in the Church and to take care of the needs of the widows.**)
- Who was Stephen? (**He was one of the seven helpers that the disciples chose to be leaders in the Church.**)

Student Page 30.1

Discuss various ways that people serve the Church today. Complete the page together.

APPLICATION

- What jobs do you have in the classroom? At home? (**Answers will vary.**)
- What talents have you received from God that help you to do your jobs well? (**Answers will vary.**)
- Think about the areas of ministry or service that people do in your church. In what areas would you like to serve when you are older? (**Possible answers: teaching Bible class, cleaning the buildings, leading worship, serving Communion, preaching God's Word, singing in the choir or worship team**)

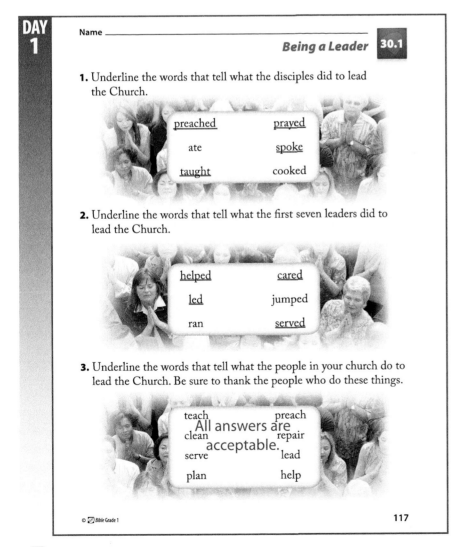

DAY 1

Name ________________________________

Being a Leader **30.1**

1. Underline the words that tell what the disciples did to lead the Church.

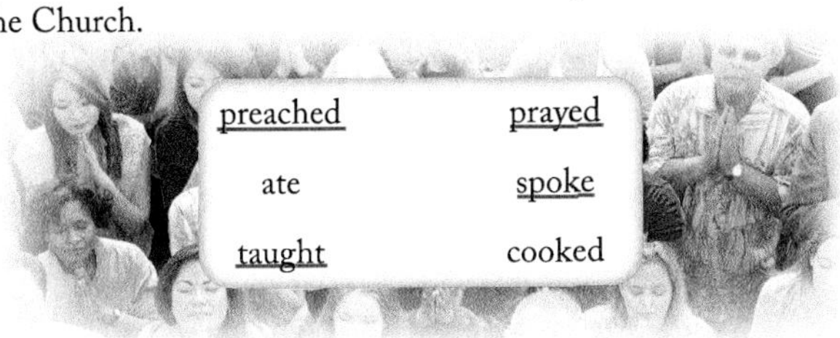

2. Underline the words that tell what the first seven leaders did to lead the Church.

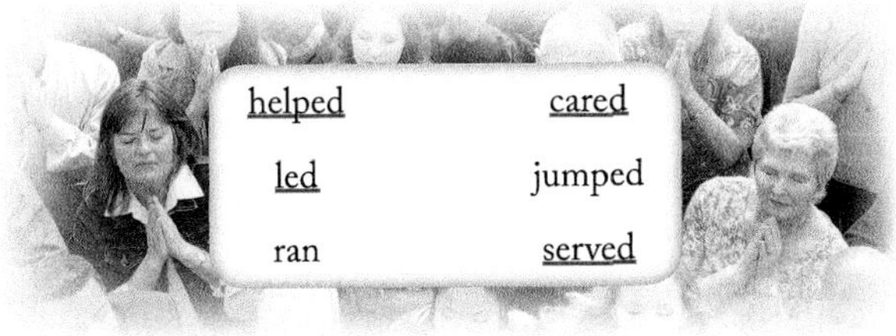

3. Underline the words that tell what the people in your church do to lead the Church. Be sure to thank the people who do these things.

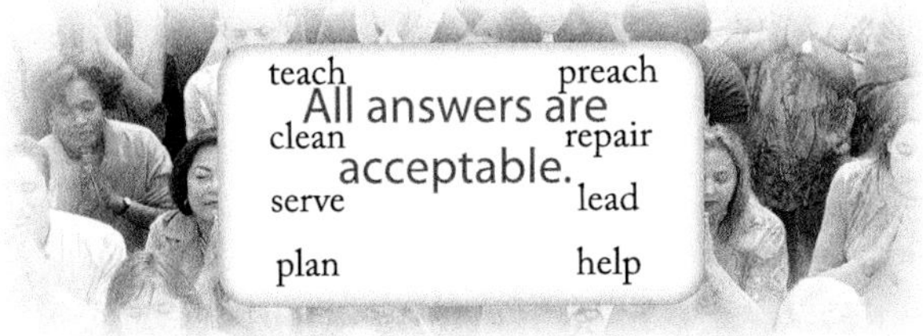

30.2 Being a Leader

Focus: Stephen Is a Servant-Leader

★ PREPARATION

Bring a bottle of SPRAY CLEANER and some PAPER TOWELS to class. (*Introduction*)

Select **VA 28A Peter and the Lame Man** and **VA 30A Stephen**. (*Directed Instruction*)

EXTENSION

2A Obtain TWO PLASTIC CUPS. Cut a slit down the side of one of the cups so that it will not hold water. Hold the good cup over a sink or DISHPAN and fill the cup with water. Explain that a cup is a type of vessel. Define a *vessel* as *a container used for holding something*. Ask students to suggest other examples of vessels. (**Possible answers: vases, bowls, pitchers**) Discuss how helpful it is to have vessels that do not leak. Pour water into the leaky cup. As the water leaks into the receptacle below, help students conclude that a broken vessel is not very useful. Hold up the two vessels and compare the two. Explain that the Lord needs "vessels" to serve Him—not cups or vases—but people who are filled with the Holy Spirit who can be used by the Lord.

2B Duplicate one copy of **BLM 30A A Vessel for Service** for each student. Have students make a face for the "vessel," color it, and cut it out. Instruct students to glue their vessel onto a PAPER BAG and stand the bag up on their desktop. Explain that God can use people to serve Him, but first they must be ready for service. Invite students to read the qualifications needed for servant-leadership on the paper strips, cut them out, and insert them into the bag.

Introduction ★

Begin the lesson by using the SPRAY CLEANER and PAPER TOWELS to clean several of the desktops in the classroom. Remark that you are a teacher and not a janitor; however, you have chosen to help your students today by cleaning desks. Inform students that you are doing this service gladly because it is more pleasant to work on a clean desktop than on a dirty one.

Remind students that the early Church needed helpers, or servants, to care for widows, orphans, and others in need (Acts 4:35). These servants not only helped the people, but they led these people to have a closer relationship with the Lord by demonstrating God's love through service.

Directed Instruction ★

Display **VA 28A Peter and the Lame Man**. Recount that Peter and John were able to heal people in the name of Jesus. The Holy Spirit gave them the power to do this. Choose a volunteer to share what Peter said and did to heal the man. (**Peter told the man to stand up and walk in the name of Jesus Christ.**) What did the man do after he was healed? (**He went into the temple and praised God.**) What happened when the religious leaders found out that Peter and John had been preaching and healing in Jesus' name? (**They arrested Peter and John and put them in prison.**)

Review that the religious leaders did not like Peter's preaching. Peter told the truth when he said that these people were responsible for Jesus' death on the cross and that God had raised Jesus to life. These religious leaders wanted the people to follow their teaching, not the true Word of God!

Choose a boy to come to the front of the room. Ask the boy to tell the class something that he considers to be one of his talents or abilities. (**Answers will vary.**) Review that one of the servant-leaders in the early Church was Stephen, who had a strong relationship with the Lord. Even though Jesus had gone to heaven, Stephen prayed often and knew God's Word. He received the same miraculous power from the Holy Spirit that Peter and John had received.

Tell the class that the boy you have called forward has many natural abilities and name some of them; however, Stephen's abilities were supernatural—Stephen's abilities came from the power of the Holy Spirit! Show the picture on **VA 30A Stephen** and ask students to recount why the religious leaders turned against Stephen. (**Stephen was preaching and healing in the name of Jesus.**) At his trial, Stephen told all the religious leaders, including the high priest, about the good news of Jesus Christ. Sadly, those leaders would not listen to Stephen's words. They took him to a place outside the city where they threw stones at him until he died.

Remind students that to *sacrifice* means *to give up something of great value.* Stephen sacrificed his life in service to the Lord. Even though God does not call many Christians to make such a great sacrifice, all service requires sacrifice. Christians sacrifice their time and share their talents and abilities when they serve. Service should not be done for selfish reasons, such as to make oneself look good in the eyes of others (Ephesians 6:5–7). When Stephen served the Church, he did so because he had a close relationship with Jesus. Stephen served to bring glory to God.

Review

- Who gave Peter, John, and Stephen the power to heal and to preach boldly? (**the Holy Spirit**)
- How did Stephen stay close to Jesus? (**Stephen prayed often and knew God's Word.**)
- What kind of attitude should Christians have when serving? (**They should have a good attitude and not serve for selfish reasons.**)
- Why did Stephen serve the Church? (**He had a close relationship with Jesus and wanted to bring glory to God.**)

Student Page 30.2

Discuss the activities that the children are doing in the pictures. Help students to spell any words that they need as they write a sentence telling about each picture. Discuss student responses.

DAY 2

30.2 *Being a Leader*

Stephen was a servant-leader. First graders can be servant-leaders!

Look at each picture. Write a sentence that tells how the child or children pictured are serving. Answers will vary, but should be related to the pictures.

1. ______________________________

____

2. ______________________________

____

3. ______________________________

____

4. ______________________________

____

118 © Bible Grade 1

APPLICATION

- Read **1 Timothy 4:12**. Godly leaders do not have to be adults. First graders can lead others in many ways. What are some of the things that you do to set an example for others? (**Answers will vary.**)
- Have you ever had to do a job that you did not want to do? Did you do the job with a good attitude? If not, how can you change your attitude the next time that you have to do a similar job? (**Answers will vary.**)

REINFORCEMENT

Stephen appeared before the Sanhedrin, the religious court of the time. The Sanhedrin consisted of two political "parties," the Pharisees and the Sadducees. Jewish leaders who were members of the sect of the Sadducees were the influential rulers. The Sadducees were wealthy aristocrats and conservative in their doctrine. Many of them were priests. They objected to unwritten traditions and liked to be able to interpret the Scriptures as they wished. They denied the existence of angels, the resurrection, and eternal life, so their views were incompatible with Christianity from the start. They were particularly insulted by Stephen's remarks at his trial (Acts 7). However, by the fall of Jerusalem in 70 AD, the Sadducees had disappeared as a political party.

30.3 Being a Leader

Focus: Stephen Is Willing and Faithful

EXTENSION

3A Place TWO SHOE BOXES on an empty desk or table. Label one box *Ready for Service to the Lord* and the other box *Not Ready for Service to the Lord*. Write each of the following words on an INDEX CARD: *kind, selfish, honest, caring, humble, prayerful, jealous, mean, unkind, forgiving, thankful, loving, faithful, willing,* and *disobedient*. Invite two or three students to work together to read the cards, decide if a godly servant should or should not have the characteristic described, and sort the cards into the appropriate box. Discuss student responses. Take the cards from the boxes, shuffle the cards, and invite other students to try the activity.

Introduction

Ask students to raise their hand if they have ever had to clean up a mess that they did not make. Invite students to share briefly about their experiences. (**Answers will vary.**) Explain that even though they may not have had a choice in cleaning up the mess, they did have a choice about the attitude that they had when doing that chore. They could have been angry or upset at having to clean up a mess that was not theirs, or they could have cleaned up the mess willingly with a desire to help. Remind students that Christian service is not only about action; it is about having an attitude that glorifies God.

Directed Instruction

Read **1 Peter 4:10–11**. Explain that Jesus wants all Christians to serve Him, but that not all Christians serve in the same way. Recount that Stephen was able to do miracles through the power of the Holy Spirit. Other leaders led the Church in different ways. Teach students that Christians ought to serve God using their own individual gifts and talents. Believers who can draw or paint well can make pictures that illustrate the Bible truth. Leaders can plan and direct service projects. Believers who are good singers can serve in the choir or lead worship.

Read **Romans 12:11**. Explain that godly leaders serve eagerly, energetically, and positively. Service should be done without grumbling or complaining. Godly leaders strive to make the most of every possible opportunity to serve.

Read **1 Samuel 12:24**. Explain that godly leaders serve faithfully and obediently, out of love for what the Lord has done for them. Recount that Peter and John obeyed Jesus' Great Commission when they continued to preach in Jesus' name, even though they had been ordered to stop.

Read **Mark 10:45**. Explain that godly leaders follow Jesus' example. Jesus did not come to the earth to be served; He came to serve others. Jesus put all His energy into service for those whom He loved. Ask students to recount some of the things Jesus did to serve others. (**Possible answers: He fed the 5,000; He healed people; He raised Lazarus from the dead; He washed the disciples' feet; He died on the cross to save all people from their sins.**) Recount that Jesus' motivation for service was His love for people and His desire to bring glory to God the Father. He wanted to provide the way for all people to no longer be separated from God. These should be the primary reasons for all Christian service.

Review

- Do all godly leaders serve others in the same way? (**No, Christians ought to serve God based upon their own gifts and talents.**)
- Do godly leaders grumble and complain about having to serve others? (**No, godly leaders eagerly serve others.**)

- Do godly leaders serve only when they will be paid for their service? (**No, Christians ought to serve faithfully and obediently, even if there is no payment involved.**)
- Whose example do godly leaders follow by their service? (**They follow the example set by Jesus.**)
- What should be the main reason for Christians to serve others? (**Christians should serve out of love for God and love for others so that others can join God's family.**)

Student Page 30.3

Read any difficult words before directing students to complete the page independently.

Notes:

APPLICATION

- Are there any ways that you serve in your church or school? How does your service glorify God? (**Answers will vary.**)
- Share some things that you could do to serve your church or school that you are not doing now. How can you start doing those things? (**Answers will vary, but should include getting advice and permission to start a new area of service.**)
- What should your attitude be when you serve? (**My attitude should be both willing and selfless.**)

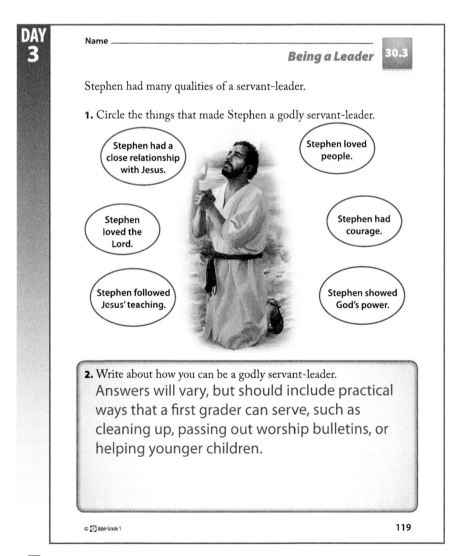

DAY 3

Name ______________________________

Being a Leader **30.3**

Stephen had many qualities of a servant-leader.

1. Circle the things that made Stephen a godly servant-leader.

- Stephen had a close relationship with Jesus.
- Stephen loved people.
- Stephen loved the Lord.
- Stephen had courage.
- Stephen followed Jesus' teaching.
- Stephen showed God's power.

2. Write about how you can be a godly servant-leader.

Answers will vary, but should include practical ways that a first grader can serve, such as cleaning up, passing out worship bulletins, or helping younger children.

30.4 Being a Leader

Focus: Stephen Is Courageous

REINFORCEMENT

The Greek word *martyrs* became associated with witnessing to the point of death and is the source of the English word *martyr*. Stephen became the first martyr of the early Church. Since that time, many other Christians have died for their faith. The Bible records that James, the brother of John, was put to death by the sword (Acts 12:2). Jesus foretold that Peter would die a martyr (John 21:18–19), and early Church tradition holds that Peter was crucified. John records that believers would overcome Satan "because of the blood of the Lamb and because of the word of their testimony, and [because] they did not love their life even when faced with death" (Revelation 12:11).

Introduction

Write the word *courage* on the board and read it together. Tell students that someone who has courage knows that he or she is facing danger, but willingly faces it anyway. Invite students to name some people who have jobs that may require courage. (**firefighters, police officers, people in the military**) Explain that it took courage for Christians in the early Church to tell others about their faith. Many of them were jailed, beaten, and even killed for their faith in Jesus.

Christians today face situations where they need to be courageous and stand firm when their faith is challenged. Invite students to listen to how one first grader displayed courage for her faith.

Directed Instruction

Read the following fictional story:

> At the end of the school year, every child at Grace Christian School received a T-shirt with the name of the school on the front. Molly, a first grader, loved her T-shirt because it reminded her of her school. She wore her T-shirt as often as she could, even during her summer vacation.
>
> One summer day, some of Molly's friends saw her at the playground. She was wearing her Christian school T-shirt. One of the girls noticed the shirt and made a comment. "Oh, you go to a Christian school," she exclaimed. "You're one of those Christians. Christians think they are better than everyone else."
>
> Molly did not know what to say. She had never heard anyone talk about Christians that way. What that girl said was not true! Molly wanted to run away! Molly went home feeling sad. She was confused. Should she stop wearing her Christian school T-shirt? She didn't want people to tease her.
>
> Molly prayed and thought about what to do. She thought about Stephen. Molly remembered how people said things about Stephen that were not true. She remembered how Stephen acted when he was on trial. Stephen told the truth! She also remembered how Stephen forgave those people who had sinned against him.
>
> Molly decided to forgive the girl who had said the untrue words about Christians. Molly skipped back to the playground, wearing her Christian school T-shirt, ready to play with everyone and treat the other girls kindly.

Review

- How did Molly feel when a girl teased her about being a Christian? (**Molly wanted to run away. She felt sad and confused.**)
- What Bible truth did Molly remember that helped her to be courageous? (**Molly remembered the Bible truth about Stephen's trial.**)

- How was Molly like Stephen? (**Stephen was courageous when he faced death for his faith in Jesus. Stephen forgave the men who threw stones at him. Molly was courageous by continuing to wear her Christian school T-shirt. She decided to forgive the girl who had made the untrue comment about Christians.**)
- How did Molly show by her actions that the girl's comment was untrue? (**Molly was ready to play with everyone. She showed that Christians do not think that they are better than others.**)

APPLICATION

- Is it easy or difficult to be a Christian? (**Answers will vary.**)
- What could you do if you found yourself in a situation where you were teased about being a Christian? (**I could talk to my parents or teacher about what to do in that situation. I could pray for the Lord's guidance.**)

Student Page 30.4

Review the directions and then tell students to complete the page.

Notes:

DAY 4

30.4 ***Being a Leader***

Read each sentence. Choose the picture of the godly leader that matches the sentence. Write the letter of that picture on the line.

A **1.** I showed courage when I faced a giant.

D **2.** I showed courage when I led an army of 300 into battle.

C **3.** We showed courage when we continued to teach and preach in the name of Jesus.

B **4.** I showed courage when I faced the false prophets of Baal.

E **5.** I showed courage when I faced the religious leaders and was stoned to death.

Trace the gray words. Read the sentence.

6. Godly leaders serve others willingly, faithfully, and courageously.

120 © Bible Grade 1

30.5 Being a Leader

Focus: Review and Assessment

★ PREPARATION

Select **VA 30A Stephen**. (*Lesson Review*)

Duplicate one copy of **BLM 30B Lesson 30 Test** for each student. (*Directed Instruction*)

Lesson Review ★

Use **VA 30A Stephen** to review the Bible truths in this lesson. Cover the following concepts:

- The early Church grew quickly. The believers lived in Judea, in and around Jerusalem. They decided to help each other by collecting money to meet the needs of the poorer people, especially the widows.
- Some of the Greek-speaking widows were not getting their fair share of the money collected.
- When the disciples heard about this, they asked the believers to choose seven helpers to make sure that all the money was given fairly to those in need.
- The seven helpers were all filled with the Holy Spirit. One of the helpers was Stephen.
- Stephen had a strong relationship with the Lord. He loved God and prayed often. Stephen did miracles through the power of the Holy Spirit and in the name of Jesus.
- The religious leaders did not like Stephen telling about Jesus. They wanted Stephen to stop preaching about Jesus.
- Some men lied about Stephen and said that he had done wrong, so Stephen was brought to trial.
- During the trial, Stephen courageously told the truth about Jesus and how the religious leaders had put the Savior to death.
- Stephen's words made some people very angry. They took Stephen to a place outside the city where they threw stones at him until he died.
- Stephen was a servant-leader. Christians lead by serving others.
- Service to the Lord should be done willingly and with a loving attitude to bring glory to God and to lead others to accept Jesus as Savior.
- Christians today are called to be courageous in taking a stand for their faith.

Directed Instruction ★

Give each student a copy of **BLM 30B Lesson 30 Test**. Read any unfamiliar words to the class and tell students to begin. After all students have completed the test, review the correct answers.

Notes:

Lesson Preparation

Witnessing to Others

31.0

Expected Student Outcomes

KNOW

Philip witnesses to an Ethiopian man.

DO

Students will:

- match words to who might have said them based on the Bible truth
- select responses that show immediate obedience
- navigate a maze to discover words that review the Bible truth of Philip and the Ethiopian man
- identify words to use in an invitation to accept Jesus as Savior

APPLY

Students will recognize the importance of obedience to God. They will invite others to come to Christ.

Lesson Outline

I. Philip and the Ethiopian (Acts 8:26–40)
  A. Relationship to God
II. Immediate obedience
  A. Relationship to God
III. Sharing the good news
  A. Sowing and reaping
  B. Importance of telling others
IV. Basics in witnessing
  A. Understand the basics
  B. Practice telling others

TEACHER'S HEART

When you read Acts 8:26–31, consider the immediate response Philip gave when the angel told him to go. Notice that Philip didn't question or ask why he needed to go—he went on his way. How many believers today would have responded with such prompt obedience to God's call?

When Philip reached the chariot, the Holy Spirit told him to stay near the chariot. Philip had to obey and be in the right place to hear the next step in his assignment. Picture the scene of Philip running up next to the chariot and then the awkwardness of not knowing what to do next. Often fear of what to say or of how someone will respond keeps Christians from starting a conversation that could lead to salvation. Philip did a wise thing—he listened to the person that he was sent to minister to. Philip then followed the Holy Spirit's prompting to help the Ethiopian man understand the plan of salvation and accept Jesus as his Savior.

Philip's example of immediate obedience and trust in the Holy Spirit's leading is one that you can model for your students. Allow God to help you grasp the joy that comes from following His direction in your life.

MEMORY VERSE

Acts 1:8

MATERIALS

Day 1:
- TM-8 Map of Israel
- VA 31A Philip and the Ethiopian
- PP-6 Tell the World About Jesus (*Extension*)

Day 2:
- Sticky notes
- VA 31A Philip and the Ethiopian

Day 3:
- Seed packet
- Globe (*Extension*)

Day 4:
- BLMs 31A–B ABCs of Faith (*Extension*)

Day 5:
- VA 31A Philip and the Ethiopian
- BLM 31C Lesson 31 Test

SONGS

I Can Obey

TEACHER RESOURCES

Hirsch, Alan, and Lance Ford. *Right Here, Right Now: Everyday Mission for Everyday People.* Baker Books, 2011.

Pilavachi, Mike, and Liza Hoeksma. *When Necessary Use Words: Changing Lives Through Worship, Justice, and Evangelism.* Regal Books, 2007.

STUDENT RESOURCES

Jander, Martha S. *Philip and the Ethiopian.* Concordia Publishing House, 2005.

Munger, Robert Boyd, and Carolyn Nystrom. *My Heart—Christ's Home: Retold for Children.* InterVarsity Press, 2010.

31.1 Witnessing to Others

Focus: Philip and the Ethiopian

MEMORY VERSE

Acts 1:8

MEMORY WORK

- Write the Memory Verse on the board and read it together. Teach students that *being a witness* means *being a person who tells others about the good news of God's plan of salvation.* Remind students of the location of each of the places mentioned by displaying **TM-8 Map of Israel**. Explain that *the end* or *the ends of the earth* are not shown on the map because the earth has no end. The phrase refers to every place on Earth. Assign four students to hold the arrow-shaped signs that you have prepared. Recite the verse again and have students with the arrow-shaped signs hold the signs over their heads as those locations are recited. Choose different volunteers to hold the signs and repeat the activity.

PREPARATION

Prepare **TM-8 Map of Israel** for display. Prepare four signs shaped like arrows. On the first sign, write *to Jerusalem*. On the second, write *to Judea*, on the third, write *to Samaria*, and on the fourth, write *to the end of the earth* or *to the ends of the earth.* (*Memory Work*)

Select **VA 31A Philip and the Ethiopian**. (*Directed Instruction*)

EXTENSION

1A Show **PP-6 Tell the World About Jesus**. Use the PowerPoint to reinforce the concepts presented in this week's Bible truth.

Introduction

Show the class two sheets of paper. Take one sheet of paper and tear it in half. Remark that it is easy to tear in half because a single thickness of paper is not very strong. Fold the second sheet of paper in half and continue folding while mentioning ways to build or strengthen a relationship, such as spending time together, listening and talking, and learning about each other. After folding the paper four or five times, try to tear the paper. Invite one or two volunteers to try to tear the paper.

Explain that if someone does not spend time with God, the relationship will not be very strong. When Christians do not spend time with God, they may miss out on things God wants them to know and do. Share that in today's Bible truth, a man learns about Jesus because a Christian had a strong relationship with God, listened, and quickly obeyed the Lord.

Directed Instruction

Display **VA 31A Philip and the Ethiopian** and read the Bible truth.

Explain that when an angel came to Philip, he was just doing some normal activities. Ask students to tell what they think he might have been doing. (**Possible answers: working in a field, praying, eating**) Invite students to share how Philip might have reacted when the angel spoke to him. (**Possible answers: shocked, scared, excited to see an angel**)

The angel was a messenger from God. Philip must have spent time learning about God and talking to God in prayer because when the angel appeared with God's message, he listened and obeyed. Philip's relationship with God made him want to do what God asked.

After Philip followed the angel's instructions, he heard from God again. Philip knew and loved God, so he was able to recognize when God was speaking to him through the Spirit of the Lord. Invite students to explain what they think Philip might have thought when he heard the Spirit of the Lord speak to him. (**Possible answers: I am glad God is speaking to me; God has a job for me to do; I will do what God is telling me to do.**)

Explain that God desires that His children spend time with Him and want to do what He wants them to do. Philip was able to help the Ethiopian man because he had spent time studying God's Word and understood what the man read in the book of Isaiah. Tell students that spending time reading the Bible and listening to Bible truths can help them build a strong relationship with God. When they spend time with God, they will be able to know what God wants them to do.

Review

- What did the angel tell Philip to do? (**The angel told Philip to get up and travel south on a certain road.**)
- After Philip obeyed the angel, what did the Spirit of the Lord tell Philip to do? (**The Spirit of the Lord told Philip to go to the chariot.**)

- What was the Ethiopian man doing? (**He was riding in his chariot and reading from the Old Testament book of Isaiah.**)
- How did Philip help the Ethiopian man? (**He explained what the man was reading and told him about Jesus. The man believed in Jesus, and Philip baptized him.**)

Student Page 31.1

Read the directions and the text as needed. Direct students to complete the page. Discuss student answers.

Notes:

APPLICATION

- How did Philip show that he had a strong relationship with God? (**Answers will vary, but should include that he trusted and followed the angel's message and the Spirit of the Lord.**)
- What are some ways you can follow Philip's example? (**Possible answers: read my Bible or listen to Bible truths, pray, go to church, tell others about Jesus**)
- How can reading the Bible help you to know what God wants you to do? (**The Bible provides me with many examples of godly behavior. It lets me know what God is like and what God would expect me to do. It gives me direction when I am faced with making a choice.**)

DAY 1

Name ______________________________

Witnessing to Others **31.1**

Philip shared the good news of Jesus with an Ethiopian man.

Draw a line to match the words with the person who said or might have said them.

I do not understand Isaiah's words. Can you explain them to me?

Do you understand what you are reading?

Who was Isaiah talking about?

Isaiah was talking about the Messiah, Jesus.

Here is some water. Will you baptize me?

Now I understand and believe that Jesus is the Son of God.

121

31.2 Witnessing to Others

Focus: Immediate Obedience

★ PREPARATION

Select "I Can Obey" from the music CDs. (*Introduction*)

Write each of the following words on a different STICKY NOTE: *parent, teacher, adult, God*. Place the sticky notes around the classroom where they can be easily seen. (*Introduction*)

Select **VA 31A Philip and the Ethiopian**. (*Directed Instruction*)

EXTENSION

2A Designate one side of the room as representing *hard to obey* and the opposite side as *easy to obey*. Read the questions below and have students move to the side of the room that shows their response. Choose volunteers to explain why they chose to answer the way they did. Ask students if it is easy or hard to obey when …

- they are tired
- they will be paid for doing something
- they do not know what the reward will be for obeying
- they would rather do something else
- no one else is obeying
- everyone else is obeying
- they do not like to do what they are asked to do
- they want to play
- they know God wants them to obey

Introduction ★

Select "I Can Obey" from the music CDs. Instruct one student to find the STICKY NOTE with the word *parent* written on it. Let that student tell something that his or her parent said to do, and the student obeyed. Continue with the sticky notes for *teacher*, *adult*, and *God*. Remind students that they will have many opportunities to show obedience every day. Encourage them to obey like Philip did.

Directed Instruction ★

Display **VA 31A Philip and the Ethiopian**. Review previous learning by asking volunteers to summarize the Bible truth for the class. Remind students that the Ethiopian man's understanding of God's Word and coming to faith were largely because Philip did not hesitate to obey. If Philip had been slow to obey, the man might never have heard the good news of God's plan of salvation because he would have been too far away for Philip to reach.

Explain to students that obedience is a choice. Mention that sometimes there is a reward involved in obedience, and they may want to quickly obey just to receive the reward. Sometimes there is no reward for obedience. On these occasions, it might be harder to obey right away.

Read the following statements and have students show how they would respond if they were in the situation mentioned. Have students stand and do quick running-in-place movements if they would immediately obey and do slow walking-in-place movements if they would obey slowly.

- You are going to go out to eat as soon as you make your bed.
- You must clean your room, but there is no reward for doing it.
- You will receive three dollars for cleaning up after a pet.
- Your neighbor asks you to help pick up trash that blew into his backyard.
- Your parent tells you to go and sit on the sofa, but you do not know why.

Discuss which items most students responded that they would obey quickly. Talk about the last statement of *sitting on a sofa without knowing why*. Let students explain why that might be something they would not obey quickly. (**Possible answers: I want to know why; I would feel silly just sitting there; I do not want to just sit on the sofa.**) Inquire as to how that statement was similar to what the angel said to Philip. (**The angel told Philip to get up and travel along a certain road, but did not explain why or what would happen.**) Explain that Philip may not have felt like going on a walk or doing something that was not fully explained to him. But Philip loved God and wanted to obey Him. Philip did not argue or question the angel, but knew God wanted him to go—so he went immediately!

Explain that when students question why they must obey, or move slowly to obey their parents or teacher, they are not showing love and respect for the person in charge. God has placed all Christians under the authority of others; even adults must obey police officers and firefighters. Proper obedience shows a strong relationship to God and a loving respect for authority.

Review

- What was Philip quick to do? (**He was quick to travel on the certain road and then to stay near the chariot out of obedience to God.**)
- What might have happened if Philip had not obeyed God right away? (**Philip would have missed a chance to help the man come to faith in Jesus.**)
- Why do you think Philip was quick to obey God? (**Answers will vary, but should include that he had a loving relationship with God and wanted to quickly obey.**)

Student Page 31.2

Read the scenarios and have students fill in the circle in front of the response that shows immediate obedience.

Notes:

DAY 2

31.2 *Witnessing to Others*

Philip obeyed the Lord right away. How should each child obey to follow Philip's example? Fill in the circle.

1. Andy's grandmother comes to pick him up from school. She calls him to come from the playground.
- ○ Andy should keep playing.
- ○ Andy should ask why he has to come right away.
- ● Andy should run over to his grandmother.

2. Amy is watching TV. Mom calls Amy to set the table.
- ○ Amy should go outside.
- ● Amy should set the table right away.
- ○ Amy should wait until the TV show is over.

3. Soo Jin wants to play with her friend, but Dad says it is time to go to church.
- ● Soo Jin should get in the car.
- ○ Soo Jin should pretend to be sick.
- ○ Soo Jin should complain about going to church.

4. Your teacher tells you to put your books away. What should you do?
Answers will vary, but should include obeying immediately.

122 © Bible Grade 1

APPLICATION

- How do you feel when you know you did not obey? (**Answers will vary, but should include feeling sad, ashamed, and afraid I'll be punished.**)
- How do you feel when you know that you did obey? (**Answers will vary, but should include feeling excited that God and my parents will be happy that I obeyed, and proud that I did what was right.**)
- Why should you obey right away? (**Possible answers: to please God, to show that I want to do what is right, to keep from being distracted, because it is the right thing to do**)
- Tell about something that you were told to do, but you did not do right away. (**Answers will vary.**) How will you change your behavior the next time you are told to do that same thing? (**Answers will vary.**)

REINFORCEMENT

Philip was likely one of the seven men listed in Acts 6:5 to fulfill the role of a deacon. After the stoning of Stephen and the beginning of persecution of the Church, Jesus' followers scattered and moved out of Jerusalem. Philip went to Samaria (Acts 8:4–8). His ministry to the Samaritans included proclaiming the Messiah and doing miracles, such as casting out demons and healing the lame. He brought joy to the area, even though Jews and Samaritans were often hostile toward each other. Acts 21:8 calls Philip *an evangelist*.

31.3 Witnessing to Others

Focus: Sharing the Good News

★ PREPARATION

Bring a SEED PACKET to class. (*Introduction*)

EXTENSION

3A Select a volunteer to spin a GLOBE. Tell him or her to point a finger at the globe until the globe stops spinning. When the globe stops, name the country in front of the student's finger. If the finger is pointing to water, choose the nearest country. Invite another volunteer to pray that someone would tell the people in that country about Jesus. Continue until all students have had an opportunity to spin the globe or pray.

3B Invite a missionary to visit your classroom. Ask the missionary to show pictures and tell stories about life on the mission field or experiences of telling others about Jesus.

Introduction ★

Display a SEED PACKET and ask students if they will find plants inside the packet. (**No, the packet only has the seeds, not the produce. The seeds will grow into the plants shown on the package.**) Explain that the seeds in the packet will grow, but they will require some care. A seed needs good soil, water, and sunlight so that it can begin to grow into a plant.

Tell students that God wants everyone to know about Him, worship Him, and grow in their faith in Him. Before that can happen, people have to hear about Him. Not everyone in the world has heard that God loves all people and that Jesus died to save them from their sins. They need to be told by someone who has already heard about Jesus. Telling people about Jesus is like planting a seed. It is the first step that a person must take in order to help someone else to come to faith in Jesus.

Directed Instruction

Recount that Philip knew about Jesus and wanted others to know about God's plan of salvation. The man in the chariot was from Ethiopia, an African country. It is not known how this man who lived so far away from Israel had heard about the one, true God, but it is clear that he worshipped God and wanted to know more about God. The Ethiopian man was studying a scroll—a type of book—containing a part of God's Word.

Ask students if they have ever read something and needed someone to explain what it meant. (**Answers will vary.**) Then ask students who they asked to help them and why they chose that person. (**Answers will vary, but should include they asked someone who would know the answer.**) Explain that the Ethiopian man knew how to read the words in the scroll, but he did not understand that God's Word was describing the Messiah. However, even though the man did not understand the words, he knew that the scroll was the Word of God. He wanted to know God, and God provided understanding.

Recount that an angel visited Philip and told him to go to the chariot. Review some of the other Bible truths studied this year that involved an angel giving a message from God. (**God sent angels to Gideon, to Mary, and to the women at the empty tomb.**) The man in the chariot did not know that an angel had sent Philip to his chariot. Ask students why they think God sent Philip to the Ethiopian man. (**God wanted the Ethiopian man to know Him and be able to tell the people in Ethiopia about Jesus.**)

Let students imagine how the Ethiopian man reacted when Philip asked if he understood what he read in Isaiah. (**Possible answers: surprised, curious, shocked, confused how the stranger knew to ask him that question**) Ask students how they think Philip felt when the man said he was reading the book of Isaiah. (**Possible answers: relieved that it was something he knew about, excited that he could use the words from Isaiah to talk about Jesus**) Explain that pastors and Bible teachers today study God's Word by using Bible reference books, websites, and many other resources. When Philip talked with the Ethiopian man, he told what he had learned about Jesus. It is important that Christians not be afraid to share God's plan of salvation with others. Just as the Spirit of the Lord helped Philip, He will help Christians as they share their faith with others.

Review

- What country did the man in the chariot come from? (**He was from Ethiopia, a country in Africa.**)
- Where was the Ethiopian man going? (**He was returning to Ethiopia.**)
- What was the Ethiopian man reading? (**He was reading from the book of Isaiah.**)
- How did Philip help the Ethiopian man? (**He explained what the man was reading and told him about Jesus.**)

Student Page 31.3

Help students mark the path through the maze and then write the words from the maze's path onto the blanks.

DAY 3

Name ____________________

Witnessing to Others **31.3**

1. Help Philip find the Ethiopian man. Then help Philip and the man get to the water for baptism. Write words from the maze to correctly complete the sentences.

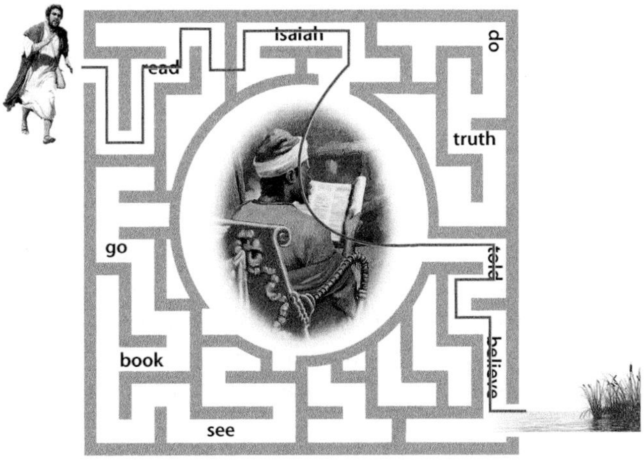

2. The Ethiopian man ___read___ the book of ___Isaiah___.

3. Philip ___told___ the Ethiopian man about Jesus.

4. The man said, "I ___believe___ that Jesus is the Son of God."

 123

APPLICATION

- How did the Ethiopian man show that he wanted to learn about God? (**He was reading the scroll of the book of Isaiah.**)
- Name some people whom the Ethiopian man might have told the things he learned from Philip. (**Possible answers: the queen of Ethiopia, his own family members, other servants, others who were as interested in learning about God as he was**)
- What should you tell others about Jesus? (**Answers will vary, but should include that Jesus is God's Son, that He died to take away their sins, that He rose from the grave, and that He wants to have a relationship with them.**)
- Missionaries are people who go to other places to witness to others about Jesus. Share a time when you were a missionary or when you witnessed to your friends. (**Answers will vary.**)

REINFORCEMENT

The Ethiopian man in the chariot held a high position as the royal treasurer in the court of Queen Candace. Her kingdom was between Aswan and Khartoum and she ruled in place of her son who was considered to be too holy to rule. The eunuch was returning from a trip to Jerusalem, and he held a copy of the prophecy of Isaiah—two unusual things for a non-Jew. It is possible that he heard teaching on Isaiah 53 while in Jerusalem and purchased a scroll. Scrolls were hand-copied documents and quite expensive, demonstrating that the eunuch was intent on studying God's Word. It was not a mere passing interest for him; he sought the Lord, and the Lord responded to his quest by sending Philip to him.

31.4 Witnessing to Others

Focus: Basics in Witnessing

EXTENSION

4A Let students find a partner and practice sharing their faith by using copies of **BLMs 31A–B ABCs of Faith** to color, cut out, and staple together as a booklet. Listen and help guide students. Remind them to ask the Holy Spirit to help them know the words to say as they tell others the good news about Jesus. Encourage students with the truth that God can use them, even while they are young, to tell others about Jesus and help people accept Jesus as Savior.

4B Teach this song to the tune of "Row, Row, Row Your Boat":
Tell, tell, tell your friends,
Tell everyone you know,
Jesus is the Lord of all,
And He loves them so.

Introduction

Invite two or three students to share facts about themselves that they could share with a new student, such as their name and age. Make the point that some facts are more important than others. Knowing someone's name is more important than knowing what color they like the best. Explain that sometimes students may meet someone and only have a short time to share some facts about themselves. In that situation, they would want to tell the most important and most helpful things. Discuss the important things for Christians to share with people who are not Christians. (**Answers will vary, but should include that Jesus died to pay for the sins of everyone, He rose again, and wants everyone to believe in Him so they can join Him in heaven.**)

Directed Instruction

Write the capital letters *A*, *B*, and *C* on the board. Explain that these letters can help students share their faith with others.

Explain that *A* stands for *Admit that we sin*. Share that Jesus never sinned or did anything that disobeyed God's rules. Review Lesson 8.2 and discuss the Ten Commandments. Encourage students to honestly admit that they have broken at least one of God's rules. It is important to explain that everyone, except Jesus, has sinned. No person—no matter how nice or how famous—has obeyed all of God's rules all of the time. Sin keeps people from God, but Jesus died on the cross to pay for the sins of everyone. Explain that no amount of money or good deeds could forgive any sins; only Jesus can pay the price for sin. Jesus died because He loves people and wants them to be part of God's family.

B stands for *Believe and repent*. Explain that it is important to believe that everything Jesus said was true. He alone has the power to forgive sins. Forgiveness comes through repentance. When people are truly sorry for the wrong things they have done and ask Jesus for forgiveness, He forgives them!

C stands for *Choose Christ as Lord*. Remind students that each person must have his or her own relationship with God. Even if a parent believes in the Lord, that does not take the place of the child's responsibility to grow in his or her own faith. The choice to respond to God's love and offer of salvation is up to each person.

Explain that Jesus gave a job to all the people who believe in Him—to tell others about Him! Pray that God would show students someone they know who does not have a relationship with God. Ask the Holy Spirit to guide students to boldly share their faith.

Review

- What does *A* stand for in the ABCs of Faith? (**Admit that we sin.**)
- What does *B* stand for in the ABCs of Faith? (**Believe and repent.**)
- What does *C* stand for in the ABCs of Faith? (**Choose Christ as Lord.**)

- Why should you tell someone about Jesus? (**Answers will vary, but should include that God's Word says all people need to hear about Jesus and believe in Him so they will no longer be separated from God.**)

Student Page 31.4

Read the sections of the invitation and have students choose the correct word from the Word Bank.

Notes:

APPLICATION

- Philip shared his faith in Jesus with the Ethiopian man. Why do you share your faith? (**I share my faith because I love God and other people. I want to obey Jesus' command to tell others about Him.**)
- Who can you tell about Jesus? (**Answers will vary.**)
- What is a good way to start a conversation about Jesus? (**Answers will vary.**)

DAY 4

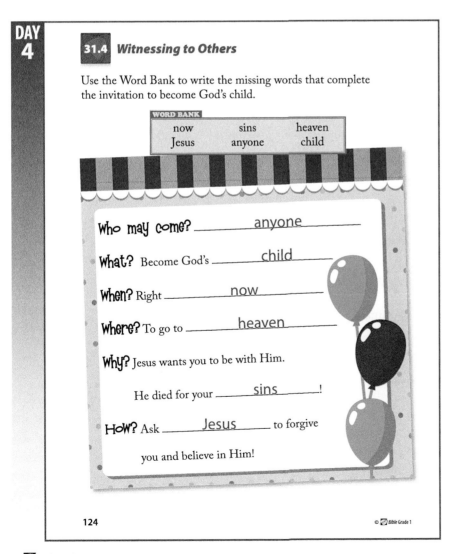

31.4 ***Witnessing to Others***

Use the Word Bank to write the missing words that complete the invitation to become God's child.

WORD BANK

now	sins	heaven
Jesus	anyone	child

Who may come? anyone

What? Become God's child

When? Right now

Where? To go to heaven

Why? Jesus wants you to be with Him.

He died for your sins!

How? Ask Jesus to forgive you and believe in Him!

124

31.5 Witnessing to Others

Focus: Review and Assessment

★ PREPARATION

Select **VA 31A Philip and the Ethiopian**. (*Lesson Review*)

Provide a copy of **BLM 31C Lesson 31 Test** for each student. (*Directed Instruction*)

Lesson Review ★

Use **VA 31A Philip and the Ethiopian** to review the Bible truths from this week's lesson. Cover the following points:

- Philip was a follower of Jesus who faithfully told others the good news of Jesus.
- An angel came to Philip and told him to get up and travel on a certain road.
- Philip immediately obeyed, even though he did not know why he should go or what would happen.
- After Philip was on the road, the Spirit of the Lord spoke to him and told him to go over to the chariot.
- In the chariot was an Ethiopian man who was in charge of the queen's money. He had been in Jerusalem to worship God even though he was not a Jew. He was reading from the book of Isaiah.
- Philip asked the Ethiopian man if he understood what he read.
- The Ethiopian asked Philip some questions about the Scripture.
- Philip got in the chariot and explained that the book of Isaiah was talking about Jesus. He told the man about Jesus and what Jesus did.
- The Ethiopian man believed what Philip said. He believed that Jesus Christ is the Son of God.
- The Ethiopian man asked Philip to baptize him in some water that was nearby. Philip agreed and baptized him.
- The Ethiopian man learned about Jesus because Philip was willing to obey God immediately.
- Philip boldly told the Ethiopian about Jesus. The Holy Spirit helps Christians living today to tell others about Jesus!
- *Being a witness* means *being a person who tells others about the good news of God's plan of salvation.*
- God wants everyone to be part of His family. Sin keeps people from Him. Jesus died on the cross to forgive sins so people can be part of God's family.
- The ABCs of Faith are: Admit that we sin; Believe and repent; Choose Christ as Lord.

Directed Instruction ★

Distribute a copy of **BLM 31C Lesson 31 Test** to each student. Read any unfamiliar words and direct students to work independently or with guidance as needed. Review answers with students.

Notes:

Lesson Preparation

Pleasing God

Expected Student Outcomes

KNOW

Ananias prays for Saul. Timothy, Aquila and Priscilla, and other believers please the Lord by their service.

DO

Students will:
- identify ways that Saul changed after he became a Christian
- complete an activity to show how Ananias and Paul served God
- select appropriate acts of service in different scenarios
- solve riddles that identify other servant-leaders in the early Church

APPLY

Students will demonstrate acts of service to God.

Lesson Outline

I. Saul's conversion (Acts 9:1–20)
  A. Saul's encounter on the Damascus road
II. Paul becomes a servant
  A. Ananias trusts God
III. Timothy serves faithfully (Acts 16:1–2, 2 Tim 1:3–6)
  A. Timothy's youth
  B. Paul encourages Timothy
IV. Early Christians serve the Church
  A. Lydia (Acts 16:11–15)
  B. Aquila and Priscilla (1 Cor 16:19, Rom 16:3–5, 2 Tim 4:19)
  C. Apollos (Acts 18:2–3, 18:24–26)

TEACHER'S HEART

When you hear the word *evangelist*, you probably picture a powerful communicator whose preaching inspires many to repent of their sins and come to faith in the Lord. Or, you may think of an evangelist as being an eloquent speaker with the seminary training necessary to deliver a thought-provoking, life-changing sermon. You may even picture an evangelist as one who takes the gospel to a previously unknown and unreached tribe of people. What you probably don't think of is a first grader!

Realize it or not, you are training evangelists every day in your classroom. Your first graders are taking the gospel into their homes and neighborhoods. You're not only teaching God's Word, but you are modeling an example of Christian conduct for your students on a daily basis. Students learn much from hearing the Word, but perhaps even more from the way they see you live it out in your life.

May the Word of Christ continue to dwell in you richly during the final weeks of this school year. Continue lifting up your students in prayer as you encourage them to be diligent in developing a close relationship with God.

MEMORY VERSE

Colossians 1:10

MATERIALS

Day 1:
- Flip chart
- Ball
- VA 32A Saul's Conversion
- Blindfold
- BLM 32A Damascus Road Sunglasses, card stock, colored cellophane (*Extension*)

Day 2:
- VA 32A Saul's Conversion
- TM-10 Books of the New Testament

Day 3:
- Bulletin board paper (*Extension*)

Day 4:
- Box of crayons
- Camping tent, Bible storybooks (*Extension*)

Day 5:
- VA 32A Saul's Conversion
- BLM 32B Lesson 32 Test

TEACHER RESOURCES

Platt, David. *Radical Together: Unleashing the People of God for the Purpose of God*. Multnomah Books, 2011.

Swindoll, Charles R. *Improving Your Serve*. Thomas Nelson, 2004.

STUDENT RESOURCES

Burgdorf, Larry. *Paul's Great Basket Caper*. Concordia Publishing House, 2009.

Rivers, Francine, and Shannon Rivers Coibion. *Bible Stories for Growing Kids*. Tyndale House Publishers, Inc., 2007.

32.1 Pleasing God

Focus: Saul's Conversion

MEMORY VERSE

Colossians 1:10

MEMORY WORK

- Invite several different volunteers to read the Memory Verse on the FLIP CHART so that students have heard the verse several times. Assemble students into a circle. Pass a BALL from one person to the next and instruct the student holding the ball to say the next word of the verse. Repeat until all students have participated. Vary the speed of the activity as students become proficient in reciting the verse. As an option, have students roll the ball across the circle to another student rather than passing it around the circle.

PREPARATION

Write the Memory Verse on a FLIP CHART. Obtain a BALL that is appropriate for indoor use. (*Memory Work*)

Select **VA 32A Saul's Conversion**. (*Directed Instruction*)

Have a BLINDFOLD on hand. (*Directed Instruction*)

EXTENSION

1A Print **BLM 32A Damascus Road Sunglasses** onto CARD STOCK. You will need one copy of the blackline master and TWO PIECES OF COLORED CELLOPHANE for each student. Assist students as needed to make sunglasses. Let students wear the sunglasses and share the Bible truth of Saul's conversion. Be sure to remind students not to look directly at the sun because the sunglasses will not protect their eyes.

Introduction

Run your hand over the top of a desk and tell students that many people who lived long ago used to think the earth was flat, just like a desktop. Explain that when ships sailed away, they seemed to disappear as if they had fallen off a flat surface, so people thought the earth was flat. Ask students to tell what shape the earth really is. (**round, a sphere**) Even though the flat-earth idea was believed by many people for a long time, it was still untrue. When people learned and accepted the truth about the earth's shape, they changed their belief.

Inform students that people sometimes believe things that are not true because they do not know the truth. Tell students to listen to how one man came to know the truth and changed his beliefs.

Directed Instruction ★ ↷

Display **VA 32A Saul's Conversion** and read the text on the back.

Remind students that it was very hard to be a Christian at the time of the early Church. Believers had powerful enemies. These enemies were the religious leaders. They should have known what the Bible said about the Messiah, but they did not believe the truth that Jesus was the Messiah or that Jesus had risen from the dead! What made them even angrier was that the disciples reminded the people that many of these same religious leaders were responsible for crucifying Jesus. These enemies of the Church wanted to stop the Church from growing. Saul was one of these leaders.

Some Christians decided to leave Jerusalem because it was too dangerous for them to live there. They moved to other countries where they were faithful witnesses for Jesus and told their new neighbors all about God's plan of salvation. Many more people heard the good news and became Christians. Ananias was one of the Christians who lived in Damascus.

Ask a volunteer to recount what happened to Saul as he was on his way to Damascus. (**A light shone from heaven and Jesus spoke to Saul. Jesus asked Saul why Saul was fighting against Him. Saul did not know who was speaking to him until Jesus identified Himself. Saul asked Jesus what to do next. Jesus told Saul to get up and go to Damascus. There, Saul would be told more. Saul got up, but he could not see.**)

Choose a volunteer to play the part of Saul. Put a BLINDFOLD over your volunteer's eyes and lead your volunteer around the classroom. As you walk, explain that Saul was blind and had to rely on his friends to lead him into Damascus. Saul could not travel quickly; he had to take things step by step. Take the blindfold off your volunteer and ask how it felt to be blind for even a short time. (**Answers will vary, but should include feeling helpless or feeling nervous.**)

Inform students that Jesus had chosen Saul to be a servant-leader in the Church, but first Saul had to develop a relationship with Jesus. It may seem strange that Saul could not see for a while, but he used that time to pray and begin to grow in his relationship with Jesus. If Saul were to become the leader that God wanted him to be, Saul would have to rely on Jesus to guide him. As long as Saul thought that he could do things his own way, he would not be a good servant-leader. Servant-leaders trust God!

Review

- What did Saul believe that was not true? (**Saul believed Christians were wrong to believe that Jesus was the Messiah.**)
- What did Saul try to do to stop the Church from growing? (**Saul tried to harm Christians and even put them to death.**)
- What did Saul hear on the road to Damascus? (**a voice, the voice of Jesus**) What did Jesus tell Saul to do? (**Jesus told Saul to get up, go into the city, and wait to be told more.**)
- How did Saul respond to Jesus? (**Saul obeyed Jesus.**)

Student Page 32.1

Read the directions and any unfamiliar words before telling students to complete the page.

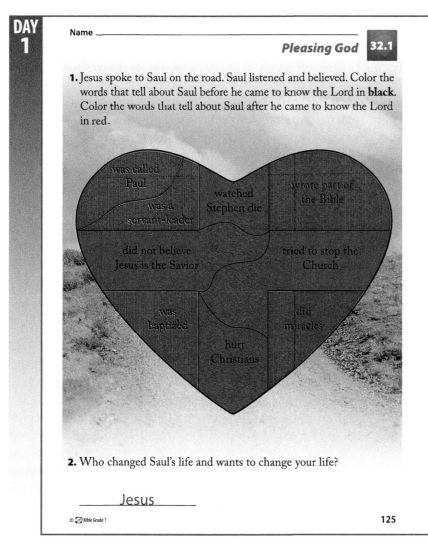

DAY 1

Name ______________________________

Pleasing God **32.1**

1. Jesus spoke to Saul on the road. Saul listened and believed. Color the words that tell about Saul before he came to know the Lord in **black**. Color the words that tell about Saul after he came to know the Lord in red.

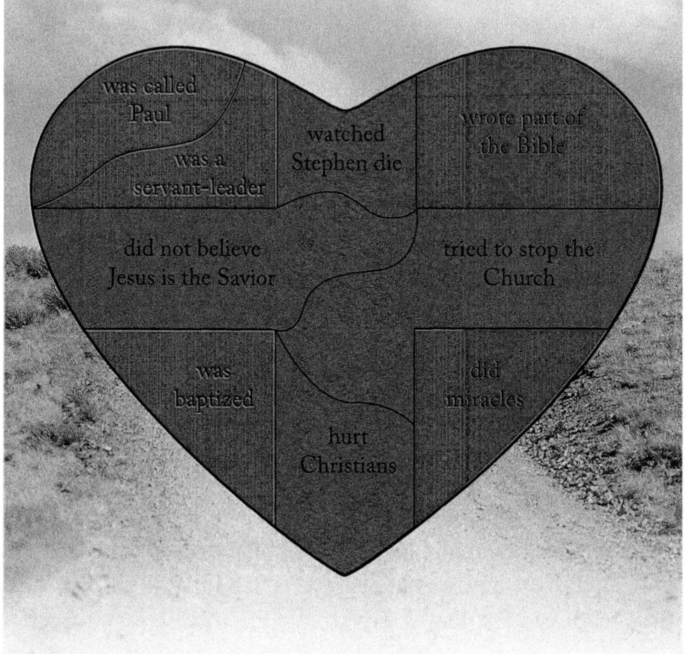

2. Who changed Saul's life and wants to change your life?

Jesus

APPLICATION

- Saul's experience on the Damascus road changed him. He behaved very differently after accepting Jesus as his Savior. Think of a misbehavior that you tend to repeat. What can you do to change your behavior? (**I can confess my sin, repent, and choose to obey the Lord in the future.**)
- Once Paul became a Christian, he wanted to serve others. Do you want to serve others? (**Answers will vary.**) Share some ways that you can serve. (**Answers will vary.**)
- Saul lost his sight for a short time and spent that time in prayer. Share about a time when you had to make a choice, so you spent time in prayer. (**Answers will vary.**)

REINFORCEMENT

The name *Ananias* means *the Lord is gracious*. Saul would likely have heard Ananias' name prior to receiving his sight and the meaning of the name would not have been lost on Saul. The Lord was truly gracious to Saul, who later described himself as being the chief of sinners (1 Timothy 1:15) and completely undeserving of God's grace. It is by God's grace alone, through faith, without anything done to deserve God's favor, that Christians are accepted by God.

32.2 Pleasing God

Focus: Paul Becomes a Servant

★ ***PREPARATION***

Select **VA 32A Saul's Conversion**. (*Directed Instruction*)

Display **TM-10 Books of the New Testament**. (*Directed Instruction*)

Introduction

Invite students to play a quick game of Simon Says to demonstrate obedience. Have students stand up, move to an open space in the classroom, and do only the actions that you preface with the words *Simon says*. Suggestions for actions are as follows: touch your nose, clap your hands, and wiggle your fingers. Have students who do an action that is not prefaced with *Simon says* sit down. Commend the students who listen well and have them return to their seats at the end of the game.

Directed Instruction ★

Display **VA 32A Saul's Conversion** and review the things that happened to Saul on the road to Damascus. Inform students that Saul was blind for three whole days! During that time, he did not eat or drink. All Saul could do was to think about what Jesus had told him and to pray.

Remind students that a Christian named *Ananias* lived in Damascus at the same time that Saul had heard the Lord's voice. Recount that Ananias received a message from the Lord. Jesus asked Ananias to do something that was really hard for Ananias to do!

Ask a few students to share things that scare them. (**Possible answers: big dogs, snakes, spiders, dark places**) Challenge those students to consider what they might do if they were asked to purposely go into a situation where they would need to face the things that they said were frightening. (**Answers will vary, but should indicate a reluctance to do as asked.**) Then ask the students what they might do if you promised to be with them in the scary situation. (**Answers will vary, but should include a greater willingness to do what they were asked to do.**)

Explain that Ananias had fears, too. He loved the Lord and trusted Jesus, but Ananias was probably afraid that the enemies of the Church would come to his house and arrest him and perhaps others. Ananias knew that Saul was working hard to arrest as many Christians as he could. It is possible that Ananias knew that Stephen had been killed for his faith in Jesus. When the Lord told Ananias to go and speak to Saul, Ananias was not ready to obey at first. Following Jesus' command was very hard for Ananias to follow! Jesus was clear in His direction to Ananias; Jesus had chosen Saul to do His work.

Ananias was a faithful servant to the Lord. He might have been afraid, but he did what Jesus had asked him to do, and Ananias believed that the Lord would be with him. Ananias placed his hands on Saul. Ananias explained that Jesus had chosen Saul to do some very important work and to bring the good news of God's plan of salvation to many, many people!

Remind students that Saul's name changed after coming to faith in Christ and being baptized. Ask a volunteer to tell what Saul's new name was. (**Paul**) Paul was a great leader in the Church and preached God's Word to many people over a large area. Display **TM-10 Books of the New Testament** to show students the books that were written by Paul.

Review

- How did Ananias demonstrate being a servant of Jesus? (**He obeyed Jesus by going to Saul, laying his hands on Saul so that Saul could see again and be filled with the Holy Spirit.**)
- Why was Jesus' command to Ananias hard for Ananias? (**Ananias was afraid of Saul! Saul had been arresting Christians and even having them put to death.**)
- How did Saul change after coming to know the Lord? (**Saul was completely changed. He was filled with the Holy Spirit and became a servant to Jesus and a leader of the Church. People began to call him Paul. Paul preached God's Word and wrote many books in the New Testament.**)

Student Page 32.2

Assist students in completing the page.

DAY 2

32.2 ***Pleasing God***

Circle every other letter, beginning with **s**, to find a message from God's Word. Write the message on the lines.

Anananias and Paul s e r v e d God

f a i t h f u l l y.

126 © Bible Grade 1

APPLICATION

- Have you ever been afraid to do something that you were told to do? Tell about that time. (**Answers will vary.**)
- What does this Bible truth teach you about Ananias? (**Answers will vary, but should include that Ananias was willing to obey Jesus even though Ananias was afraid.**)
- Why might Saul's name have been changed to Paul? (**Perhaps he became known as Paul to let people know that his life was changed by the Lord.**)

REINFORCEMENT

Paul was a very unique person!

- By birth, he was a Hebrew from the tribe of Benjamin;
- By politics, he was a Pharisee;
- By reputation, he was blameless in regard to the Law;
- By citizenship, he was a Roman;
- By the grace of God, he was a Christian.

While Paul later denounced all his credentials except for his life in Christ (Philippians 3:5–11), God used Paul's knowledge of different groups of people to prepare him for an effective ministry to much of the known world.

32.3 Pleasing God

Focus: Timothy Serves Faithfully

EXTENSION

3A Use a long sheet of **BULLETIN BOARD PAPER** to make a height chart for your class. Mark off the chart in customary or metric units. Along the side of the height chart, write the text of 1 Timothy 4:12, a verse in which Paul reminds Timothy that, despite his youth, he is to set an example for the Church. Post the height chart on the wall or a door. Measure each student's height and record it on the chart. Remind students that Timothy was probably about the same size that they are when he was six or seven years old. As Timothy listened and learned, he grew in his relationship with God.

3B Invite students to open their Bible to 1 Timothy and then to 2 Timothy. Explain that these two books in the New Testament are the letters that Paul wrote to Timothy. These two books teach Christians much about living in a way that pleases God.

Introduction

Ask students to share something specific that they learned from their parents or grandparents. (**Possible answers: a song, a poem, how to tie shoes**) Ask students how they learned what the parent or grandparent taught them. (**Learning comes through listening, observing, and practicing.**) Tell about a personal example of something a parent or grandparent taught you.

Share that today's Bible truth is about a young person named *Timothy* who learned important things from his mother and his grandmother.

Directed Instruction

Read the following Bible truth based on Acts 16:1–2 and 2 Timothy 1:3–6:

> There was a boy named *Timothy* during the time that the Church was beginning. His mother, Eunice, and grandmother, Lois, taught him about God. They taught Timothy many things about God. Timothy learned and believed that Jesus Christ was God's Son, the Messiah.
>
> When Timothy was a young man, Paul came to Timothy's town. Paul traveled to different cities to preach the good news about Jesus. Paul needed a special helper who was a faithful follower of Jesus. He needed someone dependable to take with him on his missionary journeys.
>
> The Christian leaders in Timothy's town knew that Timothy would be a good choice to join Paul as a missionary. They may have recommended Timothy to Paul because of the good example that Timothy had already set. Paul asked Timothy to join his work, and they traveled to many places, teaching and preaching about Jesus.
>
> Although Paul and Timothy traveled together, there were times when Paul left Timothy behind in a particular place. By staying behind, Timothy could help the people learn more about the Lord. Paul knew that he could depend on Timothy to lead and teach the people correctly. When Paul and Timothy were apart, Paul wrote letters to Timothy to encourage him. Because Timothy was still a young man, Paul wrote advice for Timothy about how to be wise. Paul encouraged Timothy to be a strong leader in the Church even while Timothy was young.

Remind students that Timothy's mother and grandmother equipped Timothy by teaching him God's Word. *Equipped* means *trained.* Tell students that they are now being equipped to serve God. Inform students that Timothy learned many of the same Bible truths that the students have learned this year. Not only did Timothy know about the Bible, but he trusted and loved God. Timothy pleased God by serving others and using his gifts of teaching and preaching so that others might learn about Jesus.

Paul trusted that Timothy would continue to serve God faithfully and would not give up preaching and teaching about Jesus, even if some people did not want to listen. Paul encouraged Timothy not to get tired, discouraged, or frustrated with trying to help people learn about Jesus.

Review

- Who first taught Timothy about God and Bible truths? (**Timothy's mother, Eunice, and his grandmother, Lois**)
- How did Timothy help Paul? (**Timothy traveled with Paul but sometimes stayed behind in order to teach the people in certain places more about the Lord.**)
- How did Timothy please God? (**He used his gifts of preaching and teaching to help others know the Lord.**)
- How did Paul help Timothy? (**Paul wrote letters to Timothy to give Timothy godly advice.**)

Student Page 32.3

Choose volunteers to read each scenario and the choices for answers. Encourage students to mark the answer that best demonstrates servanthood. Discuss other ways that the children in each scenario could honor God through service.

DAY 3

Name ______________________________

Pleasing God **32.3**

Timothy learned about Jesus and began serving him when he was a young boy. This pleased God!

How can these children please God by their service? Fill in the circle by the best choice.

1. Trevor's mother is a teacher, so Trevor stays after school until his mother finishes her work. Trevor can serve his mother by

O asking when they can go home.

● picking up books.

O leaving a mess in his mother's classroom.

2. Seth needs to be at his game by noon, but his dad has work to do. Seth can serve his dad by

● helping his dad with the work.

O watching TV.

O playing with toys.

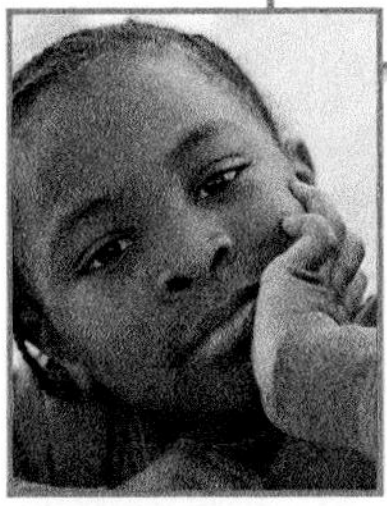

3. Ella's parents are greeters at church. Ella can serve her parents and her church by

O running around outside.

● passing out church papers.

O bothering her parents.

127

APPLICATION

- Timothy listened to Eunice and Lois as they taught him about God. Who teaches you about God? (**Answers will vary.**) What are some of the things you have learned about God from that person? (**Answers will vary.**)
- If a younger child came to you and wanted you to teach him or her about the Lord, how would you do that? (**Possible answers: I could read a Bible truth from a children's Bible; I could tell a Bible truth that I know; I could share a craft that reviews the Bible truth; I could show a Christian DVD and answer the younger child's questions about the DVD.**)
- Are you always faithful to do the jobs that you have been given? (**Answers will vary.**) Do you sometimes forget to finish your work or do a careless job? (**Answers will vary.**) What can you do to become a faithful servant? (**I can do my best, knowing that good work pleases the Lord.**)

32.4 Pleasing God

Focus: Early Christians Serve the Church

★ PREPARATION

Obtain a BOX OF CRAYONS. (*Introduction*)

EXTENSION

4A Remind students that Aquila, his wife, Priscilla, and Paul were tentmakers by profession, but they were also missionaries. No matter what a Christian's chosen profession might be, he or she should always be alert for opportunities to teach others about Jesus. Set up a CAMPING TENT in one corner of your classroom to represent Aquila, Priscilla, and Paul's vocation. Put several BIBLE STORYBOOKS inside the tent. Invite students to visit "Aquila and Priscilla's tent" to learn more about Jesus.

Introduction ★

Open a BOX OF CRAYONS. Comment on how many different colors there are. Compare the varied crayons to the Christians in the early Church. Followers of Jesus came from many different countries and took the good news of salvation to other parts of the world. These believers were all different, like the crayons, but they all had a strong relationship with the Lord. They relied on the Holy Spirit to give them the power needed to do their work.

Directed Instruction

Read the following Bible truth based on Acts 16:11–15, 18:2–3, 18:24–26; 1 Corinthians 16:19, Romans 16:3–5; and 2 Timothy 4:19:

> As Paul continued his missionary journeys, he helped many people by teaching them about Jesus' death on the cross, His resurrection from the dead, and God's plan of salvation. Some of the people helped Paul in return. Lydia, who sold purple dye and things colored purple, met Paul by a riverside. Paul and his friends spoke to Lydia and other women who were there. Lydia became a follower of Jesus. Afterwards, Lydia offered her home to Paul and his companions as a place to stay.
>
> Aquila and Priscilla, a husband and wife, were Jewish Christians who lived in Corinth. Paul had learned to make tents as a way to earn a living. Aquila and Priscilla were also tentmakers, so Paul lived and worked with them at various times. This couple led a small church that met in their home. Aquila and Priscilla had even risked their lives for Paul!
>
> Aquila and Priscilla met a Jewish man named *Apollos*. He was someone who made speeches easily, and he knew the Old Testament very well. Apollos even taught others what the Scriptures said. But he hadn't heard about Jesus. Aquila and Priscilla shared with Apollos the good news of Jesus, and he became a Christian. From that time on, Apollos spoke boldly and used the Scriptures to prove to others that Jesus is the Son of God and the Savior of the world.
>
> Ananias, Paul, Timothy, Lydia, Aquila and Priscilla, and Apollos were all faithful to tell others about Jesus. Telling people about Jesus pleases God.

Remind students that all of the people mentioned in the Bible truth were different. Lydia was a Gentile woman who sold purple dye. Aquila and Priscilla were tentmakers. Apollos was a Jewish man who could speak very well. Through these different people and many people who lived after them, the message of salvation was spread to countries around the world. This work is still continuing today; missionaries are bringing the message to people who have never heard about Jesus.

Review

- What did Lydia sell? (**purple dye and things colored purple**)
- How did Lydia help Paul? (**She offered her home as a place for Paul and his companions to stay.**)
- Who were Aquila and Priscilla? (**They were Jewish Christians who made tents.**)
- How did Aquila and Priscilla help Paul? (**They worked with Paul and risked their life to help him.**)
- Who was Apollos? (**He was a Jewish man who knew the Old Testament well. Once Aquila and Priscilla told him about Jesus, he became a Christian and preached boldly about Jesus.**)

Student Page 32.4

Assist students as needed in completing the page.

Notes:

APPLICATION

- Aquila and Priscilla risked their life helping Paul. Why might they have done this? (**Answers will vary, but should include that they had a close relationship with God, and they knew that God had important work for Paul to do. They trusted that God would keep them safe.**)
- God used many different kinds of people to spread the good news of salvation. How is God using you to reach others? (**Possible answers: I tell my friends about Jesus; I give money to help missionaries; I pray for others to accept Jesus as Savior.**)

REINFORCEMENT

Paul met Lydia by the riverside in Philippi. According to Jewish custom, there had to be 10 Jewish men who would meet together in prayer before a community could have a synagogue. If a town did not have a synagogue, then Jews would meet at the riverside on the Sabbath to pray. Paul went to the river in hopes of finding Jewish men, but the Lord led him to a Gentile woman. Lydia, like the Ethiopian man converted through Philip's preaching, was a worshipper of God but not a convert to Judaism. The Lord opened her heart to respond to Paul's message (Acts 16:14).

DAY 4

32.4 *Pleasing God*

God led many people to help the Church grow. Write the name of the servant or servants to answer each riddle. Their names are **Lydia**, **Aquila** and **Priscilla**, and **Apollos**. One name will be used twice.

1. We are tentmakers. We have a church meeting in our home.

Who are we? Aquila and Priscilla

2. I sell purple dye and things colored purple.

Who am I? Lydia

3. I am a Jewish man who knows the Bible very well. I teach others

about Jesus. Who am I? Apollos

4. I let Paul and his friends stay in my house.

Who am I? Lydia

5. Unscramble the letters below the banner to complete the sentence.

Faithful service pleases God.

s e l p e a s

128 © Bible Grade 1

32.5 Pleasing God

Focus: Review and Assessment

★ PREPARATION

Select **VA 32A Saul's Conversion**. (*Lesson Review*)

Print **BLM 32B Lesson 32 Test** for each student. (*Directed Instruction*)

Lesson Review ★

Use **VA 32A Saul's Conversion** to review the Bible truth. Cover the following concepts:

- Saul tried to stop the growth of the Church because he thought Christians were wrong about Jesus.
- Saul was going to Damascus to arrest Christians. On the way, a bright light from heaven shone around Saul.
- Saul heard Jesus speak! Saul realized that he had been wrong about Jesus. He wanted to change.
- When Saul stood up after listening to Jesus, he was blind. The men he was traveling with guided Saul to Damascus.
- Saul was blind for three days. He prayed during that time.
- A Christian named *Ananias* lived in Damascus. The Lord spoke to him and told him to go and lay hands on Saul. The Lord told Ananias that He had chosen Saul to do His work.
- At first Ananias did not want to go to Saul, but he obeyed the Lord.
- When Ananias laid his hands on Saul, Saul was then able to see and was filled with the Holy Spirit.
- People started to call Saul by the name *Paul*. Paul traveled as a missionary, preaching, performing miracles, and writing letters that became part of the New Testament.
- Eunice and Lois taught Timothy God's Word, and that Jesus was the promised Savior.
- Paul thought Timothy was a good teacher and preacher. Paul left Timothy at different places to continue preaching and teaching the people while Paul went on to start new churches.
- Lydia, Aquila and Priscilla, and Apollos were other early Christians who did the Lord's work.
- God was pleased with each of these people because they shared their gifts so the Church could continue to grow.

Directed Instruction ★

Distribute a copy of **BLM 32B Lesson 32 Test** to each student. Have students complete the exercises independently. Review the correct answers.

Notes:

Lesson Preparation

Serving God and Others

Expected Student Outcomes

KNOW
Paul and Barnabas faithfully use their gifts of service to bless others.

DO
Students will:
- review events of Paul and Barnabas' ministry in Antioch
- complete a puzzle to reinforce the Bible truth about Paul and Barnabas' service
- differentiate between faithful and unfaithful service
- use a picture key to identify missionaries

APPLY
Students will demonstrate acts of faithful service.

Lesson Outline

I. Paul and Barnabas listen to God (Acts 4:32–36, 13:13–52)
  A. The synagogue at Antioch
  B. Jealousy and rejection
II. Paul and Barnabas love others (Acts 14:8–20)
  A. Preaching and healing in Lystra
  B. Servants of the living God
III. Serving faithfully
  A. Faithful vs. unfaithful service
IV. Lottie Moon blesses others
  A. Missionary to China

TEACHER'S HEART

As you approach the end of the school year, you may feel like a marathon runner who has just passed the 25-mile marker. Only one more mile to go, but it is so tough! You can almost see the finish line, but you're running out of energy! Will you get there? If ever there was a time for someone to run alongside you to encourage you, this would be the time!

Barnabas was an encourager. He was gifted by God to be a coach, building up others in their faith. Barnabas was a faithful servant. He traveled with Paul, stood by his side, and endured many of the same trials that Paul endured. Both Paul and Barnabas were criticized, ridiculed, misunderstood, blamed, forced out of town, falsely identified as gods, falsely accused of wrongdoing, and persecuted for their faith. Yet, Barnabas kept going, kept working, and kept encouraging others. Barnabas was fueled by the Holy Spirit!

As your students are nearing the end of the school year, many of them are likely running out of energy, too. Be sure to pray for them daily, encouraging them to finish the year with enthusiasm and joy.

MEMORY VERSE

1 Peter 4:10

MATERIALS

Day 1:
- BLM 33A Memory Verse Shoes, envelopes
- VA 33A Paul and Barnabas
- PP-9 Service (*Extension*)

Day 2:
- Cardboard, shoelaces (*Extension*)

Day 3:
- Sticky notes
- BLM 33B Stoplight, paper bags (*Extension*)

Day 4:
- Sidewalk chalk (*Extension*)

Day 5:
- VA 33A Paul and Barnabas
- BLM 33C Lesson 33 Test

SONGS

Walk Like Jesus (*Extension*)

TEACHER RESOURCES

Moore, Beth. *To Live Is Christ: Joining Paul's Journey of Faith.* B&H Publishing Group, 2008.
Ramsey, William M. *St. Paul the Traveler and Roman Citizen.* Kregel Publications, 2001.

STUDENT RESOURCES

Benge, Janet and Geoff. *Christian Heroes: Then & Now—Lottie Moon: Giving Her All for China.* YWAM Publishing, 2002.
Maier, Paul L. *The Very First Christians.* Concordia Publishing House, 2001.

33.1 Serving God and Others

Focus: Paul and Barnabas Listen to God

MEMORY VERSE

1 Peter 4:10

MEMORY WORK

- Provide each student with a copy of **BLM 33A Memory Verse Shoes**. Explain that the Memory Verse is printed on shoes because service to others often involves activity. Instruct students to arrange the "shoes" in the correct order to match the Memory Verse. Invite students to mix up the shoes and repeat the activity. Give each student an ENVELOPE for storage of the shoe cutouts.

★ PREPARATION

Print one copy of **BLM 33A Memory Verse Shoes** and write a phrase from the Memory Verse on each of the shoes. Then duplicate a class set of the amended copy. Provide an ENVELOPE for each student to store the cutouts. (*Memory Work*)

Select **VA 33A Paul and Barnabas**. (*Directed Instruction*)

EXTENSION

1A Teach students the song "Walk Like Jesus" from the music CDs to reinforce the concept of evangelism.

1B Show **PP-9 Service** to reinforce the concepts presented in this week's lesson.

Introduction

Ask students to raise their hand if they have a nickname or if their parents or grandparents sometimes call them by a special name when they are at home, such as *honey* or *sweetheart*. Invite a few students to share their nicknames with the class.

Review that Jesus gave His disciple Simon the nickname *Peter*, which means *a rock*. That nickname did not describe Peter when he first began to follow Jesus, but it fit him later on as he continued to faithfully serve the Lord. Remind students that Saul was called *Paul*. Paul became a powerful leader in the early Church, but he was not the only leader in the Church. Paul had a friend named Joseph who also had a nickname. Joseph's nickname was *Barnabas*, which means *Son of Encouragement*.

Directed Instruction ★

Display **VA 33A Paul and Barnabas** and read the text on the back.

Remind students that a missionary is someone who tells others about Jesus. Not all missionaries travel to other countries, but Paul and Barnabas were two missionaries who did go to other countries. God gave each of these men special gifts. Paul was a very good speaker. He could explain the Scriptures to people in ways that they could understand and help them to realize that Jesus was the Messiah. Paul listened to God and kept on sharing the gospel, even though he faced many difficulties. Barnabas knew the Scriptures well and loved God, too. Like Paul, Barnabas spent time in prayer. He listened for direction from the Holy Spirit. Barnabas encouraged others through his actions and words.

Paul and Barnabas felt that the Holy Spirit was directing them to go preach in Antioch. Paul usually went to look for a synagogue whenever he entered a new town. This was because Paul was Jewish. Paul loved the Jewish people and wanted them to understand how God had promised in the Old Testament that He would send the Messiah. Paul used the Scriptures to prove that Jesus was the Messiah and the Son of God. Many Jews and Gentiles who worshipped God believed what Paul told them, and the Church grew.

Remind students that Paul and Barnabas experienced difficulties when they preached about Jesus. Many people listened to their teaching and chose to become followers of Jesus. However, not everyone believed that Jesus was the Savior. Some of the people who did not believe in Jesus tried to stop Paul and Barnabas from preaching.

Invite students to imagine that they are trying to shoot a basketball through a hoop, but a very tall opponent is standing right in front of the basket. It would be very hard to get the ball into the hoop! Then have students imagine that they could sit on the shoulders of a teammate. How much easier it would be to make a basket that way! In the same way, Paul was trying to preach God's Word, but some people were trying to stop him.

Barnabas was like the teammate who helped. Barnabas encouraged Paul to keep on preaching the good news.

Review

- What is a missionary? (**someone who tells others about Jesus**)
- What job did God give to Paul and Barnabas? (**to be missionaries and preach God's Word in various places**)
- Where did Paul and Barnabas go to preach in the city of Antioch? (**They went to the synagogue.**)
- Did everyone in the synagogue agree with Paul and Barnabas' preaching to the Gentiles and teaching them about Jesus? (**No, some of the Jewish people became jealous and tried to stop Paul and Barnabas from preaching God's Word to the Gentiles.**)

Student Page 33.1

Read any difficult words on the page and have students complete the exercises independently.

DAY 1

Name ______________________________

Serving God and Others **33.1**

Draw a line to match the first part of each sentence to its ending.

1. Paul and Barnabas were •   • Jesus.

2. They went to the synagogue in •   • jealous.

3. Paul told the people about Jesus, the •   • Antioch.

4. Many people believed in •   • missionaries.

5. Some people were •   • stop the missionaries.

6. The jealous people tried to •   • Messiah.

APPLICATION

- Paul and Barnabas listened to God's directions. How can you know what God wants you to do to serve others? (**I can pray, listen to Bible truths, read the Bible, and ask my parents or teacher to guide me.**)
- Paul and Barnabas traveled to different places as missionaries. Do all missionaries go to different countries? (**No, some of them share the good news in their own countries.**) Do you have to be an adult to be a missionary? (**No, I can tell my friends about Jesus right now!**)

REINFORCEMENT

Paul began the first of his three missionary journeys from Antioch in approximately 45 AD. During his trip, Paul traveled by ship and on foot in order to share the gospel with whoever would listen. He put personal comfort aside, braving robbers as well as those who tried to kill him, in order to fulfill his mission. Paul's first missionary trip took him more than 1,000 miles before coming to an end in approximately 47 AD.

33.2 Serving God and Others

Focus: Paul and Barnabas Love Others

EXTENSION

2A Assist students in making sandals similar to the ones Paul and Barnabas may have worn as they traveled from place to place telling people about Jesus. For each pair of sandals, you will need sturdy **CARDBOARD** and a **PAIR OF SHOELACES**. The laces need to be at least 54" long. Have each student find a partner and trace each other's stocking feet onto a piece of cardboard. Enlist the help of a parent to cut out the cardboard on the drawn lines and to punch holes into the soles. Thread the shoelaces through the holes so that the students can wear the sandals while indoors.

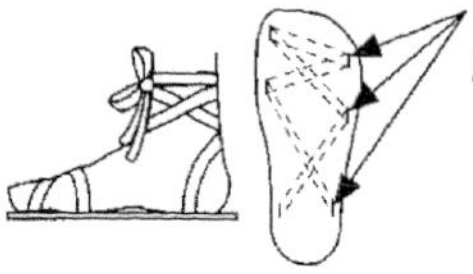

1. Punch holes.
2. Insert shoelace to wrap around ankle and foot.

Introduction

Ask students if they have ever had a bad day, a day when everything seemed to go wrong. (**Answers will vary.**) Invite a student to share briefly about his or her experience with a bad day. Explain that Paul and Barnabas were faithful to the Lord. They listened for His direction and followed His will. However, things did not always go well for them. Sometimes they experienced trouble, even though it was not their fault. Listen to how Paul and Barnabas found themselves in a bad situation.

Directed Instruction

Read the following Bible truth based on Acts 14:8–20:

After Paul and Barnabas left Antioch, they went to the town of Lystra. They preached in the synagogue and many people, both Jews and Gentiles, believed in Jesus as Savior. One day, as they were teaching, they noticed a man listening very carefully to all they taught. This man had a crooked foot and had been disabled all of his life. As the man listened, Paul saw that the man had the faith to be healed. Paul commanded this man to stand up; the man jumped up and began walking! What a miracle! The man had never walked before in his life!

The people didn't understand what had happened. They had worshipped false gods—idols—for many years and thought that Paul and Barnabas were some kind of gods who had come to heal them. The people began to worship Paul and Barnabas! This bothered Paul and Barnabas so much that they tore their clothes as a way to show how upset they were. They told the people that they were servants of the only God—the living God—and they were not gods. But even when Paul and Barnabas finished explaining the truth, they could hardly keep the Gentile people from making sacrifices to them.

Jewish leaders stirred up trouble for these faithful missionaries and convinced the people to stone Paul to death. Sadly, the people listened and took Paul outside the city where they threw stones at him until he fell to the ground. They thought they'd killed Paul. However, believers gathered around him after the stoning, and the Lord gave Paul the strength to get up. The next day Paul and Barnabas left the city and went to other towns to tell the people about Jesus. Paul and Barnabas both listened to the Lord and followed His leading.

Review

- Who was the one person who was listening very carefully to everything that Paul and Barnabas taught? (**a man with a crooked foot**)
- How did Paul know to tell the man with the crooked foot to stand up? (**Paul saw that the man had the faith to be healed.**)
- What did the people of Lystra think when they saw the man healed and walking, even though he had never walked before? (**They thought Paul and Barnabas were gods.**)

- How did Paul and Barnabas feel about being thought of as gods? (**This upset them very much; they tore their clothing to try to get the people to listen to them.**)
- What did Paul and Barnabas try to tell the people? (**They tried to explain that they were not gods, but that they were servants of the only God—the living God.**)

Student Page 33.2

Write the following Greek letters on the board: Φ, π, Ψ, Ω. Inform students that these letters are used to write the Greek language, the language spoken by Paul and Barnabas and the language in which the New Testament was originally written. Assist students in completing the page.

Notes:

APPLICATION

- Paul and Barnabas did not stay at one church for very long. Would it have been easy or hard for them to move to a new place? (**Answers will vary.**) Are you willing to try something new in order to serve God? (**Answers will vary.**)
- Some Jewish people were trying to make trouble for Paul and Barnabas again. What might have happened if Paul and Barnabas had decided to give up? (**Many Gentile people would not have heard the truth of God's Word.**)
- What have you learned from Paul and Barnabas' example? (**Answers will vary.**)

REINFORCEMENT

Paul and Barnabas worked well together. They used their individual spiritual gifts in tandem. Paul was gifted in preaching God's Word. Barnabas had the gift of encouragement. The apostles and disciples demonstrated other spiritual gifts given by the Holy Spirit as detailed in 1 Corinthians 12:1–11. The spiritual gifts allowed many to see the power of God, which resulted in salvation, healings, miracles, encouragement, understanding, and unity. Christians today exercise spiritual gifts in order to evangelize the unsaved, and build up and edify the Church.

DAY 2

33.2 *Serving God and Others*

Paul and Barnabas took God's Word to the people of Antioch and Lystra. The people who lived there spoke Greek.

1. Start at the arrow and go down. Circle the letters that are not Greek. Write them in order on the lines.

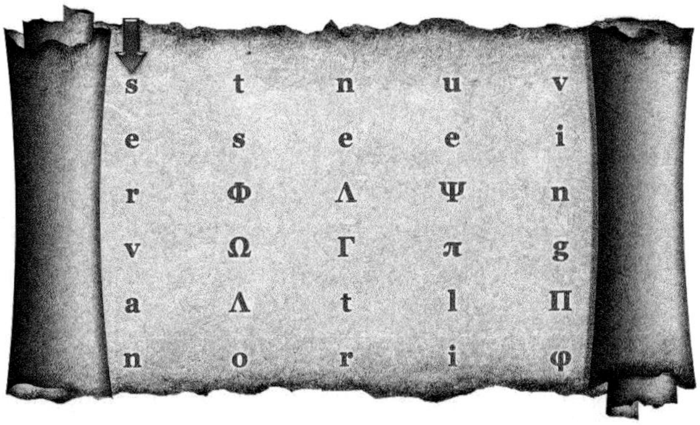

Paul and Barnabas were s e r v a n t s of the

o n e, t r u e, l i v i n g God!

2. Paul and Barnabas served people out of love for them. Tell how you will lovingly serve others.

Answers will vary.

130 © Bible Grade 1

33.3 Serving God and Others

Focus: Serving Faithfully

★ PREPARATION

Write the following phrases on STICKY NOTES: *pick up my trash, clean my room, help a new student, tell a friend about Jesus, pray for others, worship God, say bad words, leave a mess, disobey my parents, tell a lie.* (*Introduction*)

Cut sheets of green and red construction paper into pieces to make cards measuring approximately 3" × 5". Each student will need one green and one red card for an activity. (*Directed Instruction*)

EXTENSION

3A To reinforce the concept of faithful service, make a copy of **BLM 33B Stoplight** for each student. Give each student a PAPER BAG. Guide students through the activity. Tell them to take the bag home and share what they have learned with their family.

Introduction ★

Draw a large stoplight on the board, low enough for students to reach. Indicate that the lowest light is green, telling people that they may go on ahead. Explain that the uppermost light on a stoplight is red, which tells people to stop. Distribute the prepared STICKY NOTES to students and allow students time to read the phrases on the notes. Invite a volunteer to read his or her phrase aloud. Ask students if the phrase indicates behavior that is faithful service to others and should be continued, as represented by a green light, or indicates behavior that hurts relationships and should be discontinued, or stopped, as represented by a red light. Have the student put the sticky note on the correct "light" of the stoplight. Continue in the same way until all the notes have been put on the stoplight. Discuss additional ways to build relationships and honor God through faithful service. Emphasize that service can also include sincere worship, prayer for others, and the study of God's Word.

Directed Instruction ★

Distribute one GREEN CARD and one RED CARD to each student. Instruct students to hold up one of the cards at a time to indicate their response to some statements about service that you will read. The green card will signify faithful service. Let students know that faithful service is service that is done out of love and involves giving one's best to the Lord. The red card will signify unfaithful service. Unfaithful service is done for selfish reasons, or it is service done with a poor attitude. Unfaithful service does not honor God!

Have students hold up the cards to indicate their choice as to the kind of service that was being demonstrated by people in the Bible truths you have studied recently. Read the following statements:

- Peter and John healed a lame man in Jesus' name. (**green**)
- Religious leaders had Stephen stoned to death. (**red**)
- Ananias went to see Saul and prayed for him. (**green**)
- Paul wrote letters that became books in the New Testament. (**green**)
- Timothy helped new Christians know more about the Lord. (**green**)
- Lydia offered her home as a place for Paul to stay. (**green**)
- Aquila and Priscilla saved Paul's life. (**green**)
- Paul and Barnabas listened to God's direction and taught the Gentile people about the Lord. (**green**)
- The Jewish people in Antioch told Paul and Barnabas to get out of town. (**red**)
- Paul saw that a man with a crooked foot had faith in God. Paul told the man to stand up. (**green**)
- Paul and Barnabas would not let the people of Lystra worship them as gods. (**green**)
- Some jealous people convinced others to stone Paul and leave him for dead. (**red**)
- Christians gathered around Paul after he had been stoned. (**green**)

Review

- How should faithful service be done? (**Faithful service should be done out of love, not out of selfishness.**)
- Which honors God, faithful service or unfaithful service? (**Faithful service honors God.**)
- Can first graders demonstrate faithful service to others? (**Yes, they can. They should be actively involved in faithful service every day.**)

Student Page 33.3

Select volunteers to read the statements in the hearts and allow time for students to color the hearts containing correct responses. Discuss other ways that first graders can demonstrate faithful service.

Notes:

DAY 3

Name ______________________________

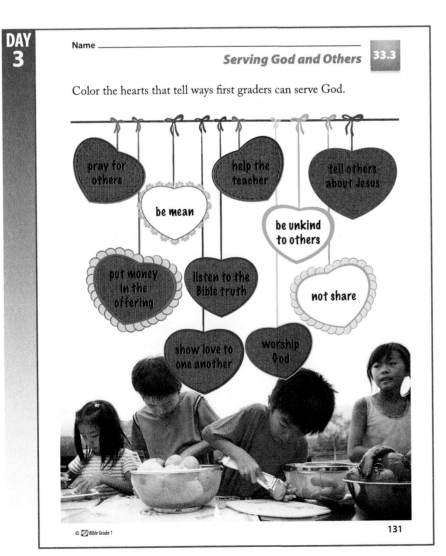

Serving God and Others **33.3**

Color the hearts that tell ways first graders can serve God.

© Bible Grade 1 131

APPLICATION

- Think about a way that you have served God recently. Tell what you did when you served. (**Answers will vary.**)
- Why did Paul and Barnabas continue to serve the Lord faithfully when they ran into so much trouble? (**Answers will vary, but should include that they had a close relationship with the Lord. They cared for the people who did not know about Jesus, and they wanted those people to know God's plan of salvation.**)
- Is it always easy to serve God faithfully? (**No, it is not always easy, but Christians often have fun when they work together to serve the Lord.**)
- Of the faithful servants that you have learned about from the Bible truths you have studied this year, who is your favorite? Why? (**Answers will vary.**)

REINFORCEMENT

In 2 Corinthians 11:16–33, Paul expressed disapproval to the Corinthians for being so easily persuaded to abandon the truth of Christ in order to follow smooth-talking false apostles. These false apostles came with impressive credentials, boasted about their pedigrees, and bragged about how they had suffered for Christ's sake. Paul called all their boasting what it was: foolishness. Paul considered his pedigree rubbish and his many sufferings for the cause of Christ to have been humiliations that made him more like Jesus.

33.4 Serving God and Others

Focus: Lottie Moon Blesses Others

EXTENSION

4A Paul and Barnabas made a good team. Lottie Moon also worked with other missionaries to lead people to faith in Jesus Christ. Encourage students to work as a team by playing the game Everyone In. This game requires drawing concentric circles on pavement with SIDEWALK CHALK. Inscribe a large circle, with a diameter of twenty feet, on the concrete or blacktop. Inside that circle, draw a second circle only ten feet in diameter, and inside that circle, draw a small circle, only five feet across. At your signal, tell students to get inside the largest circle, which will be an easy fit. Instruct them to go into the next largest circle, which will be a bit more difficult, and finally into the smallest circle. They will need to work together to fit into the smallest circle! Conclude the activity by reminding students how Christians can work together to reach people with the good news of God's plan of salvation.

Introduction

Turn off the lights and darken the classroom as much as possible. Ask students to think about some things that are difficult or impossible to do in the dark. (**Possible answers: read, write, draw, do math problems, move around**) Turn the lights back on and remark that people need light to be able to see clearly. Explain that God's Word is like light. When people know God's Word, they are able to know God and put their faith in Him.

Directed Instruction

Explain to students that many years ago, the people of China did not know God's Word. Tell students to listen as you read the following true story about a woman who took the light of God's Word to the people of China:

> Charlotte Digges Moon, nicknamed *Lottie*, was born in 1840 on a farm in Virginia. While in college, Lottie accepted Jesus as her Savior. After she graduated, Lottie became a teacher. Lottie enjoyed teaching, but she began to feel that God wanted her to become a missionary to people outside the United States. Lottie had read about the people in China who did not know the Lord because they had never heard God's Word. Lottie loved God and had a close relationship with Him. She prayed that God would allow her to go and teach Chinese women and children. After much prayer, Lottie believed God wanted her to go to China. When she was about 32 years old, Lottie Moon moved to China.
>
> Lottie loved the Chinese people and wanted them to know about Jesus. At first, the people were afraid and would not listen to her. Lottie realized that if she made friends with the women, she would have a better opportunity to tell them about the Lord. It was hard to make friends at first, so Lottie started baking cookies. The smell of the freshly baked cookies drew several of the Chinese women and children to come to Lottie's home. But Lottie knew she had to do more to get the people to trust her. She wore Chinese clothes and learned to speak Chinese. The Chinese people grew to love and respect her. Lottie was able to travel to villages and share the good news with women there. Many of them accepted Jesus as their Savior.
>
> Lottie had lived in China for years when a war broke out. During those difficult years, people suffered from famine. People were starving all around her! Lottie loved the people she served so much that she shared all of her own food with the Chinese people. Soon Lottie was so thin that she could no longer work.
>
> Lottie's American friends could see that she had to return to the United States and get some medical help. These friends put Lottie on a ship to return to the United States, but she never made it home. Lottie Moon died on Christmas Eve in 1912 at the age of 72. She had served the Lord for 39 years as a missionary to the people of China.

Explain that Lottie Moon was a blessing to the Chinese people. This means that she loved them and helped them by teaching them about Jesus and sharing her food during the time of famine. Although Christians today are not often called to give all they have, they are still to be a blessing by sharing God's Word and their love with others.

Review

- Where did Lottie Moon go to tell people about Jesus? (**to China**)
- Was Lottie Moon able to help the Chinese people? (**Yes. Because of her teaching, many Chinese people accepted Jesus as their Savior.**)
- How did Lottie Moon help the Chinese people during the war and famine? (**Lottie shared her own food with them.**)
- How was Lottie Moon a blessing to the people of China? (**She not only told the Chinese people about Jesus, she gave them food to help keep them from starving.**)

Student Page 33.4

Point out the light sources on the page. The light of God's Word is still unknown in many places in the world today. Encourage students to pray for missionaries and Bible translators around the world. Assist students as needed in completing the page.

DAY 4

33.4 ***Serving God and Others***

Use the picture key to name the person that each sentence tells about.

1. explained God's Word to an Ethiopian man.

Philip

2. wrote God's Word in the New Testament.

Paul

3. helped Paul take God's Word to the Gentiles in Lystra.

Barnabas

4. shared God's Word with people in China.

Lottie Moon

Complete the sentence.

5. I will share God's Word with Answers will vary.

132

© Bible Grade 1

APPLICATION

- How was Lottie Moon like Paul and Barnabas? (**Lottie Moon traveled to take the good news of God's plan of salvation to many people.**)
- How did Lottie Moon know that God wanted her to go to China? (**Lottie had a close relationship with God. She prayed, and God answered her.**)
- How can you be like Lottie Moon? (**I can have a close relationship with God. I can share the good news about Jesus with my friends.**)

33.5 Serving God and Others

Focus: Review and Assessment

★ **PREPARATION**

Select **VA 33A Paul and Barnabas**. (*Lesson Review*)

Print a copy of **BLM 33C Lesson 33 Test** for each student. (*Directed Instruction*)

Lesson Review ★

Use **VA 33A Paul and Barnabas** to review the Bible truth. Cover the following concepts:

- After Paul became a Christian, he went to various places as a missionary.
- Barnabas, another godly leader in the Church, was also a missionary. He went on missionary journeys with Paul.
- Paul and Barnabas went to preach in the synagogue at Antioch. At first, the people there listened. Later, some became jealous. They forced Paul and Barnabas to leave Antioch.
- Paul and Barnabas went to the town of Lystra. God gave them the ability to heal people in Jesus' name.
- A man with a crooked foot was listening carefully to Paul preach about Jesus. Paul saw that the man had faith in the Lord to be healed. Paul commanded the man to stand up, and the man walked for the first time in his life!
- The Greek people of Lystra thought that the miracle meant Paul and Barnabas were gods, similar to the false gods worshipped by the Greeks. The Greeks began to worship Paul and Barnabas!
- Paul and Barnabas explained that they were not gods; rather, they were servants of the living God—the only God!
- Sadly, some Jewish leaders stirred up trouble. They got the townspeople to take Paul outside the city and stone him. The townspeople left Paul lying there—they thought he was dead.
- Barnabas and other Christians from Lystra came to help Paul. The Lord gave Paul the strength to get up.
- The next day, Paul and Barnabas left Lystra.
- Lottie Moon was a missionary to the people of China. She was a blessing to them because, through her teaching, many Chinese people became Christians.
- First graders can serve God faithfully in many different ways!

Directed Instruction ★

Distribute a copy of **BLM 33C Lesson 33 Test** to each student. Have students complete the exercises independently. Review the correct answers.

Notes:

Lesson Preparation

Knowing God

34.0

Expected Student Outcomes

KNOW

God desires all to come to Him. He is preparing a special place for those who accept Jesus as Savior.

DO

Students will:
- complete sentences about God's creation
- sequence events of Jesus' life
- review God's plan of salvation
- write words and phrases to describe heaven

APPLY

Students will affirm that they need to accept Jesus as Savior in order to get to heaven.

Lesson Outline

I. God and His greatness
  A. Creation (Gen 1:1–2:15)
  B. Fall of man (Gen 2:16–3:24)
II. Jesus the Savior (Jn 1:29)
  A. Birth and death (Lk 1:26–2:52, Jn 19)
  B. Resurrection (Lk 24:1–49, Jn 20:1–18, 1 Cor 15:3b–8)
III. Personal decision
  A. Confession of sins (Jn 3:16, Rom 3:23, 1 Jn 1:9)
  B. Forgiveness of sins (Ps 51:7b, Jn 1:29)
IV. Heaven
  A. Gift of God is everlasting life (Jn 3:16, Rom 6:23)
  B. A place for believers (Mt 6:19–21; Jn 14:1–6; Rev 21:4, 21)

TEACHER'S HEART

You've had the incredible privilege of spending the school year with impressionable first graders. The students have learned to read, write, and solve math problems. But what is even more important, they have learned that Jesus loves them, died on the cross for their sins, and has a plan for their life.

Reflect upon special moments when your students prayed for others, when they exemplified a Christlike attitude in their work and play, when they worked diligently in service to others, or when they worshipped the Lord.

This week, students will hear God's plan of salvation once again. Be filled with anticipation as there may be several students who will come to accept Jesus as their Savior and Lord this week. Consider writing notes of encouragement to all your students over the summer vacation, mentioning that you pray for them often.

MEMORY VERSE

John 3:16

MATERIALS

Day 1:
- Read-Aloud book
- VA 1A Creation

Day 2:
- VA 17A Jesus Is Born, VA 29C Jesus' Arrest, Crucifixion, and Burial, VA 29D Jesus Is Risen
- VA 20A The Disciples Follow Jesus, VA 26A Peter Walks on Water, VA 32A Saul's Conversion (*Extension*)

Day 3:
- Baby pictures
- Card stock, stickers (*Extension*)

Day 4:
- Cookies, box, gift wrap, gift tag

Day 5:
- VA 1A Creation; VA 17A Jesus Is Born; VA 29C Jesus' Arrest, Crucifixion, and Burial; VA 29D Jesus Is Risen
- BLM 34A Lesson 34 Test

SONGS

Jesus Loves Me

TEACHER RESOURCES

Alcorn, Randy. *Heaven*. Tyndale House Publishers, 2004.
Plan of Salvation bookmarks. B&H Publishing Group, 2009.

STUDENT RESOURCES

Froeb, Lori C. *God's Creation*. Kregel Kidzone, 2008.
Growing in God. Tract. Crossway Books, 2004.

34.1 Knowing God

Focus: God and His Greatness

MEMORY VERSE

John 3:16

MEMORY WORK

- Write the Memory Verse on the board. Randomly erase a few words. Recite the verse together as a class, filling in the missing words. Continue the process until all the words have been erased.

★ PREPARATION

Choose a favorite READ-ALOUD BOOK from your classroom library. (*Introduction*)

Select **VA 1A Creation**. (*Directed Instruction*)

EXTENSION

1A Write the word *creation* vertically on the board, using lowercase letters. Brainstorm with students to think of things or animals God created that begin with each letter written on the board. Write students' suggestions opposite the appropriate letter. Read the suggestions orally with the class.

Introduction ★

Select one of the students' favorite READ-ALOUD BOOKS and hold it up for the class to see. Explain that when the author wrote the book, he or she had a purpose in mind. Authors of children's books have different purposes for writing. Some stories are written to make children laugh, to teach something about nature, or to tell an interesting tale.

Share that when God made the heavens and the earth, He had a purpose for everything He created. God made people so that they could talk with Him, worship Him, praise Him, thank Him, and bring Him glory. He wanted the first people to have a relationship with Him, just as He desires to have a relationship with all people today.

Directed Instruction ★

Display **VA 1A Creation**. Remind students that Adam was placed in the Garden of Eden to take care of all the plants and animals that God created. Ask volunteers to name the kinds of plants and animals pictured on the visual aid. (**Answers will vary.**) Read the text on the back of VA 1A.

How wonderful life would have been if Adam and Eve could have stayed in the Garden of Eden! Everything was perfect; Adam and Eve had all their needs supplied. Even better, they were able to talk to God and hear His voice! However, God could not allow Adam and Eve to stay in the Garden. This was because Adam and Eve sinned; they disobeyed God. Ask a student to recount what Adam and Eve did to commit the first sin. (**Eve listened to the devil, who had disguised himself as a snake. She ate fruit from a particular tree, even though God had said not to eat that fruit. Then Eve gave some of the fruit to Adam and he ate it, too.**) Since that time, all people have been born with a sinful nature. That means that everyone sins! Sin causes people to be separated from God.

Ask students to imagine what it would be like if they were unable to leave their seat today. Choose a volunteer to tell things that he or she could not do in that condition. (**Possible answers: go to recess, go to reading group, get a book from the classroom library, get a drink of water, play games, go home**) Explain that the Bible says that people who sin are like slaves or prisoners (Romans 6:6), and that all people deserve a terrible punishment for sin (Romans 6:23). People cannot get rid of their own sins, but because God is loving, He promised to send a savior to take away the punishment for sin once and for all.

Review

- Describe life in the Garden of Eden before Adam and Eve sinned. (**Possible answers: God walked and talked with Adam and Eve; everything was wonderful and perfect; Adam and Eve could eat from every tree except the Tree of the Knowledge of Good and Evil.**)
- Who is God's enemy? (**Satan**)

- What caused Adam and Eve to be separated from God? (**Possible answers: They sinned when they ate from the Tree of the Knowledge of Good and Evil that God said not to eat from; they disobeyed God.**)
- How did life for Adam and Eve change after they sinned? (**Possible answers: Adam and Eve could no longer walk with God and hear His voice; weeds, thorns, pain, and suffering entered the world.**)
- How did God show that He still loved Adam and Eve after they disobeyed Him? (**God promised that He would send a savior to take away the sins of the world.**)

Student Page 34.1

Read any difficult words and answer any questions. Have students complete the page independently.

Notes:

DAY 1

Name ______________________

Knowing God **34.1**

1. Use the Word Bank to complete the sentences about Creation.

WORD BANK				
people	stars	night	plants	sea

God created day and ____night____. He spoke and the sky and the ____sea____ were formed. God spoke again and dry land appeared. Grass, flowers, trees, and other ____plants____ grew. God made the sun, moon, and ____stars____ for the sky. Then God made all kinds of animals to live in the sea and on the land. Finally, God made ____people____.

2. Draw and color the rest of the tree.

God told Adam and Eve not to eat from the Tree of the Knowledge of Good and Evil, but Adam and Eve disobeyed God and ate some fruit from that tree. They sinned! They were sad!

God still loved Adam and Eve. He loves you, too!

APPLICATION

- Adam and Eve's sin broke their relationship with God. Share a time when your sin hurt a relationship with someone in your family. (**Answers will vary.**)
- What did God promise to do to restore the broken relationship? (**God promised to send a savior to take away the sins of all people.**)
- How can you have a relationship with God? (**I can accept Jesus as my Savior so that I will no longer be separated from God.**)

REINFORCEMENT

Everything in all Creation displays evidence of purposeful design. It is impossible not to see pattern and complexity in the natural world. The speed of light, the distance between the stars, the electrical attraction between atoms in a molecule, the water cycle, gravitational pull, and the interaction of plants and animals all reinforce what Paul says in Romans 1:20, "For since the creation of the world His invisible attributes are clearly seen, being understood by the things that are made, even His eternal power and Godhead, so that they (people) are without excuse."

34.2 Knowing God

Focus: Jesus the Savior

★ PREPARATION

Select "Jesus Loves Me" from the music CDs. (*Introduction*)

Select **VA 17A Jesus Is Born**, **VA 29C Jesus' Arrest, Crucifixion, and Burial**, and **VA 29D Jesus Is Risen**. (*Directed Instruction*)

EXTENSION

2A Invite three students to the front of the room. Distribute the following visual aids, one to each student: **VA 20A The Disciples Follow Jesus**, **VA 26A Peter Walks on Water**, and **VA 32A Saul's Conversion**. Have each student read the title and state how a person in the Bible truth pictured came to know Jesus the Savior.

Introduction ★

Sing "Jesus Loves Me" from the music CDs. Share about something you were promised as a child. Describe the excitement you felt when you received what had been promised; for example, a certain toy, a trip, a special day with someone, or an opportunity to play a team sport. Ask students to imagine how they might feel at receiving a promised gift from God. (**Answers will vary, but should include feeling excited or happy.**)

Directed Instruction ★

Remind students that after Adam and Eve sinned, God promised that He would send a savior to take away the sins of the world. Tell students that today they will hear, once again, how God kept His promise.

Display **VA 17A Jesus Is Born**. Remind students that God sent an angel to tell Mary she had been chosen to be the mother of the promised Savior. God was preparing to bring about His plan of salvation to save people from their sins. God chose Joseph to be Jesus' earthly father. Mary and Joseph traveled to Bethlehem. They spent the night in a stable where baby Jesus was born. Mary wrapped the baby in soft cloths and made a bed for Him in a manger. An angel announced the news of the birth of Jesus to some shepherds who went to Bethlehem and saw baby Jesus, the promised Savior of the world.

Display **VA 29C Jesus' Arrest, Crucifixion, and Burial**. Review with students that for about three years, Jesus did many miracles and taught the truth about God. He called twelve men to be His disciples. Some of the Jewish leaders did not believe that Jesus was the Son of God. They thought Jesus was gaining too many followers, so they looked for a way to kill Jesus. Judas, one of Jesus' disciples, turned against Jesus. Judas told the Jewish leaders where Jesus was praying, and they came and took Jesus to the high priest and to Pontius Pilate. The Jewish leaders demanded that Jesus be sentenced to die by being nailed to a cross, even though He had done nothing wrong. The soldiers whipped and beat Jesus. They made Him wear a crown of thorns and forced Him to carry His cross partway to Golgotha. The cross was placed between the crosses of two other men who had also been sentenced to die. Jesus died on the cross to take the punishment for the sins of all people. Followers of Jesus started to prepare His body for burial. They placed Jesus in a tomb.

Display **VA 29D Jesus Is Risen**. Jesus' followers were sad. Mary Magdalene and some of her friends went to Jesus' tomb to finish wrapping Jesus' body for burial. They noticed the large stone that had covered the entrance was rolled back. Angels appeared to the women and told them that Jesus was alive. Mary Magdalene met a Man standing in the garden and He called her name. Mary recognized that it was Jesus! Jesus later appeared to the disciples to show them that He was really alive. Jesus wants all people to know that He is alive! Whoever trusts in Him will live with Him in heaven forever.

Review

- How did God keep His promise? (**God sent Jesus to be born. Jesus died and rose from the dead.**)
- How did the soldiers treat Jesus before He died? (**The soldiers whipped and beat Him, made Him wear a crown of thorns, and forced Him to carry His cross partway to Golgotha.**)
- Who appeared to Mary Magdalene? (**Jesus**)
- What does Jesus want everyone in the world to know? (**Jesus took the punishment for sins by dying on the cross. Everyone who believes in Him will live with Him in heaven forever.**)

Student Page 34.2

Read the directions and the text on the page. Have students complete the page.

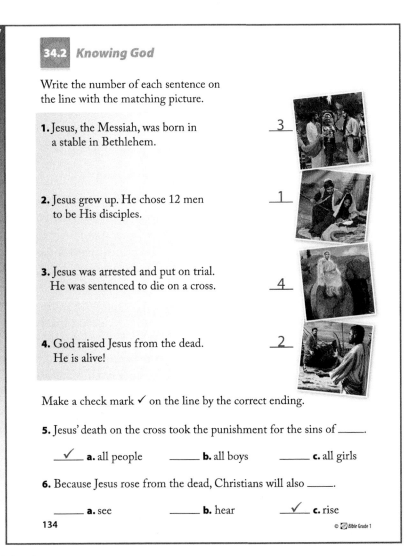

Notes:

APPLICATION

- How does knowing that Jesus died for your sins make you feel? (**Answers will vary, but should include thankful, joyful, and hopeful in anticipation of everlasting life with Jesus in heaven.**)
- God kept His promise in sending the Savior. Does God always keep His promises? How do you know? (**God always keeps His promises. The Bible tells me that this is true.**)

DAY 2

34.2 ***Knowing God***

Write the number of each sentence on the line with the matching picture.

1. Jesus, the Messiah, was born in a stable in Bethlehem.

2. Jesus grew up. He chose 12 men to be His disciples.

3. Jesus was arrested and put on trial. He was sentenced to die on a cross.

4. God raised Jesus from the dead. He is alive!

3 

1 

4 

2 

Make a check mark ✓ on the line by the correct ending.

5. Jesus' death on the cross took the punishment for the sins of ____.

✓ **a.** all people ____ **b.** all boys ____ **c.** all girls

6. Because Jesus rose from the dead, Christians will also ____.

____ **a.** see ____ **b.** hear ✓ **c.** rise

34.3 Knowing God

Focus: Personal Decision

★ PREPARATION

Collect BABY PICTURES of yourself, your children, or students. (*Introduction*)

EXTENSION

3A Distribute a half sheet of CARD STOCK to each student to make a bookmark. Give students STICKERS to decorate the bookmark and tell them to draw and color designs drawn on the bookmark as well. When complete, invite students to share their bookmarks. Instruct students to place the bookmarks in their Bible to mark John 3:16.

3B Invite students to play the game Draw Near to the Lord. When students are not in the room, hide a paper cutout of a cross somewhere in the room. When students enter the room, explain that a cross is hidden for them to find. They will know if they are near the cross when you say the name of a student who is near the cross and the word *nearer*. Name a student who is far from the cross and say the word *farther*. Continue to allow students to infer the location of the cross from your clues until students find the cross. Explain that Jesus desires all people to have a close relationship with Him. Accepting Him as Lord and Savior is the first step.

Introduction ★

Display several BABY PICTURES that you have collected. Ask students to guess who is pictured in each photograph. Explain that baby pictures are precious to people because they are reminders of the time when they were born.

Sadly, because of Adam and Eve's disobedience, all people are born sinful. People cannot do anything to get rid of their sin. They cannot pay to have their sins removed, and they cannot do enough good things to make up for their sins. Only God can take away sin. He did that by having His Son, Jesus, die on the cross to take the punishment for sin once and for all.

Directed Instruction

Write **John 3:16** on the board or have students find that verse in their Bible, read the verse silently, and mark the place. Tell students to listen for several of the words found in that verse as you read the following story:

> Landon was so glad that the school year was almost over. Last summer he spent a week at camp, and he was excited to go again this summer. During Landon's week at camp last summer, he rode a dirt bike on a steep, bumpy path for the first time. Landon learned to ride a horse, too. Most of the time the horse walked, but Landon held on tight to the reigns when the horse trotted or splashed through a puddle along the trail. Those experiences were fun, but they weren't the best part of going to camp. Nightly campfires were Landon's favorite part of his week at camp.
>
> While at a campfire one evening, Landon learned that God created the universe and put Adam and Eve in the Garden of Eden to have a close relationship with Him. God did not give His children very many rules, but He did tell them not to eat the fruit from a certain tree. Adam and Eve disobeyed God and ate from that tree. That was when sin entered the world, and Adam and Eve became separated from God. Landon learned that God sent a savior to take the punishment for sin and make a way for people to be able to have a relationship with God.
>
> Landon knew that he sinned. Sometimes he did wrong things when he was angry. Sometimes he was selfish and mean to others. Landon confessed his sins and asked God to forgive him. Landon put his faith in Jesus and trusted Jesus to forgive his sins. With a joyful heart, Landon realized his sins were gone! God forgave his sins and gave him a wonderful gift—everlasting life! His camp counselor reminded him to read God's Word and spend time in prayer every day. Landon was so happy that he shared God's love with his friends. Now Landon's friends know about God's plan of salvation.

Have students read or recite **John 3:16** chorally. Review that God's gift of salvation is available to everyone. Landon confessed his sins, repented, and accepted Jesus Christ as his Savior. Ask any student who is ready to receive the gift of salvation from God to speak to you privately.

Review

- Why did God send His only Son to die on the cross to take away the sins of people? (**God loves people and doesn't want them to be separated from Him. God wants all people to know and love Him.**)
- What does God's Word promise to those who believe in Jesus? (**everlasting, or eternal, life**)
- Who can receive God's gift of salvation? (**Anyone who realizes his or her need for a savior, confesses sin, repents, and asks God for forgiveness has God's gift of salvation (1 John 1:9).**)

Student Page 34.3

Assist students as necessary in completing the exercises.

APPLICATION

- When you accept Jesus as your Savior, one of the things that you do is to confess your sins. Do you stop sinning after becoming a Christian? (**I try not to sin now because I love Jesus, but it doesn't mean I won't sin ever again.**)
- What should you do if you sin again? (**I should confess my sin and tell the Lord that I am sorry for what I have done.**)

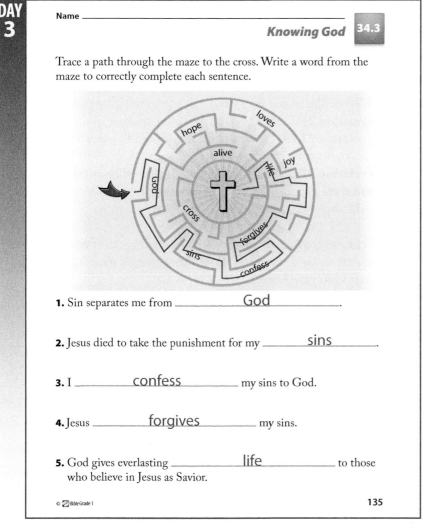

Notes:

DAY 3

Name ______________________________

Knowing God **34.3**

Trace a path through the maze to the cross. Write a word from the maze to correctly complete each sentence.

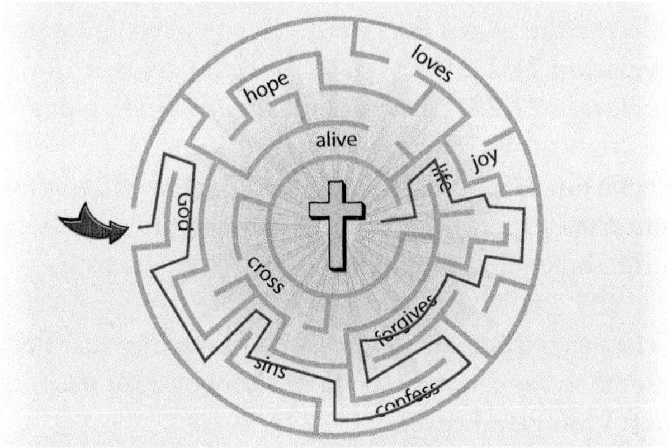

1. Sin separates me from ______God______.

2. Jesus died to take the punishment for my ______sins______.

3. I ______confess______ my sins to God.

4. Jesus ______forgives______ my sins.

5. God gives everlasting ______life______ to those who believe in Jesus as Savior.

34.4 Knowing God

Focus: Heaven

★ PREPARATION

Place a sufficient number of COOKIES for each student to have one or two inside a BOX. Use GIFT WRAP to wrap the box. Add a GIFT TAG that tells your name and the name or number of your classroom. (*Introduction*)

Draw a word web on the board so that the ovals are large enough to write in. (*Directed Instruction*)

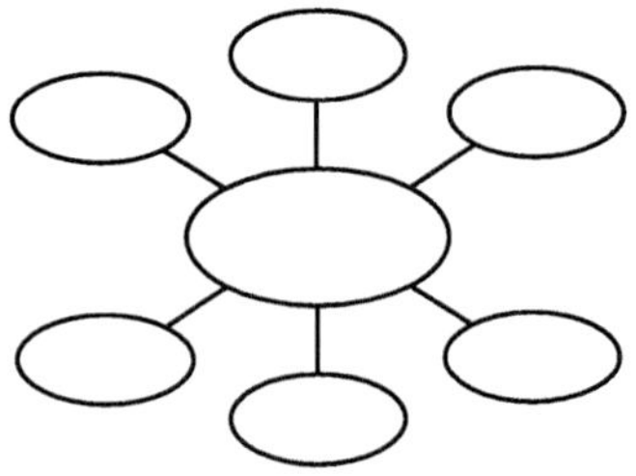

EXTENSION

4A Obtain a copy of the song "Heaven Is a Wonderful Place" by Wolfgang Koperski and teach it to the class.

Introduction ★

Display the GIFT-WRAPPED BOX OF COOKIES you have prepared. Wonder aloud what is inside the box and if the gift is for you. Read the GIFT TAG. Unwrap the gift and show the cookies. Explain that the cookies are a gift that you will all share at a later time.

Explain that the Bible tells about another kind of gift. It is not wrapped in a beautiful box, but it is even more wonderful than any earthly gift. Unlike the cookies, this gift will never end! God gives this gift to all those who believe in Him. This is the gift of everlasting, or eternal, life in heaven (Romans 6:23). Ask students to define *everlasting life*. (**living with God in heaven forever**)

Gifts are given out of love and kindness. The person receiving the gift does not do anything to deserve the gift. Everlasting life in heaven is a gift that God gives believers when they put their trust in Him. God gives believers the gift because He loves them!

Directed Instruction ★

Explain that heaven is a real place and that the Bible tells Christians quite a bit about heaven. Write the word *heaven* inside the center oval of the word web. Inform students that the outer ovals will have words that tell more about heaven. Leave the completed word web on the board.

- Read **John 3:16**. Ask students how long believers will live with God in heaven. (**Those who believe in Him will live with God in heaven forever.**) Write the words *lasts forever* in one of the outer ovals.
- Read **Revelation 21:21**. Write *street of gold* in another oval.
- Read **Revelation 21:23**. Heaven is filled with God's glory. Write *glory* in one of the outer ovals.
- Read **Revelation 21:4**. Ask students to tell what will not be in heaven. (**death, mourning or sorrow, crying, pain**) Write *no death*, *no pain*, *no crying* in the three remaining outer ovals.

Invite the class to participate in a responsive reading that describes heaven. Direct students to say *I want to go there* after you read each line.

Teacher: God is in heaven.
Students: I want to go there.
Teacher: There is no pain in heaven.
Students: I want to go there.
Teacher: There is no death in heaven.
Students: I want to go there.
Teacher: There is glory in heaven.
Students: I want to go there.
Teacher: There is no crying in heaven.
Students: I want to go there.
Teacher: The street is made of gold in heaven.
Students: I want to go there.
Teacher: There is everlasting life in heaven.
Students: I want to go there.

Review

- Describe heaven. (**Possible answers: God will be there; there will be no pain, no death, no sorrow, and no crying; there will be no need for light because God's glory lights it, the street will be made of gold.**)
- Who will be in heaven? (**The Lord God and all those who have accepted His free gift of salvation through faith in Him.**)
- Do you have to do anything to earn or pay for everlasting life in heaven? (**No, it is the free gift of God.**)

Student Page 34.4

Allow students to complete the word web using words that you have previously written on the board.

Notes:

DAY 4

34.4 ***Knowing God***

Write words that tell about heaven in each of the ovals.

Possible answers: no pain, no death, no crying, no sadness, no need for light, gold street, God is there, filled with God's glory

APPLICATION

- Should Christians be afraid of death? (**No, not at all. Death is not the end for Christians; we will live forever with Jesus in heaven.**)
- Should Christians worry about whether or not they will go to heaven? (**No, God promises that everyone who trusts in Jesus has the gift of everlasting life with Him in heaven.**)

REINFORCEMENT

Young children often have questions about heaven. They wonder if they will become angels and fly around, or if they will sit on a cloud and play a harp. They may wonder if they will see a loved one who has died. It is important to answer students' questions truthfully but simply. Explain that the Bible is clear about the fact that people do not become angels, and angels do not become people! Believers will worship God in heaven, but they will not sit on clouds. Christians will have resurrected bodies as Jesus had, and they will recognize each other even though they have been apart for many years.

34.5 Knowing God

Focus: Review and Assessment

★ PREPARATION

Select **VA 1A Creation**, **VA 17A Jesus Is Born**, **VA 29C Jesus' Arrest, Crucifixion, and Burial**, and **VA 29D Jesus Is Risen**. (*Lesson Review*)

Make one copy of **BLM 34A Lesson 34 Test** for each student. (*Directed Instruction*)

Lesson Review ★

Use **VA 1A Creation**; **VA 17A Jesus Is Born**; **VA 29C Jesus' Arrest, Crucifixion, and Burial**; and **VA 29D Jesus Is Risen** to review the Bible truths in this lesson. Be sure to review the following points:

- God created day and night, the sky, seas, dry land, plants, sun, moon, and stars, ocean creatures, birds, and animals. God created Adam and placed him in the Garden of Eden to take care of everything God created.
- Adam and Eve committed the first sin by disobeying God. Adam and Eve became separated from God. They had to leave the Garden of Eden. God promised that He would send a savior to take away the sins of the world.
- Everyone born after Adam and Eve were born with a sin nature and are sinners.
- Jesus, the Messiah, was born to take away the sins of the world.
- Jesus did many miracles and taught the truth about God. Jewish leaders arrested Jesus and put Him on a cross to die even though He had done nothing wrong. Jesus took the punishment for people's sins by dying on the cross.
- Mary Magdalene and some friends went to Jesus' tomb. The body of Jesus was not there. He was alive!
- When people confess their sins to Jesus, ask for forgiveness, and put their trust in Him, He forgives their sins and gives them the gift of everlasting, or eternal, life with Him in heaven.
- God's gift of everlasting life is free.
- Heaven is a wonderful place. There will be no death, sorrow, crying, or pain in heaven.

Directed Instruction ★

Distribute a copy of **BLM 34A Lesson 34 Test** to each student. Have students complete the test.

Notes: